Pearson New International Edition

Teaching Students with Learning Problems
C. Mercer   A Mercer P. Pullen
Eighth Edition

PEARSON®

Pearson Education Limited
Edinburgh Gate
Harlow
Essex CM20 2JE
England and Associated Companies throughout the world

Visit us on the World Wide Web at: www.pearsoned.co.uk

© Pearson Education Limited 2014

 ISBN 10: 1-292-04185-4
ISBN 13: 978-1-292-04185-8

British Library Cataloguing-in-Publication Data
A catalogue record for this book is available from the British Library

Printed in the United States of America

Table of Contents

Creating Responsive Learning Environments

Monkey Business Fotolia

From Chapter 1 of *Teaching Students with Learning Problems*, 8/e. Cecil D. Mercer. Ann R. Mercer. Paige C. Pullen.

University students recently heard the following pleas while assessing the reading skills of elementary students in general education classes. "Please teach me to read!" "Are you here to help me learn to read?" "Will you help my teacher to teach me to read?" Other youngsters refused to read or cried when they could not read the words. The university students maintained that the reading passages were too difficult until they were told that the passages were from the students' reading books and were controlled for readability. Thus, each youngster was asked to read passages at his or her respective grade level. Unfortunately, this scenario is widespread because students of all ages experience the frustration of low achievement and school failure. Moreover, these students are capable of achieving at a higher level.

Cegelka and Berdine (1995) report that 25 to 40 percent of all students are estimated to have significant academic problems. Numerous societal problems contribute to the poor school performance of youngsters. These problems include limited or no family support, poverty, increased student diversity, crime, high dropout rates, and substance abuse. Also, several school-related problems contribute to the poor achievement of students. Problems result from the practice of many educators to adopt curriculum materials that have never been field tested, adhere to one instructional approach for all students, and fail to lessen the gap between research and practice. Also, decreasing financial and community support weakens the ability of school personnel to meet the needs of all students.

This text focuses on teaching students who will experience extensive school failure if they do not receive instruction that is responsive to their needs. Educational methodology exists to help these individuals realize their learning potential and become independent and contributing members of society. The contents of this text are written within the context of four beliefs. First, all individuals are capable of learning. It is apparent that not all students are capable of learning the same thing, but most can master the basic curricula of schools. Second, the teaching talent to help all students learn according to their potential exists in most schools today. Third, the knowledge gap between what is known about effective teaching and what routinely is practiced in classrooms is enormous. Schools and educational programs can be structured to educate all students, and school administrators must act on research findings to help teachers and students. Fourth, all students need a safe, caring, and positive learning environment, and one of the best ways to care for students is to teach them in a manner that ensures success. Dr. Hiam Ginott (Milwaukee Public Schools,

1990, p. 30) reminds teachers of the need to create caring environments:

> I have come to a frightening conclusion that,
>
> I am the decisive element in the classroom.
>
> It is my personal approach that creates the climate.
>
> It is my daily mood that makes the weather.
>
> As a teacher I possess tremendous power to make a child's life miserable or joyous.
>
> I can be a tool of torture or an instrument of inspiration.
>
> I can humiliate or humor, hurt or heal.
>
> In all situations it is my response that decides whether a crisis will be escalated or de-escalated, and a child humanized or de-humanized.

The following section briefly describes many of the students who face academic achievement deficits if not provided with effective instruction in caring environments.

STUDENTS AT RISK FOR SCHOOL FAILURE

Students from all races and socioeconomic backgrounds are at risk for school failure. Efforts to respond to the needs of students who fail in school without specialized help have resulted in the creation of several programs that serve specific groups of students. Examples of such programs are special education, Title I, bilingual education, and migrant education. These programs are supported through federal legislation (e.g., the Individuals with Disabilities Education Act [IDEA] and No Child Left Behind [NCLB]), and each program includes criteria for student eligibility. The following groups of students may be at an increased risk of school failure and are likely to benefit from such programs.

Students with Disabilities

Students with identified disabilities, or those at increased risk of being identified with a disability, are at risk of school failure. Special education programs serve students with disabilities who qualify in one of the following categories as defined by IDEA: specific learning disabilities, speech or language impairments, intellectual disability, emotional disturbance, multiple disabilities, hearing impairments, orthopedic impairments, other health impairments, visual impairments, autism, deaf-blindness, and traumatic brain injury. Although it is not a separate category, students with attention-deficit hyperactivity disorders (ADHD) may be eligible for special education services under IDEA (i.e., under Other Health Impaired or other disability categories) or may be served in other federally sponsored programs (e.g., Section 504 of the Rehabilitation Act of 1973). In the 2004 reauthorization of IDEA, which is titled the Individuals with Disabilities Education Improvement Act, a new regulation allows students who are not identified as requiring special education services, yet need additional support to be successful in the general education classroom, to be eligible for *early intervening services*. Early intervening services are available for students in kindergarten through twelfth grade; however, these services are emphasized in the primary grades (i.e., kindergarten through third grade).

The learning problems for the majority of students identified for special education are categorized as mild. The learning and behavior difficulties of students with mild cognitive disabilities, learning disabilities, emotional disabilities, and ADHD are stressed in planning their respective educational programs; however, it also is important to recognize the secondary learning difficulties exhibited by students with physical or sensory disabilities. Students with physical or sensory disabilities frequently have significant problems learning academic content as well as social skills. Thus, many of these individuals need special instruction to address their learning difficulties.

Students from Low Socioeconomic Backgrounds

Students from impoverished backgrounds are at risk for academic failure, particularly in the area of literacy. Data from the National Assessment of Educational Progress (National Center for Education Statistics, 2007a) indicate that 83 percent of students from poor homes perform below the basic level of proficiency on reading tasks. A related statistic demonstrates that parents' low level of education is linked to poor academic outcomes (Shonkoff & Phillips, 2000; Stipek & Ryan, 1997).

Title I programs focus on serving students who are both low achieving and from low-income homes, and the programs are organized to be supplemental to services already available in the general education classroom. In their review of variables related to learning, Wang, Haertel, and Walberg (1993/1994) report that the home environment/parental support variable is highly related to student learning (i.e., it ranked fourth out of 28 variables). Some positive attributes of a home environment include high but realistic expectations about schoolwork, an authoritative rather than a permissive or authoritarian approach for discipline, a positive and supportive parent–child relationship, an educative atmosphere supportive of education, and daily routines and organization that facilitate doing homework (Ysseldyke, Christenson, & Kovaleski, 1994). Typically, low-socioeconomic home environments have fewer of these positive attributes, and the teacher should consider this when instructing students with learning problems who are from such environments. Borich (2007) notes that teachers of low-socioeconomic students should be warm and encouraging, and let students know that help is available; present material with an opportunity to practice what has been learned; emphasize applications before teaching abstractions; monitor students' progress at regular intervals; immediately help a student who needs help; and supplement the standard curriculum with specialized material to meet the needs of individual students.

Students from Cultural and Linguistically Diverse Backgrounds

Many students with learning problems have culturally and linguistically diverse backgrounds. It is important for teachers to value students' cultural differences and provide comfortable ways for these students to share their rich heritage with others. These activities help students respect variations among individuals and provide minority students with events that foster positive self-worth and motivation. Moreover, by becoming acquainted with the cultures of diverse learners, the teacher can adapt curriculum, instruction, and management strategies to accommodate their learning preferences and needs. Due to language differences between school and home and values that are often at odds with society's values, these students face obstacles that impede school success. For example, competition or winning in direct competition with others is a prominent value in American schools; however, cooperation or working together and being social is a value held by many African Americans, Hispanics, and Native Americans. Knowledge of the values of culturally diverse groups helps teachers adapt instruction for these students. In some cases the teacher can alter instruction to accommodate different values (e.g., use instructional games for some students and cooperative learning for others); in other situations the teacher can help the student embrace a value that is important to success (e.g., encourage the student to complete work on time through the use of advance organizers, planning, and goal setting).

Characteristics of Students at Risk for School Failure

It is apparent that disabilities, poverty, limited family support, cultural differences, language differences, ineffective teaching, and lack of educational funding contribute to the serious failures experienced by 15 to 25 percent of the school population. These youngsters all share the unfortunate experience of low academic achievement that results from problems in receiving instruction, connecting new knowledge with prior knowledge to create new learning that is organized and stored in a meaningful way, or recalling new information in such a way that it can be expressed or displayed at the appropriate time.

Although students at risk for school failure all experience academic failure without special instruction, their individual learning characteristics vary considerably. They are a heterogeneous group whose educational programs must be planned on the basis of individual characteristics and needs. In planning for students with learning problems, it helps to examine their learning characteristics. Information about some of the primary cognitive, affective, and behavioral characteristics of students with learning problems is presented in the following sections. Cognitive characteristics include cognitive and metacognitive deficits, low academic achievement, poor memory, and attention problems and hyperactivity. Affective characteristics include poor social skills, poor self-concept, poor motivation, and debilitating mood states. Adaptive behavior deficits and disruptive behavior are behavioral characteristics. Consideration of these characteristics helps teachers select, adapt, and implement techniques, strategies, and approaches that enable students with learning problems to succeed. Fortunately, numerous instructional procedures exist to help students with learning problems succeed. Frequently, one strategy works for many different students and has positive effects across cognitive, affective, and behavioral domains.

Cognitive and Metacognitive Deficits
The metacognitive and cognitive processes of students are significant influences on their learning. Metacognitive deficits are common among students with learning problems, particularly those with specific learning disabilities (Botsas & Padeliadu, 2003; Sideridis, Morgan, Botsas, Padeliadu, & Fuchs, 2006). *Metacognition* refers to a learner's knowledge (i.e., awareness) of thinking processes or strategies (such as planning, evaluating effectiveness of ongoing activities, checking the outcomes of effort, and correcting difficulties) and the ability to regulate or monitor these processes or strategies to learn successfully. In simpler terms, metacognition refers to an individual's awareness of his or her own thought processes and an ability to use those cognitive processes to learn. Knowledge about a student's metacognition appears to hold promise for designing

instruction. Instructional practices (e.g., mnemonics and think alouds) designed to help students with cognitive and metacognitive difficulties are featured throughout the text.

Low Academic Achievement
Low academic achievement occurs in all areas (i.e., language, reading, math, spelling, written expression, and content subjects) and is a primary characteristic of students with learning problems. Of these academic difficulties, language and reading problems are the most common. Many students who have reading difficulties suffer from underlying language deficits (Ehren, 2006; Wallach, 2005). It often is difficult to distinguish reading and language problems because they are so closely related.

Poor Memory
Many students with learning problems have difficulty remembering information presented visually or auditorily, and research suggests that some students with learning problems may have deficits in working memory (Martinussen & Tannock, 2006). Working memory is defined as an individual's ability to store information for a short period while engaging in tasks that are demanding cognitively (Savage, Lavers, & Pillay, 2007). Teachers frequently report that these students forget spelling words, math facts, vocabulary words, and directions. Some authorities maintain that these students do not spontaneously use techniques that facilitate memory (e.g., rehearsal or forming associations).

Attention Problems and Hyperactivity
To succeed in school, a student must recognize and maintain thought on relevant classroom tasks and must be able to shift attention to new tasks. Students with attention problems are unable to screen out extraneous stimuli and are attracted by irrelevant stimuli. Attention deficits and related behaviors received substantial coverage with the introduction of the term *attention deficit disorder (ADD)* in the 1980 *Diagnostic and Statistics Manual of Mental Disorders* (*DSM-III*; American Psychiatric Association, 1980). The current edition (*DSM-TR*; American Psychiatric Association, 2000) uses the term *attention-deficit hyperactivity disorder (ADHD)* and includes three subtypes of ADHD: predominantly hyperactive type, predominantly inattentive type, and combined type.

Poor Social Skills
Difficulties with social skills can be as debilitating as academic problems to students who have learning problems. Students with learning disabilities and students who are low achievers receive lower social skills ratings from teachers and

peers than do students who do not have learning problems (Nowicki, 2003). Examples of social skills in which some students with learning problems lack competence include greeting someone, accepting criticism, receiving compliments, saying no, and giving positive feedback. The social skills deficits of some students are caused by their inability to understand social cues. Because of their inability to interact appropriately with teachers and peers, students with social skills deficits frequently have low social status among their peers.

Poor Self-Concept Faced with repeated failure and low academic achievement, students with learning problems often have low self-esteem. Rather than learning and developing attitudes about tasks they can do, youngsters with learning problems often learn what they cannot do. The focus on what they cannot do also leads to greater levels of anxiety, particularly toward test taking. Although some students with learning disabilities have a low self-concept regarding academics, their self-concepts related to other areas (e.g., affect, family, physical, and social) do not differ from the self-concepts of their high-achieving peers and peers without disabilities (Montgomery, 1994).

Poor Motivation Given the repeated academic failure that many students with learning problems experience, it is not surprising that they are less motivated to perform than their peers without disabilities. When early attempts to succeed in school meet with failure, it is common for students to believe that success is beyond their abilities and efforts. Consequently, many develop a learned helplessness and lose their intrinsic motivation to prove their competence. Thus, they become externally motivated because they believe that success is dependent upon external factors and beyond their control (Smith, 2004).

Debilitating Mood States Little research on the mood states of students with learning problems exists; however, some research on students with learning problems offers noteworthy findings. This research indicates that students with learning disabilities have higher levels of depression than students without disabilities (Maag & Reid, 2006), and these difficulties may be more common among girls than boys (Heath & Ross, 2000). Also, research indicates that the rates of depression among individuals with intellectual disabilities are significant (McGillivray & McCabe, 2007; McGillivray, McCabe, & Kershaw, 2008). In addition, students with learning problems are at increased risk of suicidal thoughts, loneliness, and social rejection (Al-Yagon, 2007; Hallahan, Kauffman, & Pullen, 2009; Margalit, 2006).

Adaptive Behavior Deficits Students with learning problems frequently exhibit adaptive behavior deficits that interfere with academic achievement and social relationships. Adaptive behavior "consists of social and practical intelligence that people have learned so that they can function in their everyday lives" (Hallahan et al., 2009, p. 147). Adaptive behavior is a multidimensional variable and includes problem solving, social coping, relationships, pragmatic language, and production (i.e., how one produces work).

Disruptive Behavior Disruptive behavior may be the result of social skills deficits or frustration over lack of academic success. Disruptive behavior generally includes acts that interrupt or interfere with appropriate activities. Disruptive behavior inhibits the learning or work of others and requires the teacher or supervisor to stop productive events and deal with the disruption. The behavioral problems of numerous students with learning problems are well documented (Hallahan et al., 2009). Some students display disruptive aggressive behavior toward others (e.g., fighting and acting out). Their low tolerance for frustration often leads to outbursts that include name calling, sarcasm, or swearing. These behavioral problems frequently lead to disruptive events in inclusive classrooms and prompt educators to view the behavioral difficulties of students with learning problems as serious deterrents to their school success. One behavior that is very disruptive to the teaching–learning process is high absenteeism. Teachers must constantly make plans to help absent students catch up on their learning and work. Moreover, the academic progress of absent students is impeded.

INDIVIDUALIZED EDUCATIONAL PROGRAMS

Meeting the needs of a diverse group of students is a formidable task for both general and special education teachers. Primary and elementary teachers are faced with helping youngsters acquire basic skills, develop independent learning strategies, and explore careers. While teaching more than 100 students daily, secondary teachers are faced with helping adolescents acquire specific vocational skills, learning strategies, and academic knowledge. These teachers must be able to alter the type and amount of instruction. Altering the *type* of instruction may involve recording reading passages on tape or teaching the student a strategy for writing a paragraph. Altering the *amount* of instruction entails providing more extensive teacher modeling of concepts, using elaborated feedback, or providing more independent practice.

Individualized instruction refers to instruction that enables the student to work on appropriate tasks or content over time under conditions that motivate. This individualized approach does not imply that each student must be taught one to one. It *does* mean, however, that students receive daily instruction tailored to their educational needs. It can occur within various instructional arrangements, including seatwork, small groups, peer teaching, and large groups. The teacher matches the learner, the task, and instructional interventions to ensure optimal student growth.

Some specific components of individualized instruction consist of instructional objectives based on assessment, variable entry points into the curriculum, variable pacing, active participation of the learner in decision making, a variety of instructional arrangements (e.g., large groups, small groups, and cooperative learning) as a function of the task and learning level, and criterion-referenced evaluation of the learner. An *individualized educational program (IEP)* outlines the plan (i.e., the outcomes, curriculum, teachers' responsibilities, schedule, and settings) that facilitates individualized instruction.

As mentioned previously, the Individuals with Disabilities Education Act is aimed at special education. IDEA reauthorizes Public Law (PL) 94-142 (adopted in 1975), and it incorporates the amendments to PL 94-142, including PL 99-457 (adopted in 1986), PL 101-476 (adopted in 1990), PL 105-17 (adopted in 1997), and PL 108-446 (adopted in 2004). Essentially, IDEA guarantees a free, appropriate public education for all individuals with disabilities through age 21. Although PL 94-142 primarily deals with educational programs, PL 99-457 and PL 101-476 include mandates and incentives to provide services for infants, toddlers, and their families. Moreover, the amendments provide guidelines for assisting adolescents to make transitions from secondary school to postschool settings. The law provides the following four basic educational rights for students with disabilities.

1. A thorough, nondiscriminatory assessment of the parameters of the specific disability, with no single measure being the only criterion for evaluation
2. The right to a free, appropriate public education tailored to the needs of each individual
3. Placement in the "least restrictive environment," with maximum emphasis on enhancing participation in the general education curriculum and placing the youngster with a disability in a program with youngsters without disabilities when possible
4. The provision of supplementary aid and services to help ensure the success of the educational program

An IEP must be designed and implemented for each student (i.e., age 3 through 21) with a disability. The legislative intent of the IEP is to serve three primary functions: management, communication, and accountability (California Department of Education, 1994). The management function exists because the IEP is a planning tool designed to ensure that eligible students receive appropriate services based on the individual needs of the student. The communication function exists because the IEP requires a multidisciplinary team to work together to develop a written plan that details appropriate services and learner outcomes. Accountability exists because student progress toward specified objectives must be monitored and periodically reviewed. According to the 2004 reauthorization of IDEA, the IEP must state the following:

- The student's current levels of academic achievement and functional performance, which often is abbreviated as PLOP (present level of performance)
- Annual academic and functional goals along with how to monitor the child's progress toward meeting the annuals goals
- The special education and related services and supplementary aids and services based on peer-reviewed research to be provided to the child, and program modifications or supports for school personnel
- The extent, if any, to which the child will not participate with nondisabled children
- The individual accommodations that are necessary to measure the academic achievement and functional performance
- If applicable, reasons the child cannot participate in regular assessments and a description of the alternate assessment that will be administered
- The projected date for the beginning of services, as well as the frequency, location, and duration of those services
- Postsecondary goals based on transition assessments when the child is 16 years of age

Moreover, Public Law 99-457 provides an *individualized family service plan (IFSP)* for infants and toddlers (i.e., birth through age 2) with disabilities.

The IFSP documents the early-intervention services required by these children and their families.

The IEP and the IFSP both require that the written plan be developed by a multidisciplinary team, which includes the parents, and be based on a multidisciplinary assessment of unique needs. At the IEP meeting, a multidisciplinary team typically determines at least one short-term objective for each annual goal. The goals are major statements, and parental permission must be given for one to be added or deleted, whereas short-term objectives are steps taken to obtain a stated goal and can be added at the teacher's discretion. It is a good practice for the special education teacher to work with a student and his or her teachers for several sessions before the IEP conference. During this time, the special education teacher can determine realistic objectives and specific teaching techniques. The specific components of the IEP are described in more detail in the following sections.

Components of an IEP

Levels of Performance On the IEP, level-of-performance data must be precise enough to aid the teacher in formulating initial objectives. Norm-referenced or criterion-referenced evaluation instruments are designed to provide such data. In a norm-referenced evaluation, a student's performance is compared with others' scores; in a criterion-referenced evaluation, a student's performance is described in terms of fixed criteria. Evaluating student progress with standardized achievement tests is common. However, this practice is not warranted because standardized tests do not directly assess the content included in a student's curriculum and, thus, student learning and teacher effectiveness are being evaluated according to content that the teacher has not taught. Criterion-referenced instruments and informal measures seem to be more suitable than tests that primarily yield comparative scores. These instruments typically include systematic skill sequences and provide information that directly leads to objectives (e.g., instruct student in sums-to-9 facts). Currently, curriculum-based measurement is the best practice for evaluating student performance and progress on IEPs. Levels of performance may be assessed in the following areas: social adaptation, emotional maturity, prevocational–vocational skills, psychomotor skills, and academic achievement. Formal and informal assessment devices are discussed in Chapter 3, and specific tests are presented in each of the respective curriculum area chapters. In addition, scope and sequence skills lists in reading, spelling, handwriting, written expression, and math are provided in the Appendix.

PEARSON
myeducationlab

Go to the Assignments and Activities section of the Topic IEP's in the MyEducationLab for your course and complete the activity entitled The IEP as a Whole. As you watch the video and answer the accompanying questions, notice how the components of an IEP come together.

Annual Goals Annual goals must be tailored to individual needs—academic and otherwise—and must encompass the entire spectrum of short-term objectives in each specified area. They must be measurable and describe what the student should be able to do at the end of the school year. Although teachers are not held accountable if the IEP is implemented as written and the student does not achieve the projected growth, they are responsible for setting realistic expectations and providing systematic instruction toward these goals. Annual goals that are likely for a student with mild disabilities include the following:

- Student will read fourth-grade-level material fluently with comprehension.
- Student will learn the multiplication facts through 9.
- Student will work independently and complete assigned current tasks.

For the teacher who uses a scope and sequence skills list to identify instructional objectives and to monitor progress, the process of writing annual goals may be less time consuming. By coding the scope and sequence skills list, the teacher simply can write the annual goals using the code. For example, a student's present level of performance may be reading skill No. 3.14, and the annual goal may be to reach reading skill No. 4.26. In this approach, the short-term objectives become the skills listed between 3.14 and 4.26. When using coding, the teacher must ensure that parents understand the organization of the instructional objectives.

Short-Term Objectives Short-term objectives must be listed and described in specific, measurable terms. These objectives help boost present levels of performance toward annual goals. As noted previously, this task is much simpler if criterion-referenced evaluation measures are used, because the mastery of specific skills is targeted readily on a continuum of listed competencies. Short-term objectives that are likely to be used with some students with mild disabilities are as follows:

- Student will recognize and say the sounds of the initial consonants *r* and *w* 100 percent of the time.
- Student will correctly write his or her name within 30 seconds.

- Student will read the next story in his or her reader at 150 correct words per minute with 90 percent comprehension.

Description of Services   A statement of the specific services and materials provided for the student includes who teaches the student, what content is included in the instructional program, and what materials are used. Also, because IDEA requires that the student be educated in the least restrictive environment, the extent of the student's participation in the general education program must be established. For example, the plan may state that the student functions in the general education classroom for all but an hour a day. The role of the general education teacher then is noted (e.g., the child will sit in the front of the general education classroom and will use individualized spelling tapes developed jointly by the general education teacher and the special education teacher).

Dates of Service   The plan outlines the projected dates for initiation and the anticipated duration of services.

Evaluation   The use of objective criteria and frequent assessment are encouraged. However, the law requires only an annual evaluation to determine whether the annual goals are being achieved. Evaluation procedures are presented in Chapter 3 and in each of the respective curriculum area chapters.

Participants in IEP Meetings

The law specifies who must participate in IEP meetings: (1) a representative of the schools, other than the child's teacher, who is qualified to provide or supervise special education, (2) the student's teachers (a special education teacher and a general education teacher), (3) one or both parents, (4) the student, when appropriate, (5) an individual who can interpret the instructional implications of evaluation results, and (6) others at the discretion of the parent or school personnel.

Schools must follow certain procedures regarding parental participation to ensure the presence of parents at the meeting. Specific steps include the following:

1. Notify parents early enough. The purpose, time, and location of the meeting and the persons who will be in attendance should be included in the notice.
2. Schedule the meeting at a mutually agreed upon time and place.
3. If neither parent can attend, use other methods to ensure parental participation, such as telephone calls or home visits.

4. If a meeting is held without a parent in attendance, document attempts to involve the parents (e.g., telephone calls, copies of correspondence, and records of home visits).
5. Provide a copy of the student's IEP to the parent upon request.

Finally, the law states that, when appropriate, the student is to participate in the planning of his or her IEP. Although the participation of the student in the meeting often would be minimal, it may be especially effective to include the secondary level student in the planning of a program.

myeducationlab

Go to the Building Teaching Skills and Dispositions section of the Topic IEP's in the MyEducationLab for your course and complete the activity entitled Conducting or Participating in an IEP Meeting. As you work through the learning unit, consider the contributions and purposes of each stakeholder in the meeting.

Using the IEP

The IEP is a substantial improvement over past planning strategies used by many educators; however, it is not sufficient for delivering an individualized program. The components of diagnostic prescriptive teaching (i.e., an individualized programming approach) and the IEP both require assessment of the student's current level and specification of goals and objectives. However, only prescriptive teaching specifies the teaching tasks inherent in the objectives (such as antecedent events, student responses, consequent events, and daily evaluation for each task).

Although the IEP is recognized as a major step toward the improvement of educational services for students with learning problems, the accompanying data management system can be quite burdensome to the teacher. Developing, writing, and monitoring the IEP require a great deal of teacher time, although a computer offers an excellent tool to help educators manage it. Computer-generated IEPs are often of higher quality and take significantly less time to write.

The following are computer applications in IEP management.

- *Create new IEPs.* A computer can be used to develop an IEP (e.g., store and retrieve demographic data, test scores, annual goals, short-term objectives, and other data). Most software programs used in IEP development produce official forms; contain databases that maintain histories of student needs, goals, interventions, and objectives; and serve as authoring resources by offering banks of commonly used IEP goals and objectives (Belson, 2003).

- *Monitor procedural safeguards.* A computer can be used to provide the steps in the IEP process (e.g., receipt of parental consent for assessment, notification of IEP meeting, and annual review date) and the respective status regarding each step.
- *Update records.* A student's IEP can be displayed readily and modified easily on a computer. For example, progress on short-term objectives can be added. Moreover, the updated or existing record can be printed quickly for parents, teachers, or multidisciplinary team members.
- *Analyze and interpret test data.* Test results can be scored and analyzed on a computer. Computer programs are available that include scoring and analysis for the *Wechsler Intelligence Scale for Children—IV,* the *Kaufman Assessment Battery for Children—II,* and the *Woodcock-Johnson III Tests of Cognitive Abilities* and *Tests of Achievement.*
- *Monitor academic progress.* A list of curriculum skills can be programmed, and student progress can be monitored.

Computer applications to IEP management are obviously extensive. Some school districts have developed their own IEP management programs tailored to their specific needs.

EDUCATIONAL SERVICES AND RELATED PRACTICES

Selecting the appropriate school setting for serving students with learning problems is a complex and important task. This decision affects the quality of instruction provided and determines who does the teaching and who becomes the student's peer group. In essence, the placement decision significantly influences the student's attitude, achievement, and social development. In making the placement decision, educators are required by law to select the setting that represents the student's least restrictive environment.

Least Restrictive Environment

According to IDEA, the term *least restrictive environment* (*LRE*) means that, to the extent appropriate, students with disabilities should be educated with students without disabilities. The IEP committee collectively decides the student's least restrictive environment by determining the setting that best meets the student's social and educational needs. Selecting the student's "most

enabling environment" is a more positive way of conceptualizing LRE. Historically, students with disabilities were pulled out of general education classrooms and placed in self-contained classes. LRE is based on the premise that placing youngsters who have disabilities with youngsters who do not results in improved academic and social development for students with disabilities and reduces the stigma associated with being educated in segregated settings.

The least restrictive principle stresses the need for using a continuum of services sensitive to diverse needs. Figure 1.1 presents a core of necessary alternatives to serve a heterogeneous population of students with disabilities. The three major categories of services are general class, special class, and special school. The alternatives are arranged in the figure from bottom to top in the order in which segregation, labeling, and severity of need of the recipients usually increase. According to the U.S. Department of Education (2009), in the 2004–2005 school year, the percentages of students with learning disabilities ages 6 through 21 served in various educational environments were as follows: 52.1 percent in general education classrooms for most of the day (i.e., less than 21 percent of the day in other settings), 35.4 percent in separate rooms for 21 to 60 percent of the day (e.g., resource rooms), 15.8 percent in separate classrooms, and 1.0 percent in separate environments (i.e., public and private separate schools, hospital/homebound programs, or public or private residential facility).

Although students with learning disabilities receive a majority of their instruction in the general education classroom, these youngsters have a wide range of needs. Student needs must be determined on an individual basis, and placement decisions should be based on need rather than philosophies insensitive to the unique needs of the individual. General and special educators must work together to determine the appropriate placement and instructional plans for each student.

In establishing objectives for a student with learning problems, it is important to adopt a tentative commitment to a program level and to not consider placement in any program as permanent or terminal. When feasible, a student needs to move from the more restricted setting to the most integrated placement. Many schools are now implementing response to intervention (RTI) programs that allow for various levels of support. In this model, students receive instruction in a tiered framework usually comprising three tiers. With each tier of instruction, the level of support becomes more intensive. This model allows educators to provide these youngsters with programs that continuously respond to their

FIGURE 1.1

Continuum of educational placements for students with disabilities

Source: From *Students with Learning Disabilities* (p. 130), 7th ed., by C. D. Mercer and P. C. Pullen, 2009, Upper Saddle River, NJ: Merrill/Pearson. Copyright 2009 by Pearson Education. Reprinted by permission.

unique needs. In the RTI model, the general education teacher provides the Tier 1 and Tier 2 instruction in the general education classroom. If a student needs more intensive support, he or she may receive a portion of the instruction outside the general education setting. General education class-based services and related practices, which most frequently involve students with learning problems, are presented next.

The General Education Class

A high percentage of students who have the ability to learn the basic curriculum spend most of their time in general education classes. In this placement, the student spends most of the day with youngsters of the same age.

The key to success for the student with disabilities placed in the general education classroom is the general education classroom teacher. Factors that deserve consideration include the teacher's attitude toward having a student with a disability in the classroom, the teacher's

judgment of the student's capacity to make progress, the teacher's ability to deal with peer acceptance problems, and the teacher's skill in dealing with the emotional behavior and problems that may result from the student's inability to compete academically with other students. Unfortunately, many teachers have negative feelings regarding students with learning problems. For example, attitudinal surveys of general education classroom teachers regarding students with disabilities suggest high levels of rejection and low levels of attachment (Cook, Cameron, & Tankersley, 2007).

myeducationlab

Go to the Assignments and Activities section of the Topic IEP's in the MyEducationLab for your course and complete the activity entitled Access to the General Education Classroom.

In the RTI model, general education teachers also are responsible for implementing individualized instruction and administering ongoing progress monitoring assessments. Individualized instruction should address the unique needs of the individual, and appropriate modifications and accommodations are likely to be required. It is apparent that the general education classroom teacher has an enormous responsibility, and it is important that these teachers receive preparation and useful support (e.g., teacher assistance teams or coaching). Moreover, a student with a learning difficulty should not be placed in a general education classroom with a teacher who does not believe that the student will profit.

Special Materials and Consultation Occasionally, a teacher can manage with the help of additional materials such as a supplementary reading series, learning strategy materials, computer-assisted instruction, content enhancement materials, or manipulative materials for math. To be successful, the teacher must have a reasonable student–teacher ratio (e.g., mid-20s-to-1 or lower), especially in the earlier grades. The special education teacher or other service provider also may be provided with limited consultation. Consultation may consist of demonstrating the use of materials or equipment, performing an assessment, developing specific learning strategies, or providing an in-service program. Collaborative consultation is a service that should be inherent in all general class-based service alternatives. (Consultation skills are discussed later in this chapter.)

Itinerant Services General education teachers sometimes have students in class whose difficulties are not severe enough to warrant resource room instruction or special-class placement. In such cases, an itinerant teacher usually visits the schools periodically and focuses on teaching skills and special materials. These consultation services range from daily to biweekly visits, with the classroom teacher still having the basic responsibility for the student. Obviously, the itinerant teacher must carefully schedule visits to avoid interrupting the activities of the general education classroom teacher. Occasionally, itinerant services are bolstered by volunteers or teacher paraprofessionals.

Resource Room Assistance Many students with learning problems spend the majority of the day in a general education class and go to the resource room for a specified period of time (e.g., 45 to 60 minutes) each day. The resource room teacher works closely with numerous teachers to coordinate the instructional programs of the students. The resource room teacher typically provides daily services to about 20 to 30 students with disabilities and their respective teachers; thus, the role demands a highly competent, personable individual.

Resource room teachers should provide the following support services to general educators.

1. Attend parent conferences
2. Meet informally to discuss student progress
3. Provide remedial instruction in the resource room
4. Provide information on behavioral characteristics
5. Provide academic assessment data
6. Schedule meetings to evaluate student progress
7. Provide materials for the classroom
8. Suggest materials for the classroom
9. Provide written reports of students' activities and progress

Because many of these services require consultation from resource room teachers, in-service and preservice programs should emphasize the development of consultation skills.

Most students with learning disabilities are served in one of three types of resource room models: categorical, cross-categorical, or noncategorical. Categorical programs serve only students with learning disabilities. Cross-categorical programs serve exceptional students from several categorical areas (i.e., educable mentally retarded, emotionally disabled, and learning disabled). Noncategorical programs meet the educational needs of students with mild learning problems, whether classified as disabled or not. These programs are becoming more common; the national trend for teacher certification also is increasingly noncategorical in nature (Katsiyannis, Zhang, & Conroy, 2003).

From a review of the research, Smith (2004) reports that some research supports the effectiveness of resource room services in increasing the attending behavior and academic achievement of the students served. Moreover, she notes that teacher and student perceptions of progress and personal-social adjustment of students attending resource rooms do not appear to diminish. Smith, however, notes that the resource room model has several disadvantages associated with pulling students out of their general education classes, including the following:

- The student may miss valuable lessons in the general education class while attending the resource room.
- The student may miss some enjoyable activities (e.g., music, physical education, and art) in the general education class while attending the resource room.

- The student may feel stigmatized for leaving the general education classroom to receive special help.
- The resource room teacher and the general education classroom teacher may fail to coordinate instruction.

To deal with these disadvantages, push-in models as opposed to pullout models are being developed. In the push-in models, the resource room teacher provides instruction in the general education classroom. The resource room teacher's activities may include working with an individual student, team teaching with the general education teacher (i.e., by teaching the entire class independently or together), and teaching small groups of students in certain content areas. When the resource room teacher works with *all* students periodically, the stigma associated with having a teacher only for students who have learning problems is decreased. As previously mentioned, these integrated arrangements have yielded equivocal academic gains with less cost than resource room programs.

Reintegration of Students

To meet the requirements of educating students with learning problems in their least restrictive or most enabling environment, educators must constantly evaluate each student's needs and progress to determine whether a placement change is appropriate, especially if the student's needs appear to warrant a less restrictive service model. Thus, for students in more restrictive placements, educators frequently must examine the feasibility of reintegrating each student successfully into the general education classroom. Critics maintain that too many students with disabilities are identified, labeled, and placed in special education settings without appropriate emphasis given to changing these students' programs or returning these students to general education. Furthermore, recent legislation ensures that students receive instruction that is based on scientific research. The intent of the law is to eliminate students being over-identified as a result of poor instruction. The RTI model provides the framework to ensure that each student receives evidenced-based instruction before placement in an alternate program or setting.

Educators need to consider the social consequences of integrating students who have disabilities with students without disabilities. Essential social skills should be taught to students with disabilities to ensure that students without disabilities will not be negative toward them. Social skills that are considered critical to successful functioning in elementary general education settings include competencies related to interacting positively with others, obeying class rules, and displaying proper work habits. Although there are numerous similarities among the competencies needed to succeed in elementary and secondary settings, the expectations for success in the higher grades often are more stringent regarding classroom decorum and behavior.

Ellett (1993) surveyed secondary teachers to determine student skills and behaviors that they considered necessary for success in general education classrooms. She developed the following rank ordering of student competencies (i.e., skills or behaviors) important to success in secondary classes.

1. Follows directions in class
2. Comes to class prepared with materials
3. Uses class time wisely
4. Makes up assignments and tests
5. Treats teachers and peers with courtesy
6. Completes and turns in homework on time
7. Works cooperatively in student groups
8. Completes tests with a passing grade
9. Appears interested in content
10. Takes notes in class
11. Scans a textbook for answers and information
12. Volunteers to answer questions in class
13. Writes neatly
14. Is able to give oral reports and speeches

It is apparent that academic and social skills criteria provide placement teams with critical information for determining whether the student is ready to be reintegrated into the general education classroom.

Specific guidelines for reintegration include the following:

- Help students and parents adjust to modifications or a reduction of special education services.
- Include the respective teachers and solicit their observations of the student in relation to placement decisions.
- Use fading techniques when changing placements.
- Be sure the new classroom teacher can make the necessary minor adjustments (Ellett, 1993).
- Make certain the exiting criteria include the same variables used in identifying and placing the student.

Obviously, dismissal from a special education program originates from a reevaluation of the student's needs and progress. The IEP format offers the teacher an excellent opportunity to examine the possibility of reintegration. If observations indicate that a change is warranted, the teacher can initiate a meeting or reevaluate the existing IEP.

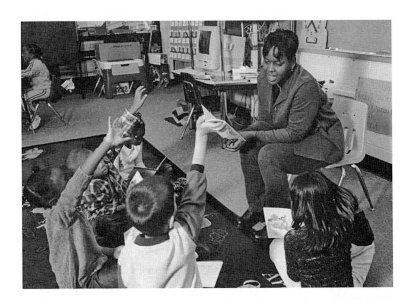

Success in learning is the key variable in any classroom setting.
T. Lindfors/Lindfors Photography

MOVEMENT FROM MAINSTREAMING TO INCLUSION

When Public Law 94-142 was passed in 1975, it mandated that students with disabilities be provided services in their least restrictive environment. Restriction was interpreted in terms of the amount of time students were educated in classes with their peers without disabilities. Thus, the term *mainstreaming* developed from the least restrictive environment concept and referred to the practice of integrating students with disabilities socially and instructionally into general education classrooms as much as possible. Mainstreaming was implemented in collaboration with the continuum of special education placement options listed previously in this chapter. Although some students with mild disabilities remained in part-time and full-time special classes, the most popular service delivery format was the resource room. Most students with mild disabilities attended the resource room for one or two periods a day and remained in general education classes for the remainder of the day. In the resource room, the students received special help as outlined in their IEPs. The dual system of general education placements supported with selected special education placements continued without serious challenges until 1986. Beginning in 1986, the Regular Education Initiative (REI) promoted the position that students with disabilities be educated in general education classes without pullout special education services.

The Regular Education Initiative

Madeleine Will, Assistant Secretary for the Office of Special Education and Rehabilitative Services in the Reagan administration, and other educators (Reynolds, 1989; Stainback & Stainback, 1987; Wang, Reynolds, & Walberg, 1986) promoted a system of service delivery to special education students referred to as the Regular Education Initiative. The REI included major revisions in how services are provided to students with learning disabilities. It maintained that a dual system of general and special education is not necessary and that students with learning disabilities can be served more effectively within the general education setting. In essence, the REI recommended that the continuum of special education service alternatives be eliminated and that students with learning disabilities, as well as other special education students, be served totally within the general education classroom.

The REI emerged because Will (1986) and several of her colleagues (Wang et al., 1986) maintained that negative consequences occur when special education students are separated from their peers without disabilities to receive instructional services. Specifically, Will offered the following statements as a rationale for the REI.

- Some students with learning or behavioral problems who need special services do not qualify for special education.
- Students are stigmatized when placed in special education settings that separate them from their normally achieving classmates.
- Special education students usually are identified after they develop serious learning problems; therefore, the emphasis is on failure rather than prevention.
- The special education system, with its eligibility requirements and rigid rules, may not lead to cooperative school–parent relationships.

The REI stimulated much debate and discussion among special educators. It was agreed that general and special educators need to coordinate their services and educate special education students according to their least restrictive environment; however, there was much concern about completely changing the current continuum of services available through special education. During the latter part of the 1980s, the REI position became part of the inclusion movement.

The Inclusion Movement

During the early 1990s, the REI position gained substantial momentum within the context of inclusion. The inclusion movement, however, highlighted the social value of inclusive classes and the need to place individuals with severe disabilities in general education classes (Fuchs & Fuchs, 1994). Also, the inclusion movement stressed strong opposition to the continuum of placements. Likewise, opposition to educating students with and without disabilities in general education classes without the continuum of alternative placements increased. This section examines the relative positions on where students with disabilities should be educated.

PEARSON
myeducationlab

Go to the Assignments and Activities section of the Topic Inclusive Practice in the MyEducationLab for your course and complete the activity entitled Exploring Inclusion. As you watch the video and answer the accompanying questions, note how the goals of the inclusion movement are being carried out.

The Inclusion Position Sapon-Shevin notes that inclusion embraces the vision that all students be served in their neighborhood schools in the general classroom with individuals their own age (O'Neil, 1994/1995). These inclusive schools are restructured to be supportive, nurturing communities that meet the needs of all individuals within them, with substantial resources and support for students and teachers. Sapon-Shevin maintains that little evidence exists to support the education of students in segregated settings. She espouses that inclusive schools are based on the belief that the world is an inclusive community with people who vary not only in terms of disabilities but in race, class, gender, and religious background. To prepare students to live in an inclusive world, it is important for them to learn and grow within communities that are similar to the world they will live in as adults. Sapon-Shevin believes that educators should begin with the assumption that all students are included and their needs will be met in inclusive settings.

The Continuum of Alternative Placements Position During the mid-1970s, the consensus of advocates for students with disabilities was that students with disabilities should be part of general education classes. This viewpoint was incorporated into Public Law 94-142 with the least restrictive environment mandate. This mandate was retained in the Individuals with Disabilities Education Act of 1990. However, Yell (1995) notes that results of litigation show that IDEA supports the continuum of placements rather than forcing the placement of students with disabilities in the general education classroom. He states, "At times, the mainstream will be the appropriate placement; however, IDEA and case law interpreting the LRE mandate are clear that for some students with disabilities, the appropriate and least restrictive setting will not be the regular education classroom . . . The most important placement factor must be the individual needs of the student" (p. 402).

The need for a continuum of alternative placements is based on the assumption that options ranging from full-time placement in general education classrooms to placement in special residential schools or hospitals are essential to meet the diverse needs of students with disabilities. Kauffman notes that educators must justify every placement decision, inclusive or otherwise (O'Neil, 1994/1995). He states, "Sure, we ought to meet special needs in a regular class when that's possible. But there isn't anything wrong with meeting special needs outside the regular class if that is required. In fact, the law and best practice say we must consider both possibilities" (O'Neil, 1994/1995, p. 7).

In essence, the continuum of alternative placements position assumes that students with disabilities need optional placements to learn in a manner commensurate with their potential. Prescriptive educations are needed to help them become independent and productive members of society. An inspection of the two positions reveals that both support the idea of educating students in general education classes. The inclusion position adopts a general education class placement only, whereas the continuum of alternative placements position recommends the continuation of placement options.

Rationale for Inclusion

Statements of the rationale for inclusion include the following:

• Many inclusionists believe that placing students in integrated or inclusive settings is morally right. Stainback, Stainback, East, and Sapon-Shevin (1994) state that many educators think that grouping students homogeneously based on a common characteristic is inappropriate for moral reasons involving equality.

- Both identification and consequent labeling of students within special education categories harm students. Labels lower students' self-esteem and cause others to develop biased viewpoints (e.g., lower expectations) toward them. Inclusion decreases the need to label.
- The efficacy of placing students categorically identified in special education placements apart from general education has not been established.
- According to Sapon-Shevin, placing students outside general education lessens schoolwide efforts to develop responsible inclusive settings for serving students with disabilities (O'Neil, 1994/1995).
- Through collaboration among special educators, general educators, parents, and other service providers, the educational needs of all students can be met in general education classes.
- Placing students with and without disabilities together provides educators with opportunities to teach youngsters to understand and appreciate individual differences. Sapon-Shevin notes that these experiences help prepare students to function in inclusive societies (O'Neil, 1994/1995).

There is a great deal of conviction and passion surrounding the inclusion movement. Baker, Wang, and Walberg (1994/1995) state, "As schools are challenged to effectively serve an increasingly diverse student population, the concern is not *whether* to provide inclusive education, but *how to implement* inclusive education in ways that are both feasible and effective in ensuring schooling success for all children, especially those with special needs" (p. 34). Moreover, Sapon-Shevin believes that "inclusion is much bigger than special education, much bigger than individual classrooms; it's even much bigger than the school. Inclusion really calls for a fundamental restructuring of the school districts and the schools" (O'Neil, 1994/1995, p. 9).

Rationale for Continuum of Alternative Placements

Statements of the rationale for continuum of alternative placements include the following:

- The general education class placement and the continuum of placements apart from general education are necessary to meet the intense and diverse needs of students with disabilities.
- The history of special education documents the enormous efforts that parents, legislators, educators, and organizations have expended in securing these varied and intense service delivery alternatives. Inclusion threatens the loss of service options that advocates have spent years obtaining.

- The availability of the continuum of alternative placements has been mandated by law since 1975. The mandate reflects the wishes of many parents, educators, and legislators, and the loss of these service options violates the civil rights of students with disabilities (Kauffman & Hallahan, 1995).
- Research regarding the continuum of placements has serious methodological problems and was conducted so long ago that it has little relevance to current practices in special classes (Hallahan & Kauffman, 1994).
- General education teachers are not prepared to work with students who have disabilities. In many cases, the present system does not provide quality education to general education students; thus, in its present form, it would not incorporate the educational needs of students with learning and achievement problems.
- Many general educators do not support inclusion. Albert Shanker (1994/1995), president of the American Federation of Teachers, questions how teachers can meet the extraordinary demands of teaching in an inclusive classroom when they already are overburdened with overcrowded classes, persistent social problems, a diversity of learners, and a lack of training to teach students with various disabilities.
- There is no clear evidence that inclusion is appropriate for all students with disabilities, and evidence of its benefit for average and above-average students is lacking.

Research on the Inclusion and Continuum of Alternative Placements Issue

A solid research base has not been established regarding the efficacy of service alternatives to students with disabilities. Methodological problems, conflicting research results, and the changing demographics (e.g., increasing diversity) of America's schools make it difficult to interpret and apply earlier studies to today's schools.

The Adaptive Learning Environments Model (ALEM) was developed as a program to demonstrate the feasibility of inclusion. The ALEM is a large-scale, full-time inclusion program in which students who are nondisabled, disabled, and at risk are integrated in the general education classroom. While its advocates (Reynolds, Wang, & Walberg, 1987; Wang & Zollers, 1990) report that the ALEM is successful, other researchers (Bryan, 1988; Fuchs & Fuchs, 1988) are less positive and believe that it is premature to endorse a merger of general and special education. Kauffman and Hallahan (1993) note that the ALEM has not been effective in meeting the needs of students with mild-to-moderate disabilities.

Efficacy of Inclusion From 1989 to 1993, the Office of Special Education and Rehabilitative Services supported four research projects to study the education of students with mild disabilities within the general education classroom. The four projects were led by the following researchers: Sharon Vaughn and Jeanne Schumm at the University of Miami; Keith Lenz, Jean Schumaker, and Don Deshler at the University of Kansas; Sue Gordon, Maureen Riley, and Catherine Morocco at the Education Development Center in Newton, Massachusetts; and Lynn Fuchs and Douglas Fuchs at Vanderbilt University. The research teams represented varying philosophical positions, used different research methodologies, and involved hundreds of elementary and secondary teachers from numerous curriculum areas. Amazingly, from this kaleidoscope of differences emerged a common core of vital findings about some of the challenges that teachers face when they attempt to educate a class of academically diverse students. The Joint Committee on Teacher Planning for Students with Disabilities (1995) reports the following four common themes.

Theme 1:   *Teachers are sensitive to and concerned about at-risk students in their classes.* The researchers found that teachers were greatly concerned about students in their classes who struggled to meet academic demands. These attitudes existed among elementary and secondary teachers. Unfortunately, many of the teachers were perplexed about what to do when some students failed to keep up with the rest of the class.

Theme 2:   *Specific instructional procedures and tools are workable and effective for most students in general education classrooms.* Several planning strategies and instructional approaches were developed by the researchers for use in general education classrooms. The researchers found that when teachers were given sufficient instruction and opportunities to receive feedback regarding their applications, they were able to incorporate the strategies and approaches successfully into their instructional activities. Teachers were satisfied with the new procedures, and the majority of students, including high, middle, and low achievers, benefited. The following procedures highlight some of the features of the varied instructional approaches.

- Teachers viewed students from a holistic perspective and shared the results of their teaching and discussed ways to meet unique needs of diverse students.

- Teachers used self-questions to guide them in planning and structuring lesson content in ways that enable all students to learn.
- Teachers used classwide peer tutoring and curriculum-based measurement to afford more opportunities for individually focused intensive instruction.
- Teachers selected the critical content and used graphic organizers to structure the content in learner-friendly ways.

Theme 3:   *Consideration must be given to the complex realities of the general education classroom setting when planning a program to meet the needs of students with disabilities.* Instructional procedures that were most readily adopted were those most easily incorporated into the flow of existing routines and those perceived as benefiting all students in the classroom. Some of the realities facing general education teachers included pressure to cover a lot of content, raise the performance level of learners, teach large groups, prepare for multiple classes with little planning time during the school day, and work with other teachers and staff without much time for collaboration. Pressure escalates when parents and community leaders claim that instructional programming for inclusive classrooms risks compromising the quality of education for students without disabilities.

Theme 4:   *Some students with mild disabilities did not benefit from the adjustments made in the general education classroom.* A few students across all projects did not benefit from the instructional procedures. The researchers offered the following as plausible explanations for the lack of achievement.

- The instructional procedures lacked the power to influence the performance of certain students.
- The classroom teacher lacked the training to individualize instruction for unique learners.
- Because of the pressure to cover the content in the curriculum, the classroom teacher did not have sufficient time for the students to achieve mastery.
- The demands of the class were so extensive that the teacher overlooked the difficulties of students with disabilities and assumed that learning had occurred.
- The students with disabilities were absent frequently.

Basically, the demands of the inclusive classroom were so extensive that teachers had neither the time nor the energy to ensure that all students mastered the skills or content. The numerous pressures combine to create a difficult setting within which teachers are able to meet the needs of students with disabilities who have unique, and often severe, learning deficits.

The researchers from the four projects overwhelmingly reached the following consensus: "In order for students with disabilities to be successfully included in the general education classroom, educators need to think in terms of 'supported inclusion,' not simply 'inclusion'" (Joint Committee on Teacher Planning for Students with Disabilities, 1995, p. 5). The researchers provide the following set of instructional conditions to implement supported inclusion.

- Teachers must be philosophically committed to meeting the needs of all students in the general education classroom.
- Teachers must have time to plan and think about the needs of diverse learners.
- Teaching practices that meet the needs of all students must be incorporated into the instructional program.
- General education teachers must collaborate with special education teachers to assess, teach, and monitor student progress.
- Short-term, intensive instruction from a special education teacher needs to be available for some students with disabilities.
- Sustained instruction in basic skills or learning strategies that cannot be provided in general education classes must be available to some students with disabilities.

In essence, supported inclusion promotes the process of educating as many students as possible in the general education class. For those students who fail to make acceptable progress in the general education class, however, short-term and long-term instruction in alternative settings is recommended.

More recent research appears to show additional implications for serving students with mild disabilities; however, the research results are conflicting regarding the efficacy of inclusion. For example, Rea, McLaughlin, and Walther-Thomas (2002) studied the outcomes for middle school students with learning disabilities in inclusive and pullout programs and found that students served in inclusive classrooms earned higher grades, achieved higher or comparable scores on standardized tests, committed no more behavioral infractions, and attended more days of school than students served in the pullout program. However, Klingner, Vaughn, Hughes, Schumm, and Elbaum (1998) examined the academic progress of elementary-level students with and without learning disabilities placed full-time in general education classes and report that although some students with learning disabilities made considerable gains over the school year, others showed no improvement. Also, fewer low- and average-achieving students improved than students with learning disabilities. Moreover, in their study of students' perceptions of inclusion and resource room settings, Vaughn and Klingner (1998) found that the majority of students with learning disabilities preferred to receive specialized instruction outside of the general education classroom for part of the school day. Also, a literature review indicates that when students with disabilities are placed in inclusive settings, their teachers are unlikely to alter their whole-group instructional strategies in favor of specific individualized adaptations (Scott, Vitale, & Masten, 1998). It appears that to meet the needs of all students with disabilities, a range of educational models must be provided and the placement of each child individually according to his or her unique needs must be considered.

Perspective on the Movement from Mainstreaming to Inclusion

Although inclusion has theoretical appeal and promising directions, existing realities remind professionals and parents that it is premature to eliminate the continuum of alternative placements. Educators have not yet widely implemented the rapidly accruing knowledge and technology about teaching in general or special education settings. The proverbial gap between research and practice is larger than ever. No more structural changes in the current system are needed until the quality of instruction in all settings is improved.

There is evidence that students with disabilities, as well as other students with learning problems, are not making acceptable progress. It is apparent that business-as-usual is not acceptable in either general or special education settings. Changes in the delivery of services to problem learners are needed to improve the quality of instruction at the classroom level, and they must be implemented according to a systematic plan. Keogh (1994, p. 68) provides insight into the change process:

> We are now in a time of enormous change, and the potential for progress is real. At the same time, there are many threats to progress, some from social/political and economic conditions, others from conflicts and dissensions within our profession. Real progress requires that we address both policy and research issues. As a start I . . . suggest that we are forced to think.

Citizens, educators, and parents all want schools in which every student receives an appropriate education in a safe and caring environment. All individuals also want a society whose diverse members value one another's rights and cultures. To accomplish these visions, educators must maintain the passion for ideals but retain the wisdom that comes from an awareness of the realities of educating a diverse population with limited funds. It is not a time for segregation through fanaticism and bitterness. Division fueled by antagonism weakens the educational profession and makes it vulnerable to funding cuts and movements not in the best interests of students or teachers. It is time to work together toward the shared goal of educating all students. Also, it is time to realize that many individuals feel strongly about both the inclusion ideas and the need for a continuum of alternative placements. Keogh (1994) challenges educators to stop and think. Thinking is enhanced through listening; thus, educators should listen and then think about what parents and peers are saying during these troubled times in special education. The following quotes deserve attention and thought.

- According to Kauffman (1994), "Hirschman (1986) observed that many who become impatient with the social welfare programs of government—of which general and special education are examples—offer radical reform or restructuring as the solution to problems that are correctable through patient, deliberate improvements within the current structure. The popular, structuralist approach to reform, however, typically leads to disappointment because only the structure changes; actual treatment, the hardest thing to change, is not modified as the structure changes" (p. 617).
- Sapon-Shevin states, "I have never, ever met a parent of a child with disabilities who did not hope that the child would someday have friends and connections with the broader community" (O'Neil, 1994/1995, p. 7).
- Morse (1994) notes, "Special education is declared a caring profession, yet little is said about the rehabilitative function of teacher caring as an essential special education ingredient, even in the discussion of the increasing number of children stultified by not being cared for . . . Caring by consultation requires even more imaginative extension. Yet caring is what many special children most need" (p. 538).
- Brandt (1994/1995) concludes, "I endorse the testimony of numerous pioneering educators and satisfied parents that it works—under the right conditions. But I also concede that conditions are often far from right in many schools. Looking at the arguments for and against inclusion . . . I think of Tevye in the musical *Fiddler on the Roof* saying, 'He's right—but she's also right'" (p. 3).
- Wilmore (1994/1995), an educator and parent of a child with disabilities, states, "Every committee must think, What if this child were my child? Think about the child's tomorrows. Think about what we

do now that will affect those tomorrows. We can't afford to make mistakes" (p. 62).

PROGRAM FACTORS AND LEAST RESTRICTIVE ENVIRONMENT

In School A, placing a student with learning disabilities in an inclusive program may be the least restrictive environment, whereas in School B, part-time placement in a resource room would be the least restrictive environment for the same student. This scenario exists because the quality of services varies across districts, schools, teachers, and placements. School A has several general education teachers who are excellent at tailoring instruction to meet the needs of the student with learning disabilities. School B has a learning disabilities resource teacher who does an excellent job of teaching students to achieve academic gains and use learning strategies to become more independent learners. Unfortunately, the general education teachers at School B are not sensitive to the instructional needs of students with learning disabilities. It is apparent that some general education teachers receive students with learning problems and tailor instruction appropriately, while other teachers respond negatively to inclusion. In a study of teachers' attitudes toward students with disabilities in their inclusive elementary classrooms, Cook, Tankersley, Cook, and Landrum (2000) report that students with disabilities were significantly overrepresented both in concern nominations ("If you could devote all your attention to a child who concerns you a great deal, whom would you pick?") and in rejection nominations ("If your class were to be reduced by one child, whom would you be relieved to have removed?").

Bender, Vail, and Scott (1995) report that teachers with less positive attitudes toward inclusion use effective instructional strategies for students with learning problems less frequently. Adaptive instruction used in inclusive settings should include the following instructional features to promote successful inclusion.

- An instructional match is maintained for each student.
- Individualized pacing for achieving instructional goals is maintained.
- Student progress is monitored, and continuous feedback is provided.
- Students are involved in the planning and monitoring of their learning.
- A broad range of techniques and materials is used.
- Students help one another to learn.
- Students are taught self-management skills.
- Teachers engage in instructional teaming.

To enable access to the general education curriculum, King-Sears (2001) provides guidelines for helping teachers determine how accessible their general education curriculum is for students with mild to moderate disabilities and includes suggestions for strengthening the curriculum and making curriculum modifications. When the instructional and social needs of students with disabilities are met in inclusive settings, it is the most appropriate placement. The question of what constitutes an effective inclusive program is becoming increasingly important. Fortunately, several researchers are investigating the factors of effective inclusive environments. Ysseldyke and Christenson (2002) developed the *Functional Assessment of Academic Behavior* to help educators evaluate learning environments. This scale was developed, in part, on empirically based teaching practices that facilitate positive student outcomes for learners with mild disabilities.

This section features program factors that promote the successful inclusion or successful academic achievement of students with mild disabilities. Topics include teachers teaching teachers, the special education or at-risk teacher, and teacher–parent collaboration.

myeducationlab

Go to the Assignments and Activities section of the Topic Inclusive Practice in the MyEducationLab for your course and complete the activity entitled Inclusion and the Least Restrictive Environment.

Teachers Teaching Teachers

The Individuals with Disabilities Education Act has had a widespread effect on the identification, instructional, and placement practices in special education. For example, collaboration between general education teachers and special education teachers is required. The addition of the response to intervention model (RTI) in the identification and intervention process in the 2006 IDEA regulations has solidified the general educator's importance in collaborating with special education teachers. It is the responsibility of educators to employ the interactive framework established by IDEA to ensure that all students are educated in the least restrictive environment and that all students have received intervention based on scientific research before a change of placement is made.

In addition to the need for general and special education teachers to collaborate to meet the diverse needs

of students with disabilities, there are other compelling reasons for working together. For example, the information explosion necessitates a need for shared expertise. Also, the increasing trend toward site-based management implies that administrators, teachers, parents, and community members must be able to make responsible decisions concerning school quality. Various special education/general education "teaching teams" have emerged to meet the challenge of educating students with disabilities in the general education classroom. Moreover, Robert Fulghum (1988) reminds us of the importance of helping one another: "And it is still true, no matter how old you are—when you go out into the world, it is best to hold hands and stick together" (p. 6).

A teachers-helping-teachers approach focuses on meeting the needs of students with disabilities within the general education class before considering formal special education services and more segregated placements. Much of the promise of these activities rests on the assumption that, in a supportive and trusting environment, teachers can support and teach one another to individualize instruction better. Consequently, as teachers become more competent, the general education setting improves for students with disabilities and referrals to special education decrease.

Strategies for Increasing Consultation Time
Specific strategies for increasing consultation time have been implemented successfully at the elementary, middle, and secondary school levels (West & Idol, 1990). These strategies include the following:

- Create times when large numbers of students can be brought together for grade-level or schoolwide activities under the supervision of a few teachers.
- Have the principal regularly teach one period a day.
- Cluster students working on similar assignments into larger groups under the supervision of a few teachers.
- Hire a permanent substitute who "floats" from classroom to classroom as needed.
- Designate a specific time each week for staff collaboration.
- Designate one day each month or one day per grading period as "Collaboration Day."
- Extend the school day for about 20 minutes twice weekly to provide collaboration periods for teachers.

West and Idol (1990) note that numerous different and creative strategies have been used to support collaborative consultation. Developing strategies to create time for consultation requires more than administrative and logistical support. The collegial problem-solving process must be valued by both teachers and administrators (West & Idol, 1990). Finally, some of the components that are needed to develop and maintain effective consultations include adequate time, administrative support, combining the strengths of professionals, and the use of language that all participants understand (Olson, Platt, & Dieker, 2008).

Collaborative Consultation

Collaborative problem solving aimed at preventing student learning and behavioral problems offers a viable alternative to the overused and costly refer–test–place paradigm. The most apparent needs are for more collaboration with general education teachers and other special program teachers, the coordination of special education with other programs and services, and an improved relationship between general and special education.

West and Idol (1990) point out the differences between consultative and collaborative relationships. In consultative relationships, one professional confers with another to seek guidance. In collaborative relationships, two or more professionals work together with parity and reciprocity to solve problems. When collaborative consultation initially was conceptualized as a special education service model, the following definition emerged (Idol, Paolucci-Whitcomb, & Nevin, 1986, p. 1):

> Collaborative consultation is an interactive process which enables people with diverse expertise to generate creative solutions to mutually defined problems. The outcome is enhanced, altered, and different from the original solutions that any team member would produce independently. The major outcome of collaborative consultation is to provide comprehensive and effective programs for students with special needs within the most appropriate context, thereby enabling them to achieve maximum constructive interaction with their nonhandicapped peers.

In essence, mutual empowerment is an important goal of educational collaboration.

The major goals of collaborative consultation are to prevent behavioral and learning problems, ameliorate learning and behavioral problems, and coordinate instructional programs (West, Idol, & Cannon, 1988). For collaborative consultation to be most effective, a formal set of problem-solving stages is recommended. The most commonly accepted stages (Idol et al., 1986; West et al., 1988) include the following:

Stage 1: *Goal/entry*. Roles, objectives, responsibilities, and expectations of the consultant and consulter are negotiated.

Stage 2: *Problem identification*. The problem is defined clearly and discussed until all members have a mutual understanding of the problem.

Stage 3: *Intervention recommendations*. Interventions are generated and prioritized in the expected order of implementation. Written, measurable objectives are developed to detail specific interventions for each aspect of the problem, establish criteria to determine whether the problem has been solved, and spell out the roles of the student and respective team members and identify appropriate resources needed for delivering interventions.

Stage 4: *Implementation recommendations*. Implementation is provided according to established objectives and activities. Timelines and respective personnel responsible for selected interventions are specified. In the collaborative model, the consultant typically assumes a modeling role that phases out as the consulter gains expertise and confidence with the intervention.

Stage 5: *Evaluation*. The success of the intervention strategies is assessed. This assessment includes measures of the student, consultant, consulter, and system change.

Stage 6: *Redesign*. The intervention is continued, modified, or discontinued based on the evaluation of the intervention strategies.

West and Idol (1990) report that team consensus is reached at each stage before going to the next step. Moreover, they note that adherence to the stages allows for a systematic and efficient approach to solving problems.

Collaborative consultation may occur as a simple problem-solving process in a variety of contexts. Educational reforms are being suggested and demanded to provide learners who have disabilities with appropriate educational programs in their least restrictive environments. Many educators are calling for general and special educators to work together more closely to serve students with learning and behavioral problems. Consequently, many team approaches have been developed in which collaborative consultation may occur. Some models include assistance teams (Chalfant & Pysh, 1989), coaching (Showers, 1985), peer collaboration (Pugach & Johnson, 1988), and cooperative teaching (Bauwens & Hourcade, 1995).

Assistance Teams

Assistance teams provide an opportunity for professionals to work together to solve problems and develop strategies and working plans for students with academic or behavioral difficulties. Various models exist and may be called *teacher assistance teams*, *intervention teams*, or *problem-solving teams*. Regardless of the name, these models focus on a team approach to problem solving and are an integral part of the RTI process (Kovaleski & Glew, 2006). The following steps are comprised in most assistance team models: identification of a problem and the request for a team; analysis and statement of the academic or behavioral problem; collection of baseline data and setting of a specific measurable goal; design and implementation of an evidence-based intervention; ongoing monitoring of student progress toward the goal; and evaluation of the responsiveness to the intervention (Bahr & Kovaleski, 2006). These steps have remained a part of the problem-solving team approach from earlier iterations of prereferral teams to the current practices in response to intervention (RTI).

Early research on the teacher assistance team (TAT) (Chalfant & Pysh, 1989) demonstrated that reductions were noted in the number of inappropriate referrals to special education and an increase in the resolution of many students' problems. Furthermore, teachers who were part of the teams were generally satisfied with the process and their involvement on the teams. A large-scale study of more than 1,700 schools in Pennsylvania demonstrated that instructional support teams can be implemented district-wide and that the implementation of instructional support teams results in improved learning for students and decreased referrals to special education (Kovaleski & Glew, 2006).

It has also been noted that the team problem-solving approach is beneficial to minority students (Gravois & Rosenfield, 2006) and English language learners (Ortiz, Wilkinson, Robertson-Courtney, & Kushner, 2006). Minority students, including those who are culturally and linguistically diverse, are represented disproportionately in special education. Support teams may offer teachers the necessary support and expertise to provide appropriate intervention and prevent the misidentification of a disability. In a study examining the use of intervention teams, the number of minority students referred for special education services was reduced significantly (Gravois & Rosenfield, 2006).

Coaching   *Peer coaching* is a form of professional development that includes an instructional coach who provides one-on-one support to a peer teacher. Most coaches focus on a specific content area (e.g., mathematics coach or reading coach). The peer coach, who typically is an experienced teacher, models lessons to demonstrate specific teaching techniques, observes and provides feedback, and assists in planning and assessment. In particular, to be most effective, coaches should assist their peer teacher in using progress monitoring assessments to make data-based instructional decisions (Denton,

Swanson, & Mathes, 2007; Jorissen, Salazar, Morrison, & Foster, 2008). The ultimate goal of peer coaching is to affect student learning or behavior outcomes. To realize this goal, specific coaching aims are to (a) improve the teacher's content knowledge, (b) increase empirically validated teaching strategies, (c) build the teacher's knowledge and skill in using assessment data to make instructional decisions, and (d) engage the teacher in reflective, inquiry-based teaching (Driscoll, 2008).

Peer coaching in reading has increased dramatically in recent years as a result of the No Child Left Behind Act (Moss, Jacob, Boulay, Horst, & Poulos, 2006). Although coaching is becoming common practice in schools, it is unclear whether the model results in significant improvements in student outcomes (Denton et al., 2007; Peterson, Taylor, Burnham, & Schock, 2009).

Peer Collaboration   One way of enhancing general education teachers' abilities to design and adapt educational interventions for students with learning problems is through peer collaboration (Pugach & Johnson, 1988). Peer collaboration is based on the assumption that when general education teachers work together using a systematic problem-solving strategy, they can develop appropriate instructional and behavioral interventions for all of their students.

Peer collaboration involves pairs of teachers who engage in a highly structured dialogue about a problem involving a single student, a group of students, or a whole class. The structured dialogue includes opportunities for self-questioning, summarizing, and predicting with regard to the specific problem concerning the teacher. Each teacher in the dyad has a specific role. The Initiator is the teacher who shares the problem and ultimately solves the problem. The Facilitator guides the partner through each step in the dialogue to arrive at a solution. Table 1.1 presents the four steps included in the peer-collaboration process.

According to Pugach and Johnson (1988), as this process is repeated systematically, the general format of the dialogue becomes an internalized problem-solving strategy. Peer collaboration can provide general classroom teachers with a strategy to accommodate students with disabilities in the inclusive classroom. In a synthesis of their research on peer collaboration, Pugach and Johnson (1990) report that classroom teachers exhibited the following behaviors as a result of training in the peer-collaboration process.

- The focus of problem identification shifted away from the student to factors directly under the teacher's control.

TABLE 1.1
Steps included in the peer-collaboration process

Problem Description and Clarifying Questions
In this step, the Initiator provides the partner with a short, written description of the problem. Next, the Facilitator reads the problem and asks the partner whether there are any clarifying questions to be asked. For example, the written problem might be "Robert fails to complete classroom and homework assignments." The Initiator might ask questions such as, "When does the behavior occur?" or "Are there any occasions when he does complete his work?" The Facilitator also can guide the process by asking, "Are there questions you could ask yourself about his classroom and homework assignments?" The purpose of this type of probing is to lead the Initiator to a general area of the problem rather than suggest specific areas for examination. The goal is to enable the Initiator to "recognize a pattern of behavior and form a summary" (Pugach & Johnson, 1988, p. 76).

Summarizing
After the problem is clarified, the Initiator summarizes the problem. The summary includes the clarified behavior pattern of the student, the teacher's response to the behavior, and the relevant factors in the classroom environment under the teacher's control.

Interventions and Predictions
During this step, at least three possible interventions are proposed by the Initiator, and predictions are made regarding potential outcomes for each intervention. The role of the Facilitator is to help the partner arrive at an intervention that is practical and minimally disruptive to the teacher and the class.

Evaluation Plan
During the last step in the process, a reasonably simple plan is developed to document and evaluate the effectiveness of the intervention. For example, in Robert's case, the Initiator may realize that a check-off sheet for Robert to mark as he completes assignments may help him complete his work. The intervention also can include a special notebook in which Robert records all of his homework assignments. His performance on both tasks should be monitored daily for 2 weeks. Finally, the Initiator and the partner may agree to meet in two weeks to discuss whether to continue the intervention or begin the peer-collaboration process again.

- The teachers generated potential interventions for all problems targeted in a peer-collaboration session.
- The teachers effectively resolved over 85 percent of the problems targeted through peer collaboration.
- The teachers felt significantly more confident in their ability to manage classroom problems.
- Positive attitudes increased toward their class as a whole.

Cooperative Teaching The term *cooperative teaching* has been used interchangeably with *co-teaching* or *collaborative teaching*. Cooperative teaching appears to be a viable model for integrating students with disabilities into the general education setting. Bauwens and Hourcade (1995, p. 46) provide the following definition.

> Cooperative teaching refers to a restructuring of teaching procedures in which two or more educators possessing distinct sets of skills work in a coactive and coordinated fashion to jointly teach academically and behaviorally heterogeneous groups of students in educationally integrated settings, that is, in general classrooms.

Using their definition as a framework, Bauwens and Hourcade discuss three different configurations of cooperative teaching: team teaching, complementary instruction, and supportive learning activities.

In a *team-teaching* arrangement, two teachers share instructional responsibility for a common body of content-area knowledge. The general and special educator jointly plan and instruct the same academic content to all students. Negotiation is a critical feature of this process. The teachers negotiate how the content will be presented, the time frames for instruction, and specific responsibilities for each part of the unit or lesson. In *complementary instruction*, the general educator has primary responsibility for teaching specific content areas, while the special educator teaches specific strategies or skills (e.g., notetaking, summarizing, or identifying main ideas in reading) to students who need additional instruction. In contrast to the team-teaching arrangement, in which teachers share equal responsibility for the same content, the complementary instruction arrangement features separate but related responsibility for instruction. Finally, in the *supportive learning activities* arrangement, the general and special educators collaboratively determine the major content and instructional goals for any lesson. The teachers jointly identify activities to support and extend the lesson. Within the supportive learning activities arrangement, the general educator primarily is responsible for teaching the content; however, the special educator reinforces and enriches the content by implementing supportive learning activities. For example, the special educator may have expertise in computer applications to extend the mathematics unit on decimals and percents. Moreover, the special educator can enrich and support content areas through the use of interest centers.

For cooperative teaching, or co-teaching, to be implemented well, the general education teacher and the special education teacher must have a good working relationship and the two teachers must share a common or compatible philosophy and approach to the instructional process. Research on the effectiveness of co-teaching is limited; however, in a study of the perspectives of students with and without learning disabilities and their parents regarding this teaching model, Gerber and Popp (1999) found a high level of satisfaction with reports of positive results in academic grades and in self-esteem. Concerns include poor communication of the philosophy of the model to parents and the lack of continuation of the program across grade levels. In another study, Walther-Thomas (1997) reports that the benefits of co-teaching for elementary and middle school students with disabilities include positive feelings about themselves as capable learners, enhanced academic performance, improved social skills, and stronger peer relationships. The most persistent problems reported involve scheduled planning time, student scheduling, caseload concerns, administrative support, and staff development opportunities. Moreover, Rice and Zigmond (2000) note that secondary school teachers stress the importance of schoolwide commitment to inclusion principles as an important factor in the success of co-teaching.

Because many schools employ cooperative teaching arrangements to educate all students in inclusive educational programs, Salend, Gordon, and Lopez-Vona (2002) provide guidelines and strategies to examine the experiences and perceptions of cooperative teaching teams, to validate successful collaborative practices, and to identify practices in need of revision. Also, after intensive study of collaborative teaching in elementary, middle, and high school programs, Gerber and Popp (2000) offer recommendations addressing service delivery, administrative issues, and communication issues as well as training recommendations for new teachers and administrators, indirectly involved personnel, parents, and university program administrators.

Communication Skills for Collaboration In addition to being familiar with various models for collaboration, teachers need to use effective communication skills to implement collaboration successfully. Parity, shared responsibility, accountability, and mutual goals cannot be mandated. These characteristics result from reciprocal relationships among volunteers who value collaboration and believe it can work to help students and themselves. Idol and West (1991) provide the following principles of successful collaborative consultation skills.

- Create an atmosphere of mutual trust and respect so that team members feel safe in sharing information.
- Provide nonevaluative feedback when others are speaking.
- Use jargon-free language when sharing ideas.
- Be aware that nonverbal body language can communicate positive or negative messages.
- Give and receive feedback willingly and effectively, without confrontation.

Adapting and modifying teacher–teacher and teacher–student interactions and teaching repertoires demands considerable risk-taking by teachers. General and special educators who share responsibility for modifying their instruction to meet the diverse needs of students with disabilities need to establish a trusting relationship to help support their efforts toward change. Training in the principles given in Covey's (1989) *The Seven Habits of Highly Effective People* and Covey, Merrill, and Merrill's (1994) *First Things First* provides an excellent foundation to help individuals develop and maintain collaborative relationships that foster positive changes.

myeducationlab

Go to the Assignments and Activities section of the Topic Collaboration in the MyEducationLab for your course and complete the activity entitled Devoting Time to Collaboration. As you watch the video and answer the accompanying questions, consider the best ways to make time for collaboration.

The Special Education or At-Risk Teacher

Although numerous variables (e.g., funding, support, and cooperation) affect the quality of instructional services provided to students with disabilities, the teacher remains the most important influence in program quality. To deliver direct services, the special education or at-risk teacher must demonstrate the most effective empirically based assessment and teaching practices discussed in the remaining chapters of this text. To deliver indirect services, the teacher needs effective consultation skills to work with general education teachers of students with disabilities, school-based assistance teams, and parents. Because more students with disabilities are being educated in the general education classroom, the trend is moving toward using consultative services to help students succeed. Generally, the research on the outcomes of consultation appears promising for reducing referrals to special education and helping students achieve in general education classrooms (Heron & Kimball, 1988; Idol, 1988; Polsgrove & McNeil, 1989). Heron and Kimball report that "the data currently available justify consultation as an appropriate service for facilitating the education of all students in the least restrictive environment, and it is clear that the database regarding the efficacy of specific consultation practices continues to emerge" (p. 27).

Consultation Collaborative consultation represents an increasingly popular process regarding how numerous experts view the dynamics of problem solving in consultation. Special education teachers as well as general education teachers need training to become efficient in collaborative consultation. West and Cannon (1988) worked with a 100-member interdisciplinary expert panel to generate consultation competencies needed by general education and special education teachers to meet the educational needs of students with disabilities in general education classrooms. The panel identified 47 essential competencies in nine categories. The categories receiving the highest ratings were interactive communication; personal characteristics; equity issues, values, and beliefs; collaborative problem solving; and evaluation of consultation effectiveness. Staff development competencies were rated as important but not essential. Categories that received ratings indicating less importance to the consultation process were consultation theory and models, consultation research, and system change.

Idol (1988) recommends that a consulting teacher should have completed a supervised practicum experience in school consultation and should have knowledge of all types of exceptional learners, all special education service delivery models, the history of special education, and special education legislation and legal rights of exceptional persons. In addition, Idol notes that a consulting teacher should have demonstrable skills in using assessment techniques (e.g., curriculum-based assessment, criterion-referenced testing, classroom observation, and standardized tests); applying basic remediation techniques for academic skill deficits (e.g., study skills strategies); applying basic behavior management techniques for individuals as well as groups of students; applying accommodation techniques to special needs learners in general education settings (e.g., materials modification, principles of reinforcement, and computer-assisted instruction); transferring learned skills from supportive service pro-

grams to the classroom; measuring, monitoring, and evaluating academic and behavioral progress in students; and using effective communication and working collaboratively with other adults.

Viable knowledge regarding consultation is increasing, and it needs to be part of a special education teacher's preservice and staff development training. Tindal, Shinn, and Rodden-Nord (1990) provide a model that includes consideration for realistic school-based variables that influence the consultation process. This model includes 11 variables that are organized within three dimensions—people, process, and procedural implementation.

People Variables
1. Consultant background and skills—history, experiences, knowledge, resources
2. Consulter background and skills—history, experiences, knowledge, resources, teacher tolerance
3. Client background and skills—history, experiences, knowledge, resources
4. Administrator background and skills—history, experiences, knowledge, resources

Process Variables
5. Problem-solving relationship between consultant and consulter—problem identification and problem remediation
6. Theoretical perspective of consultation—behavioral, organizational, mental health
7. Stage in consultation—problem identification, problem corroboration, program development, program operationalization, program evaluation
8. Activity structure—assessment, assessment/direct intervention, assessment/indirect intervention, indirect service to system

Procedural Implementations Variables
9. Type of data—judgments, observations, tests
10. Program intervention—context, materials, interactive techniques
11. Evaluation strategies—qualitative, quantitative (i.e., individual-referenced, criterion-referenced, norm-referenced)

Tindal et al. note that the model should be used to help teachers consider important variables as they implement consultation in applied educational settings.

Teacher–Parent Collaboration

Students with learning problems are more successful when parents and teachers work collaboratively. When parents are involved with their child's education at school, the home becomes the supportive foundation

TABLE 1.2
Questions and answers for parents about RTI

What Is RTI?
RTI stands for response to intervention. It is based on the premise that all students receive excellent classroom instruction based on scientific research. Students who are not benefiting from the classroom instruction based on assessment receive more intensive intervention implemented in tiers (e.g., Tier 1, Tier, 2, and Tier 3).

What Is Tiered Instruction?
Programs and practices based on scientific research are provided to all students. This instruction is considered **Tier 1 instruction.** Students who are not making adequate progress receive additional support. The additional support is considered **Tier 2 Instruction.** Tier 2 is more intensive and could include small-group or one-on-one instruction. Each tier provides more intensive support; students who do not make progress may be referred for further evaluation and possible placement in special education.

What Is the Parents' Role in the RTI Process?
Parents have a right to be notified before special education evaluations are implemented. Depending on the RTI model that is employed in the school or district, evaluations could occur at various points in the process (e.g., after Tier 2 or Tier 3). Although it is not required that parents be notified until the student is evaluated for special education, it is best to include parents as a part of the process as early as possible.

Source: Adapted from *Students with Learning Disabilities* (p. 451), 7th ed. by C. D. Mercer and P. C. Pullen, 2009, Upper Saddle River, NJ: Merrill/Pearson. Copyright 2009 by Pearson Education. Reprinted by permission.

that the student needs to face the daily challenges encountered (Mercer & Pullen, 2009). In a survey of the 20 variables most highly rated by a team of experts as being important for learning in children, three variables involving parents emerged (Reynolds, Wang, & Walberg, 1992). These experts report that to promote learning, parents should show affection for their child, display interest in their child's schoolwork, and expect academic success.

Foremost, parents should provide the child with a home environment of warmth, acceptance, and understanding. The child needs and deserves a comfortable place to retreat from the pressures, demands, and frustrations of daily living. When parents are involved and cooperative, the home becomes the supportive foundation that the child needs to face the changing demands of school. Teachers and parents should recognize their roles as complementary and supplementary and view their relationship as a partnership to foster the child's progress. In addition, training for both parents and school personnel results in more efficacious collaborative relationships (Whitbread, Bruder, Fleming, & Park, 2007).

Establish Cooperation Teachers and parents often harbor attitudes about each other that inhibit mutual cooperation. These attitudes sometimes manifest themselves through teacher blaming or parent blaming. Such dissonance benefits no one. Its sources should be identified and strategies should be pursued to promote a cooperative and working relationship.

Initial progress toward cooperation hinges on development of mutual respect. In general, parents prefer a teacher who approaches them as individuals, treats them with dignity, and conveys a feeling of acceptance. A parent does not want to be treated as simply a parent of a child with disabilities.

Many obstacles can inhibit cooperative parent–teacher relationships. However, the common goal should enable both to transcend the obstacles and work together. The following selected activities may foster teacher–parent cooperation.

- Provide parents with information about important processes, such as response to intervention (see Table 1.2).
- Provide parents with training on how to tutor their child.
- Invite parents to volunteer in the classroom.
- Develop an informative and consistent communication system between the teacher and the parents regarding homework. Initiate communication regularly, communicate about a problem early enough to resolve it, follow through on what is said, and communicate clearly (Jayanthi, Nelson, Sawyer, Bursuck, & Epstein, 1995).
- Communicate frequently through home notes, phone messages, progress reports, parent–teacher conferences, parent nights, e-mail, and at-school events.
- Ask parents to help with academics by reading to their child, signing homework, asking about their child's school day, helping their child practice math facts or spelling words, and taking their child to the library.

- Invite parents to go on field trips or visit the classroom.
- Focus on listening to parents in an effort to gain understanding and show respect.
- Help parents become informed advocates for their child.
- Provide transportation and child care services for parents to attend school meetings or events.

Develop Culturally Responsive Relationships

The changing demography in the United States challenges educators to develop techniques for effectively engaging linguistically diverse parents. The number of language minority students (i.e., students whose first language is other than English) and students with limited English proficiency (LEP) is growing rapidly (Garcia, Jensen, & Scribner, 2009). It is estimated that nearly 11 percent of students in American schools are considered English language learners (Snipes, Soga, & Uro, 2007). Some major factors that influence these parents' involvement are length of residence in the United States, English proficiency, availability of support groups and bilingual staff, and prior experience. Moreover, teachers should learn about the family's customs, values, concerns, and expectations. Wilson and Hughes (1994) offer the following techniques for engaging these parents.

- Employ an interpreter for parent conferences.
- Print all signs, school communications, and notes in the language spoken by the family.
- Send parents a large amount of written and visual information over an extended time.
- Videotape some class activities and share them with the parents.

Parent–Teacher Conferences

Parent–teacher conferences create an environment in which parents feel they are working cooperatively with school personnel. Many school districts encourage the special education teacher to meet with the parents before the child begins receiving special education services. Early meetings with parents may help to reduce attendance problems and discipline problems, as well as to facilitate good future communication.

The initial parent–teacher conference is extremely important, and the preparation for this meeting often determines its success (Jordan, Reyes-Blanes, Peel, Peel, & Lane, 1998). To prepare, the teacher should examine the child's records and review pertinent information such as present status (i.e., chronological age, grade, class, and previous teacher), physical appearance and history, educational status, personal traits, and home and family characteristics. The teacher should also identify objectives for the meeting and develop an appropriate agenda. The conference time should be convenient for all attending, and the meeting place should be arranged to promote communication.

Successful conferences typically consist of six parts: (1) establishing rapport, (2) obtaining pertinent information from the parents, (3) providing information, (4) collaborating with parents to reach a consensus on a plan, (5) summarizing the conference and planning follow-up activities, and (6) evaluating the conference (Kroth & Edge, 1997; Salend, 2001). Starting with neutral topics and providing a comfortable seat help establish rapport. To obtain information, the teacher should state the purpose of the conference, ask open-ended questions, recognize parents' feelings by responding empathetically, and avoid irrelevancies (such as marital problems). To provide information, the teacher should start with positive statements about the child's behavior and provide samples of work when possible, avoid educational jargon, and share anticipated plans. To collaborate with parents, the information presented by both parties must be considered. Active listening and flexibility facilitate reaching a consensus on a plan. To summarize the conference, the teacher should briefly review the main points concerning the student's progress, restate the activities that will be implemented to deal with identified weaknesses and problems, and answer any questions. The teacher and parents should discuss and agree on follow-up strategies and schedule another meeting, if necessary. The conference should end on a positive note, and the teacher should thank the parents for their input and interest and offer to be available for any future questions concerning their child. Finally, evaluation consists of noting each person's satisfaction with the meeting. Sample questions include: Was a folder of the student's representative work prepared for the parents? Was the teacher able to explain the academic remediation strategy to the parents? Was the teacher able to provide an adequate report of social and emotional progress? Was the teacher able to solicit and respond to questions raised by the parents?

Listening is the key to communication, and both parties must listen. A good listener gains much information that often can help solve problems. Parents like to talk to a teacher who listens sympathetically, calmly, and nonjudgmentally. Active listening involves increased levels of responding, body animation, and questioning. Eye contact is a basic component of good listening, whereas fatigue, strong feelings, too much talking, and environmental distractions deter active listening. Simpson (1996) notes that to facilitate the communication process, the effective listener must demonstrate skills in attention, acceptance, and empathy, as well as use specific listening strategies (e.g., door-opening statements, clarifying statements, restating content, reflecting affect, silence, and summarizing). He states that "the professional who attempts to respond to parents prior to listening to them, or the educator who too hastily assumes the position of 'telling' parents what to do or 'answering' their questions when they simply desire the opportunity to talk, will rarely offer the most satisfactory conferencing relationship" (p. 120).

Parents are major stakeholders in their child's educational program and, because of the emotions involved, it is not uncommon for a teacher to encounter parental criticism or anger. Jones and Jones (1995) provide the following helpful techniques for teachers to deal with parental criticism and confrontation.

- Maintain a calm and pleasant manner.
- Use active listening and avoid becoming defensive. Look genuinely interested during the process. These behaviors defuse emotions.
- Ask what the parent wishes to accomplish.
- Set a time limit if necessary and give consideration to scheduling another meeting.
- Ask the parent whether the student is aware of the problem of concern.
- Be honest and rely on specific data.
- Let the parent know specifically what will be done to deal with the problem.

Parents as Teachers
From generation to generation, parents transmit customs, unique family habits, and traditions. Society expects parents to teach values and social skills, but should parents teach academics? The literature is mixed on the general effectiveness of parental tutoring. Some experts claim it is effective, whereas others question it. Basically, it is an individual decision that can be made intelligently if selected guidelines are followed.

Each individual must decide about home tutoring. A basic consideration is whether tutoring can be accomplished without depriving any family member of the resources (e.g., time, money, and activities) that should be directed toward maintaining a well-balanced life. Essentially, home tutoring is feasible if the overall experience is pleasant for the child and the parent.

If the decision is made to engage in parental tutoring, attention must be directed toward doing a good job. Guidelines include the following:

- Give simple instructions and precisely convey the requirements of the task.

- Be flexible regarding the length of the session. Sometimes the child will not attend to the work for a concentrated period of time. In these instances, settle for 2 to 5 minutes of concentrated work instead of insisting on completed work at the risk of creating frustration and tension.
- Maintain a tutoring log of the child's performance or a written record of observations (e.g., types of errors, questions asked, and rate of responses) made during the tutoring. These observations can be shared with the teacher and may assist in making future plans. Keeping a record of the child's progress is often helpful.
- Do not extend formal tutoring indefinitely. Periodically halt the tutoring. Supplement or replace it by incorporating the remedial tasks in everyday chores and games.
- Make an effort to select the best time for the session. Many parents report that immediately following the evening meal is a good time. Also, choose a place for the session that does not restrict the activities of the other family members and is not too distracting. Tutor at the same time and place to establish an expectation for the activity.
- Identify appropriate levels and make sure the child can complete the task. Tutoring sessions should be success oriented. Work should be challenging but not too difficult.
- Limit the length of the tutoring session to about 15 minutes for children up to grade 6 and up to 30 minutes for older students (Cummings & Maddux, 1985).
- Use creative techniques in reviewing and teaching new material, and practice activities in ways that reduce boredom.
- Let the child know when a mistake has been made but do so in a positive or neutral manner. Provide encouragement and praise the learner for trying.
- Give the child time to become familiar with the task materials. Provide the child with an overview or introduction before beginning formal instruction.
- Encourage the child to make judgments or choices on the basis of evidence rather than by guessing or appealing to authority. Give the child time to think about the problem.
- Make sure that the tutoring sessions are pleasant for both the parent and the child.

Perspective on Teacher–Parent Collaboration
With the trend toward more parental involvement in identification, placement, and educational programming, school personnel must prepare themselves to

work more closely and effectively with parents. The teacher must be supportive, sensitive, and informative during crucial parental adjustment periods. Both parties must realize that the optimal growth of the child will emerge only from a pilgrimage of problem-solving ventures. Frustration and hard work surely will accompany the search for services; however, joy likely will accompany the solution. This process beckons the teacher and the parent to develop precise assessment techniques and gather information about resources, techniques, and materials.

INSTRUCTIONAL VARIABLES RELATED TO STUDENT LEARNING

Numerous factors related to student achievement are outside of the direct control of the teacher; however, the quality of instruction within the classroom remains a major factor in student learning. Teachers and teacher educators have a responsibility to examine the research and apply the findings as they develop teacher practices. The instructional variables that follow highlight the major findings of selected research in general and special education. When a teacher incorporates these practices into daily instruction, the likelihood of improving the achievement of students increases.

Focus on Time for Learning

Successful teachers maintain a strong academic focus. Effective teachers instruct students to spend more time working directly on academic tasks in texts, workbooks, instructional materials, and peer-mediated instruction. They assign and hold students responsible for more homework and test students more frequently.

The importance of an academic focus also receives support from research on engaged time. *Engaged time* is the time a student actually spends performing an academic task (e.g., writing, reading, or computing). An extensive study of teaching activities that make a difference in student achievement was conducted as part of a 6-year Beginning Teacher Evaluation Study funded by the National Institute of Education through the California Commission for Teaching Preparation and Licensing. One of the major contributions of the study is its emphasis on academic learning time—that is, the time a student spends engaged in academic tasks of appropriate difficulty (Denham & Lieberman, 1980). As expected, the study found that academic learning time is related to student achievement. Specifically, Fisher et al. (1980) report that the time allocated to a content area is associated positively with learning in that area,

and the engaged time that students spend successfully performing reading or mathematics tasks is associated positively with learning. Thus, a cornerstone of good teaching is establishing appropriate academic instructional objectives and designing intervention programs that maximize opportunities for the student to work successfully on tasks related to the objectives (Howell & Nolet, 2000). Unfortunately, students' engaged time in many classrooms is relatively low, particularly for students who are at risk for learning or behavioral disabilities (Montague & Rinaldi, 2001).

Haynes and Jenkins (1986) examined the instruction that special education students receive in resource rooms. One of their findings revealed that the amount of reading instruction per day varied from class to class. One class received about 58 minutes a day, and another class received about 17 minutes a day. As expected, the students who spent more time in reading instruction learned more about reading. In an observation of 230 elementary students with mild disabilities, Rich and Ross (1989) found that noninstructional time (e.g., transitions, housekeeping, wait time, and free time) accounted for almost 3 hours of the school day. Moreover, researchers report that achievement and academic engagement time are greater during teacher-directed behavior than during independent work (Sindelar, Smith, Harriman, Hale, & Wilson, 1986).

The finding that academic learning time is related positively to more student learning is consistent in the research for both general education students and students with learning problems (Reynolds, 1992). To foster a positive and productive learning environment, students should spend as much time as possible engaged in meaningful academic tasks.

Gettinger (1991) found that students with learning disabilities required significantly more time to achieve mastery on a reading comprehension task than students without learning disabilities. In essence, students with learning problems need ample time for learning, high rates of success, and strategies on how to learn and retain relevant information. Greenwood (1991) used classwide peer tutoring with at-risk elementary students to increase time on academic tasks over a five-semester period. The peer tutoring group achieved academic gains that were superior to a control group of comparable students.

Researchers claim that achievement is improved in two ways: by increasing the student's learning time and by decreasing the time a student needs to learn. Instructional factors that increase engaged time or decrease time needed for learning a specific skill include relevant learning tasks, effective classroom management, clearly

TABLE 1.3
Suggestions for increasing engaged time

General Suggestions for Increasing Engaged Time
Schedule more instructional time.
Teach students to make transitions quickly.
Use effective teaching techniques.
Strive to motivate students.
Be organized and prepared.
Increase teacher instructional interactions with students.
Maintain a balance between teacher-led and seatwork time.

Suggestions for Increasing Engaged Time During Teacher-Led Instruction
Use signals to remind students to attend.
Be enthusiastic.
Maintain a brisk pace.
Illustrate content with interesting metaphors or stories.
Ask questions frequently and involve all students.
Praise students for effort and being on task.
Highlight the importance of content and its relation to daily life.

Suggestions for Increasing Engaged Time During Independent Work
Use a variety of seatwork activities, instructional games, self-correcting materials, and computer-assisted instruction.
Teach students to work independently.
Use peer tutoring pairs and classwide peer tutoring.
Make independent work relevant and meaningful.
Use cooperative learning groups.
Praise students for doing seatwork.
Check independent work for progress.
Monitor independent work through scanning and moving around the classroom.
Give clear and concise directions.
Evaluate independent work.
Post student work in the classroom.
Give independent work at each student's instructional level.

stated learning expectations, timely and specific feedback, teacher–student interaction, reinforcement for learning, and continuous monitoring to meet instructional objectives. Table 1.3 suggests ways to increase both instructional and engaged time.

Ensure High Rates of Student Success

The need for students to experience high levels of success has substantial research support. In this research, *success* refers to the rate at which the student understands and correctly completes exercises and assignments (Borich, 2007). Success is defined according to the difficulty level of the materials. In high success, the student understands the task and makes occasional careless errors. With moderate success, the student partially understands the material and makes numerous mistakes. In low success, the student does not comprehend the material. Student engagement in academic work is related highly to rate of success (i.e., instruction that produces moderate-to-high success rates results in increased achievement). Apparently, during high success more content is covered at the

learner's appropriate instructional level. The positive relationship between achievement and high success rate is documented, especially when the instruction is didactic or expository.

One of the primary findings of the Beginning Teacher Evaluation Study (Fisher et al., 1980) is that learning improves most when students have a high percentage of correct responses during teacher questioning and seatwork. A reasonable success rate appears to be at least 80 percent during instruction and 90 percent at the end of a unit. Ideally, the task should maintain an appropriate level of challenge (i.e., require effort to succeed). Fisher et al. (1980, pp. 17–18) highlight this point:

Common sense suggests that too high a rate of high-success work might be boring and repetitive and could inhibit the development of persistence. Probably, some balance between high success and more challenging work is appropriate. Also, we found that older students and/or students who were generally skilled at school learning did not require as high a percentage of time at the high-success level. Apparently these students had learned problem solving—how to take a task they did not

TABLE 1.4
Selected instructional features that promote student success

Area	Instructional Feature
Content	Is useful or relevant
	Is clearly specified
	Is instructionally organized for easy learning
Assessment	Enables appropriate placement
	Provides frequent feedback regarding programs
	Leads to the establishment of realistic but high goals
Learning Experience	Allows ample time for learning
	Provides support to facilitate learning
	Lets students actually experience high rates of progress
	Reinforces achievements and efforts
Self-Regulation	Permits students to work independently
	Permits students to self-monitor their progress in some lessons
	Allows students to participate in goal setting and the selection of some activities
Collaboration	Includes peer teaching
	Includes collaboration in group activities

Source: From Students with Learning Disabilities (p. 181), 7th ed., by C. D. Mercer and P. C. Pullen, 2009, Upper Saddle River, NJ: Merrill/Pearson. Copyright 2009 by Pearson Education. Reprinted by permission.

completely understand and work it out. Such students are able to undertake the challenge of more difficult material, as long as they eventually experience success . . . When students worked with materials or activities that yielded a low success rate, achievement was lower.

Borich (2007) claims the research suggests that students need to spend about 60 to 70 percent of their time on tasks that allow almost complete understanding with occasional careless errors. Instruction that promotes high success not only contributes to improved achievement but also fosters increased levels of self-esteem and positive attitudes toward academic learning and school. The need for appropriate instructional matches and the continuous monitoring of student progress is apparent. Lack of success can lead to anxiety, frustration, inappropriate behavior, and poor motivation. In contrast, success can improve motivation, attitudes, academic progress, and classroom behavior.

Although many variables contribute to student success, the degree to which an appropriate instructional match is accomplished for each student must be viewed as the cornerstone of teaching that promotes high rates of success. The teacher's ability to diagnose relevant student characteristics (e.g., skill level, prior knowledge, strategy use, interests, and motivation) and task factors (e.g., level of difficulty, time to achieve mastery, and relevance) influences the quality of the instructional match (Christenson, Ysseldyke, & Thurlow, 1989). In essence, the teacher must match the learning task to the student's aptitude (i.e., diagnostic teaching function) to develop

an instructional program that ensures student success. As presented in Table 1.4, Wang (1987) highlights some of the features of learning environments that promote successful learning outcomes. Borich (2007) notes that moderate-to-high success rates not only help learners achieve mastery of lesson content but also provide a foundation for students to become independent learners and engage in higher order thinking. This development becomes more likely when explicit instruction is coupled with strategies or self-directed instruction.

Provide Positive and Supportive Learning Environments

It is well known that students learn more when the school and classroom environments are positive and supportive (Pianta, LaParo, Payne, Cox, & Bradley, 2002). For example, an academic focus with a humanistic orientation increases student achievement. The teacher is the key individual who influences the tone of a classroom. The teacher arranges physical (e.g., lighting, temperature, and seating) and academic (e.g., scheduling, method of lesson presentation, test dates, and homework) variables and establishes the affective nature (e.g., encouragement, competitiveness, and cooperation) of the classroom. Teacher expectations, encouragements, evaluations, attentiveness, and attitudes greatly influence students' perceptions of themselves as learners. Because many students with learning problems have negative perceptions of their academic abilities, general and special education teachers must create and maintain a supportive classroom setting for them. When the teacher is cheerful, supportive, and enthusiastic, students tend to feel more comfortable and model those actions and attitudes. This can result in a pleasant, productive learning environment for all learners.

Teachers easily can notice when things go wrong in the classroom, but *effective* teachers comment on positive classroom happenings. Sprick (2001) notes that learning is greater and behavior is more appropriate in classrooms in which teachers attend more to positive events than to negative events. Specifically, he reports that teachers who maintain a 3:1 ratio of attention to positive over negative events are likely to have a well-managed classroom and be able to devote more attention to teaching than attending to violations of rules. Goodlad (1984) found that teachers with positive styles used about 10 percent of their time handling behavior problems, whereas teachers with predominantly negative styles spent about 42 percent of their time managing students' inappropriate behavior. Sprick reports that, unfortunately, most classroom teachers attend to negative events three times more often than they attend to positive events.

Several educators (Borich, 2007; Brigham, Scruggs, & Mastropieri, 1992) maintain that teacher enthusiasm is an important aspect of teacher effort, is positively correlated to student achievement, and helps establish a positive and supportive learning environment. Brigham et al. examined the effects of teacher enthusiasm on the learning and behavior of junior high school students with learning problems. Their results indicate that enthusiastic presentations yield higher academic achievement and lower levels of off-task behavior. They characterize enthusiastic presentations according to eight elements: (1) varied, uplifting, and rapid vocal delivery; (2) dancing, wide-open eyes; (3) frequent, demonstrative gestures; (4) dramatic and varied body movements; (5) varied, emotive facial expressions; (6) varied word usage; (7) ready animated acceptance of ideas and feelings; and (8) exuberant overall energy level. Conversely, they describe five elements of unenthusiastic teacher behavior: (1) standing or sitting in the same place, (2) speaking in a monotone or inexpressive voice, (3) making infrequent eye contact, (4) using few animated facial expressions, and (5) generally interacting less with students. Borich maintains that no one can sustain a heightened level of enthusiasm for a long time without becoming emotionally fatigued. He states that a proper level reflects a balance of gesturing, eye contact, vocal inflections, and movement, which signals to most students the teacher's vigor, involvement, and interest.

Alderman (1990) notes that a positive learning environment and student learning are enhanced when teachers believe that *all* students can learn and that teachers can make a difference. Christenson et al. (1989) state that a positive learning environment is built upon the use of realistic expectations for student learning, the development of instructional plans that consider student characteristics and needs, the use of reinforcement for student productivity, the use of active monitoring of student progress, and the belief that all students will experience academic success. Alderman notes that in a positive classroom, errors are viewed as a natural and important part of the learning process rather than as an indication that the student lacks ability. Moreover, a positive approach is enhanced by the appropriate use of reinforcement for desirable academic, on-task, and social behaviors. The positive effect of reinforcement on academic achievement and work behaviors is well established (Lovitt, 1995). The teacher may consider the following questions to examine his or her potential influence on creating a positive and supportive learning environment.

- Am I enthusiastic most of the time?
- What is my attitude toward students?
- What is my attitude toward peers?
- Do I support all students?
- Do I admit mistakes and remain comfortable?
- Do I change my opinion with new information?
- Am I happy?
- Is my job fulfilling?
- Do I take care of my physical and emotional health?
- Am I a good listener?
- Do I laugh and smile much?

Students' descriptions of good teachers (Lovitt, 1977) reflect the importance of being positive. The students in Lovitt's study noted that good teachers compliment students, let students come to them for assistance, help all students, use good manners, trust students, join in class humor, explain more than once, and ask students for help. The students were concerned with fair play, inclusion in the action, and getting work done in a quiet and orderly room. They wanted their teachers to be real people with senses of humor. When the teachers behaved more like this, the academic performance of the students improved: "As the teacher did more things that pleased the students, they did more to please the teacher" (Lovitt, 1977, p. 94).

Plan and Maintain a Motivational Environment

The initial step in preventing classroom behavioral problems is to keep students motivated and, thus, engaged in the learning process. *Motivation* is used to describe what focuses or energizes a student's attention, emotions, and activity. It explains why students choose certain activities over others (e.g., do homework or talk on the telephone). Motivators can be internal or external, and they represent things or events that influence choices. Internal motivators come from within the individual (e.g., the desire to read a sports magazine). External motivators come from within the environment (e.g., parental pressure to do homework). When both internal and external sources motivate in the same direction, the effect is powerful. Thus, to motivate effectively, the teacher should be aware of a student's internal motivators, such as interests, needs, and aspirations, and external motivators, such as peer influence or teacher approval.

Many students with learning problems lose their motivation for learning as a result of a history of frustration and school failure. When teaching students with limited motivation, the teacher should plan systematic procedures to increase motivation. Van Reusen and Bos (1994) examined the effects of motivation strategy instruction on the participation of secondary students with learning disabilities in planning their IEPs. This instruction required the students to examine their strengths and limitations and identify their needs and aspirations. The purpose of the motivation strategy instruction was to involve the learners in key aspects of the learning process and increase the students' commitment to learn. Compared with students with learning disabilities who did not receive the motivation strategy training, the treatment group identified more goals and communicated more effectively during their IEP conferences. These findings highlight the importance of involving students with learning disabilities in the planning of their educational program. Specifically, the motivation strategy instruction helped the teachers and students recognize needs, interests, and aspirations that were important for motivating these students.

Setting realistic instructional goals and determining specific mastery criteria are important to student motivation. Clifford (1990) encourages teachers to establish learning goals that represent a moderate success probability. She notes that students often attribute success with easy tasks to task ease, and attribute success with extremely difficult tasks to luck. Clifford states, "It is only success at moderately difficult . . . tasks that we explain in terms of personal effort, well-chosen strategies, and ability; and these explanations give rise to feelings of pride, competence, satisfaction, persistence, and personal control" (p. 22). Similarly, Alderman (1990) notes that the linking of success to one's own efforts is critical for the development of motivation in students.

Once goals are established, student motivation is enhanced by monitoring progress toward these goals and delivering feedback on how to correct errors through learning strategies and study skills (Porter & Brophy, 1988; Wang, 1987). Table 1.5 features strategies for motivating students as suggested by Alderman (1990), Brigham et al. (1992), Brophy (1987), Christenson et al. (1989), Porter and Brophy (1988), and Salend (2008).

TABLE 1.5
Strategies for motivating
students to learn

Plan for Motivation
Create a supportive and positive environment.
Program for success by maintaining a match between task and student capabilities.
Develop meaningful learning outcomes.
Relate content to students' interests and their daily lives.
Use metaphors, anecdotes, stories, and examples to embellish understanding.

Motivate Through Appropriate Expectations
Communicate positive expectations.
Communicate challenging expectations.
Teach goal setting and help students link efforts to outcomes.

Use Extrinsic Incentives for Students Who Require Them
Praise sincere effort.
Reward good or improved performances.
Point out pragmatic values of learning.
Structure appropriate competitive activities.
Provide students with many opportunities to respond.
Provide immediate feedback to student responses.
Periodically use a game format.

Recognize and Provide Intrinsic Motivation
Teach self-management.
Involve students in planning selected instructional activities.
Provide ample time for students to achieve mastery.
Give students choices in selecting activities or topics.
Allow students to complete products.
Use fantasy or simulation activities.
Challenge students with higher order thinking activities.
Use cooperative learning and peer tutoring.
Discuss rationales for learning specific skills and content.
Induce students to develop their own motivation.
Encourage students to move from extrinsic to intrinsic motivators.
Use activities that arouse curiosity.

Use Strategies to Promote Motivation
Teach basic social skills.
Model interest in learning.
Project intensity.
Be enthusiastic about content and learning.
Be enthusiastic when presenting and interacting.
Use advance organizers to establish attending and importance.
Use explicit modeling to teach understanding.
Use a variety of independent learning activities (e.g., self-correcting materials
and computer-assisted instruction).
Model metacognition through "think alouds" while problem solving.
Minimize anxiety during learning activities.
Monitor progress and adjust instruction accordingly.
Vary grouping arrangements.
Use culturally relevant materials and examples.
Use students' names, experiences, hobbies, and interests in lessons.

Source: From *Students with Learning Disabilities* (p. 184), 7th ed., by C. D. Mercer and P. C. Pullen, 2009, Upper Saddle River, NJ: Merrill/Pearson. Copyright 2009 by Pearson Education. Reprinted by permission.

Planning and Organizing Instruction

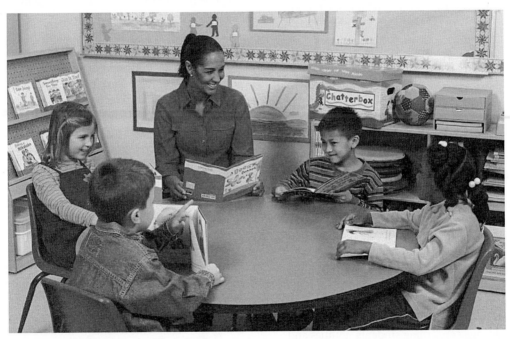

David Mager/Pearson Learning Photo Studio

From Chapter 2 of *Teaching Students with Learning Problems*, 8/e. Cecil D. Mercer. Ann R. Mercer. Paige C. Pullen.

Chapter 1 focuses on creating responsive educational environments within the context of student needs and characteristics, teacher–teacher collaboration, and teacher–parent collaboration. Moreover, it promotes the adoption of a philosophy that embraces research concerning instructional variables that promote learning. Whereas Chapter 1 concerns macro-factors such as human resources and legal requirements, Chapter 2 focuses on micro-factors such as planning and organizing the many details that accompany teaching. Arranging the classroom, selecting instructional materials, developing homework guidelines, and scheduling are only a few of the details that teachers must plan and organize.

When instruction engages student attention and participation continuously without interruptions, digressions, and diversions, it usually is the result of extensive teacher planning. Given the importance of teacher planning, it is imperative that teachers receive recognition and support for planning activities. In a report on teacher planning, Lenz, Deshler, and Schumaker (1990) provide helpful information about teacher planning.

- The time that teachers spend planning after school hours varies greatly. The average amount of planning time is 76 minutes.
- The average time teachers spend planning during the summer is 59 hours.
- Many teachers report that their most productive planning occurs in unstructured settings (e.g., driving a car, walking the dog, or taking a shower). Teachers generally agree that during-school planning involves "top structure" planning (i.e., scheduling, determining class structure, and responding to administrative tasks), whereas "deep structure" planning (i.e., how to clarify a difficult concept or develop a motivating activity) is accomplished away from school.
- Teachers report that the biggest obstacles to planning for an academically diverse class are insufficient time, lack of opportunity to develop or discover motivating and ability-appropriate materials and activities, and lack of knowledge concerning students' abilities and academic history.

This chapter presents planning and organizing instruction in the areas of physical arrangements, instructional arrangements, scheduling, classroom equipment, and material organization.

PHYSICAL ARRANGEMENTS

The decisions a teacher makes regarding the physical arrangements of a classroom have an important effect on the success of instructional activities and classroom management. Cegelka and Berdine (1995) note that

physical arrangements influence the time students spend in active learning, the time students spend attending, and the amount of disruptive behavior. Thoughtfully designed classrooms enable teachers and students to access materials easily and move around the room without creating congestion. Also, in well-designed classrooms teachers easily can see the students and, in turn, students easily can see and hear teacher presentations. In planning physical arrangements it is helpful to consider the arrangement of students, materials, and special areas.

Arrangement of Students

When selecting an arrangement for students, it helps to begin by determining where the teacher will present whole-class instruction. The position of the chalkboard and overhead projector screen usually determines the best location for teacher presentations. The following considerations in arranging students are important.

- *Arrange students so that they easily can see and hear teacher presentations.* The students should readily see any content presented visually (e.g., on the chalkboard or dry erase board, overhead projector screen, or Smart Board) and easily hear the teacher.
- *Arrange students so that the teacher has easy access to any student.* Easy access helps the teacher provide individual help, offer private feedback, and prevent crisis situations.
- *Arrange students so that the teacher easily sees the students.* This enables the teacher to monitor the students by frequently scanning the classroom. Scanning increases on-task behavior and is especially important during student-directed activities. Sprick (1991) reports that scanning is an important factor in teaching, and effective teachers typically scan the classroom about once every 15 seconds.
- *Decide whether desks are to be arranged in clusters or rows.* Options on arranging student desks include using isolated desk areas, clusters, rows, or combinations. Because placing desks in clusters tends to promote socialization and interactions among students, many educators (Emmer & Evertson,

2009) suggest placing student desks in rows, especially at the beginning of the school year. Moreover, students should neither sit with their backs to major instructional areas nor face distractions (e.g., windows, doorways, or other students).

- *Place difficult-to-teach or off-task students in the middle of the room near the front.* These students need more monitoring than other students; placing them close to the teacher helps the teacher monitor their attention and behavior.

Arrangement of Materials

The appropriate location of materials facilitates the flow of instructional activities and improves classroom management. In arranging materials, the following considerations are important:

- *Keep frequently used materials easily accessible.* Although the specific materials frequently used by the teacher and the students depend on the academic area or subject being taught, basic items usually include paper, markers, rulers, scissors, chalk and erasers, transparencies and water-soluble pens, masking tape, glue, and a stapler. To help students maintain the materials that they supply, it is helpful to send a list home for parents, and the teacher should have an ample supply of items needed by students. Frequently used materials should be arranged on accessible bookshelves and in cabinets.
- *Ensure that high-traffic areas are free of congestion.* High-traffic areas are usually around group work places, the pencil sharpener, the trashcan, the teacher's desk, certain bookshelves, computers, doorways, and student desks. These high-traffic areas should not be close to each other and should be easily accessible.

Arrangement of Special Areas and Centers

An important consideration in planning the arrangement of a classroom is to designate selected areas for specific activities (e.g., math area, language area, or study area). In many classrooms, space is needed for small-group instruction, centers, and individual work. Several types of areas are presented next.

Academic Areas It is sometimes necessary to divide instructional spaces in the academic areas. In the elementary grades, these areas typically include reading, math, language, handwriting, spelling, and subjects such as science, social studies, and health. Each area provides room for several students and a space for storing materials. In the intermediate and secondary grades, fewer academic areas are specified in a classroom; however, instructional areas may be set up for various branches of a particular subject. For example, an English teacher may have areas for literature, grammar, listening, and free reading.

Teacher Areas The teacher needs spaces for small-group and large-group instruction. In addition, the teacher needs an area for storing materials and personal articles. The teacher's space should provide a good vantage point for monitoring the ongoing activities in the room.

Individual Student Areas Each student needs a place to store materials, to sit during whole-class or cooperative learning activities, and to work on independent seatwork. Typically, students are assigned a desk. It often is helpful to provide students who are highly distractible or having a difficult day with a quiet work area, such as carrels or desks located away from the flow of activity. However, it is important that such carrels be viewed as a positive place to learn, not as punishment.

Audiovisual Area It is helpful to designate areas or listening centers for using audiovisual materials (e.g., DVD or CD players). A separate designated space also is needed for computers that are available for student use. Many classrooms do not provide a separate audiovisual area. In these situations, some space may serve dual functions (e.g., a reading area/listening station).

General Considerations

In planning a classroom arrangement, the total effect should be pleasant and inviting. Teachers must take the resources and space available and arrange the class to suit their style and the content being taught. A sample general education classroom floor plan, which can be modified to fit teacher needs, is presented in Figure 2.1. This arrangement of a general education classroom provides a good vantage position for the teacher, easy access to students, a small-group instruction area, and a whole-class presentation format that allows the students to see the teacher at the chalkboard or material on the overhead projector screen.

Class Size The limited research that exists on the effects of special-education class size indicates that

FIGURE 2.1

Sample floor plan for a general education classroom

smaller student–teacher ratios result in more positive student outcomes than do larger ratios (Forness & Kavale, 1985). The research in general education is more extensive. In a survey of teachers' perceptions of class size, Englehart (2006) reported that on-task behavior decreased as class size increased. Teachers believed this to be the case because of the lack of close proximity to all of their students. Mueller, Chase, and Walden (1988) present results from Program Prime Time in Indiana concerning the effects of a reduced class size in primary grades. Specifically, they report that a reduced class size in primary grades results in a less hectic atmosphere, better teacher morale, more individualized

instruction, and improved student achievement, particularly by at-risk students and students with learning problems. In a synthesis of the research on the effects of class size, Robinson (1990) found that the most positive effects of small classes (i.e., 22 or fewer students) occur in kindergarten through third grade and especially benefit the achievement of at-risk students; the positive effects of class size on student achievement decrease as grade levels increase; reducing class size has little effect on student achievement if teachers continue to use the same instructional methods in smaller classes as they used in larger classes; and reductions in class size have small positive effects on achievement

FIGURE 2.2
Instructional arrangements

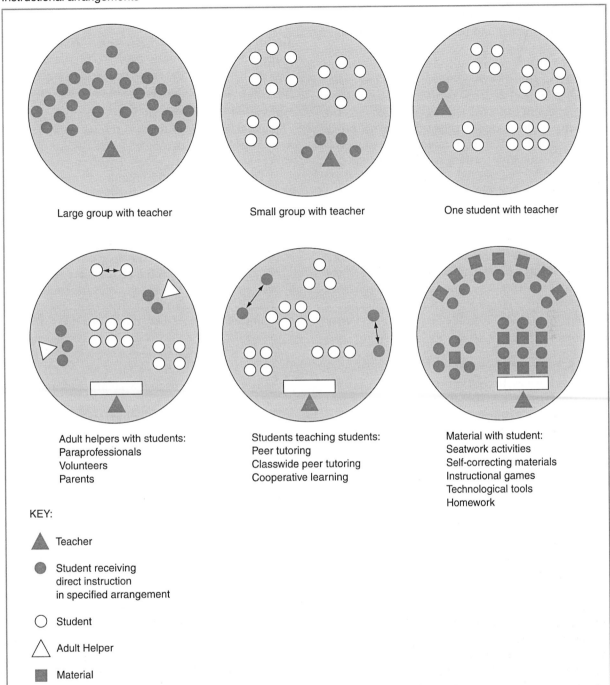

Large group with teacher

Small group with teacher

One student with teacher

Adult helpers with students:
Paraprofessionals
Volunteers
Parents

Students teaching students:
Peer tutoring
Classwide peer tutoring
Cooperative learning

Material with student:
Seatwork activities
Self-correcting materials
Instructional games
Technological tools
Homework

KEY:

▲ Teacher

● Student receiving
direct instruction
in specified arrangement

○ Student

△ Adult Helper

■ Material

when compared to many less-costly learning interventions and strategies. The improved learning of at-risk students and students with learning problems in smaller classes is likely the result of the teachers having the opportunity to respond to the students' individual instructional needs.

INSTRUCTIONAL ARRANGEMENTS

Six basic instructional arrangements that are available to teachers are presented in Figure 2.2. The large-group instruction, small-group instruction, and one student with teacher arrangements are teacher directed and require continuous teacher participation. Adult helpers with students, students teaching students, and material with student require indirect teacher involvement and periodic teacher participation. Careful use of these six instructional arrangements is a key factor in individualizing instruction for a class of students with diverse needs. For example, when a teacher uses small-group instruction or the one student with teacher arrangement, the remaining students can be engaged meaningfully in learning activities through indirect teacher involvement (e.g., students teaching students or material with student). The skillful orchestration of these arrangements helps the teacher maintain student participation and attention.

Large-Group Instruction

The large class sizes that exist in many schools necessitate large-group instruction. When the content is appropriate for all students, large-group instruction can be an effective way of presenting new content or discussing pertinent information. Typically, the large-group format is appropriate for such activities as story telling, presenting show and tell, discussing interesting events, taking a field trip, brainstorming, playing a game, or viewing videotapes. If the teacher uses effective presentation strategies such as demonstration, modeling, and guided practice and supplements them with cooperative learning, small-group instruction, follow-up direct instruction, or engaging seatwork activities, large-group instruction can be effective for teaching academics and social skills to students with diverse needs. In a response to intervention (RTI) framework, much of the Tier 1 instruction is provided in a large-group format.

Advantages and Disadvantages of Large-Group Instruction
Large-group instruction is time efficient and prepares students for the type of instruction that primarily is used in secondary schools, community colleges, and universities. Also, experiences in large groups may help students with disabilities make the transition from special to general education settings. Moreover, general education and special education teachers who co-teach may share the responsibilities of teaching the large group. The primary disadvantage of large-group instruction is that it does not allow for the teacher to deal easily with the diverse abilities and skill levels present in most classrooms. In large groups, questions may go unanswered, distracted students may remain off task, and students who need more intensive instruction may fail to receive it. For high-ability students, large-group instruction frequently moves too slowly, whereas for low-ability students, it usually moves too quickly. In either situation, behavioral problems are likely to result because of boredom or frustration.

Guidelines for Large-Group Instruction
Large-group instruction is more likely to accommodate students with different learning needs and rates if the following guidelines and techniques are used.

- *Keep instruction short.* Suggested amounts of time for large-group instruction according to grade level include: kindergarten or first grade—5 to 15 minutes; second or third grade—5 to 20 minutes; fourth or fifth grade—5 to 25 minutes; sixth or seventh grade—5 to 30 minutes; and eighth through twelfth grade—5 to 40 minutes.

- *Use questions to involve students in the lesson.* Teachers should ensure that each student has opportunities to participate frequently. Choral or group responses are good ways to involve all students simultaneously. It is helpful to use signals to cue students for group responses so that leaders and followers are eliminated. Also, teachers should guard against calling on the same students too often. Positive participation is enhanced if the teacher asks high-ability students the most difficult questions and offers less demanding questions to low-ability students.

- *Use lecture–pause routines.* The lecture–pause procedure involves the teacher lecturing for 6 to 12 minutes and then pausing for about 3 minutes to allow students divided into groups of three to follow the RAP procedure:

  R—*Read* your notes or questions.

  A—*Ask* other students about your notes (e.g., spellings, missing information, or questions about the content).

  P—*Put* corrections or answers to questions in your notes.

- *Encourage active participation among lower performing students while maintaining the involvement of higher achieving students.* Heads Together (Kagan, 1989/1990) is a teacher-questioning strategy that combines elements of teacher-directed and peer-mediated instruction. Students are placed into four-member learning teams, each consisting of one high achiever, two average achievers, and one low achiever. The students number themselves 1 through 4 and sit together during teacher-directed lessons. When the teacher directs a question to the entire class, the teams "put their heads together" to determine the best answer. The teacher then asks, "How many Number (1s, 2s, 3s, or 4s) know the answer?" After one randomly selected student responds, the teacher asks whether other students with the selected number agree with or want to expand on the answer. Because students are given time to discuss possible answers before responding and it is not known which group member will be selected to respond, it is more likely that everyone, including low achievers, will know the correct responses.

- *Use visual aids to promote understanding of lecture material.* Diagrams are useful, especially in helping students understand relationships. Concept diagramming and story mapping are visual diagramming approaches that are used frequently.

- *Maintain a lively pace.* A lively pace helps maintain student attention. Because thinking time is always faster than speaking time, it is important to keep the lecture moving at an appropriate pace to hold interest.

- *Use frequent "change-ups."* "Change-ups" are anything the teacher does to vary the presentation. Selected change-up activities include varying voice levels, varying rate of talking, illustrating a point with a story, telling a joke, having students follow a sequence of directions (such as look at ceiling, floor, windows, and chalkboard), and allowing students to stand up to stretch.

- *Determine the rules for behavior during presentations.* Mnemonics, such as SLANT, are excellent for reminding students of behavioral expectations during lectures. The SLANT mnemonic reminds students to *sit* up straight, *lean* forward in your desk, *act* interested, *nod* occasionally to signal understanding, and *track* the teacher with your eyes.

- *Determine the rules for behavior during discussions.* Rules for discussions are imperative to prevent call-outs and put-downs. A good rule for discussions is, "Raise your hand to request to ask a question or answer a question."

- *If students misbehave, praise students who follow the rules.* This reinforces students for appropriate behavior, communicates teacher expectations, and provides a model for misbehaving students.

- *Use flexible grouping.* With flexible grouping, the teacher instructs the large group by using direct instruction procedures, such as descriptions and demonstration, but individualizes guided instruction and independent practice. The small groupings for individualized instruction would differ from lesson to lesson because different students would need various levels of help as a function of the lesson content. Flexible grouping is an important aspect of RTI models; typically the general educator provides Tier 2 instruction within the flexible grouping format.

- *Use participation buddies to promote student involvement.* In this technique (Fister & Kemp, 1995), the teacher divides students into teams of two and asks the class a question. Each student is instructed to think of the answer and then share it with his or her buddy. The partners then can share their answers with the class.

- *Use response cards to promote participation.* Each student is given a card with *True* on one side and *False* on the other side. The teacher makes a statement and asks the students to decide whether it is true or false. After a few seconds, the teacher instructs the students to show their answers by placing their cards on their chests with *True* or *False* displayed. Then the teacher gives the correct answer, discusses it, and praises students for participating. This activity can be modified by presenting multiple-choice items on an overhead or handout and asking students to display (or signal) their card answers (i.e., *a*, *b*, *c*, or *d*) to specific questions.

- *Use Ask, Pause, and Call.* The teacher can *ask* a question, *pause* for several seconds to allow thinking time, and *call* on an individual or group for the response (Fister & Kemp, 1995).

- *Use signals to avoid surprise call-ons.* The teacher can prearrange a subtle cue (e.g., standing near the student's desk) that lets certain students know in advance that they will be called on next to answer a question or read a passage (Fister & Kemp, 1995).

Small-Group Instruction

The small-group arrangement typically consists of three to seven students and represents a major format for teaching academic skills. Although it can be a highly effective arrangement for all students, small-group instruction is especially recommended for students with learning problems. As described earlier, in an RTI model, teachers use this format to provide much of the Tier 2 instruction. In establishing small groups for instruction, the teacher attempts to group students who have similar instructional needs in a specific academic area. Groups can be based on placement in a reader or on need for instruction in selected phonics rules, paragraph writing, or specific math facts. To accommodate different rates of learning, the composition of the groups should remain flexible. If a student makes rapid progress, it may be advisable to place the student in a different group for instruction. Decisions to move students should be based on data collected through ongoing progress monitoring.

Foorman and Torgesen (2001) note that providing small-group instruction is the most practical method for increasing instructional intensity for students at risk for reading failure. Moreover, the results of a meta-analysis of grouping practices and reading outcomes for students with disabilities indicate positive effects of small-group and student-pairing grouping practices compared to whole-class instruction (Elbaum, Vaughn, Hughes, & Moody, 1999). Also, in an examination of general education classroom practices, Slavin (1988) reports that research on within-class instructional grouping in mathematics clearly supports grouping for instruction. Specific findings indicate that the effects are greater for low achievers than for average and high achievers. To improve the effectiveness of instructional grouping, the students can be placed in a semicircle facing the teacher. Distractible students tend to perform better when they are in the middle of the group and about 2 feet from the teacher.

Advantages of Small-Group Instruction It is difficult to meet the learning needs of a heterogeneous group of students during large-group instruction, and small-group instruction provides an effective alternative. Moreover, small-group instruction is especially important for students who are learning basic skills in reading, writing, and math; thus, small-group instruction occurs more frequently during the elementary grades. Compared with large-group instruction, specific advantages of small-group instruction include the following:

- Students are able to participate more during the instruction.
- Teachers are able to provide more instruction, praise, and feedback.
- Students are able to progress at their own rates (i.e., both high achievers and low achievers are able to progress at rates commensurate with their abilities).
- Small-group instruction typically is less boring.
- Teachers using small-group instruction are able to monitor the progress of students better and make teaching modifications.
- Small-group instruction provides students with language differences with a more comfortable setting for participating and asking for clarification.
- The small-group arrangement is especially important for students with learning and behavioral problems because many of these students lack the skills to work and learn independently. They frequently have difficulty recognizing relationships, making associations, remembering information, using or activating an effective learning strategy, or discovering new knowledge. Thus, they need and prosper

from the direction, structure, and intensity of the teacher-directed small-group setting (Cegelka & Berdine, 1995).

- A small-group follow-up can be helpful to students who do not learn sufficiently during large-group teacher presentations. The teacher can extend an invitation to a teacher-directed small-group follow-up session (e.g., "Please join me at the table if you need help with the seatwork assignment") so that certain students can meet while other class members work on the assignment independently or in cooperative groups (Cegelka & Berdine, 1995).
- Small-group instruction may have an advantage over one-on-one instruction because a student with learning problems may, through observation, learn a skill that is being taught to another group member (Ledford, Gast, Luscre, & Ayres, 2008).
- Small-group settings provide the opportunity to increase the intensity of intervention for students who have moved to Tier 2 in an RTI model.

Disadvantages of Small-Group Instruction Most of the disadvantages of small-group instruction involve teacher preparation time and managing students doing their seatwork while others are participating in a small group. Compared with large-group instruction, specific disadvantages of small-group instruction include the following:

- Students are required to do more seatwork.
- Teachers must do more planning (e.g., a reading teacher must plan small-group lessons as well as seatwork activities for students when they are not in their small group).
- Teachers must organize more instructional variables (such as grouping students, managing transitions, and monitoring seatwork activities while teaching).
- Teachers must provide more instruction in the respective academic or content area.

Guidelines for Small-Group Instruction Because the rewards in student learning and motivation can be substantial when small-group instruction is used, the teacher should approach small-group instruction positively. The advantages of small-group instruction can be attained and the disadvantages minimized if effective guidelines are followed.

- *Establish rules for small-group instruction.* In addition to reminding students that general classroom rules apply in small-group lessons, the teacher should have some specific rules for these lessons (e.g., "Always bring your materials—pencil, book, and workbook—to small-group lessons" and "Wait quietly for the teacher to begin the lesson"). Also, if the teacher previously has not developed the rules and behavioral expectations for making the transition of going to small-group instruction, then this routine needs to be taught. Finally, it is important to remind students who are out of the group to follow the classroom rules regarding seatwork.

- *Make the groups as homogeneous as possible.* Grouping the students according to ability and skill helps the teacher tailor instruction for the students in the group. Because the lowest performers need more intense instruction (i.e., more elaboration, examples, praise, feedback, and practice), it helps to keep their group as small as possible.
- *Maintain flexible groupings.* To ensure that students progress at their own rates, it helps for the groupings to remain flexible. For example, a student who makes rapid progress may be placed in a different instructional group.
- *Locate the small group in an area that allows the teacher to scan the entire class.* When working with a small group, the teacher should be able to see the rest of the class. It also helps to select a location that minimizes distractions for the students. For example, students in the small group should sit where they do not see other students doing seatwork. Seatings away from high-traffic areas such as the pencil sharpener, wastebasket, or audiovisual center also reduce potential distractions.
- *Place the students in a semicircle so that their shoulders align with the shoulders of the students beside them.* This alignment provides an equal opportunity for all students to participate in the group activities. When a student's shoulders are several inches behind the others, he or she tends to feel outside of the group. There can be two semicircle rows of students when there are nine or more students in the group. Students in the back row sit in chairs; those in the front row sit on the floor. For sitting on the floor not to be aversive, it can be presented as a privilege (e.g., "Because Tonya, Greg, and Jason have done such a nice job of attending to the lesson today, they get to sit on the floor mats next time.").
- *Use motivation activities during small-group work.* Motivation techniques include providing much positive praise during the initial small-group session, using descriptive praise, using group praise (e.g., occasionally conduct a group handshake), using some choral responding to involve everyone, and maintaining enthusiasm and a lively pace during the lesson.

myeducationlab

Go to the Assignments and Activities section of the Topic Planning/Organization in the MyEducationLab for your course and complete the activity entitled Determining What to Teach and How to Teach It.

One Student with Teacher

Intensive tutorial teaching frequently is used to help students with learning problems learn a new skill. In addition, one-to-one instruction is appropriate for students who are learning skills that are different from the rest of the class. One-to-one tutoring is a powerful instructional arrangement, and it can be used to intensify interventions in Tier 2 or Tier 3 of the RTI framework. In the one-to-one arrangement, the student has the opportunity to ask questions, explain reasoning or strategies, receive instructional feedback, correct errors, and prevent further learning problems with specific skills or content. One-to-one teaching can be used spontaneously with group methods of instruction to prevent or relieve frustration. When teachers observe students having difficulty during group instruction or seatwork, they can give them attention at the first opportunity.

Often, 3 to 5 minutes is just the amount of time needed to help a student understand a concept, receive corrective feedback, understand directions, and feel motivated to continue working. When one-to-one instruction is scheduled daily for students with learning problems, the students know they will have some time with the teacher to receive help. Elementary teachers and resource room teachers have fewer students or are with them for a longer time; thus, it is easier for them than for intermediate and secondary level teachers to offer one-to-one instruction. When teachers use one-to-one instruction, they must plan such activities as seatwork, peer tutoring, computer-assisted instruction, or cooperative learning activities for the rest of the class.

Adult Helpers with Students

The use of volunteers and paraprofessionals in classrooms has increased substantially during the last decade. With class sizes increasing and students with special needs becoming more prevalent, it is logical for educators to turn to paraprofessionals as a supportive instructional arrangement. Furthermore, paraprofessionals provide vital, cost-effective services to teachers and students. Traditionally, paraprofessionals have been used for clerical tasks, but their roles as instructors are increasing. Several researchers who investigated the effectiveness of using paraprofessionals or volunteers for tutoring found significant positive results for students (Brown, Morris, & Fields, 2005; Pullen, Lane, & Monaghan, 2004). Paraprofessionals and volunteers provide a powerful resource for increasing the engaged learning time of students with learning and behavioral problems. For recruiting volunteers and paraprofessionals, it is helpful to contact parent–teacher associations, service organizations, parents, church groups, and senior citizen groups. School personnel should interview potential paraprofessionals thoroughly to ensure that they understand the roles and responsibilities of the position and are suitable for the job.

Planning and Implementing Paraprofessional Programs

To plan and implement an effective paraprofessional program, the following factors should be considered.

- *Roles of paraprofessionals.* To maximize the benefits of paraprofessionals, it is important to identify the strengths of the individual and match his or her skills to the needs of the classroom teacher. In addition, the classroom teacher should explain each assistant's roles and responsibilities clearly. Unfortunately, many paraprofessionals are not provided with written job descriptions or clear expectations of their roles (Mueller, 2002; Riggs & Mueller, 2001). An inventory can be created to assist in identifying paraprofessional skills and teacher/student needs. Such an inventory can serve the two purposes of (1) matching the paraprofessional's strengths to teacher needs and (2) helping to clarify roles and expectations of the paraprofessional. Figure 2.3 provides a sample inventory with primary category headings along with suggested tasks for each category. The classroom teacher lists on the inventory the categories and tasks for which paraprofessional help is needed. The paraprofessional then reviews the tasks and indicates those tasks that he or she can perform independently, those for which supervision is needed, and those for which additional training is needed.
- *Training paraprofessionals.* Paraprofessionals and volunteers need training to prepare them for their respective roles. The following activities should be included in their training: (1) Tour the school and meet key school personnel; (2) explain the need for confidentiality and the rules that govern it; (3) review the dress code and appropriate standards of behavior; (4) review the communication system; (5) demonstrate how to operate equipment related to instruction and special needs of students; (6) discuss schedules, school events, emergency procedures, and absences; and (7) introduce training in instructional procedures

regarding presentation techniques, guided practice, corrective feed-back, encouragement, and independent practice activities. Skills in instructional procedures can be developed and refined through ongoing in-service, readings, videos, and collaboration with teachers and other paraprofessionals.

- *Collaboration.* After the teacher and paraprofessional clarify role expectations, it helps to outline the specific tasks of the paraprofessional, determine the skills needed to do the tasks, and provide training or demonstration of the procedures or strategies needed to do the tasks. Daily meetings are helpful to review the day, plan the next day, and make needed modifications in activities or duties. One of the most important aspects of these meetings is for the pair to maintain communication and a collaborative framework for evaluation, training, and problem solving. Also, the teacher should recognize the contributions of the paraprofessional.
- *Working with culturally and linguistically diverse students.* In some settings it is helpful to have paraprofessionals who speak languages other than English or who understand diverse cultures. These qualifications enable the paraprofessional to assist non-English-speaking students or students from diverse backgrounds. Miramontes (1991) developed a Multilingual/Multiethnic Instructional Services team to coordinate services to students from culturally and linguistically diverse backgrounds. In this model, paraprofessionals assist in developing and providing instructional programs, incorporate students' primary languages and cultures in their program, serve as positive ethnic and linguistic role models, and provide school–community liaison services.

PEARSON
myeducationlab

Go to the Assignments and Activities section of the Topic Collaboration in the MyEducationLab for your course and complete the activity entitled Sharing Responsibilities. As you watch the video and answer the accompanying questions, note the effect collaboration has on planning.

Students Teaching Students: Peer Tutoring

The students-teaching-students instructional arrangement provides teachers with a viable resource of instructional support and offers students the opportunity for intensive practice on academic tasks tailored to individual needs. It features students working independently and thus frees the teacher to work with other students individually or in small-group sessions. In a general education classroom of heterogeneous learners,

FIGURE 2.3
Inventory of paraprofessional roles and responsibilities

Paraprofessional Roles and Responsibilities Inventory

Read through the following categories and tasks. Mark each task with one of the following codes:

I	I can implement this task independently.
T	I can implement this task but will need some training or specific instructions.
PD	I need formal professional development training before I am able to implement this task.
U	I feel uncomfortable with this task.

Response to Intervention

_____ Conduct progress-monitoring assessments including curriculum-based measurement (CBM).

_____ Implement small-group or one-to-one instruction using _____ *(name specific program or strategy, e.g., Great Leaps Reading Program).*

_____ Administer informal assessments.

_____ Supervise independent work time of students in Tier 1 while classroom teacher implements Tier 2 intervention with a small group.

_____ Reinforce concepts presented by the classroom teacher during Tier 1 instruction to students requiring additional support (i.e., Tier 2) in a small group format.

Clerical Tasks

_____ Take attendance.

_____ Create materials using word processing software.

_____ Record grades in online grading system.

Behavior Management

_____ Observe and record social behaviors.

_____ Provide positive reinforcement to students.

_____ Assist students in implementing self-monitoring of attention.

_____ Devise contingency contracts.

Classroom Organization

_____ Prepare manipulative materials for instructional lessons.

_____ Make instructional games and activities.

_____ Locate instructional materials.

_____ Make bulletin boards.

_____ Develop and manage learning centers.

_____ Create self-correcting materials.

Other Instructional Support

_____ Listen to students read and provide reinforcement and corrective feedback.

_____ Supervise independent work time.

_____ Modify written materials.

---

instructional arrangements that allow students to practice needed skills or learn subject content independently are critical to the academic success of students with learning problems. Although students-teaching-students occurs in a multitude of formats, most peer instructional arrangements feature either peer tutoring or cooperative learning.

Description of Peer Tutoring Tutorial instruction (e.g., parents teaching their children or older siblings instructing younger siblings) was probably the first pedagogy among primitive societies. As early as the first century A.D., Quintilian in his *Institutio Oratoria* discussed teaching settings in which older children tutored younger children. Today, a basic definition of peer tutoring is *an instructional arrangement in which the teacher pairs two students in a tutor–tutee relationship to promote learning of academic skills or subject content.* The teacher determines the academic task and provides the instructional materials. Although peer tutoring is used to foster social skills, positive relationships, and self-esteem for both students, the emphasis is usually on the learning progress of the tutee. Peer tutoring is most frequently used to teach, practice, or monitor basic skill areas such as spelling words, math facts, oral reading, and vocabulary. To maintain effective peer tutoring, the teacher monitors behavior and praises both the tutor and the tutee for performing their respective duties.

Research on Peer Tutoring   Several studies have focused on the effectiveness of peer tutoring for students with a wide range of learning problems and in various content areas. Levin, Glass, and Meister (1984) examined the effectiveness of peer tutoring in terms of reading and math outcomes and found that peer tutoring produced more than twice as much achievement as computer-assisted instruction, three times more than reducing the class size from 35 to 30 students, and almost four times more than lengthening the school day by 1 hour. Moreover, Elbaum et al. (1999) report strong support for the efficacy of student pairing for students with disabilities during reading instruction. Osguthorpe and Scruggs (1986) reviewed studies in which special education students served as tutors. They found that tutees who received instruction from special education students made academic gains in a variety of content areas. In addition, many of the tutors benefited academically and socially from being the tutor. These findings encourage both general and special education teachers to set up many different tutor–tutee pairs to promote social integration as well as academic gains among students with and without learning problems.

Scruggs and Richter (1985) reviewed 24 studies in which students with learning disabilities were involved in tutoring interventions. They note that investigators favored the use of peer tutoring, and most studies support the continued use of tutoring with students with learning problems. Other studies have investigated the comparative effects of peer tutoring for students with and without learning problems. The educational implications from the peer-tutoring research are similar for students in general education and special education. Tutor and tutee benefits in academics (i.e., achievement gains across academic and content areas) are reported for students with and without learning problems, whereas the effect of peer tutoring on the enhancement of social skills and self-concept remains inconclusive for students both with and without learning problems (Cohen, Kulik, & Kulik, 1982; Osguthorpe & Scruggs, 1986). Moreover, the research indicates that peer-tutoring program variables are more important to student achievement than are student variables such as age, ability, grade, and training. Relevant program variables include structured settings, lower order target skills, teacher-developed achievement measures, and programs of shorter longitudinal duration. Because of the effect of program variables, it is not surprising that both students with and students without learning problems benefit from peer-tutoring programs of similar design and content.

Peer tutoring appears to hold much promise. It can improve academic skills, foster self-esteem, develop appropriate behaviors, and promote positive relationships and cooperation among peers. It benefits both tutor and tutee, and once the program is designed it requires less of the teacher's time than most instructional arrangements. Also, it is tailor-made to help students with learning problems achieve in general education settings.

Programming Guidelines for Peer Tutoring
The development and implementation of a successful peer-tutoring program require the consideration of numerous factors. The following 12 steps represent best practices from the research and literature regarding the factors involved in planning and implementing peer tutoring.

1. *Determine goals of peer tutoring.* Although peer tutoring is used primarily to help students with academic achievement, some educators report that it is effective for improving socialization skills, classroom behaviors, self-concept, and interpersonal relationships. Appropriate goals include the following:

   - Provide tutees with an opportunity to practice and learn a targeted academic skill (e.g., spelling words, math facts, and word recognition) until mastery is achieved.
   - Provide tutees with an opportunity to review and learn subject content (e.g., definitions of science terms and identification of countries on a map).
   - Provide tutors and tutees with an opportunity to develop appropriate social skills (e.g., giving encouragement, giving corrective feedback, clarifying directions or subject matter, and providing cues and prompts).
   - Provide tutors with an opportunity to review or practice recently learned skills or content.
   - Enhance the self-concepts of tutors and tutees by making positive statements about their skills or abilities and by providing them with success experiences in both social and academic areas.

2. *Target skills or content for the peer tutoring pairs.* When the entire class is working on skills (e.g., spelling words) or content (e.g., presidents of

the United States) presented in a recent lesson, the teacher may have each pair working with the same content. In other situations, peer tutoring provides students who need extra practice with the opportunity to receive it. Generally, the content or skills targeted should include material the teacher already has presented to the students. In selecting content and skills, it is helpful to consider the following research findings.

- Peer tutoring has resulted in academic gains for tutors and tutees within most academic areas.
- Gains in math have been greater than in other academic areas for tutors and tutees.
- Peer-tutoring pairs seem to achieve best when working on lower level skills such as spelling words or math facts.
- Peer tutoring appears to work better on multiple skill activities such as number of words written or read correctly than on singular skill activities such as decoding skills.
- The targeted skills and content should be similar to those used in the classroom.
- Student gains usually are more evident on curriculum-based measures than on standardized tests.

3. *Select materials.* In addition to paper and pencils, materials needed for a peer-tutoring program usually include the following:

- Directions for tutor and tutee
- An academic task presented on flash cards, a worksheet, or pages in a textbook
- An assessment sheet on which the tutor can record correct and incorrect responses
- Scoring procedures if tutee performance is to be evaluated

A sample tutor instruction sheet for flash cards is presented in Table 2.1, and a sample tutor record sheet is provided in Figure 2.4.

4. *Design procedures for tutor and tutee.* The procedures instruct the tutor how to present the academic task, score the tutee responses, provide feedback for correct and incorrect responses, and record the total performance score of the tutee. The procedures instruct the tutee how to respond (e.g., written, timed, or verbal) to the academic task. Finally, the procedures detail the rewards for the tutor and tutee for the achievement of specified goals (e.g., tutee passes a weekly quiz on the tutoring content with 90 percent accuracy or achieves 80 percent accuracy during the session).

TABLE 2.1

Sample tutor instruction sheet for flash cards

Step 1: At the beginning of the tutoring session, get the folder of tutor materials.

Step 2: Sit directly opposite and facing the tutee.

Step 3: Ensure that the tutor materials include record sheets, flash cards, blank cards, and pencils.

Step 4: Ask whether the tutee is ready to begin.

Step 5: Remove the record sheet, pencil, and flash cards from the folder.

Step 6: Hold up the flash cards one at a time with the card facing the tutee.

Step 7: Instruct the tutee to read aloud the number fact or word.

Step 8: Count to three silently. If the tutee does not respond or responds incorrectly, say, "The answer is_____. Say it." After the tutee repeats the answer, place the card at the bottom of the stack.

Step 9: If the tutee does not respond or responds incorrectly, mark a "–" next to the number fact or word in the first trial column of the record sheet.

Step 10: If the tutee responds correctly, mark a "+" next to the number fact or word, and say, "Good job," "Great," or "Super." Place the card on the table.

Step 11: After the tutee attempts all of the cards, present them again, and mark a "+" or "–" in the second trial column of the record sheet.

Step 12: Present the cards a third time, and mark a "+" or "–" in the last trial column of the record sheet.

Step 13: Look at the data sheet. If there are three "+"s for a number fact or a word, provide a blank card and a pencil and instruct the tutee to write the number fact or word. Have the tutee file this card in the tutee's mastery box.

Step 14: Ask the tutee to move the marker on the Ladder of Success chart to the correct spot according to how many number facts or words the tutee has learned.

Step 15: Place the materials back in the folder and return the folder to its place.

FIGURE 2.4
Sample tutor record sheet

Tutor Record Sheet

_____

Tutor _____   Date _____

Tutee _____

Mark either a "+" or a "−" depending on the tutee's response (+ = correct; − = incorrect)

Math Fact or Word	Trial 1	Trial 2	Trial 3	Math Facts or Words Not Learned
1				
2				
3				
4				
5				
6				
7				
8				
9				
10				

How did you feel about today's session?

_____

Do not write below this line

_____

Percent correct _____   Percent incorrect _____

Number learned _____   Number not learned _____

---

5. *Assign tutor–tutee pairs.* Several configurations of tutor–tutee assignments are used in peer tutoring. Across-class tutoring involves students from one class going to another class to tutor. Across-class tutors are usually older or high achievers. Pullout tutoring involves the tutee going to a specialized setting to work with a tutor from another class. These two arrangements require administrative support and scheduling among the classes involved. A third type of tutoring, intraclass tutoring, yields good results and requires less schoolwide planning. Intraclass tutoring involves students within the same class serving as tutors and tutees for each other. The tutoring interaction may be either one way or reciprocal. In reciprocal tutoring, the tutor and tutee exchange roles during the tutoring session so that each has an opportunity to serve as teacher and learner. Unless there are students who have chronic problems with each other, tutor–tutee assignments can be random. After a specified time (such as 1 week to 1 month), the tutor–tutee assignments are randomly changed (e.g., tutors or tutees select names of a partner from a container). Low achievers can act as tutors for high achievers when the tutoring materials include the correct answers for the tutor. This enables the tutor with learning problems to check the answer and provide feedback to tutees who are high achievers. This format enables a heterogeneous group of students to tutor each other and engage in reciprocal tutoring.

6. *Train tutors.* Tutor training procedures are included in most peer-tutoring programs. The duties of tutors typically include introducing new material,

FIGURE 2.5
Sample tutor checklist

Tutor							
Date	Date	Date	Date	Date	Date		Collects material
							Goes to work space
							Describes lesson to partner
							Praises correct responses
							Shows enthusiasm
							Provides corrective feedback
							Uses positive manner
							Follows directions without assistance
							Speaks in a quiet voice
							Keeps records
							Replaces material at end of session

presenting items, correcting errors, prompting and praising correct answers, testing and recording progress, and assigning points for progress. Tutor training procedures consistently include a combination of the following: an orientation to the rationale and goals of tutoring, a description of the materials and procedures, teacher demonstration of tutoring skills, tutor imitation and role playing of procedures with feedback, intermittent guidance when needed, and praise for following the procedures correctly. In essence, tutor training follows the direct instruction sequence (i.e., use an advance organizer, describe the behavioral expectations, demonstrate the behavioral expectations, and so on) used to teach behavioral expectations such as classroom rules. Sample guidelines for helping the tutor succeed include the following:

- Make the relationship with your partner positive because it is the most important part of any tutoring program.
- Greet your partner as you would a good friend. Be friendly and open. Make your partner feel at ease. Call your partner by name.
- Listen carefully to your partner. Be interested. Ask questions.
- Be patient. Be respectful. Build confidence by helping your partner succeed.
- Believe in your partner! You will both succeed and you will both be learning. Remember, everyone is different and everyone learns at an individual pace.

Figure 2.5 presents a sample tutor checklist for the teacher to use for training and feedback.

7. *Train tutees.* A primary task of the tutees is to try their best to do the tasks presented by the tutor. Specific duties include following directions, receiving feedback appropriately, and maintaining attention. Tutees typically are trained with the same direct instruction sequence used to teach tutors.

8. *Teach social skills used in peer tutoring.* For peer tutoring to occur in a positive and supportive environment, the teacher should teach social skills such as accepting a partner, giving and accepting corrective feedback, and praising a partner. Each of these skills is taught through the direct instruction sequence. Teacher demonstrations of nonexamples (such as rudeness or put-downs) and discussions of how those behaviors make people feel help teach the importance of good social skills, as do teacher demonstrations and role playing of how to greet a partner with a smile and a gesture (such as a high-five).

9. *Review rules.* The teacher reminds the students that the classroom rules apply during peer tutoring. Rules to emphasize during peer tutoring are "Make transitions quickly" and "Use whisper voices." Again, the behavioral expectations for these rules are taught using the direct instruction sequence.

10. *Schedule the peer-tutoring sessions.* Most researchers recommend about 20 minutes for one-way tutoring sessions and 30 minutes for reciprocal sessions. Positive achievement results primarily from two or more sessions weekly.

11. *Conduct a tutoring session.* In addition to planning the peer-tutoring program and adapting curriculum materials, teachers must supervise the sessions, evaluate progress, and make periodic revisions. Initially the teacher needs to supervise the peer-tutoring sessions closely and provide corrective and positive feedback. Once the students become proficient in their respective tutor–tutee

roles, the teacher can scan the tutoring sessions while working with a small group or individual students. Some educators report good results when the teacher periodically meets with tutor–tutee pairs to discuss progress. Also, researchers have found that tutor and tutee performance contingencies positively affect maintenance of effective peer-tutoring interactions as well as academic achievement (Greenwood, Carta, & Hall, 1988). Suggestions for managing misbehavior during peer-tutoring sessions include the following:

- Ignore misbehavior unless it persists.
- If misbehavior is chronic, reassign the pair to other partners.
- Do not get involved in minor disputes.
- Praise pairs for appropriate behavior.
- For persistent misbehavior, implement owing-time consequences.
- Develop a signal (e.g., tap a note on a toy xylophone) to remind the class to work quietly.

12. *Evaluate the peer-tutoring program.* The achievement of tutees can be evaluated by examining the daily progress sheets completed by tutors. Weekly quizzes on the skills or content covered in peer tutoring also help monitor progress. Social skills progress can be monitored through systematic observation of the tutoring pairs, and affective domains can be evaluated through interviews or questionnaires.

With appropriate planning, student training, and teacher support, peer tutoring can be a viable instructional alternative. To maintain the tutors' involvement, their efforts can be recognized by activities such as displaying their pictures on bulletin boards, allowing them to meet before school, offering awards, providing reinforcing events such as meetings with faculty or administrators, publishing articles about the program, and having the principal recognize tutors.

Students Teaching Students: Classwide Peer Tutoring

Peer-mediated instructional programs deserve consideration from general education and special education teachers. Classwide peer tutoring enables the teacher to engage all students in a classroom simultaneously in a variety of academic tasks. It involves restructuring the classroom so that pairs of students work together on academic activities.

Description of Classwide Peer Tutoring *Class-Wide Peer Tutoring* (Delquadri, Greenwood, Whorton, Carta, & Hall, 1986; Greenwood, Delquadri, & Carta,

1997) was developed at the Juniper Gardens Children's Project in Kansas City, Kansas, and is designed to help students with mild disabilities improve their basic skills. *ClassWide Peer Tutoring* is an integrated behavior management and direct instruction procedure based upon reciprocal peer tutoring and group-oriented reinforcement contingencies (e.g., cooperative learning). The method includes three features to increase on-task behavior and amount of practice of academic skills: (1) Peers are used to supervise responding and practice; (2) a game format is used that includes points and competing teams to motivate students and maintain interest; and (3) a weekly evaluation plan ensures gains in individual and class progress. The teacher trains students to be effective tutors by carefully explaining and demonstrating error-correction procedures and the point system to be followed in the tutoring sessions. Corrective feedback is given during supervised practice opportunities.

The *ClassWide Peer Tutoring* system features the following basic arrangement.

1. Daily tutoring slots of about 30 minutes are required. Each student tutors for 10 minutes and then receives 10 minutes of tutoring. An additional 10 minutes are spent counting points and posting results.
2. On Monday the tutor–tutee pairs for the week are selected. The students of each pair sit next to or across from each other and begin a 10-minute tutoring session. For example, if the task is spelling, the tutor monitors the spelling and awards two points for each word written correctly. The tutee earns one point for correctly respelling a word after the tutor has detected an error and gives the correct spelling. The tutor marks points on a Tutoring Point Sheet. At the end of 10 minutes, the tutoring roles are reversed.
3. During the tutoring sessions, the teacher moves among the students and awards bonus points for correct tutoring behavior.
4. After the second 10-minute session, each student counts the number of points earned as both tutor and tutee. The class is divided into two teams by having students draw from a container that holds squares of two different colors. The point totals for each student are recorded in one of two team columns on a chart. The team earning the highest number of points is the winning team for the day or week. The composition of the two teams changes periodically.
5. On Friday the teacher conducts a more intensive assessment of each student's progress on the skills from that week.

Peer-Assisted Learning Strategies (PALS), which was developed at George Peabody College of Vanderbilt University and formally is known as Peabody Classwide Peer Tutoring, is a research-based instructional alternative that extends the Juniper Gardens Children's Project model so that students engage in strategy-based reading practice and intensive math practice. In PALS Reading (Fuchs, Fuchs, & Burish, 2000; Fuchs, Mathes, & Fuchs, 1996), which originally was developed for grades 2 through 6, students in the class are paired such that each pair includes a higher- and a lower-performing student. Each pair is assigned to one of two teams for which the pair earns points for completing reading activities correctly and demonstrating appropriate tutoring behavior. Three major reading activities are included during three weekly 35-minute sessions: partner reading, paragraph shrinking, and prediction relay. In partner reading, students take turns reading aloud, correcting errors, and retelling what they read. In paragraph shrinking, students take turns reading the paragraph aloud, correcting errors, and stating the main idea of each paragraph in ten or fewer words. In prediction relay, students take turns predicting what happens next, reading the next passage aloud, correcting errors, verifying predictions, summarizing the text, and making more predictions.

Because reading problems begin before second grade and extend beyond sixth grade, downward and upward extensions of PALS Reading have been developed for kindergarten, first grade, and high school (Fuchs et al., 2001). In Kindergarten PALS (Mathes, Clancy-Menchetti, & Torgesen, 2001), each 20-minute lesson (i.e., three sessions per week) includes class and pair games that teach pronunciation, letter knowledge, and phonological and phonemic awareness. Sound Play includes activities in rhyming, isolation of first sounds, ending sounds, blending sounds, and segmenting words into sounds, and Sounds and Words activities include What Sound? and What Word? In First Grade PALS (Mathes, Torgesen, Allen, & Allor, 2001), a higher-achieving student is paired with a lower-achieving student and 35-minute sessions are conducted three times a week. Each lesson is preceded by 3 minutes of teacher-directed instruction on new letter sounds and sight words and a segmenting and blending activity. Sounds and Words includes activities in letter-sound correspondence, blending, sight words (including a speed-reading game), and reading decodable words and sight words in short stories. After students have been doing Sounds and Words activities independently for 4 weeks, partner reading is added. The upward extension of PALS, which is for high school students, incorporates the same activities and team structure as PALS for

students in grades 2 through 6; however, students switch partners frequently, a more adult motivational system is incorporated, and expository text of material useful in students' lives is used.

In PALS Math (Fuchs, Fuchs, Karns, & Phillips, 1996), two primary procedures are used: coaching and practice. During coaching, the tutor asks scripted questions and uses correction procedures to guide the tutee in solving three math problems. The tutee completes the next three problems with guidance and explains the process. The students change roles at the middle of the worksheet. During practice, the students work independently on a mixed-problem worksheet and then score each other's work. PALS Math is designed for students in grades 2 to 6 and involves 40-minute sessions that are conducted two or more times a week. A computer program determines which students should be paired together to work on specific math skills.

Research on Classwide Peer Tutoring The *ClassWide Peer Tutoring* program was developed over an 8-year period and has been field-tested extensively. Intervention studies have been conducted at the elementary and the secondary level and have included students with mild and moderate disabilities as well as nondisabled low-achieving students. Research data indicate that *ClassWide Peer Tutoring* improves students' engagement in academic tasks, increases academic achievement gains, and enhances cooperative peer relations (Kamps et al., 2008; Maheady, Harper, & Mallette, 1991, 2001; Simmons, Fuchs, Fuchs, Hodge, & Mathes, 1994; Utley, Mortweet, & Greenwood, 1997). Recently, research has demonstrated that *ClassWide Peer Tutoring* also can be useful as a part of the RTI framework. McMaster, Kung, Han, and Cao (2008) examined the efficacy of a peer-tutoring model (i.e., Kindergarten PALS) as a Tier 1 intervention for kindergarten students who were English language learners. Children who participated in the peer-tutoring intervention performed better on measures of early reading (i.e., phonemic awareness and letter knowledge) than children in the control group. McMaster and her colleagues recommend the use of the peer tutoring model as an effective way to implement Tier 1 instruction and prevent the need for more intensive levels of Tier 2 or Tier 3 intervention.

PALS for instruction in reading and math was combined with curriculum-based measurement and field-tested in inclusive classrooms with outstanding results. Efficacy studies were conducted for two successive years in general education classrooms that included students with learning disabilities. The studies involved more than 150 teachers and 3,500 students. Each study yielded impressive statistically significant outcomes (Joint Committee on Teacher Planning for Students with Disabilities, 1995). Results of additional PALS research on oral reading fluency, reading comprehension, and math measures include increased academic on-task time, academic growth, and positive reports about tutoring from students and teachers (Fuchs, Fuchs, & Kazdan, 1999; Fuchs, Fuchs, Phillips, Hamlett, & Karns, 1995; Mastropieri et al., 2001; Mathes & Babyak, 2001). Workshops and training materials are available that enable teachers to instruct their students to implement curriculum-based measurement and classwide peer-mediated instruction. (For information, contact Lynn Fuchs or Douglas Fuchs at Vanderbilt University, Box 328 Peabody, Nashville, TN 37203; 615/343–4782.)

Programming Guidelines for Classwide Peer Tutoring   To develop and implement a successful classwide peer-tutoring program, the following guidelines are presented:

- Provide social skills training to those students who need it to work together cooperatively. Useful skills include accepting a partner, encouraging and praising your partner, taking turns, using quiet voices, and stopping activity on signal. Demonstrating and reinforcing these skills greatly enhances the success of peer tutoring.
- For partner reading, pair a high-level reader with a low-level reader and use the following sequence: (1) The high-level reader reads aloud for 5 minutes, (2) the low-level reader reads the same text aloud for 5 minutes, and (3) the low-level reader sequences the major events of what has been read for 1 minute if in second or third grade, or for 2 minutes if in fourth, fifth, or sixth grade.
- For paragraph shrinking, pair a high-level reader with a low-level reader and use the following sequence: (1) For 5 minutes, the high-level reader continues reading new text in the story, stopping after each paragraph to summarize the paragraph, and (2) for 5 minutes, the low-level reader continues with new text, summarizing each paragraph.
- For prediction relay, pair a high-level reader with a low-level reader and use the following sequence: (1) Continuing with new text, the high-level reader reads aloud for 5 minutes, stopping after each page to check the previous prediction, summarize the page, and predict what will happen on the next page; and (2) the low-level reader continues to read new text aloud for 5 minutes, stopping after each page to check the previous prediction, summarize the page, and make a prediction.

- For lower level skills such as spelling or math facts, use scoring similar to basketball. The student who announces the word or math fact responds to a correct answer by saying "Two points" and circles two points on a score sheet. For an incorrect response, the announcer says, "Sorry, Partner, the correct spelling (or math fact) is _____. Go for a foul shot." The partner then practices writing the word (or math fact) correctly three times. To encourage the practice of foul shots (i.e., error correction), the teacher periodically gives bonus points for players writing the word or math fact correctly three times.
- Assign each pair of students to one of two class teams and pool together the weekly points of the pairs of students to get a weekly team score. When team total scores are announced, it is important to celebrate each team's score and minimize competition. Moreover, the weekly spelling or math test scores for each team can be compiled and recorded. Each team can be encouraged to beat last week's score or set new records.
- Use classwide peer tutoring two or three times a week.
- Avoid long-term pairing of students who do not get along with each other. Teams may be changed weekly or biweekly.

---

myeducationlab

To enhance your understanding of PALS and peer tutoring, go to the IRIS Center Resources section of the Topic Assessing and Teaching Literacy and Language in the MyEducationLab for your course and complete the Module entitled PALS: A Reading Strategy for Grades 2–6.

Students Teaching Students: Cooperative Learning

Cooperative learning represents another instructional arrangement in which peers work independently. Because of its success with diverse groups of students (Mainzer, Mainzer, Slavin, & Lowry, 1993) and the independent nature of their work, it represents a viable approach for promoting successful inclusion. During the last decade, cooperative learning has enjoyed increasing popularity and enthusiastic support from general educators and special educators.

Description of Cooperative Learning   There are many forms of cooperative learning, but they all involve students working in teams or small groups to help one another learn (Slavin, 1991). Because cooperative learning provides students with an opportunity to practice skills or learn content presented by the teacher, it supplements teacher instruction. Cooperative learning emphasizes team goals, and team success is achieved only if each individual learns. A basic definition of cooperative learning is *an instructional arrangement in which small groups or teams of students work together to achieve team success in a manner that promotes the students' responsibility for their own learning as well as the learning of others.* According to Johnson and Johnson (1994), five basic elements need to be included in each lesson for small-group learning to be cooperative: (1) interdependence—the students work toward a common goal with each student's efforts helping both the individual and the team; (2) promotive interaction—the students promote their peers' learning through praise, help, support, and encouragement; (3) individual accountability—each student is responsible for learning the required material and contributing to the group; (4) interpersonal and small-group skills—students learn collaborative skills including social skills, decision-making, communication, and conflict-management skills; and (5) group processing—the students discuss and assess how well they are achieving their goals and working together.

The Student Team Learning model includes the most extensive practices used in cooperative learning. The methods in this model emphasize that team goals can be achieved only if each member achieves selected academic objectives. Slavin (1991) notes that the concepts of team reward, individual accountability, and equal opportunities for success are central to all methods in the model. Team rewards are earned when a team achieves at or above a predetermined criterion level. Because all teams that achieve criterion are successful and rewarded, teams are not in competition for an all-or-nothing reward. Individual accountability is featured because team success depends on the individual learning of all team members. Team success is evaluated by the composite performances (e.g., scores) of team members on a quiz of material assigned to the group. This relationship of individual performance to team performance fosters activities that involve team members helping one another learn the targeted academic content. Equal opportunities for success are provided because each team member helps the team by improving on past performance. This challenges low, average, and high achievers to do their best because their respective performances all are valued by the team.

Student Teams-Achievement Divisions (STAD) (Slavin, 1978, 1986) and Teams-Games-Tournament (TGT) (DeVries & Slavin, 1978; Slavin, 1986) are two cooperative learning methods in the Student Team Learning model that are adaptable across subject areas and grade levels. In STAD, a heterogeneous group of four students are assigned to a team. After the teacher presents a lesson, the team works together to ensure that all students have mastered the lesson. Then the students take individual quizzes without peer help. The students' quiz scores are compared with their past averages, and points are awarded if their performances meet or exceed their earlier efforts. The points are totaled to yield a team score, and teams that meet criteria are rewarded (e.g., they receive certificates). This cycle of activity usually takes three to five class periods. STAD works best with academic material that has single correct answers (e.g., math computations and map skills). TGT uses the same teacher presentation, group assignment, and teamwork format as STAD. The quizzes, however, are replaced with weekly tournaments. In these tournaments students compete with players from other teams to earn points to add to their respective team scores. Students compete at three-member tournament tables with others who have similar skill levels on the target skills. The winners at the tournament tables each earn the same number of points for their teams. All students have an equal opportunity for success because low achievers competing with other low achievers can earn as many points as high achievers competing with high achievers. As with STAD, TGT takes three to five classes and is most appropriate with content featuring single answers.

In addition to STAD and TGT, two comprehensive curricula exist for specific content and grades. Team Assisted Individualization (TAI) (Slavin, Madden, & Stevens, 1990) is designed for mathematics in third through sixth grade, and Cooperative Integrated Reading and Composition (CIRC) (Slavin, Stevens, & Madden, 1988) is designed for reading in third through fifth grade. Also, Bilingual Cooperative Integrated Reading and Composition (BCIRC), an adaptation of CIRC, is designed to help Spanish speakers make a transition to English reading instruction. Studies examining the efficacy of CIRC and BCIRC indicate that both have potentially positive effects for students (Institute of Education Sciences, 2007a, 2007b).

Research on Cooperative Learning Most research on cooperative learning focuses on the Student Team Learning techniques developed at Johns Hopkins University. In a synthesis of research on cooperative learning, Slavin (1991) reports the following:

- The most successful approaches for improving academic achievement include group goals and individual accountability. In these settings, groups are rewarded based on the performances of the respective team members.

- In studies featuring group goals and individual accountability, the achievement effects of experimental/control comparisons consistently favor cooperative learning. Specifically, in 37 of 44 studies of at least 4 weeks' duration, the significantly positive effects favor cooperative learning, whereas none favor traditional methods.
- The positive achievement effects of cooperative learning appear consistent across grades (i.e., 2 through 12), subject areas, and school settings (i.e., rural, urban, and suburban).
- Effects are equally positive for high, average, and low achievers.
- The positive effects of cooperative learning are reported consistently in affective areas (e.g., self-esteem, intergroup relations, attitudes toward school, and ability to work cooperatively).

Slavin et al. (1990) report excellent results in math achievement and affective measures with Team Assisted Individualization for students with academic disabilities in general education settings. Likewise, Cooperative Integrated Reading and Composition groups for reading and writing yield excellent outcomes for students without disabilities as well as students with academic disabilities in general education settings (Slavin et al., 1988). Slavin (1989/1990) states, "Cooperative learning seems to be an extraordinary success. It has an excellent research base, many viable and successful forms, and hundreds of thousands of enthusiastic adherents" (p. 3).

Programming Guidelines for Cooperative Learning Team goals and rewards, individual accountability, and equal opportunities appear to be the essential components of a cooperative learning program. The following guidelines adapted from those presented in peer tutoring are appropriate for planning and implementing cooperative learning.

- Determine goals of cooperative learning.
- Target selected skills or contingent lessons for the teams.
- Select materials, including the quizzes or tournament questions.
- Design procedures for team members to help one another.
- Assign students of varying achievement levels to the same teams.
- Train teams to help one another.
- Teach social skills for teamwork.
- Review classroom rules and teach new rules.
- Schedule the cooperative learning sessions for 3 to 5 days a week.
- Conduct a cooperative learning session.
- Evaluate the cooperative learning program.

In addition to the general guidelines for cooperative learning, guidelines specifically for students with disabilities also should be considered. In a review of research on cooperative learning, results for students with learning disabilities were not always positive (McMaster & Fuchs, 2002). The following are a set of guidelines to ensure the success of students with learning problems when implementing cooperative learning techniques.

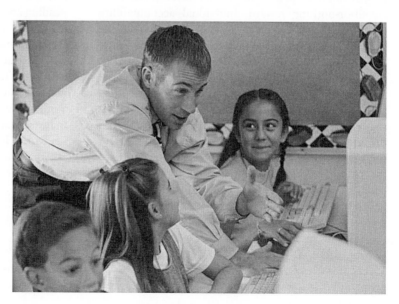

Technological tools can provide individualized instruction and immediate reinforcement of student responses.
Getty Images, Inc.–Photodisc/Royalty Free

- Provide adequate teacher or peer support.
- Select group members carefully to ensure appropriate support of student learning.
- Monitor student progress using formative assessment to ensure that academic goals are achieved.
- Make certain that the student with learning disabilities has a role conducive to learning, rather than an ancillary role that does not produce learning outcomes (Vaughn, Bos, & Schumm, 2007).

Material with Student: Seatwork Activities

Learning Considerations   From a learning perspective, the material-with-student or independent seatwork arrangement provides the student with opportunities to practice skills that the teacher has presented. Practice helps the student move through the learning sequence that begins with acquisition and progresses to the higher levels of proficiency, maintenance, and generalization. For many students with learning problems, the mastery of skills and content requires extensive practice.

From a review of the research on practice, Dempster (1991) reports the following findings that have implications for classrooms.

- Given equivalent practice time, two or more opportunities with the same material are more effective than a single opportunity.
- Spaced practice promotes better learning than massed practice.
- Relative to massed practice, the effectiveness of spaced practice increases as the frequency of the practice activity increases.
- Cumulative questions or tasks promote effective learning.
- Frequent, spaced practice seems to produce a more elaborate understanding of the topic than massed practice.

Direct classroom implications of Dempster's (1991) findings include the following suggestions for planning effective practice.

- Incorporate spaced reviews or practice (including questions from previous and current lessons) into a variety of activities (such as discussions, seatwork, peer tutoring, and homework).
- Organize lessons so that a brief time is used to review the main points of the previous day's lesson. Include review tasks or questions on seatwork activities.
- Once or twice a month, conduct a comprehensive practice session featuring discussions and seatwork.

Teacher Considerations   From a teacher's perspective, a material-with-student arrangement not only provides students with opportunities to improve achievement but also allows the teacher some freedom to work with small groups or individual students. Although planning seatwork activities and teaching students to work independently is time consuming, it is worth the effort. Well-designed material-with-student activities can make the school year pleasant and productive. Guidelines for planning and implementing an effective independent seatwork program include the following:

- *Ensure that the independent work assignments are tailored to the student's instructional level.* Preceding independent practice with demonstration or guided practice is a good way to ensure that the assignment is instructionally appropriate.
- *Use a variety of independent seatwork activities.* Varying the activities provides the teacher with alternatives and tends to increase student motivation and on-task time. Suitable activities include self-correcting materials, instructional games, computer-assisted instruction, and tape recorder–assisted instruction. These activities are presented in this chapter and in the curriculum area chapters throughout the text.
- *Consider work folders for daily assignments.* A work folder is a flexible system of communication between the teacher and the individual student. Work folders can be used to communicate the day's assignments. They provide a place for keeping charts and completed work and for giving feedback. After students have used the work folders for a while, they can enter the room, pick up their folders, and begin work without teacher intervention. A check-off sheet can be placed in the folders to help students determine which tasks are completed and which need to be studied.
- *Prepare some cushion activities to accommodate students finishing their work at different times.* Activities include starting another assignment, writing on the computer, working in a learning center, listening to a recording, assisting another student, or reading a book or magazine.
- *Modify the format of worksheets to improve learner friendliness.* Because some students become anxious when given a full worksheet of problems to complete, it helps to divide worksheets into fewer problems. This enables students to complete as much work (e.g., two short worksheets) without feeling overwhelmed. Also, a full worksheet can be divided into sections and students can be encouraged to work on one section at a time.

- *Design procedures that enable students to ask questions while doing independent seatwork.* Procedures that prevent constant interruptions from students while the teacher is working with a small group include (1) assigning student helpers to answer questions, (2) developing a signal (e.g., a desk sign that signifies that the student has a question) that allows the student to continue working until help arrives, and (3) designating an area of the room where one student at a time can go when he or she has a question.
- *Ensure that students understand the instructions for their seatwork activities before starting small-group instruction.* This is especially important when new assignments or a new format (e.g., self-correcting material or computer) are used.
- *Use the direct instruction teaching sequence to teach the behavioral expectations for independent seatwork.*

Material with Student: Self-Correcting Materials

Students spend much classroom time working with instructional materials on their own; thus, the materials used should not lead to frustration, failure, and the practicing of errors. To some degree, a material serves as a teacher. The more teacher functions it can serve, the more useful it is. Inexpensive materials can provide instructions, present a stimulus or task, and provide feedback about correctness of student responses.

Self-correcting materials give the student immediate feedback without the teacher being present. Self-correcting materials are especially useful with students with learning problems who have a history of academic failure. It is important to reduce their failure experiences, particularly public failures. When the student makes a mistake with a self-correcting material, it is a private event—no one else knows. Only the student sees the error, and the error can be corrected immediately. Furthermore, if immediate feedback is not provided, mistakes will be practiced until the teacher corrects the student at a later time. With self-correcting materials, the student is corrected immediately and practices only the correct response.

Self-correcting materials help students maintain attention to academic tasks. The student can approach each response with a game-playing attitude: "I bet I get this one right!" When self-correcting materials are used, some cheating should be expected at first. Although many students initially enjoy beating the system, eventually it becomes more fun to select an answer and see whether it is correct. If cheating persists, a checkup test or posttest on the featured content can be administered. The student soon realizes that cheating on the material will not help on the checkup test.

There are many ways to make self-correcting materials, including the use of answer keys, matching cards, puzzles, pocket calculators, and computers. The materials should be simple so that a demonstration enables students to use them. The best use of these materials is to provide practice or drill on areas that the teacher already has introduced.

Students should not be required to use the same self-correcting material for a long time. The teacher should vary the content periodically, exchange materials with another teacher, give students a choice of which material they wish to use, have students make their own content for the self-correcting device, or put away selected materials for a while. By changing self-correcting materials from time to time, the teacher can maintain student interest and involvement.

The remainder of this section provides examples of feedback devices that can be used to make self-correcting materials. Some of the self-correcting materials are presented with construction guidelines, while others are simple to make. The same device or material often can be used with different content. Throughout this book, self-correcting materials are presented in the different curriculum areas.

Flap A flap can be made of any flexible material such as cloth, vinyl wallpaper, construction paper, or thin cardboard. When using this device, the student can bend the flap up or to the side to reveal the answer to the question or problem. Figure 2.6 illustrates an Answer Box with a flap to provide feedback.

Windows Small windows can be cut in materials to provide feedback. The correct answer can be in the window or, when two or more windows are used, the items in the windows can match to show a correct response. Spinning Wheels in Figure 2.7 illustrates the use of windows to provide feedback.

Stylus Feedback can be provided by using a stylus with certain types of stimulus cards. The Poke Box in Figure 2.8 illustrates the use of a stylus.

Matching Cards Sets of cards are prepared with the problem or question on one card and the answer on another card. The back of the set of cards contains a match of some sort or a picture completion. After selecting an answer to a problem, the student turns over the cards. If the appropriate answer is chosen, the objects, numbers, colors, or pictures on the back will either match or fit together to complete a picture.

FIGURE 2.6
Answer Box

Outside view

Inside view

Block of wood

Stack of cards

Answer Box

Instructional objective: See math fact or problem—say answer; see math fact or problem—write answer; see contraction words—write contraction; see percentage problem—write answer.

Feedback response: A flap is placed over the mouth. When the flap is raised, the answer is revealed. Vinyl wallpaper is flexible and serves as a good flap.

Materials: A cardboard box (e.g., cigar or school supply box); 3" × 5" index cards; contact paper or lamination; a small wooden block, about 3" × 3½".

Construction: Cut out three squares in the lid of the box so that they form two eyes and a mouth. Cut a section out of the right side of the box so that the index cards can be fed into the box from the side. Paint the box inside and out. Laminate a picture of a face on the box and place the eyes and the mouth over the squares. Place a flexible flap over the mouth. Prepare index cards with problems and answers so that the problem appears in the "eyes" and so that the flap over the mouth can be lifted to reveal the answer. For math problems, use a grease (or overhead projector) pencil to write the math operation (i.e., +, −, ×, ÷) in the space between the "eyes."

Directions: The student inserts a stack of selected cards into the Answer Box. Then the student responds (orally or by writing) to the problem presented in the two windows. The student lifts the flap over the mouth to reveal the answer and check the response.

Modifications: The card formats can be varied to present a variety of math problems and reading tasks. Possible card formats include the following:

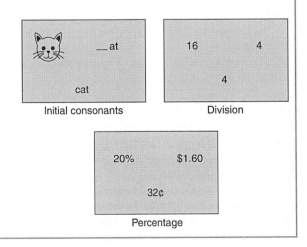

Initial consonants

Division

Percentage

FIGURE 2.7
Spinning Wheels

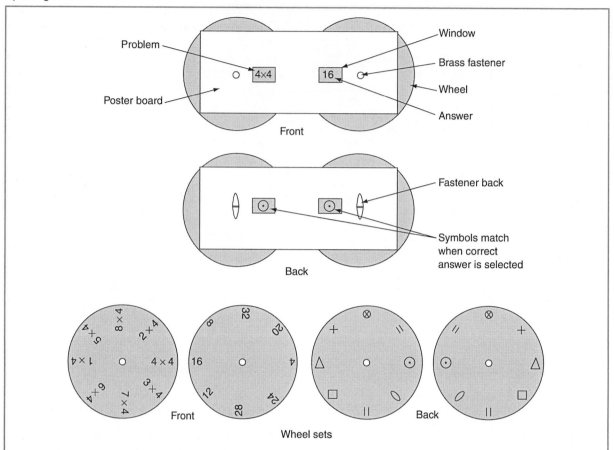

Front

Back

Wheel sets

Spinning Wheels

Instructional objective: Any objective in which a matched pair can be devised (i.e., problems on one wheel and the correct answers on another wheel) can be selected. See math problem—select answer; see picture—select word; see picture—select initial sound.

Feedback device: Windows provide feedback. When a correct match is obtained in the front windows, the objects, symbols, or numbers match in the back windows. Thus, to check an answer the student looks at the back windows.

Materials: Poster board; brass fasteners; small pictures or symbols.

Construction: Cut two horizontal pieces of poster board with matching dimensions. Cut two windows on the same horizontal line in each piece so that the windows line up with each other when the pieces are placed together (i.e., back to back). Decorate and laminate each piece and make the center holes for the fasteners. Cut circles with dimensions that enable the outer 1" ridge to pass through the windows when the center of the wheel is lined up with the poster board hole. Write, draw, or paste problems on one wheel and put answers on a corresponding wheel. Write, draw, or glue symbols, objects, or numbers on the back of each wheel set.

Directions: The student selects a wheel set that presents an appropriate task. The student places the wheels between the two rectangular pieces, lines up the holes, and inserts the brass fasteners. The student then rotates the task wheel until a problem is presented in the window. Next, the student rotates the other wheel and selects one of the answers that passes through the window. Once an answer is selected, the student flips over the material and checks to see whether the answer is correct. A correct answer yields matching objects in the two windows on the back.

Modifications: The teacher can make numerous wheel sets and code them according to skill area. Wheels that are to be used together (i.e., a wheel set) should have matching codes. The tasks that can be placed on the wheels are almost limitless. The size of the material can be varied to accommodate different-size windows.

Time

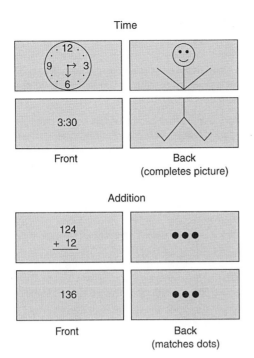

Front

Back
(completes picture)

Addition

Front

Back
(matches dots)

Answer on Back   A problem is presented on one side of a stimulus card, and the answer is placed on the other side.

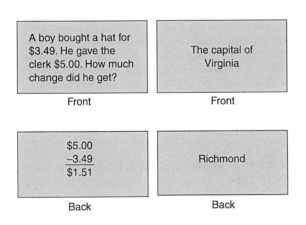

Front

Front

Back

Back

Tab   A tab is pulled from a pocket in the learning material to reveal an answer or answers.

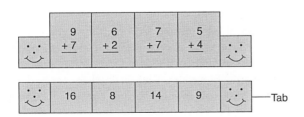

Pocket   Pockets can be made easily by stapling envelopes to the back of the learning material. Pockets usually hold some type of answer key. In addition, pockets can be coded to provide feedback. For example, library card pockets can be used for sorting stimulus cards. A code is on the back of the stimulus card and the library pocket. If a card is placed in the correct pocket, the codes match. Many instructional targets can be taught with this format. For example, if the stimulus cards show words from the categories of noun, pronoun, verb, and adjective, there would be a pocket corresponding to each category.

Holes   Problems are written on one side of a card or sheet, and a hole is punched beside or underneath each item. The answer to each problem is written on the back of the card next to or under the hole. The student sees the problem, writes or says the answer, puts a pipe cleaner or pencil in the hole, and turns over the card to check the response. This format can be used for teaching opposites, plurals, synonyms, word problems, and so on. Manila folders can be used to make this material.

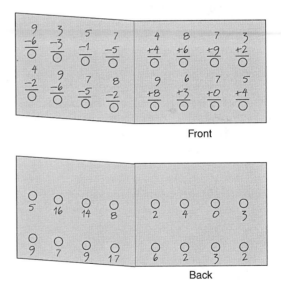

Front

Back

Clips   Clips such as clothespins or paper clips can be used to provide feedback. For example, a cardboard pizza wheel can be divided into segments with a task stimulus presented in each segment. Responses are made by clipping clothespins to the edge of the segments. To check answers, the board is turned over to see whether the code on the pizza board matches the code on the clothespin.

FIGURE 2.8
Poke box

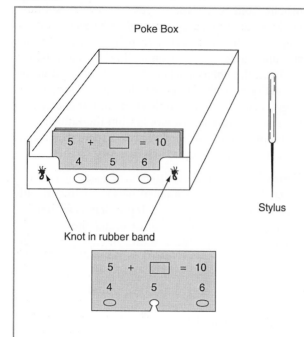

Poke Box

Stylus

Knot in rubber band

Poke Box

Instructional objective: Any instructional target that features a multiple-choice answer format can be used with the Poke Box. See math problem—choose or write answer; see sentence—choose missing word; see paragraph—choose title.

Feedback response: The student inserts a stylus in one of the holes below the answers and pulls the card to see whether it comes out of the box. If the correct hole is selected, the card is removed easily from the box because the area below the correct answer is cut and offers no resistance to the stylus.

Materials: A cardboard or wooden box big enough to hold 3" × 5" or 5" × 8" index cards; a large rubber band; a thin stick or poker; index cards.

Construction: Cut the front end of the box so that most of the index card is visible, but leave a horizontal strip at the bottom of the box about 1" high. Using a hole punch or drill, make three evenly spaced holes across the front of the box about ½" from the bottom. At each end of the front of the box, drill or punch a hole that extends beyond the dimensions of the index cards. Insert a broken rubber band from the inside of the box on both sides, and tie the ends in knots on the outside of the box. (The rubber band holds the cards and pushes them to the front of the box.) Paint the box inside and out. Make holes in the index cards so that they line up with the holes in the box. Cut out one answer slot on each card. Attach the stylus to the box. Prepare index cards with problems or questions on top and possible answers beneath. Line up the answers with the appropriate holes. To prevent a student from tearing the card by pulling too hard on an incorrect choice, strengthen the holes with gummed reinforcers.

Directions: The student says, writes, or chooses the answer to the problem card. Then the student pokes the stylus in the hole representing the answer. If the choice is correct, the problem card can be pulled up and out of the box and the next problem card is presented.

Modifications: The size of the box can vary so that large cards can be used. Some Poke Boxes feature 8" × 11½" cardboard cards. The large space provides room for short stories and multiple-choice comprehension questions. The teacher can put the problem or story on a separate worksheet and put the answer selections on the cards.

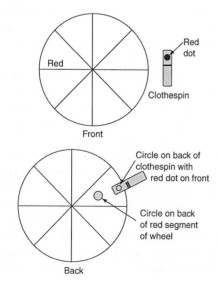

Strips in a Folder   Strips are cut in one side of a manila folder, which is then laminated. Worksheets containing problems and answers are inserted into the folder so that only the problem is presented. The student uses a grease pencil or a felt-tip pen to write the responses under each problem. Then the worksheet is pulled upward, and the answers appear in the strip.

Material with Student: Instructional Games

Once students with learning problems understand the concept involved in a new skill or strategy, they need practice to achieve mastery or automaticity. Instructional games help students maintain interest during practice. Familiar game procedures such as checkers, cards, dice, spinners, and start-to-finish boards are useful. Game content can be individualized for students by putting

Worksheet

Folder with
strips cut out

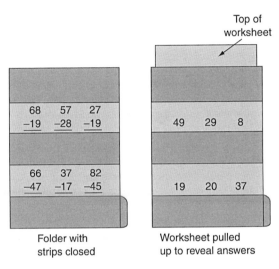

Top of
worksheet

Folder with
strips closed

Worksheet pulled
up to reveal answers

questions on cards and requiring players to answer a question on a card selected from his or her personalized stack (e.g., multiplication facts for one player and word meanings for another player). If the question is answered correctly, the student gets to take a turn (e.g., roll dice or spin a spinner) in the game. To maintain a high level of academically engaged time, students should maintain a good pace during games. A fast pace is facilitated by limiting the number of players to two or three for games in which students take turns or by setting a limit on response time.

Some students with learning problems do not like games because they are concerned that they do not possess the knowledge or skills needed to win in a game format. Games are only motivating when students think that they have a good chance of winning. Students are more likely to think they can win if the game features content or skills at the students' independent practice level. Also, cooperative game formats should be used until the students have the maturity to handle competitive games.

The games should be individualized for student needs. If a game has many uses, it saves the gamemaker's time and helps the student learn new skills in a familiar format. Games can be made self-correcting, or an answer key can be provided. This allows students to play the game without direct teacher supervision. Chance factors (e.g., lose a turn, take an extra turn, and skip two spaces) boost interest, and familiar formats (such as a game board) allow students to play independently.

Manila folders are good game boards because they are sturdy and conveniently sized, have tabs for easy reference, and are easy to store in a file cabinet. Rules are readily available if written on the back of each folder. Lamination makes the game board more durable and attractive. The teacher can purchase kits with blank laminated boards that have established routes for markers to travel, unmarked spinners, and blank playing cards. Several publishers market these materials. Finally, the teacher may wish to make a rough draft of a game and test it before making the finished product.

Two teacher-made instructional games are presented next (Figure 2.9 and Figure 2.10). In addition, games involving cards, dominoes, chips, dice, and so on are presented in the curriculum area chapters.

Material with Student: Technological Tools

Technological tools can be used in classrooms to promote learning for all students. However, the key to enhancing student learning is not the technological tools themselves; it is how the teacher uses the tools to promote student learning. King-Sears and Evmenova (2007) suggest three premises for integrating technology into instruction. First, using instructional technology can prepare students with disabilities for careers that require technological skills. As technology increases in schools and in businesses, it is clear that postschool success will require some level of technological skills. Second, technology improves the learning process rather than being the primary focus of the learning. In other words, technology should not be used for the sake of technology, but should be used to enhance student learning. Finally, technology changes quickly; thus, the teacher is required to stay current on the technological tools that are beneficial to student learning.

When selecting technology to enhance student learning, the teacher should follow several guidelines. As with any instructional tool, the teacher should consider the evidence base on the specific technology. Many new technologies may appear to provide benefit to students and may, perhaps, be marketed by vendors as researched based; however, these claims are sometimes unsubstantiated, and thus, the teacher

FIGURE 2.9
Simple game-board format

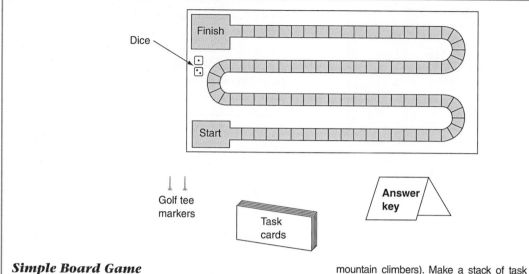

Simple Board Game

Instructional objective: Any instructional task that can be presented on a card and performed in a few seconds is suitable.

Feedback device: Answer key and peer correction provide feedback.

Materials: Poster board (or a manila folder); index cards; golf tees; dice; tasks for the cards.

Construction: Draw a segmented road, race track, rocket path, football field, mountain path, or any other start-to-finish sequence on poster board. Decorate the board to accent the game theme (e.g., racing cars, football, joggers, or mountain climbers). Make a stack of task cards with an accompanying answer key. For example, if the task card says 4 × 4 = ___, the answer key would read 4 × 4 = 16.

Directions: A player rolls the dice, picks up a task card, and says an answer. If no player challenges this answer, the player moves the marker the number of spaces indicated on the dice. If the answer is challenged, it is looked up on the answer key. If it is correct, the player gets another turn. If it is incorrect, the marker is not moved and the challenger takes a turn.

Modifications: Omit the challenge factor, or mark spaces so that when a player lands on them a chance card (e.g., *Move back three spaces* or *Take an extra turn*) is picked up.

should select technologies carefully (Blackhurst, 2005). Also, the technological tool should be selected based on alignment with curriculum outcomes (King-Sears & Evmenova, 2007). When the teacher considers this guideline, a high-technological device (i.e., electronic or computerized) may not be the most effective or efficient way to teach a concept or skill; a low-technological tool (e.g., a chart and markers) may be sufficient and, in fact, most effective. Finally, in addition to matching the curricular goal, the technological tool should match individual student needs. This is particularly true when selecting assistive technologies for students with disabilities. An assistive technology is a tool that aids a student in meeting personal IEP goals (Blackhurst, 2005). Like other technological tools, assistive technological devices may be considered high, medium, or low technology. Table 2.2 provides examples of various instructional and assistive technological tools that can be used to enhance the learning outcomes of students.

The computer can be used as a tool for classroom management as well as classroom instruction. With computer-managed instruction, teachers can more efficiently develop individualized educational programs and keep records. Computers can store sequences of instructional objectives and student performance information, track student progress, and generate proper forms and required recordkeeping data.

Computer-assisted instruction, or CAI, refers to software that is designed to provide instruction. The computer offers some unique advantages in instructing students with learning problems. Attributes of CAI that appear useful in helping students achieve include the following:

• Instruction is individualized by branching students to items appropriate for them.

FIGURE 2.10
Mystery Detective Game

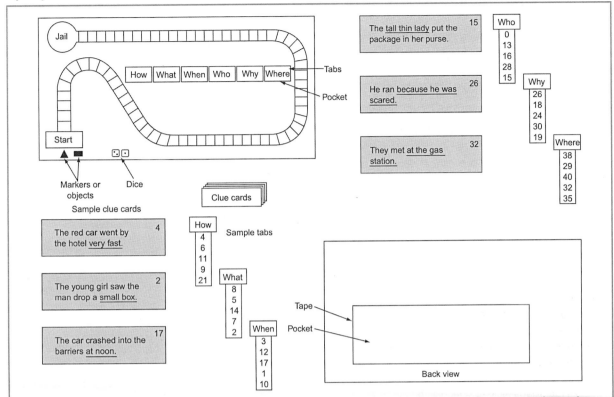

Mystery Detective

Instructional objective: Reading comprehension. See sentence clue card—select the meaning of underlined portion in terms of how, what, when, who, why, or where.

Feedback device: Tabs with numbers that match those on the clue cards are used to provide feedback. For example, a number on a *What* card will be on the tab labeled *What*. Thus, a correct response results in a number match between the card and the tab.

Materials: Poster board for game board, tabs, and clue cards; dice; pictures or drawings for decoration; objects to move from start to jail.

Construction: Cut a slot in the poster board and tape an additional piece of cardboard to the poster board to form a pocket with the slot at the top. Cut six tabs of a length that exposes the name of the tab but not the numbers when inserted fully in the pocket. On the game side of the board draw a "start-to-jail" winding, segmented road. Make a stack of sentence clue cards. Underline a portion of each sentence that corresponds to one of the how, what, when, who, why, or where questions. Place a number in the right top corner of each clue card. Do not repeat the numbers. Make six tabs, one for each of the questions. On each tab list the numbers that match the clue cards. Laminate the material to increase its durability.

Directions: A player rolls the dice and picks up a clue card. The player determines whether it is a how, what, when, who, why, or where clue and selects one of the tabs. If the number on the sentence clue card is on the tab chosen, the player's marker is moved the number of spaces indicated on the dice. If the number on the sentence clue card is not on the tab, the player's marker is not moved. The next player does the same thing, and the first player whose marker is put in jail wins.

Modifications: Use this game format to practice syllabication by labeling each tab with a number to indicate the number of syllables on corresponding word cards. Instead of using the pocket on the game board, put each tab in an envelope or in a separately constructed pocket. To make the game more exciting, mark "Trouble" or "Good News" on certain squares. When a marker lands on a marked square, the player picks up a card and does the activity on the card (e.g., *Go ahead three spaces*).

TABLE 2.2
Instructional and assistive high-, medium-, and low-technological tools

---

High Technology

Voice Recognition Software (VRS)—VRS converts speech directly into text. This software can be used to assist students with learning problems to improve their written expression skills. Students who are English language learners also benefit from the use of voice recognition software.

Handheld Computer Devices (iPods)—These devices can be used for a variety of purposes, including gaining access to information online, polling and testing students, displaying animations of scientific processes, and supporting language lessons (Rosenberg, 2009).

Computer-Assisted Instruction (CAI)—Some drill-and-practice programs have yielded small but positive effects on learning.

Distance Education—With distance education, students in remote locations have access to learning opportunities. Learners can gather in a remote location at a site that has a satellite and experience live video feeds. Students also can use their own computers at home to access distance education online.

Computerized Adaptive Testing (CAT)—With CAT, the test questions vary according to the test taker's responses. An incorrect answer is followed by an easier question, whereas a correct response generates a more difficult question. Initial studies report that CAT provides more accurate results regarding a person's knowledge level in less time than traditional test formats.

Medium Technology

Calculators—Features can include arithmetic, algebraic, and trigonometric functions, as well as plotting and graphing capabilities that allow the student to view computation results in graphic form.

Presentation Software—Overhead projectors and other audiovisual technologies effectively support lectures and demonstrations. A computer combined with a large-screen monitor or LCD display panel is a powerful medium for presenting visual material. Adding multimedia capability permits enhancements such as sound, graphics, and video images.

Laser Videodiscs—Laser videodisc programs enable the learner to interact with print and still or moving images. These programs do not require a computer, but utilize disc players with remote controls and bar-code readers that select and present images.

Pen-Based Computing—Data are entered through pen-based applications that use touch-screen icons and handwriting recognition, instead of through a keyboard.

Low Technology

Post-It Notes—Students can use various reading strategies, such as making connections in text, using post-it notes.

Chart Paper and Markers—At times, concepts can be illustrated using charts and markers as effectively as using a high-technology option.

Graphic Organizers—Graphic organizers are useful for helping students organize their thoughts before writing narrative or expository text.

- Tasks are analyzed and presented in meaningful sequences.
- Progress is at the student's own rate.
- Reinforcement of individual student responses is immediate.
- Fluency programs enable the student to increase the rate of correct responses.
- Animation, sound effects, and game-playing situations make drill and practice multisensory and motivating.
- Programs that simulate real-life experiences allow the student to make decisions and see the consequences.
- Strategies related to problem solving can be adapted for the computer through such programs as adventure games and software that teaches how to program.
- The computer can be programmed to use the student's name when giving lessons. A computer is nonjudgmental and allows the student to make mistakes in a nonthreatening environment.

- Students need to learn how to use technology to succeed in the future.

Educational software can differ in method or mode of delivery as well as in quality. Six modes of delivery include the following:

1. *Drill and practice.* Computer-assisted drill and practice supplements other forms of instruction. It is designed to integrate and consolidate previously learned material.
2. *Tutorial.* The role of teacher is assumed by the computer, and material is presented in a programmed learning format. The student moves from one step to the next by answering questions and can be branched to remedial or review segments as well as to more advanced levels of the program.
3. *Educational games.* Games are designed to develop general problem-solving methods and strategies while maintaining interest and motivation.
4. *Simulations.* Simulations attempt to model the underlying characteristics of a real phenomenon so that its properties can be studied. They can incorporate many game features but are intended to model some reality.
5. *Problem solving.* The computer can be used to solve real-world problems. For example, students can write computer programs to test possible solutions to a variety of problems.
6. *Word processing.* A word processor is a tool for writing instruction. Ease of correcting errors, availability of spelling and grammar checkers, elimination of the need to rewrite after revisions are made, and use of a printer that produces neat copies help teach writing to students with learning problems.

Although limited information exists concerning how computers can best be applied in the classroom, it is apparent that the use of appropriate software can motivate students with learning problems through individualized instruction and needed academic practice. Belson (2003) notes the following three advantages of using technology with students with learning problems: computers make individual attention possible, computers present students with tasks that interest and engage them, and computers give students greater control over their learning and encourage more risk-taking.

Three specific criteria can be used for evaluating software to use in teaching students with learning problems. First, software should use the computer's capacity to present the materials better than traditional methods. Voice synthesis, interaction, animation, and response monitoring are features of successful CAI. Moreover, to transcend traditional methods, CAI programs should use the student's knowledge base, provide guided and independent practice, give corrective feedback, present material in steps that facilitate learning, provide clear lesson overviews and goals, conduct periodic performance evaluations, and finish with a summary and review of the lesson's main points. The second criterion for good software is that the teacher must be able to modify or adapt the program to develop appropriate instructional matches for individual learners. The third criterion is that the CAI program should include a way to collect student response data so that teachers can monitor student progress. Actually, the teacher should expect software to report graphic representations of progress on easily generated printouts.

In addition to the many general uses of the computer for students with learning problems, specific applications also are suited to these students. For students who have difficulty maintaining on-task attention, computer programs can promote attention with color cueing, animation, underlining, and varying print sizes. For students who respond impulsively, the computer can provide cues or hints to inhibit impulsive responding. For those who take a lot of time to respond (i.e., reflective responders), computer programs can be tailored to allow extra response time. In addition, bilingual word-processing programs can be helpful to students from linguistically diverse backgrounds, and interactive computer technology can promote communication between students from economically diverse backgrounds.

Majsterek and Wilson (1993) reviewed several CAI studies that focused on teaching basic skills to students with learning problems. They conclude that CAI with well-designed software based on sound educational principles and tailored to the learning needs of students with learning problems can produce equivalent or slightly less than equivalent learning with less teacher time than traditional instruction. Other reports of CAI (Hasselbring, Goin, & Bransford, 1988; Woodward & Carnine, 1988) conclude that student achievement usually is greater when CAI supplements rather than replaces teacher-directed instruction. In general, an increasing number of research studies indicate that computer-based instruction improves student performances in word recognition, spelling, vocabulary knowledge, math computation, and reasoning skills (Okolo, Bahr, & Rieth, 1993; Okolo, Cavalier, Ferretti, & MacArthur, 2000).

Future successful technology-assisted instruction depends on a closer working relationship between educators and software manufacturers. Various software programs for language, reading, spelling, written expression, math, learning strategies and study skills, and transition education are presented in their respective chapters.

Material with Student: Homework

Homework continues to be a widely practiced activity in schools. In fact, the amount of homework has increased in recent years, particularly for younger students (Cooper, Robinson, & Patall, 2006). Olympia, Sheridan, and Jenson (1994) define *homework* as academic work assigned by teachers that extends the practice of academic skills into other environments. Cooper et al. note that homework implies completion during nonschool hours, but in actuality most students have options to do the work during study hall, library time, or subsequent classes. An important aspect of homework includes programming for academic skill generalization through working in numerous environments. In general, a homework activity must be teacher-directed, include only previously taught skills, be an extension of schoolwork, be evaluated, be based on instructional objectives appropriate to the student, and occur outside school hours.

Cooper and Nye (1994) conclude that homework accounts for about 20 percent of the total time typical students spend on academic tasks. Bursuck et al. (1999) note that 1996 national data indicate that more than half of all eighth and twelfth graders and nearly half of all fourth graders report at least 1 hour or more of homework every night and more than two-thirds of all students report at least 30 minutes of homework every night. Moreover, students with learning disabilities generally spend more time completing homework and require more support than do students without disabilities (Harniss, Epstein, Bursuck, Nelson, & Jayanthi, 2001).

High rates of achievement are related to the amount of time students are actively engaged in academic tasks. Homework represents a viable method to help students with learning problems engage in academic tasks and improve achievement. The positive relationship of homework to achievement has been well documented for students with learning problems (Jenson, Sheridan, Olympia, & Andrews, 1994). Minimally competent students can compensate for lower ability through increased home study. Specifically, it helps them move through the acquisition, proficiency, maintenance, and generalization stages of learning (Mims,

Harper, Armstrong, & Savage, 1991) and provides an opportunity for the teacher to control the temporal aspects of practice (i.e., spaced versus massed practice) that are most effective for learning (Dempster, 1991).

From a synthesis of research on homework in general education, Cooper (2001) reports that homework positively affects achievement but that the effect varies considerably across grade levels. In essence, he notes that the effects of homework are substantial for secondary students and minimal for elementary students. For middle school students, the effects are good but are only about half as beneficial as for secondary students. In a follow-up meta-analysis 5 years later (Cooper et al., 2006), similar results were noted. Cooper (2001) also reports that the optimal amount of homework varies across grade levels.

Although there is a limited amount of research on homework practices, Patton (1994) highlights 35 recommended practices from the available research and literature. He discusses practices in the areas of management (e.g., involve the parents and evaluate assignments), assignments (e.g., ensure a reasonable chance of completion and high rate of success), student competencies (e.g., help students with self-management skills), and parental involvement (e.g., provide parent training or homework assistance). Patton notes that 14 of the recommended practices have empirical validation, 25 have literature-based support, and 5 have field-based support. It is apparent that research is limited, but a validation base for effective practices is emerging.

In a survey of homework practices of 88 teachers of students with learning disabilities, Salend and Schliff (1989) found that most teachers (i.e., 80 percent) use homework regularly but fail to use quality practices consistently. They report that 85 percent of the teachers experience problems in getting students to complete their homework. Salend and Schliff note that students' low motivation may be related to the failure of the learning disabilities teachers to give feedback on homework (i.e., 43 percent do not discuss or review homework), incorporate homework into grading policies (i.e., 42 percent do not regularly grade homework), or involve parents in the homework process (i.e., only 41 percent solicit feedback from parents). From the limited research on the effects of homework on students with learning disabilities, it appears that quality practices are related to positive student achievement.

In a review of the literature on homework for students with learning disabilities, Cooper and Nye (1994) indicate that homework practices should emphasize simple and short assignments, careful monitoring and reward for homework completion, and parental involvement. Bryan and Sullivan-Burstein (1998) found that three strategies to increase homework completion include giving students real-life assignments (i.e., connecting homework to events or activities in the home) plus reinforcement, using homework planners, and graphing homework completion. Moreover, in a national survey of special education teachers on solving communication problems about homework, Bursuck et al. (1999) report the following top-ranked recommendations: (a) General education teachers should require that students keep a daily assignment book; (b) parents should check with their child about homework daily; (c) school administrators should provide release time to communicate with parents on a regular basis; (d) school personnel should establish homework hotlines so that parents can call when questions or problems arise over homework assignments; (e) students should keep a daily assignment book; (f) school personnel should schedule after-school sessions where students can go to get extra help on their homework; and (g) special education teachers should provide general education teachers with information about the strengths and weaknesses of students with disabilities. These recommendations are the same as those of a similar survey of general educators (Epstein, Munk, Bursuck, Polloway, & Jayanthi, 1999). The following additional guidelines promote best practices in homework.

- *Assign a reasonable amount of homework.* Cooper (2001) offers the following general ranges for frequency and duration of homework assignments: first through third grade—three to four 10- to 30-minute assignments per week; fourth through sixth grade—three to four 40- to 60-minute assignments per week; seventh to ninth grade—four to five 70- to 90-minute assignments per week for all subjects combined; tenth through twelfth grade—four to five 100- to 120-minute assignments per week for all subjects combined. An alternative guideline is for all homework assignments to last as long as 10 minutes multiplied by the student's grade level (e.g., 40 minutes for fourth graders, 80 minutes for eighth graders, and 120 minutes for twelfth graders). The purpose of homework at the elementary level is to help students develop good study habits, practice newly acquired skills, and realize that learning can take place in nonschool environments. For students in seventh to twelfth grade, homework becomes essential to academic achievement and school success. To regulate the amount of time students spend on homework,

the teacher should check with students or parents periodically about how much time homework is taking. For example, it is not uncommon for students with learning disabilities to spend twice as much time doing an assignment as students without disabilities (Jenson et al., 1994). Weintraub and Graham (1998) note that, on the basis of handwriting alone, it generally will take 50 minutes for students with learning disabilities to do what normally achieving students do in 30 minutes. Thus, Cooper (2001) suggests that homework assignments for students with learning disabilities should be short and should focus on reinforcement of skills and class lessons rather than on extension (i.e., transfer of previously learned skills to new situations) or skill integration (i.e., the application of separately learned skills and concepts to produce a single product, such as science projects or creative writing). Accommodations for students with learning problems include the following: (1) separate large assignments into smaller chunks; (2) provide more time to complete the assignment; (3) offer incentives for completing homework to students who are distractible, off-task, or impulsive; and (4) organize student groups that can work together. For example, O'Melia and Rosenberg (1994) report good progress on homework completion through cooperative homework teams. Moreover, teachers who work in teams need to plan together on assigning homework. Because students take classes from different teachers in the upper grades, the teachers should work cooperatively to develop appropriate amounts of homework.

- *Make homework an integral part of the learning process.* Nicholls, McKenzie, and Shufro (1994) compared perspectives of students with and without learning problems on the relevance of homework. Most students with learning problems viewed homework as an imposition and remotely related to life skills, whereas most students without learning problems viewed homework as important and related to life skills. When the teacher discusses the rationale for homework and informs students of the specific objectives (such as mastery of skills) of each assignment, students are able to appreciate homework's value. When teachers discuss, review, explain, and evaluate homework assignments with students who have learning problems, homework becomes an effective learning activity. A feeling of ownership of the assignment is promoted when students recognize the value of homework. Homework should not be busy work or used as punishment.

- *Plan homework assignments at the student's instructional level.* Teachers must ensure that assignments represent an appropriate match between the student's ability or skill level and the difficulty level of the assignment. This instructional match usually is maintained when the teacher assigns homework to practice or review material that the student has been taught.

- *Make sure the student understands the assignment.* Understanding the purpose and instructions for the assignment is critical (Jenson et al., 1994). When the assignment is similar to classwork, clarity is facilitated. When the assignment is new or different, the teacher should demonstrate the task and provide some guided practice on a portion of the assignment. Understanding also is facilitated when directions are clear and simple and when students are asked to explain the task.

- *Evaluate homework.* Teachers should evaluate all homework assignments and maintain a cumulative record of the results. Assigning a grade encourages students to complete assignments and develop a sense of responsibility. Moreover, for students who do not test well, homework provides an opportunity to improve their grades and display their skills and knowledge (Mims et al., 1991).

- *Reinforce the completion of homework.* Teachers should indicate that homework is important to help students learn and develop responsibility. Students should be encouraged when they complete their homework. Encouragement may be private (e.g., verbal praise, note sent home, sticker, or high grade) or public (e.g., bulletin board display of work or display of names with homework stars). Also, the entire class or teams of students can be encouraged when each member has completed the assignment or improved in the number of assignments completed.

- *Involve parents in homework.* In a study of parents of students with learning disabilities, Kay, Fitzgerald, Paradee, and Mellencamp (1994) examined parental perspectives on homework. They found that parents felt inadequate to help with homework. The parents desired more information on how to help their children with homework and wanted a two-way communication system that would help them become partners on their child's instructional team. Initially, the teacher should send a letter to parents regarding homework policies and practices. Because letters do not always represent a functional medium of communication to homes, it may be necessary for the teacher to discuss homework in parent conferences, at PTA meetings, during parent nights at school, or on the telephone. Information for parents should include the purpose of homework, the expected frequency of homework, the approximate amount of time assignments should take, homework evaluation procedures, effects of homework on grades, and suggestions for parents on how to help with homework. Tips regarding parental involvement include the following:

  - Schedule a specific time and place for homework.
  - Supervise the homework session by periodically checking with the student to determine progress, rather than overseeing every task.
  - Provide an environment conducive to learning. The area needs to be well lighted and free of distractions.
  - Provide the student with appropriate materials.
  - Sign and date completed homework assignments.
  - Encourage and praise the student for doing homework.
  - Share with the teacher any concerns involving the amount of work or the difficulty level of the assignments.

- *Facilitate homework through effective support systems.* To improve homework completion rates as well as homework quality, Hughes, Ruhl, Schumaker, and Deshler (2002) present a comprehensive assignment completion strategy designed for independently recording and completing assignments. In addition, Frith (1991) suggests using peer tutoring for checking and assessing homework and for giving corrective feedback, using computer-assisted instruction for students who have access to computers, encouraging parents to support the value of homework with their actions and words, and developing monitoring systems (such as graphs or checklists) for homework.

In his concluding remarks concerning homework, Frith (1991, p. 49) states:

For maximum usefulness, homework assignments need to be made in the context of a strong support system that includes assistance from teachers and peers as well as parents. A strong support system will increase positive impressions that students have toward homework, especially when it might appear that these assignments are imposing on their free time. Regardless of perspective, homework is certainly important, and it should be viewed as an integral component of the instructional program—not only in regular education but in special education as well.

SCHEDULING

Schedules are vital for accomplishing instructional goals in an organized manner. They indicate which activities will occur and when they will occur. Most students with learning problems need the organization and routine typical of systematic scheduling. Furthermore, scheduling greatly affects the pace of instruction. It ensures that enough classroom time is spent in high-priority curriculum areas and that enjoyable activities are interspersed with less appealing activities.

A well-planned daily schedule greatly aids the teacher in providing effective instruction and collaboration; however, developing an appropriate schedule is hard work. A teacher needs knowledge and skills in individualized programming, assessment for teaching, instructional approaches and techniques, curriculum materials, and classroom management. Scheduling techniques presented in this section include general scheduling techniques, scheduling at the elementary level, scheduling at the secondary level, and scheduling in the resource room.

General Scheduling Techniques

The following suggestions and techniques apply to improving scheduling practices in various program settings (e.g., resource room and general education classroom) and at all grade levels.

- *Schedule for maximum instructional time.* To allocate academic time, teachers should plan time to practice new skills within a demonstration-practice-feedback-mastery paradigm, build planning time into the schedule and adhere to it, consider time needed for transitions and setups, and pace the instruction quickly during sessions allocated to academics.
- *Proceed from short work assignments to longer ones.* At first, some students may be unable to work on a seatwork assignment for a long period (such as 30 to 45 minutes). The teacher can break the task into short lessons that the student can manage independently. When task complexity, rather than time, is a problem for the student, it may be helpful to break the task into steps. Eventually, time and task complexity can be increased as the student develops academic and self-management skills.
- *Alternate highly preferred with less preferred tasks.* In scheduling, it often helps if a less preferred activity is followed by a highly preferred activity. For example, if reading is preferred over math, math is scheduled first and followed by reading. If none of the academic

subjects is preferred, it may be necessary to use nonacademic activities (such as art, recess, music, and physical education) as preferred activities.

- *Provide a daily schedule for each student.* A daily schedule provides needed structure for students with learning problems. It also presents them with expectations and a sequence of events in advance. Developing a daily schedule is easier if students understand that events will occur at the same time each day. This is accomplished by giving students a schedule form, perhaps on a card or chalkboard, which specifies the time of events for the day. On assignments that are progressive (such as assignments in a text or workbook, or long-term writing, art, or science projects), students can record the starting point for the next day on the schedule. When scheduling changes are needed, the teacher explains the new events or assignments.
- *Schedule assignments that can be completed in a school day.* Students need the opportunity to begin each day with a "clean slate." They then do not have to worry about yesterday's incomplete or incorrect work. To make sure students are able to complete their work, the teacher should be certain assignments are at the student's instructional level, make initial assignments short and increase them gradually, provide leeway time for completing work, reinforce on-task behavior, provide answer keys and self-correcting materials, and make some assignments continuous (i.e., weekly), with daily aims and a completion date specified.
- *Provide time cues.* The schedule designates the time allotted for each assignment. Many students with learning problems have difficulty managing their time and need reminders or cues. Several techniques can be used as time reminders. For example, the teacher can cut sections that are the same size as the face of the classroom clock out of circular pieces of cardboard. When these circular pieces are placed on the clock face, they display blocks of time on the clock (e.g., a circle with ¼ section cut out displays a 15-minute block of time). The student receives time cues by observing the proportion of time exposed on the clock and the location of the minute hand in that exposed section. Secondly, the teacher can set a kitchen timer for the amount of time allotted to an activity. The timer can be used occasionally with an individual student on a given activity. The sound of the timer ticking and the movement of the dial remind the student to continue working.
- *Schedule activities in a complementary manner.* In an individualized program, teachers must organize student activities and plan time to provide individual

assistance. Because some subjects require more teacher assistance than others, it often helps if the entire class is not working on the same subject at the same time. Math, spelling, and handwriting usually require less teacher assistance than reading. Thus, a teacher may be able to provide more individual assistance if part of the class is scheduled to work on math while others are working on reading.

- *Plan a variety of activities.* Sometimes academic instruction is more effective if one activity is not too long and if a variety of activities are planned. Many teachers organize a 45-minute instructional period into three 15-minute segments. A sample math lesson can include the following activities: direct teacher instruction, listening station for recorded instruction, or self-correcting material activity. In this plan, students are divided into three groups and rotated through the activities. The option of working in an interest center can be added for students who complete their work early.

- *Consider alternative schedules.* To reduce instructional fragmentation, discipline problems, and student failure, some schools redesign the traditional school schedule to include block scheduling (Canady & Rettig, 1995). For example, parallel-block scheduling with a 100-minute time block is used at the elementary level, and a four-block schedule with 90-minute time blocks is used at the middle school level. Another middle school method is to reorganize the 180-day school calendar to a 75–75–30 plan in which courses end after two 75-day terms; during the final six weeks, students are enrolled in specialized courses that provide enriching activities or additional learning time to master grade-level objectives. At the secondary level, block scheduling can include a 4 × 4 semester plan (i.e., four 90-minute blocks for 90 days) or a Day 1/Day 2 schedule so that students have fewer classes daily and fewer class changes. These scheduling approaches attempt to address students' differing needs for learning time and improve the quality of time that students spend at school.

Scheduling at the Elementary Level

General education and special education elementary teachers often teach the same students for a large portion of the school day. Moreover, in cooperative or team-teaching situations in inclusive classrooms, the general education teacher and the special education teacher need to plan the schedule together. This requires scheduling a variety of activities: opening exercises, reading, math, recess, art, and so on. The following four steps can be used to schedule entire school days.

1. *Analyze the day's events.* The first step in developing a daily schedule is to analyze the daily events and determine how much time the teacher is responsible for planning. This time is affected by nonacademic school activities and supportive instructional services. After the teacher has determined the amount of time students are at lunch, resource room instruction, physical education, art, and so on, the teacher knows how much time must be scheduled. In a 6-hour school day, the classroom teacher probably needs to schedule 4½ to 5 hours. Planning 4½ to 5 hours of daily instruction for 180 days a year is a sizable project.

2. *Plan opening exercises.* Opening exercises usually require 15 to 20 minutes; they develop rapport and prepare students for the day's activities. The teacher can use this time to observe the attitudes, moods, and physical appearance of the students. Common activities for opening exercises include collecting lunch money; taking attendance; recognizing special days (such as birthdays and holidays); discussing the schedule of activities for the day; and discussing current events, weather, or the date. For the young student who cannot read, pictures can be used to designate activities.

Picture	Activity
25¢ 10¢	Collect lunch money
☼	Recess
2 + 2 = 4	Math

myeducationlab
Go to the Assignments and Activities section of the Topic Planning/Organization in the MyEducationLab for your course and complete the activity entitled Morning Routine. As you watch the video and answer the accompanying questions, consider the ways in which opening exercises impact students' days.

3. *Schedule academic instruction.* Although many students are more alert and easier to motivate in the morning than in the afternoon, some students with learning problems are more alert in the afternoon. Therefore, it helps to plan some intensive learning activities in the afternoon. Also, because students function at different academic levels, students should be divided into small groups for academic instruction.

4. *Plan closing exercises.* Closing exercises usually require 10 to 15 minutes; they are designed to tie together the school day in a pleasant, orderly manner. Some closing activities include cleaning up, returning materials, determining what to take home, reviewing the day's activities, and discussing the next day's major events. The teacher should strive to finish the day in a positive manner with each student.

The sample schedule presented in Table 2.3 stresses systematic and small-group academic work in reading and math in the morning and group-oriented activities in the afternoon. The schedule also provides time to complete unfinished work. This extra time permits slower students to finish their work and other students to work ahead or select interesting activities. The teacher can use this time to provide individual attention or conduct assessments. These flexible time periods reduce pressure and enable the teacher to individualize instruction. Often it is easier to assign math or spelling seatwork than reading seatwork; thus, the teacher may wish to give math or spelling seatwork to students when they are not receiving small-group reading instruction.

Scheduling at the Secondary Level

A typical secondary school schedule includes a homeroom period, five or six class periods, and a lunch period. Class periods are about 50 minutes, and the

TABLE 2.3
Sample schedule

Time	Activity		
8:30	Opening exercises		
8:50	Setting up and beginning work		
9:00	Reading period (small groups)		
	Group A	*Group B*	*Group C*
9:00	Group with teacher	Listening center	Paper-pencil task
9:15	Listening center	Paper-pencil task	Instructional game
9:30	Paper-pencil task	Instructional game	Group with teacher
9:45	Instructional game	Group with teacher	Listening center
10:00	Recess		
10:20	Math period (small groups)		
	Group 1	*Group 2*	*Group 3*
10:20	Paper-pencil task	Cooperative learning group	Group with teacher
10:35	Cooperative learning group	Group with teacher	Criterion test, timing, or math game
10:50	Group with teacher	Criterion test, timing, or math game	Paper-pencil task
11:05	Criterion test, timing, or math game	Paper-pencil task	Cooperative learning group
11:20	Prescribed and selected activities including: choosing a free activity, going to the library, using an interest center, working on unfinished tasks, performing timings, taking a test, or playing an instructional or recreational game. The teacher can use this time to work with students who have been absent or out of the room, provide feedback, and give individual attention.		
11:45	Story time, handwriting, or content area (e.g., science or social studies)		
12:00	Lunch		
12:30	Spelling, language arts (involving classwide peer tutoring on Tuesdays and Thursdays)		
1:00	Physical education, music, art, or motor development		
1:30	Recess		
1:45	Content area (e.g., science, social studies, geography, career education, or citizenship)		
2:05	Prescribed and selected activities		
2:20	Closing activities		
2:30	Dismissal		

teacher usually has one period for planning. Because a fixed schedule of periods exists at the secondary level, it may seem that teachers do not need to do much daily scheduling. However, because lessons must fit into 50-minute segments, planning is essential to ensure efficient use of instructional time.

In scheduling, an opening exercise may be limited to an explanation of the activities for the period, and a closing exercise may simply consist of allowing time to put away materials. Some secondary classes are structured so that students enter the room, get their work folders, and begin working. The teacher moves from group to group, or individual to individual, offering assistance and reinforcement. In this arrangement, opening activities are omitted, but time is scheduled for returning folders.

In planning for a period, it may be a good idea to divide students into groups and schedule appropriate activities for each group. With this format a teacher may rotate through the groups. Some content is taught adequately to the whole group; however, when this arrangement is used, the teacher must ensure that all students understand the lecture material (e.g., by taking questions from students). The teacher should expect students with learning problems to need additional help during seatwork. This help can be provided by a classmate, special material, an aide, or the teacher.

The following general scheduling considerations can be used with adolescents who have learning problems.

- If there is flexibility in scheduling electives, students can select courses in which they have a good opportunity to succeed. Scheduling that results in a heavy load or an unsympathetic teacher can cause serious difficulties for a learner with problems.
- A course load must reflect student needs. There should be a balance between demanding and less-demanding courses. Course substitution also can be used. If the school offers less-demanding courses that satisfy required credits, the student with learning problems can avoid courses in which he or she is likely to be unsuccessful.
- Expanded course offerings are used in some settings to accommodate the student with learning problems. In these situations the special education staff teaches some content areas in a different setting.

Scheduling in the Resource Room

The resource room teacher is faced with a tedious and time-consuming scheduling task, primarily because students participate in more than one instructional setting with two or more teachers. The following issues complicate resource room scheduling.

- The student's academic, emotional, and social needs must be considered when determining the best time to schedule resource room instruction. If the student leaves the general education class for the resource room during an academic lesson, will needed academic instruction be missed? If the student leaves during a nonacademic activity (such as art, physical education, or music), will the student resent missing a desirable activity?
- Classroom teachers usually have preferred times for sending students to the resource room.
- Students who come to the resource room at a specified time may have different instructional needs. For example, one student may need help with a specific math skill, whereas another student may need to work on reading comprehension.
- In some situations it is helpful if the resource room teacher teaches in the general education class setting.
- Because students are participating in parallel and complementary instructional programs, with different teachers working on the same instructional objectives, the resource room teacher must schedule time for conferring with classroom teachers.

Despite numerous scheduling difficulties, the resource room program remains an important instructional model for serving students with learning problems. The following techniques and suggestions are helpful in resource room scheduling.

- Students may come to the resource room at different times, depending on the day. For example, they may come at a certain time three days a week and at another time two days of the week. With this schedule the students do not consistently miss a given subject or activity in the general education class.
- A resource room teacher may choose to provide instruction in the various academic areas at fixed times during the day. With this type of schedule, reading, math, handwriting, and spelling are taught at a specified time, and students may come to the sessions they need. Thus, a student may come to the resource room for a half-hour of instruction one or more times daily to receive help in problem areas.
- To maximize the efficient use of time, the resource room teacher must encourage and reinforce being on time and making a quick transition from task to task.
- To decrease the likelihood that students will disrupt the general education classroom when they return from the resource room, the resource room teacher may give students an assignment to work on until

the general education classroom teacher can involve them in the ongoing activities. Also, the teacher may assign a student the responsibility of helping the returning student to begin work.

CLASSROOM EQUIPMENT

Instructional equipment can be used to meet the specific needs of students with learning problems. For example, audiovisual equipment can be used to instruct students with specific modality preferences, and manipulative devices often help to hold the attention of a distractible learner. Use of a tape recorder, overhead projector, and small-item materials is presented in this section. The use of computers and computer software is discussed in the section on technological tools.

Tape Recorder

Cassette recorders have several advantages. They are simple to operate, the recorder and tapes are small and easy to store, and tapes are relatively inexpensive. Headphones enable individual students to operate a recorder without distracting classmates. Instructional applications of a tape recorder include the following:

- A tape can be made of reading material (e.g., literature, stories, and magazines). The student can read along with the tape to practice reading. Thus, the tape can provide feedback, increase speed, and help the student identify and practice difficult words.
- In a language activity, the student can use a tape recorder to make a tape of a story. Later, the student can write the story from the tape with a peer, aide, or teacher.
- Oral directions can be put on tape to accompany seatwork activities. The student who has difficulty with oral directions can play the tape until the directions are understood.
- Spelling tapes are useful for practice and taking tests. One commonly used format gives the spelling word; the word used in a sentence; and a pause, a beep, and the word spelled correctly. The pause can be eliminated by having the student stop the tape recorder to write the word and then start it to check the spelling.
- Stories, facts, or a report of an event can be recorded. News programs, commercials, telephone messages, weather reports, and teacher-made content can be used. The student listens and then responds to comprehension questions. For example, a weather report is taped and the student is required to answer the following questions: High temperature? Low temperature? Any rain? Forecast for tomorrow? What season is it?

- One-minute samples of instrumental music can be taped for students to use in conducting timings. The tapes usually begin with the word "start" and end with the word "stop." The teacher may prefer to use only the words and omit the music. In place of a kitchen timer, tapes of different time spans can be used to mark the end of any timed activity.
- Correction tapes can be used to provide feedback to students who have completed math seatwork.
- Music can be recorded on tapes for students to listen to when they have completed an assignment. Also, pleasant background music can be played while students are engaged in activities such as cleaning up, settling down after recess, free-choice, seatwork, or art.
- At the secondary level, class lectures and discussions can be taped. These tapes can be used to help students review or understand the material.

Overhead Projector

An overhead projector is readily available to classroom teachers and is used to display an image on a screen from a transparency. Transparencies can be teacher-made or purchased. They allow the user to write on, color in, and point at specific details while discussing them. Overhead projectors can be used to project images on light-color surfaces without darkening the room. Because an overhead projector greatly accents the visual image, it aids students who are easily distracted by extraneous visual stimuli. The teacher can block out all stimuli that do not relate to the item being studied or completed.

Guidelines for effective use of transparencies on an overhead projector include the following:

- Prepare transparencies ahead of time.
- Type or write in clear, bold lines on plain paper. Put the paper through a copy machine and copy on a transparency film for plain paper copiers. Also, a transparency can be made from information on a computer by printing on a transparency film in a laser printer.
- Make letters at least ¼″ high. Orator or bulletin type from a primary typewriter projects adequately.
- Simplify and be concise. Use a maximum of six or seven lines of copy and six or seven words per line.
- Use simple graphic drawings. Have diagrams ready ahead of time rather than using teaching time to put complicated illustrations on a transparency.
- Emphasize key points by capitalizing, underlining, circling, and boxing.
- Use color for clarity, emphasis, and variety. The acetate background itself can be a color instead of clear. Also, colored pieces of acetate can be attached in key spots, or color markers can be used on the acetate.

- Turn the projector off and on to shift students' attention.
- Use the revelation technique (i.e., covering the visual with a sheet of paper and revealing items one at a time) to avoid distractions and keep the class interested. Students who are taking notes may appreciate being shown the complete visual first as an overview before the masks are applied.
- Use the techniques of overlays and masking (i.e., revelation) to break down a whole into its component parts.
- Locate the screen so that everyone in the room can see it clearly. Position it as high as possible, and tilt it forward to project an appropriate image.
- When writing while talking, check the screen periodically to be sure the students are seeing what is being discussed. Write clearly.
- Keep extra markers or pencils on hand.
- Use transparencies in place of a chalkboard to focus attention, thereby saving time and space because the lesson can be used again. Also, class control and eye contact can be maintained better than at a chalkboard.

Uses of an overhead projector include the following:

- Class schedules and homework assignments can be put on an overhead to save chalkboard space for student and teacher use throughout the day. To check on the schedule or finish copying a homework assignment, the student can turn on an overhead projector and complete the task.
- An overhead projector can be used for administering many kinds of tests: computation facts, word problems, cloze spelling tests, fill-in-the-blank items, and multiple-choice items.
- An overhead projector can be used to display the category being discussed. Words, phrases, sentences, poems, drawings, and pictures are useful stimuli in facilitating relevant interactions.
- An overhead projector is useful for playing reading comprehension and spelling games. The teacher gradually exposes the letters of a word, the definition of a word, a sentence, or a paragraph. The students attempt to respond correctly with the fewest cues possible. With the letters of a word, students attempt to finish spelling the word; with the definition, they identify the word that matches the definition. In the sentence task, students try to complete the sentence correctly. The paragraph task involves providing a title for the paragraph. It often helps to divide students into teams and allow each group to give a response as another cue is presented.

- A spinner can be made on a transparency, placed on an overhead, and used for a variety of instructional activities and games. The teacher or student spins it, and it points to letters, numbers, words, or math facts. The spinner can be used to determine the number of points a specific task item is worth, select a math problem (i.e., by pointing to it), select one word at a time until the student can make a sentence, or select a letter for the student to sound out or add to previous letters to spell a word. These games are suitable for the student–teacher pair, two or more students, or a large group divided into teams.
- The overhead projector can be used to develop experience stories with small groups of students. In this activity, the group contributes to the story while the teacher writes it on the transparency.
- Students can use the overhead projector to display stories developed in language experience activities. The stories can be read to the class or copied by selected students. In addition, the class can help the student title the story.
- It often is easier for the teacher to lecture while using an overhead projector than while using a chalkboard. It is easier to point to or uncover material on an overhead than to write on a chalkboard. With an overhead, the teacher does not need to write and talk simultaneously or have students wait while the teacher writes.
- Many students enjoy writing on a transparency and seeing it presented on a screen. This activity is especially useful in practicing handwriting.
- An overhead projector can be used to project figures, pictures, letters, or numbers on a black chalkboard. The student can trace over the projected images to practice handwriting or develop fine motor skills, or this activity can be used as reinforcement.

Small-Item Materials

Inexpensive materials that are useful in a classroom include the following:

- *Miniature chalkboard.* One side of a piece of three-ply cardboard, about 15″ × 18″, can be painted with several coats of chalkboard paint (available at school supply and paint stores). Also, the smooth side of a Masonite board can be painted and the rough side can be used as a flannelboard. These boards can be made for students to use at their desks. In addition, small whiteboards can be written on with wet-erase Vis-à-Vis markers and used as miniature writing boards.
- *Flannelboard.* A heavy piece of cardboard can be covered with flannel. Also, as mentioned, the rough side of a piece of Masonite can be used for a flannelboard.

Figures for the board can be made from foam-backed material or felt. Flannelboards are available commercially in various sizes, and some have easel backs. Uses include presenting vocabulary or spelling words, listing important rules, displaying parts of an outline, displaying graphs and fractions, presenting pictures representing difficult concepts, and displaying map outlines.

- *Game materials.* Materials commonly used with game boards can be collected and stored in an accessible location. Golf tees, Playskool characters, and items from old games are good markers; dice and spinners are good number indicators. Manila folders are excellent for drawing start-to-finish game-board formats and are easy to store.

- *Construction materials.* Various materials should be collected, such as pictures (e.g., of specific sounds, story starters, and so on), school supply or cigar boxes, oatmeal boxes, egg cartons, shoe boxes, water-base marking pens, plastic term-paper holders, tobacco or coffee cans, tongue depressors, library card holders, poster board, oak-tag paper, wooden cubes, pizza discs, envelopes, and clothespins. These and other materials are useful for constructing instructional materials. The instructional games and self-correcting materials presented in this chapter and the instructional activities featured throughout the curriculum area chapters require many of these items.

- *Typewriter.* A manual typewriter can stimulate learning and be fun to use (e.g., in practicing spelling and typing stories). Also, a typewriter is helpful for students with handwriting difficulties.

- *Stopwatch.* Many academic tasks (e.g., oral reading and math facts) are timed to measure fluency and monitor progress. Students can use a stopwatch to time themselves or their peers, and results of timings can be recorded on charts to enhance motivation.

- *Durable coverings.* Materials used frequently can be covered with a transparent adhesive material or with plastic spray. The student can mark on the material and wipe off the markings with a damp cloth. Also, a consumable workbook can be protected for repeated use. The teacher can trim two pieces of acetate to the size of the workbook, lay the acetate on the inside of each cover, and tape it to the cover along the outer edge. To do the work on a page, the student simply flips the acetate over the page and uses a crayon or grease pencil. This can be erased, leaving the workbook blank so that it can be used by another student. Another method is to cut cardboard into $8'' \times 11''$ pieces and tape acetate to it, either along the left side only or along both the sides and the bottom, forming a pocket to hold worksheets.

- *Magnetic board.* A magnetic board can be used for students to respond on, to present tasks, or to display work. Work or tasks are displayed easily by taping a paper clip to the back of the stimulus card or worksheet. The paper clip clings to the magnetic board and holds up the material.

- *Tracing screen.* A wire screen with a cardboard edge makes an excellent tracing screen. When paper is placed over the screen and written on with a crayon, the letters become raised and can be used for tracing.

- *Mirror.* A door-mounted or full-length mirror is excellent for teaching grooming and self-concept activities. The mirror provides direct feedback to a student about appearance.

MATERIAL ORGANIZATION

To plan and deliver individualized instruction in a systematic and continuous manner, a great deal of organization is needed. For the beginning teacher, the development of a system is a large undertaking; however, without it much frustration and anxiety can result. For example, without a system of filing instructional materials that accounts for storage and retrieval, the beginning teacher can spend hours trying to locate needed materials. Thus, one of the initial jobs for a teacher is to develop a filing and storage system and refine it with use.

Before the first day of teaching, the teacher begins to make bulletin boards, instructional games, worksheets, interest centers, overhead transparencies, and special project activities. A filing system helps the teacher organize and add to these materials. In addition, the system can be refined as the teacher develops priorities.

Table 2.4 presents a general filing system. The categories would change depending on the subjects being taught. As it develops, the system would become more specific. For example, numerous subcategories would be listed under phonics as materials and activities are collected and developed (e.g., individual consonant sounds, blends, vowel sounds, and digraphs). In the academic areas, a highly specific filing system can be developed from scope and sequence skills lists, commercial programs, or curriculum guides. By making the system open-ended, the teacher can add categories as needed. New ideas or materials collected from teachers, books, in-service meetings, university classes, or commercial programs can be filed into the system readily and used when needed.

TABLE 2.4
Sample categorical outline for a filing system

I. Academic Areas
  R. Reading
      R–1 Phonological awareness materials and activities
      R–2 Print awareness materials and activities
      R–3 Phonics materials and activities
      R–4 Vocabulary materials and activities
      R–5 Comprehension materials and activities
      R–6 Literature-based materials and activities

  M. Math
      M–1 Readiness materials and activities
      M–2 Quantity materials and activities
      M–3 Place value materials and activities
      M–4 Addition materials and activities
      M–5 Subtraction materials and activities
      M–6 Multiplication materials and activities
      M–7 Division materials and activities
      M–8 Fractions materials and activities
      M–9 Percentages materials and activities
      M–10 Word problem materials and activities
      M–11 Money materials and activities
      M–12 Algebra materials and activities

Other academic areas (e.g., language, spelling, science, and social studies) would be developed according to subareas and specific skills.

II. Management and Motivation Areas
      B.B. Bulletin boards
      I.C.   Interest centers
      L.C. Learning centers
      C.R. Classroom rules
      S.   Scheduling materials (e.g., forms)
      E.C. Evaluation center materials (e.g., charts, forms, stopwatches, and logs)
      G.   Games
      A.V. Audiovisual materials
      S.C. Self-correcting materials
      R.M. Reinforcement materials
      C.A. Classroom arrangement materials
      C.S. Computer software and CD-ROMs
      C.M. Computer manuals

Teaching Students and Managing Instruction

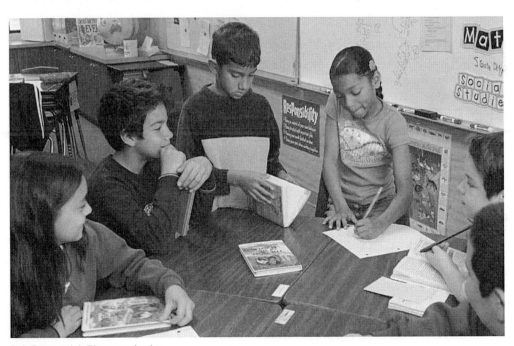

Bob Daemmrich Photography, Inc.

From Chapter 4 of *Teaching Students with Learning Problems*, 8/e. Cecil D. Mercer. Ann R. Mercer. Paige C. Pullen.

The first chapter of this text, "Creating Responsive Learning Environments," stresses the need to understand the characteristics and needs of learners, maximize the use of human resources (e.g., teachers, parents, and students), identify and plan for students with mild disabilities according to federal legislation, and recognize some factors that promote school success for learners with mild disabilities. The second chapter, "Planning and Organizing Instruction," considers physical arrangement of the classroom, instructional arrangements (e.g., large-group instruction, students teaching students, and material with student), and logistical factors such as scheduling, homework practices, and use of classroom equipment. The third chapter, "Assessing Students for Instruction," discusses the importance of assessment within the context of instruction and learning. Monitoring student performance, alternative grading, and test modifications are featured topics. These three chapters set the stage for the focus of this chapter—interactive teaching and factors that directly influence it.

Interactive teaching begins when the teacher and the students are engaged with one another to promote student learning. The intensity of interactive teaching is apparent when one realizes that the typical elementary teacher probably participates in 1,000 daily interactions and, according to Goldberg (1990), makes about 5,000 daily decisions. Interactive teaching is the hub of the instructional process and demands careful planning and skillful orchestration and implementation. Furthermore, interactive teaching is the cornerstone of response to intervention approaches to instruction.

A CONTINUUM OF INSTRUCTIONAL CHOICES

Classes that include students with mild disabilities typically also include average achievers, high achievers, low achievers, and culturally diverse learners. These students bring a kaleidoscope of prior knowledge, personal needs, and cultural experiences to the classroom. This diversity necessitates that teachers use instructional procedures that make it possible for all students to learn. Too often, however, educators become narrowly focused on a single perspective of teaching and learning. For example, a teacher who is a social constructivist may dismiss highly behavioral approaches. Likewise, a teacher who is a behaviorist may refuse to try constructivistic approaches. In either case, instructional choices are reduced and learners are denied the instructional options they need.

Mather and Roberts (1994) underscore the need to recognize individual differences and to select an instructional method or a combination of methods that helps a student achieve. Although a single instructional method is seldom effective for all students in a classroom, some educators cling to a particular method, insisting that all students will succeed if it is implemented correctly. Mather and Roberts note that the notion of teaching "harder" using a previously unsuccessful method is similar to "shouting English to a non-English speaker" (p. 55). Neither is likely to create enhanced results. Instead, teachers should select methods of instruction to match student needs, implement ongoing progress monitoring of student achievement, and use student data to make decisions about continuing, modifying, or discontinuing the individual's program. Program decisions should be based on student needs and achievement rather than on educational ideologies.

This section focuses on two instructional approaches that have been characterized as mutually exclusive: explicit teaching and implicit teaching. These two broad, yet distinct, approaches encompass most commonly used teaching practices (Mercer, Lane, Jordan, Allsopp, & Eisele, 1996). From a pragmatic perspective, they appear compatible, and both are needed to address the needs of students in a diverse classroom.

Explicit teaching is instruction in which the teacher serves as the provider of knowledge. Explicit teaching is based on the belief that when learning is complex and difficult for learners, the teacher must provide extensive support to students and transmit knowledge that facilitates learning. Skills and concepts are presented in a clear and direct fashion that promotes student mastery. In explicit instruction, the teacher provides an explanation or model of a skill or concept, guides students through application of the skill or concept in a variety of situations, and provides many opportunities for independent application that will ensure mastery and generalization. Explicit instruction emphasizes student mastery, and its principles are compatible with behavioral theory, direct instruction, task analysis, product-oriented effective teaching research, and exogenous constructivism.

Implicit teaching is an instructional ideology that assumes that students are naturally active learners who construct new personalized knowledge through linking prior knowledge and new knowledge. An authentic context augments the development of this knowledge as students make connections between classroom activities and real-world problem solving (Cobb, Yackel, & Wood, 1992; Englert, Tarrant, & Mariage, 1992). Thus, in implicit instruction, the teacher facilitates student learning and creates situations in which students can discover new knowledge and construct their own meanings. Skills and concepts are learned through exposure in meaningful contexts. In implicit instruction, the teacher guides students only as much as is necessary for them to build their own understandings. Scaffolding, or teacher support through questioning and explaining, is provided only as needed. A community of learners is developed in which students collaborate to discover alternative ways to solve problems and construct new knowledge. Implicit instruction emphasizes the thinking processes involved in learning; it is compatible with holistic theory and social constructivism.

Between the explicit and implicit extremes is *dialectical* or *interactive teaching,* which is based on the belief that knowledge is a collaborative enterprise and that instruction should include both explicit and implicit methods. In these collaborative interactions, the teacher provides instruction (e.g., offering metacognitive explanations, modeling cognitive processes, asking leading questions, and providing encouragement) as necessary to guide student discovery. A key feature of this supportive instruction is that the dialogue between the teacher and the students provides the learners with the support and guidance they need to achieve a goal efficiently.

Table 4.1 provides a continuum of explicit-to-implicit instructional choices with descriptive components. The continuum includes Moshman's (1982) three levels of constructivism: exogenous, dialectical, and endogenous. These three levels parallel explicit, interactive, and implicit instruction.

Explicit and implicit approaches are viewed by many educators as incompatible and dichotomous. Heshusius (1989, 1991) and Poplin (1988) criticize the explicit approaches employed by many special educators as being too reductionistic and mechanistic.

They believe that an implicit approach to teaching is better suited to the construction of knowledge by learners. In contrast, Engelmann (1988) and Liberman and Liberman (1990) insist that learners need explicit instruction to master many basic concepts and develop problem-solving and higher order thinking. They view implicit teaching as ineffective and inefficient for many learners.

The student population's increasing diversity compels educators to view student learning needs along a continuum. Student factors and content factors influence the appropriateness of instructional options along the continuum. Most educators favor explicit teaching when students with moderate-to-mild disabilities are the target population. This position is understandable when the characteristics of these learners are considered. Students with histories of problems in automaticity, metacognitive strategies, memory, attention, generalization, proactive learning, and motivation cannot plausibly engage in efficient self-discovery learning (i.e., implicit teaching).

Howell and Nolet (2000) provide guidelines regarding student factors when selecting an instructional approach. They suggest using a more implicit approach when the student has an adaptive or flexible motivational system, has significant prior knowledge of the task or concept, and encounters consistent success with the content. They recommend a more explicit approach when the student has a rigid motivational pattern, lacks significant prior knowledge, or encounters repeated failure on the task.

In addition to student characteristics, the nature of the content of instruction guides educators in their selection of instructional approaches. Howell and Nolet (2000) provide guidelines regarding curriculum or content factors when selecting an instructional approach. They recommend a more implicit approach

TABLE 4.1

Explicit-to-implicit continuum of instructional choices

Explicit Instruction	Interactive Instruction	Implicit Instruction
Much direct teacher assistance	Balance between direct and nondirect teacher assistance	Nondirect teacher assistance
Teacher regulation of learning	Shared regulation of learning	Student regulation of learning
Directed discovery	Guided discovery	Self-discovery
Direct instruction	Strategic instruction	Self-regulated instruction
Task analysis	Balance between part-to-whole and whole-to-part	Unit approach
Behavioral	Cognitive/metacognitive	Holistic
Exogenous constructivism	Dialectical constructivism	Endogenous constructivism

when the task is simple, well defined, conceptual in nature, and able to be completed by a general problem-solving strategy. On the other hand, an explicit approach is more appropriate when the task is complex, is poorly defined, has missing information, or requires a task-specific strategy. Explicit instruction is warranted if the content is critical to subsequent learning or requires a high level of proficiency. If time is limited or if a priority on mastery exists, then an explicit approach works best. Finally, a hazardous task requires explicit instruction. For example, a person learning to operate heavy equipment needs specific information regarding correct procedures and possible hazards, rather than self-discovering such information. In Figure 4.1, student factors and curriculum factors that should be considered when selecting teaching practices are placed along a continuum of instructional choices.

Setting Demands of an Implicit Learning Environment

An implicit learning environment places substantial demands on the learner. The following list highlights some of the most pertinent demands and their relationship to certain learning characteristics of students with learning problems (Mercer, Jordan, & Miller, 1996).

- Learners must have sufficient prior knowledge to construct new and appropriate meaning from understanding connections between prior learning and new information. Many students with learning problems exhibit severe learning discrepancies in academics. Thus, many of these students have inadequate amounts of prior knowledge.
- Learners must attend to teacher presentations, teacher–student interactions, and student–student interactions regarding academics. Many students with learning problems have difficulty sustaining attention to relevant visual or auditory stimuli.
- Learners must use cognitive and metacognitive processing to acquire, remember, and construct new knowledge in a manner that is authentic to their lives. Students with learning problems typically exhibit cognitive and metacognitive deficits that hinder information processing (Torgesen, 1990). Specifically, some of these students are described as having difficulty in assessing their abilities to solve problems, identifying and selecting appropriate strategies, organizing information to be learned, monitoring problem-solving processes, evaluating problems for accuracy, and generalizing strategies to appropriate situations.
- Students must be active participants in their own learning. Many students with learning problems

FIGURE 4.1
Student and curriculum factors for selecting teaching practices along a continuum of instructional choices

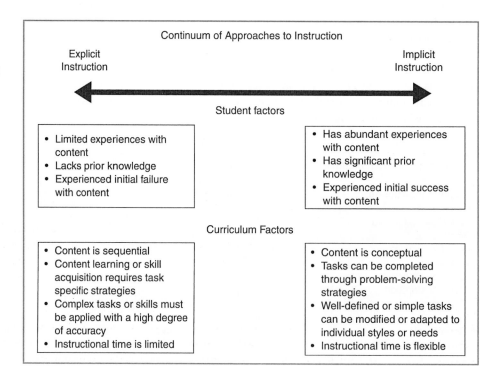

have histories of academic failure that contribute to the development of learned helplessness in academics. It is postulated that such learned helplessness results from students repeatedly trying to read words or solve problems when they have little or no understanding of content or concepts. This lack of understanding fosters the student's dependency on the teacher and thus promotes the belief that external help is needed to read words or solve problems correctly. Repetition of this event promotes and strengthens learned helplessness.

- Students must engage in group discussions to work in cooperative learning arrangements. These collaborative and cooperative events help establish a community of learners and require oral language skills (e.g., presenting organized information, making persuasive arguments, and participating in debates) and appropriate social skills (e.g., listening, taking turns, and respecting others' opinions). The use of language is extensive, and the language demands of cooperative group activities increase in each grade level. Also, social skills deficits among individuals with learning problems are high.

- To become self-regulated learners, students must recognize their own learning characteristics, develop their own metacognitive strategies, and maintain a proactive attitude about learning. Many students with learning problems have been described as *passive learners,* and the term refers to students who are cognitively passive because they typically do not participate actively or self-regulate their own learning. Also, many of these students are characterized as having motivational deficits due to their passivity.

Examination of the setting demands and prevalent characteristics of students with learning problems demonstrates that many such students lack the attributes, skills, and knowledge needed to succeed in an implicit setting. These and other students at risk for school failure require much teacher support and direction to begin moving toward becoming self-regulated lifelong learners. The teaching practices on the explicit end of the continuum of instructional choices (such as directed modeling, teaching to mastery, scaffolding, think alouds, and the use of mnemonics) can serve as a springboard to help students become more proactive and successful learners. The range of teaching practices along this continuum provides a framework for educating a diversity of learners. Explicit teaching or teacher-directed learning is needed immediately to help the more immature learners, whereas implicit teaching helps mature learners (e.g., those with rich prior

knowledge, proactivity, and social acumen) continue their growth.

Research Base for a Continuum of Instructional Choices

Research conducted across curriculum areas indicates that students of diverse abilities respond differently to instruction. The findings of this research provide a foundation for an instructional continuum.

Language   Instructional choices in the field of language and communication are needed and, during some developmental stages, certain choices are clearly better than others. For example, direct, explicit instruction was compared with milieu teaching (i.e., an approach that combines student-directed activities with teacher prompts) and was found to be more effective for instruction in advanced linguistic skills (Yoder, Kaiser, & Alpert, 1991). In contrast, explicit instruction was not as effective as milieu teaching for early vocabulary instruction.

Recent research indicates that vocabulary interventions have differential effects on students' vocabulary acquisition. For example, in a shared storybook intervention, students with a high level of vocabulary knowledge learned more vocabulary incidentally than did those with low levels of vocabulary (Pullen, Tuckwiller, Konold, Maynard, & Coyne, 2010; Tuckwiller, Pullen, & Coyne, 2010). Students at risk for school failure who received additional explicit Tier 2 instruction made greater vocabulary gains than the students in the comparison condition (Pullen et al., 2010). Coyne and his colleagues (Coyne, Simmons, Kame'enui, & Stoolmiller, 2004) found that students with lower receptive vocabulary made greater gains in vocabulary taught explicitly than students who had higher levels of receptive vocabulary. In another study of shared storybook reading, incidental exposure was not as effective as storybook reading combined with explicit instruction in vocabulary (Maynard, Pullen, & Coyne, 2010).

Reading   Stanovich (1994) asserts that the selection of an appropriate approach to reading instruction depends upon the learner and the skill. With skills close to perceptual input systems (i.e., specific information such as phonological relationships and vocabulary), the need for explicit instruction is great. On the other hand, as the type of skill moves away from perceptual input systems (i.e., less specific information such as inferential comprehension), implicit instructional approaches become more powerful.

According to Stanovich (1994), explicit instruction and teacher-directed strategy training are more effective for teaching word recognition skills, especially for at-risk students, students with learning disabilities, and students with special needs. Numerous researchers have demonstrated that explicit instruction helps students at risk for learning problems acquire reading and spelling skills (Lyon, 1995a; Moats, 2000). Moreover, programs for such students have improved reading skills using explicit instruction (Slavin et al., 1994).

Results from a study of various teaching methods in reading (Juel & Minden-Cupp, 2000) support Stanovich's (1994) assertions. Juel and Minden-Cupp compared students whose teachers implemented explicit, phonics-based reading instruction with students whose teachers used trade books and more implicit teaching methods. The effects of the reading instruction varied based on student factors. For example, students who were at risk for reading failure did not perform well in trade book classrooms; however, their more capable peers made excellent progress. Likewise, students with low levels of literacy at school entry made more progress in the explicit, phonics-based classrooms. This study supports the differentiation of instructional practices.

Writing   Like learning to read, learning to write is a complex process that requires the integration of several skills (Baker, Chard, Ketterlin-Geller, Apichatabutra, & Doabler, 2009; Graham, 2006). Many students with learning and behavioral problems struggle learning to write effectively (Baker et al., 2009; Gersten & Baker, 2001; Lane, Graham, Harris, & Weisenbach, 2006). Graham and Harris (1994) note that by the end of the primary grades, average-achieving students often have reached a level of fluency in the mechanics of writing that provides freedom in getting thoughts on paper (i.e., planning and content generation). Students with special needs do not reach this level of fluency as early as other students (Graham, 1990).

The incidental methods of whole language and process approaches may be insufficient for students at risk for learning failure. Graham and Harris (1994) explain that students with special needs require more than frequent, meaningful, authentic writing to achieve good writing skills. To help students plan compositions and regulate writing behavior, Self-Regulated Strategy Development (SRSD) combines explicit strategy instruction with explicit instruction in self-regulatory procedures (Harris & Graham, 1996, 1999; Harris, Graham, & Mason, 2003; Mason, 2009). In a recent meta-analysis, Baker et al. (2009) indicate that SRSD is an effective strategy for students with or at risk for learning disabilities. Furthermore, SRSD met the strict criteria to be considered an evidence-based practice

using the quality indicators for research (Gersten et al., 2005; Horner et al., 2005).

Math   The findings of mathematics research indicate that students can benefit from instruction that includes both explicit and implicit methods (Mercer, Jordan, & Miller, 1994). The literature supports explicit methods such as description of procedures, modeling of skills (i.e., the teacher uses "think alouds" or describes the thinking process as problems are solved), use of cues and prompts, direct questioning of students to ensure understanding, and practice to mastery. In mathematics problem solving, explicit instruction in transferring knowledge to novel problems as well as self-regulated strategy instruction are validated practices, particularly for students with learning problems (Fuchs et al., 2008; Fuchs et al., 2006). Although explicit teaching has been deemed effective for students with learning problems, implicit instruction may also be appropriate. For example, implicit methods such as linking information to prior knowledge, reflection on learning, interactive discourse about concepts, and discovery methods also are recommended.

Science   Scruggs and Mastropieri (1994) point out the lack of attention in research to implicit science instruction for students with special needs. They describe their continuing research in special education classrooms that use an inquiry (i.e., implicit) approach to science. Scruggs and Mastropieri conclude that students with mild disabilities can construct scientific knowledge but that they need much support to succeed. Teachers must provide highly structured coaching and behavioral management techniques. Palincsar, Magnusson, Collins, and Cutter (2001) present findings of a 2-year design experiment that investigated the experiences and outcomes for special needs students in guided inquiry science instruction in upper-elementary-grade inclusive classrooms. They report that advanced strategies focusing on monitoring and facilitating student thinking (e.g., miniconferencing), supporting print literacy (e.g., providing a glossary of terms), and improving work in small groups (e.g., manipulating group membership) resulted in significant learning gains for all students.

Perspective on a Continuum of Instructional Choices

The description of research across curriculum areas provides support for teaching along a continuum of explicit to implicit strategies. Response to intervention (RTI) frameworks allow for the combination of instructional choices. For example, Tier 1 instruction may be more implicit and taught in large-group settings. For students with learning problems, this instruction may not be robust enough to improve student outcomes. Small-group instruction that is more explicit may result in increased learning outcomes for students with disabilities. Early research on this model is promising (e.g., see Fuchs et al. [2008] for research on mathematics instruction and Pullen et al. [2009] for research on vocabulary instruction). Rather than choosing one instructional approach, selecting approaches to meet individual needs will result in success for all learners.

Struggles to advance a single instructional paradigm occur almost exclusively at the university level and, fortunately, the ideological extremes are seldom found in actual classrooms. Educational researchers must remember the needs of individual students and individual teachers. Restricting the range of instructional choices in the name of paradigmatic purity serves no useful purpose. Educational research should support the implementation of instructional practices that are most appropriate to meet individual educational needs. Accepting a broader view of instructional practice is a good place to start. The following personal story provides an interesting perspective on the need to consider a range of viewpoints in constructing a responsive learning environment.

Several years ago, Ann and I took a snow skiing lesson in Utah. Our ski instructor was wonderful. His experiences included teaching skiing to many individuals with physical disabilities. When the lessons began, I was fearful, anxious, and excited. The skiing equipment, the slopes, the ice, the ski lifts, and gravity were all intimidating. During the process of the lessons, I had the following experiences:

1. During the first 10 minutes of instruction, I went backward down the little knoll we were on and could not get up. Ann laughed, and the ski instructor smiled.
2. When approaching the ski lift, I tried to hurry and fell down on the path under the lift. The operator stopped the ski lift and instructed a person to help me get up. Ann laughed from her vantage point on the ski lift above me, and the ski instructor smiled.
3. Upon exiting the ski lift, I saw Ann and the ski instructor sprawled on the ground. I was unaware that skiing was required to exit the lift; however, I made an incredible move to avoid hitting my wife and the instructor. Unfortunately, I did not see the person on the top of the slope about to launch down the mountain. I joined this person with force, and we proceeded to tumble down the slope. Ann looked concerned, and the ski instructor enjoyed a hearty laugh.

The instructor worked with Ann and me for several hours. He explicitly taught us how to fall, get up with skis on, turn, traverse a slope, and snow plow to slow down. He described, modeled, and gave corrective feedback and encouragement. Slowly, I gained confidence, but I continued to work hard at skiing. Finally, the instructor said, "If I could stop you from thinking so much about all the techniques, I could help you discover the ease and joy of skiing." Then he told me to stop looking at my skis and to look at the mountain across the valley and ski down the mountain. He told me that I was ready and could do it. I tried it, and I skied down the mountain without looking at my skis. What an exhilarating experience! The techniques that the instructor had taught seemed to develop naturally. He was indeed a gifted teacher.

When reflecting about the ski instructor's teaching, I realized that he had used a continuum of explicit and implicit instruction. Initially, he taught me the basics explicitly and gave me confidence. As I learned, he became more implicit. In the end, he challenged me to discover skiing at a more advanced level.

Just as I was challenged by skiing down the mountain, students of all ability levels are challenged by academic concepts that often are difficult to understand and attain. However, the use of both explicit and implicit instructional components has the potential to help a diversity of learners acquire and use academic skills and content. Educators should teach students how to fall, get up, self-correct, and discover the mountains of fun that learning can provide. They should teach them how to use the equipment (e.g., computers, rulers, calculators, objects, and books), explore concepts, correct errors, slow down and think, collaborate, and discover the joys of learning.

The curriculum area chapters of this text provide a wealth of activities, strategies, and techniques that can be used within the context of the explicit-to-implicit instructional continuum. Because most students with learning problems need much teacher assistance, explicit and interactive instruction are emphasized. For example, the Direct Instruction Model developed at the University of Oregon and the Strategic Intervention Model developed at the University of Kansas Center for Research on Learning are included as effective instructional practices that respectively represent explicit and interactive instruction.

SYSTEMATIC TEACHING STEPS

Teaching styles are developed individually, but they should not be based on whims, biases, or personal opinions. Teachers and teacher educators have a responsibility to examine the research and apply the findings as they develop teacher practices. Greenwood, Arreaga-Mayer, and Carta (1994) found that students in classrooms in which teachers used research-based interactive teaching practices had higher academic engagement times and achievement scores than students in classrooms in which teachers used other methods. To ensure appropriate academic progress, teachers must use well-designed lessons with students who have learning problems. Components from a lesson design for students with disabilities that is based on effective teaching research are discussed and organized in terms of (1) opening the lesson, (2) conducting an interactive presentation, (3) closing the lesson, and (4) using continuous teaching components. The information included in the tables in this section provides competencies for various systematic teaching activities. When a teacher incorporates these practices into daily instruction, the likelihood of improving the achievement of students increases.

Opening the Lesson

The first task in opening a lesson is to gain the students' attention. This usually is accomplished through verbal cueing such as "Let's get started," "Eyes on me," or "Time to start." Verbal statements frequently are more effective if they are followed by teacher "wait time" to permit follow-through and eye contact with students. The use of a focusing activity can help capture students' attention. This activity, which is especially useful for beginning the day's first lesson, can involve asking a high-interest question related to current events. For example, when the teacher asks, "Does anyone know what surprising event happened at the beach yesterday?" the students quickly may become engaged in a discussion about whales beaching themselves. After a brief discussion on whales, the teacher can shift students' attention to the lesson. Nonverbal cues are another technique for gaining students' attention (e.g., the teacher stands in a specific area and visually scans the class, or the teacher points to a poster that says *Look at the teacher and listen*). Throughout the day the teacher must redirect students' attention from one activity to another. In doing this, the teacher should announce the transition clearly and ensure that students know her or his expectations. Specific expectations are taught readily by teaching students a mnemonic that cues expected behaviors (e.g., the SLANT mnemonic, which is presented later in this chapter).

Once the students are attending, the teacher helps them connect the lesson to prior knowledge (e.g., the previous lesson or related experience). This procedure usually includes such statements as "Last time, we learned to solve multiplication problems by using objects" or "Yesterday we practiced finding words within words." Also, it helps to ask questions that allow students to demonstrate their skill or knowledge level. For example, the teacher can ask, "In a multiplication problem such as *27 × 4*, what does the *4* represent?" or "What words can you find in the word *together*?"

Next, the teacher introduces the target skill, strategy, or knowledge for the lesson and provides a rationale for learning it. Included in this step is a focus on setting goals (e.g., "Today we are going to learn to solve multiplication problems by drawing. Drawing the problems will help you understand multiplication better and enable you to solve them without using objects."). Such statements introduce the skill and the goal as well as provide a rationale for learning. The use of anchoring activities can help connect the lesson content to real-world situations. Anchoring activities involve having the class discuss the relevancy of the skill, strategy, or content within an authentic context. Technology, such as multimedia presentations and video, also can be used as part of anchoring instruction. The use of anchoring instruction has been linked to increased participation, academic engaged time, and comprehension of content for students with learning disabilities (Rieth et al., 2003). Mercer, Jordan, and Miller (1996) note that authenticity may be accomplished by discussing the skill, strategy, or content within the context of school activities (e.g., passing tests), community events (e.g., computing the best price of an item), or future demands (e.g., getting a job or graduating from secondary school). Finally, it helps for the students to identify their objectives by evaluating their current learning status and predicting learning outcomes. Having students identify what they know, what they will learn, and how they know whether they have learned provides a nice context for guiding their learning process. Table 4.2 lists a summary of competencies for opening a lesson.

Conducting an Interactive Presentation

The interactive presentation is the heart of the instructional process and actively involves the teacher presenting and interacting with the students. To do this, the teacher uses explicit modeling and guided practice to teach new material. These procedures are essential in helping most students with learning problems to succeed in school.

Explicit Modeling The purpose of explicit modeling is to "paint pictures" for learners in such a way that understanding is ensured. The teacher instructs the students to watch, listen, and think while the teacher models. Through teacher "think alouds," learners observe metacognitive processes used in learning skills, content, or strategies. Two excellent procedures are used in modeling: (1) The teacher asks a question and provides the answer; the students hear and observe

TABLE 4.2
Competencies for opening a lesson

Gain students' attention by using verbal or nonverbal cues, or introduce a high-interest focusing topic.
State expectations for each transition, and consider using a mnemonic device (e.g., SLANT) to teach expectations.
Connect the lesson to prior learning or knowledge.
Review and reteach if prior knowledge is insufficient.
Identify the lesson's target skill, strategy, or content.
Provide a rationale for learning the skill, strategy, or content.
Discuss the relevance of the skill, strategy, or content until an authentic context is realized. Authenticity may be achieved within the context of school activities, community events, or future demands.
Have students identify what they know and set goals indicating what they expect to learn.

TABLE 4.3
Competencies for explicit modeling

Provide step-by-step demonstrations of covert and overt procedures involved in learning new information or applying strategies.
Use think alouds to model covert processes involved in learning strategies or problem solving (e.g., the teacher asks a question aloud and answers it aloud while describing covert and overt processes).
Provide examples and nonexamples to show distinctive and nondistinctive concept features.
Maintain a lively pace while modeling, but allow enough time for students to understand the content or strategy.
Model with enthusiasm.
Model task-specific learning strategies (i.e., perform the task) and self-instructions (e.g., self-monitoring or problem solving) to help students achieve.
Prompt student involvement with questions and check understanding during modeling.
Correct student responses and help students expand responses.
Note organization, relationships, and clues in the new material that elicit learning strategies.

the teacher think aloud while modeling the strategy. (2) The teacher asks a question and the students help provide the answer; the teacher and the students perform the strategy together, and the teacher continues to provide modeling. The opportunity to observe and experience these thought processes helps learners activate their own thinking processes. Thus, explicit modeling becomes essential for immature learners (e.g., those who have limited prior knowledge or are passive learners) to acquire and use essential knowledge. For example, Montague (1992) used explicit modeling of cognitive and metacognitive strategies to teach students with learning disabilities to solve word problems successfully. The specific cognitive strategies modeled included the following: (1) *read* for understanding, (2) *paraphrase* in your own words, (3) *visualize* a picture or diagram, (4) *develop* a plan to solve the problem, (5) *estimate* the answer, (6) *compute,* and (7) *check* to make sure everything is right. Table 4.3 lists a summary of competencies for explicit modeling. Teacher modeling is a key to academic success for many students. Just do it!

Guided Practice After explicit modeling and before independent practice, the teacher directs the active participation of students in guided practice. Guided practice primarily consists of the teacher prompting students and checking their work. Prompts enable the teacher to help students perform the task so that initial practice will be successful. Prompts consist of asking leading questions, repeating and rephrasing lesson content, pointing to a specific word or number, providing examples and nonexamples, giving feedback, doing tasks partially, doing a task with students, and providing manual guidance. After students perform the task with prompts, the teacher checks whether they can work successfully without prompts. The teacher constantly monitors student progress and gives corrective feedback until students are ready to work independently. If students have difficulty, the teacher may repeat the model, prompt, and check procedures in quick succession.

The teacher should use a continuum of assistance to determine how much support students need and what kind of prompts and cues are necessary. For example,

TABLE 4.4
Competencies for conducting guided practice

Provide clear directions and expectations for tasks used during guided practice.
Use prompts to ensure student success. For example:

Ask leading questions (e.g., "Did you check your work?").
Point and cue (e.g., point to a word or number, and cue students to think aloud).
Give examples and nonexamples.
Model the task.
Repeat the directions or rephrase lesson content.
Provide wait time.
Instruct students to check their work.
Do the task with students.

Use prescriptive prompts to guide successful learning.
Reduce assistance when students are successful, and increase assistance when students have difficulty.
Check student work continuously to ensure success.
Provide instruction based on student errors (e.g., repeat the model, prompt, and check sequence for students who are having difficulties).
Summarize students' accomplishments, and encourage them to enter independent practice.

some students may need little assistance after appropriate modeling and, thus, minimal monitoring and feedback to complete the task. Other students may need to be reminded to complete certain steps in the task, or they may need more explanation about some aspect of the task. The teacher provides more or less explicit instruction during guided practice, based upon individual student needs. As students demonstrate accuracy in the skill, the teacher decreases the amount of assistance. Table 4.4 presents a summary of competencies for conducting guided practice.

Closing the Lesson

In closing a lesson, the teacher summarizes the lesson's skills or concepts and connects them to future learning. The typical components of a closing are (1) a review of the lesson content, (2) a preview of the next lesson, and (3) the introduction and assignment of independent practice (Archer, Gleason, & Isaacson, 1995).

Review   During review, the critical information presented in the lesson is summarized. Also, the teacher checks student understanding with a final practice or by questioning students. For example, the teacher might ask students to solve a math problem by drawing it, and then monitor their work to check for understanding. The teacher also can determine student understanding through questions (e.g., "What is the first step in drawing a math problem?").

Preview   The preview consists of introducing the next lesson. It provides students with a meaningful temporal context for their learning (e.g., what they are learning and doing, and what they will learn and do).

Also, expectations concerning how they can apply their accumulating knowledge are discussed.

Independent Practice   The teacher acknowledges how much students have learned in the lesson and informs them that they are now ready for independent work. Independent work is designed to assist students to master the lesson's skill, strategy, or content. Thus, practice activities should relate to the lesson's objectives. A recommended success level during independent practice is 90 to 100 percent. Students can complete independent practice in class and as homework, and they can work individually or in small groups. Table 4.5 presents competencies for conducting independent practice. An interactive presentation culminates with independent practice and involves three phrases: "I do it" (i.e., teacher modeling), "We do it" (i.e., guided practice), and "You do it" (i.e., independent practice). When a student experiences difficulty, any of these three phases may be used to ensure success.

Using Continuous Teaching Components

Although interactive teaching follows a linear sequence of teacher activities (e.g., advance organizer to independent practice), teachers constantly are engaged in a multiplicity of thoughts and behaviors during interactive presentations. For example, while conducting guided practice, a teacher may be making mental notes on how to improve the lesson, assessing student progress, adapting directions to help individual students, providing feedback, and enhancing the lesson's authenticity to promote generalization. This section features some of the teaching components that

TABLE 4.5
Competencies for conducting independent practice

Review the task and describe the assignment and the criteria (e.g., neatness, accuracy, and promptness) used to evaluate it.

Explain the rationale of the assignment and its importance.

Ensure that students understand the assignment through questioning and reviewing homework and previous assignments.

Demonstrate strategies and procedures for completing independent practice activities.

Maintain records of students' performance and provide results of evaluations to students.

Provide for error-correction activities during seatwork.

Praise or reinforce students for independent work effort and assignment completion.

Circulate among students to monitor progress and assist students.

Frequently scan the classroom to see whether students are working.

Ensure that students experience high rates of success during seatwork.

Hold students accountable for independent work.

Have students complete missed assignments and correct errors.

Ensure that independent work relates to academic goals.

Provide peer tutoring and cooperative-learning group arrangements for students who are mature enough to interact appropriately.

Provide a variety of independent practice activities (e.g., instructional games, self-correcting materials, computer-assisted instruction, tape recorder–assisted instruction, and quality homework practices).

Instruct students to generalize and apply knowledge across settings and situations.

occur throughout the interactive teaching presentation. The skillful use of these components increases the likelihood of academic success of students who have learning problems.

Monitoring Progress and Providing Feedback

Monitoring progress involves the teacher frequently checking on students' behavior and academic work and adapting instruction to ensure that an appropriate instructional match is being maintained. Active and frequent monitoring is a key to student learning. Active monitoring includes checking to see whether students understand the task requirements and the procedures needed to complete the task correctly. To check understanding, the teacher asks each student to demonstrate how to complete the task. When the student performs the task, the teacher is able to note errors and help the student make corrections. Because these procedures enable the teacher to catch errors before extensive practice, high success rates are maintained. Moreover, active teacher monitoring (e.g., moving rapidly around the classroom, checking work, and interacting substantively with students) increases the on-task academic responses of students with learning problems. In a review of programs for at-risk students, Slavin and Madden (1989) report that the most effective programs involve frequent assessment of student progress so that programs can be modified according to individual needs. In essence, the most effective teachers maintain a productive flow of activity through continuous scanning and monitoring.

A significant finding of the Beginning Teacher Evaluation Study (Fisher et al., 1980) is that academic feedback is positively associated with student learning. Feedback serves two important functions: (1) It helps students distinguish between correct and incorrect responses, and (2) it informs students of their progress. Rieth and Evertson (1988) note that all major reviews of effective teaching cite feedback as among the most essential teacher behaviors for promoting positive learning outcomes. Teachers should give frequent positive feedback, persistent feedback to students who respond incorrectly, and supportive responses to high and low achievers to enhance the academic performance of their students. Moreover, in a synthesis of research on good teaching, Porter and Brophy (1988) report that good teachers monitor students' understanding through regular appropriate feedback. Wang (1987) reports that feedback strongly promotes mastery of content and skills for further learning, ability to study and learn independently, ability to plan and monitor learning activities, motivation for continued learning, and confidence in one's ability as a learner.

In a review of academic monitoring procedures, Fuchs (1986) reports that when students' academic programs were monitored systematically and developed formatively over time, the students achieved an average of .7 standard deviation unit higher (i.e., equivalent to 26 percentage points) than students whose programs were not monitored systematically. According to Ysseldyke and Tardrew (2007), ongoing progress monitoring in mathematics leads to increased teacher individualization of instruction and improved achievement outcomes for students. In addition, Baechle and Lian (1990) report that direct feedback significantly improved the performance of students with learning problems in interpreting metaphors. Moreover, Collins, Carnine, and Gersten (1987) note that basic and elaborative feedback significantly improved student performance on reasoning-skill tasks. In a comparison of basic and elaborative feedback, they found that elaborative feedback produced the greatest skill acquisition. Kline, Schumaker, and Deshler (1991) report excellent results with elaborated feedback in the teaching of academic-specific learning strategies to adolescents with learning problems. In a math strategies program, Mercer and Miller (1991–1993) indicate that the following elaborated feedback sequence is effective in teaching students with learning problems to acquire, retain, and apply basic math facts.

1. Grade the student's work.
2. Praise the student for the correct responses.
3. Chart the results on a graph and discuss the progress toward the mastery criteria.
4. Note the incorrect responses.
5. Point out error patterns and demonstrate correction procedures, if needed.
6. Instruct the student to correct errors using rules and information taught in the lesson.
7. Praise the student for error corrections.

Interestingly, when kindergartners are questioned about their abilities (e.g., "Who can draw?" "Who can sing?" "Who can dance?"), most will respond enthusiastically with "I can!" However, when college students are asked the same questions, many do not respond affirmatively, or they give responses that are timid and tempered with qualifiers (e.g., "I can draw a tree"). It is unfortunate that, after years of schooling, college students fail to exhibit the confidence and enthusiasm that kindergartners display. A plausible reason for their timidness is that they have a history of being punished for incorrect responses, which has resulted in a loss of confidence and a fear of risk-taking.

Teacher reactions to incorrect responses influence student achievement and self-esteem. Rather than seeking help from other students, the student who responds incorrectly should participate in correcting the answer. The teacher can prompt a correct response (e.g., pause, repeat the question, rephrase the question, or provide a clue) or give the answer and ask the student to answer the question again. Thus, the student always finishes with a correct response, and the teacher praises the student for listening. The teacher should view errors as teaching opportunities, and the learner should view errors as learning opportunities. Perhaps these orientations will produce more confident adult learners.

Although the literature is replete with studies that document the importance of feedback, studies analyzing the behavior of general education and special education teachers report low frequencies of feedback to special education students (Rieth & Evertson, 1988). Table 4.6 presents competencies for monitoring progress and providing feedback. Curriculum-based measurement provides teachers with a viable method of monitoring student progress and providing systematic feedback.

Promoting Generalization   As the emphasis on teaching students to be independent learners and active problem solvers increases, generalization is becoming an instructional focus of effective teaching. *Generalization* refers to the occurrence of relevant behavior in different, nontraining situations (i.e., across subjects, settings, people, behaviors, or time) without the scheduling of the same events that were present in the training conditions (Stokes & Baer, 1977). For example, generalization to new situations occurs when a student demonstrates proficiency in math facts and continues to respond quickly and accurately when these facts are embedded in calculation problems.

Ellis, Lenz, and Sabornie (1987a) report that various types of generalization are stressed throughout the instructional process. Specifically, they identify the following four levels.

1. *Antecedent generalization* involves changing negative student attitudes that may eventually affect generalization behaviors.
2. *Concurrent generalization* involves learning the skill well enough to be able to generalize it.
3. *Subsequent generalization* involves applying the skill to various situations, contexts, and settings.
4. *Independent generalization* involves the student using self-instruction (e.g., cognitive behavior modification) to mediate generalization.

These levels reflect the student's progress during learning. Ellis et al. report that two types of generalization can occur at each level.

1. In *stimulus generalization,* the learned skill is used in conditions that are different than those encountered in training. This leads to the transfer of skills to different settings.
2. In *response generalization,* the newly learned skill is combined with previously learned skills to

TABLE 4.6
Competencies for monitoring progress and providing feedback

Competencies for Monitoring Progress

Monitor progress continuously to maintain an instructional match between the instructional task and the student's ability, skill, and existing knowledge.

Monitor to check understanding of task demands by asking the student to perform a sample task.

Monitor to ensure high rates of success.

Use a systematic recordkeeping system to monitor progress.

Use the results of monitoring to initiate interventions to improve student learning.

Check homework, grade and comment on homework, and return homework quickly.

Competencies for Giving Feedback

Give frequent positive feedback for student successes.

Provide informative feedback (e.g., note error patterns and highlight positive features) to students when making written or verbal corrections.

Involve students in setting instructional goals and discuss performance in terms of goals.

View errors as teaching opportunities and reteach (e.g., provide modeling or guided practice) on the basis of student performance.

Correct careless errors immediately.

Require students to correct errors and remember what to do when they encounter similar problems.

Praise students for error correction.

Use student performance data to make instructional decisions (e.g., repeat lesson, move to next lesson, or change lesson).

Acknowledge correct responses quickly and continue with the lesson or ask another question.

Repeat the part of the response that is correct when a student hesitates but answers correctly, and explain why the response is correct.

Reteach when a student answers incorrectly due to lack of knowledge.

---

produce a different, nontrained skill. Essentially, the skill is adapted for use with different stimuli. For example, a student learns the concept of place value and uses it to regroup in addition problems.

The Learning Strategies Curriculum developed at the University of Kansas Center for Research on Learning is one of the few curriculums that systematically incorporates generalization training within the teaching sequence.

Attributional retraining is a technique that has been used successfully to teach students with learning problems to generalize (Borkowski, Weyhing, & Carr, 1988). Students with learning problems tend to attribute academic success to ease of task or luck, and attribute failure to low ability (Ellis, 1986). These misconceptions highlight the need for attributional retraining. Once students learn that successes are the result of their own efforts, they are more likely to feel in control of their learning and develop more independent learning behaviors.

Independent generalization is the product of highly developed metacognitive processes involving self-evaluation, self-monitoring, self-recording, self-goal setting, and self-reinforcement (Ellis et al., 1987a). These metacognitive skills reflect a thinking process that is acquired through self-instructional training

(Borkowski, Estrada, Milstead, & Hale, 1989). During the acquisition of a skill, the concept of "thinking for yourself" is incorporated into the instructional program. Preparing students with learning problems to use metacognition requires them to develop a system of self-questioning. For example, students can ask themselves the following questions as they begin and proceed through an academic task.

1. Why am I learning this?
2. What am I supposed to learn?
3. What do I already know about it?
4. What ideas are important?
5. How is the information organized?
6. How am I going to learn it?
7. How am I going to remember it?
8. Where am I going to use it?
9. When am I going to use it?
10. How do I apply it?

When students use these self-questions, they actively participate in their learning tasks. They are developing generalization skills by considering how, when, and where they will apply the knowledge they are gaining.

Pressley and Harris (1990) note that teachers must help students realize that generalization of a strategy leads to improved performance. Furthermore, teachers

TABLE 4.7
Competencies for promoting generalization

Have students discuss the rationale for using content or strategy.
Have students identify settings for using content or strategy.
Identify cues in settings that remind students to use content or strategy.
Enlist assistance of other teachers to encourage generalization of content or strategy.
Identify metacognitive processes needed to remember and apply content or strategy.
Set goals to use content or strategy in different contexts.
Teach content or strategy to mastery.
Relate content or strategy use to students' personal lives.
Use a variety of activities in teaching content or strategy (e.g., different teachers, peer instruction, and various practice activities).
Teach content or strategy that is likely to be reinforced or useful in students' natural environments.
Enlist parental help to encourage use of content or strategy at home.
Use a variety of formats (e.g., objects, pictures, media, and computer-assisted instruction) to teach content or strategy.
Encourage students to use content or strategy in their daily lives.
Point out to students that successes are related to their own efforts.
Encourage students to engage in self-management through self-recording, self-evaluation, and self-reinforcement activities.
Provide students with problem-solving instruction through metacognitive strategies (e.g., use of mnemonics that key strategy use).
Teach students to set goals and monitor progress toward their goals.

must help students know when and where a learned strategy can be used profitably. Table 4.7 presents competencies for promoting generalization.

Fostering Independence

The practice of teaching students to become independent learners has emerged as a viable component in effective teaching research (Porter & Brophy, 1988; Pressley & Harris, 1990; Wang, 1987). Wang notes that self-responsibility for one's own learning and behavior is enhanced when academic tasks are perceived as important to functioning in society, ample time is allowed for mastery, and effective study skills are used. Moreover, she reports that student involvement in instructional activities and decisions (e.g., goal setting, selection of practice activities, self-monitoring of progress, and lesson completion through independent study) fosters independent learning. Knapp, Turnbull, and Shields (1990) discuss the balance between teacher-directed and learner-directed instruction to foster independent learning: "The key is to strike the right balance between teacher direction and student

myeducationlab

Go to the Teacher Talk section of the Topic Classroom and Behavior Management in the MyEducationLab for your course to listen to Teacher of the Year Lewis Chappelear of California talk about Letting Students Be Themselves.

responsibility, so that students understand what they are doing (and why) and that, over time, their capacity for self-regulated learning increases" (p. 6).

Students with learning problems typically have difficulty with self-management (Niesyn, 2009; Rooney & Hallahan, 1985). Consequently, many lack self-control strategies that are fundamental to achieving success at school and home. Self-management is an essential component of the independent behavior needed to succeed as a student and as an adult. When students work independently, the teacher can perform essential teaching activities more freely. In essence, it allows students to do independent practice.

Numerous approaches exist for teaching self-management, and research demonstrates that students with learning and behavior problems can learn to implement these strategies effectively (Landrum, Tankersley, & Kauffman, 2003; Lane et al., 2006; Mooney, Ryan, Uhing, Reid, & Epstein, 2005). Three useful techniques for teaching self-management are self-recording, self-evaluation, and self-reinforcement. The steps for teaching each of these three techniques are (1) provide the rationale, (2) demonstrate and model, and (3) practice with feedback (Hughes, Ruhl, & Peterson, 1988). Each technique can be used alone or in combination with related techniques.

Self-recording involves counting and recording one's own behavior, on the assumption that such actions will influence one's behavior. For example, the daily recording of one's weight is likely to influence one's intake of calories or fat grams. Event and interval recording are appropriate for most self-recording situations. The steps for teaching self-recording include the following:

1. *Provide the rationale*—This step involves selecting a behavior that needs changing (e.g., the need to complete more seatwork) and discussing how self-recording can be used to change it.
2. *Demonstrate and model*—In this step a recording form and a method of observation are selected. The teacher demonstrates self-recording by using the observation method and recording the results on the form. Next, the student performs self-recording and receives feedback until understanding is certain.
3. *Practice with feedback*—In this step the student practices self-recording with prompts and corrective feedback. As the student becomes proficient in self-recording, the teacher reduces prompts, praise, and feedback.

Self-evaluation is the component of self-management that teaches the student to judge his or her level of success. The following steps for teaching self-evaluation are used.

1. *Provide the rationale*—The importance of evaluating one's work is discussed. The notion that evaluation enables the student to determine whether his or her performance is satisfactory is stressed. Also, the point is made that it helps the student to know whether more effort is needed.
2. *Demonstrate and model*—In this step a self-evaluation form is selected. It usually requires the student to mark digits (e.g., 0, 1, and 2) that correspond to a grading scale of poor progress (0), some progress (1), and good progress (2). The teacher demonstrates using the form and has the student model the behavior to ensure that he or she understands the process.
3. *Practice with feedback*—The student practices self-evaluation with teacher feedback until proficiency is achieved.

Self-reinforcement is a technique for self-management that involves the student reviewing his or her progress to determine whether reinforcement has been earned. The steps for teaching self-reinforcement include the following:

1. *Provide the rationale*—This step focuses on teaching the importance of earning reinforcement by helping the student identify appropriate reinforcers. The rationale establishes standards of performance for the earning of reinforcements, and it specifies when and how the student is to be rewarded.
2. *Demonstrate and model*—The teacher uses mock data, recording sheets, and a reinforcement menu to demonstrate self-reinforcement. The teacher tells the student when reinforcement criteria are met and selects the reward. The student performs the same behavior with teacher feedback until understanding is apparent.
3. *Practice with feedback*—The student practices self-reinforcement by using self-recording and self-evaluation. Students are encouraged to give praise subvocally when selecting the reinforcer (e.g., "I worked hard and now I get a reward."). The teacher provides corrective and positive feedback until the student becomes proficient by self-reinforcement.

myeducationlab

To enhance your understanding of independence, go to the IRIS Center Resources section of the Topic Classroom and Behavior Management in the MyEducationLab for your course and complete the Module entitled SOS: Helping Students Become Independent Learners.

Hughes et al. (1988) used a combination of self-recording, self-evaluation, and self-reinforcement to help learners with mild disabilities improve their independent work behavior during seatwork. They note that some generalization to other times occurred among their students.

Individualized instruction is easier to organize and carry out if students are involved in managing their own programs. Students may participate in the following activities involving self-management.

- Select activities from a list designed to help them achieve objectives.
- Manage their own work schedules using check-off sheets.
- Use audiovisual equipment independently.
- Select instructional materials and return them to the proper place.
- Tutor one another when feasible.
- Ask for adult help when necessary.
- Self-correct work.
- Administer timings on probes for targeted behaviors.
- Model appropriate learning and social behavior for one another.

- Develop techniques for modifying their own behavior.
- Find solutions to social conflicts without teacher intervention.

The major approach for teaching students to become independent learners is strategy instruction. According to Deshler and Lenz (1989, p. 205),

> A strategy is an individual's approach to a task. It includes how a student thinks and acts when planning, executing, and evaluating one's performance on a task and its outcomes . . . In other words, a strategy is seen as a "tool" that can be used by learners to facilitate their analysis of the demands of a given problem, to help them make decisions regarding the best way(s) to address the problem, and to guide their completion of the task, including a careful monitoring of the effectiveness of the process along the way.

Pressley and Harris (1990) state that strategies are procedures for accomplishing academic tasks. Examples of strategies include clustering information to memorize it, using self-questioning to enhance reading comprehension, and using a first-letter mnemonic strategy to remember information (e.g., using _Daddy_, _Mother_, _Brother_, and _Sister_ to remember the _divide_, _multiply_, _bring down_, and _subtract_ steps in division).

Techniques and procedures of effective strategy instruction begin with matching student abilities and needs to the strategy selected for instruction. Once the match is determined, the teacher points out the benefits of the strategy and discusses (with student input) how and when to use it. The heart of effective strategy instruction is teacher modeling. During the modeling, the teacher thinks aloud as the strategy is applied to meaningful academic tasks. The student then is given ample opportunity to practice the strategy on tasks that gradually increase in difficulty level. The teacher remains supportive as control of strategy use is transferred gradually to the student. Finally, the student is encouraged to transfer strategy use across settings (e.g., special education setting, general education setting, and homework) and content subjects (such as using a reading strategy in social studies and science). During the transfer phase, the student needs to realize and acknowledge the benefits of using a strategy. The learning strategies developed at the University of Kansas Center for Research on Learning have been used successfully throughout the nation with adolescents who have learning problems. Table 4.8 presents competencies for fostering independence.

Using Questions

Asking questions during presentations and follow-up discussions is a key part of the teaching process. The purpose of teacher questioning is multifaceted and frequently can determine how well students with learning problems succeed. Questions are used to involve the student, promote learning, monitor student progress and adjust instruction, and manage the flow of the lesson. Questions can be used to help involve the student by gaining her or his attention and stimulating interest and curiosity. Moreover, they can lead the student to reflect on prior learning and self-evaluate progress. Thus, questions often are useful in beginning a lesson or discussion. Questions also can be used to promote learning. For example, review questions help students remember prior knowledge and link it to new information. Recall questions help students rehearse basic information and promote memorization of important details. Questions reinforce

TABLE 4.8

Competencies for fostering independence

Stress the importance of instructional content (i.e., skills, content, or strategies) and its relevance to daily functioning.
Allow ample time to reach mastery.
Encourage generalization.
Teach effective study skills.
Involve students in goal setting and point out how their errors relate to goal achievement.
Help students connect their degree of effort to positive and negative consequences.
Encourage students to be proactive about learning (e.g., set goals).
Provide students with strategies that foster independent learning (e.g., using mnemonics, clustering information to memorize it, and using self-questioning to ensure comprehension).
Model metacognitive or regulatory self-statements to help students self-instruct, self-monitor, and self-evaluate.
Model being a learner.

specific concepts and prompt students to recall and apply the information.

Sequential questions can lead students to discover connections; divergent questions can promote higher order thinking. Questions enable the teacher to monitor student progress because student responses readily indicate whether students are acquiring and understanding the lesson content. Student responses also help the teacher diagnose students who need additional help on instructional modifications. Finally, questions enable the teacher to adjust the flow of the lesson. If student responses indicate that the lesson is easy, the pace can be increased; when student responses indicate that the lesson is difficult, the pace can be decreased.

Both convergent and divergent questions can be used in the instructional process. Convergent questions limit the answer to a single response or to a small number of responses and usually relate to content the learner previously has read or heard (e.g., "What is the tallest mountain in North America?"). Convergent questions are direct or closed questions and begin with verbs such as *define, describe, identify, summarize, paraphrase,* or *rephrase.* Convergent questions elicit responses relating to the acquisition of facts, rules, and action sequences. About 80 percent of all classroom questions are convergent (Borich, 2007). These lower-level cognitive questions encourage student participation and promote factual knowledge.

Divergent questions are open-ended questions with several correct responses (e.g., "What role do you think sports play in building self-discipline?"). These questions require higher-level cognitive responses than convergent questions and begin with verbs such as *relate, distinguish, differentiate, formulate, compose, produce, justify,* or *decide.* Divergent questions call for responses that relate to the acquisition of concepts, patterns, or abstractions, and they elicit a variety of appropriate responses. About 20 percent of all classroom questions are divergent (Borich, 2007). Students with learning problems have more difficulty with divergent questions than convergent questions. To prepare students with learning problems to answer divergent questions, they need to be given a foundation of concepts and knowledge through explicit instruction. Table 4.9 provides competencies for using questions when instructing students with learning problems.

TABLE 4.9
Competencies for using questions

Use review questions to ensure that students know prior content.
Use questions with specific and concrete examples that are familiar.
Use step-by-step questions that gradually become more complex.
Use questions that rephrase or review the answers to previous questions.
Provide students with wait time (i.e., 3 to 5 seconds) after asking a question.
Provide one or two probable answers in a question to guide students in the appropriate direction.
Use questions and answers in a game format (e.g., the class gets a point when a student responds correctly, and the teacher gets a point when the teacher provides the correct response).
Use questions to individualize instruction (e.g., ask more convergent questions than divergent questions to low achievers).
Use questions to increase lesson clarity (e.g., "What are you going to do when you have read the story?").
Use questions to check for understanding.
Use rapidly paced questions in basic skill instruction in which short, factual answers can encourage learning and students are responding quickly.
To maintain group attention, call on a student after, rather than before, a question.
Promote higher order thinking through questions with more than one correct answer.
Promote higher order thinking through questions that encourage application (i.e., questions with *apply* and *use*), analysis (i.e., questions with *relate* and *distinguish*), synthesis (i.e., questions with *formulate* and *create*), and evaluation (i.e., questions with *justify* and *appraise*).
Use convergent questions that elicit correct answers about 75 percent of the time.
Respond to incorrect answers in a sensitive and helpful manner.
Use divergent questions that encourage students to respond with substantive answers (i.e., including incorrect, incomplete, and "I don't know" answers) about 25 percent of the time.
Instruct students to construct questions.
Attend to who is answering questions correctly during discussions.
Call on nonvolunteers and ask students to elaborate on other students' answers.
Wait or pause for about 3 seconds after asking a question and calling on a student to enable the student to offer a substantive response (e.g., give a correct or incorrect answer, ask for clarification, or say "I don't know").

CLASSROOM MANAGEMENT

Managing student behavior and teaching are simultaneous and ongoing activities. When teachers plan instruction according to their students' abilities and effectively use the systematic teaching steps to deliver instruction, most management problems disappear. Management primarily involves getting students to work on tasks independently or in small groups, or to attend to teacher-directed lessons or discussion. If students perceive a task as worthwhile and one that they can do successfully, getting them to attend or engage in it is fairly easy. On the other hand, if the task is perceived as too difficult or irrelevant, it is almost impossible to get students to work on it for more than a few minutes. Thus, successful management begins with good teaching.

Classroom Tone

The teacher has the power to invite or not invite each student to learn. The teacher's attitudes, attentiveness, enthusiasm, support, and expectations strongly influence how students feel about themselves as learners. Thus, the teacher creates the affective tone of the classroom and sets the stage for learning. Teacher behavior significantly influences student behavior. To maximize the positive aspects of teacher influence, the teacher must be a good role model. The following questions help the teacher assess his or her potential to influence students in a positive way.

- Do I strive to maintain good physical health?
- Do I strive to maintain good emotional health?
- Do I treat students with respect?
- Do I enjoy teaching?
- Do I behave confidently (e.g., in walking and talking)?
- Do I have a positive attitude toward students and peers?
- Do I accept the challenge of educating all learners?
- Do I change my position when a compelling reason exists to do so?
- Am I happy?
- Am I effective at helping students learn?
- Do I listen to students and peers well?
- Do I have a sense of humor?

Classroom Rules

Because it is not possible for the teacher to conduct quality instruction or for students to work productively without guidelines for behavior and procedures, all effectively managed classrooms have rules and procedures. Rules and procedures help students function in the complex social and emotional environment of the classroom. Classroom rules are essential for establishing the expected behaviors of students and the teacher. Rules help structure the learning environment and provide students with guidelines to follow, and they offer the teacher a framework for reinforcing behaviors.

PEARSON **myeducationlab**

Go to the Building Teaching Skills and Dispositions section for the Topic Classroom and Behavior Management in the MyEducationLab for your course and complete the activity entitled Establishing Classroom Rules and Routines.

Rule Guidelines   Numerous educators (Emmer & Evertson, 2009; Rademacher, Callahan, & Pederson-Seelye, 1998) offer the following guidelines for planning and establishing rules for classrooms.

- *Select the minimum number of rules.* It is difficult to remember and enforce a large number of rules. Usually, four to six rules are sufficient for operating a classroom efficiently. Suggested rules for primary students include the following:

  - Always try your best.
  - Raise your hand to say something.
  - Get along with your classmates.
  - Work quietly during seatwork.
  - Listen when the teacher or someone else is talking. Sample rules for older students include the following:
  - Bring essential materials to class.
  - Be in your seat and ready to work when the bell rings.
  - Respect and be polite to others.
  - Be quiet and stay seated when someone is talking.
  - Respect the property of other people.
  - Obey all school rules.

- *State the rules positively.* Negatively stated or "don't" rules imply that the teacher expects students to misbehave. Moreover, a positively stated rule automatically excludes many misbehaviors and includes many desired behaviors. For example, the rule "Respect and be polite to others" excludes numerous misbehaviors (such as teasing, name calling, butting in line, and hitting classmates) and includes many appropriate behaviors (e.g., sharing materials, saying "thank you," saying "please," and talking quietly). Positively stated rules provide nonthreatening, assertive expectations without making the teacher appear to be a dictator.

- *Determine consistent consequences for rule fulfillment or infraction.* For example, students who obey rules earn free time and students who break rules lose recess time. To ensure understanding, the positive and negative consequences for following or breaking rules should be described explicitly to all students (Gunter, Coutinho, & Cade, 2002). Rules without consequences have little effect on behavior; thus, consistent teacher follow-through is critical. Also, rules and their consequences should be applied in an equitable manner; bending the rules for specific students or situations should be avoided.
- *Tailor rules to individual classroom goals and to individual teaching styles.* For example, encourage students to work independently and allow a certain level of noise during seatwork.
- *Include school rules within class rules.* This reminds students that school rules apply in the classroom.
- *Display a set of the rules where the students and the teacher easily can see it.* Posted rules provide a visual reminder to students about how to act appropriately, and the teacher can refer to a specific rule when reminding a student of expected classroom behavior.

The presentation of rules should be done as soon as possible after the teacher is responsible for a new group of students. Rule presentations usually begin with a group discussion concerning the need for rules. This discussion helps students understand the need for the rules, have a sense of ownership of the rules, and assume responsibility for their own behavior. Student involvement often is promoted by the teacher soliciting reasons for having rules and why particular rules are important. Typical student responses may include that rules protect individual and group rights, prevent violence, and permit normal activities to take place. After this general discussion, the rules are presented one at a time. The following steps are helpful in presenting specific rules.

1. *Present each rule and discuss why it is important*— The teacher may solicit discussions from the students regarding the usefulness and importance of each rule.
2. *Clarify each rule and the expected behaviors associated with it*—The teacher should give and recognize examples and nonexamples of behaviors associated with each rule. The teacher may model behaviors associated with the rule and ask students to demonstrate appropriate rule-based behaviors.
3. *Once a rule has been presented and discussed, immediately begin to reinforce students for appropriate rule-based behaviors*—(e.g., "I liked the way you raised your hand when you wanted to say something.").

4. *Discuss the consequences for breaking the rules*— For example, initial failure to obey rules may result in the teacher ignoring the student until the rules are followed. Continued misbehavior may result in loss of recess time.

Teaching Behavioral Expectations for Rules and Classroom Routines

Generally it takes the teacher from 1 to 2 weeks to communicate the behavioral expectations for rules and classroom routines. During these beginning weeks, the teacher should teach students what is expected in performing classroom routines such as checking attendance, arriving late to class, leaving the room as a group or individually, bringing materials to class, using the pencil sharpener, participating in group discussions, completing seatwork, making transitions (e.g., changing from one content area to another, moving from small groups to individual work, and getting ready for lunch), performing peer tutoring, using classroom equipment, turning in seatwork and homework, and responding to classroom interruptions. These routines occur frequently, and appropriate behaviors should be established as quickly as possible. Teachers and classrooms are unique, and each teacher must clarify behavioral expectations for numerous situations: What is expected during seatwork? Is talking allowed? What is expected during whole-class discussions? What do students do to get teacher help? What are the procedures for making transitions from one activity to another (such as from lunch to academic work)? These activities occur many times during a school day, and explicitly teaching students what is expected saves the teacher many hours of corrective feedback during the school year.

For teaching the appropriate behavior regarding classroom rules and routines, it is helpful to use the following direct instruction teaching format.

1. *Use an advance organizer*—In this step the teacher links the lesson to previous discussions about rules and reminds students of the need for rules and routines. The teacher notes that rules and routines maintain both students' rights and a productive environment. Next, the teacher introduces a specific behavioral expectation (e.g., "Raise your hand if

myeducationlab

Go to the Simulations section for the topic Classroom and Behavior Management in the MyEducationLab for your course and take part in the simulation entitled Creating Classroom Behavioral Expectations.

you have something to say.") or a class of behavioral expectations associated with a routine (e.g., making the transition from reading to math activities). Finally, the teacher and the students briefly discuss the rationale for the lesson's behavioral expectations.

2. *Describe the behavioral expectations*—In this step the teacher explicitly describes the specific behaviors required to perform the target activity appropriately. For example, in presenting how to make the transition from seatwork to small-group reading, the teacher describes the steps (e.g., get reading materials out of your desk, stand up and quietly push your chair under your desk, walk to your reading group without disturbing your classmates, quietly pull out your chair at the reading table, be seated, and patiently wait for the teacher to begin reading). Some teachers help students remember the behaviors by using mnemonics. In teaching behavioral expectations for teacher lectures, the SLANT mnemonic is useful.

   S—*Sit* up straight.
   L—*Lean* forward in your desk.
   A—*Act* interested.
   N—*Nod* occasionally to signal understanding.
   T—*Track* the teacher with your eyes.

3. *Demonstrate the behavioral expectations*—In this step the teacher models the behaviors. For example, in teaching the routine of making a transition from seatwork to small-group reading, the teacher performs each behavioral activity while talking aloud about it. A good technique for demonstrating the behavior is for the teacher to ask a question and then answer it: "What's the first thing I need to do to get ready for reading group? Let's see, I need to get my reading materials together." Then the teacher gets each material while talking about it: "I need my reading book, a pencil, and some paper."

4. *Conduct guided practice with feedback*—In this step the teacher instructs the students to model a target behavior (e.g., raising hand or using quiet voices) or a class of behaviors within a routine (such as going to a reading group). When the students exhibit the behaviors, the teacher provides positive and corrective feedback.

5. *Conduct independent practice with feedback*—In this step the students perform the behavior(s) per instructions without models, cues, or prompts, and the teacher provides positive praise for correct procedures and gentle verbal corrections for incorrect

behaviors. It is helpful to tell students how the activity or routine should proceed prior to the event. At the conclusion of a routine or activity, the teacher tells students how well they performed: "You did a great job of making transitions to reading groups today. I'm so proud of you."

6. *Maintain behavioral expectations*—Once the formal lesson on a specific behavior or class of behaviors (i.e., routine) is conducted, the teacher continues to teach the behavioral expectations during daily events. For example, during the first 2 weeks, the teacher uses descriptive praise for correct behavior (e.g., "You did a great job raising your hand for help and waiting quietly for me to come to you.") and gentle verbal reprimands for correction. These reprimands simply involve restating the rule: "Please remember to raise your hand if you want my help or attention" or "Please remember to bring your reading book and pencil to reading group." Descriptive praise and gentle verbal reprimands help clarify the behavioral expectations and indicate a teacher's commitment to them. Once the behavioral expectations are understood and most students are behaving appropriately (e.g., in 2 to 3 weeks), the teacher gradually reduces the amount of reinforcement for correct behaviors and implements consequences for students who consistently do not behave appropriately.

Engaging Students

Students with learning problems often have difficulty attending or maintaining on-task behavior. Techniques exist to help these youngsters engage in schoolwork. Fister and Kemp (1995) provide several activities to promote engagement. The You–Me Game involves putting a You–Me chart on the chalkboard. Each time students use predetermined steps for attending (e.g., SLANT), the teacher records a tally for the students on the *You* side. When students fail to use the attending strategy, the teacher quickly marks a point under the *Me* side and says "I got you!" Another technique Fister and Kemp provide is Participation Budding, which promotes student participation. Students choose or are assigned partners, and the teacher poses a question to the class. Each student thinks about the answer and then turns to his or her assigned buddy to share the answer. The partners then share the answers with the rest of the class.

Table 4.10 provides a list of competencies for managing instruction and students' behavior in the classroom. These competencies are organized into three areas: communicating expectations, engaging interactions, and instructing for engagement.

TABLE 4.10
Competencies for managing instruction and behavior

Communicating Expectations
Establish a positive, expectant, and orderly classroom environment.
Maintain a positive classroom environment through enthusiasm, encouragement, and a positive disposition.
Establish rules that involve respect for others.
Clearly state what behaviors are expected and what behaviors are not tolerated.
Introduce and discuss rules, procedures, and consequences for following rules and breaking rules.
Post rules, discuss rules, and provide rationale for rules.
Establish classroom routines and procedures to promote flow of activities.
Hold students accountable for work and keep records of progress.
Communicate expectations and provide structure for learning (e.g., instructional groupings, prescriptive seatwork, accessible materials, and support for working).

Engaging Interactions
Use task-specific and descriptive praise.
Use a hierarchy of reinforcers to adapt to level of student maturity (e.g., food, objects, tokens, points, praise, activity, or sense of mastery).
Maintain a 3:1 ratio of teacher attention to positive classroom events versus negative classroom events.
Provide positive reinforcement for appropriate behavior or effort, successful task completion, and the learning of new or difficult material.
Gradually shift reinforcement from appropriate behavior to learning accomplishments.
Provide students with verbal reminders to follow rules.
Use nonverbal signals when feasible to direct students in a manner that does not disrupt the class.
Deliver specific praise contingently.
Engage in frequent positive and supportive interactions.
Reinforce student accomplishments.
Frequently scan the classroom.
Arrange the classroom to facilitate smooth transitions and ease of student monitoring.

Instructing for Engagement
Ensure that students have the ability or skills to acquire the targeted content or perform the strategy or procedure being taught.
Correct student behavior in a way that helps students understand the appropriate behavior for the situation.
Instruct students to understand and follow rules through demonstrating, modeling, giving examples and nonexamples, reinforcing students for following rules, correcting students for not following rules, and applying consequences for students who break rules.
Foster self-management in students through self-monitoring, self-recording, and self-evaluating.
Provide explicit instruction in classroom routines.
Provide more teacher-led instruction than independent work.
Use metaphors, anecdotes, and concrete examples to help students connect new content with their existing knowledge.
Circulate throughout the classroom to check the accuracy of work and progress of students.
Engage students in talk about their own thinking.
Ask students to interact with one another and collaborate on problem-solving tasks.

ACCOMMODATING STUDENTS WITH LEARNING PROBLEMS IN GENERAL EDUCATION CLASSROOMS

Teaching students with learning problems in inclusive settings is challenging. Both general education and special education teachers seek accommodations that foster the learning and management of a class of heterogeneous learners. Schumm and Vaughn (1995) note the importance of identifying accommodations that are reasonable to ask of teachers in inclusive settings. This section features accommodations that appear reasonable. They are organized according to accommodations involving materials, interactive instruction, and student performance.

Accommodations Involving Materials

Students spend a large portion of the school day interacting with materials. Most instructional materials give teachers few activities or directions for teaching a large class of students who learn at different rates and in various ways. This section provides material accommodations that enhance the learning of diverse students. Frequently, paraprofessionals, volunteers, and students can help develop and implement various accommodations. Material accommodations include the following:

- *Use of audio recording.* Many problems with materials are related to reading disabilities. The use of audio recording often is an excellent aid in overcoming this problem. Directions, stories, and specific lessons can be recorded on tape, a computer, or an audio file for an MP3 player. The student can replay the audio to clarify understanding of directions or concepts. Also, to improve reading skills, the student can read the printed words silently as they are presented on the audio file.

- *Clarify or simplify written directions.* Some directions are written in paragraph form and contain many units of information. These can be overwhelming to some students. The teacher can help by underlining or highlighting the significant parts of the directions. Rewriting the directions is often helpful. For example:

  Original directions: This exercise will show how well you can locate conjunctions. Read each sentence. Look for the conjunctions. When you locate a conjunction, find it in the list of conjunctions under each sentence. Then circle the number of your answer in the answer column.

  Directions rewritten and simplified: Read each sentence and circle all conjunctions.

- *Present small amount of work.* The teacher can tear pages from workbooks and materials to present small assignments to students who are anxious about the amount of work to be done. This technique prevents students from examining an entire workbook, text, or material and becoming discouraged by the amount of work. Also, the teacher can reduce the amount of work when it appears redundant. For example, the teacher can request the student to complete only odd-numbered problems or items with stars by them, or can provide responses to several items and ask the student to complete the rest. Finally, the teacher can divide a worksheet into sections and instruct the student to do a specific section. A worksheet is divided easily by drawing lines across it and writing *go* and *stop* within each section.

- *Block out extraneous stimuli.* If a student is distracted easily by visual stimuli on a full worksheet or page, then a blank sheet of paper can be used to cover sections of the page not being worked on at that time. Also, line markers can be used to aid reading, and windows can be used to display individual math problems.

- *Highlight essential information.* If an adolescent can read a regular textbook but has difficulty finding the essential information, the teacher can mark this information with a highlight pen.

- *Locate place in consumable material.* In consumable materials in which students progress sequentially (such as workbooks), the student can make a diagonal cut across the lower right-hand corner of the pages as they are completed. With all the completed pages cut, the student and teacher readily can locate the next page that needs to be corrected or completed.

- *Provide additional practice activities.* Some materials do not provide enough practice activities for students with learning problems to acquire mastery on selected skills. Teachers then must supplement the material with practice activities. Recommended practice exercises include instructional games, peer teaching activities, self-correcting materials, computer software programs, and additional worksheets.

- *Provide a glossary in content areas.* At the secondary level, the specific language of the content areas requires careful reading. Students often benefit from a glossary of content-related terms.

- *Develop reading guides.* A reading guide provides the student with a road map of what is written and features periodic questions to help him or her focus on relevant content. It helps the reader understand the main ideas and sort out the numerous details related to the main ideas. A reading guide can be developed across paragraphs, pages, or sections.

Accommodations Involving Interactive Instruction

The task of gaining students' attention and engaging them for a period of time requires many teaching and managing skills. Teaching and interactions should provide successful learning experiences for each student. Some accommodations to enhance successful interactive instructional activities are as follows:

- *Use explicit teaching procedures.* Many commercial materials do not cue teachers to use explicit teaching procedures; thus, the teacher often must adapt a material to include these procedures. Simmons, Fuchs, and Fuchs (1991) provide an instructional template to help teachers include explicit teaching steps within their lessons (i.e., present an advance organizer, demonstrate the skill, provide guided practice, offer corrective feedback, set up independent practice, monitor practice, and review). The following template reminds teachers of steps to use before, during, and after instruction.

Before Instruction

- Note time allocated for instruction (e.g., total instructional time and estimated time for teacher-directed instruction).
- Determine lesson objective (e.g., The student will be able to . . .).
- List preskills to review (e.g., "Before we begin, let's review . . .").

During Instruction

- Frame lesson (e.g., "Today we're going to learn . . ."; "This is important because . . .").
- Present target skill (e.g., "Listen and watch as I show you . . .").
- Guide practice (e.g., "Let's try this one together.").
- Correct errors and provide feedback (e.g., correct response—"That's right"; hesitant response—"Good" and repeat rule or procedure; and incorrect or no response—use prompts on process errors and model correct response on factual errors).
- Prepare for independent practice (e.g., "Let's do the first one together.").

After Instruction

- Monitor independent practice (e.g., circulate throughout the room and provide feedback to students through brief interactions).
- Review new skills (e.g., review skills at the end of the lesson and systematically throughout the instructional year).
- *Repeat directions.* Students who have difficulty following directions often are helped by asking them to repeat the directions in their own words. The student can repeat the directions to a peer when the teacher is unavailable. Lewis and Doorlag (2006) offer the following suggestions for helping students understand directions.
  - If directions contain several steps, break down the directions into subsets.
  - Simplify directions by presenting only one portion at a time and by writing each portion on the chalkboard as well as stating it orally.

- When using written directions, be sure that students are able to read and understand the words as well as comprehend the meaning of the sentences.
- *Maintain daily routines.* Many students with learning problems need the structure of daily routines to know and do what is expected.
- *Provide a copy of lecture notes.* The teacher can give a copy of lecture notes to students who have difficulty taking notes during presentations.
- *Provide students with a graphic organizer.* An outline, chart, or blank web can be given to students to fill in during presentations. This helps students listen for key information and see the relationships among concepts and related information.
- *Use step-by-step instruction.* New or difficult information can be presented in small sequential steps. This helps learners with limited prior knowledge who need explicit or part-to-whole instruction.
- *Combine verbal and visual information.* Verbal information can be provided with visual displays (e.g., on an overhead or handout).
- *Write key points or words on the chalkboard.* Prior to a presentation, the teacher can write new vocabulary words and key points on the chalkboard or an overhead transparency.
- *Use balanced presentations and activities.* An effort should be made to balance oral presentations with visual information and participatory activities. Also, there should be a balance between large-group, small-group, and individual activities.
- *Use mnemonic instruction.* Mnemonic devices can be used to help students remember key information or steps in a learning strategy. In a review of the literature, Wolgemuth, Cobb, and Alwell (2008) strongly support the use of mnemonic strategies for students with disabilities across settings.
- *Emphasize daily review.* Daily reviews of previous learning or lessons can help students connect new information with prior knowledge.

Accommodations Involving Student Performance

Students vary significantly in their ability to respond in different modes. For example, students vary in their ability to give oral presentations, participate in discussions, write letters and numbers, write paragraphs, draw objects, spell, work in noisy or cluttered settings, and read, write, or speak at a fast pace. Moreover, students vary in their ability to process information presented in visual or auditory formats. The following accommodations involving mode of

FIGURE 4.2
A graphic organizer

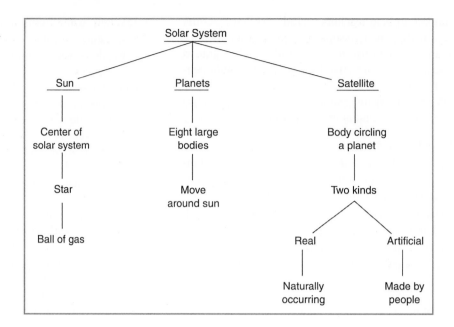

reception and expression can be used to enhance students' performance.

- *Change response mode.* For students who have difficulty with fine motor responses (such as handwriting), the response mode can be changed to underlining, selecting from multiple choices, sorting, or marking. Students with fine motor problems can be given extra space for writing answers on worksheets or can be allowed to respond on individual chalkboards.
- *Provide an outline of the lecture.* An outline enables some students to follow the lesson successfully and make appropriate notes. Moreover, an outline helps students to see the organization of the material and ask timely questions.
- *Encourage use of graphic organizers.* A graphic organizer, as illustrated in Figure 4.2, involves organizing material into a visual format. To develop a graphic organizer, the student can use the following steps: (1) List the topic on the first line, (2) collect and divide information into major headings, (3) list all information relating to major headings on index cards, (4) organize information into major areas, (5) place information under appropriate subheadings, and (6) place information into the organizer format.
- *Place students close to the teacher.* Students with attention problems can be seated close to the teacher, chalkboard, or work area and away from distracting sounds, materials, or objects.

- *Encourage use of assignment books or calendars.* Students can use calendars to record assignment due dates, list school-related activities, record test dates, and schedule timelines for schoolwork. Students should set aside a special section in an assignment book or calendar for recording homework assignments.
- *Reduce copying activities.* Student copying activities (e.g., copying information from the chalkboard) can be minimized by including the information or activity on handouts or worksheets.
- *Have students turn lined paper vertically for math.* Lined paper can be turned vertically to help students keep numbers in appropriate columns while computing math problems.
- *Use cues to denote important items.* Asterisks or bullets can denote questions or activities that count heavily in evaluation. This helps students spend time appropriately during tests or assignments.
- *Design hierarchical worksheets.* The teacher can design worksheets with problems arranged from easiest to hardest. Early success helps students begin to work.
- *Allow use of instructional aids.* Students can be provided with letter and number strips to help them write correctly. Number lines, counters, and calculators help students compute once they understand the mathematical operations.
- *Display work samples.* Samples of completed assignments can be displayed to help students realize expectations and plan accordingly.

- *Use peer-mediated learning.* The teacher can pair peers of different ability levels to review their notes, study for a test, read aloud to each other, read directions or word problems in math, write stories, or conduct laboratory experiments. Harper and Maheady (2007) point out the various effective teaching components that are included in peer-mediated learning, including increased opportunities to respond, immediate feedback, and active engagement of students.
- *Encourage note sharing.* A student can use carbon paper or a notebook computer to take notes and then share them with absentees and students with learning problems. This helps students who have difficulty taking notes to concentrate on the presentation.
- *Use flexible work times.* Students who work slowly can be given additional time to complete written assignments.
- *Provide additional practice.* Students require different amounts of practice to master skills or content. Many students with learning problems need additional practice to learn at a fluency level.
- *Use assignment substitutions or adjustments.* Students can be allowed to complete projects instead of oral reports or vice versa. Also, tests can be given in an oral or written format. For example, if a student has a writing problem, the teacher can allow her or him to outline information and give an oral presentation instead of writing a paper (Cegelka & Berdine, 1995).

The accommodations listed in this section provide a framework for helping students with learning problems achieve in general education classrooms. Throughout this book, activities, techniques, and strategies are presented that embellish these accommodations. The planning and teaching chapters (Chapters 1 through 3) and the curriculum area chapters (Chapters 6 through 14) provide more detailed accommodations.

SELECTING CURRICULUM

Curriculum primarily involves what is taught in the school and consists of learning outcomes that society considers essential for success. A curriculum is established before students enter the school, and it represents what society values as important for becoming a productive citizen and successful individual. If the curriculum accurately represents what is important, it should not be altered, because students deserve an opportunity to acquire this valued knowledge and skills. To accommodate some students with learning problems, it is necessary to prioritize the content to ensure that the most important content is mastered. This position is highlighted in the belief that "less is more."

Specifically, it refers to covering highly valued content extensively so that students achieve understanding and mastery. Another way of accommodating students with learning problems is to focus on how to teach the curriculum. Although some curriculum materials simply present objectives and activities, most materials influence how to teach through their organization, sequencing, and activities. Other materials provide extensive directions in how to teach (e.g., teacher scripts). Students with learning problems learn better when instruction follows research-supported interactive teaching activities (e.g., explicit modeling, corrective feedback, and monitoring of progress), which were presented earlier in this chapter. Because only a low percentage of published curriculum materials are field tested and validated before marketing, educators need to select curriculum materials carefully. This section presents some factors to consider when selecting curriculum materials or designing a curriculum for students with learning problems.

Material Selection Factors

Given the large number of commercial materials, selection often is difficult. Educators who are making decisions on curriculum material selection should consider effective curriculum material design practices.

Curriculum Materials Should Promote Best Instructional Practices The extensive research findings regarding teaching practices (Englert et al., 1992) should be incorporated in curriculum materials. For example, procedures should be included that help the teacher provide good advance organizers, clarify objectives, model concepts explicitly, provide meaningful examples, teach generalization, give helpful feedback, tie the content to something important, and accommodate learner diversity. Teachers deserve to have materials that remind or guide them to use best practices. Teachers are constantly required to adapt, modify, or restructure curriculum materials to include best teaching practices. For many students with learning problems, these teacher procedures represent the difference between success and failure.

Curriculum Materials Should Foster Learner Understanding Many students have experienced the arduous task of memorizing information (e.g., dates, facts, and math formulas) that becomes isolated cognitively (i.e., it does not connect with anything meaningful or relevant). Baker, Simmons, and Kame'enui (1994) note that content needs to be presented in relation to "big ideas." These big ideas are concepts or strategies that facilitate efficient learning across a range of examples. The big ideas serve as anchors through which "small ideas" can be connected and understood. Baker et al. suggest that big ideas are especially useful in teaching content areas. For example, they suggest the big idea of using the problem––solution–effect sequence to teach history. This sequence provides a generalizable strategy for understanding historical events and their interrelatedness. When faced with a *problem,* people throughout history have used moving, inventing, dominating, accommodating, or tolerating to *solve* it. Attempts to solve the problem produce *effects* that often produce another problem; thus, the cycle continues. This cyclical approach helps learners understand history because meaning is clearer and historical events are associated more readily to current events.

Prater (1993) discusses the importance of teaching concepts effectively to students with learning disabilities. She reports that such students have difficulty learning concepts through observation and experience, and thus need explicit concept instruction to succeed in school and life. Prater presents the following sequence of steps that are well grounded in theory and empirical evidence for teaching students to understand concepts.

1. Define the instructional objectives.
2. Analyze the task used for demonstrating knowledge of the concept.
3. Define the concept and label it.
4. Select the number and sequence of examples and nonexamples.
5. Elaborate the defining attributes.
6. Provide immediate feedback.

Materials that feature these steps are noteworthy. Moreover, metaphors, multiple examples, demonstrations, think alouds, and tying content to something relevant also facilitate understanding.

Curriculum Materials Should Guide the Assessment of Relevant Prior Knowledge

The assessment of prior knowledge needed to learn something new should be featured in curriculum materials. This assessment can guide the review of prerequisite knowledge or the teaching of important prerequisite content. Also, continuously monitoring student progress helps the teacher know when to reteach, review, or introduce new material. The curriculum area chapters in this text present assessment formats and procedures that help assess prior knowledge and learning progress.

Curriculum Materials Should Guide Mastery Learning

Most students with learning problems do not succeed with the spiral curriculum approach of exposing specific content to students, and then moving on to a new topic without regard for how well the students learned the original material. This "spray and pray" approach usually results in frustration and minimal learning. Curriculum materials that include goal setting and mastery criteria and feature explicit presentations of new content followed by meaningful and varied practice activities help teachers determine whether individual students are achieving mastery.

Curriculum Materials Should Promote Generalization

Although teaching for generalization is presented in the section of this chapter on using continuous teaching components, the influence of curriculum materials on generalization should be examined. Features such as multiple examples, big ideas, meaningfulness, mastery learning, and application activities that specifically require the learner to connect the new knowledge to daily living foster generalization.

Recently, much has been written about making content more meaningful through authentic learning and integrated instruction. *Authentic learning* is meaningful to the student and is based on the assumption that learners connect prior knowledge with new knowledge to construct meaning (Newmann & Wehlage, 1993). Also, authentic learning assumes that the learner uses a systematic or disciplined strategy to construct meaning that results in discourse, products, or performances that have value beyond success in school. Baker et al. (1994) note that curriculum materials featuring conspicuous strategies (i.e., general steps that students follow when solving a problem) aid students with learning problems, especially when the strategies are explicit, concise, and generalizable. Newmann and Wehlage (1993) present five standards that are basic to authentic learning: (1) Higher order thinking is required, (2) depth of knowledge is obtained (i.e., mastery), (3) learning is connected to the world beyond the classroom, (4) substantive conversation occurs, and (5) social support for student achievement is provided. *Integrated* or *unit instruction* promotes generalization by teaching a concept across subject areas. For example, to teach likenesses and differences among people, students can measure heights and weights of people in math, read stories about individuals with disabilities in reading, and examine the likenesses and differences of people's hair with a microscope in science. A curriculum structure that promotes authentic learning standards or teaches concepts across subject areas enhances generalization.

Curriculum Materials Should Provide Guidelines for Learner Diversity Curriculum materials offering viable suggestions for students who learn at different rates help a teacher meet the needs of diverse learners. Materials that include best teaching practices greatly reduce student frustrations and minimize learning diversity. Materials that provide for mediated scaffolding help teachers respond to a wide range of learners. _Mediated scaffolding_ refers to personalized guidance, instruction, assistance, and support that a teacher, peer, task, or material provides to a learner. It is temporary guided instruction that gradually is removed as the learner acquires skills. Mediated scaffolding may be included in materials through sample teaching scripts, additional examples, metaphors or anecdotes, and meaningful practice activities. Finally, materials that offer suggestions for cooperative learning, computer-assisted instruction, peer-mediated instruction, instructional games, and grouping arrangements help teachers plan and respond to diverse learners. In essence, the curriculum material should be designed to reach all students and challenge advanced achievers to higher order thinking. It appears more prudent to teach low and average achievers well and challenge high achievers than to frustrate low achievers while focusing primarily on high achievers.

Guidelines for Designing a Curriculum

From his research and review of curriculum and practice activities, Carnine (1989) provides the following guidelines for designing a curriculum that is most likely to increase accuracy and decrease instructional time to mastery.

- _Introduce information cumulatively._ This procedure avoids memory overload by introducing new pieces of information one at a time. Each new piece of information is presented after the previous piece has been learned. For example, a student can learn one continent at a time until all seven are learned.
- _Build retention._ To increase memory and decrease the likelihood of errors, a review of difficult material should occur within a couple of days of initial learning. Moreover, students need practice in discriminating a newly learned concept from similar concepts. Supervised practice is important in the initial stages of discrimination practice. Solving problems involving the multiplication and division of fractions is an example of discrimination practice.
- _Separate confusing elements and terminology._ When similar symbols are to be taught (such as 6 and 9, + and ×, or b and d), the teacher should introduce one symbol at a time. Once students learn a symbol or term, then the teacher can introduce the similar one.
- _Make learning more meaningful by stressing relationships._ First, the teacher should stress the relationship of components to the whole. For example, the teacher can instruct students to use their knowledge of sound–symbol correspondence to decode words, or the teacher can point out how a comprehension strategy can be applied to books across subject areas. Second, the teacher should stress the application of known information to unknown information. For example, the teacher can point out that the multiplication of 5s involves counting by 5s or that the commutative property of addition (i.e., $a + b = c$, $b + a = c$) applies to multiplication.
- _Reduce processing demands._ Processing demands are decreased by teaching a strategy or algorithm first and

A well-planned lesson leads to student engagement and learning. iStockphoto.com then teaching the information in increasingly difficult stages. For example, teaching letter–sound correspondences first reduces the processing requirements for decoding words, and teaching addition (i.e., easiest information) before multiplication decreases the processing demands of learning multiplication.

- *Require faster responses.* Requiring faster responses helps students develop automatic responses.

PLANNING UNITS AND LESSONS

A lesson that maintains students' attention and participation and proceeds smoothly without interruptions, digressions, and diversions usually has been carefully planned. Effective teaching and classroom management do not "just happen." In planning for academically diverse classes, teachers focus on developing interesting activities that motivate and encourage student involvement. Many teachers report that their most productive planning occurs in unstructured settings (e.g., driving a car, walking the dog, or taking a shower). Teachers generally agree that during-school planning involves "top structure" planning (i.e., scheduling, determining class structure, developing units, and responding to administrative tasks), whereas "deep structure" planning (e.g., how to clarify a difficult concept within a lesson or develop a motivating activity) is accomplished away from school.

The planning of units and lessons is germane to effective instruction. Units and lessons provide the framework for structuring teaching to accomplish short- and long-range learning outcomes. Lenz, Bulgren, Schumaker, Deshler, and Boudah (1994) define a unit of instruction as *a chunk of content that is distinguishable from a previous chunk of content through a closure or transition activity* (e.g., a test or project).

Schumm, Vaughn, and Leavell (1994) provide a format for planning units for teachers to use in planning instruction for diverse classes. Their planning pyramid framework, which consists of three levels, includes a structure that enables the teacher to differentiate outcomes according to students' learning characteristics. This enhances the teacher's proficiency in planning units to promote learning for all students. Level 1 represents the basic concepts, content, or skills that the teacher wants all learners to master. The information at this level is critical for understanding the content of the unit and is usually more general than information in Levels 2 and 3. The functional teacher question at this level is "What do I want *all* students to learn?" Level 2 represents a higher level of information than Level 1. It focuses on information that the teacher

considers next in importance for understanding or applying the content or skills. The functional teacher question at this level is "What do I want *most* students to learn?" Level 3 represents supplemental information that is more complex or detailed. The functional teacher question at this level is "What information may *some* students learn?" A student's mastery of information at the different levels is not determined by abilities. Because a student's prior knowledge and interests vary across topics, a student's learning will vary across topics. Access to information at all levels should be available to all students.

The following questions pertaining to the topic, the teacher, and the students provide guidelines for helping the teacher use the level format to plan units (Joint Committee on Teacher Planning for Students with Disabilities, 1995).

- What prior knowledge do the students and do I have of this topic?
- How interesting is the topic to individual students and to me?
- How many new concepts are introduced, and how complex are they?
- How can I relate this material to previous instruction?
- Have I taught this material before?
- What resources are available to me for this unit?
- Will students' communication skills make comprehension of a particular concept difficult?
- Will students with reading difficulties be able to function independently while learning about the concept from the text?
- Will students with behavioral or attention problems be able to concentrate on this material?
- Will my students have the vocabulary they need to understand this concept?
- What experiences have my students had that will relate to this concept?
- Is there some way to relate this concept to the cultural and linguistic backgrounds of my students?

Planning Routines for Units

The level format for planning units can be combined readily with unit planning routines to develop a unit responsive to the needs of diverse learners. Lenz et al. (1994) discuss unit planning routines that help teachers become explicit with students about learning outcomes, the relationship of chunks of information, and activities that will facilitate learning. They note that these unit planning routines help students with learning problems to understand and retain information. The routines involve thinking about the content of a unit, the outcomes

FIGURE 4.3
A unit organizer

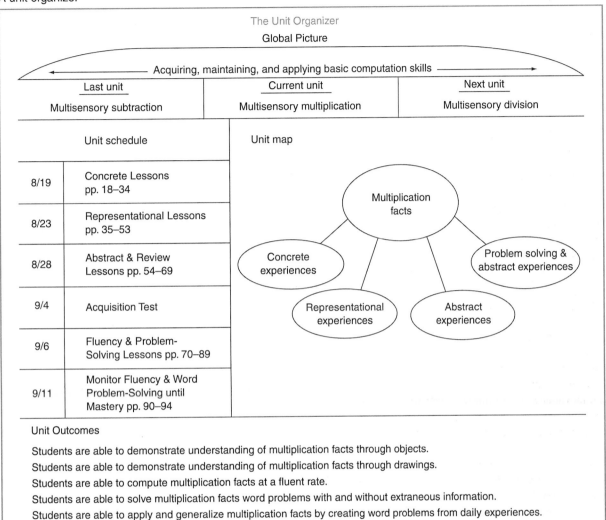

The Unit Organizer
Global Picture

Acquiring, maintaining, and applying basic computation skills

Last unit	Current unit	Next unit
Multisensory subtraction	Multisensory multiplication	Multisensory division

Unit schedule

8/19	Concrete Lessons pp. 18–34
8/23	Representational Lessons pp. 35–53
8/28	Abstract & Review Lessons pp. 54–69
9/4	Acquisition Test
9/6	Fluency & Problem-Solving Lessons pp. 70–89
9/11	Monitor Fluency & Word Problem-Solving until Mastery pp. 90–94

Unit map

Multiplication facts

Concrete experiences

Problem solving & abstract experiences

Representational experiences

Abstract experiences

Unit Outcomes

Students are able to demonstrate understanding of multiplication facts through objects.
Students are able to demonstrate understanding of multiplication facts through drawings.
Students are able to compute multiplication facts at a fluent rate.
Students are able to solve multiplication facts word problems with and without extraneous information.
Students are able to apply and generalize multiplication facts by creating word problems from daily experiences.

of the unit, and the development of a graphic device to display the organization and relationship of the unit content. The unit organizer in Figure 4.3 features the use of a unit planning routine for teaching multiplication facts. The suggested order for planning a unit, as illustrated in Figure 4.3, is to title the current unit, provide the title of the last unit, determine the next unit, indicate the global picture, draw the unit map, list the unit outcomes, and determine the unit schedule. Lenz et al. offer an excellent routine for planning units of content in inclusive classrooms at the secondary level.

Lesson Planning Format

The planning format for lessons is similar to the unit planning format. It helps the teacher explicitly determine what will be taught and how it will be taught. This planning adds essential details to the teaching of the lessons within a unit. The lesson planning format features teacher planning to determine what all students will learn, what most students will learn, and what some students will learn (Schumm et al., 1994). These levels are identical to those previously presented in the format for planning units. Schumm et al. (1994) provide the following sequence to guide the development of the lesson planning format.

1. Identify content according to the three levels (i.e., what all will learn, what most will learn, and what some will learn).
2. Use the following questions to guide the "context" of instruction.

   • Are there scheduled interruptions (e.g., holidays or special events) that may alter instructional time?

- How will the class size affect instruction of the lesson?
- Do the students work well individually, in small groups, or in pairs? Which students need to be grouped together?
- What resources exist to teach this lesson?
- What methods will be used for motivation?
- What instructional strategies and adaptations can be implemented to promote learning for all students?
- What learning strategies are needed to help students master these concepts?
- What independent work and homework assignments are appropriate for this lesson?
- How will student learning be monitored? How will student learning be assessed at the end of the lesson and at the end of the unit?

3. Develop an agenda for the lesson.
4. List needed materials.
5. Determine seatwork and homework assignments.
6. Determine what method will be used to evaluate student learning.

The lesson plan design that includes the systematic teaching steps in Table 4.11 could be adapted readily to include the three levels of content in the lesson planning format. The differentiated learning outcomes (i.e., Levels 1, 2, and 3) can be incorporated in the lesson by adapting instruction during the modeling, guided practice, independent practice, feedback, and generalization steps. Advanced students (i.e., students working on content at Level 3) could develop a booklet of multiplication problems encountered in their daily lives or could solve more complex problems by applying the strategies they have learned. Students with learning difficulties in multiplication (i.e., students working on content at Level 1) could receive extra modeling or guided practice, more independent practice activities with computers, or more time to achieve mastery.

POSTINSTRUCTIONAL ACTIVITIES

Information regarding the relationship between competent teachers and involvement in postinstructional tasks is limited. However, it is assumed that the following postinstructional activities improve teaching effectiveness: reflecting on one's actions and students' responses; staying current on subject matter and educational issues by reading journals, texts, or professional organization literature; taking advanced education courses; and interacting with colleagues to coordinate teaching plans (Reynolds, 1992). It also is recognized that postinstructional activities combine with planning activities.

Teacher Reflection and Collaboration

One of the primary activities of postinstruction involves the process of reflecting about teaching. Brandt (1991, p. 3) highlights the importance of reflecting in the following passage.

> Everyone needs opportunities for self-renewal, but those responsible for developing other human beings need them most of all. Thinking deeply about what we are doing leads us to ask better questions, break out of fruitless routines, make unexpected connections, and experiment with fresh ideas.

Reynolds (1992) reports that competent teachers reflect on their teaching to find out what teaching behaviors are successful and unsuccessful with students. This process helps teachers refine their teaching practices. Reynolds notes that reflection occurs during as well as after interactions with students. During interactions, teachers gather information from student comments, actions, and written work to determine levels of student understanding. These multiple forms of assessments provide information that enables teachers to reflect on what practices are effective or ineffective and to improve their teaching. Reynolds notes that as teachers gain experience and become more competent, their reflections change from concerns about classroom management, the quality of their explanations, how they respond to questions, and student participation to concerns about student understanding and instructional events that seem especially noteworthy. With experience, teachers seem to develop a system for organizing, understanding, and using the enormous amount of information gained from experience. Because of the learning differences of students, the focus on student understanding is important in guiding teachers to make adjustments that enable all students to succeed.

One of the primary techniques for fostering teacher reflections is journal writing. Smyth (1989) suggests the following questions to guide reflections that are applicable to teacher journal writing.

- What do I do? (Elicits description of practice.)
- What does this mean? (Elicits principles of instruction.)
- How did I come to be this way? (Elicits awareness beyond the classroom and situates practices in a broader cultural milieu.)
- How might I do things differently? (Elicits action.)

TABLE 4.11
Math lesson design for teaching diverse learners

Step 1:	**Introduce the lesson**
	Use a focusing activity to gain student attention.
	Connect the lesson to previous learning or lesson.
	Identify the target skill, strategy, or content.
	Provide a rationale for learning the skill, strategy, or content.
	Discuss the relevancy of the skill, strategy, or content until an authentic context is realized. Authenticity may be achieved within the context of school activities, community events, or future demands.
Step 2:	**Describe and model the skill or strategy**
	The teacher requests the students to attend while the teacher demonstrates the skill or strategy. To help students understand the demonstration, the following two procedures are used.
	Procedure 1: The teacher asks a question and then answers the question. The students hear and observe the teacher think aloud while modeling metacognitive strategies.
	Procedure 2: The teacher asks a question and the students help provide the answer. The students participate by answering the question and solving the problem. The teacher and the students perform the strategy together, and the teacher continues to provide modeling.
Step 3:	**Use scaffolding to guide practice and interactive discourse**
	Procedure 1: The teacher guides students through problem-solving strategies without demonstration unless it is required. Guidance is provided as needed and the following supportive techniques are used.
	• The teacher asks specific leading questions and models if necessary (e.g., "What is the first step in solving a problem?").
	• The teacher provides prompts regarding declarative knowledge (e.g., "Use a variable [letter] to represent the unknown in the word problem.").
	• The teacher provides cues regarding procedural knowledge (e.g., "Remember to isolate the variable in solving the equation.").
	Procedure 2: The teacher instructs students to do the task and reflect on the process and product. The teacher provides support on an as-needed basis and uses fewer prompts and cues. The students are encouraged to become more independent.
Step 4:	**Conduct independent practice to mastery**
	Students are encouraged to reflect (i.e., estimate, predict, check, and create) and work without teacher assistance. Activities include group projects to explore multiple ways to solve problems (e.g., using objects, pictures, drawings, and algorithms) or the creation of authentic contexts for solving problems (e.g., conducting a survey and using math to present and describe the results). A variety of practice arrangements are used, including cooperative learning, peer tutoring, instructional games, self-correcting materials, and computer-assisted instruction.
Step 5:	**Provide feedback**
	Procedure 1: Focus on successes. Discuss student performance or product in terms of a predetermined learning goal. Tie student efforts and thinking processes to success.
	Procedure 2: Focus on error correction. View errors as opportunities for the teacher to teach and for the students to learn. Ask students to note errors and correct. If needed, guide their correction through questions, metaphors, and modeling. Also, have students work together to correct errors.
Step 6:	**Teach generalization and transfer**
	Reflect on applications of new knowledge across settings and situations.
	Encourage students to create meaningful math word problems related to new knowledge.
	Have students work on more difficult problems. For example, if they have learned multiplication facts 0 to 81, have them attempt problems such as 12×6 using the strategies they have learned. With word problems, challenge students to solve those involving more than one operation. Have students collaborate to solve the challenging problems.

Although reflection is often a private or individual event, it is facilitated through collaborative activities. Working together with colleagues often helps teachers gain personal insights and create synergistic solutions. The following collaborative questions can foster reflection.

- Will curriculum-based assessment allow teachers to assess the progress of students in a manner that provides insight into effective instructional activities and learner differences?
- How can teachers more effectively involve parents in school activities?
- How can teachers effectively combine elements of whole language instruction with phonological awareness instruction to improve reading instruction?

An additional collaborative/reflective activity involves establishing an educators' forum to focus on school problems.

Mohlman, Sparks-Langer, and Colton (1991) report that educators can foster professional growth through performing microteaching followed by writing in reflection journals, conducting self-analysis of video- and audiotapes, conducting action research projects, and collaborating about student learning and teaching. They note that case studies of teaching and learning events that highlight specific context, practices, content, and ethical and moral dilemmas help teachers develop a valuable repertoire of ideas, skills, and attitudes. Finally, Mohlman et al. indicate that teachers need time to understand, interpret, and personalize information from research, theories, and experts.

PERSPECTIVE ON INSTRUCTIONAL COMPONENTS

When teachers examine the many instructional components that are recommended for good teaching, it is understandable if they feel a little overwhelmed. The instructional components related to positive student outcomes represent a formidable list to incorporate into daily teaching practices. Fortunately, the growing knowledge base about effective teaching can enlighten educators about best teaching practices; however, a unifying theory or framework to organize the knowledge base and guide the application of best teaching practices is missing. The examination of teaching in terms of planning, interactive teaching, and postinstructional activities helps organize the many components of teaching into a manageable framework for improving the practice of teaching. If one considers that many of the supported instructional practices are interrelated, the task of effective teaching becomes more reasonable. For example, the competency involving monitoring student progress is inherent in several planning activities (e.g., provide time for learning, ensure success, and strive to motivate), interactive teaching activities (e.g., monitor progress and give feedback), and postinstructional activities (e.g., reflect on student learning and activities that are effective or ineffective).

When examining all the aspects of good teaching, it is nice to remember that students can bring much joy to teaching. It helps if the teacher appreciates students and expects to enjoy their freshness, humor, questions, and ideas.

Perhaps the most important source of knowledge about good teaching is the students. In a paper on "The Good Teacher" presented at a conference titled "Education from Cradle to Doctorate," Clark (1989) notes that students' thoughts and stories about good teachers almost invariably concern four fundamental human needs: (1) to be known, (2) to be encouraged, (3) to be respected, and (4) to be led. Moreover, he discusses the voices of students concerning good teaching (pp. 18–19):

> In the language of children, their good teachers nurture them by treating them as intelligent people who can become even more intelligent, by taking the time to learn who we are and what we love, treating us fairly by treating us differently, by explaining why he teaches and acts as he does, by telling stories of her own life outside school and listening to ours, by letting me have a bad day when I can't help it. The good teacher is both funny and serious. We can laugh together, and this makes me feel happy and close. She puts thought into surprising us in ways that we will never forget. He draws pictures that show how ideas are connected; we don't feel lost or afraid that we will be sent away or humiliated. The good teacher loves what he is teaching, but does not show off or put distance between us and him. The good teacher sets things up so that children can learn how to learn from one another. She knows how to be a friend while still a responsible adult . . . The good teacher puts people first, say the children. The good teacher acts from love and caring, and is loved and cared for in return.

Promoting Social, Emotional, and Behavioral Development

Anthony Magnacca/Merrill

From Chapter 5 of *Teaching Students with Learning Problems*, 8/e. Cecil D. Mercer. Ann R. Mercer. Paige C. Pullen.
Copyright © 2011 by Pearson Education. All rights reserved.

Students with learning problems often have difficulty with social skills and emotional development and with maintaining appropriate behavior. Problems in social skills result in difficulty interacting with others, whereas emotional difficulties generally involve problems within oneself (e.g., low self-concept). Students with behavioral problems often disrupt others or undermine their own learning progress. Problems in these areas frequently overlap; for example, a student with a poor self-concept regarding academics may withdraw from social interactions during academic activities and engage in off-task behavior (e.g., daydreaming) throughout the school day. Although it is not always apparent whether social, emotional, or behavioral problems contribute to a student's academic difficulties, they usually interfere with learning and thus limit academic success. On the other hand, learning difficulties can contribute to social, emotional, and behavioral problems by causing the student to face excessive academic failure and frustration.

In addition to treatment for academic deficits, educational plans must consider the social, emotional, and behavioral characteristics and needs of students with learning problems. Through appropriate instruction, the teacher can help students improve their social, emotional, and behavioral development. Table 5.1 includes profiles of students and related interventions for selected social, emotional, and behavioral characteristics.

ASSESSMENT OF SOCIAL, EMOTIONAL, AND BEHAVIORAL DEVELOPMENT

Assessment of social, emotional, and behavioral development involves the use of various types of measurement and evaluation procedures. In addition to student behavior in the classroom, a thorough assessment of social, emotional, and behavioral factors considers student self-concept and attitudes as well as behavior outside the classroom. To provide a broad and natural picture of the student, an ecological assessment includes an evaluation of the student's behavior and status in the various environments in which he or she functions. Currently, no single test can yield a comprehensive, reliable, valid, and useful assessment of social skills or emotional and behavioral problems. Thus, several instruments and procedures are required to assess social, emotional, and behavioral development. Helpful information may be obtained from teachers, parents, students, and peers as well as from records of social, developmental, and educational history.

During assessment of social, emotional, and behavioral development, the type of behavior and its frequency, intensity, and duration should be considered. When assessment consists of a combination of various methods, contexts, and sources of data, the social, emotional, and behavioral problems of students can be identified and can lead to appropriate educational interventions.

For students displaying serious behavioral problems, the Individuals with Disabilities Education Improvement Act of 2004 requires a functional behavioral assessment (FBA), a behavior intervention plan (BIP), and a manifestation determination review for students with disabilities who are removed from school for more than ten cumulative school days. An FBA, which is a comprehensive and individualized approach to identify the functional relationship between behaviors, antecedents, and consequent events, can also be an effective assessment technique for dealing with students who have persistent patterns of minor behavior problems that may indicate more severe problems in the future. The FBA includes two processes: (1) descriptive analysis uses multiple sources (such as interviews, checklists, behavior rating scales, and direct observation) to describe and predict problem behavior, and (2) functional analysis is used to test and confirm hypotheses about the function of the problem behavior. The results of the FBA lead to the development of a BIP, which must address the behavior that led to the student's removal. Also, a manifestation determination review must be conducted to determine if there is a causal relationship between a student's disability and the misconduct for which the student is being disciplined.

This section presents several techniques and measures available to assess social, emotional, and behavioral development. Included are commercial observer-rater instruments, commercial measures of adaptive behavior, self-report instruments, sociometric techniques, and naturalistic observations.

Commercial Observer-Rater Instruments

With the commercial observer-rater instruments, an observer (e.g., teacher, guidance counselor, social worker, school psychologist, or family member) completes either a checklist or a rating scale. Checklists generally are used to record the presence or absence of specific characteristics or behaviors. Rating scales are designed to indicate the frequency of a particular behavior or the degree to which certain characteristics are present. Teacher ratings frequently are used to assess behavioral problems in classrooms. These ratings usually are conducted with published checklists, scales, or questionnaires. These formats are most useful for general screening and initial identification of student behavioral problems, as well as for measuring student progress over time. Table 5.2 provides

TABLE 5.1
Profiles of students and related interventions for selected social, emotional, and behavioral characteristics

---

Social Skills Deficits

Nobody seems to like Barry. He often is called rude or inconsiderate. For example, he may continue to relate the details of a neighborhood rumor even though the face of one of his classmates is red with embarrassment, or he thoughtlessly may interrupt a serious conversation between two adults. He cannot tell when his listeners have lost interest. To help Barry identify critical social and nonverbal cues, his teacher involves him in role playing and games such as charades. A social skills curriculum is used, too.

Poor Self-Concept

Melanie, a secondary school student, has faced repeated failure and frustration throughout her school years. She has few friends and seldom initiates social interactions or takes part in school activities. When given an academic task, Melanie frequently responds, "That's too hard for me. I can't do it." Melanie's English teacher, who has taken an individual interest in her, has minimized her anxiety about failure through the use of support and success techniques. The teacher is helping Melanie attribute her failures to insufficient effort and praises her for effort regardless of the accuracy of her responses. She also uses Melanie as a peer tutor to enhance her feelings of self-worth.

Dependency

As a young child, Brad was very dependent on his mother. She gave him excessive attention and assistance. Now, he frequently turns to his teacher with requests such as "Help me" or "Show me how." Brad's teacher is trying to provide him with appropriate academic tasks and success experiences and is reinforcing him for effort. Brad also works independently with self-correcting materials and computer software programs that provide him with immediate feedback without the teacher being present.

Loneliness

Tessa usually works, plays, and eats alone. She sits quietly at her desk, staring into space, rather than working or participating in discussions. She seldom willingly joins group activities or even initiates a conversation. She does not share and frequently makes negative comments that reduce the likelihood of further interaction (e.g., "You sure are dumb. Don't you know how to do anything right?"). Tessa's teacher is providing her with much support and praise and gradually is encouraging various interpersonal relationships. Peer teaching and instructional games in which Tessa is paired with a competent, accepting student are providing Tessa with appropriate peer contact. The teacher systematically reinforces any group participation or positive social interaction.

Disruptive Behavior

Larry is often out of his seat or yelling across the room. He starts fights over minor incidents, such as tripping or butting in line. Larry's teacher is using social skills training and behavior modification techniques to reduce his disruptive behavior. She reinforces and praises him for appropriate behavior and ignores him as much as possible when he is being disruptive. When she must reprimand him, she does so quietly so that others cannot hear.

Hyperactivity

Richard's mother describes her son as having been in a state of perpetual motion since he was very young. It seems impossible for him to sit still for even a few minutes. At mealtime, he quickly stuffs his food in his mouth and is then once again on the go. In the classroom Richard also is easily excitable and constantly in motion. For example, he frequently is out of his seat, shuffling papers, moving his feet or legs, or tapping his pencil on his desk. Richard's activity level causes him to have frequent accidents (e.g., while riding his bicycle), and he sometimes unintentionally hurts a classmate when playing too rough on the playground. Richard takes Ritalin every morning under his doctor's prescription, and his classroom teacher structures Richard's daily work schedule according to his attention span, reinforces him when he is less active, and frequently allows him to perform tasks that permit him to move about the room.

Distractibility

According to her teacher, Amy is highly distractible and has a short attention span. She can work on an assignment for a short time, but she is diverted quickly by any noise or motion in the room. She stares out the window or daydreams, and her assignments go uncompleted. Her teacher uses a carrel to isolate Amy from potentially distracting auditory and visual stimuli. She also encourages Amy to use verbal mediation (i.e., quietly talking to herself about what she is doing) while performing a task and gives her praise for on-task behavior.

Impulsivity

Jane's impulsivity is evident in class. She is usually the first person to complete and hand in a worksheet, always without checking the accuracy of her responses. Jane's grades in math especially have been affected by her tendency to respond impulsively, even though she usually can correct a wrong response when given the opportunity. She talks out of turn, and without thinking says things that may hurt someone's feelings. Jane's teacher is encouraging her to pause before acting or speaking. In math, her teacher has Jane estimate the answers and check her work. Also, through contingency contracts, Jane is reinforced according to an accuracy criterion (i.e., percent correct) for each task.

Source: From *Students with Learning Disabilities* (pp. 392–393), 7th ed., by C. D. Mercer and P. C. Pullen, 2009, Upper Saddle River, NJ: Merrill/Pearson. Copyright 2009 by Pearson Education. Reprinted by permission.

TABLE 5.2
Observer-rater instruments

Instrument	Ages	Respondent
Behavior Assessment System for Children—Second Edition (Reynolds & Kamphaus, 2004)	2–21 years	Teacher, parent, student

The system provides teacher, parent, and self-reports, as well as a structured developmental history and observed classroom behavior of the student. The teacher rating scale includes items (such as "Bullies others" and "Adjusts well to new teachers") related to adaptive and problem behaviors in school settings, whereas the parent rating scale pertains to behaviors exhibited in community and home settings. The teacher and parent scales use a 4-point rating scale of frequency. The self-report measure of personality includes short true–false and multiple-choice statements concerning personal thoughts and feelings. Children ages 6 to 7 provide yes-or-no answers to questions asked by the examiner who records responses on a checklist. Additional student information is obtained on the development history survey of social, psychological, developmental, educational, and medical areas, and a student observation system is used to code and record maladaptive and adaptive behaviors. Two computerized formats for easy scoring and reporting are available. In addition, the *BASC-2 Behavioral and Emotional Screening System* (Kamphaus & Reynolds, 2007) can be used to screen for behavioral and emotional issues in children and adolescents ages 3 to 18. The norm-referenced screening system consists of brief forms that can be completed by teachers, parents, or students in about 5 to 10 minutes.

Instrument	Ages	Respondent
Behavior Evaluation Scale—3 (McCarney & Arthaud, 2005)	4–19 years	Teacher, parent

The scale yields behavioral information about students according to five subscales: learning problems, interpersonal difficulties, inappropriate behavior, unhappiness/depression, and physical symptoms/fears. The school version includes 54 items representing behaviors easily observed and documented by educational personnel, and the home version includes 52 items representing behaviors exhibited in and around the home environment. Each version can be completed in about 15 minutes. A computer program converts raw scores to standard and percentile scores.

Instrument	Ages	Respondent
Behavior Rating Profile—2 (Brown & Hammill, 1990)	6–18 years	Teacher, parent, student, peers

Six independent measures of behavior are included: teacher rating scale, student rating scale (school), parent rating scale, student rating scale (home), sociogram, and student rating scale (peer). The three student rating scales are embedded in a 60-item true–false format, and the parent and teacher rating scales each contain 30 items that the respondents classify on a 4-point scale. The sociogram provides information about the student's sociometric status within the classroom. The results of the profile can be used to identify students whose behavior is perceived to be deviant and to identify specific settings in which behavioral problems are prominent. Also, the profile can be useful in identifying persons whose perceptions of a student's behaviors are different from those of other respondents.

Instrument	Ages	Respondent
Conners—Third Edition (Conners, 2008b)	6–18 years	Teacher, parent, student

The *Conners 3* combines teacher, parent, and student reports to provide a comprehensive evaluation of student behaviors. The three norm-referenced rating scales (i.e., parent, teacher, and self-report) are available in long- and short-term versions, and administration time is 20 minutes for long forms and 10 minutes for short forms. The following empirical and rational scales are included: hyperactivity/impulsivity, executive functioning, learning problems, aggression, peer relations, family relations, and inattention. In addition, symptom scales assess attention-deficit hyperactivity disorder, oppositional defiant disorder, and conduct disorder. Screener items uncover anxiety and depression; impairment items indicate if problems are affecting schoolwork/grades, friendship/relationships, and home life; and critical items identify students with severe behavior problems who need immediate attention. Computer scoring and assessment, feedback, and progress reports are available. The *Conners Comprehensive Behavior Rating Scales* (Conners, 2008a) is similar to the *Conners 3* in terms of the three rating scales; however, it assesses a wider multitude of disorders and a wide range of emotional, behavioral, and academic problems as well as the student's potential for violence.

Instrument	Ages	Respondent
Devereux Behavior Rating Scale—School Form (Naglieri, LeBuffe, & Pfeiffer, 1993)	5–18 years	Teacher, parent
The scale is especially effective as a screening device to identify the existence of behaviors that fall within the normal range and behaviors that indicate a severe emotional disturbance. Two 40-item versions, one for children ages 5 through 12 years and one for adolescents ages 13 through 18 years, feature separate sets of appropriate items. The four subtests focus on interpersonal problems, inappropriate behaviors/feelings, depression, and physical symptoms/fear. Administration time is about 5 minutes, and item-level scores help identify specific problem behaviors.		
Revised Behavior Problem Checklist (Quay & Peterson, 1996)	5–18 years	Teacher, parent, anyone familiar with the student
A checklist is used to rate problem behaviors that are classified according to six domains: conduct disorder, socialized aggression, attention problems–immaturity, anxiety–withdrawal, psychotic behavior, and motor tension–excess. The 89 items can be administered in about 20 minutes.		
Scale for Assessing Emotional Disturbance (Epstein & Cullinan, 1998)	5–18 years	Teachers, parent, anyone familiar with the student
The standardized, norm-referenced scale is based on the federal terminology for identifying students with emotional disturbance. Student functioning is measured in seven areas: inability to learn, relationship problems, inappropriate behavior, unhappiness or depression, physical symptoms or fears, social maladjustment, and overall competence. The 52-item scale can be completed in less than 10 minutes, and information from the scale is useful in understanding the emotional and behavioral disorders of students.		
Social-Emotional Dimension Scale—Second Edition (Hutton & Roberts, 2004)	6–18 years	Teacher
This 72-item norm-referenced rating scale can be used to identify students who are at risk for problematic behaviors that may interfere with academic functioning. The test kit also includes a 15-item screener and a structured interview form for functional assessment of behavior. Administration time is 20 to 30 minutes.		
Social Skills Improvement System Rating Scales (Gresham & Elliott, 2008)	3–18 years	Teacher, parent, student
There are three rating forms (i.e., teacher, parent, and student) that evaluate a broad range of behaviors. The social skills scale on all three forms evaluates positive social behaviors (such as communication, cooperation, assertion, responsibility, empathy, engagement, and self-control). The problem behavior scale on the teacher and parent forms measures behaviors that can interfere with the production of social skills (such as externalizing, bullying, and hyperactivity/inattention). The academic competence scale on the teacher form is an index of reading achievement, math achievement, and motivation to learn. Items on each scale are rated according to perceived frequency and importance. *SSIS ASSIST* software provides computerized scoring and reporting, and an intervention guide provides instructional units on communication, cooperation, assertion, responsibility, empathy, engagement, and self-control.		

nine instruments to use in assessing social, emotional, and behavioral development.

Traditionally, teacher ratings of social skills have received less attention than emotional and behavioral problems; however, Gresham and Elliott (2008) authored an instrument that involves teacher ratings of social skills (see Table 5.2). The teacher version of the *Social Skills Improvement System Rating Scales* (Gresham & Elliott, 2008) features items that represent a broad range of behaviors (e.g., positive behaviors such as stay calm when teased, respects the property of others, and follows classroom rules, as well as problem behaviors such as fights with others, gets distracted easily, and acts sad or depressed). Another dimension of the *Social Skills Improvement System Rating Scales* involves the teacher specifying whether each behavior is critical, important, or unimportant for the classroom system. These ratings indicate which behaviors are most important for social skills intervention. Teacher ratings are valuable for identifying students and problematic behaviors that can be assessed further through naturalistic observations.

Parental ratings also have been used extensively to rate children's atypical behaviors and adaptive behavior. Eight of the behavior rating instruments included in Table 5.2

are suitable for parental use. Parental ratings of social skills have received limited attention, but the *Social Skills Improvement System Rating Scales* (Gresham & Elliott, 2008) includes a version for parents to rate their children's social skills on cooperation, assertion, self-control, and responsibility. An important feature of the instrument is the inclusion of a frequency dimension and an importance dimension for each social skill rated.

Commercial Measures of Adaptive Behavior

Adaptive behavior refers to the way an individual adjusts to the demands and changes in the physical and social environment. The interview technique frequently is used to obtain information from parents about the student's current nonacademic functioning, whereas teachers typically respond on written questionnaires concerning the student's social and emotional behavior. Adaptive behavior assessment scales generally include items for measuring personal self-sufficiency, independence in the community, and personal and social responsibility. Four measures of adaptive behavior are presented in Table 5.3.

Self-Report Instruments

Self-report techniques allow students to report on their own specific behaviors. Self-report procedures obtain information directly from the students; thus, the information is totally subjective. Its validity depends on the willingness of students to report the information and on their ability to understand and perform the task. Some commercial self-report instruments have built-in lie scales to screen for defensiveness and unrealistic levels of social desirability. Commercial self-report instruments are presented in this section, as are the Q-sort technique and various informal techniques.

Commercial Self-Report Instruments Self-report measures are the primary means for assessing students' self-concepts and for identifying areas that cause students anxiety or concern. Students respond directly to test items concerning themselves. Table 5.4 includes five commercial self-report instruments for assessing self-concept. Self-report instruments have several weaknesses because of the potential for bias, the desire to give responses that please, social desirability, and reading-level difficulties (Gresham & Elliott, 1989). Consequently, self-report measures of students' social skills are not used as widely as sociometrics, teacher ratings, and other measures. However, the self-report version of the *Social Skills Improvement System Rating Scales* (Gresham & Elliott, 2008) represents an attempt to develop a reliable and valid self-report measure of social skills. According to Elliott and

his colleagues, the use of such a system is a critical component in identifying appropriate interventions for students and evaluating the outcomes of the interventions (Elliott, Gresham, Beddow, & Frank, 2008).

Q-Sort Technique The Q-sort technique is a procedure for investigating self-concept that can be used to identify areas for behavior modification. The technique focuses on determining the degree of discrepancy between an evaluation of the "real" self and the "ideal" self. The procedure offers a way to select specific social, emotional, and behavioral problems for intervention.

The student is given a set of cards containing statements that must be sorted onto a continuum. A sample list of 25 statements suitable for elementary school students is presented in Table 5.5, and Figure 5.1 shows the behavior sorting continuum. The sorting continuum contains nine categories from *most like me* to *most unlike me*. The student is given descriptor cards to sort along the continuum. In sorting the items, the student may place only the number of cards indicated on the sorting box. First, the student is asked to complete a *real sort* by sorting the items onto the continuum to best reflect her or his own beliefs about her or his classroom behavior. After the responses of the real sort are recorded, the student is asked to complete an *ideal sort* in which the same items are arranged on the continuum to indicate how she or he would *like* to be in daily classroom activities. During sorting, the student may rearrange the cards as many times as needed. The teacher compares the student's responses on the real sort with the responses on the ideal sort and notes items that differ greatly (i.e., by four or more points). These items can become target behaviors for intervention.

The behavioral Q-sort also can be administered to parents or teachers. Thus, comparisons can be made between others' perceptions of the student's school behavior (i.e., both real and ideal) and the student's own perceptions. The teacher's rating of the student's behavior can be compared with the student's own rating. When the comparisons on a specific behavior (such as "Pays attention to work") are very different, that behavior can be selected for examination and intervention.

Informal Self-Report Techniques Informal self-report techniques provide a general idea of a student's problems. Each student who participates should be assured that the information provided is confidential and that only honest answers help the teacher. Wallace, Larsen, and Elksnin (1992) note that teacher-developed measures of self-concept are generally as reliable and valid as those of widely used research instruments. Four frequently used informal self-report

TABLE 5.3
Measures of adaptive behavior

Instrument	Ages	Respondent
AAMR Adaptive Behavior Scale—School (Lambert, Nihira, & Leland, 1993)	3–18 years	Teacher, parent, anyone familiar with the student

The school edition covers social and daily living skills and behaviors. Part I evaluates personal independence in daily living (e.g., independent functioning, self-direction, and responsibility). Part II measures social maladaptive behaviors (e.g., conformity, trustworthiness, and self-abusive behavior). The scale domains are grouped into five factors: personal self-sufficiency, community self-sufficiency, personal-social responsibility, personal adjustment, and social adjustment. The responder must circle the highest level of functioning demonstrated by the student, answer "yes" or "no" to a series of statements, or rate the statements in each item as occurring never, occasionally, or frequently. Testing time is 15 minutes, and the scale yields standard scores and percentiles for each domain.

Adaptive Behavior Assessment System— Second Edition (Harrison & Oakland, 2003)	Birth–89 years	Teacher, parent, anyone familiar with the individual

The checklist yields scores for 10 areas of adaptive skills: communication, community use, functional academics, home or school living, health and safety, leisure, self-care, self-direction, social, and work. Parent forms are available for ages birth to 5 years and 5 to 21 years, teacher forms are available for ages 2 to 5 years and 5 to 21 years, and the individual or the individual's caregiver can fill out an adult form for ages 16 to 89 years. Respondents can complete the checklist in about 15 to 20 minutes, and *Scoring Assistant* software is available.

Scales of Independent Behavior—Revised (Bruininks, Woodcock, Weatherman, & Hill, 1996)	Infant–adult	Teacher, parent, student, anyone familiar with the student

The instrument provides a noncognitive measure of adjustment in social, behavioral, and adaptive areas. It assesses functional independence and adaptive behavior in motor skills, social interaction and communication skills, personal living skills, and community living skills. Also, an optional problem behavior scale focuses on externalized, internalized, and asocial maladaptive behaviors. Each scale can be administered using either a structured interview or checklist procedure. Administration time is 45 to 60 minutes for the full-scale form and 15 to 20 minutes for the short form or early development form.

Vineland Adaptive Behavior Scales—Second Edition (Sparrow, Cicchetti, & Balla, 2005)	Birth–90 years (survey interview form, parent/ caregiver rating form, expanded interview form); 3–21 years (teacher rating form)	Teacher, parent, anyone familiar with the student

The *Vineland–II* includes four forms: The survey interview form is administered to a parent or caregiver using a semistructured interview format; the parent/caregiver rating form covers the same content as the survey interview form but uses a rating scale format; the expanded interview form provides an in-depth alternative to the survey interview form; and the teacher rating form uses a questionnaire format completed by the teacher or day-care provider. The scales assess adaptive behavior in four domains: communication, daily living skills, socialization, and motor skills. The survey and expanded forms also measure maladaptive behavior. Standard scores and percentiles are available for each area, and *Vineland–II ASSIST* software provides helpful score conversion.

techniques are checklists, questionnaires, interviews, and autobiographies.

In a teacher-made checklist, students are asked to indicate which behaviors or descriptions they believe apply (such as "Has a lot of friends," "Finishes classwork," and "Gets mad quickly"). Checklists are easy to administer and can give the teacher some insights concerning how the students view themselves. For example, students are presented with a list of adjectives and are instructed to check all words they consider to be descriptive of themselves. Sample items include the following:

_____ absent-minded	_____ noisy
_____ athletic	_____ friendly
_____ lonely	_____ cooperative
_____ intelligent	_____ quiet
_____ popular	_____ happy

TABLE 5.4
Self-report instruments

Instrument	Ages
Culture-Free Self-Esteem Inventories—3 (Battle, 2002)	6–18 years
The set of self-report inventories includes three age-appropriate forms (i.e., primary, intermediate, and adolescent) that provide a global self-esteem quotient. The intermediate and adolescent forms provide self-esteem scores in four areas (i.e., academic, general, parental/home, and social), and the adolescent form provides an additional score on personal self-esteem. Yes–no responses can be either written or spoken, and a defensive measure assesses the extent of guarded responses. The test can be administered to individuals or groups in 15 to 20 minutes.	
Multidimensional Self-Concept Scale (Bracken, 1992)	9–19 years
The instrument includes six 25-item scales in the following areas: social, competence, affect, academic, family, and physical. Each area can be assessed independently. The test yields standard scores and can be administered to individuals or groups in about 20 minutes. The manual provides specific recommendations for improving self-concept.	
Piers-Harris Children's Self-Concept Scale—Second Edition (Piers, Harris, & Herzberg, 2002)	7–18 years
The scale covers six areas of self-concept, including physical appearance and attributes, popularity, freedom from anxiety, behavioral adjustment, intellectual and school status, and happiness and satisfaction. The student responds with "yes" or "no" to 60 descriptive statements (e.g., "I am good looking" and "My classmates make fun of me"), which are written at a third-grade reading level. Suggested administration time is 10 to 15 minutes.	
Self-Esteem Index (Brown & Alexander, 1991)	8–18 years
The norm-referenced measure indicates how individuals perceive and value themselves. The index includes four scales: academic competence, family acceptance, peer popularity, and personal security (e.g., physical appearance and personal attributes). The student classifies each item on a scale ranging from *always true* to *always false*. In addition to a global self-esteem score, the four scales yield standard scores and percentile ranks. Administration time to groups or individuals is about 30 minutes.	
Tennessee Self-Concept Scale—Second Edition (Fitts & Warren, 1996)	7 years and older
The scale is designed to measure self-concept and provides scores in 15 areas, including identity, behavior, satisfaction, physical self, moral self, personal self, family self, social self, and academic/work self. Each descriptive statement (e.g., "I have a healthy body" and "I have a lot of self-control") is answered on a 5-point scale from *completely false* to *completely true*. The child form, written at a second-grade reading level, can be used with 7- through 14-year-old students, and the adult form, written at a third-grade reading level, is designed for individuals 13 years of age and older. Each form requires about 10 to 20 minutes to complete.	

Several kinds of questionnaires are designed to obtain information about a student's personal, social, and emotional behaviors. The yes–no or true–false format is useful and easy to administer:

1. Are you usually very friendly?   Yes   No
2. Do you get mad often?   Yes   No
3. I usually like to be by myself.   True   False

Questionnaires using open-ended questions or sentence completion require students to complete the statements. Thus, students express themselves in their own words. Such a format requires more time and ability on the part of the students, but it often yields more meaningful information than the yes–no or true–false format. Sample items from a sentence completion questionnaire include the following:

1. I work best when _____.
2. I get angry when _____.
3. When I feel lonely I _____.

Specific information also can be obtained from students through interviews. They provide an opportunity

TABLE 5.5
Elementary-level school items on the behavioral Q-sort

Social Emotional/Behavioral Items	Academic/Study and Work Habits
1. I smile a lot at school.	14. I concentrate on my work.
2. I am a good friend to others.	15. I work slowly.
3. I poke or hit my classmates.	16. I finish my work on time.
4. I leave my seat without permission.	17. I read during my free time.
5. I play with my pencil or other things when I am working.	18. I ask my teacher for help when I need it.
6. I make noises that bother others.	19. I am a good speller.
7. I fidget in my seat.	20. I am a good reader.
8. I follow directions.	21. I am good at mathematics.
9. I make noises with objects like pencils.	22. I lose track of my work or homework.
10. I talk to my friends during work time.	23. I read because it is fun.
11. I call out when my teacher is talking.	24. I work hard until I finish a task.
12. I wander around the room when I should be working or studying.	25. I am quiet during work time.
13. I rock in my chair.	

FIGURE 5.1
Behavior sorting continuum

for students to express opinions and feelings about themselves and others. Interview techniques can be extended into daily conversations, providing a flexible and ongoing source of information. In an interview, the teacher should relate the discussion questions to the student's particular area of difficulty. The interview is most effective when conducted in private, and rapport reflecting an honest interest in the student is established. Interview questions should be kept to a minimum and should be broad instead of specific to require the student to develop a topic or express an opinion. If the teacher receives proper consent, the interview can be recorded so that it is available for later study. If recording is not possible, notetaking during the interview should be minimal but immediate.

In autobiographies, students give written accounts of their lives or reveal their feelings about themselves and others. Personal experiences, ambitions, or interests can be described. Students who have difficulty in expressive writing can record oral presentations. The type of autobiography depends upon the student's age and maturity. Students can be asked to respond to specific questions or be given a topic, such as "Things That Upset Me." Autobiographical material then can be analyzed for present or potential problem areas.

Sociometric Techniques

Sociometric techniques are commonly used to assess social skills and related problems. Sociometric methodology typically is grouped into three categories: peer nominations, peer ratings, and peer assessment. A sociogram provides a visual record of the group's social structure.

Peer Nominations This procedure involves asking students to nominate peers according to *nonbehavioral* criteria (such as preferred work partners, best friends, or preferred play partners). These criteria are viewed as nonbehavioral because they refer to activities (e.g., play) or attributes (e.g., best friend) rather than specific behaviors (e.g., asks for the opinion of others). Thus, nominations assess attitudes and preferences for engaging in selected activities with peers. Peer nominations can be fixed choice (i.e., the student nominates a limited number of peers) or unlimited choice (i.e., the student nominates as many peers as desired). It helps if a printed list of the names of all class members is provided, and responses should be kept secret. Nominations can be weighted (i.e., the order of nominations is considered with weights assigned in a rank-order manner) or unweighted (McConnell & Odom, 1986). Peer nominations also can be keyed to negative criteria (e.g., least preferred play partner). Research suggests that positive and negative nominations are not at opposite ends of the same continuum, but measure two distinct dimensions of sociometric status (Gresham & Reschly, 1988; McConnell & Odom, 1986).

Coie, Dodge, and Coppotelli (1982) and Dodge (1983) have generated empirical support for the peer nomination approach. Coie and his colleagues provide a classification system for peer nominations that identifies five sociometric status groups: popular, neglected, rejected, controversial, and average. These groups are then evaluated in terms of *liked most* and *liked least*. These techniques provide a detailed description of the social status of a student in a peer group and identify behavior correlates for each sociometric group. For example, rejected students exhibit high rates of aggressive and disruptive behaviors and low rates of cooperative, peer-reinforcing behaviors, whereas neglected students display high rates of shy, withdrawn, and fearful behaviors and low rates of positive social interactions (Dodge, 1983).

Peer Ratings

In a peer rating, *all* students in a classroom rate one another on a Likert-type scale according to *nonbehavioral* criteria. These criteria are similar to peer nominations in that areas such as *play with* and *work with* preferences are used. A student's score on a peer rating is the average rating received from peers. Gresham and Elliott (1989) note that these ratings tend to indicate a student's overall acceptance level within the peer group. Peer ratings feature several advantages over peer nominations. First, every student in the class is rated rather than only a few students. Second, a student's rating scores are more reliable because they are based on a larger number of raters. Third, peer ratings typically do not involve the use of negative criteria, thereby reducing ethical objections to sociometric assessments. Disadvantages of peer ratings include stereotypical ratings (i.e., giving many peers the same rating) and central tendency errors (i.e., rating peers in the middle of the scale) (McConnell & Odom, 1986).

Peer Assessment

In peer assessment, students are asked to nominate or rate peers on several *behavioral* characteristics. Students hear or read behavioral descriptions and then nominate or rate individuals according to the descriptions. One of the more popular peer assessment techniques is the *Guess Who?* technique (Kaufman, Agard, & Semmel, 1985). In this technique, students nominate peers who fit behavioral descriptions involving such dimensions as disruptive behavior, smartness, dullness, and quiet/good behavior.

Sociogram

Responses from a sociometric questionnaire indicating the number of times each student is chosen may be recorded on a tally sheet, or a *sociogram* can be constructed to provide a visual record of the social structure within the class. Figure 5.2 shows a sociogram of ten fourth-grade students who were asked to write the names of two classmates with whom they would most like to play. In this example, for the most part, girls preferred to play with girls, and boys with boys. Among the girls, Alice, Debby, and Judy seem to have a close relationship. None of these girls chose other classmates. Joan did not receive any choices, and Kim was selected as first choice only by Joan. Kim was the only girl to choose a boy. Among the boys, Bob and Steve were mutual choices, as were Ken and John. Adam received no choices, and John was the only boy to choose a girl.

The information obtained from the sociogram can help to identify isolates as well as leaders and can give the teacher a basis for congenial, effective group activities. In addition, the social preferences discovered provide insight about which social patterns should be changed and which should be encouraged. In this example, activities involving Adam and either Ken or Steve may be a positive for Adam, who in general is an isolate. Among the girls, situations should be planned to foster relationships outside of the clique. Different patterns probably will be revealed for different activities or settings. A student may be selected by several classmates as their choice for a study partner, but may receive no choices for social activities.

Information also can be provided through peer nomination techniques, in which each student responds to statements about attitudes or behavior by naming classmates (e.g., "Which students are very popular?" or "Which students are selfish?"). Sociograms can be scored (rather than mapped) based on combinations of positive and negative nominations, and the social status of students can be identified as popular (i.e., high number of positive nominations and low number of negative nominations), rejected (i.e., high number of negative nominations and low number of positive nominations), controversial (i.e., high numbers of positive and negative nominations), and neglected (i.e., no evaluations).

FIGURE 5.2
A sociogram

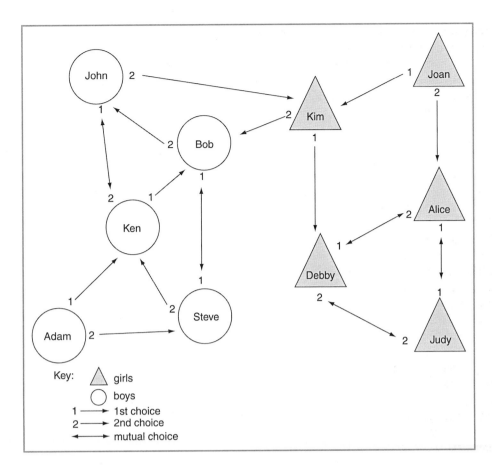

Overall, sociometric assessment can be an important component in evaluating students with learning problems. Gresham and Elliott (1989) maintain that the Coie et al. (1982) system offers the best reliability and validity.

Naturalistic Observations

Direct observation provides an in-depth study of possible problem behaviors identified by rating scales, checklists, and interviews. Moreover, defining target behaviors, observing and recording their frequency in the natural environment, and analyzing the data represent the most direct and ecologically valid assessment of students' social skills and related behaviors (Elliott, Gresham, & Heffer, 1987). Naturalistic assessment allows for a functional analysis of the antecedent events, behavioral sequence, and consequences that may influence inappropriate social behavior or decrease prosocial behaviors. Because problem behaviors serve a purpose for the student, an analysis of the behavior and its surrounding events helps the teacher determine the purpose or function of that behavior (e.g., getting attention, escaping or avoiding a demand, or getting something tangible).

This approach promotes the use of operationally defined social skills or behaviors and the development of systems for measuring and recording target behaviors. The collection of frequent data provides a sensitive index to variations in student behavior. Direct observation of social, emotional, and behavioral development includes observing the behavior, the teacher–student interaction, and the environment. The primary difficulty with naturalistic observation is that the student might not act naturally in the context in which observation occurs. If the observer suspects the student is not behaving naturally, role-play assessment may be useful.

Observation of Behavior Direct, systematic observation of student behavior can provide information and insights about the student's social and emotional skills. Many teachers have training in personality development and work with students for several hours each day in different situations; therefore, they usually are highly qualified to observe and assess behavior. If behaviors are *described* and reported as responses seen or provided (such as "Gets out of seat," "Butts in the cafeteria line," or "Calls Bill a sissy during math seatwork") instead of as interpretations (such as "hyperactive," "disruptive," or "impulsive"), the validity of teacher observations increases. The teacher should observe the conditions under which the behavior occurs and record the frequency of occurrence. Careful observation may reveal, for example, that out-of-seat behavior occurs only during math, or that singing in class occurs when the student is sitting near Maria. The target behavior also can be measured by duration (i.e., how long the student exhibits the behavior) or by a time sampling, in which the student is observed during certain periods for specified lengths of time.

In addition to the behavior itself, the teacher also should note the events that occur immediately before and immediately after the behavior and serve to reinforce it. Information about the surrounding conditions may enable the teacher to choose management strategies. For example, a student's swearing might receive the reinforcement of attention from peers (e.g., laughter). The teacher could concentrate on eliminating peer reinforcement and encouraging peer attention to desirable responses. Finally, daily measurement of behavior can provide feedback on the success of strategies used to resolve the behavior.

Observation of Teacher–Student Interaction

Flanders (1970) presents the *interaction analysis system* for measuring the interactions between the teacher and the students in the entire class. Flanders specifies ten behavior categories: Seven involve teacher's verbal behavior (e.g., praising or encouraging students, asking questions, and criticizing); two involve students' verbal behavior (e.g., responding to the teacher); and one is for silence or confusion. Teacher–student interactions are observed, and behaviors are recorded every 4 seconds. Data are collected for several days during short observation periods. A simplified version of the Flanders technique involves the use of a videotape or audiotape recorder instead of a trained observer. The teacher can interpret the recordings made during the day and can categorize the verbal interactions according to Flanders's ten categories. By using this assessment device, the teacher can identify verbal patterns of student–teacher interactions in the classroom.

Sprick (2001) developed a system for monitoring teacher–student interactions that focuses on the frequency of teacher responses to negative events and positive events. He suggests that a 3:1 positive-to-negative ratio is needed for effective interaction and classroom management. Other variables noted include nonverbal interactions, sincerity of praise, variety of language used to praise, and distribution of attention to individual students.

More recently, the *Classroom Assessment Scoring System* (Pianta, La Paro, & Hamre, 2008) was introduced as a research-based observational assessment of classroom quality across three domains: emotional support, classroom organization, and instructional support. The primary focus of the emotional support domain is on teacher–student interactions. Observations fall into four dimensions including positive climate, negative climate, sensitivity, and regard for student perspectives. Pianta and Hamre (2009) suggest that the use of standardized observation of teacher behaviors, including teacher–student interactions, holds promise for improving teacher quality and student outcomes.

In teacher–student interactions, a teacher occasionally may overreact to a certain behavior. Teachers must show understanding and awareness to control inappropriate reactions.

Observation of Environment

In assessing social, emotional, and behavioral development, the teacher should observe the student in different environments. The teacher then can consider the environment's influence in starting or maintaining the problem behavior. Some observation can be made outside the school setting; however, the teacher mainly should observe in-school environments (such as art class, physical education class, lunchroom, and playground). Perhaps the target behavior surfaces only in certain settings or instructional conditions. The student may become disruptive when required to remain seated for a long time during a lecture; however, when allowed to move about or participate in class discussions, his or her behavior may be acceptable. Also, a student may exhibit anxiety and withdraw when required to read orally in front of the class or to compute timed math problems, but be quite comfortable when working alone in untimed situations or in small-group activities. Thus, teacher observation of various environments can help determine the adjustments needed to improve the student's instructional program.

Role-Play Assessment

This approach elicits a student's behavior in response to staged social interactions (such as receiving criticism), and the student's performance is recorded. Advances in role-play methodology (Dodge, Pettit, McClaskey, & Brown, 1986) have improved their generalizability to naturalistic observations. Moreover, role-play assessments enable the observer to determine whether the student has a social skill acquisition deficit (i.e., does not possess the skill) or a social skill performance problem (i.e., does not desire to perform the skill).

GENERAL TECHNIQUES FOR PROMOTING SOCIAL, EMOTIONAL, AND BEHAVIORAL DEVELOPMENT

The development of social, emotional, and behavioral attributes is complex because these affective domains are interdependent. Improvement in one domain frequently has a positive effect on the others. For example, positive reinforcement can help a youngster behave more appropriately, and when other students respond positively and accept the youngster, his or her self-concept improves. Fortunately, several techniques can develop positive attributes in social, emotional, and behavioral domains. *Positive behavioral support* is a term that includes comprehensive, multicomponent interventions that focus on the remediation of deficient contexts that are documented by functional assessments to be the source of the problems. This approach to managing problem behaviors matches supportive strategies to the needs of the student to reduce or eliminate the inappropriate behavior. Through the use of preventative, proactive, and educative behavioral intervention strategies, the teacher can help students learn positive responses that result in responsible behaviors and academic success. The general techniques featured in this section include teach for success, focus on promoting proactivity, promote cooperation, teach self-management, model target behaviors and attributes, and focus on motivation through behavior modification. Activities for increasing on-task behavior also are provided.

Teach for Success

Many students with learning problems have low self-concepts, attention deficits, social skills deficits, or emotional problems. Because these affective problems can lead to aggressive, disruptive, or withdrawal behavior, students with learning problems may become difficult to manage in the classroom. Moreover, some of these students are overly negative about themselves. Sprick (2001) notes that acting out, misbehaving in a manner to get caught, and giving up or withdrawal are common manifestations of a poor self-concept. Educators agree that effective behavior management must

begin with preventive techniques and that these techniques start with good teaching. Most behavioral problems of students with learning difficulties probably can be prevented with effective instruction. The development of positive social, emotional, and behavioral attributes through teaching is fundamental to a student's school success, motivation, and future learning.

Teach Effectively Effective teaching leads to academic progress, which is critical if a student with learning problems is to develop a positive self-concept regarding learning. Sprick (2001) states, "There is nothing more important for any student than believing he or she is able to learn, grow, and be successful. When in doubt about what to do to improve a child's self-concept, teach!" (Book E, p. 8). Although all instructional variables related to student learning likely would lead to improvements in the social, emotional, and behavioral attributes of students with learning problems, those of note include ensuring high rates of student success, monitoring progress and providing feedback, and providing positive and supportive learning environments. Table 5.6 highlights some of the variables that are the most important in teaching difficult-to-teach students.

Provide Feedback The importance of feedback to success is well documented; however, the type of feedback that improves a student's social, emotional, and behavioral development needs examination. First, positive feedback or reinforcement should be contingent on student performance (i.e., students should be praised for accomplishing tasks that require a reasonable amount of effort). Second, noncontingent feedback or praise can signal to students that the teacher thinks they cannot do better work; thus, students receive the message that they lack ability, which lowers their opinion of their learning capabilities. Third, students often view criticism or corrective feedback as positive when high achievers receive it (Weinstein, 1982). This feedback indicates that the teacher believes the students can do better; thus, it communicates a positive opinion about the teacher's view of a student's potential. Consequently, corrective feedback can help improve the self-concepts of students with learning problems. Furthermore, corrective feedback may communicate that the teacher cares about a student.

Focus on Promoting Proactivity

Many students with learning problems live a reactive existence and maintain an external locus of control. Essentially, they believe that they have little control over what happens to them. Thus, fate, bad luck, and

TABLE 5.6
Variables related to effective instruction of difficult-to-teach students

Instructional Variables	Specific Emphasis
Preinstructional Variables	
Arrangement of classroom space	Arrange classroom to facilitate smooth transitions and ease of student monitoring.
Rules and procedures	Communicate expectations and provide structure for learning.
Managing student academic work	Hold students accountable for work and keep records of progress.
Assessment	Use criterion-referenced measures to match tasks to students and monitor performance in terms of instructional objectives.
Communication of learning goals	Communicate rationales for academic tasks and clearly state learning goals.
Pacing decisions	Maintain a lively instructional pace but allow enough time for much practice. Presentation-demonstration-practice-feedback cycles appear to be most effective.
Time allocations	Plan as much time as possible for academic learning.
Instructional Delivery Variables	
Engagement time	Maintain substantive interactions with students and provide feedback. Reinforce students for being on task and for work completed.
Success rate	Maintain high rates of success because success is related to student achievement and motivation.
Academic learning time	Facilitate the amount of time students are engaged in high rates of success or appropriate goals.
Monitoring	Circulate throughout the room to check the accuracy and progress of students.
Postinstructional Variables	
Testing	Regularly administer informal criterion-referenced measures (e.g., curriculum-based assessment) to assess student progress or plan instruction.
Academic feedback	Provide immediate feedback on academic work to promote learning. Praise and corrective feedback are most effective when used together.

Source: From *Students with Learning Disabilities* (p. 414), 7th ed., by C. D. Mercer and P. C. Pullen, 2009, Upper Saddle River, NJ: Merrill/Pearson. Copyright 2009 by Pearson Education. Reprinted by permission.

good luck are guiding forces in their lives. This reactive existence causes individuals to believe that the conditions in their lives are out of their control, which is a terrible way to live. These students need to learn that they can control many of the events or consequences in their lives. Proactivity is based on the following belief: I can control events in my life through my own efforts (e.g., I study and I get good grades; I behave appropriately and people treat me well). A proactive or internal locus of control is much more empowering than a reactive existence. The following three techniques promote proactivity: (1) set goals, (2) give responsibility, and (3) engage in self-appreciation.

Set Goals When a student reaches goals that require considerable effort, self-worth is improved. Individuals feel good about themselves when they work hard to achieve a worthwhile goal. Goal ambitiousness is related positively to school success. In contrast, goals that are too easy often lead students to believe that the teacher thinks they are not capable of higher level achievements. Consequently, these low teacher expectations frequently lower students' beliefs about their learning potential. The teacher must stress that the students' own efforts were essential in reaching a goal. The teacher should constantly pair effort with positive or negative consequences.

Give Responsibility Students with poor affective attributes often are pleased when the teacher thinks they can accept responsibility. Giving students responsibility demonstrates a level of trust in their ability to act maturely. Some responsibilities include caring for a class pet, taking messages to the office or other classes, conducting a lunch count, tutoring other students, leading the line, making a bulletin board, using equipment, and grading papers.

Engage in Self-Appreciation Self-depreciation tends to lower a student's self-worth. Conversely, self-appreciation or positive self-talk can help improve self-worth. The teacher should reinforce students for making appropriate positive comments about themselves. Students can make lists of their positive attributes and periodically refer to them.

Promote Cooperation

To develop positive social, emotional, and behavioral attributes, students should work in a community of cooperative learners. The following three techniques promote cooperation: (1) promote positive interactions among students, (2) use peer tutoring, and (3) use cooperative learning.

Promote Positive Interactions Among Students

Teaching students to be positive with one another benefits individual students. If the students can learn to interact positively, they will receive pleasant and friendly reactions in return. The teacher can pair students with learning problems with popular students for social group activities or on teams in instructional games so that the paired students share positive and pleasant experiences. Sprick (2001) recommends three techniques for promoting positive interactions: (1) modeling positive interactions in daily teaching, (2) practicing positive interactions through role playing specific situations, and (3) reinforcing positive interactions as they occur throughout the school day.

Use Peer Tutoring

Peer tutoring typically involves pairing a competent student with one who has difficulty in a particular academic area. In addition to improving academic skills, a successful peer tutoring program can enhance self-esteem, encourage appropriate behavior, and foster positive and cooperative relationships among peers. Moreover, peer tutoring can help students with disabilities achieve in inclusive settings. For example, if assessment reveals that a student has no friends or is not accepted by peers, peer tutoring can be a strategy for enhancing positive interactions. Using information from a sociometric device, such as a sociogram, the teacher can pair a student with a preferred tutor. The student thus will be likely to model the appropriate behavior. The teacher should train the student tutor in teaching and reinforcement techniques. Tutoring sessions should have easy-to-use materials and a set routine. Self-correcting materials and instructional games provide excellent materials for peer teaching arrangements.

Use Cooperative Learning

Cooperative learning is an instructional arrangement in which small groups or teams of students work together to achieve team success in a manner that promotes the students' responsibility for their own learning as well as the learning of others. In cooperative learning, team goals are emphasized, and team success is achieved only if each individual learns. Regarding research findings on cooperative learning, Slavin (1991) reports that positive achievement effects are consistent across grades, subject areas, and school settings; effects are equally positive for high, average, and low achievers; and positive effects are reported in affective areas (e.g., self-esteem, intergroup relations, and ability to work cooperatively).

myeducationlab

Go to the Assignments and Activities section of the Topic Promoting Social and Emotional Development in the MyEducationLab for your course and complete the activity entitled Circle Time.

Teach Self-Management

Many youngsters with learning difficulties cannot solve problems and make decisions effectively, which affects their performance adversely at school, home, or work. Issues related to problem solving, interpersonal relations, and generalization learning can be viewed within the context of self-management skills (Shapiro, 1989). Self-management typically is divided into three components: self-monitoring, self-evaluation, and self-reinforcement. Each component requires specific instruction.

Several researchers report success using self-management training with students who have mild disabilities (Hughes, Ruhl, & Peterson, 1988; Sander, 1991; Shapiro, 1989). Shapiro concludes that self-management instruction appears to be a promising approach for teaching students with learning problems to be more independent learners and citizens. Moreover, McDougall (1998) reports that research on self-management techniques indicates that behavioral self-management can be used successfully by students with disabilities to enhance their social and academic performance in general education settings.

Model Target Behaviors and Attributes

The saying "Don't do what I do, do what I say" is not appropriate for helping youngsters with learning problems develop social, emotional, and behavioral attributes. These youngsters need models to imitate and emulate regarding social skills (e.g., listening, giving encouragement, and saying "no"), emotional states (e.g., being positive and proactive), and appropriate behavior (e.g., being considerate of others and respecting property). Cognitive behavior modification is a procedure that frequently involves modeling to help youngsters internalize appropriate thinking processes related to affective behavior.

Teach Cognitive Behavior Modification

Cognitive behavior modification analyzes the thinking processes involved in performing a task. Meichenbaum

123

(1977) discusses self-instructional training as a method to encourage appropriate responses and discourage inappropriate responses. The following sequence can be used.

1. Instruction by another person (e.g., an adult model such as the teacher performs a task while talking aloud)
2. Overt self-instruction (e.g., while performing a task, the student speaks or whispers self-instructions)
3. Covert self-instruction (e.g., the student guides performance through private speech)

Thus, inner speech is considered to be an aspect of the thinking process, and the student is encouraged to verbalize before acting. Language is thought to enhance thinking and, in turn, affect behavior. In the classroom the student can be taught to use the following self-verbalizations: questions about the task (e.g., "What does the teacher want me to do?"), answers to the question (e.g., "I'm not supposed to talk out in class."), self-instruction to guide the student through the task (e.g., "First I raise my hand and wait for the teacher to call on me."), and self-reinforcement (e.g., "I really did well that time!").

In cognitive modeling, the teacher should model not only strategies for performing a task but also actions and language appropriate for dealing with frustrations and failures. In addition to self-instruction, the student can be taught to use images (e.g., thinking of sitting in the classroom during recess as an image to reduce out-of-seat behavior).

Set Up Models in the Classroom

In modeling, students learn appropriate behaviors by observing and imitating others. When students observe one of their peers being rewarded for desirable behavior, they tend to follow the example of the model. Thus, they learn behaviors that have positive consequences. Likewise, unacceptable behavior can be discouraged when students watch others receive punishment for such behavior. In addition, the teacher can call attention to behavior that should be modeled: "I like the way Jimmy raised his hand instead of talking out, so I will answer his question first."

In using modeling to influence a specific behavior, the following steps are helpful: (1) Select the behavior, (2) select the model, (3) give the model and the observer directions concerning their roles, (4) reinforce the model for exhibiting the behavior, and (5) reinforce the observer for imitating the behavior. The modeling process can have three effects on students: (1) New behaviors may be learned from the model, (2) previously acquired behaviors may be strengthened as the students observe similar desirable behaviors of the model being reinforced, or (3) previously acquired behaviors may be weakened as the students observe the model receiving punishment for similar unacceptable behaviors.

Focus on Motivation Through Behavior Modification

Given their failures and difficulties in acquiring information, many students with learning problems understandably lack motivation to work in school. In particular, early reading failure is linked to a lack of motivation to read and decreased reading practice (Morgan, Fuchs, Compton, Cordray, & Fuchs, 2008). Whereas many normally achieving students are motivated to achieve for intrinsic reasons (e.g., mastery, task completion, and enjoyment of learning new information), students with learning problems often need extrinsic reinforcers to help motivate them to work and behave. Some students with learning problems even require punishment or negative consequences to help them reduce off-task and disruptive behavior. Although some students need external reinforcers and negative consequences to work and behave, the goal of effective teachers is to help these youngsters become mature or intrinsically motivated learners. This section covers behavior modification techniques that can be used to help motivate and manage students with learning problems.

The basic premise of behavior modification is that behavior is learned and is a function of that behavior's consequences. According to Wallace and Kauffman (1986), "Behavior modification refers to any systematic arrangement of environmental events to produce specific changes in observable behavior" (p. 21). Thus, it is a highly structured and systematic approach that results in strengthening, weakening, or maintaining behaviors.

After identifying and collecting baseline data on a target behavior, the teacher must observe events that happen just before the student's behavior (i.e., antecedent events) and just after the behavior (i.e., subsequent events). These events are then manipulated, and various reinforcers or rewards are used to elicit a change in the behavior. A *reinforcer* is any event that follows a behavior and results in maintaining or increasing the probability or rate of the behavior. *Positive reinforcement* means adding something pleasurable or positive to the environment (i.e., consequences that increase the probability that the behavior will occur again), whereas *negative reinforcement* means withdrawing something unpleasant or negative from the environment (i.e., avoidance of a negative consequence by performing a behavior). Reinforcement results in strengthening or increasing the target behavior.

Various social or tangible reinforcers can be used (e.g., praise, hugs, treats, and free time). The following hierarchical order of the level of reinforcers moves from extrinsic reinforcers (i.e., reinforcement from outside the performance of a task) to intrinsic reinforcers (i.e., reinforcement directly from performing a task).

Extrinsic reinforcers
1. Primary reinforcers (e.g., sleeping, eating, and drinking—necessary for survival)
2. Tangible reinforcers (e.g., food items, pencils, and certificates)
3. Token reinforcers or points with backup items or activities (e.g., chips that can be exchanged for a preferred item or activity when a certain amount is earned)
4. Social approval (e.g., gestures, touch, and verbal expressions)
5. Project or activity (e.g., running errands, being a line leader, getting free time, and playing a game)

Intrinsic reinforcers
6. Task completion
7. Feedback or result
8. Acquisition of knowledge or skill
9. Sense of mastery or accomplishment

Extrinsic reinforcers initially can be used to encourage a student to exhibit appropriate behavior or perform a task. The teacher gradually should withdraw material reinforcers and stress activities and events. As competence in a task increases, the need for extrinsic reinforcement eventually will decrease and intrinsic reinforcers will provide motivation.

Praise is a social reinforcer and is one of the most effective and convenient positive reinforcers teachers can use to manage student behavior. Paine, Radicchi, Rosellini, Deutchman, and Darch (1983) report that effective praise has the following important features.

- Good praise adheres to the "if—then" rule, which states that *if* the student is behaving in the desired manner, *then* (and *only* then) the teacher praises the student.
- Good praise frequently includes students' names.
- Good praise is descriptive.
- Good praise conveys that the teacher really means what is said (i.e., it is convincing).
- Good praise is varied.
- Good praise does not disrupt the flow of individual or class activities.

Moreover, Witzel and Mercer (2003) note that contingent verbal praise should focus on the value and the relevance of the task being rewarded in order to build intrinsic motivation. For example, when praising a student for completing a math assignment, the teacher should point out that this will help the student perform well on future math tests.

In using reinforcement techniques, the teacher must remember that reinforcement immediately following the behavior is most effective. In addition, attention can act as a reinforcer for inappropriate behavior. For example, when the teacher frowns or speaks sharply, the student may interpret this as reinforcing attention. Thus, the teacher should be careful not to reinforce inappropriate behavior with attention. The teacher should shift from reinforcing everyday appropriate behavior to reinforcing academic effort as soon as possible. Behaviors such as raising a hand to talk or appropriate lining up for lunch eventually should become routine and be maintained without a great deal of teacher praise. Contingent reinforcement of academic learning promotes a higher level of functioning and improves achievement.

The *schedule of reinforcement* (i.e., the plan of conditions under which reinforcement occurs) can be either continuous or intermittent. On a *continuous schedule*, the desired behavior is reinforced every time it occurs. On an *intermittent schedule*, reinforcement is given according to either an *interval* (i.e., reinforcers given at certain times) or a *ratio* (i.e., reinforcers given after a specific number of responses).

Shaping refers to reinforcing steps toward the target behavior. The goal is broken down into an ordered sequence of steps or tasks, and reinforcement is given to those behaviors that come close to the desired behavior. The desired behavior thus is shaped by gradually increasing the requirement for reinforcement until the target behavior is obtained.

Punishment, as opposed to reinforcement, refers to presenting something negative or withdrawing something positive following the behavior. This results in decreasing the undesirable response. Kame'enui, Darch, and Colvin (1995) maintain that punishment is an important part of management, but only as a transition tool. Thus, punishment is a temporary transitional intervention that enables the teacher to deal with nonproductive behavior until the student or students return to productive behavior. Various punishment strategies are associated with different degrees of "hassle" for the teacher or class. Punishment used alone is ineffective with many students, and punishment techniques that are powerful enough to rely on as a primary management strategy are not available to teachers. Moreover, punishment can have negative side effects (e.g., low morale, revenge, and negative feelings), and the more punishment is used in the classroom the less effective it becomes. Thus, punishment should be used as infrequently as possible, and strategies that produce the least disruption should be selected. Some mild punishment techniques include ignoring, gentle verbal reprimands, quiet time, owing time, and nonexclusionary time out. Once punishment is selected, Sprick (2001) recommends the following guidelines.

- Punishment must change the behavior in the desired direction.
- Punishment always should be used in conjunction with a reinforcement plan.
- Punishment always should be administered calmly.
- Punishment should be used discriminately.
- Once a punishable behavior is targeted, it should be punished consistently.

Paine et al. (1983) provide a step-by-step management system that combines positive reinforcement, a warning technique, and response cost (i.e., loss of a reinforcer contingent on inappropriate behavior). It includes the following steps.

1. When a student misbehaves, praise nearby students who exhibit correct behavior. Once praise is given to several students, wait a brief time (e.g., 30 seconds) to see whether the misbehaving student responds. If the student responds by giving the correct behavior, praise that student.
2. If the student fails to respond positively, talk to her or him in an unemotional manner. Indicate that the student is receiving a warning and instruct her or him to begin work. The warning is more effective when it is delivered near the student and eye contact is established. The teacher should avoid getting into a conversation while giving the warning. After a short time, praise the student if she or he begins correct behavior.
3. If the student does not respond to the warning, calmly remind her or him about the warning, and then write her or his name on the chalkboard and put a mark next to it.
4. If the student fails to comply, place another mark by her or his name. This should be done without comment. Moreover, continue to praise other students for appropriate behavior.
5. At this point, if the student fails to comply, repeat step 4.
6. Use predetermined consequences for unacceptable behaviors. Unacceptable behaviors and resulting consequences should be explained at the beginning of the school year.

7. Have each mark after a student's name represent a loss of privileges. One mark could stand for 5 minutes taken from recess, two marks means 10 minutes are lost, and so on. The consequence can be similar for everyone or varied for different students. The marking system is only effective if students lose privileges that they value.
8. Finally, be sure not to give the student extra attention when she or he misses time from recess or stays after school. Consequences of the marking system should not be reinforcing in any way.

Because punishment is a transition strategy, it is best to examine and use it within the context of a management plan that focuses on stabilizing and maintaining a productive learning environment. Variables such as academic success, good teaching, motivation, and prevention of nonproductive behavior must be considered to manage a classroom effectively.

Apply Consequences with Adolescents In managing secondary students, structure and consistency are essential. The likelihood of power struggles and defiance of authority is greater with adolescents. Thus, both teacher and student must function in a structured environment in which expectations (i.e., rules), consequences, and routines have been established clearly. Effective techniques with secondary students include token economies, contingency contracting, verbal feedback, mutual goal setting, and self-control training. Moreover, the importance of involving adolescents in curriculum and management decisions is stressed throughout the literature.

Suggestions for managing consequences with adolescents include the following:

- Stress the natural consequences of behavior. For example, the natural consequence for stealing is arrest, for being tardy is detention, and so on. Thus, if a rule is broken, the stated consequence is applied. This helps reduce power struggles between the student and teacher because the student is likely to view the teacher as a person who follows rules rather than as an authority figure who maliciously applies punishment.
- Use conditioned reinforcers (such as points) with adolescents. They are administered easily or withheld with a minimum of teacher verbalization.
- Consider using peer interactions as reinforcers for adolescents.
- Develop a continuum of consequences for managing inappropriate behaviors. Public reprimands should be avoided because they increase the probability of

further conflict. Use little verbal interaction and eye contact when administering a negative consequence. Response cost is a good beginning step in dealing with inappropriate behavior. Time out is another effective consequence with adolescents.

Activities for Increasing On-Task Behavior

Some social, emotional, and behavioral problems result in lowered academic performance. A student with low frustration tolerance may become overwhelmed easily when attempting to complete academic tasks requiring great effort. The problem behaviors of task avoidance and task interference also hamper the completion of academic work. The student who seldom completes timed assignments within his or her capabilities may have a problem with slowness. The following activities are suggested for increasing on-task behavior.

- Allow the student who avoids academic tasks to choose from a variety of activities within a skill area. This will allow the student to think he or she selected the work rather than having it determined by the teacher. Also, consider letting the student complete academic tasks in various ways, such as using a red pen or working in a different area of the classroom. A variety of stimuli (e.g., tape recorder, computer, and manipulative materials) can be used to maintain the student's attention to the task.
- Shortly after assigning an academic task, provide a reward for students who have started the work and completed several problems. This will encourage the student who avoids tasks to become more involved. Rewards also can be given upon task completion to encourage the student to work steadily to finish an assignment.
- To increase speed in performing academic tasks, have the student work against a timer and chart progress. For example, the number of addition problems completed correctly during a specific time can be recorded on a graph each day. As progress is made in the student's rate of work, the difficulty of the tasks can be increased.
- To discourage slowness in work, devise a contingency contract. The student and teacher can agree that if a specific part of an academic task is completed within a certain amount of time, the student will not have to complete the remainder of the assignment. The contract also should specify an accuracy criterion (such as 85 percent or more correct responses) to discourage the student from rushing incorrectly through the task. Thus, accurate work performed in a reasonable amount of time is rewarded.

- When a student shows a task interference behavior, such as looking out the window, move physically closer so that the student is aware of your presence. Also, pair the student with a productive worker and use modeling to elicit appropriate behavior.
- Prepare a series of tasks at different levels of difficulty. Allow the student with low frustration tolerance to complete the first task at his or her own pace. Gradually introduce time limits. Record the student's progress and reward steps of progress. After the student has mastered the first task at various time intervals, repeat the procedure with a more difficult task.
- Provide the student who avoids tasks with an incentive to start working: Give the student a worksheet with the first few problems already completed.
- Present academic tasks in game formats, such as start-to-finish races or card playing.
- Use self-correcting materials, which provide immediate feedback and reduce the practicing of errors. The student may avoid academic tasks to avoid failure; however, with self-correcting materials, failure is not publicly known, and the student can immediately correct responses.
- Use a spinner to provide reinforcement after the student completes an academic assignment. The spinner can be divided into several different-size pie-shaped sections, with the more preferred reinforcers on the smaller wedges and the less costly reinforcers on the larger areas. The student spins the spinner and receives the reinforcer listed on the selected spinner section. This adds reinforcement variety as well as an element of unpredictability, and thus serves as a "mystery motivator."
- Use assistance cards to help manage requests for assistance (Paine et al., 1983). Fold a 9" × 12" piece of construction paper into a triangular shape with two 4" sides and a 2" base. Tape the triangle together and write "Please Keep Working" on one side and "Please Help Me" on the other side. When help is needed, the student places the side stating "Please Help Me" toward the front of the room, thus leaving the side stating "Please Keep Working" facing the student. Provide each student with a work folder that occupies the student until the teacher is available to help. Frustration is reduced and success is increased if the work folder includes self-correcting material. The work folder should include tasks relating to the student's instructional needs (e.g., practice in a specific skill). The assistance card enables the student to request help without raising a hand or disrupting engaged academic

time. The supplementary work folder enables the student to continue to work productively on another academic task in which immediate teacher assistance is not required. Also, the assistance card reminds the student to keep working.

- Use feedback charts for managing student behavior. Paine et al. (1983) note that feedback charts give the student a visible display of progress and also generate valuable data to help make educational decisions. The chart is displayed where all students can see it and is divided into four areas. For example:

Begins assigned activities promptly	Follows directions
Completes work or works entire time	Receives less than two warnings

Each student receives a blank card divided into four squares. Throughout the day, the teacher marks each square with plus marks (+) when the student performs the desired behavior. At the end of a specified time period, the student may be allowed to trade the marks for free time, playing a game, and so on. The teacher may use separate cards for different academic periods. Also, a group chart can be made and laminated so that it can be used repeatedly.

	Math		Reading		Language	
Alan	+		+		+	
			+			
Elise	+	+	+			+
	+		+			
Clayton		+	+		+	+
		+	+		+	+

- Have the student who does not complete homework earn the privilege of being allowed to do homework at home (Lieberman, 1983). Place the student on a 5-day probation during which the student must stay after school and complete homework assignments within an agreed-upon time period. Then have the student alternate doing homework at home and at school every other day for 5 days. Finally, the student can be allowed to do all homework at home. However, if any assignments are not completed at home, the student is placed on probation for another 5 days. Thus, for the student the positive consequence is earning the privilege to do homework at home, as opposed to the negative consequence of staying after school for not completing homework.

SOCIAL DEVELOPMENT INTERVENTIONS

Among affective domains, social competence has received extensive attention in the educational literature. Social competence is a global construct that involves the interaction of personality development variables and social interaction factors (Bender, 2008). A socially competent individual can perceive situations in which social skills can be used, can discriminate which social skills are appropriate for a given situation, and can perform the appropriate social skills in such a way that there is a high likelihood of positive consequences. Given the low social competence of many individuals with learning problems and the extensive social demands of adult living, it is apparent why social competence receives so much attention. Social skills, a component of social competence, are discrete behaviors that are learned and performed in interactive situations, and they have been the focus of many intervention studies involving students with learning problems.

Social Skills Training

Several procedures have been used to improve the social skills performance of students with learning problems (Elksnin & Elksnin, 1998; Schumaker & Hazel, 1984). One technique involves the manipulation of antecedent and consequent events associated with the target social behavior. For example, environmental events can be changed in an effort to increase the probability of future occurrence of appropriate social behaviors while decreasing the probability of occurrence of inappropriate behaviors. Approaches of this technique include the use of cooperative goal structures, the delivery or the withholding of particular consequences contingent upon the occurrence of social responses, the application of group contingencies, and the use of home-based contingency management systems. Another technique that has been used to reduce the rate of inappropriate social behaviors is cognitive training aimed at teaching self-control of personal behaviors (e.g., self-recording and self-evaluation of behaviors).

Interpersonal social skills also can be increased through direct instruction. Schumaker and Hazel (1984) discuss four types of instructional interventions that have been used to facilitate the acquisition of social skills.

1. *Description* involves primarily oral techniques in which the teacher describes how to perform a skill appropriately.
2. *Modeling* involves demonstrations of the social skill either by live models or by film, audiotape, or pictorial models.
3. *Rehearsal* involves verbal repetition of required skill steps to ensure that the students have memorized the steps in sequence and can instruct themselves in what to do next, and structured practice (e.g., role-play activities) whereby the learner attempts to perform the skill.
4. *Feedback* involves verbal reinforcement following rehearsal to inform the students about what steps they performed well and what behaviors need improvement.

Frequently, combinations of these procedures are included in social skills training interventions.

A social skills curriculum also can be used. A basic principle of social skills instruction is that behaviors chosen for instruction should be those valued by persons important in the learner's environment. In an analysis of social behaviors selected for individualized educational programs, Pray, Hall, and Markley (1992) found that academically related social skills (e.g., task-related skills such as following directions or being on task) were much more prominent than interpersonal skills (e.g., making conversation or accepting authority). In a similar vein, Mellard and Hazel (1992) maintain that nonacademic characteristics may have more effect than academics on the employment of an individual with learning problems. Thus, Pray et al. and Mellard and Hazel recommend more emphasis on interpersonal skills for these students. To foster peer interaction, attention should be given to areas such as informal conversation and play skills. The following social skills curriculum consists of four main areas.

1. *Conversation skills* include using body language, greeting others, introducing oneself, applying active listening, answering questions, interrupting correctly, asking questions, saying good-bye, and conversing.
2. *Friendship skills* include making friends, saying thank-you, giving compliments, accepting thanks, accepting compliments, joining group activities, starting activities with others, and giving help.
3. *Skills for difficult situations* include giving criticism, accepting being told "no," accepting criticism, fol-

lowing instructions, responding to teasing, resisting peer pressure, and apologizing.
4. *Problem-solving skills* include negotiating, giving rationales, persuading, problem solving, getting help, and asking for feedback.

Sugai and Fuller (1991) provide an excellent decision model for examining a social skills curriculum. Their model addresses background, assessment, and instruction and features insightful questions to ask in each area.

Bender and Wall (1994) note that the research indicates that social skills training has successfully helped students with learning problems; however, most of this research has focused on short-term outcomes. Research is needed to demonstrate that social skills training generalizes to the daily settings of employment, significant-other relationships, and recreation (Bender & Wall, 1994; Mellard & Hazel, 1992). In a meta-analysis of 53 studies on social skills training, Forness and Kavale (1996) found that the average amount of social skills training tended to be 30 hours or less (i.e., fewer than 3 hours per week for less than 10 weeks) and had a relatively modest effect. They suggest that longer interventions may be needed to improve long-standing social problems and result in generalization and long-term effects. Moreover, to design and produce more effective social skills training interventions, Gresham, Sugai, and Horner (2001) recommend that social skills training must be more frequent than 30 hours of instruction over 10 to 12 weeks, and that the intervention must be directly linked to the individual's social skills deficits.

myeducationlab

Go to the Assignments and Activities section of the Topic Promoting Social and Emotional Development in the MyEducationLab for your course and complete the activity entitled Explicit Social Skill Instruction. As you watch the video and answer the accompanying questions, think about the importance of teaching social skills.

SOCIAL DEVELOPMENT ACTIVITIES

The socially immature student lacks the ability to get along with peers and lacks other social skills common to his or her age group. The student may engage in antisocial behavior, failing to recognize his or her responsibilities and the rights of others. Social withdrawal may result from lack of academic success. The following activities are presented to help students who are socially immature.

- Pair a withdrawn student with a competent, socially mature peer for various activities. They must cooperate in completing an academic task together or being a team during a game. Thus, in these situations, success or failure is shared by both students.

- If one student frequently teases another, ask the teased student to ignore the one doing the teasing and reward him or her each time no response is made to the teasing. Thus, the student who is teasing receives attention neither from the teacher nor the peer for the inappropriate behavior. Also, self-recording can be used to reduce teasing. Give the student a slip of paper with lines for name and date, and spaces in which the student is to mark each time he or she teases. The marking should be monitored. Self-recording inappropriate behavior may help the student decrease teasing.
- Use the socially withdrawn or rejected student in peer teaching situations as either the tutor or tutee. A sociogram can indicate an appropriate match. Peer tutoring encourages appropriate peer contacts in a secure and structured activity.
- Use modeling techniques to teach various social skills. Praise the model for appropriate social behavior in the presence of the socially immature student.
- Encourage the withdrawn student to use an audio recorder when he or she feels like talking. Tell the student that if he or she would like to share feelings, the teacher will be glad to listen. The teacher can respond on a recorder if the student prefers. This is a first step in encouraging a withdrawn student to talk and discuss feelings.
- Use role playing to present a variety of possible social situations. Discuss several different mature reactions to specific problems. Thus, the student is presented with a choice of solutions to use when coping with similar social occurrences.
- When a student frequently is aggressive toward a peer, ignore the aggressive student and pay attention to the victim. Reinforce cooperative and peaceful behavior in the presence of the aggressive student and reward the student for appropriate behavior.
- Encourage the student to develop a vocabulary that expresses feelings. Glue pockets on a large piece of tagboard, and on each pocket illustrate a face showing a different expression (e.g., smiling, frowning, and serious). Write words expressing feelings (e.g., *sad, cheerful, troubled, anxious, pleased, miserable,* and *nervous*) on index cards. Instruct the student to match each word to a picture expressing that emotion. The correct face can be drawn on the back of each card so that the student can check the response. Another activity with feeling words is to provide a list of words

and ask the student to write each word in a way that shows the emotion:

Afraid	*afraid*
Shy	shy
Excited	EXCITED
Jumpy	*jumpy*

Secondary students can increase their vocabulary to include feeling words that can be divided into the categories of *unpleasant* and *pleasant*:

Unpleasant	*Pleasant*
Ambivalent	Accomplished
Betrayed	Confident
Condemned	Ecstatic
Distraught	Fascinated
Dubious	Gratified
Exasperated	Infatuated

- Have each student express his or her mood or feeling at different happenings. Write events on index cards (e.g., *It's time to go to school; I don't know what to do; I don't have any money; My teacher smiles at me;* and *It's my birthday*). Use a piece of tagboard with pockets labeled with various moods. Each student selects a card, reads it aloud, tells how the described event makes him or her feel and why, and places the card in the pocket that corresponds to the feeling. Also, take pictures of students showing various emotions during classroom situations. These photographs can be displayed with captions telling the emotion shown and the situation in which it occurred: *Kevin is very proud. He is wearing his badge for captain of the safety patrol.* By observing the pictures, students may become more sensitive to facial expressions.
- Conduct class meetings during which the students discuss any question that seems relevant to them at the time. This opportunity for personal involvement is especially appropriate for secondary students. The teacher should keep the discussion moving and see that everyone is given an opportunity to participate as much as possible.

INSTRUCTIONAL GAMES IN SOCIAL DEVELOPMENT

Many activities can be presented in a game format to stimulate interest and involvement. Games also promote positive peer relations and enable the teacher to work on specific social behaviors (e.g., cooperating, taking turns, or expressing feelings). The following games are designed to promote appropriate social behaviors.

Best and Worst Game

Materials: Paper and pencil.

Directions: The teacher describes a social situation and instructs each student to write down what would be the *best* and the *worst* thing to do in response to that event. Each student reads his or her response, and the choices presented are discussed. The student with the best response, which is decided by the presenter of the problem, gets to describe the next social incident and lead the discussion.

Socialization Game

Materials: Start-to-finish board; dice; set of cards containing personal questions; markers.

Directions: A game board is used to improve social skills by giving the players an opportunity to talk freely about feelings, relationships, or activities. Each player rolls the dice and moves that number of spaces on the board. The player then must take a card and respond to the question by explaining the answer to the other players. The first player to reach the finish space wins.

Sample questions: When do you like to be alone? If you could be anyone in the world, who would you be and why? What happened on the happiest day of your life? What would you do if you didn't go to school?

Decision Game

Materials: Five parallel lines marked on the floor with masking tape.

Directions: The teacher explains to students that the five lines from right to left represent *absolutely right*, *somewhat right*, *undecided or neutral*, *somewhat wrong*, and *absolutely wrong*. The teacher tells a story or describes a situation and then asks students to move to the line that indicates their decision about the story or situation. Each student should explain why he or she moved to a particular line.

Sample story or situation: John saw William take two quarters from the teacher's desk and put them in his pocket. He told William to return the money but William refused to do so. John then went to the teacher and told her William had taken the money. Was the decision to tell the teacher right or wrong?

COMMERCIAL SOCIAL DEVELOPMENT PROGRAMS

Various commercial programs are designed to help students get along with others. The following programs can be used to promote the social development of students with learning problems.

Skillstreaming the Elementary School Child; Skillstreaming the Adolescent

These two manuals provide a program for teaching prosocial skills based on a structured learning method that involves modeling (i.e., demonstrating the behavioral steps that make up specific skills), student role playing (i.e., reviewing, rehearsing, and performing each of the skill steps), performance feedback (i.e., evaluating the role play), and transfer training (i.e., developing assignments for using the skills in real-life situations). In *Skillstreaming the Elementary School Child* (McGinnis & Goldstein, 1997), 60 specific prosocial skills (such as asking for help, dealing with group pressure, and accepting consequences) are presented within the content areas of dealing with feelings, classroom survival skills, alternatives to aggression, friendship-making skills, and dealing with stress. *Skillstreaming the Adolescent* (Goldstein & McGinnis, 1997) presents 50 prosocial skills (such as starting a conversation, setting a goal, and standing up for a friend) within the content areas of beginning and advanced social skills, dealing with feelings, alternatives to aggression, dealing with stress, and planning skills. A video program is available illustrating the concepts and training procedures contained in the books.

The Waksman Social Skills Curriculum for Adolescents

The Waksman Social Skills Curriculum for Adolescents (Waksman & Waksman, 1998) includes a 9-week, 18-lesson format that uses reproducible worksheets to teach appropriate assertive behavior skills to students ages 10 to 15 years who display social skills deficits, behavior disorders, hyperactivity, and emotional problems. The program includes lessons on getting along with peers, teachers, and family members; expressing feelings appropriately; accepting criticism and compliments; social problem solving; peer pressure/refusal skills; tension and anger management; communicating effectively; and assertiveness and self-concept enhancement. The lessons, which can be used with individuals or groups of students, contain specific goals, objectives, worksheets, homework assignments, and instructions.

The Walker Social Skills Curriculum

The ACCEPTS Program (Walker et al., 1983) is a social skills curriculum that teaches classroom and peer-to-peer social skills to students in kindergarten through sixth grade. The 28 classroom competencies and social skills are presented in five areas: (1) classroom skills (e.g., listening to the teacher and following classroom rules), (2) basic interaction skills (e.g., eye contact, listening, and taking turns), (3) getting-along skills (e.g., using polite words, sharing, and assisting others), (4) making-friends skills (e.g., good grooming, smiling, and complimenting), and (5) coping skills (e.g., when expressing anger, when being teased, and when things don't go right). *The ACCESS Program* (Walker, Todis, Holmes, & Horton, 1988) teaches peer-to-peer skills, skills for relating to adults, and self-management skills to students at the middle- and secondary-school levels. The 30 social skills are presented in three areas: (1) relating to peers (e.g., interacting with the opposite sex, being left out, and handling group pressures), (2) relating to adults (e.g., disagreeing with adults, working independently, and developing good study habits), and (3) relating to yourself (e.g., being organized, using self-control, and feeling good about yourself). The curriculum is designed for use by both general and special education teachers and can be taught in one-to-one, small-group, or large-group instructional formats.

EMOTIONAL DEVELOPMENT INTERVENTIONS

The emotional development of individuals with learning problems is an area that warrants study and the development of related interventions. This section features selected interventions to promote emotional development and includes bibliotherapy, attribution retraining, life-space interviewing, reality therapy, techniques for improving mood states, and projective techniques.

Bibliotherapy

Bibliotherapy is a teaching technique that uses reading materials to help students better understand themselves and their problems. Characters in the books learn to cope with problems and situations similar to those faced by the students. Through identifying with the character, students release emotional tensions and achieve a better understanding of themselves and their problems. Also, characteristics, attitudes, values, and situations in reading selections can serve as models for the students.

Hoagland (1972) notes that for bibliotherapy to be effective, students must move through three phases during or immediately after reading a book: (1) *identification*—the students must become personally involved and must identify themselves or see a situation similar to some of their own situations, (2) *catharsis*—the students must release emotional tensions regarding the problems, and (3) *insight*—through empathizing with the character or plot, students must reach a better understanding that tempers their emotional drives.

Forgan (2002) presents a lesson plan based on a teaching framework for bibliotherapy and problem solving that contains the four elements of prereading, guided reading, postreading discussion, and a problem-solving/reinforcement activity. To discuss a book with a student, Cianciolo (1965) suggests the following steps.

1. Retell the story and emphasize incidents, feelings, relationships, and behavior.
2. Discuss changes of feelings, relationships, and behaviors.
3. Identify similar events from the student's life or other reading selections.
4. Explore the consequences that occurred.
5. Generalize about the consequences or helpfulness of alternative behaviors.

The student should begin to realize that many other people have experienced the same problem and that there is more than one way to solve a problem.

Books chosen for a bibliotherapeutic program should focus on a particular need and should be written on the student's level. The selections also should depict realistic approaches and have lifelike characters. Altieri (2008), Sridhar and Vaughn (2000), Forgan (2002), and McCarty and Chalmers (1997) present numerous books on various topics that are appropriate for bibliotherapy. Also, suitable books can be selected from various bibliographies that are cross-indexed by theme and age level. Creative activities (e.g., art, drama, writing, and role playing) can be used in conjunction with bibliotherapy. Sridhar and Vaughn note that bibliotherapy can improve reading comprehension, enhance self-esteem, and improve behavior for students with learning and behavior problems. They also report that studies indicate that bibliotherapy is effective for developing assertiveness, attitude change, and self-development. Although research on bibliotherapy is minimal, the approach seems to help some students with learning problems by providing them with reading materials relevant to their own social and emotional needs.

Attribution Retraining

Attributions refer to a person's beliefs concerning the causes of events. Students have different ideas about why they succeed and fail. Those who believe in an internal locus of control explain the outcomes of their actions on the basis of their abilities or efforts. In contrast, persons with an external locus of control believe that factors outside their control, such as luck or task difficulty, determine their fates.

Students with learning disabilities are more likely than normally achieving students to believe that their successes are a function of external factors (Chapman & Boersma, 1979; Pearl, Bryan, & Donahue, 1980). Bryan (1986) notes that it would seem advantageous to induce such students to have more positive and self-serving expectations of their academic successes. As students with learning problems experience many academic failures, they are likely to lack confidence in their intellectual abilities and doubt that anything they do will help them overcome their difficulties. Thus, they may lessen their achievement efforts, especially when presented with difficult material. In other words, repeated failure can lead students to believe that they are not capable of overcoming their difficulties, and students' beliefs about their abilities can affect their achievement efforts and accomplishments.

Attribution retraining studies (Schunk, 1981; Shelton, Anastopoulos, & Linden, 1985) have found that teaching students to attribute their failures to insufficient effort can result in increased persistence and improved performance when confronted with difficulty. In these studies, students are engaged in academic tasks and are given feedback emphasizing the importance of their effort. In a review of attribution retraining research, Bryan (1986) reports that attribution retraining sessions have been shown to be somewhat successful in changing attributions and persistence behavior. Fowler and Peterson (1981) found that prompting and reinforcing students for verbalizing the appropriate effort attributions can be more effective than simply telling students, when they fail, that they need to try harder. In a recent study, students who received attribution retraining in combination with strategy instruction showed improvement in reading comprehension (Mastropieri, Berkeley, Scruggs, & Marshak, 2008). Unlike students who received strategy instruction without reattribution training, the students who received the combined intervention maintained the reading comprehension improvement in a follow-up assessment 6 weeks later. In addition to stressing effort as a determinant of a student's difficulties, it also can help to teach students to attribute their failures to ineffective task strategies (Licht, 1984). Bryan (1986) notes that teachers should convey to students with learning problems that they are learning new skills and that determined application of the new skills can help them overcome their difficulties.

Ellis, Lenz, and Sabornie (1987b) suggest the following instructional sequence in attribution retraining.

1. Teach students to make statements that reflect effort.
2. Teach students to attribute difficulty to ineffective strategies.
3. Arrange for students to have success with newly learned strategies.

Life-Space Interviewing

Life-space interviewing is a verbal strategy for intervention that can be used in the classroom to manage a crisis or an everyday problem. This technique attempts to structure a situation so that the student works out the problem independently. The interview is designed to be free of judgment. The teacher is simply a listener and helper as the student makes decisions about how to handle the problem.

Morse (1971) outlines the following steps in life-space interviewing.

1. All students involved in the specific incident are allowed to give their own impressions of the occurrence without interruption.
2. The teacher listens and, without casting judgment, asks questions to determine the accuracy of each student's perception.
3. If the students cannot resolve the problem agreeably, the teacher may have to suggest an acceptable plan to deal with it.
4. The students and the teacher work together to develop a plan for solving similar problems in the future.

The classroom teacher may best use life-space interviewing to provide emotional first-aid at times of unusual stress. Thus, the technique is used to reduce students' frustration and anxiety by giving them support during an emotional situation; change behavior and reinforce behavioral and social rules; enhance self-esteem; and assist students to solve their own everyday problems by expanding their understanding and insight into their own and others' behavior and feelings. For example, after a fight on the playground, the teacher can engage in life-space interviewing to allow students to release frustration and anger. The teacher provides support and helps students view all sides of the situation and the rights of others.

Long, Wood, and Fecser (2001) use the term *life-space crisis intervention* to emphasize that a crisis always evokes verbal intervention. They note that the key to success or failure in obtaining a therapeutic outcome of a crisis is the quality of the adult's verbal intervention. The teacher's attitude and behavior as interviewer influence the effectiveness of life-space interviewing. The teacher should be polite to the student and should maintain eye contact. Asking *why* questions should be avoided, and the interviewer should try to reduce any apparent guilt feelings. In addition, the teacher should encourage the student to communicate and ask questions as they work together to develop a plan of action for present or future use. The life-space interview technique is time-consuming and requires sensitivity and emotional control from the teacher. However, it can help students see the consequences of behavior and find ways to deal with a problem. Moreover, in a review of interventions for students with emotional and behavioral disorders, life-space crisis intervention was found to have evidence for improving outcomes for students (Ryan, Pierce, & Mooney, 2008).

Reality Therapy

Reality therapy, developed by Glasser (1965), is used to manage behaviors by teaching students to behave responsibly and to face reality. An interview technique similar to life-space interviewing is used in an attempt to help students make sound decisions when confronted with a problem. In reality therapy, all students are assumed to be responsible for their own behavior, and inappropriate behaviors are not excused because of unconscious motivations. During interviews the student receives emotional support, and no judgments are made of the present behavior. The teacher and the student jointly develop a plan to increase the student's responsible behavior, and the student is encouraged to make a commitment to carry out the plan. The student is expected to realize the consequences of irresponsible behavior, and no excuses are accepted. Thus, the morality of behavior is emphasized, and the student is taught socially accepted ways to handle problems.

Glasser (1965) presents a three-step format for applying reality therapy. The first step is to help the student identify the problem. This is accomplished by asking questions such as "What happened?" and "Where are you going?" The second step is to help the student develop value judgment by asking questions such as "Is the behavior helping you?" or "Is the behavior against the rules?" The third step is to involve the student in carrying out a plan to correct the inappropriate behavior (e.g., "What can you do about it?"). An application of reality therapy is featured in the following scenario.

Teacher:	Michael, what just happened?
Michael:	Nothing.
Teacher:	I thought I saw you push Susan.
Michael:	Yeah, maybe I did.
Teacher:	Tell me about it.
Michael:	I was running to get in line and she got in my way.
Teacher:	Well, I'm sure you didn't push her on purpose, but is pushing students against the rules?
Michael:	Yeah.
Teacher:	What do you think should be done?
Michael:	I don't know.
Teacher:	Why don't you sit over there at the reading table for a couple of minutes and think about what you can do to solve the problem.
Michael:	Okay.

(5 minutes later)

Teacher:	Got an idea?
Michael:	Yeah, I think I should line up after the others for the rest of the week.
Teacher:	Does that help Susan?
Michael:	No.
Teacher:	What can you do to help Susan?
Michael:	I can tell her I'm sorry and let her line up in front of me tomorrow.
Teacher:	Can you do that?
Michael:	Yeah.
Teacher:	Fine, I think that's an excellent plan.

Techniques for Improving Mood States

Some students with mild disabilities are susceptible to loneliness or depression (Maag, 2002; Pavri & Monda-Amaya, 2000). Pavri and Monda-Amaya (2000) report that students rated self-initiated strategies (e.g., engaging in a solitary activity or seeking companionship) as most helpful in dealing with loneliness. To treat depression, intervention techniques such as social skills training, self-control training, and attribution retraining frequently are used; however, Maag (2002) suggests a contextually based approach for treating depression and offers ten specific strategies (e.g., exaggerate helplessness, make deliberate mistakes, and be perfect) that direct students to display a particular behavior or symptom of depression but alter the circumstances or situations in which it occurs. Moreover, the following are some tentative suggestions for dealing with temperament, suicide, and general personality variables.

Temperament Some students with learning problems have a temperament that predisposes them to be less task persistent or display less social flexibility; thus, educators should strive to develop interventions that lessen the negative effects of their temperament. Because little intervention research exists in this area, the following suggestions should be regarded as tentative.

- Reward on-task behavior, and discuss the positive consequences of completing tasks.
- Teach the student to self-monitor on-task and off-task behavior.
- Include the student in selecting some tasks to do.
- Lessen social inflexibility by helping the student make transitions among activities (e.g., periodically cue the student about a transition prior to its occurrence).

- Reward smooth transitions and discuss their positive outcomes.
- Involve the student in role-play games or situations in which students must take turns.

Suicide Bender (2008) offers the following suggestions for dealing with suicide concerns.

- Take suicide-related drawings and comments (such as "I hope I die") seriously and keep records of their occurrence.
- Elicit confirmation regarding a student's suicidal signals (e.g., "Do you think about hurting yourself often?").
- Affirm a commitment to life when responding to a student's concerns (e.g., "I see how that can upset you, but isn't it nice that you have your friend to enjoy each day with?").
- Have the student stay with someone if his or her thoughts or actions seem serious.
- Seek professional help in dealing with the student.

Personality Variables The following suggested interventions focus on dealing with personality variables and increasing self-determination (Bender, 2008).

- Separate the student's problem from the person and do not criticize the student personally.
- Provide opportunities for the student to be proud (e.g., encourage sharing a special interest or talent when the content or situation is appropriate).
- Constantly point out the relationship between the student's efforts and outcomes, and encourage the student to set goals for learning. These activities may help the student develop an internal locus of control.
- Display the student's work on bulletin boards and arrange situations where outsiders (such as the principal or other teachers) are able to encourage or praise the student.

Projective Techniques

The teacher can use various projective techniques to encourage students to project or express their feelings and emotions. Creative activities, such as role playing and puppetry, provide an opportunity for the student to express feelings and reduce frustrations with few constraints.

Role Playing In role playing, students assume the role of a character and act out a brief episode that involves a problem. The role-playing process includes four steps.

1. A specific problem is identified (i.e., classroom problems or conflicts or other relevant situations).
2. After the problem is described, the roles must be established and assigned to various students. Volunteers should be sought; students should not be forced to play a role.
3. The actual role playing takes place and should be brief. The same situation can be repeated several times with different students to present many solutions to a single problem.
4. A discussion follows, which focuses on the role or behavior rather than the student portraying it.

Thus, through role playing, the student faces reactions of other people and learns ways to cope with similar situations.

Puppetry Puppets can help students experience different events and express feelings and emotions. Fairy-tale characters (such as king, witch, giant, and animal) can be used to represent human emotional experiences. Students can make hand puppets and a stage. The puppet theater provides a nonthreatening atmosphere in which students can express their feelings freely as they engage in problem solving. After the puppet show, other solutions to the problems presented can be discussed.

EMOTIONAL DEVELOPMENT ACTIVITIES

Activities for Improving Reactions to Authority Figures

Some students respond inappropriately to school personnel or authority figures. The student may resist coming to school and frequently may challenge the authority of the teacher and principal by arguing constantly and disobeying school rules. This negative reaction needs to be changed to promote a healthy attitude toward school and authority figures. The following activities are suggested for improving students' reactions to authority figures.

- Provide the student with positive reinforcement for attending school. For example, give the student a special treat or plan a rewarding activity each day the student arrives on time. Special privileges, snacks, and activities can be made contingent on regular school attendance.
- Pair the student who is absent frequently with a well-liked peer who has regular attendance. (Use a sociogram to determine a good match for modeling purposes.) With the teacher's guidance, the model can plan to meet the student at school for various activities and thus encourage attendance.

- Allow class members to establish some of their own rules of behavior and consequences for disobeying a rule. Discuss the need and reasons for the rules. When some rules are made by peers, students may be less inclined to challenge the teacher's authority.
- Give the student who repeatedly disobeys rules and instructions several courses of action from which to choose. When possible, avoid conflict and "show-downs" in which the student is forced to obey. Sometimes a peer can explain an assignment or rule to a student who resists adult authority and the student will comply.
- Ignore or walk away from the student whenever he or she argues with you or disobeys instructions. Isolation also can be effective in dealing with the student who argues. Reinforce obedient behavior and positive language through praise and attention.
- Invite various authority figures in the community to speak to the class and share some of their problems and experiences during their school years. Such sharing can make a positive impression on the student who shows a negative attitude.
- Use an "emotion box" in the classroom. Give the class members several forms that ask for name, date, emotion, and reasons. Ask students to complete a form and place it in the emotion box whenever they react strongly to an event in the classroom. Through this method the teacher can gain understanding about each student's reasons for undesirable and negative behaviors.
- To foster a positive attitude toward authority figures, ask the student "planned interest" questions every day (e.g., "What did you do last night?" "Did your team win its ball game?"). Also, remember the student on special days (e.g., birthday). A teacher's genuine interest in individual students encourages a positive feeling toward school attendance and authority figures.

Activities for Enhancing Self-Concept

Self-concept refers to a person's perception of his or her abilities and of how others important to the person feel about him or her. A person with a poor self-concept has feelings of inferiority and inadequacy and may express these feelings (e.g., "I can't do that"; "I'm not very smart"). Such a student may lack self-confidence and be reluctant to interact with others. The student may resist academic work due to fear of failure. The following activities are suggested to enhance self-concept.

- To make the student feel special and important, select the student to be "Student of the Week." Have the student sit in a special chair and wear a badge. Each day ask the student's classmates to write something special about her or him. They may write positive statements about the student's abilities or personal attributes. Also, the classmates can decide on other special activities they can do for the student (e.g., write a story about the student or play the student's favorite game at recess).
- To develop self-awareness, have students collect items that tell something about themselves (e.g., magazine pictures, small objects, and photographs). Encourage each student to make a collage of these items on tagboard. The center of the collage can contain a picture of the student, with the items arranged around the photograph. The students can share with others what the items represent and why they were chosen.
- Write short, personal notes to the student to provide encouragement and to let him or her know you are interested. Also, have brief conversations with the student, and provide extra encouragement when he or she is trying a new task or suffering from a disappointment.
- Use the student as a tutor in peer tutoring situations. This may boost self-esteem, and it also shows that the teacher has confidence in the student's ability to handle the task.
- Make some academic tasks look more difficult than they really are. The student will gain self-confidence when successfully completing a task perceived as very difficult. For example, a simple math worksheet to practice subtraction facts can be replaced by a worksheet that appears to contain very difficult problems but really requires the same basic skills. For example, the problem

$$\begin{array}{r} 394876 \\ -173472 \\ \hline \end{array}$$

requires the same basic skills as

$$\begin{array}{cccccc} 3 & 9 & 4 & 8 & 7 & 6 \\ -1 & -7 & -3 & -4 & -7 & -2 \\ \hline \end{array}$$

- Provide success activities and limit failure as much as possible. For example, before requiring participation in oral reading, have the student review difficult words or listen to the story on a tape recorder. Also, using self-correcting materials keeps incorrect responses private and gives the student a chance to correct responses immediately. Provide verbal praise and correct wrong responses without hurting the student's feelings (e.g., "You're almost right," "Let's do it together," and "Nice try").

- Help the student compile a personal scrapbook. Include pictures or drawings of family, friends, and pets. If possible, take photographs in class. The scrapbook can include written accounts of trips, interests, and favorite activities.
- Set realistic goals with the student on selected tasks. Record the student's daily progress toward the goal. When the goal is achieved, point out the progress to make the student feel proud of the accomplishments.
- Emphasize the importance of student effort on academic tasks and teach the student to attribute successes and failures to amount of effort. This may result in increased persistence on difficult material and reduce doubts of intellectual ability.

INSTRUCTIONAL GAMES IN EMOTIONAL DEVELOPMENT

Activities to promote emotional development can be presented in a game format. Because games often stimulate interest and motivation, they frequently engage students with emotional difficulties. The following game promotes emotional development.

Personality Game

Materials: Start-to-finish game board; cards with personality traits written on them; markers.

Directions: The cards are placed face down on the playing board (see Figure 5.3). The first player takes the top card and reads it aloud. If the player thinks the card describes him or her, the player's marker is moved forward five spaces. However, if the player believes the statement on the card does not apply, but the majority of the group thinks it does (or vice versa), the player's marker is moved back three spaces. If neither the player nor the others believes the card applies, the player's marker is not moved. The players may tell why they think a trait is or is not descriptive of their personality. After each turn the card is placed face down in the discard pile. If a blank card is picked, the player must make up a trait. Players may choose the top card from either the original card pile or the discard pile. The purpose of the game is to help students better understand themselves. The first player to reach the finish space is the winner.

Sample cards: I am impatient; I joke around a lot; I am kind to animals; I don't ever like school.

COMMERCIAL EMOTIONAL DEVELOPMENT PROGRAMS

Various programs and materials are available to help students deal with emotional problems. The following programs can help students understand themselves better and develop appropriate strategies for dealing with personal problems.

The Passport Program

The Passport Program: A Journey Through Emotional, Social, Cognitive, and Self-Development, developed by A. Vernon (published by Research Press), is designed to help students

FIGURE 5.3
Personality game board

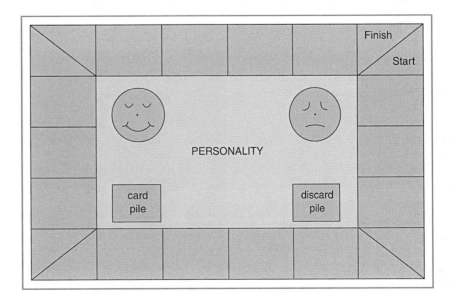

learn positive mental health concepts by developing self-acceptance, personal relationship skills, and problem-solving and decision-making strategies. Each of the three volumes (i.e., grades 1–5, grades 6–8, and grades 9–12) includes learning activities that cover emotional development, social development, cognitive development, and self-development. The activities are designed for use in the classroom or in small-group settings and include games, stories, role plays, reading and writing activities, and discussion questions. The program is grounded in developmental theory and the principles of Rational Emotive Behavior Therapy.

Thinking, Feeling, Behaving

Thinking, Feeling, Behaving, developed by A. Vernon (published by Research Press), is an emotional education curriculum based on the principles of Rational Emotive Behavior Therapy. The curriculum consists of one volume for youngsters in first through sixth grade and one volume for adolescents in seventh through twelfth grade. Each volume includes 90 field-tested activities arranged by grade level and organized into the categories of self-acceptance, feelings, beliefs and behavior, problem solving/decision making, and interpersonal relationships. The activities are designed for use in small-group settings and include simulation games, stories, role plays, written activities, brainstorming, and art activities. The curriculum is appropriate as a preventive or remedial program to help students learn to use positive health concepts in overcoming irrational beliefs, negative feelings and attitudes, and the negative consequences that may result.

BEHAVIORAL DEVELOPMENT INTERVENTIONS

Discipline and fighting rank among the top problems facing public schools (Rose & Gallup, 2006). Whelan (1996) maintains that broken social bonds, inordinate amounts of stress and conflict, the observation of violent behavior in relationships, and substance abuse are primary reasons that youngsters face conflicts in school and are disruptive. Although many of the causes of disruptive behavior are beyond the parameters of the educational system, these conditions do not lessen the educator's responsibility to ameliorate discipline problems. Whelan maintains that one of the primary reasons that discipline problems remain a top concern is many educators fail to use effective and efficient classroom management procedures.

If the techniques featured in this chapter in the sections on interventions (i.e., general techniques for promoting social, emotional, and behavioral development; social development interventions; and emotional development interventions) are applied, disruptive behavior should diminish to the extent that it is not a problem. In essence, when applied within a classroom community that values cooperation, feelings, and property, using the techniques listed in this chapter should diminish or eliminate chronic disruptive behavior. The primary techniques include academic success through good teaching, the use of motivation techniques, the occasional use of mild consequences, social skills instruction, self-regulation instruction, and sensitivity to personality variables. If these techniques are unsuccessful, more intense management techniques should be used. Kame'enui et al. (1995) note that three levels of intervention are needed for managing mild to severe behavioral problems. The first level of intervention is for mild behavioral problems, and 80 percent of students respond to routine instructional management at this level. At the

Students can be rewarded for appropriate behavior in creative ways. EyeWire Collection/Getty Images–Photodisc/Royalty Free

second level of intervention, another 15 percent of students present persistent problems and require ongoing attention and a strategic intervention plan. The third level of intervention is for the remaining 5 percent of students who exhibit severe and chronic behavioral problems.

A management approach grounded in teaching students appropriate behavior, responsibility, and self-regulation will succeed with almost all students. This section includes reinforcement and punishment perspectives and procedures that help with students requiring strategic management plans and vigilance.

Positive Reinforcement Plan

Knowledge and application of reinforcement principles can help manage a classroom. Many teachers apply these principles in a natural way, without taking the time to write a behavior modification plan specifying the target behavior, consequent events, schedule of reinforcement, and so forth. However, some students' behavior does not change unless a highly systematic behavior modification plan is developed and applied.

Figure 5.4 presents a record of a behavior modification plan to increase staying-in-seat behavior. The teacher used a time-sampling technique to record whether the student stayed seated during seatwork activities. Observation sessions were 30 minutes long, and the teacher used a recording sheet marked off with a row of ten squares. The teacher looked at the student every 3 minutes and recorded a "+" if the student was seated and a "−" if the student was not. As Figure 5.4 shows, the student's percentage of staying-in-seat behavior was low during baseline$_1$. However, when the teacher began giving the student praise and attention for appropriate in-seat behavior (in sessions 11 through 20), the level of the desired behavior increased greatly. When praise and attention were withdrawn in baseline$_2$ (sessions 21 through 25), the student's staying-in-seat behavior sharply diminished. However, when praise and attention were provided again (in sessions 26 through 35), the level of the appropriate behavior quickly increased. Thus, the teacher was able to note the effects of teacher attention on modifying the student's out-of-seat behavior.

Contingency Contracting

Contracts between a student and the classroom teacher can help to motivate the student toward desirable behavior changes. A *contract* is an agreement—verbal or written—between two parties. The term *contingent* means that there is a relationship between what one does and the consequences. In behavior modification,

FIGURE 5.4

Record of a behavior modification plan to increase staying-in-seat behavior

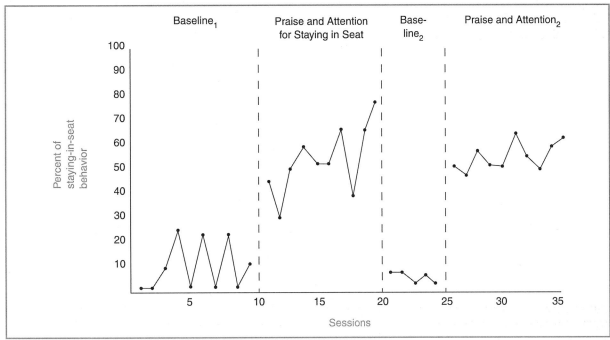

contingency contracting is based on the Premack Principle (Premack, 1959), which states that the frequency of a less preferred activity increases when it is followed by the opportunity to engage in one that is preferred. For example, if the student would rather play outside than sit quietly in the classroom, the contingency contract might state that sitting quietly for a certain amount of time will be followed by outside play.

The following steps are involved in writing a contingency contract.

1. The teacher outlines the specific behavior required of the student.
2. The teacher identifies the reinforcement for which the student will work. This reinforcement should be available to the student *only* for performing the specified behavior. The required behavior or the consequent reinforcement can be determined through student–teacher discussions.
3. The teacher specifies the terms of the contract, which should include the amount or type of behavior required and the amount or type of reward.
4. The teacher watches for the specified behavior to occur and then rewards the student according to the terms of the contract.

A sample contingency contract is presented in Figure 5.5.

A contingency contract should represent an agreement between the student and the teacher. The terms should be stated clearly in a positive manner and should be fair for both the student and the teacher.

After both parties have signed the contract, the conditions should be monitored frequently to assess progress. In addition, all parts of the contract should be followed systematically, and the student should receive reinforcement as soon as the contract is completed.

Various types of contracts can be used. The agreement may or may not specify a time limit within which the required behavior must be performed. Intermittent reinforcers can be used in long-term contracts, and steps toward the desired behavior can be rewarded. Contracts also can include agreements between the student and other school personnel or parents. Group contracts can be used in which the entire class agrees to behave in a certain manner or perform a specified task by a designated date, and the teacher agrees to reward students who fulfill the agreement. Contingency contracting thus can promote desirable social or academic actions by involving students in managing their own behavior.

Token Systems

Token reinforcement systems are used widely in behavior modification and have been validated empirically for increasing desired behaviors of students with disabilities (Alter, Wyrick, Brown, & Lingo, 2008). These systems have three basic characteristics: (1) Behaviors to be reinforced are stated clearly, (2) procedures are devised for giving out a reinforcing stimulus (i.e., token) when the target behavior occurs, and (3) a set of rules is explained to govern the exchange of tokens for reinforcing objects or events.

FIGURE 5.5
A sample contingency contract

CONTRACT

Beginning date: _10/21_____

Ending date: _10/25_____

STUDENT: I agree to _finish my math seatwork during math period on Monday, Tuesday, Wednesday, and Thursday._

Signed _Timmy_____

TEACHER: I agree to _give Timmy free time during math period on Friday._

Signed _Mrs. Jackson_____

A *token* is an item given to a student immediately after a target behavior occurs. Usually the tokens have little intrinsic value, but they acquire value when they can be exchanged for a desired object or activity. Tokens can consist of play money, trading stamps, poker chips, stars, or any other object that is easy to dispense and store. These tokens can be accumulated and then exchanged for a desired object or activity. A classroom store can be established where, at designated times, each student may purchase reinforcers by trading in earned tokens. Objects (e.g., balloons, comics, jewelry, sports trading cards, pennies, coloring books, and magazines) and activities (e.g., playing a game, listening to records, coloring, and watching a filmstrip) can be available in the store. A reward menu can be posted, listing the store items and their costs (e.g., listening to records for 10 minutes = 10 tokens; purchasing a baseball trading card = 15 tokens).

Token systems have several advantages. First, they avoid boredom because tokens can be traded for a variety of reinforcing objects or events. Second, a token system is useful with students who generally do not respond to social reinforcement. Third, tokens are administered easily, and the number can be adjusted to reflect the time and energy required to perform the target behavior. Fourth, token systems help students appreciate the relationship between desirable behavior and reinforcement. Students learn that behavior has consequences, which is likely to enhance self-control.

Blackham and Silberman (1980) stress that a token system must be developed and applied thoughtfully. They also report that problems should be expected at first, and the teacher will have to refine the system. Blackham and Silberman suggest guidelines for planning and using a token system.

- The target behaviors that earn tokens should be specified clearly. For example, individual behaviors can be posted on a student's desk. Rules governing group behavior contingencies should be reviewed frequently.
- The reinforcers that the tokens are exchanged for must be appealing and available *only* within the token system.
- The number of tokens earned must match the effort required for performing the target behavior. If a student has great difficulty staying on task during math seatwork, the reward for staying on task must be sufficient to encourage on-task behavior.
- If possible, the teacher should keep a record of the number of tokens each student and the group earn. This type of record often provides an additional incentive to students.
- If *response cost* (i.e., token fines) is used, the conditions under which tokens are earned and lost must

be specified clearly. Awarding and taking away tokens always must be related to student *behavior.* Arguments about token loss should be avoided.

- A scheduled token exchange at the end of the day usually works best.
- The system should be devised so that there is self-competition rather than competition with others.
- A well-planned token system gradually should withdraw material reinforcers and stress reinforcing activities and events. Also, praise should be combined with the tokens so that social reinforcement eventually can be used alone to maintain desirable behaviors.
- The token system should be simple, functional, and not distracting to the learning process. In school, check-mark tokens are often the easiest to use. Each student is given a card, and the teacher puts checks on it as they are earned. A special pen can be used to distinguish these checks. Other students cannot use a student's card, whereas tangible tokens might be traded or stolen.

Extrinsic Reinforcement

Many disruptive or aggressive students need extrinsic reinforcers to establish the habits of appropriate behavior. Once these habits are developed in caring environments, effort should be made to help them become intrinsically motivated. Table 5.7 provides some advantages and disadvantages of several extrinsic reinforcers.

Sprick (2001) provides the following guidelines for changing a behavior during spontaneous interventions.

- Reinforce students who are doing the behavior in an appropriate manner.
- When a misbehaving student begins to behave, reinforce the student.
- Provide fun activities for the whole class.
- Provide fun activities for a student who improves in behavior or academic performance.

Sprick recommends the following modifications when the behavior improves.

- Require more of the desired behavior for the same amount of reinforcement.
- When the behavior has reached the appropriate level of success, reinforce less frequently and less immediately.

myeducationlab

Go to the Assignments and Activities section of the Topic Promoting Social and Emotional Development in the MyEducationLab for your course and complete the activity entitled Conflict Resolution by Students.

TABLE 5.7
Advantages and disadvantages of extrinsic reinforcers

Type and Definition of Reinforcer	Advantages	Disadvantages
Tangible—a physical object given for appropriate behavior Examples: popcorn, crackers, stickers, pencils, books, coupons, and mazes	Are very desirable Are highly reinforcing	Must be purchased May teach incorrect associations Should be paired with praise Are temporary and should be switched to social praise as soon as possible
Token—an item, given for appropriate behavior, that can be exchanged at a later time for rewards (e.g., toys, food, or games), which may be displayed in a classroom store Examples: points, poker chips, stars, trading stamps, and play money	Are a concrete means for immediate reinforcement Provide a record of accomplishments Do not interfere with class routines	Require much organization Require planning, time, and energy to use Require an assortment of backup items May not generalize Create dependency on concrete reinforcement
Social—a social behavior provided contingent on appropriate behavior Examples: gestures (e.g., smile, wink, thumbs up, and eye contact), verbal approval (e.g., praise and encouragement), and touch (e.g., hug, shoulder pat, handshake, and high-five)	Easy to use Require little teacher effort Are always available Rarely cause criticism Are powerful reinforcers	Are sometimes not powerful enough
Activity—an action that students get to do as a reward for appropriate behavior Examples: eat lunch with teacher, run errands, have free time, lead the line, pass out books, and use the computer	Are readily available Can be combined with social reinforcers Can be built into class routines	May delay gratification May interrupt other activities

- When delayed reinforcement has successfully maintained the desired behavior, begin to modify the reinforcement by using a less powerful reinforcer or one closer to intrinsic reinforcement.
- When the behavior has been maintained successfully with a less powerful reinforcer, switch from a continuous reinforcer to an intermittent reinforcer.

Punishment

Unfortunately, some people tend to equate discipline with punishment. An effective classroom management plan, however, focuses on prevention or proactive strategies and minimizes the use of punishment. Sprick (2001) and Whelan (1996) maintain that an emphasis on punishment is inappropriate for the following reasons.

- Punishment focuses on decreasing an inappropriate behavior rather than on teaching an appropriate behavior.
- Punishment can be self-defeating and result in such complications as poor self-image or revenge.
- Students may become anxious and learn to lie, cheat, or steal to avoid punishment. Also, anxiety interferes with learning.
- Punishment is effective only while the threat is present, and it does not eliminate the desire to engage in misbehavior.

Overall, effective classroom management does not stress punishing the misbehavior but emphasizes its correction. When misbehavior occurs, the teacher works with the student to solve it.

Although punishment is not a preferred approach, it is needed periodically as a transition strategy for students who frequently engage in misbehavior. Kame'enui et al. (1995) note that punishment serves as a transition strategy to restore a safe and productive learning environment. Some of the advantages of punishment highlight its usefulness as a transition strategy. For example, punishment can be powerful if used effectively, and, although the behavior change may be temporary, punishment can reduce disruptive behavior rapidly. Also, punishment can provide information to the misbehaving student and other students about what is acceptable and unacceptable.

Punishment Prevention Strategies Some generic prevention strategies are discussed in the general techniques section of this chapter. Most of these strategies focus on good teaching and effective intervention skills. This section presents some low-energy strategies that help prevent the need for punishment. Punishment prevention strategies include the following:

1. *Ensure the task is appropriate*—The task must be within the student's ability to perform if the student tries.
2. *Give more attention to appropriate behavior than to inappropriate behavior*—The teacher should maintain a 3:1 attending ratio for positive events versus negative events in the classroom (Sprick, 2001).
3. *Reinforce students who are following the rules*—This provides examples of acceptable behavior to all students.
4. *Use gentle verbal reminders*—A gentle verbal reminder involves reminding the student of the rule that is not being followed. The reminder is delivered in an instructional manner: Eye contact is limited, body language is relaxed, voice is calm, and it happens quickly and in a matter-of-fact manner. In delivering a gentle verbal reminder, the teacher might say, "Please remember to raise your hand if you wish to speak." Giving a gentle verbal reminder provides all students with an example of unacceptable behavior.
5. *Use proximity control*—The teacher can move to stand near the student who is misbehaving or is about to misbehave. Also, students who are prone to misbehave should be seated close to the area where the teacher spends the most time.
6. *Discuss the problem with the student*—The teacher should discuss the misbehavior with the student at a neutral time. The discussion may simply involve requesting the student to stop the misbehavior. More involved discussions usually focus on a problem-solving approach in which the pair discusses appropriate alternative behaviors or creative plans for the situation.
7. *Use a precorrection strategy for teaching appropriate behavior*—Colvin, Sugai, and Patching (1993) note that correction is reactive, focuses on consequences, stresses misbehavior, and deals with immediate events, whereas precorrection is proactive, stresses appropriate behavior, focuses on antecedents, and deals with future events. They maintain that correction often leads to more misbehavior, whereas precorrection enhances appropriate behavior. A seven-step precorrection plan is featured in Table 5.8.
8. *Ignore mild misbehavior*—The teacher should ignore behavior that is mildly disruptive (e.g., talking to others) if it does not occur frequently. Guidelines for teachers to use when ignoring misbehavior include the following:

- Ignore only what you feel comfortable ignoring.
- Ignore behavior that is displayed primarily for teacher attention.
- When ignoring, pretend the student is not present.

TABLE 5.8

Seven-step precorrection plan

Precorrection Steps	Example
1. Identify context for the predictable behavior.	Students enter the classroom immediately after lunch. (Predictable behavior: Students talking loudly, laughing, and moving around before following teacher directions.)
2. Specify expected behavior.	Students should enter the room quietly, go quickly to their desks, and begin a specified task.
3. Modify the context.	The teacher meets students at the classroom door, waits until they are quiet, and then allows them to go to their desks to begin work.
4. Conduct behavior rehearsal.	The teacher reminds students before lunch of the expected behavior following lunch. A student can be called on to explain the expected behavior.
5. Provide strong reinforcement for expected behavior.	The teacher tells the students that if they follow the teacher's requests, they will have an additional break or an extra 5 minutes at recess.
6. Prompt expected behavior.	The teacher gives a signal at the door to be quiet and points to the activity on the chalkboard. The teacher praises students who are beginning work.
7. Monitor the plan.	The teacher times how long it takes for all students to begin work and counts how many students begin the task within 10 seconds.

- Prior to ignoring, tell the class or student that you will use ignoring.
- Be aware that effective ignoring usually results in an increase in the misbehavior before the misbehavior decreases.

Punishment Strategies Punishment strategies may be viewed on a continuum from least intrusive (i.e., least energy consuming) to most intrusive (i.e., most energy consuming). Kame'enui et al. (1995) provide a low-energy to high-energy continuum of punishments that features the following sequence: verbal reprimands, quiet time, owing time, nonexclusionary time out, exclusionary time out, and third-party sanctions. Figure 5.6 displays a continuum of preventive strategies and punishment strategies.

Punishment strategies include the following:

1. *Verbal reprimands*—Reprimands conducted calmly and briefly can be effective and unobtrusive. Guidelines for implementing verbal reprimands include the following:

- During the reprimand, specify the inappropriate behavior.
- Pair the reprimand with a consequence.
- When reprimanding, stand close to the student or talk so that others do not hear.
- Follow reprimands with reinforcement.

2. *Quiet time*—Quiet time allows the student to think about the misbehavior and its consequences and to consider appropriate alternative behaviors. To implement quiet time, the following procedures are used.

- Instruct the student immediately to stop the inappropriate behavior.
- Instruct the student to remain quiet.
- Enforce quiet time for 1 or 2 minutes.
- Instruct the student to resume the assigned task.
- Reinforce appropriate behavior.

3. *Owing time*—This strategy is based on the rationale that misbehavior uses learning time and this

FIGURE 5.6

A continuum of preventive strategies and punishment strategies

High energy	Request suspension Send note to parents Send student to the principal or counselor Send student to another teacher's room

Punishment Strategies:
- Third-party sanctions
- Exclusionary time out
- Nonexclusionary time out
- Owing time
- Quiet time
- Verbal reprimands

Preventive Strategies:
- Ignoring
- Precorrection
- Discussion of problem
- Proximity control
- Gentle verbal reminders
- Reinforcement of others
- Attending ratio
- Appropriate tasks

Low energy

time must be paid back. Guidelines for implementing owing time include the following:

- Specify behaviors that lead to owing time.
- Prior to implementing owing time, discuss the rationale for the strategy and how it will be conducted.
- Determine the amount of time the student owes. Requiring the student to pay back the amount of time that the misbehavior took away from learning deserves consideration.
- Specify when the student will pay back time.
- Determine what learning activity the student will engage in during payback time.

4. *Nonexclusionary time out*—Time out is a procedure in which access to sources of reinforcement is removed. Some examples of nonexclusionary time out are student's head on desk, lights turned off, removal of materials from student, and removal of student from group but allowing student to watch (i.e., contingent observation).

5. *Exclusionary time out*—This procedure is more obtrusive than nonexclusionary time out and involves the student moving to a new location. Examples of exclusionary time out include placing the student in another part of the room, having the student sit in a chair in the corner of the room, and having the student sit in a chair outside the classroom door. Finally, seclusion time out involves placing the student in a specially designed isolation room for a short period of time. Guidelines for implementing exclusionary time out include the following:

- Always administer time out calmly.
- Specify punishable behaviors.
- Establish time-out procedures and locations for exclusionary and seclusion time outs.
- State inappropriate behavior and direct the student to take a time out.
- Lead younger children to the time-out area.
- Keep track of time for exclusionary and seclusion time outs. Recommended time is 3 minutes or less.

6. *Third-party sanctions*—Third-party sanctions are high cost in energy and time and involve other school personnel or parents. Third-party sanctions include the following:

- *Send student to another teacher's room.* Prior to using this strategy, the following procedures are arranged with another teacher: The student enters the new class without disruption and goes to a designated seat; students in both classrooms are instructed to ignore the student at all times, and after a specified time, the student returns to the original class without disruption.
- *Send student to the principal or counselor.* This strategy results in instant removal from the room; however, it may be reinforcing and communicate that the teacher has lost control.
- *Send note to parents.* An advantage of this strategy is that it keeps parents informed; however, the note may result in severe punishment by the parents, or the student may be reinforced by the attention.
- *Request suspension.* The teacher should be aware of the school policies and procedures for suspension. Disadvantages of suspension are that it may be reinforcing, it may negatively affect the student's self-image, and it does not teach appropriate behavior.

General Guidelines for Punishment

The following are general guidelines for using punishment effectively.

- Specify acceptable and unacceptable behavior.
- Be as consistent as possible in implementing punishment.
- Always implement punishment with a concurrent plan of positive reinforcement.
- Administer punishment calmly and quickly (e.g., limit the consequence statement to no more than 3 seconds).
- Establish punishment for as few behaviors as possible.
- Always treat students with respect.
- Monitor punishment to ensure that it is decreasing the target misbehavior.

Techniques for Managing Surface Behaviors

Long and Newman discuss techniques for managing surface behaviors (e.g., laughing, passing notes, talking out of turn, humming, and pencil tapping) (Maag, 2001). The following strategies for responding to minor misbehaviors can help prevent the buildup of behavior problems.

1. *Planned ignoring*—Many behaviors will stop if they are ignored rather than given teacher attention.
2. *Signal interference*—The use of a cue (such as finger snapping) can alert the student to stop a particular behavior.

3. *Proximity control*—Some disruptive behavior can be prevented by the teacher's presence in the area of potential trouble.

4. *Interest boosting*—Some behaviors can be managed when the teacher shows a genuine interest in the student as an individual (e.g., pay specific attention to the student's work).

5. *Tension reduction through humor*—A humorous remark by the teacher can release tension in an emotional situation.

6. *Hurdle lessons*—The teacher can lessen frustration by providing individual academic assistance (e.g., offering to help with a specific task).

7. *Support from routine*—A familiar routine can provide support to the student.

8. *Direct appeal to value areas*—The teacher needs to be aware of the student's personal values to appeal to them.

9. *Removing seductive objects*—Items that distract the student can be removed from the classroom to avoid provoking disruptive behavior.

10. *Antiseptic bouncing*—The student can be removed from the classroom without punishment (e.g., ask the student to run an errand).

BEHAVIORAL DEVELOPMENT ACTIVITIES

Disruptive behavior in the classroom includes actions that interfere with instruction or activities of an individual or a group. Inappropriate talking out and out-of-seat behaviors frequently disrupt the classroom. Moreover, the use of sarcasm, swear words, and temper tantrums are disturbing behaviors that need to be modified. The following activities focus on managing disruptive behavior.

• As much as possible, ignore disruptions and reward the student's complying behaviors. For example, when a student talks out during class, completely ignore the student and do not respond to what is said; however, when the student raises a hand during class, immediately recognize the student and praise the behavior. This is effective only if teacher attention is reinforcing. It may be necessary also to control peer attention to the inappropriate behavior.

• Ignore out-of-seat behaviors and give verbal praise to students who remain in their seats. Students who remain seated during work periods can be rewarded by being allowed to participate in a game involving movement (e.g., musical chairs or kickball).

• Use a timer to see how long an active student can stay seated. Time the student at various intervals during the day and reward the student for remaining seated during the interval. Record progress on a graph so that the student competes to improve the behavior. As the student progresses, gradually increase the time interval for staying seated.

• Give periodic breaks that allow the active student out-of-seat time. The student may be given errands to run, during which the student can move around or leave the room.

• Devise contingency contracts in which the student agrees to stay seated for a period of time; if the student does so, the teacher agrees to reward the student with some free out-of-seat time (such as extra recess). Likewise, a student can agree in a contract not to talk out during class for a specific amount of time in return for the reward of free talking time.

• Cut out a figure of the student that includes a large pocket and tape it to the wall. Whenever the student behaves appropriately, place a chip or token in the figure's pocket. When the student engages in an inappropriate behavior (e.g., out of seat, talking out, or use of swear words), remove a chip from the pocket. At the end of each day the chips can be traded for a reinforcing activity (e.g., free time, playing a game, or watching a filmstrip).

• To reduce swearing, suggest to the student other words that can be used (e.g., *darn*, *heck*, or *shoot*). Provide reinforcement every time the student refrains from swearing and uses another word.

• Use a graph to record the number of swear words or sarcastic remarks made by the student during a specific time period. This will call attention to the inappropriate remarks. Have the student compete to improve progress, and reinforce the student for improved behavior.

• When a student begins a temper tantrum, immediately remove the student to a time-out area in which the student is isolated from the teacher and peers. When the student is able to remain quiet, allow him or her to return to the classroom. In this way, the student receives little attention for inappropriate behavior. Also, be aware of the chain of behavior that leads the student to an outburst or tantrum. Apply time out or another management technique before the chain has gone too far.

• At the beginning of the day, make 15 numbered marks on the chalkboard. Explain to the class that they have an opportunity to have a 15-minute recess at the end of the day. However, for each disruptive behavior, one mark is erased from the board. At the end of the day, give the class the number of minutes of extra recess remaining on the board. Instead of recess, the minutes can be used in a special game, story time, or field trips.

INSTRUCTIONAL GAMES IN BEHAVIORAL DEVELOPMENT

Game formats can be used to enable the teacher and students to focus on appropriate behaviors (e.g., staying on task, raising a hand to talk, or remaining seated). The following games are designed to promote behavioral development.

Picture Puzzle Game

Materials: A large picture of something the student is interested in or wants, which is cut into pieces.

Directions: Encourage appropriate behavior over a period of time by rewarding the student with a requested item or activity. The student and teacher agree on the desired behavior to be reinforced and the type of reward. Each time the student shows the desired behavior, the teacher provides a piece of the picture puzzle. Each time inappropriate behavior is observed, the teacher takes away a puzzle piece. When all the puzzle pieces to the picture are received, the student is reinforced by receiving the reward.

Work Around the Circle

Materials: Classroom chairs arranged in a circle; a timer.

Directions: Set a timer to ring at various times during intervals of from 1 to 4 minutes. When the timer rings, each student who is working may move to the next chair. Students who are caught not working must remain in their seats for that turn. Thus, students who are working appropriately rotate around the circle. When a student has completed the circle, the teacher should check the assignment and give the student free time until all students have worked their way back to their own seats.

The Principal's Game

(Paine et al., 1983)

Materials: Timer; chalkboard area for recording points.

Directions: Use this game to improve the behavior of a disruptive class of students. Begin by telling students they need to work harder and that there is a game that can help them. In the game, teams are formed according to seating clusters or rows (i.e., one team for each row or cluster). A timer is set to ring six times during the class or day. Each time it rings, the teacher determines which teams are following classroom rules and working. If all team members are working, the whole team receives a point; however, if one or more members are not working, no points are awarded. To win, a team must receive a minimum of five points, and it is possible for all teams to win. At the end of the day or class, invite the principal to come into the room and recognize the winning teams and praise their work. In addition to the principal, other significant people (e.g., counselor, another teacher, local sports figure, or parent) can be asked to visit and recognize winning teams.

Behavior Monopoly

Materials: A game board similar to a Monopoly board that has a variety of reinforcers (including some booby prizes) written in the squares; a die; student markers.

Directions: Use the game board (see Figure 5.7) to provide the student with some type of reinforcement. Randomly identify a student displaying an appropriate behavior. Allow the student to roll the die and move the marker on the board. The student receives the reinforcer indicated on the space where the marker lands. The marker is left on that space so that it can be moved the next time the student gets to play.

Suggested Chance Cards: Arm wrestle with teacher; Hop on one foot for 5 seconds; Send note to a friend; Hug the teacher; Pick up trash.

Speed Chase

Materials: Poster board with large speedometer dial drawn on it; cardboard arrows, each of which has a student's name on it; various small prizes.

Directions: Allow groups of students to compete to see who can complete the most classwork accurately during the day. After the teacher has checked an assignment, each student attaches an arrow to the speedometer to indicate the number of items the student performed correctly on the task. The speed on the speedometer increases according to the number of correct items on each assignment. At the end of the day, the student with the highest speed wins and picks a prize.

Modifications: Rather than competing in all subject areas for an entire day, students can record their speed in one subject area for several days. Also, the speedometer can be used to record specific behaviors during the day, such as staying in seat or raising a hand instead of talking out. Two students who need to change the same behavior can compete. Each time the student displays the appropriate behavior, the teacher moves the student's arrow on the speedometer; the arrow is moved *back* for inappropriate behavior. The student with the highest speed at the end of the day wins the speed chase.

The Lottery

(Paine et al., 1983)

Materials: Prerecorded tape with randomly spaced "beeps"; tape recorder; space on chalkboard for recording checks by students' names.

Directions: Hold a daily lottery in which students work for the opportunity of having their names drawn at random. During the day, play a tape with six randomly distributed "beeps." Students who are following classroom rules

FIGURE 5.7
Behavior Monopoly
game board

Pick chance card	Trip to water fountain	Listen to record	Teacher's helper today	Read a magazine
Get two snacks		BEHAVIOR MONOPOLY		Free pick
Trip to library				10 seconds of applause
Choose prize				Throw darts at target
Go back 5 spaces	Have picture taken	Line leader		5 minutes free time

(e.g., on task, seated, and quiet) when the beep sounds receive a check by their names on the chalkboard. Students who receive five or six checks in a day are eligible for the daily drawing. At the end of the day, two names are selected from the qualifying students. The principal or teacher phones the respective parents and tells them about their child's good behavior.

Good Behavior Game

Materials: Tally chart.

Directions: Divide the class into two teams and explain that talking out and out-of-seat behaviors are going to be recorded. Whenever a student engages in either behavior, place a mark on the tally sheet for the student's team. At the end of the day, the team with the fewest marks wins. If both teams have fewer than six marks, the whole class wins. The members of the winning team receive a previously agreed upon reward. If both teams win, reward the entire class with a 30-minute special project period.

Timer Game

Materials: Timer; point chart; prizes.

Directions: Set the timer to ring at least once during a range of from 1 to 40 minutes. Each student who is seated when the timer rings is awarded five points. Each student's earned points are recorded on a point chart. At the end of a specified time period, the points may be traded in for prizes such as snacks or privileges.

COMMERCIAL BEHAVIORAL DEVELOPMENT PROGRAMS

Various commercial materials help the teacher focus on managing the behavior of disruptive students. The following commercial programs are designed to promote behavioral development.

Cooperative Discipline

Cooperative Discipline, developed by L. Albert (published by Pearson), provides a realistic, positive approach to discipline and classroom management. The system affirms students but insists that they share responsibility for their behavior. The program offers effective strategies for dealing with aggressive and difficult students, and it features a conflict resolution process that resolves teacher–student and student–student problems. *Cooperative Discipline*, which is available in either an elementary or secondary package, develops a classroom climate based on caring, clear limits, consistency, and respect. The materials include a teacher's handbook, an overview video, an implementation guide, and ten posters.

The Teacher's Encyclopedia of Behavior Management; CHAMPs

The Teacher's Encyclopedia of Behavior Management (Sprick & Howard, 1995) provides practical, positive solutions to common classroom problems in kindergarten through ninth grade. More than 100 specific problem behaviors, such as absenteeism, blaming others, sloppy work, fighting, and cheating, are included. For each misbehavior, up to six detailed step-by-step plans are offered to present effective interventions that teachers can choose from or modify to fit the origin, duration, and severity of the actual situation. A companion book, *CHAMPs* (Sprick, Garrison, & Howard, 1998), assists teachers in designing a classroom management plan that overtly teaches students to behave responsibly. Eight modules (such as organization, expectations, motivation, and correction procedures) focus on varying aspects of classroom organization and behavior management. The implication steps and procedures are supported by school effectiveness research literature related to classroom and behavior management.

PERSPECTIVE ON SOCIAL, EMOTIONAL, AND BEHAVIORAL DEVELOPMENT

Academic difficulties clearly cause frustration, anxiety, low self-concept, and mood swings. The degree to which these academic learning problems contribute to social, emotional, and behavioral aberrations is difficult to ascertain. An understanding of academic and social, emotional, and behavioral problems is complicated further by the position that such problems can interfere with academic learning. Certain educators continue to debate the academic deficiency/behavioral disorder relationship. Which occurred first? Which caused the other? Does the student primarily have emotional disabilities or learning problems? Moreover, some students exhibit social or emotional disabilities yet maintain excellent academic progress. These conditions and their related questions are complex, and until precise causes and valid diagnostic procedures are developed, they will continue to generate controversy. Meanwhile, perhaps the best strategy involves the direct treatment of target behaviors and the placement of youngsters in settings that provide earned success, reasonable structure, and sensitive support. This chapter offers information (i.e., assessment practices and intervention procedures) aimed at facilitating an appropriate education for students with learning problems who also have social, emotional, or behavioral problems.

The disintegration of the family and its supportive structures combines with increasing crime, violence, child abuse, and substance abuse to remind educators that perhaps at no other time in the history of civilization has it been more important for school personnel to provide safe and caring environments for students. Whelan (1996, p. 309) discusses the need for intervention and treatment to help students develop prosocial styles of relating to others:

> The schools cannot do it alone. Schools must use an interagency approach, involving all of the social service disciplines, in order to proactively respond to the problems and to provide assistance at every point in the student's life. Why should the schools be responsible for prevention and intervention programs? Because normal and dysfunctional behavior grow from the same roots, we prevent and remedy student behavior problems by meeting developmental needs. Thus, according to Brendtro and Long (1995), the four "A's" of reclaiming school ethos are

> attachment: Positive social bonds are prerequisites to prosocial behavior,

> achievement: Setting high expectations means refusing to accept failure,

> autonomy: True discipline lies in demanding responsibility rather than obedience, and

> altruism: Through helping others, young people find proof of their own self-worth.

Assessing and Teaching Language

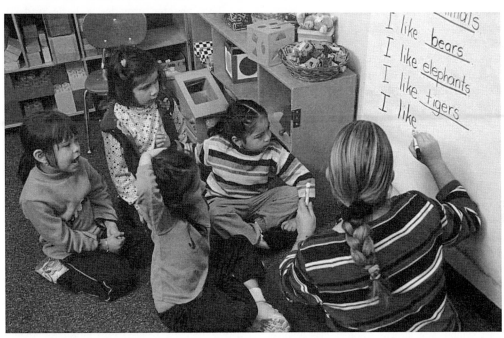

T. Lindfors/Lindfors Photography

From Chapter 6 of *Teaching Students with Learning Problems*, 8/e. Cecil D. Mercer. Ann R. Mercer. Paige C. Pullen. Copyright © 2011 by Pearson Education. All rights reserved.

Oral language is a learned behavior that enables people to transmit their ideas and culture from generation to generation. The ability to communicate through language is perhaps an individual's most vital and complex characteristic. It is through speech and language that people make sense of and respond to their environment. A communication problem can be devastating because it directly affects the individual as well as others in the immediate environment as attempts are made to transmit ideas, facts, feelings, and desires. Language also is related directly to achievement and adjustment in school because it forms the basis for formulating questions, comprehending information, and facilitating understanding in new learning situations. In addition to being part of the academic curriculum, language is a medium through which information is taught and acquired.

Language is defined as "a socially shared code or conventional system for representing concepts through the use of arbitrary symbols and rule-governed combinations of those symbols" (Owens, 2008, p. 4). In contrast, *speech* involves the actual mechanics or motor act of verbal expression. Thus, whereas speech includes spoken utterances to convey meaning, language indicates a person's knowledge of the linguistic concepts on which speech is based. Moreover, language comprises receptive skills (i.e., understanding) and expressive skills (i.e., use) and includes both written and oral forms.

A variety of terms may be used with youngsters who do not acquire language at a normal rate. Terms such as *specific language impairment, language delay,* and *language disorder* generally are used with students who are having difficulty learning language in the absence of any intellectual, sensory, or emotional problems. The American Speech-Language-Hearing Association (1992, p. 949) provides the following definition of *language disorder:*

> A language disorder is the impairment or deviant development of comprehension and/or use of a spoken, written, and/or other symbol system. The disorder may involve (1) the form of language (phonologic, morphologic, and syntactic systems), (2) the content of language (semantic system), and/or (3) the function of language in communication (pragmatic system) in any combination.

The term *language disorder* generally is used when a student exhibits difficulty learning language or is learning language in a nontypical sequence. However, the initial manifestation of a language disorder is generally a delay in language development. Thus, in practice, the distinction is not clear, and the terms *language disorder* and *language delay* often are used interchangeably. As Lahey (1988) states, "It is not always easy to determine whether a child's system is qualitatively different from that of any non-language-impaired child at some point in development" (p. 21).

Students with severe language impairments usually are identified at an early age and receive speech or language therapy through a prekindergarten or developmental program. A greater number of students possess a more subtle language problem and begin to show difficulties as they grow older. As curriculum demands increase in about the third or fourth grade, these students lack the language foundation required to build academic skills. Teachers often describe such students as having difficulty maintaining attention, following directions, and using the right words when speaking. Other students are identified when they begin to have difficulties in academic subjects such as reading and writing. These students need an informed classroom teacher who can identify and understand their language problems and help them receive appropriate intervention.

This chapter provides a basic understanding of language disorders in students with learning problems. Theories of language acquisition and the major components of language are discussed. Language difficulties at various stages in a student's life are included, as well as a discussion of issues involving the language skills of bilingual and culturally diverse students. Moreover, assessment techniques, service delivery models, and teaching strategies are provided. Finally, language activities, instructional games, self-correcting materials, commercial programs, and computer software programs are described.

Although certain language skills are discussed separately in this chapter, they should be understood in the context of their interactiveness and pervasive impact on a student's learning and academic success. Language is viewed as interacting with other cognitive constructs and is best assessed and remediated as a whole in social communication rather than as isolated language skills. To ensure academic success for students with language problems, the teacher and language specialist should consult each other and work cooperatively.

THEORIES OF LANGUAGE ACQUISITION

Theories of language acquisition fall within three major camps: behavioristic, nativistic (or psycholinguistic), and interactionistic (or cognitive). The behavioristic position (Skinner, 1957) relies on learning principles to explain language acquisition. Braine (1971), Jenkins and Palermo (1964), and Staats (1971) are proponents of the behavioristic position. Behaviorists believe that the infant begins with no knowledge of language but possesses the ability to learn it. The child learns through reinforcement of imitation. Reinforcement of babbling (including parental attention and delight) and the shaping of vocal behavior account for the initial stages of learning. Behaviorists emphasize environmental influences and the universal laws of learning, namely operant conditioning principles.

Chomsky (1965), Lenneberg (1967), and McNeil (1970) are proponents of the nativistic position. Chomsky claims that the child possesses an innate capacity for dealing with linguistic universals. The child generates a theory of grammar to help understand and produce an infinite number of sentences. Lenneberg states that the child is biologically predisposed to learn language as the brain matures. Nativistics believe that humans are "prewired" for language development and that the environment simply triggers its emergence. Language programs that teach rules for sentence transformations represent the nativistic model.

Piaget (1960), the major proponent of the interactionistic position, theorizes that the child acquires language through the interaction of perceptual-cognitive capacities and experiences. The child's environment and neurological maturation determine learning. Language and thought thus develop simultaneously as the child passes through a series of fixed developmental stages requiring more and more complex strategies of cognitive organization. Interactionists consider the capacity for language to be innate; however, unlike the nativist, the interactionist believes the child must internalize linguistic structures from the environment and must become aware of communication's social functions. Thus, language programs in the interactionistic model are based on two ideas: (1) Meaning is brought to a child's language through interaction with the environment, and (2) the child uses speech to control the environment. Intervention approaches based on this model emphasize natural language teaching rather than structured exercises and drills.

On the one hand, the biologists (Lenneberg, 1967) and the linguists (Chomsky, 1965) view the child as a product of the maturation process. Biologists and linguists believe that, unless physical or mental complications occur, the child's development is predetermined. This view places heavy emphasis on the child, who is considered to be biologically prepared or linguistically preprogrammed to develop language. On the other hand, behaviorists stress the influence of the environment. The child's development depends largely on the individuals in the child's environment who respond to his or her behavior. The interactionistic position emphasizes the child's active interactions with the environment as he or she learns to talk.

Primarily through the work of Wiig and Semel, language intervention has focused on the linguistic model, with direct concern about language functioning through analyzing comprehension and performance according to the components of language (such as phonology) and their rules. The linguistic model has served as the basis for the creation of many language programs. These programs usually focus on a particular language skill that the student should possess. Although the content of these programs is similar (i.e., phonemes and morphemes), some are founded in behavioral theory, some in nativism, and some in interactionism.

COMPONENTS OF LANGUAGE

Language refers to "a code whereby ideas about the world are expressed through a conventional system of arbitrary signals for communication" (Lahey, 1988, p. 2). Speakers and listeners both are involved in oral language because language is heard as well as spoken. A speaker's use of this arbitrary vocal system to communicate ideas and thoughts to a listener is referred to as *expressive language,* or *production.* In this process the listener uses *receptive language,* or *comprehension.* Students with expressive language difficulties may be reluctant to participate in verbal activities, whereas students with receptive language problems may have difficulty following directions or understanding content presented orally.

To assess and plan instruction for language problems, the teacher needs to be familiar with the components of language (see Table 6.1). A common classification system organizes the components of language according to form (i.e., phonology, morphology, and syntax), content (i.e., semantics), and use (i.e., pragmatics). These language components are distinct but interrelated and interactive.

Form: Phonology

Phonology is the system of rules governing sounds and sound combinations; a *phoneme* is a unit of sound that combines with other sounds to form words. A phoneme is the smallest unit of language and is distinguished from the other language components in that a phoneme alone, such as /s/ or /b/, does not convey meaning. However, when interchanged in a word, phonemes significantly alter meaning (e.g., *sat* to *bat*). The rules governing phonemes focus on how sounds can be used in different word positions and which sounds may be combined. For example, standard English does not have a sound for the combination /zt/.

The English language consists of about 44 phonemes, classified as either vowels or consonants. Vowels are

TABLE 6.1
Components of language

Component	Definition	Receptive Level	Expressive Level
Phonology	The sound system of a language and the linguistic rules that govern the sound combinations	Discrimination of speech sounds	Articulation of speech sounds
Morphology	The linguistic rule system that governs the structure of words and the construction of word forms from the basic elements of meaning	Understanding of grammatical structure of words	Use of grammar in words
Syntax	The linguistic rule system that governs the order and combination of words to form sentences, and the relationships among the elements within a sentence	Understanding of phrases and sentences	Use of grammar in phrases and sentences
Semantics	The psycholinguistic system that patterns the content of an utterance, intent, and meanings of words and sentences	Understanding of word meanings and word relationships	Use of word meanings and word relationships
Pragmatics	The sociolinguistic system that patterns the use of language in communication, which may be expressed motorically, vocally, or verbally	Understanding of contextual language cues	Use of language in context

Source: From *Students with Learning Disabilities* (p. 210), 7th ed., by C. D. Mercer and P. C. Pullen, 2009, Upper Saddle River, NJ: Merrill/Pearson. Copyright 2009 by Pearson Education. Reprinted by permission.

categorized according to where they are produced in the mouth. The tongue may be moved up, down, forward, or backward in producing vowels. These different tongue positions are used to classify vowels as high, mid, or low (i.e., the position of the highest part of the tongue) and front, central, or back (i.e., the location of the highest position) (Owens, 2006). For example, the long /e/ sound is classified as high front because the tongue blade is high in the front of the mouth. The tip of the tongue is down for all vowels. Consonants are classified according to place and manner of articulation. For example, the phoneme /f/ can be described by place (e.g., labiodental—lower lip touches upper incisors) and manner (e.g., unvoiced fricative—narrow constriction through which the air must pass, creating a hissing noise).

Jacobson and Halle (1956) propose three principles that influence the order of phoneme acquisition.

1. Children learn first to distinguish sounds that have the fewest features in common, such as oral-nasal (e.g., /p/, /m/), labial-dental (e.g., /p/, /t/), and stop-fricative (e.g., /p/, /f/).
2. Development of front consonants such as /p/ and /m/ precedes the development of back consonants such as /k/ and /g/.
3. Phonemes that occur infrequently among the languages of the world (such as the English short /a/ in *bat*) are the last to be acquired, even though they may be frequent in the child's native language.

Owens (2006) notes that vowels are acquired by the age of 3, whereas consonant clusters and blends are not acquired until age 7 or 8. However, there are individual differences, and the age of acquisition for some sounds may vary by as much as 3 years.

Phonological Deficits Problems in phonology frequently appear as articulation disorders, most commonly in the child who is developmentally delayed in consonant acquisition. The child may omit a consonant (such as saying "oo" for *you*), substitute one consonant for another (such as saying "wabbit" for *rabbit*), or distort a consonant. An example of a consonant distortion is the lateral emission of air in the production of /s/ in which the air escapes over the sides of the tongue (rather than the tip), resulting in a noticeably slushy quality to the sound.

In addition to problems in expression, problems in reception also can occur, such as discrimination difficulty. For example, the child may hear "Go get the nail" when the command was actually "Go get the mail." The child cannot tell the difference between /n/ and /m/, and thus does not respond correctly. Phoneme discrimination errors can occur in comprehension of consonants (e.g., /p/ for /b/ and /d/ for /t/), consonant blends (e.g., /pr/, /fr/, and /kr/ confused with /pl/, /fl/, and /kl/), and vowels (e.g., confusion of vowels produced with the tongue in a forward position such as in *pit, pet,* and *pat*) (Wiig & Semel, 1976).

Various researchers examine the relationship between phonological disorders and academic reading performance. Ackerman, Dykman, and Gardner (1990) note that students with reading disabilities tend to articulate sequences more slowly than do students without disabilities. Ackerman et al. claim that the slow-speaking student has greater difficulty sounding out and blending polysyllabic words and comprehending what is read. Moreover, Pehrsson and Denner (1988) add that many students with language disorders have organization problems, which may inhibit their ability to remember what they have read. Students with a limited phonological repertoire (i.e., unintelligible speech) who are experiencing difficulties in reading, spelling, and writing present concerns for the teacher regarding the priorities and content of appropriate intervention.

Form: Morphology

A *morpheme* is the smallest unit or segment of language that conveys meaning. Two different types of morphemes exist: free and bound. A free morpheme is one that has meaning and may stand alone. Root words, for example, are free morphemes (e.g., *car, teach,* and *tall*). A bound morpheme is one that may not stand alone (e.g., affixes). Prefixes and suffixes are bound morphemes that change the meaning of the root word to which they are attached (e.g., *cars, teacher,* and *tallest*). Bound morphemes are either derivational or inflectional. *Derivational* suffixes change word class; for example, the verb *walk* becomes a noun, *walker,* with the addition of the suffix *-er. Inflectional* suffixes change the meaning of a word; for example, the addition of the inflectional *s* to the word *boy* changes the meaning to "more than one boy."

A further distinction can be made between two broad classes of words in a language: content words and function words (Lahey, 1988). Similar to root words, content words convey meaning when they stand alone; they generally carry the meaning in sentences. Function words or connective words (e.g., pronouns, articles, prepositions, and conjunctions) join phrases or sentences together. The meanings of connective words vary according to the context or words that they connect.

Morphological Deficits Students who are delayed in morphological development may not use appropriate inflectional endings in their speech. An elementary school student may not use the third-person *s* on verbs (e.g., "He walk"), may not use *s* on nouns or pronouns to show possession (e.g., "Mommy coat"), or may not use *-er* on adjectives (e.g., "Her dog is small than mine"). Older elementary and middle school students who are delayed in morphology may lack more advanced morphemes of irregular past tense or irregular plurals (e.g., they may use such forms as *drived* for *drove* or *mans* for *men*). Such students exhibit inconsistency regarding morphology usage (e.g., they vacillate in the use of *bringed, brang,* and *brought*).

Students with morphological problems may not acquire and understand word formation rules at the same rate and complexity as their peers with normal language development. Disorders in form or morphology also include difficulties learning the language code and linking it to what already is known about the environment. Wiig and Semel (1984, p. 303) list the following areas in which specific morphological deficits can be found in many students with language problems.

1. The formation of noun plurals, especially the irregular forms (*-s, -z, -ez,* vowel changes, *-ren,* etc.).
2. The formation of noun possessives, both singular and plural (*-'s, -s'*).
3. The formation of third person singular of the present tense of verbs (*-s*).
4. The formation of the past tense of both regular and irregular verbs (*-t, -d, -ed,* vowel change).
5. The formation of the comparative and superlative forms of adjectives (*-er, -est*).
6. The cross-categorical use of inflectional endings (*-s, -'s, -s'*).
7. Noun derivation (*-er*).
8. Adverb derivation (*-ly*).
9. The comprehension and use of prefixes (*pre-, post-, pro-, anti-, di-, de-*).

Some differences in inflectional endings are observed in students who speak African American English. The teacher should be aware that some inflectional endings reflect a student's cultural difference rather than a developmental delay. Examples of inflectional differences in African American English include "John cousin" instead of "John's cousin," "fifty cent" instead of "fifty cents," and "She work here" instead of "She works here."

Form: Syntax

Syntax is a system of rules governing how words or morphemes are combined to make grammatically correct sentences. Rules of syntax specify word, phrase, and clause order; sentence organization; and the relationships between words, word classes, and other sentence elements (Owens, 2008). Moreover, syntax specifies which word combinations are acceptable or grammatical and which word classes may appear in noun and verb phrases (e.g., adverbs modify verbs). Thus, syntax frequently is referred to as *grammar*.

Rules of grammar emerge between 18 and 24 months of age, as evidenced in a child's production of two-word sentences. The child does not change abruptly from single words to grammatical two-word sentences. There is a transition period in which a distinction can be made between two-word utterances and two words in grammatical form. Braine (1976) claims that in this transition period the child often is groping for a pattern that later is replaced by a correct grammatical form.

Wood (1976) outlines six stages in the acquisition of syntax. Stages 1 and 2 are described better with semantic rules of grammar, whereas the last four stages describe syntactic structure. Stage 3 typically begins when the child is 2 to 3 years old. At this age, the child's sentences contain a subject and a predicate. For example, in Stage 2, the child says, "No play," but in Stage 3 says, "I won't play." Stage 4 begins around 2½ years of age and continues to about 4 years of age. In this stage the child begins to perform operations on sentences, such as adding an element to basic sentences through the process of *conjunction*. For example, "where" can be added to the simple sentence "Daddy go" to form "Where Daddy go?" The child also can *embed* (i.e., place words within the basic sentence). For example, the sentence "No glass break" becomes "The glass didn't break." In Stage 4 the word order is changed to ask a question. For example, the question, "Man is here?" is changed to "Is the man here?" During this stage, sentences remain simple. Between 2 and 3 years of age, the child does not combine simple sentences but says them next to each other (e.g., "John bounced the ball; John hit the lamp"). Between 3 and 4 years of age the child combines simple sentences with the conjunction *and* (e.g., "John bounced the ball and hit the lamp.").

Stage 5 usually begins between 3½ and 7 years of age. In this stage the child uses complete sentences that have word classes typical of adult language: nouns, pronouns, adverbs, and adjectives. The child also becomes aware of differences within the same grammatical class. This awareness is evident in the child's use of different determiners and verbs with singular and plural nouns. For example, *this* is inappropriate for use in the sentence, "This chairs are heavy." The proper determiner (i.e., singular or plural) and appropriate verb for expressing plurality must be used. This same principle applies to prepositional phrases. For example, the sentence, "We cried to the movie" is not grammatically correct because an inappropriate prepositional phrase is used. In essence, in this stage the child learns the appropriate semantic functions of words and assigns these words to the appropriate grammatical classes.

Wood's Stage 6 begins when the child is about 5 years of age and extends until 10 years of age. The child begins using complex sentence structures and learns to understand and produce sentences that imply a command (e.g., "Give me the toy."), a request (e.g., "Please pass the salt."), and a promise (e.g., "I promise to stop."). Implied commands are the easiest to acquire but often are confused with requests. The promise is difficult for children to understand, and this type of verb may not be mastered until age 10 (Wood, 1976).

Syntactic Deficits Children who have delay in syntax use sentences that lack the length or syntactic complexity expected for their age. For example, a 6-year-old child who uses a mean sentence length of three words may say, "Where Daddy go?" instead of "Where did Daddy go?" Additional deficits in the processing of syntax include problems in comprehending sentences (such as questions or sentences that express relationship between direct and indirect objects), negation, mood (such as inferences of obligations signified by auxiliary verbs *must, have to,* and *ought*), and passive sentences (Wiig & Semel, 1976, 1984).

Students with language problems may have difficulty processing syntactic structures of increased complexity such as embedded sentences, *wh* questions, interrogatives, and negative sentences. Wiig and Semel (1984) include deficits in memory and recall, difficulties using strategies to enhance memory, and decreased selective attention as being related to deficits remembering spoken messages. Students with language problems also may tend to rely on basic sentence structures and exhibit little creativity and use of novel or interesting sentences (Simon, 1985).

Content: Semantics

Semantics refers to language meaning and is concerned with the meaning of individual words as well as the meaning produced by combinations of words. For example, the word *cup* means "a container from which to drink" and refers to an object in the child's world. An example of meaning attached to combinations of words is the phrase "Daddy's cup." These words add the meaning of possessiveness in relationship to one another (i.e., the cup belongs to Daddy). Receptive semantics refers to understanding language, whereas expressive semantics refers to producing meaningful discourse.

According to Lahey (1988), language content (i.e., semantics) has three categories. One category involves general objects (e.g., cars, ball, Mommy, and juice). The second category involves general actions (e.g., throwing, hitting, and kicking). The third category involves relations between objects (e.g., Michael and his computer, me and my puppy, and Debbie and her car) and relations between events (such as the causal relation between going swimming and getting wet). The particular message is called the *topic* (e.g., rescue heroes), and the more general categorization of the message is called the *content* (e.g., toys). Consequently, because youngsters from different cultures talk about different topics, they do not have the same vocabulary even though their content is often the same.

Wood (1976) outlines several stages of semantic acquisition. In Stage 1, a child develops meanings as he or she acquires first words. Wood refers to these first words as one-word sentences. The meanings of these sentences are determined by the context in which they are spoken. An 18-month-old child may use the word *doggie* quite frequently, but the context in which the child says the word may differ and imply different meanings (e.g., "There is a doggie," "That is my doggie," "Doggie is barking," or "Doggie is chasing a kitty").

At about 2 years of age, the child begins to produce two-word utterances with meanings related to concrete actions (such as "Doggie bark" or "My doggie"). In Stage 2, the child conveys more specific information verbally and continues to expand vocabulary and utterance length. However, until about the age of 7, the child defines words merely in terms of visible actions. To a 6-year-old child, a fish is "a thing that swims in a lake" and a plate is "a thing you can eat dinner on." Also, during this stage, the child typically responds to a prompt word (such as *pretty*) with a word that could follow it in a sentence (such as *flower*). Older children, around 8 years of age, frequently respond with a verbal opposite (such as *ugly*) (Brown & Berko, 1960).

In Stage 3, at 8 years of age, the child's word meanings relate directly to experiences, operations, and processes. If a child's neighbor owns a horse, the child may include this attribute in the word meaning of *horse* in addition to the attributes of "animal," "four-legged," and "a thing that can be ridden." When asked where horses live, the child may respond, "At the Kahns'." By an adult definition, this answer is not correct. The child's vocabulary is defined by the child's experiences, not those of adults. At 12 years of age, the child begins to give dictionary-like definitions for words (Wood,

1976). When asked to define *bear*, the child might respond, "a large, warm-blooded animal that hibernates in the winter." At this time the child's word definitions approach the semantic level of adults.

Semantic Deficits Developmental delay in word meaning (i.e., semantics) is observed in youngsters who use or understand a limited number of words. The limited vocabulary may be in specific areas, such as adjectives, adverbs, prepositions, or pronouns. Students may have a longer response time when selecting vocabulary words or have difficulty retrieving or recalling a specific word (i.e., dysnomia). The student with retrieval difficulties often attempts to participate in classroom discussions but has no apparent response when called on to answer. Vocabulary difficulties may be evident in an inability to use specific words when describing objects or events (e.g., "that thing over there" or "the thing you use to write with").

Semantic delay also is evident when students assign a narrow set of attributes to each word so that each word has limited meaning. Students with semantic deficits often fail to perceive subtle changes in word meaning that follow from changes in context and may not perceive multiple meanings of frequently used words (Wiig & Secord, 1994). This leads to incomplete understanding and misinterpretations of what is heard or read. In addition, students may have figurative language problems and tend to interpret idioms, metaphors, and proverbs literally (Wiig & Semel, 1984). These problems have important classroom implications when considered with research findings by Lazar, Warr-Leeper, Nicholson, and Johnson (1989). Their study of math, reading, and language arts teachers in kindergarten through eighth grade revealed that 36 percent of all teacher utterances contained at least one multiple-meaning expression. Indirect requests, which were 27 percent of the utterances, occurred most frequently. Moreover, at least one idiom occurred in 12 percent of the utterances, and more idiomatic expressions were used as grade level increased. Thus, older students with language problems may become increasingly unable to follow teacher directions or understand classroom discourse. The following middle school classroom discussion exemplifies this problem. The teacher asked the students whether the expression "my father hit the roof" meant that the father literally hit the roof. One student, interpreting the nonverbal contextual cues, proudly responded, "No, it doesn't mean he literally hit the roof. It means he hit the roof with his broom or something long!"

Additional semantic difficulties experienced by students with language problems include understanding linguistic concepts (e.g., *before/after, if/then, many, some,* and *few*), perceiving logical relationships among words (e.g., comparative, possessive, spatial, and temporal), and comprehending verbal analogies (e.g., sandwich is to eat as milk is to drink) (Wiig & Semel, 1984). Moreover, students may misuse transition words (i.e., conjunctions such as *although* and *if* and phrases such as *in addition*) and avoid making complex sentences and signaling logical relationships among two arguments in sentences or sentence sequences (Wiig & Secord, 1994).

Use: Pragmatics

Pragmatics refers to the use of language to affect the behavior of others or to relay information; thus, it "concentrates on language as a communication tool that is used to achieve social ends" (Owens, 2008, p. 22). Pragmatics comprises two broad functions: controlling or influencing the listener's action (e.g., "Give me the doll.") and influencing attitudes (e.g., "I think Jane would make a good class president."). These functions also are referred to as the *speaker's intent.* Language is used in social contexts to convey a variety of intentions such as requesting, asserting, and questioning. An individual's language use based on an understanding of how language works in social interactions also is referred to as *communicative competence.* Wilcox (1986) describes communicative competence as "the ability to convey effectively and efficiently an intended message to a receiver.... This requires not only knowledge of the conventional communicative code, but also knowledge pertaining to socially appropriate communicative behaviors" (p. 644).

One pragmatic function that occurs after 3 years of age is the indirect request or hint (Ervin-Tripp & Mitchell-Kernan, 1977; Leonard, Wilcox, Fulmer, & Davis, 1978). Indirect requests frequently are used (e.g., "My mother always lets me have cookies before lunch."). Leonard et al. studied 4-, 5-, and 6-year-old children's understanding of three types of indirect requests: affirmative construction (e.g., "Can you shut the door?"), responses with a negative element (e.g., "Can't you answer the phone?"), and affirmative construction with a negative intention (e.g., "Must you play the piano?"). The 4- and 5-year-old children understood the first two types of requests but not the third type. The 6-year-old children understood the third type of request but made mistakes. Leonard et al. interpret the mistakes to mean that understanding was not complete.

The situation affects the form of the message within the pragmatics of language. The characteristics of the message that increase the likelihood that the message will be accepted as well as understood are referred to as *pragmatic presuppositions.* In adult speech these presuppositions appear as tendencies to be polite and indirect in requests. Children as young as 4 and 5 years of age show these pragmatic presuppositions when they talk politely as they make a request. Pragmatic presuppositions develop as the child matures and learns not to interrupt the speaker, talk at the wrong time, or speak too loudly for the situation.

Pragmatic Deficits   Delay in pragmatics is evident when students do not use functions that are expected for their developmental age. For example, a student with a developmental age above 8 years who seriously answers "Yes" to the indirect request "Must you play the piano?" and continues to play the piano, rather than ceasing to play, may be developmentally delayed in understanding indirect requests. Moreover, a student may have difficulty determining when the listener does not understand what he or she is saying and thus continue with the manner of presentation rather than adapt the speech to the listener's needs. Also, a student may enter conversations in a socially unacceptable fashion or fail to take turns when conversing. The student may either monopolize a conversation or expect the other speaker to do most of the talking with little feedback to indicate listening. Other examples of problems with language use include difficulty staying on a topic during conversation (i.e., topic maintenance), inappropriate facial expressions and body posture, immature speech, and difficulty interpreting verbal and nonverbal communication cues (Simon, 1985; Wiig & Semel, 1984). Finally, a student may have difficulty choosing the right linguistic content (i.e., gauging complexity according to the listener), using questioning strategies, and interacting well verbally in a group (Wiig & Semel, 1984). Difficulties with communicative competence are particularly frustrating because they can persist into adulthood and affect the student's academic, vocational, and social performance (Schumaker & Deshler, 1984).

LANGUAGE DIFFICULTIES

Students with language problems display a wide variety of difficulties, although many of the deficits initially may be subtle. The teacher should be aware of the potential language difficulties so that students can be identified and receive appropriate services as early as possible. In spite of early intervention, many language problems are long term and require intervention that changes with the varying needs of the student. This section presents the language difficulties typically found in three age groups of students: preschool and kindergarten, elementary, and secondary. It is important to keep in mind that language is interactive and that many of these difficulties may not occur in isolation. Furthermore, because language difficulties generally do not disappear without intervention, the same deficits may span several age categories.

Preschool and Kindergarten Students

Young students with language problems are a diverse group, so it may be difficult to differentiate them from their normally developing peers. However, various researchers (Bernstein, 1993; Wiig & Semel, 1984) discuss the difficulties common to this age group. Readiness skills such as counting, naming colors, naming the days of the week, and using scissors often are delayed. The child may be unable to follow simple directions, follow the story line in a book or movie, or enjoy listening to stories. In addition, the period of normal acquisition for articulation and sound development may be delayed, so that the child exhibits immature-sounding speech. The mean length of utterances and vocabulary may be similar to that of a younger child. Word-finding difficulties and an inability to name common objects also may be noted. As a result, the child may exhibit sound substitutions such as "buzghetti" for "spaghetti." The child may produce fewer functionally appropriate and accurate responses, say phrases such as "you know" or "that thing over there," or describe rather than name objects. In addition, the child may be unable to make one-to-one correspondence between letters and sounds and have difficulty discriminating between sounds.

Furthermore, young children may have difficulty responding accurately to certain types of questions. Parnell, Amerman, and Harting (1986) note that questions regarding nonobservable persons, actions, or objects are the most difficult for young children. In an evaluation of nine *wh-* forms, *why, when,* and *what happened* were the most difficult.

Young children with language problems also may demonstrate significant deficits in symbolic, adaptive, and integrative play as compared with their linguistically matched peers. They frequently play by themselves or exhibit more nonplay and parallel play than do their peers (Roth & Clark, 1987). Behaviorally, children with language problems may have attention deficits, need additional time to understand information and formulate ideas for expression, and have a poor tolerance for frustration.

Elementary Students

A student with a language problem may exhibit a variety of difficulties in the first grade, such as a limited ability to identify sounds, difficulty analyzing and synthesizing sound sequences, and problems segmenting words into grammatical units. Temporal and spatial concepts, as well as abstract concepts such as *before-after, neither-nor, some, if/then,* and *few,* may pose particular difficulty (Snyder, 1986; Wiig & Semel, 1984). These concepts often are presented in sentences of increased length and complexity that are particularly problematic for students with subtle processing problems. The student may be seen as obstinate or noncompliant, when actually the directions are misunderstood.

In the early elementary grades, the use of manipulatives begins to decrease, and the student must gain information from the teacher's verbal presentation. As the language complexity increases with each grade advance, the student must keep up with the demands of the instructional language as well as absorb the curriculum content. By fourth grade, most of the curriculum content is presented in print, and the student with language problems may have particular difficulty making the transition from narrative to expository writing.

Word finding (i.e., retrieval) difficulties still may exist, but the deficits may not be as evident because the student begins to use strategies involving circumlocution (i.e., talking around the word), fillers, and descriptors (Vaughn & Bos, 2009). German (1984) adds the manifestation of secondary characteristics such as tapping and saying "I know it." She claims that students with retrieval problems generally have difficulty with three indices: response time, error index or word selection process, and substitution types. Students generally do not perform similarly across the three areas, and situations often occur in which the student's speed is affected although the correct word eventually is recalled.

Problems stemming from the relationship between phonological disorders and reading achievement begin to emerge in elementary school. Students with reading problems often articulate sequences more slowly than do their peers who do not have reading difficulties. As a result, the slow-speaking student tends to have greater difficulty sounding out and blending polysyllabic words and comprehending what is read (Ackerman et al., 1990). Requirements for comprehension also change because multiple-meaning words emerge and students are required to draw conclusions and make inferences. Deficits in text comprehension lead to problems in reading independence and mastery of content material. Thus, students with language problems may have difficulties participating in group discussions, sharing ideas on a topic, and developing ideas that follow earlier learning.

Students in elementary school also may be deficient in expressive or oral language. In a study that examined children's discourse or ability to tell a story, Merritt and Liles (1987) found that the stories told by students with language problems contained fewer story episodes and fewer main and subordinate clauses than the stories told by their peers without language problems. In addition, the students with language problems had significant difficulty integrating critical parts of a story, and these difficulties continued after maturity and intervention. Merritt and Liles conclude that students with language problems may have difficulty forming verbal abstractions and performing the logical operations needed to interpret and understand complex concepts. The students also had difficulty formulating and expressing spoken language; such problems often are reflected in academic difficulties.

Finally, elementary students with language problems continue to exhibit difficulties in their use of language. In academic settings, this often is reflected in the student's social skills. Such students may exhibit some of the same behaviors as they did when they were younger, such as failing to adjust to their listener's needs and having difficulty joining an ongoing conversation. In addition, they may misinterpret social cues, fail to think of others' thoughts and feelings, and be unable to predict the consequences of their behavior. Also, students at this level may be able to formulate a question but have difficulty functionally using requests to obtain new information (Schwabe, Olswang, & Kriegsmann, 1986).

Secondary Students

Adolescents who have language problems exhibit a variety of difficulties that tend to become more subtle. They tend to be passive learners and often appear to lack the metacognitive strategies necessary to perform complex academic tasks. At the secondary level, the teacher is faced with the challenge of designing interventions to assist students in overcoming or compensating for their language disabilities so that they can meet the increased demands of secondary school.

Many adolescents with language problems lack the ability to use and understand higher level syntax, semantics, and pragmatics in both production and processing. Secondary students are expected to organize their time and complete assignments and, thus, they must follow both oral and written instruction to complete work independently. However, receptive and expressive language difficulties affect their ability to learn effectively. This creates problems in gaining information from class lectures and textbooks, completing homework, following classroom rules, demonstrating command of knowledge through test taking, expressing thoughts in writing, passing minimum competency exams, and participating in classroom discussions. Some adolescents learn strategies to compensate for their language difficulties, whereas others need additional services or support. As students mature, the teacher must be aware of the changing curriculum demands. For example, intervention may change from a content-oriented approach to a functional approach in which the student is taught strategies to deal with everyday situations.

Problems in comprehension of auditory language also are persistent in adolescents and result in short-term memory problems and a decrease in the understanding of linguistic relationships (Riedlinger-Ryan & Shewan, 1984). Frequently, adolescent students with language problems have difficulty organizing information and correctly associating or categorizing it for later retrieval. Thus, they often are unable to retain and synthesize complex information because they lack the ability to organize or categorize it. Poor organization and categorization result in other problems, such as poor notetaking, test-taking, and study skills, as well as difficulty integrating information.

Difficulties also may persist in language use in the awareness of social cues, interpretation of the motives and emotions of others, and use of appropriate language. Because adolescents frequently are aware of their difficulties, behaviors such as aggression, frustration, lack of motivation, withdrawal, and inattention may arise (Hazel & Schumaker, 1988; Seidenberg, 1988; Wiig & Semel, 1984).

BILINGUAL AND CULTURALLY DIVERSE STUDENTS

Bilingual students know and use more than one language. Many bilingual students speak Spanish as their first language and acquire English as a second language. A student who displays inadequate skills in understanding and speaking English has limited English proficiency. Unfortunately, some students with limited English proficiency or nonstandard dialects are misdiagnosed as having learning or language impairments because of their difficulty on culturally biased standardized tests (Payne & Taylor, 2006). As a result, alternative assessment procedures are recommended for diagnosing language and learning problems for bilingual or culturally diverse students (Caesar & Kohler, 2007). As the bilingual population in the United States increases, the teacher must distinguish between students who are unfamiliar with the language and culture and students with a true language problem. Bilingual students with language problems may need services somewhat different from those for students whose primary language is standard English. Salend and Fradd (1986) note that bilingual students have the following needs.

- Access to teachers who are proficient in English as well as in the student's native language.
- Use of nonbiased assessment and instruction to formulate appropriate individualized educational programs.
- Exposure to curriculum and alternative instructional strategies that promote the academic and social relevance of instruction.

Several factors should be considered when assessing bilingual students. To determine whether the student has limited English proficiency or a language problem, assessment should be conducted in the student's primary language to examine writing, reading, listening, and speaking skills. Language assessments should include both quantitative measures (i.e., formal tests) and qualitative measures (e.g., observations, adapted test instruction, and a language sample). It also helps to interview significant people in the student's life with the same cultural background to determine how effectively the student communicates in the primary language. Interviews can yield important information regarding the language spoken at home, attitudes toward the two languages and cultures, the parents' educational level, and a profile of the community where the student lives (Kayser, 1989).

Salend and Salinas (2003) recommend that the assessment plan for second-language learners should include data collection relating to the student's performance in both the native and secondary languages through the use of informal and standardized tests, language samples, observations, questionnaires, and interviews. Comparisons of the student's performance in each language can indicate the student's language proficiency, language dominance, language preference, and code switching (i.e., use of words, phrases, expressions, and sentences from one language while speaking another language). Moreover, to determine if a student's problems are due to language difficulties, a learning disability, or lack of exposure to effective instruction, Salend (2008) suggests that the following factors should be considered in assessing second-language learners.

1. Length of residence in the United States.
2. School attendance patterns.
3. School instructional history (e.g., language of instruction in native country).
4. Cultural background.
5. Performance in comparison to peers (e.g., comparison of student's language skill, learning rate, and learning style with those of other students from similar experiential, cultural, and language backgrounds).
6. Home life (e.g., language or dialect spoken at home).
7. Health and developmental history.

Gersten and Woodward (1994) discuss two major instructional approaches advocated for bilingual students. In programs with a native-language emphasis, the student receives academic instruction in the primary language, whereas in sheltered English or structured immersion programs, English is used for the majority of the teaching day. Most studies indicate little or no difference in achievement between students taught with these two bilingual approaches. In both approaches, second-language instruction should be relevant rather than only a series of drills on grammar and usage. Gersten and Woodward note that many second-language programs have moved toward the increased use of natural language to promote comprehension and use of English.

Another group of culturally diverse students speaks nonstandard English by using dialects related to geographic regions or race and ethnicity. Dialectical differences may be evident in the student's pronunciation of speech sounds or in variations in morphology and syntax. For example, in African American English the use of the verb *to be* (as in "he be running") is different from standard English. As with bilingual students, language assessment of culturally diverse students should include the collection of spontaneous speech samples in naturalistic settings or interviews with other students who speak the dialect. Thus, the student's cultural background is considered and he or she is compared with others in the same language community to determine the existence of a language problem.

Students who exhibit normal production of their own primary language or dialect should not be identified as having a language problem. These students simply are producing an acceptable language variation. However, many students with limited English proficiency or dialectical differences are identified as having a language problem such as a phonological deficiency. For example, a Spanish-speaking youngster may say "cheap" for "chip," and a youngster learning African American English may say "birfday" instead of "birthday." Owens (2008) presents the major phonemic and grammatical contrasts between standard

American English and African American English, Latino English, and Asian English. Adler (1988) raises the following questions regarding these students: Should only standard English be taught to these students? If the dialect is rule-governed and nonstandard, rather than substandard, should the student be taught to speak "correctly" if the dialect is consistent with what is spoken in the community in which the student lives? Finally, should only English be taught to young nonstandard-speaking students, or should they be allowed to retain the social dialect of their cultural peers and parents? Alder notes that the current belief appears to support teaching the use of language that is relevant to school talk (i.e., standard English) as well as everyday talk (i.e., nonstandard English). This is difficult to accomplish, however, because it requires a change in the current system and collaborative interaction between families and teachers in language arts and English.

To promote learning and language acquisition, Salend and Salinas (2003) suggest the use of numerous strategies for differentiating instruction for second-language learners. Selected strategies include the following:

- Use simple vocabulary and short sentences, and limit the use of idiomatic expressions, slang, and pronouns.
- Use gestures, facial expressions, voice changes, pantomimes, demonstrations, rephrasing, visuals, props, manipulatives, and other cues to communicate and convey the meaning of new terms and concepts.
- Use modeling and hands-on experiences to preview and teach new vocabulary, phrases, idioms, structures, and concepts.
- Supplement oral instruction and descriptions with visuals such as pictures, charts, maps, graphs, and graphic organizers.
- Give regular summaries of important concepts and check students' understanding frequently.
- Correct students indirectly by restating their incorrect comments in correct form.

To provide appropriate educational programs for bilingual and culturally diverse students, linguistic and cultural differences must be differentiated from learning difficulties. Although changes in the service delivery to bilingual and culturally diverse students are beginning to emerge, the teacher must assume the responsibility of providing quality assessment and intervention to these students to assist in the prevention of instructional problems related to a lack of English proficiency.

ASSESSMENT OF LANGUAGE SKILLS

The heterogeneity of students with language impairments and language problems makes the assessment task especially difficult, because no two students exhibit the same strengths and weaknesses. The speech and language evaluator must know not only what areas to assess but also how to interpret the findings and help make the necessary adjustments in the student's curriculum. Although most classroom teachers never conduct an in-depth assessment of a student's language skills, they should understand the implications of a language evaluation because language pervades the curriculum. In the past, speech and language assessments were viewed as separate from the curriculum and the sole responsibility of the speech and language pathologist. However, this trend is changing, with emphasis being placed on the teacher and the speech and language specialist *sharing* the responsibility for diagnosing problems and designing intervention programs to improve a student's receptive and expressive language skills. After becoming familiar with the basic principles of language development, the teacher undoubtedly will identify numerous youngsters who exhibit language problems in the classroom and would benefit from systematic assessment and instruction in the use of spoken language.

Language assessment should be viewed not as a single isolated event but as an ongoing process throughout a student's education. The five major reasons for language assessment are as follows:

1. To identify students with potential language problems.
2. To determine a student's language developmental level.
3. To plan educational objectives and design appropriate intervention programs.
4. To monitor the student's progress.
5. To evaluate the language intervention program.

The last three of these assessment functions are most relevant to daily instructional planning. The first of these three functions is *planning objectives*. The assessment information describes the student's language. This description is used in planning objectives that relate directly to the problem. The assessment of a morphological disorder, for example, should be specific: "The student does not use *s* on regular nouns to indicate plurality." The teacher then can plan the objective: "The student will use plural *s* on regular nouns with 90 percent accuracy when naming pictures of plural regular nouns." *Monitoring the student's progress* involves the teacher determining daily or weekly whether the student is reaching short-term instructional objectives. The sample objective of 90 percent accuracy of plural *s* when naming pictures of plural regular nouns requires an assessment procedure of counting responses. Finally, in *program evaluation*, the teacher assesses the student's progress with the materials and techniques used in the program. This information allows the teacher to determine whether she or he needs to change materials or techniques to achieve the educational objective.

Thus, language assessments of school-age youngsters should be educationally relevant and provide both diagnostic information and intervention strategies. To accomplish this goal, two levels of information should be included in the assessment: the content-oriented level and the process-oriented level. The content-oriented level examines the actual content the student has learned and identifies specific areas that require intervention (e.g., a syntactic deficit in the use of present progressive tense). The process-oriented level examines how skills are learned or acquired (e.g., the use of a strategy such as clustering digits to remember a phone number).

Language development assessment is an evaluation of the student's receptive and expressive language skills. The components assessed include phonology, morphology, syntax, semantics, and pragmatics. The teacher can assess all of these components or decide to assess only one or two specific components. An experienced examiner obtains information or observes the student before deciding what to assess. The information gathered can include various observations (e.g., the student is difficult to understand, the student has difficulty understanding what others say, the student uses short sentences, the student uses few words, or the student cannot start and maintain a discussion topic).

The student who is difficult for others to understand, but who understands what others say and uses many words and long sentences, may have problems in phonology. Thus, assessment should begin in this area. The student who uses only a few words needs to be assessed in semantics, and the student who uses short sentences needs assessment in semantic relationships and syntax. The *Pragmatic Language Observation Scale* (Newcomer & Hammill, 2009) can help teachers assess the daily classroom spoken language behaviors of students ages 8 through 17. This norm-referenced 25-item rating scale consists of statements that relate to specific spoken language behaviors (e.g., "Pays attention to oral instructions" and "Expresses thoughts clearly") and the teacher rates each statement on a 5-point scale.

Language assessment includes the use of formal and informal assessment procedures. Quantitative or formal measures are used when the examiner needs to determine the student's developmental level and obtain a standardized score or classify the student. These measures include observable behaviors and result in a numerical score or an assigned classification. If the examiner wants to determine specific teaching objectives, informal measures are used. Qualitative or naturalistic measures are based on the assumption that behaviors vary across different settings, and their purpose is to determine the relevant behaviors or skills evident in the setting being examined. Assessment of both language developmental level and teaching objectives should include both types of tests. School speech and language specialists are experienced in administering and interpreting formal and informal measures of language. The teacher who is unfamiliar with these tests should consider working with the school speech and language specialist in assessing language.

Formal Language Assessment

In a formal language assessment, standardized instruments are used to compare a student's performance with pre-established criteria to determine the existence of a speech or language problem. On these instruments, a student's raw score is converted to a standardized score, language age or mental age, age equivalent, or, occasionally, a grade equivalent. Students whose scores are much lower than the scores of other students their age usually are referred for additional testing or are placed in speech and language therapy.

Some language tests provide a comprehensive measure of all language functioning. This type of test assesses receptive and expressive language in many components. For example, the *Clinical Evaluation of Language Fundamentals—4* (Semel, Wiig, & Secord, 2003) assesses morphology, syntax, semantics, and pragmatics. Other tests are designed to measure specific components of language. For example, the *Test of Early Language Development—3* (Hresko, Reid, & Hammill, 1999) assesses receptive and expressive skills in syntax and semantics. Some tests are more specific and measure only receptive or expressive skills in one component. For example, the *Peabody Picture Vocabulary Test—Fourth Edition* (Dunn & Dunn, 2007) assesses receptive semantic skills.

Screening Tests In many school districts, students are given a speech-and-language screening test when they enter preschool or kindergarten. The screening provides a general overview of a student's performance in a particular area, which can be compared with the performance of a student of the same age or grade who

TABLE 6.2
Selected language screening measures

Test	Component Measured	Receptive/Expressive	Age Norms
Adolescent Language Screening Test (Morgan & Guilford, 1984)	Phonology, morphology, syntax, semantics, pragmatics	R, E	11–17 years
The dimensions of language use, content, and form are screened by seven subtests: Pragmatics, Receptive Vocabulary, Concepts, Expressive Vocabulary, Sentence Formulation, Morphology, and Phonology. Administration time is less than 15 minutes.			
Clinical Evaluation of Language Fundamentals—4: Screening Test (Semel, Wiig, & Secord, 2004)	Syntax, semantics	R, E	5–21 years
The screening test identifies the need for an in-depth diagnosis of language. The test includes parallel items from *CELF—4,* and the brief form is easy to administer and score. It screens receptive, expressive, grammatical, and semantic skills in about 15 minutes.			

is developing normally. Many school districts use standardized or formal screening instruments, whereas other districts devise informal assessment instruments to identify preschool and kindergarten students who may have potential language problems. Table 6.2 presents two formal language screening tests that assess receptive and expressive language in various components. Students who score below an acceptable level on a screening test usually are referred for a comprehensive evaluation.

One advantage of a screening is that it requires little administration time and, thus, allows a large number of students to be evaluated. When all students are screened at the beginning of their formal education, speed is an obvious concern because so many students must be evaluated. However, because of factors such as social and emotional development, participation in a preschool program, family environment, and cultural influences, only a few language skills should be expected to have been mastered by all 4- or 5-year-old children. Thus, a disadvantage to screening young children is that the screening often cannot detect subtle language problems. To illustrate, a youngster may receive high scores (i.e., 80 to 90 percentiles) in both processing and production on a language screening test administered at the beginning of first grade. However, because subtle language problems were not detected at the initial screening and intervention was not made available, the student may experience academic difficulties later when faced with a more abstract and demanding fourth-grade curriculum. Thus, ideally, several speech and language screenings should be administered (e.g., kindergarten, third grade, sixth grade,

and ninth grade); however, time constraints on public school clinicians force them to give a screening test only one time. Consequently, many students with language problems are not identified at an early age.

Diagnostic Tests Diagnostic tests measure one or more specific language components including receptive or expressive language. As presented in Table 6.3, comprehensive tests measure a wide range of language skills, whereas other diagnostic tests assess specific speech and language components. In a comprehensive diagnostic evaluation, it generally is advisable to administer a test that provides an overall view of the student's understanding and use of language. The specific test often is determined by the student's age or level of functioning. If the examiner notices that the student has difficulty formulating words and sentences, an additional test should be administered to measure the student's ability to understand and use words (e.g., the *Test of Word Knowledge*) or apply syntactic skills (e.g., the *Test of Early Language Development—3*). If the student's speech intelligibility is reduced, the examiner may administer a test of phonology to obtain additional information (e.g., the *Goldman-Fristoe Test of Articulation—2*). The assessment provides an overall view of the student's language skills as well as additional information concerning reported or observed areas of concern.

Although standardized language tests do not provide information regarding academic or therapeutic interventions, they do target the student's specific strengths and weaknesses. The examiner's role is to interpret the assessment information and transform it to academically relevant instructional skills and interventions.

TABLE 6.3
Selected diagnostic language measures

Test	Component Measured	Receptive/Expressive	Age Norms
Comprehensive Measures			
Bankson Language Test—2 (Bankson, 1990)	Morphology, syntax, semantics, pragmatics	R, E	3–6 years

This instrument is organized into three general categories. Semantic knowledge includes body parts, verbs, nouns, functions, prepositions, and opposites and categories. Morphological and syntactic rules include pronouns, verb usage and tense, plurals, comparatives and superlatives, questions, and negation. Pragmatics includes controlling, ritualizing, informing, and imagining. A 20-item short form also is available to screen children for language problems.

Test	Component Measured	Receptive/Expressive	Age Norms
Clinical Evaluation of Language Fundamentals—4 (Semel, Wiig, & Secord, 2003)	Morphology, syntax, semantics, pragmatics	R, E	5–21 years

This test features a multi-tiered assessment process to evaluate a student's language performance and language abilities. Four core subtests determine if a problem exists and whether the student qualifies for services. The next level of assessment focuses on the nature of the disorder by examining receptive and expressive modalities; determining language strengths and weaknesses; and evaluating language structure, content, and memory. Additional testing with supplemental subtests (i.e., Phonological Awareness, Rapid Automatic Naming, Number Repetition, Familiar Sequences, and Word Associations) determines what critical clinical skills or behaviors underlie the disorder. Finally, the Observational Rating Scales and Pragmatic Profile provide descriptive measures of a student's language performance at school and home. Administration time is 30 to 60 minutes, and *Scoring Assistant* software is available.

Test	Component Measured	Receptive/Expressive	Age Norms
Comprehensive Assessment of Spoken Language (Carrow-Woolfolk, 1999a)	Morphology, syntax, semantics, pragmatics	R, E	3–21 years

This research-based oral language assessment battery is individually and orally administered. Fifteen tests measure language processing skills (i.e., comprehension, expression, and retrieval) in four language structure categories: lexical/semantic (i.e., knowledge and use of words and word combinations), syntactic (i.e., knowledge and use of grammar), supralinguistic (i.e., comprehension of complex language such as nonliteral language, inference, and ambiguous sentences), and pragmatic (i.e., awareness of appropriate language in a situational context). Reading or writing ability is not needed to respond to test items; only a verbal or pointing response is required. Each of the 15 tests can be used as a stand-alone test, and administration time for the core battery is 30 to 45 minutes. Supplemental tests also are included to provide additional diagnostic data.

Test	Component Measured	Receptive/Expressive	Age Norms
Oral and Written Language Scales: Listening Comprehension and Oral Expression (Carrow-Woolfolk, 1995a)	Syntax, semantics, pragmatics	R, E	5–21 years

Neither scale on this individually administered test requires reading by the student. On the Listening Comprehension scale, a verbal stimulus is read aloud by the examiner, and the student responds by pointing to one of four pictures. Administration time is 5 to 15 minutes. On the Oral Expression scale, the student is shown a picture while a verbal stimulus is read aloud by the examiner, and the student responds orally by answering a question, completing a sentence, or generating one or more sentences. Administration time is 10 to 25 minutes.

Test	Component Measured	Receptive/Expressive	Age Norms
Test of Adolescent and Adult Language—4 (Hammill, Brown, Larsen, & Wiederholt, 2007)	Syntax, semantics	R, E	12–24 years

Designed to assess receptive and expressive aspects of spoken and written vocabulary and grammar, the test includes six subtests: Word Opposites, Word Derivations, Spoken Analogies, Word Similarities, Sentence Combining, and Orthographic Usage. Group or individual administration time is about 1 hour.

Test	Component Measured	Receptive/Expressive	Age Norms
Test of Language Development— Primary: 4 (Newcomer & Hammill, 2008)	Phonology, syntax, semantics	R, E	4–8 years
Test of Language Development— Intermediate: 4 (Hammill & Newcomer, 2008)	Syntax, semantics	R, E	8–17 years

The *TOLD–Primary: 4* has nine subtests: Picture Vocabulary, Relational Vocabulary, and Oral Vocabulary assess the understanding and meaningful use of spoken words; Syntactic Understanding, Sentence Imitation, and Morphological Completion assess differing aspects of grammar; Word Articulation, Word Analysis, and Word Discrimination measure the abilities to say words correctly and to distinguish between words that sound similar. The *TOLD–Intermediate: 4* contains six subtests: Sentence Combining, Word Ordering, and Morphological Comprehension assess different aspects of grammar; Picture Vocabulary, Relational Vocabulary, and Multiple Meanings measure the understanding and use of word relationships, the knowledge of abstract relationships, and the knowledge of different meanings for a word.

Measures of Specific Components

Test	Component Measured	Receptive/Expressive	Age Norms
Boehm Test of Basic Concepts—3 (Boehm, 2000)	Semantics	R	5–7 years

Fifty pictorial items, in multiple-choice form, are arranged in approximate order of increasing difficulty and divided into two booklets. The test is read by the teacher, and students mark their answers in the test booklets. The test measures understanding of 25 basic concepts relating to space, quantity, and time, and it can be administered individually or to small groups in 30 to 45 minutes. The directions for administration include English and Spanish instructions.

Test	Component Measured	Receptive/Expressive	Age Norms
Comprehensive Receptive and Expressive Vocabulary Test—2 (Wallace & Hammill, 2002)	Semantics	R, E	4–89 years

The Expressive Vocabulary subtest includes 25 items that encourage and require the student to converse in detail about a particular stimulus word. The Receptive Vocabulary subtest consists of 61 items in which the student must point to the picture of the stimulus word said by the examiner. The subtest includes 10 plates with six pictures on each plate, and the words associated with each plate relate to a particular common theme and are spaced evenly across all grade levels. Two forms are available, and the test can be individually administered in 20 to 30 minutes.

Test	Component Measured	Receptive/Expressive	Age Norms
Goldman-Fristoe Test of Articulation—2 (Goldman & Fristoe, 2000)	Phonology	E	2–21 years

The first subtest, Sounds in Words, consists of pictures that elicit the student's articulation of the major speech sounds in the initial, medial, and final positions. In the second subtest, Sounds in Sentences, the student is asked to retell a short story based on a picture cue. The third subtest, Stimulability, determines whether misarticulated phonemes are articulated correctly when the student is given maximum stimulation. The student is asked to watch and listen carefully while the sound is pronounced in a syllable, used in a word, and used in a sentence.

Test	Component Measured	Receptive/Expressive	Age Norms
Peabody Picture Vocabulary Test— Fourth Edition (Dunn & Dunn, 2007)	Semantics	R	2–90+ years

Stimulus pictures are presented to the student, who points to the picture among four choices that best represents the corresponding stimulus word spoken by the examiner. There are two forms of 228 items each; the items are arranged in increasing order of difficulty.

Test	Component Measured	Receptive/Expressive	Age Norms
Test for Auditory Comprehension of Language—3 (Carrow-Woolfolk, 1999b)	Morphology, syntax, semantics	R	3–9 years

The test is individually administered and measures auditory comprehension of vocabulary, grammatical morphemes, and elaborated phrase and sentence constructions. There are 142 test items in which the student looks at a set of three pictures and points to the one that best represents the meaning of the word, phrase, or sentence spoken by the examiner. No oral responses are required, and administration time is 15 to 25 minutes.

(continued)

TABLE 6.3
(continued)

Test	Component Measured	Receptive/Expressive	Age Norms
Test of Early Language Development—3 (Hresko, Reid, & Hammill, 1999)	Syntax, semantics	R, E	2–7 years

This individually administered test provides information directly related to the semantic (i.e., content) and syntactic (i.e., form) aspects of language. The items can be administered in about 15 to 45 minutes and assess receptive and expressive language using a variety of semantic and syntactic tasks. Manipulatives are included in a storage box.

Test of Pragmatic Language—2 (Phelps-Terasaki & Phelps-Gunn, 2007)	Pragmatics	E	6–18 years

For a comprehensive analysis of social communication in context, each test item establishes a social context, and the items are designed to provide information within six components of pragmatic language: physical setting, audience, topic, purpose (i.e., speech acts), visual-gestural cues, and abstraction. After the examiner provides a verbal stimulus prompt and displays a picture, the student responds to the social problem and situation presented.

Test of Word Finding—2 (German, 2000)	Semantics	E	4–12 years
Test of Adolescent/Adult Word Finding (German, 1990)	Semantics	E	12–80 years

These two tests both contain naming sections in picture-naming nouns, picture-naming verbs, sentence completion naming, and picture-naming categories. The adolescent test has an additional section in description naming. Each test also includes a comprehension section to determine whether errors are due to word-finding problems or poor word comprehension. The adolescent form also includes a brief test that provides a 10-minute assessment of word-finding abilities.

Test of Word Knowledge (Wiig & Secord, 1992)	Semantics	R, E	5–17 years

This test evaluates the student's ability to understand and use vocabulary words. Level 1, for students ages 5 to 8, includes subtests in expressive vocabulary, word definitions, receptive vocabulary, word opposites, and synonyms (optional). Level 2, for students ages 8 through 17, includes core subtests in word definitions, multiple contexts, synonyms, and figurative usage, as well as supplementary subtests in word opposites, receptive vocabulary, expressive vocabulary, and conjunctions and transition words. All stimuli are presented through visual and auditory modes to accommodate students with poor reading skills or auditory memory problems.

Informal Language Assessment

Informal assessment procedures generally are combined with standardized tests to provide descriptive information regarding a student's language ability. Although standardized measures are used widely, the emphasis on including some type of informal assessment is consistent with the theoretically based descriptive approach that is critical of viewing language as a series of independent objectives. Standardized instruments can determine the need for services; however, they often are too narrow to assess a student's baseline performance or the communicative skills needed for academic achievement in the classroom. Moreover, many formal tests use a small number of items to assess a particular skill, and using a small sample can lead to incorrect conclusions about the student's skill level. Thus, informal assessment often is used to affirm or refute the results of formal measures. Also, many formal measures do not give enough specific information to plan educational objectives. Therefore, informal language measures often are used to determine specific instructional objectives. Another common use of informal measures is to monitor a student's daily or weekly progress. Unlike formal measures, which are designed to assess a student over a long period of time, informal measures lend themselves to daily or weekly assessment.

The teacher may wish to interview the student's parents to obtain a case history as a form of informal assessment. This technique gives the teacher insight into the history of the student's language development. In addition, it provides information regarding the student's communicative functioning in environments other than the school setting and can result in suggestions for appropriate assessment and intervention techniques.

Larson and McKinley (1995) provide general and supplemental case history forms as well as a learning style questionnaire designed for preadolescent or adolescent students.

The current emphasis in language assessment stresses the informal evaluation of a student's language within the context in which it occurs. The goal of informal language assessment is to provide insight into how the student uses communication from a functional viewpoint in a variety of settings. Specific areas to examine include the intention or purpose of language, the social communicative context, and the physical setting. Various informal techniques that include the use of spontaneous, imitative, or elicited language can be used, depending on the type of information desired.

Informal Tests of Phonology   Phonology can be assessed informally by analyzing the student's production of phonemes in single words. The examiner makes a list of all the consonant phonemes and collects pictures to depict words that contain each phoneme. There should be a picture to elicit a word with the consonant in the initial position and a picture to depict the consonant in the final position. For example, a picture of a pot will elicit initial /p/, and a picture of a map will elicit final /p/. The examiner shows the student each picture and says, "Tell me the name of each picture." A notation is made if the student says the word incorrectly, and the results are recorded on a checklist. This type of assessment requires careful, experienced listening for accurate results. Only the error sounds are recorded; for example, a /b/ sound is recorded to indicate that the student said "bot" for *pot*. Also, comments that describe the error are recorded; for example, a substitution of /b/ for /p/ is recorded as an error in voicing. The examiner lists all the phoneme errors and determines which phonemes should have been mastered at the student's developmental age. These phonemes can become targets for the student's educational objectives.

After analyzing the phoneme profile and selecting a target phoneme, the examiner should collect baseline data on the target phoneme in the student's spontaneous speech. The examiner also needs to monitor change in the student's speech after corrective instruction has begun. Informal assessment is the primary tool used to gather baseline data on the target phoneme and to monitor change in the student's speech.

Direct observation of the production of a phoneme can be used to obtain baseline data and to monitor the student's progress. The examiner engages the student in spontaneous speech with pictures or toys as stimuli to elicit speech from the student. Older students may respond to prompts such as "Tell me about your weekend." The examiner's talking should be kept to a minimum so that the student is allowed to talk. During a 3-minute sample, the examiner counts the student's correct and incorrect productions of the target phoneme. The target phoneme's frequency can be observed by charting the correct and incorrect responses. Accuracy is computed by dividing the number of correct target phonemes the student said by the total number of target phonemes said (i.e., correct and incorrect).

One aspect of receptive phonology that is assessed readily by informal measures is auditory discrimination. The examiner may want to verify whether the student has difficulty discriminating between two particular sounds that were confused on a formal measure. For example, the student may have confused /p/ with /b/, and the examiner may assess these sounds further with a criterion measure. The measure can consist of a list of consonant-vowel-consonant words in which only one phoneme is different (e.g., *pin—bin* or *cup—cub*). Two words are said in word pairs, and the student is asked whether the words are the same or different. The examiner records the results on a checklist and scores the responses for accuracy. Accuracy levels can be used to indicate whether the student needs help in learning to discriminate these sounds. Accuracy of 90 percent or above is a good indication that the student already can discriminate these sounds.

Informal Tests of Morphology   Informal measures of morphology can determine the mastery level of each morpheme in a hierarchy. The examiner can use Brown's (1973) rank ordering of morpheme acquisition to make sentences that assess each morpheme. Pictures are presented with the sentences to assess the use of each morpheme. If the objective is to assess use of the present progressive morpheme *ing*, the examiner may show a picture of girls playing and say, "The girls like to play. Here they are _____." The student says the missing word, "playing." When assessing the use of the morpheme *in*, the examiner may show a picture of a baby sleeping and ask, "Where is the baby? The baby is _____." The student says the missing words, "in bed."

The examiner records the results as correct or incorrect on a checklist. Analysis of the results helps the teacher determine which morphemes are mastered and which need to be taught. Also, assessing the morphemes in a hierarchical order indicates to the teacher which morpheme to teach first.

Another informal assessment of morphology is a measure of accuracy of a specific morpheme in a student's conversational speech. Mastery of a morpheme is indicated by 90 percent accuracy in a student's conversational speech (Brown, 1973). It would be time consuming to obtain a daily or weekly conversational sample with enough occurrences of a specific morpheme to determine accuracy. An informal assessment that is less time consuming is to have the student respond to the prompt, "Tell me about this picture." First the examiner shapes the response by showing the student a picture depicting a person jumping and asks, "What is the person doing?" If the student does not describe the action (i.e., by saying "jumping" or "jump"), the examiner can prompt the student: "Say *jumping.*" After the student gives two correct responses (i.e., description of action) to two different pictures and the question "What is the person doing?" the instruction can be changed to "Tell me about this picture." The examiner can show a series of 20 pictures, each of which elicits the present progressive *ing* form of a word. As each picture is presented, the examiner says, "Tell me about this picture." The examiner records the number of correct and incorrect responses on a checklist. The accuracy percentage is determined by dividing the correct responses by the total number of pictures. If the accuracy is 90 percent or above, the morpheme is mastered and does not need to be taught. Accuracy below 90 percent indicates that the morpheme is not mastered and may require teaching. The examiner should note whether mastery of the morpheme is expected at the student's developmental age.

An informal measure of receptive morphology is to have the student point to a picture that depicts a morpheme. The examiner says a sentence with a specific morpheme and asks the student to point to the correct picture. For example, to assess the irregular past tense of *eat,* the examiner can show a picture of a girl who has finished eating and a picture of a girl eating. The examiner says, "The girl ate." The student must point to the correct picture of the girl who has finished eating. Sequencing picture cards (such as those produced by Lakeshore) can be used with this task. The examiner records the results on a checklist by marking each irregular past tense verb as correct or incorrect. The results are analyzed to determine which morphemes the student has mastered receptively. The examiner may recommend that the student master a morpheme receptively before he or she is taught to use that morpheme expressively.

Informal Tests of Syntax   Expressive syntax can be assessed informally by analyzing the student's spontaneous speech for use of grammatical forms. Spontaneous speech or language is a student's unrehearsed verbal expression that occurs naturally in real-life settings and situations. The examiner can obtain and record a spontaneous sample of the student's speech using the guidelines presented in the next section on informal tests of semantics. If the sample is used only for grammatical analysis, the guidelines can be modified so that a tape recorder is used without recording the context of each utterance. After recording, the examiner transcribes the sample and lists each utterance on a checklist, as shown in Figure 6.1. Each

FIGURE 6.1
Syntactic analysis of utterances

Student's Name: Michael Jordan Date: 3/15 Utterances	present progressive *ing*	is	plural regular s, es	possessive s	I, me, mine, my you, yours	irregular past	he, him, his she, her, hers	am, are, was, were	not	can't, don't	and	but	because	reversal of copula (is it)	who, what	where
1. What this is?		X													X	
2. That all of it?																
3. This a wall.																
4. I gonna tell you.					X											
5. Yeah, but her not in today.							X		X			X				
6. Car go up and car go down.																
7. Car go sideways.																

utterance is analyzed for the grammatical forms used, and a list is compiled of the grammatical forms that were not used. Each form is compared with norms for the student's developmental age. If the particular form is expected for the student's developmental age, a teaching objective can be planned to teach it.

An alternative informal assessment of syntax involves sentence repetition. The examiner says each sentence, and the student repeats it. In an imitation task that is long enough to tax the memory, the student frequently translates the adult sentence into the student's own language system and repeats the sentence using the student's own language rules (Salvia & Ysseldyke, 2010). Thus, imitation tasks can elicit language forms that the student did not attempt in spontaneous speech. To increase the accuracy of the examiner's judgment, the evaluation session can be recorded on tape so that the student's responses can be checked. The examiner records the student's responses on a checklist and analyzes them for critical syntactic features. Omitted syntactic features should be included in the student's educational objectives.

Informal Tests of Semantics   Some tasks that assess semantics are complex (such as the areas of logical relationships, cause-and-effect relationships, and verbal problem solving), so informal procedures may be difficult to devise. However, for areas such as verbal opposites, categorization, and classification of words, informal testing is useful.

For the assessment of verbal opposites, the examiner can use a set of cards that display pictures of pairs of opposites. When paired correctly, the cards in each set illustrate two opposites (e.g., *near* and *far*). The examiner mixes the cards and asks the student to sort them into sets of opposites. The examiner observes as the student makes set combinations, and the results are recorded on a checklist. Analysis of the incorrect sets helps the teacher determine which opposites to include in teaching objectives for the student.

An informal assessment of word categorization involves having the student say words in the same category. The examiner says a word and asks the student to say as many words as possible in the same category. The words can fall into the category because of similar function or physical attribute. The examiner lists the words on a checklist as the student says them. The results are analyzed to determine whether the student can say several words in a category or whether the student says a word that is an opposite, says a rhyming word, or tends to repeat the stimulus word.

A word association task can be used to measure word classification. Young children tend to respond to a stimulus word with a word that precedes or follows the stimulus word according to the rules of syntax. This is called a *syntagmatic* response. For example, if the stimulus word is "apple," the young student may respond with "eat" or "red." Youngsters shift to a response in the same grammatical category around the age of 6 to 8 years. This type of response is called *paradigmatic*. For example, if the stimulus word is "apple," the older student may respond with "orange," "banana," or another fruit. The examiner says the stimulus word, notes which kind of response the student makes, and records the response under that category (i.e., syntagmatic or paradigmatic) on a checklist. The checklist shows whether the student is categorized as a younger child with syntagmatic responses or as an older student with paradigmatic responses. The student may have responses in both categories but have most responses in one category.

Another area of semantics that can be assessed by informal measures is semantic relationships. This area can be assessed if the student's language utterances are three or fewer words. If a student uses more words, a syntactic analysis is more appropriate. Semantic relationships can be assessed informally by analyzing the student's spontaneous speech. The examiner observes the student playing or interacting with someone, codes or transcribes the conversation, and analyzes it according to error pattern. Various objects such as clay, toys, and games can be used to stimulate communication.

The following steps for obtaining a speech or language sample can be used.

1. Set up a partially structured play situation in which the student interacts with a familiar adult.
2. Use toys that the student is familiar with and that are likely to elicit a variety of responses.
3. Record the student's speech on videotape. Continue the sampling until 50 to 100 intelligible utterances are obtained. If videotape equipment is not available, record the sample on a tape recorder and have an observer record the context of each utterance.
4. Avoid talking excessively or structuring the student's verbal responses by asking questions such as "What is this?" or "What color is the doll's dress?"
5. Transcribe the tape as soon as possible.
6. List each utterance (i.e., any meaningful speech segment preceded and followed by a pause). Analyze each word in the utterance for semantic form and list each word under the appropriate category. Several two- and three-word utterances are analyzed in Figure 6.2. The two-word utterance "that

FIGURE 6.2

Format for semantic analysis of a language sample

Student's Name _Lisa Walker_   Date Collected _4/3_

Total Number of Utterances _11_

Relationship Components	Demonstrative		Attribute			Possession	Conjunction
	Nomination	Notice	Recurrence	Nonexistence	Descriptive		
Two-word grammatical	That ball	Hi Mommy	More cookie	allgone cookie	Big ball pipe	Daddy	Milk cookie
Three+-word grammatical							
Nongrammatical one-word utterances							

Relationship Components	Action			Location			
	Agent	Action	Object	Agent	Action	Object	Location
Two-word grammatical							
Three+-word grammatical	Mommy	drink	milk	Daddy Mommy	sit put	car doll	here here bed
Nongrammatical one-word utterances							

ball" is listed under demonstrative because *that* plus a noun is used to point out an object or person. "More cookie" is listed under attribute because *more* modifies the noun, and "Daddy pipe" is listed under possession because it refers to Daddy's ownership of the pipe. "Milk cookie" is listed under conjunction because it refers to milk *and* cookie. The three-word utterance "Mommy drink milk" is placed in the action category (i.e., agent—Mommy; action—drink; object—milk).

7. After listing each utterance in the appropriate category, analyze the checklist to determine which semantic relationships the student did or did not use. The forms that the student did not use can be included in teaching objectives of semantic relationships. For example, if the student used three-word utterances but did not use action-object-location forms, this may be an appropriate teaching objective.

After the student's language sample is analyzed for semantic grammar, the mean length of utterance in morphemes is computed. Brown (1973) suggests the following sequence.

1. Transcribe the language sample.
2. Start the analysis on the second page of the transcription and count the first 100 utterances. Count only fully transcribed utterances, including utterance repetitions.
3. Count each morpheme in the 100 utterances. Do not count fillers (i.e., "mm" or "oh") or repetitions, but do count "no," "yeah," and "hi." Count as single morphemes all compound words, proper names, idiomatic duplications (e.g., *night-night, choo-choo,* and *see-saw*), irregular past tenses of verbs (e.g., *got, did, went,* and *saw*), diminutives (e.g., *doggie*), and catenatives (e.g., *gonna, wanna,* and *hafta*). Count as separate morphemes all auxiliaries (e.g., *is, have, will, can, want,* and *would*) and inflections (e.g., possessive *s*, plural *s*, third-person singular *s*, regular past *ed*, and progressive *ing*).
4. Compute the mean length of utterance by dividing the total number of morphemes by 100.

FIGURE 6.3
Checklist of pragmatic functions

Utterances	Instrumental	Protest	Request	Acquire Information	Metalinguistic	Give Information	Label	Imitate	Answer	Initiate/Terminate Social	Entertain	Other
Student's Name _Julie Bates_ Date _2/12_												
1. Drink milk	X											
2. No milk		X										
3. Shoes on			X									
4. Car							X					
Question asked: "Where is the ball?" 5. Ball chair									X			
6. Daddy come?			X									

The mean length of utterance gives the examiner a quick measure of growth over an extended time period. Many research studies report students' semantic development in terms of this measure rather than chronological age. For example, the agent-action-object semantic form may be reported as occurring in students with a mean length of utterance of three words, rather than in students of any specific chronological age.

Informal Tests of Pragmatics Pragmatics can be assessed informally by analyzing a sample of the student's spontaneous speech to determine which pragmatic function was used. The first step is to obtain a videotaped language sample from the student. (Guidelines for obtaining a language sample are presented in the semantics section of this chapter.) If videotape equipment is not available, an observer can record what happened just before and just after each utterance. The second step is to transcribe the tape and list each utterance on a checklist, as shown in Figure 6.3. The examiner classifies the pragmatic function of an utterance by analyzing the events before and after it. For example, the student's utterance may be "Throw ball." The examiner notes that before the utterance the examiner was holding the ball and the student's arms were extended to catch the ball, and also notes that the examiner threw the ball to the student after the utterance. The utterance is classified as a request and a mark is put in the *Request* column. The examiner analyzes the checklist for each function the student did or did not use and then lists the functions that the student did not use. For example, it may be noted that the student did not use a protest function, such as "No shoes," to mean "Don't put on my shoes." The teacher can select from the pragmatic functions that were not used to determine appropriate teaching objectives.

In older students, informal assessment of pragmatics includes measures of speaking with inappropriate loudness, talking at inappropriate times, interrupting the speaker, and using indirect requests. These behaviors can be assessed by counting and recording them in several situations and on different days. A teacher may want to count and record these same behaviors in a speaker of the same age who is not delayed in pragmatics. The teacher can select a student who talks to other students and contributes during group activities, rather than a student who is quiet or has little to say. Three situations are chosen, such as group instructional time, independent work time, and lunch or playground time. The teacher counts the number of times each student interrupts other speakers, talks too loudly, and talks when the student should be listening, reading, or working. The results are recorded on charts, and the teacher compares the results of the two students. A significant difference in the two students' behaviors signifies a possible teaching objective. An appropriate objective is to decrease interruptions by increasing skills in determining when a speaker is finished talking.

Indirect requests can be assessed informally in students whose developmental age is 8 years and above by asking the student to state the implied direct requests. For example, the examiner says, "Tell me what I want you to do when I say, 'Can you close the door?'" The student says, "You want me to close the door." The examiner then says, "Tell me what I want you to do in each of the following sentences." The examiner reads indirect requests listed on a checklist and puts a check in a column to indicate whether the student's response is correct or incorrect. The results are analyzed to determine the number of errors made and the forms with which the student is having the most difficulty (i.e., the affirmative: "Can you . . .?"; the negative: "Can't you . . .?"; or the affirmative with negative intention: "Must you . . .?"). These forms of indirect requests can become teaching objectives for the student.

Curriculum-Based Measurement In curriculum-based measurement, curriculum contexts and content are used to determine appropriate language interventions by identifying activities and skills that may help the student develop more effective communicative skills. The goal is to make functional changes relevant to the student's communicative needs within the academic setting. Sample language contexts and skills can include expository test comprehension, the ability to follow oral directions, narrative comprehension and production, and use of language to complete math problems. Additional activities may include written expression, silent and oral reading, and listening comprehension of written language. Nelson (1994) discusses the philosophy and methods of curriculum-based language assessment and intervention for students with language problems.

LANGUAGE SERVICE DELIVERY MODELS

Pullout Therapy Model

The most common language service delivery model is the pullout therapy model, in which the language specialist takes students from their classes and instructs those with similar difficulties in homogeneous groups. Many teachers admit that this model presents various problems and can result in ineffective and inefficient services. Students often dislike this model because they do not like to be singled out as different. This becomes particularly important as peer pressure increases during adolescence. Many adolescents also do not want to continue with the same methods and activities as they had during speech instruction in elementary school, and they lack motivation to achieve because speech and language therapy is not a class they register for in their normal schedule.

The pullout method also causes students to miss course work while they are out of the classroom. This is especially devastating to students with learning problems, who can least afford to miss classroom instruction. As attempts are made to formulate a pullout schedule, the language specialist is faced with numerous scheduling concerns, such as from which subject and how often to pull the student as well as how to handle special events, tests, and absences. Scheduling problems are compounded further by the number of students who need services and the inability to provide the intensity required by certain students.

A final problem associated with the pullout model involves fragmentation of services. Because students generally are seen for therapy in a separate classroom, the services often are isolated from general classroom content and, thus, may not be consistent with classroom goals and expectations. Disagreement regarding responsibility for certain content and type of instruction increases when language goals seem irrelevant to the student's functioning or needs in the general classroom, or when the goals are derived without regard to content in the curriculum. This fragmentation of services frequently results in resentment on the part of the general classroom teacher and often hinders students who need instructional consistency to achieve academic success.

Classroom-Based Language Models

Classroom-based models involve a new delivery of traditional services, and some school systems use them in an attempt to improve the services to students with language problems and to integrate therapy goals with the student's academic needs. In spite of their differences, all classroom-based models emphasize the need for collaborative consultation between the classroom teacher and the language specialist so that resulting interventions are meaningful and relevant to natural occurrences in the classroom. The American

Speech-Language-Hearing Association (1991) Committee on Language-Learning Disorders presents a model for collaborative service delivery for students with language-learning disorders. In the collaborative service delivery model, the team members (i.e., language specialist, teacher, parents, and student) work together closely to plan and implement each student's educational program. The team devises all treatment goals, assessment methods, intervention procedures, and documentation systems to enhance the student's academic and social functioning in the school environment. The team members share responsibility for educational goals, and all services and instruction take place in the classroom. The five major types of classroom-based language models include team teaching; self-contained classroom teaching; one-to-one intervention; staff, curriculum, or program development; and consultation.

Team Teaching In this classroom-based model, the language specialist teaches with the general or special classroom teacher. The key to this format is that the language specialist actually teaches a portion of the curriculum. The curriculum goals and objectives as well as the methods and materials to be used are established jointly by the members of the professional team. Services can be rendered in a variety of settings, including the general classroom with the general education teacher or a self-contained classroom or a resource room with a special education teacher.

Self-Contained Classroom Teaching In this service-model format, the language specialist teaches in a self-contained language class. This format is common with younger students, and the language specialist is responsible for teaching content areas including reading, math, science, and social studies to students who need particular interventions in language processing and production. At the middle- and secondary-school levels, some language specialists offer a separate course that focuses on writing, reading, or other language areas that are difficult for students with language problems to deal with in the general curriculum.

One-to-One Intervention The language specialist can provide one-to-one intervention to particular students in the classroom. In this approach, the language specialist must maintain close contact with the classroom teacher to provide appropriate interventions to each student regarding specific content areas, study skills, writing, and vocabulary. Classroom textbooks and materials are used to maintain relevance to ongoing classroom activities.

Staff, Curriculum, or Program Development The language specialist can aid students indirectly by providing staff, curriculum, or program development to a school or district. For example, the specialist can plan community programs to increase student and parental awareness of the school's language objectives. The language specialist also can participate in curriculum development and evaluation or present in-service workshops to teachers or parents that focus on the effect of language on academic success. This service delivery format requires a fundamental change in the focus of the language specialist from providing direct service to students to educating those responsible for teaching the students.

Consultation The language specialist can serve as a consultant to the various professionals who interact with students, such as general or special education teachers, psychologists, physicians, nurses, social workers, or counselors. In this model, the language specialist consults with persons who provide language interventions to the student, and an effort is made through the consultation to determine methods to improve the student's communication. An additional benefit of the consultation format is that students who do not qualify for direct services under school district guidelines benefit indirectly from the suggestions of the consultant as they affect educational and social concerns in the classroom.

Strategies-Based Model

A strategies-based service delivery model focuses on teaching specific learning strategies to students and is especially appealing to language specialists who work with middle and secondary school students. One of the major differences between the strategy-based model and a classroom-based model is that students are able to register for and receive a grade for the course work. The use of strategies involves increasing the student's understanding and use of metacognitive and metalinguistic skills. These skills focus on improving the student's awareness and use of strategies that enhance learning. In essence, a change is made from teaching students *what* to learn to teaching students *how* to learn.

Based on the perspective that many students with language problems show delays in metalinguistic maturation and strategic language use, Wiig (1990) discusses the need for emphasizing different reasoning strategies in language intervention. This approach to language intervention is process oriented rather than product oriented and is implemented collaboratively between language specialists and classroom teachers.

One of the most widely researched and developed approaches to learning strategies is the Strategies Intervention Model developed by Don Deshler and his colleagues at the University of Kansas Center for Research on Learning. Although this model is quite specific, it is based on principles applicable to strategy training in general. Deshler and Schumaker (1986) state that the ultimate goal of learning strategies is to enable students to analyze and solve novel problems in both academic and nonacademic settings. Their approach to teaching learning strategies to adolescents is based on three rationales.

1. The development and application of learning strategies or metacognitive skills are appropriate for older students who are more proficient in these skills.
2. Adolescents who learn how to learn are in a better position to learn new skills in the future.
3. Students should accept responsibility for their learning and progress.

To design relevant instruction, the language specialist must determine what curriculum demands the student is failing to meet. Student involvement and mutual goal setting also should be established to maximize motivation toward learning, and activities should be designed to promote generalization. Motivation can be enhanced by broadening the student's understanding of the skill and its application to a variety of settings. To facilitate generalization, the learning-strategies model stresses the importance of cooperative planning and consultation between the language specialist, general and special education teachers, and personnel of other support services.

TEACHING LANGUAGE SKILLS

Many teachers who use direct teaching methods for remediation of reading and math problems undoubtedly select this technique for teaching language skills. With this format, the teacher directs the learning and dictates the lesson's content, pace, and sequencing. Often the student is allowed little opportunity to engage in spontaneous conversations during this highly structured skills approach. Conversely, some teachers believe that learning should be student centered, with the student dictating the lesson's content, pace, and sequencing.

The teacher controls minimally and emphasizes social interaction so that communication can occur along the lines of normal conversation. To teach new concepts, the responsive interaction approach emphasizes adult expansions or modifications of the youngster's utterances, whereas elicited prompts are used in milieu teaching. It may be advantageous to use a combination of approaches based on the characteristics of the learner, the instructional context, and the skills being taught. For example, milieu teaching may be effective for teaching early vocabulary, whereas direct instruction can be used for teaching more abstract language skills.

When designing appropriate language intervention, the phonological, syntactic, semantic, and pragmatic aspects should be considered, as well as the student's cognitive skills and social environment. The following general principles focus on meeting a student's language needs.

- The language specialist should be aware of young students with language disorders who are dismissed from language services, because academic problems may resurface later due to a breakdown in the language system and increased curriculum demands.
- Language screenings should consist of more than one test and be sensitive to subtle forms of language disorders.
- Students suspected of having learning problems should receive routine language evaluations that emphasize language and auditory processing.
- School officials should consider service delivery alternatives to the traditional pullout model, and language specialists should focus on both contextualized and decontextualized aspects of language.
- Professionals should collaborate to devise a coordinated program for students with language problems rather than implement a variety of isolated programs.
- The delivery of instruction in learning strategies should be language sensitive.
- The curriculum in language intervention should be relevant to the general curriculum, respond to setting demands, reflect areas of academic concern, integrate spoken and written language systems, and focus on generalization.
- The individual strategy preferences of students with language problems should be considered, and students should be encouraged to determine which strategies are successful in a given situation.

- Intervention should encourage student accountability and responsibility.
- Effective interventions from other disciplines should be applied.

Moreover, especially when working with young children, the following specific techniques for teaching language may be helpful.

- Teach language in a context.
- Follow the sequence of normal language development.
- Use specific and effective teaching strategies when introducing a new concept.
- Vocalize thoughts or describe actions.
- Describe what others are doing using parallel talk.
- Use modeling to provide practice on a specific language skill.
- Use expansion to show how an idea can be expressed in a more complex manner.
- Use elaboration to demonstrate how to provide more information.
- Use structured programs to provide adequate practice and feedback regarding performance.
- Use everyday activities to provide skill practice within a context.
- Recognize the relationship of comprehension and production.
- Systematically plan for and teach generalization.

Because language is interactive, the teacher should be creative when implementing teaching methods, because an activity designed to focus on a particular skill also may be useful in other areas. The remainder of this section presents strategies for increasing language comprehension, strategies for increasing language production, and imitation and modeling strategies.

Strategies for Increasing Language Comprehension

The following strategies may improve listening skills and increase the comprehension or understanding of students with language problems.

- If the student frequently has difficulty following directions or understanding information of increased complexity, establish eye contact and maintain attention prior to presenting information. Cue the student to listen by using silent pauses or instructions to listen to or look at the teacher. This helps to establish a mental set for listening.
- Ask the student to repeat or paraphrase directions or instructions to the teacher or a peer to ensure comprehension.

- To facilitate listening, arrange classroom seating to limit distractions from doorways and windows and to maximize the use of visual aids.
- When introducing a new concept or skill, use vocabulary that is familiar to the student and explain new vocabulary words by using familiar terms.
- Present new concepts in as many modalities as possible (e.g., auditory, visual, and kinesthetic), and use gestures to augment verbal presentations.
- To increase understanding of the relationship between semantic role and word order, encourage young children to act out sentences (e.g., "Mommy kiss baby") or manipulate objects and talk about their movement.
- Explain to students that listening is an active process that requires them to behave in certain ways, and teach them to identify specific behaviors associated with good listening (e.g., look, think about what is said, and repeat to yourself). Model effective listening skills by being attentive to students.
- Use introductory statements (such as "These are the main points" or "Before we begin") to provide an organizational framework and help students prepare for a task.
- Be sensitive to the students' linguistic sophistication and adjust the rate and complexity of instructional language accordingly. Use structurally simple and relatively short sentences of not more than 5 to 10 words and limit the number of new and unfamiliar vocabulary words presented in a single lesson to five or less (Wiig & Semel, 1984).
- Teach specific memory strategies (e.g., visual imagery, clustering and grouping information, and forming associations) to help students organize, categorize, and store new information for later retrieval.
- To enhance students' recall and memorization of new vocabulary, use the keyword method, in which familiar words are associated with each new concept or word (Mastropieri, Scruggs, & Fulk, 1990).
- Engage adolescents in concrete problem-solving activities to identify those who have difficulty thinking symbolically or using reasoning in nonsymbolic events (Moses, Klein, & Altman, 1990).

Strategies for Increasing Language Production

The following strategies focus on improving the production or expressive skills of students with language problems.

- Expect students to speak occasionally in incomplete sentences because this is normal for discourse.

- Regardless of the effectiveness of a student's communication, convey that the message is important. React first to the content of a student's message because it is most important in the communication process, and then correct the syntax error.

- When attempting to expand a young child's utterances, provide one or two additional words to the child's spontaneous utterance for the child to repeat rather than impose adult structures that are difficult to imitate. Explain that the reason for the expansion of the utterance is not to correct what the youngster is saying but to give a more complex way of expressing thought.

- Teach language in various natural settings (e.g., classroom, cafeteria, and playground) rather than only in isolated groups. Also, teach language skills in connection with other curriculum content.

- Act as a good language model, and ask students to imitate what they hear. Imitation is frequently a good measure of language skills because students tend to imitate only the forms they know and not necessarily what they hear.

- Use structured language programs that provide adequate opportunities to practice a new skill as well as interactive activities for applying the skill to relevant contexts.

- Comment or elaborate on students' ideas to demonstrate how more information can be expressed and how concepts can be associated.

- Use activities such as role playing and charades to improve a student's use of language in different contexts and to enhance the ability to recognize the importance of nonverbal skills such as eye contact, facial expressions, and gestures. Also, model and reinforce appropriate turn-taking in conversations.

- When a student has difficulties with word retrieval, examine indices such as response time, error index (i.e., word-selection process), and substitution types (German, 1984).

- Use semantic training to improve a student's word-retrieval skills, and include strategies such as categorizing or classifying words and using associative clues.

- To improve a student's verbal expression, encourage storytelling activities in which the student must name all of the objects or pictures, tell what is happening, and create an ending.

- Teach generalization of language skills through three phases: an orientation phase in which the student becomes aware of the different contexts applicable, an activation phase in which practice is provided in a variety of situations, and a maintenance phase in which periodic probes are conducted to ensure proficiency is maintained (Deshler & Schumaker, 1986).

Imitation and Modeling Strategies

Two frequently used language-skills teaching strategies are imitation and modeling. In these strategies, the student gives a response that is similar to that of a model. In imitative behavior that is mimicry, the student gives a one-to-one, literal matching response for each stimulus statement. In contrast to mimicry, modeling involves acquiring an abstract language rule without giving an immediate response to the stimulus. For example, the student observes the teacher modeling a rule several times before being required to use the rule. This strategy is apparent in the following method of teaching the use of s on singular verbs: The teacher models 20 different singular subject–verb sentences that describe pictures (such as "Dog runs," "Boy walks," and "Cat plays"). After the teacher models these sentences, the student is requested to describe the pictures.

To use modeling with problem solving, the teacher can use a puppet as a model and place visual stimuli, such as toys or pictures of objects and people, in front of the model (i.e., puppet). The teacher tells the student to listen carefully and determine which sentences earn reinforcers for the model. The model produces 10 to 20 utterances that describe the visual

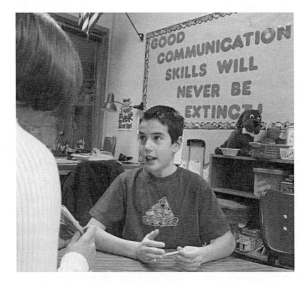

Informal assessment of a student's oral language skills can help determine specific instructional objectives.
Patrick White/Merrill

177

stimuli and deliberately gives 25 percent of the responses incorrectly. The teacher then presents the same visual stimulus to the student and encourages a response that earned a reinforcer for the model. The student and model take turns responding until the student has produced three consecutive appropriate responses that were presented previously by the model. At this point the student is presented with new visual stimuli and is required to produce unmodeled utterances.

The teacher can use imitative mimicry at one point with a student and gradually move to more spontaneous responses. When using this strategy, the teacher needs to structure the event preceding the student's response (i.e., the antecedent event). The antecedent event can have varying degrees of cueing. A teacher can use total cueing in the antecedent event (e.g., "What do you want? Tell me, 'I want an apple.'") or partial cueing in the antecedent event (e.g., "Is this a ball or an orange?"). Partial cueing also can include pointing to or looking at items to help the student make a correct response. Minimal cueing can be used when the student is ready to generalize a rule. For example, the teacher can say "What's happening? What's he doing?"

The expansion model is a modeling technique frequently used by parents for language intervention. With this technique, the youngster's response is expanded by the parent or teacher. For example, the youngster says, "Car go," and the parent or teacher immediately gives the expanded model, "The car is going." The expansion model can be used during any interaction with a youngster; however, shared storybook reading is a particularly useful time to employ this technique (Pullen & Justice, 2003). In shared storybook reading, the adult prompts the child to be an active participant as a story is read aloud. As the adult and child talk about the story and the illustrations, the parent or teacher uses expansion modeling, which maximizes the benefit of reading aloud.

LANGUAGE ACTIVITIES

After carefully selecting a language program, the teacher may decide to supplement to meet the specific needs of certain students. Some teachers prefer to plan a complete individualized program rather than use an available commercial program. To supplement or design an individualized program, the teacher must plan teaching activities. One advantage of planning activities is that the teacher can select and vary teaching methods and materials to fit individual students' needs.

Direct teaching activities are designed to meet specific objectives. They must, however, be supplemented with independent learning and reinforcing activities. Self-correcting materials are a good choice for independent learning of a skill, and instructional games frequently are used to reinforce newly acquired skills. Various teaching activities are presented in this section, and instructional games and self-correcting materials are described in the following sections. Activities, games, and self-correcting materials that are appropriate for use with secondary students are presented near the end of each section.

1. ***To teach* is + *verb* + ing (is jumping):** For each picture, say a model sentence that includes *is* plus verb plus *ing*. The teacher can show a picture of a girl jumping rope and say, "The girl is jumping." The teacher models ten different sentences with pictures. The student is not encouraged to respond during the modeled sentences. After the modeled sentences, the teacher shows the pictures again and asks the student to tell what is happening in each picture. After successful completion of this task, the teacher shows ten new action pictures and for each new picture, says, "Tell me what's happening."

Modification: The teacher can use modeling to teach semantics, morphology, syntax, and so forth by varying the stimulus and the modeled response. For example, the morphological form of singular pronouns plus the inflectional verb ending *s* (e.g., "She walks") can be taught by using action pictures with singular subjects and changing the model to "She walks," "He runs," "He jumps," and so on.

2. ***To teach plural morpheme s on regular plural nouns:*** Use modeling with problem solving to teach language rules. Show a puppet 20 pictures that depict 20 plural nouns. The puppet names each picture and misses 25 percent of them. The teacher reinforces each correct response with a chip. After the modeling of 20 pictures, the teacher asks the student to name the pictures. After the student correctly responds to these pictures, the teacher presents 20 new pictures and asks the student to name them.

Modification: Modeling with problem solving also can be used to teach semantics, phonology, syntax, and so on. For example, to teach a syntactic rule of *they* + *are* + verb + *ing*, present pictures depicting action with a plural subject (such as children playing) and say to the puppet, "Tell me what's happening in each picture." The puppet responds using the form of *they* + *are* + verb + *ing* for each picture (e.g., "They are playing."). The puppet randomly makes 25 percent of the responses incorrect (e.g., "They play"). The teacher reinforces the correct responses with a chip. After the modeling, the teacher says, "You give the puppet a chip for each correct sentence." After successful completion of this task, the teacher says to the student, "You tell me what's happening in each picture."

3. **To teach possessive pronouns (her, his, their):** Prepare small cards with mounted pictures of a single girl, a single boy, and several children. Mount pictures of objects on separate cards. Attach the cards to rings and group all the people pictures together on one set of rings and all the object cards on another. Attach the rings and card sets to a folded cardboard stand. The student or teacher flips each card separately to form phrases (e.g., *her hat, his ball, their house,* and so forth). Coloring books and computer clip art are good sources of pictures.

Modification: A third set of color cards can be used in which each card is shaded a different color. The student is required to say phrases such as "Her dress is red," "His hat is yellow," or "His ball is blue."

4. **To teach classification of associated words:** Have the student sort various association pictures using the following procedure (see Figure 6.4).

- Mount individual pictures of objects commonly associated with each other on small cards. Select pictures such as ball and bat, cup and saucer, and shoe and sock from reading-readiness workbooks.

- Make a card holder with strips of tagboard stapled to a large piece of tagboard.
- Place a picture in each slot down the left side of the card holder.
- Have the student place the remaining pictures and tell how the two objects are associated.

Modification: Matching pictures and pictures that depict opposites can be used. Also, the activity can be made self-correcting by putting matching shapes on the backs of associated pictures. After sorting the pictures, the student can check the work by looking at the backs of the cards to determine whether the shapes match.

5. **To teach ed on regular verbs (walked, jumped):** Have the student describe an activity as he or she is performing it. For example, the student says, "I am jumping" as he or she is jumping. Upon completion, have the student say, "I jumped very high" or "I jumped over the box." This activity can be extended by using small objects that can perform movement; for example, a doll can be made to jump, walk, or hop. Also, this activity can be used to teach irregular verb forms such as *ate, drank,* and *fell.*

6. **To teach the prepositions in, on, out of, in front of, in back of, and beside:** Use hula hoops and physical activity to teach prepositions. Tell the students to move in relation to the hoops (e.g., "Stand in the hula hoops."). At first the teacher announces and performs the activity with students; then gradually the teacher only announces the activity. Finally, the teacher has students themselves talk during the activity. For example, students say, "The hula hoop is beside me" when they move their hoops by their side.

FIGURE 6.4
Association pictures mounted in a card holder

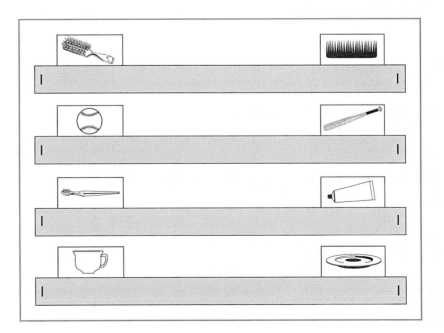

Modification: The teacher can stand in some kind of relation to the hoop (e.g., in the hoop) and ask, "Where am I?" The students answer, "You are in the hula hoop." Each student then can have a turn standing in relation to the hula hoop and asking, "Where am I?"

7. ***To teach classification of part/whole relationships:*** Cut out of flannel the parts of two complete objects such as a truck. Have one truck put together on the flannelboard before beginning. Ask the student to complete the second truck by saying, "Put on the part of the truck that is the wheel," "Put on the part of the truck that is the door," and so on.

Modification: This activity also can be used to teach functional relationships. For example, ask the student to put on the part of the truck that opens to let people inside, or the part of the truck that turns to change the truck's direction.

8. ***To teach classification by function:*** Collect pictures of objects used for one function. For example, to show a bath, collect pictures of a bathtub, soap, washcloth, and towel. Have the student sort the pictures according to function. For example:

- *Sandwich:* bread, knife, peanut butter, and jelly
- *Bath:* tub or shower, washcloth, towel, and soap
- *Washing dishes:* dishes, soap, sink, sponge, drainer, and towel
- *Building:* lumber, nails, hammer, sandpaper, paint, screws, and tools

Modification: This task can be made more difficult for older students by making the functional relationships more complex (e.g., *Dressing for a party:* washing hair, fixing fingernails, brushing hair, and brushing teeth).

9. ***To classify objects that belong to the same class (animals, foods, houses, vehicles):*** Prepare a large card with four sections. In one section put a picture of a house; in the second section put a picture of an animal; in the third, a picture of a vehicle; and in the fourth, a picture of food. Collect and mount pictures of animals, foods, houses, and vehicles. Have the student sort the pictures in the four areas. An area can be made with a color or shape so that the student can sort objects or pictures according to these attributes.

10. ***To teach synonyms:*** Ask a student to call out a word for which he or she knows at least one synonym. Then ask the next student to "match" the word by providing a synonym of it. Use a game format in which the student receives one point for each correct synonym named. If unable to think of any synonyms, the student can challenge the first player to state the synonym he or she had in mind. Any failure in this task is penalized by one point. A player fails to score a point if he or she is unable to think of a synonym, and a player is penalized one point if he or she responds with a word that is not a synonym of the word proposed by the preceding player. The object is to squeeze as many synonyms out of the original word as possible. If a player can think of only one or two synonyms, the opponent can earn points by naming some others. When the possibilities of a given word have been exhausted, a new word is used.

Modification: This activity also can be used with antonyms. For example, if *big* is the given word, an appropriate response might be *little.* Then the next player must give an antonym of *little* (e.g., *large*) without using the original word, *big.* A point is scored for each correct antonym (or synonym of the original word) given.

11. ***To increase auditory discrimination between two phonemes:*** Draw a ladder on a piece of paper. Provide a marker and tell the student to move the marker when he or she hears two different words. Say some word pairs that consist of the same word and some that are different words. When the student consistently moves the marker only for two different words, change the task by having the student listen to words that are different by only one phoneme, such as *pair–fair.* The student moves the marker when he or she hears two different words. Some suggested pairs differing in only one phoneme are *pair–fair, purr–fur, put–foot, pork–fork,* and *pay–day.*

Modification: The activity can be modified according to how the student signals that two sounds are the same or different. The student can raise a hand, tap a pencil, move a space on a game board, or pick up a chip.

12. ***To teach negatives:*** Model a sentence without a negative and then immediately model a sentence containing a negative. For example, the teacher says, "Some for John. None for John." The student imitates the two sentences. When several sentences with negatives have been modeled correctly, the teacher only presents a sentence without a negative. The student responds by saying a sentence with a negative. A recommended sequence of negatives is as follows:

- no
- none
- nothing else
- no more
- not enough
- don't
- let's not
- we'll not
- do not
- don't do
- is no more
- does not
- is not
- did not
- nothing is
- will not
- was not

Modification: This technique can be used to teach morphology. For example, to teach plural *s* on regular nouns, the teacher can present sets of two pictures and two modeled responses, such as "one kite—two kites, one cat—two cats." After the student correctly repeats several modeled responses, the teacher presents a picture of one cat and says, "One cat." Then the teacher presents a picture of two cats, and the student says, "Two cats."

13. ***To extend the use of linguistic forms to other environments:*** Have a student act as a speaker to describe an object to a listener such that the listener can select a similar object from several objects placed in front of him or her. The speaker and listener sit back-to-back. Place three objects in front of the listener (e.g., key, comb, and ball) and one similar object (such as a comb) in front of the speaker. The speaker describes the object, and the listener is encouraged to ask questions until he or she can select the correct object.

Modification: A block-building activity can be used in which two students are seated back-to-back. The speaker and listener each have an identical set of six blocks that vary in shape, color, or size. The speaker builds a construction using all of the blocks and provides enough information so that the listener can duplicate the construction.

14. ***To use language as an effective communicator:*** Use an over-the-shoulder activity in which the speaker is the encoder and the listener is the decoder. The encoder stands behind the decoder and talks over the decoder's shoulder to tell the decoder what to do next. The encoder must give information so that the decoder understands, and the information must be revised if the decoder does not understand. For example, the encoder may say, "Put the red triangle on top of the blue square." The decoder places the triangle above the square so that it touches the top of the square. The encoder then may say, "You have put the triangle on top of the square like a roof on a house. Instead, lay it on top of the square like a blanket." The encoder must keep revising the instructions until the decoder completely understands the message.

Modification: The encoder can draw a simple design and then talk over the decoder's shoulder to tell how to draw the same design. The decoder can stand at the chalkboard while the encoder looks at his or her own design and the one the decoder is drawing.

15. ***To teach the classification of where, when, and what phrases:*** Write the word *where* next to the word *place*. Tell the student that *where* refers to place. With the student, list a few phrases that refer to place. Write the word *what* next to the word *thing*. Tell the student to list some phrases that refer to things. Write the word *when* next to the word *time*. Tell the student that *when* usually refers to time. The student needs a broader concept of time than time on a clock. Time can refer to the hour, parts of a day, events of a day (such as breakfast,

school, and bedtime), day of the week, and so on. Have the student list some time phrases. For practice, provide a worksheet with the three headings of *Where*, *What*, and *When* and have the student list the following phrases under the appropriate heading.

- on the playground
- tomorrow morning
- beside your bed
- the blue car
- on a rainy day
- her pretty dress
- my broken cup
- behind the school
- a small coat
- at my house
- before lunch
- after school

Modification: This activity also can be used to classify *who*, *why*, and *how* phrases. Classification of these phrases can be made self-correcting by putting the phrases on cards in a Poke Box (described in Chapter 2) with the multiple-choice words of *When*, *Where*, and *What* (or *Who*, *Why*, and *How*).

16. ***To teach vocabulary likenesses:*** Write the following verbs and objects on the chalkboard.

kicking	swing
pushing	house
sewing	ball
building	dress

Ask the student to tell how to pair the action words and objects. Then ask the student to tell how *kicking* the *ball* is like *pushing* a *swing*. (Help the student conclude that when you kick a ball it goes away from you, and when you push a swing it also goes away from you.) Ask the student how *sewing* a *dress* is like *building* a *house*. (Again, help the student conclude that when you build or sew you make a complete item out of parts.) Then provide a worksheet with incomplete sentences and ask the student to select the best word to complete each sentence. For example:

- *Sweeping* is to *broom* as *hitting* is to _____. (bat, ball, catch)
- *Sleeping* is to *bed* as *sitting* is to _____. (table, chair, desk)
- *Smiling* is to *happy* as *crying* is to _____. (anger, tears, sad)
- *Eating* is to *food* as *drinking* is to _____. (thirst, water, cup)
- *Writing* is to *pencil* as *painting* is to _____. (paper, canvas, brush)

Modification: This vocabulary task of comparison of likenesses can be modified to include items based on part/whole relationships (e.g., *fingers* are to *hands* as *toes* are to *feet*).

17. ***To teach the use of relative clauses:*** On the chalkboard give the student several examples of sentences that contain relative clauses. Then give the student a practice sheet with several sets of two sentences. Ask the student to combine each set of two sentences into one sentence by using a relative pronoun. For example:

- The boy broke the window. The boy ran away. (who)
- Read the book. The book is about dogs. (that)

- The boy who broke the window ran away.
- Read the book that is about dogs.

Modification: The sentences can be combined with conjunctions such as *and, but, because,* and *so.* For example, the following sentences can be combined with *but:*

- Bob eats breakfast every day. Bob is always hungry at lunch.
- The puppy plays outside. The puppy likes to sleep in the house.

- Bob eats breakfast every day, but he is always hungry at lunch.
- The puppy plays outside, but he likes to sleep in the house.

18. *To use the conjunctions* **and, but, because,** *and* **so:** Use the cloze procedure with multiple-choice items. Make a list of sentences that require the use of a conjunction. Leave a blank space and give multiple choices. For example:

- I don't want ice cream _____ I would like a dessert. (or, but)
- You should take a bath _____ you are dirty. (because, but)
- You must finish your homework _____ you can play outside. (but, so)

Modification: The cloze procedure with multiple-choice items can be used to teach semantics, morphology, or other forms of syntax. For example, the following sentence requires an inflectional ending (*-ed*) on a regular verb:

The boy _____ to school this morning before breakfast. (walk, walked)

19. *To teach paraphrasing:* Use a game format in which the students are divided into two teams. Have the first player on Team A tell the first player on Team B to do something (e.g., "Touch your nose."). The Team B player performs the action and then tells the first player on Team A to do the same thing; however, the Team A player must give the command using different words (e.g., "Put your finger on your nose"). If both players perform correctly, both teams get a point. If the player on Team B is unable to say the same command in different words, only Team A gets the point. The game continues in this manner, and the team with the most points at the end of the game wins.

Modification: The students can be required to paraphrase a short paragraph. This can be a written or oral task. For example:

Mary woke up early because she had to arrive at school before the bell rang. She needed to go to the library before school so she could return an overdue book.

Paraphrased paragraph:

Mary had to return an overdue book to the library before school began. Therefore, she needed to wake up earlier than usual.

20. *To teach employment vocabulary words to secondary students:* Cut out job ads from the newspaper and collect job application forms. Read the ads and application forms to the class and determine what words and phrases they know (such as *experience, minimum wage, waitress, waiter, good working conditions, apply in person,* and *references required*). Define the words the students do not understand. With each student, role play a job interview and use the vocabulary on the job applications.

Modification: Vocabulary words can be selected from credit applications, checkbooks, classified ads, or driver's license applications.

INSTRUCTIONAL GAMES IN LANGUAGE

His, Her, or Their

Objective: To teach the use of the possessive pronouns *his, her,* and *their.*

Materials: Game board with start-to-finish format; one stack of picture cards depicting objects; one stack of picture cards depicting people, which should include at least one picture of a boy, one picture of a girl, and one picture of several children; a spinner; markers.

Directions: The stack of object pictures and the stack of people pictures are placed face down on the game board, and each player places a marker at the start position. Each player in turn spins the spinner, notes the number on which it lands, and picks up from each stack the number of cards shown on the spinner. The player turns over the cards and makes as many pronoun and object combinations as possible (e.g., *her hat, his hat, their hat, their ball, her house,* and *his shoe*). For each combination said, the player moves the marker ahead one space and puts the used cards face down on the bottom of each stack. The players take turns, and the one who moves to the end of the game board first is the winner.

What Goes Together

Objective: To teach classification by association.

Materials: Set of 40 playing cards composed of association pictures (e.g., a card illustrating a shoe and a card illustrating a sock).

Directions: Six cards are dealt to each player (i.e., two to four players), and the remaining cards are placed face down in the center of the players. Each player combines any association sets in his or her hand and lays them face up on the table. Then each player in turn takes a card from the deck, discards one from his or her hand, and places it face up next to the deck. After the first discard, each player can select a card either from the deck or from the discard pile. The first player who displays three association sets wins. (The criteria for winning can be varied to suit the students and the situation.)

The Deck

Objective: To teach opposite words.

Materials: Deck of cards composed of pictures depicting opposite words (e.g., a card illustrating the word *up* and a card illustrating the word *down*).

Directions: An equal number of cards is dealt to each player until all cards are dealt. Each player combines any sets of opposites in his or her hand and lays them face up on the table. Then each player draws a card in turn from another player's hand. When a player has a set of opposite pictures in his or her hand, the player lays them on the table. The game continues until one player wins by pairing all the cards in his or her hand.

Whose Is It?

Objective: To teach the use of possessive personal pronoun *mine* and the possessive -*'s*.

Materials: Two matching sets of 12 pictures.

Directions: The dealer lays three pictures from the first set of cards face down in front of each of the four players. The dealer then lays the entire second matching stack of cards face down on the table. The dealer turns the first card in the stack face up and asks, "Whose is it?" The first player guesses whose stack contains the matching card by saying, "Mine," "John's," or "Mary's." The player must use the possessive -*'s* or possessive pronoun *mine*. Whoever the player guesses must turn over his or her cards; that is, if the player says, "John's," John must turn over his cards for everyone to see. If the card matches one in John's stack, the player who selected John gets a chip. If it does not, the card is placed face down on the bottom of the deck, and John turns his cards back face down on the table. The dealer turns the next card from the stack face up and asks the next player, "Whose is it?" The player who makes the most correct guesses receives the most chips and wins.

Say the Whole Sentence

Objective: To teach sentence construction.

Materials: Deck of cards of matching pairs with several of the pairs having only one attribute different from other pairs (e.g., three pairs of Christmas trees—one set with blue lights, one set with red lights, and one set with green lights).

Directions: Six cards are dealt to each player, and the remaining cards are placed face down in a stack on the table. Each player combines any matching sets in his or her hand and lays them face up on the table. Each player in turn asks for a card from another player by using all the attributes (e.g., "Do you have a Christmas tree with green lights?"). If the other player has that card, it is given to the first player. If the other player does not have the requested card, the first player takes a card from the deck. The first player who matches all of his or her cards wins the game.

Phonetic Bingo

Objective: To teach phoneme identification.

Materials: Cards that have five numbered columns, with each column containing five letters; discs.

Directions: Each player receives a bingo card containing letters. The caller calls out a column number and a phoneme, such as 2/p/. If that particular phoneme is in the appropriate column on the card, the player places a disc over that letter. The winner is the first player to cover five letters in a row. A list of the called-out letters can be kept to check the winning card.

1	2	3	4	5
p	d	g	t	v
g	v	p	v	t
b	t	d	g	p
t	g	b	p	b
d	p	t	d	g

Fishing for Blends

Objective: To teach /s/ blends.

Materials: Fish-shaped cards displaying /s/ blends: *st*, *sk*, *sw*, and *sl*.

Directions: The cards are placed face up in the center of the students. The caller calls out a word containing an /s/ blend, such as *skate*. The players take turns finding the correct blend from the group of fish cards. If the correct card is picked, the player gets to keep the card. When all the cards are gone from the center, the player with the most "fish" wins.

Two-Way Words

Objective: To improve use of homonyms.

Materials: Set of 20 index cards with a pair of homonyms written on each card; answer key that lists the definition of each homonym.

Directions: Two pairs of partners sit across from each other, and the dealer deals five cards to each of the four players. The first player selects one of his or her cards, makes a statement that includes either of the homonyms on the card, and then repeats the homonym (e.g., "She wore a plain dress—plain"). The player then challenges his or her partner to make a statement that includes the other homonym on the card but gives no further clues. When the partner makes a statement (e.g., "We were in the plane."), the dealer refers to the answer key to see whether the response is correct. If the response is questionable, the dealer can ask for another statement that gives additional information concerning the meaning of the homonym (e.g., "We were flying above the clouds in the plane."). If the partner's statement is correct, the player can place the card in the middle of the table. If the partner's statement is not correct, the player must keep the card for another turn. The next player challenges his or her partner in the same way, and the partner pairs take turns. A player can challenge only his or her own partner and must use his or her own cards. The first partner pair to have all their cards in the middle of the table wins the game.

Sentence Game

Objective: To teach sentence construction.

Materials: A start-to-finish game board; a deck of cards displaying stimulus pictures; a spinner; markers.

Directions: Each player places a marker at the start position, and the picture cards are placed face down. The first player spins the spinner and moves the designated number of spaces. Then the player selects a card from the deck and must say a sentence using the word or words illustrated in the picture. If the sentence is complete and correct, the player remains on the square. If the word or words are not used correctly, the player moves back one square at a time and picks up another card until able to produce a correct sentence. The first player to reach the finish square wins.

Can You Answer with a Question?

Objective: To teach the use of *who, what,* and *where* questions.

Materials: A game board with categories and points (i.e., similar to Jeopardy game); question cards corresponding to the categories and point levels (i.e., the words range in difficulty according to their point value) with the answers written on the back of each card.

Directions: The first player chooses a category and point value from the game board. The player is presented with a word from the chosen category and must define the word with a question. For example, the category may be *Clothes,* and the word on the card may be *shoes.* The correct answer on the back of the card is, "What do you wear on your feet?" Object categories require a *what* question. If the player selects from a place category, the answer must be in the form of a question that uses *where.* For example, if the category is *Community Places* and the word is *library,* the answer is "Where do we get books?" If the student selects from a person category, the answer must be in the form of a question that uses *who.* For example, if the category is *Community Helpers* and the words are *police officer,* the answer is "Who catches criminals?"

Suggested categories: (1) What—Clothes (e.g., hat, shoes, and dress); Animals (e.g., dog, cat, and bird); Sports Equipment (e.g., ball, bat, and glove); (2) Where—Community Places (e.g., bank, post office, and school); Fun Places (e.g., restaurant, zoo, and theater); Travel Depots (e.g., train station, airport, and bus station); (3) Who—Community Helpers (e.g., firefighter, police officer, and mail carrier); Family Member (e.g., mother, father, and sister); School Personnel (e.g., principal, teacher, and librarian).

Build a Sentence

Objective: To teach combining independent clauses with conjunctions.

Materials: Thirty (30) flannel-backed cards with independent clauses written on the front of each card; 13 flannel-backed cards with conjunctions written on the front of each card; a flannelboard.

Directions: The flannelboard is placed in the middle of the table, and the cards are dealt to the players. The first player lays down a card containing an independent clause, such as *She was late.* The second player lays down a card containing a conjunction, such as *because.* The third player must lay down a clause to complete the sentence, such as *she missed the bus.* Then the next player begins a new sentence. A player loses a turn if the player does not have an appropriate card to play. The first player who uses all of his or her cards wins the game.

Suggested clauses: She went to bed; She was tired; Mary stayed home; He made a good grade; John went to the store; He studied; She watched television; He brought some ice cream; He washed dishes; He bought a ticket; Father fussed; Mother cooked supper.

Suggested conjunctions: because; and; since.

Prefix Bingo

Objective: To teach the prefixes *in, re, un,* and *non.*

Materials: Bingo cards with various root words that can be combined with the prefixes *in, re, un,* or *non;* a spinner, with four sections, that has a prefix in each section; markers with one prefix printed on each marker (see Figure 6.5).

Directions: The first player spins the spinner, notes on which prefix it lands, and picks up a marker with that prefix on it. The player places the prefix marker on a root word with which it can be combined. The player loses a turn if the spinner lands on a prefix that cannot be combined with a root word on his or her card. The first player whose markers are in a row (i.e., vertically, horizontally, or diagonally) wins the game. The winning card is checked to make sure the prefix on each marker can be combined with the root word on which it is placed.

Modification: This game can be modified by using suffixes, such as *ful, less,* and *ly.*

Deal a Sentence

Objective: To teach sentence construction.

Materials: Fifty-five (55) word cards containing words from the following grammatical categories: noun (9), pronoun (9), verb (15), adjective (12), article (3), conjunction (3), preposition (3), and adverb (1).

Directions: Each player receives five cards, and the remaining cards are placed face down in the center of the players. Each player organizes his or her hand to determine whether

FIGURE 6.5
Prefix Bingo game
card and spinner

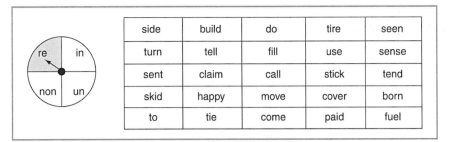

side	build	do	tire	seen
turn	tell	fill	use	sense
sent	claim	call	stick	tend
skid	happy	move	cover	born
to	tie	come	paid	fuel

there is a sentence. Then each player selects one card from the deck and discards one card face up. The first player to make a sentence wins the hand. The number of hands played can vary according to the time available, and the player with the most points at the end of the time period wins. Another option is for the first player to earn a predetermined number of points to be the winner. Scoring can be one point for a declarative sentence, two points for using *not* in a sentence, three points for a sentence with a conjunction, and four points for a question.

Suggested words: Nouns—ball, dress, boy, girl, book, house, doll, bike, dog; Pronouns—I, you, she, he, him, they, them, it, we; Verbs—is, are, was, were, made, can, go, should, may, do, see, ride, walk, run, am; Adjectives—big, round, pretty, small, sad, happy, little, red, fast, slow, fat, funny; Articles—a, an, the; Conjunctions—and, but, or; Prepositions—to, at, with; Adverb—not.

Conjunction Square

Objective: To teach sentence construction using conjunctions.

Materials: A checkerboard with a conjunction written on each square; a stack of cards with a sentence printed on each card; checkers.

Directions: The player makes a checker move (i.e., according to the rules of the game of checkers) and takes two sentence cards. The player must combine the two sentences on the cards with the conjunction on which the checker lands. The player must make a correct sentence to keep the move. If unable to make a sentence, the player must move the checker back to its previous position. The players continue taking turns and making sentences until one player wins the checker game.

SELF-CORRECTING LANGUAGE MATERIALS

Opposites

Objective: To teach classification of word opposites.

Feedback device: Windows in the back of the Spinning Wheels show matching symbols to indicate picture or word opposites.

Materials: Spinning Wheels (described in Chapter 2); a worksheet that has one picture in the left column and two pictures on the right—one of which illustrates the opposite

of the picture on the left—corresponding to the pictures on the Spinning Wheels; an acetate overlay (see Figure 6.6).

Directions: The student places the acetate overlay over the worksheet, selects the picture that is the opposite of the one in the left column, and marks an *X* on that picture. After completing the worksheet, the student checks the work with the Spinning Wheels. The student turns the wheels so that the selected picture opposites appear in the windows, and then the student turns over the wheels to see whether matching symbols appear in the back windows.

Modification: This activity can be used to teach same, different, or associated words by changing the items or pictures on the Spinning Wheels.

Time Slot

Objective: To increase skills in using verbs relating to time.

Feedback device: Symbols or line drawings on the back of the verb cards match the line drawing on the envelope with the appropriate verb form.

Materials: Three envelopes for present-, past-, and future-tense verbs with a different line drawing or symbol on each envelope; a set of cards with pictures depicting the time associated with various verb tenses (see Figure 6.7).

Directions: The student looks at each card to determine which verb tense the picture illustrates. The student then places each card in the envelope that denotes the answer. After sorting all the cards, the student takes the cards out of the envelopes and checks to see whether the symbol on the back of each card matches the symbol on the front of the envelope in which it was placed.

Modifications: The activity can include several syntactic forms such as *are* + verb + *ing* or *has* + verb + *ed*. A different line drawing or symbol should be assigned to each syntactic form. Also, the activity can be modified further by using words instead of pictures and labeling the envelopes with the name of the verb tense.

Flip-Siders

Objective: To teach classification by association.

Feedback device: Matching colors or symbols are on the back of pictures that are associated.

FIGURE 6.6
Worksheet for Opposites

FIGURE 6.7
Envelopes and cards
for Time Slot

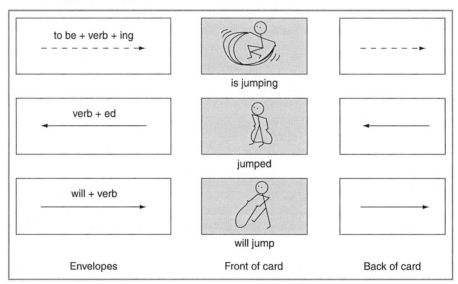

Materials: Flip-sider cards that contain pictures of associated words (such as a sock and a shoe) and have matching colors or symbols on the back of associated pictures.

Directions: The student looks at each picture and finds the picture associated with it. The student combines the pictures and turns over the cards. The pictures that are associated have the same color or symbol on the back.

Modifications: Flip-siders can be used to teach opposites, verb tenses, and phoneme recognition. Also, the material can be modified for secondary students by combining associated pictures that illustrate cause-and-effect relationships (e.g., pictures showing a student studying and a report card with good grades, or an accident and an ambulance).

Make a Question

Objective: To teach the interrogative reversal.

Feedback device: The pieces of the puzzle strip fit together when the sentence is in question form.

Materials: A worksheet with declarative sentences; a set of puzzle pieces for each sentence that fit together when the sentence is in the form of a question.

Directions: The student rewrites each sentence on the worksheet into an interrogative reversal to ask a question. After completing the question, the student puts the corresponding puzzle pieces together to check the answer.

- The girls are at home.

- She is very tall.

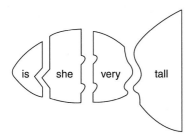

When Did It Happen?

Objective: To teach the past-tense morpheme *ed*.

Feedback device: A tab pulled from a pocket in the material reveals the correct answer.

Materials: An audio recording of sentences that contain the morpheme *ed*; a card that contains the sentences and has a smiling face to circle to indicate correct use of *ed* and a frowning face to circle to indicate incorrect use of *ed*; a tab containing the answer key that fits in a pocket in the card; an acetate overlay (see Figure 6.8).

Directions: The student places the acetate overlay over the card, listens to the sentence on the audio recording, and circles the appropriate face on the answer card to indicate correct or incorrect use of *ed*. A pause on the recording is given after each sentence to allow the student time to circle the answer and pull the tab from the pocket to see whether the answer is correct. The numbers next to the faces on the tab correspond to the numbers of the sentences.

Modifications: The activity can be used to teach *is* or *ing* by making an audio recording with sentences that require *is* or *ing*. The activity can be modified further for older students by using written sentences, each of which the student must judge as grammatically correct or incorrect.

Word Endings with Meanings

Objective: To teach the suffixes -*less* and -*ful*.

Feedback device: The correct answer is revealed under a flap.

Materials: A laminated card that contains incomplete sentences that require a root word and the suffix -*less* or -*ful*; a laminated card illustrating a tree with roots at the bottom and the same number of branches at the top of the tree: (1) two numbered leaves on each branch are cut so that each leaf will fold back to reveal an answer underneath, (2) holes are punched in each corner of the card and a sheet of paper is attached to the back of the card with brass fasteners, (3) under each numbered leaf a suffix is written that fits the respective sentence, and (4) root words are written along the tree roots with a grease pencil (see Figure 6.9).

Directions: The student is given a laminated card that contains incomplete sentences requiring a root word and a suffix. The student circles the correct suffix with a grease pencil. After completing the sentences, the student lifts the leaves on the tree card to see the correct answers.

Modification: A sheet containing different prefixes and suffixes can be attached to the back of the tree card, and a corresponding worksheet can be provided.

Make It Say a Sentence

Objective: To teach sentence order.

Feedback device: An answer key in an envelope attached to the back of the card provides the answers.

Materials: A card containing scrambled sentences that contain conjunctions; an envelope on the back of the card; an answer key; paper.

Directions: The student looks at each scrambled sentence on the card and unscrambles the words. The student writes the

FIGURE 6.8
Card and tab for When Did It Happen?

		Right	Wrong
1. Yesterday the boy walked to the store.		☺	☹
2. At lunch the girl look at the clerk.		☺	☹
3. Last week the boy jump over the fence.		☺	☹
4. The dog chewed the ball.		☺	☹
5. John played all afternoon.		☺	☹

1. ☺
Tab

FIGURE 6.9
Cards for Word Endings with Meanings

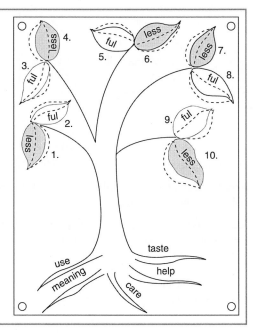

1. The broken car is use(ful/less) until it is fixed.
2. The basket is use(ful/less) to carry groceries.
3. I learned a lot from the meaning(ful/less) speech.
4. The poor directions were meaning(ful/less).
5. The student was vey care(ful/less) and wrote a neat letter.
6. The student was care(ful/less) and spilled paint on her dress.
7. She felt help(ful/less) when she couldn't start her car.
8. The neighbor was help(ful/less) when she loaned me her telephone.
9. The flower arrangement was pleasing and taste(ful/less).
10. The food was very bland and taste(ful/less) to me.

unscrambled sentences on paper and checks the work by looking at the answer key in the envelope on the back of the card.

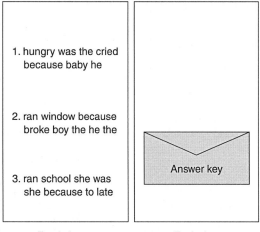

1. hungry was the cried because baby he

2. ran window because broke boy the he the

3. ran school she was she because to late

Answer key

Front view   Back view

Modifications: This self-correcting device can be used with many tasks, such as making grammatical judgments, changing declarative sentences into interrogative sentences, and using conjunctions. The cloze procedure for completing sentences with conjunctions can be adapted to this procedure by putting sentences on a card with an answer key attached. For example:

She went to the store _____ she needed to buy some groceries. (because, and)

She is going to buy milk _____ bread. (since, and)

Does It Mean the Same Thing?

Objective: To teach similarity of deep structure in two sentences.

Feedback device: An answer key on the back of the card provides the correct answers.

Materials: A card with sentence pairs, with some having the same meaning (i.e., deep structure) and others having different meanings; an acetate overlay; an answer key on the back of the card (see Figure 6.10).

Directions: The student reads each set of sentences and decides whether the meaning of both sentences is the same or different. The student places the acetate overlay over the response section of the card and circles *same* or *different* to indicate the answer. After completing the task, the student turns over the card and places the acetate overlay over the answer key. The circles on the overlay should match the words circled on the answer key.

Modifications: Acetate overlays and marked answer keys can be used with sentences that use a cloze procedure with multiple choices. For example:

He heated the water _____ made coffee. (and, because)

This procedure also can be used with grammatical judgments. For example:

Yesterday he walk to school.

_____ Correct _____ Incorrect

FIGURE 6.10
Card and acetate overlay for Does It Mean the Same Thing?

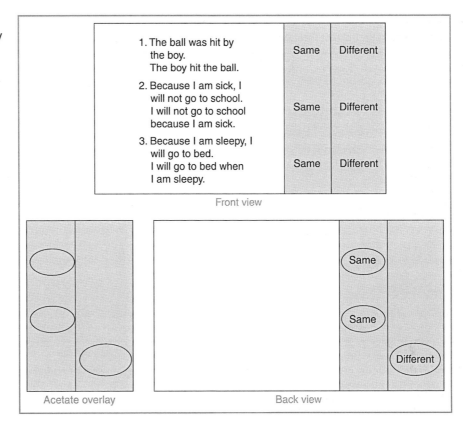

1. The ball was hit by the boy.
   The boy hit the ball. Same Different

2. Because I am sick, I will not go to school.
   I will not go to school because I am sick. Same Different

3. Because I am sleepy, I will go to bed.
   I will go to bed when I am sleepy. Same Different

Front view

Acetate overlay

Back view

Same

Same

Different

Descriptors

Objective: To increase use of effective communication skills.

Feedback device: The correct responses are provided on the back of the stimulus card.

Materials: Cards with a small object mounted on the front of each card and a list of six descriptive categories pertaining to the object written on the back of each card; a tape recorder.

Directions: The student looks at the object on the card and records six different sentences describing the object on a tape recorder. After recording the six sentences, the student turns over the stimulus card, listens to each of the recorded sentences, and checks the appropriate descriptive category used on the back of the card.

Modification: This material can be modified for younger students by using a picture of an object with two attributes (e.g., a small, red car). The student records a descriptive sentence on a tape recorder. Then the student turns over the picture card to the answer key, listens to the recording, and checks each attribute used. Answers can be coded for nonreaders—a color to indicate color category and a small object to indicate size category.

☐ Name (pencil)

☐ Color (blue)

☐ Function (write, draw)

☐ Size (long, thin)

☐ Material of construction (wood, lead)

☐ Characteristics (point, eraser)

Indirect Requests

Objective: To identify indirect requests.

Feedback device: An answer key is provided on the back of the response card.

189

FIGURE 6.11

Response card for Indirect Requests

	Indirect Request	Question			Indirect Request	Question
1.	_____	_____		1.		X
2.	_____	_____		2.	X	
3.	_____	_____		3.	X	
4.	_____	_____		4.	X	
5.	_____	_____		5.		X
6.	_____	_____		6.		X
7.	_____	_____		7.	X	
8.	_____	_____		8.	X	
9.	_____	_____		9.	X	
10.	_____	_____		10.		X

Front of response card	Back of response card

Materials: A tape recording of various indirect requests and questions; a response card with an answer key provided on the back of the card; an acetate overlay (see Figure 6.11).

Directions: The student places the acetate overlay over the response card and listens to the taped sentences. The student decides whether each sentence is a question or an indirect request and marks the answer on the overlay. After completing the task, the student turns over the response card and places the acetate overlay over the answer key to check the responses.

Taped sentences

1. What time is it?
2. Can you shut the door?
3. Won't you stop that?
4. Can't you finish your work?
5. When does the bus arrive?
6. Is the water running?
7. Must you just sit there?
8. Must you slurp your milk?
9. Can't you sit still?
10. Did the dog run away?

Modification: The taped sentences can be changed to questions and statements. The student identifies each sentence as a statement or question.

COMMERCIAL LANGUAGE PROGRAMS

Numerous commercial language programs and materials are available to help students having difficulty with language. Selection of a program for intervention is influenced by two primary factors: the population the program serves and the theoretical model on which it is based. The theoretical model describes normal language acquisition and includes the content the student learns, the sequence in which the student learns, and how the student learns. Because language is interactive, no single program is appropriate for use alone, and the teacher should select programs based on the language needs of individual students. Thus, the selection of programs and materials for classroom use should reflect the developmental ages of the students for whom they are selected as well as the purpose of the intervention. The following selected commercial language programs may be useful for teaching language skills to students with language problems.

Language for Learning; Language for Thinking; Language for Writing

Language for Learning, Language for Thinking, and *Language for Writing,* developed by S. Engelmann and J. Osborn (published by SRA), present a highly structured approach to language intervention. The programs are designed for students in pre-kindergarten through fifth grade and focus on expressive and receptive language and cognitive development. In *Language for Learning,* students learn commonly used vocabulary and practice using complete sentences, answering questions, and following oral directions. Efficacy studies of *Language for Learning* support its use for improving receptive language skills, including vocabulary, grammatical morphemes, and elaborated sentences and phrases (Benner et al., 2002; Waldron-Soler et al., 2002). *Language for Thinking* adds new content, which includes making inferences, sequencing and retelling exercises, and determining meanings of sentences. *Language for Writing* gives students oral practice in using words and syntax they will later apply to writing, teaches the vocabulary students need to describe features of their writing, and helps students learn to use grammar and punctuation to make their writing clear.

Lindamood Phoneme Sequencing Program for Reading, Spelling, and Speech

The *Lindamood Phoneme Sequencing Program for Reading, Spelling, and Speech* (Lindamood & Lindamood, 1998) presents step-by-step sensory-cognitive procedures to develop the ability to identify and sequence individual sounds and their order within words. Activities focus on the lip, tongue, and mouth actions that produce speech sounds. Phonemic awareness is brought to a conscious level, and activities progress from single phonemes through multisyllabic words. Students are taught to use sensory information from feeling, hearing, and seeing to develop a feedback system that promotes self-correction in speech, reading, and spelling. Both a classroom version and clinical version are available, and manipulatives, static-cling letters and mouth pictures, a videotape, and an audiocassette are included. A magnetic kit that includes magnetic tiles and pictures and a magnetic board is available for use as an alternate practice material. The program is designed for students in kindergarten through adult age. Lindamood programs have substantial empirical support. Studies examining the Lindamood programs demonstrate improved outcomes for students at risk for disabilities and with identified learning disabilities (Sadoski & Willson, 2006; Torgesen et al., 1999; Torgesen et al., 2001).

Peabody Language Development Kits

The *Peabody Language Development Kits,* developed by L. M. Dunn, J. O. Smith, L. N. Dunn, and K. B. Horton (published by Pearson), provide a multilevel program for developing oral language and cognitive skills in young children. Level P, for 4- to 5-year-old preschoolers, provides practice in labeling language, constructing sentences, and thinking logically. Level 1, for 5- to 6-year-old students, focuses on brainstorming and problem solving to prompt divergent thinking and oral expression. The kits stress overall language development rather than specific psycholinguistic processes. The activities at each level emphasize the skills of *reception* through sight, hearing, and touch; *expression* through vocal and motor behavior; and *conceptualization* through divergent, convergent, and associative thinking. Picture card decks, puppets, a sound book, story posters, and a teacher's manual are included in the kits. The teacher's manual has descriptions of daily lessons and specifies a teacher script as well as appropriate materials and activities.

Teaching Morphology Developmentally

Teaching Morphology Developmentally, developed by K. G. Shipley and C. J. Banis (published by PRO-ED), is a developmental program for teaching word formation that is designed for students whose language age is between 2½ and 10 years. The 522 color stimulus cards can be used to teach more than 1,000 vocabulary words and 700 bound morphemes. Specific morphemes include present progressives, plurals, possessives, past tenses, third-person singulars, and derived adjectives (i.e., comparative-superlative and irregular forms). Reproducible lists of curriculum items, pretest and posttest forms, and suggestions for developing behavioral objectives are included in the instructional manual.

COMPUTER SOFTWARE PROGRAMS IN LANGUAGE

Computer-assisted instruction can be used to improve students' speech and language skills. As well as enhancing motivation, computers appear to facilitate both social and cognitive interactions (Clements, 1987). Moreover, the use of computers tends to stimulate social use (Lipinski, Nida, Shade, & Watson, 1986), produce more positive and varied facial expressions and smiling (Hyson, 1985), and produce more spoken words per minute when compared with traditional activities such as blocks, art, or games (Muhlstein & Croft, 1986). Also, speech synthesizers provide speech for "talking" programs, and headphones can facilitate individual use. The following software programs focus on language skills.

Parts of Speech

Parts of Speech (produced by Optimum Resource) is designed to help students in third through ninth grade increase grammar and vocabulary skills. Students identify nouns, pronouns, adjectives, verbs, adverbs, conjunctions, prepositions, and interjections from word lists and from within sentences and paragraphs. The 32 leveled lessons use a variety of timed and untimed activities and present more than 1,000 graded words. The teacher can customize the program by adding new words and exercises. Progress reports are available, and worksheets can be printed for later use.

Picture Gallery

Picture Gallery (produced by Psychological Corporation) is a series of CD-ROM products for use by language specialists who use visual stimuli in an educational setting. The collection features thousands of color digitized photographs that can be used to create picture sets according to each student's needs. Five CD-ROMs are available: articulation and phonology, thematic units, early concepts, advanced vocabulary, and morphology. The items can be used to facilitate the acquisition or remediation of speech or language skills.

ItemWriter Language Software

ItemWriter Language Software (produced by Academic Communication Associates), which is designed for students reading at or above the second-grade level, includes five programs.

In *Completing Analogies,* students complete sentences by picking the appropriate word from a group, and in *Identifying Synonyms and Antonyms,* students select words that have the same meaning or the opposite meaning as each stimulus word. *Drawing Conclusions* includes exercises in inferential reasoning in which students select the conclusion that can be derived logically from a statement. Students respond "yes" or "no" to factual or opinion questions in *Answering Yes–No Questions,* and students finish incomplete phrases or provide the beginning of a phrase in *Completing Familiar Phrases.* Each program feature real speech, and the lessons can be customized with the creation of individualized item sets.

LanguageLinks: Syntax Assessment and Intervention

LanguageLinks (produced by Laureate Learning Systems) is a comprehensive software series designed to help prekindergarten through eighth-grade students acquire language. The program takes students from the early two-word development stage through the mastery of a broad range of syntactic forms. There are six levels that include over 75 essential grammatical forms in developmental order. The software begins with an assessment to determine where to begin training, and then the program tracks performance and automatically guides the student through the curriculum. Student performance can be reviewed at the end of each lesson, and comprehensive reports can be printed.

Vocabulary Development

Vocabulary Development (produced by Optimum Resource) is a comprehensive vocabulary-building program for students in third through ninth grade that provides practice in recognizing synonyms, antonyms, homonyms, multiple meanings, prefixes, suffixes, and context clues. The program includes more than 400 words in 44 multilevel lessons at six progressive difficulty levels. The student automatically is advanced to the next level upon mastering the previous one. The teacher can create exercises and set difficulty levels to expand the use of the program. Practice sheets and test masters can be printed, and the program keeps records of student progress. An additional program, *Vocabulary Development 2,* provides a more complex structure that allows students to apply experience and context to generate meanings for unfamiliar words and to more accurately define known words.

Words and Concepts Series

The *Words and Concepts Series* (produced by Laureate Systems) is designed to enrich vocabulary, strengthen language comprehension, increase understanding of word relationships, and encourage concept development. The three programs in the series use a core vocabulary of 40 nouns in six related language units: vocabulary, word association, categorization, word identification by function, concept of same/alike, and concept of different. Most of the activities have three levels of difficulty, and the computer can be set to work on one level or branch among the levels according to the progress of the student. In addition, there are three *CONCENTRATE!* programs, which are based on the classic card game, that reinforce the skills trained in the *Words and Concepts Series. CONCENTRATE!* can be played by students independently or in pairs to enhance word knowledge, provide recreational enjoyment, foster cooperative play, or build short-term memory skills.

Assessing Reading

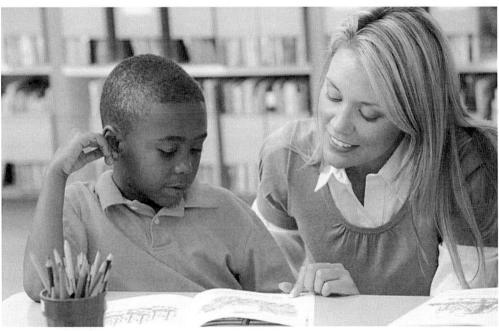

Monkey Business/Fotolia

From Chapter 7 of *Teaching Students with Learning Problems*, 8/e. Cecil D. Mercer. Ann R. Mercer. Paige C. Pullen.

The number of students in the United States who have reading difficulties is alarming. According to the National Center for Education Statistics (2007b), reports from national assessments of reading progress indicate that in 2007 approximately 34 percent of fourth-grade students read below a basic level of achievement (i.e., little or no mastery of reading knowledge and skills necessary to perform work at grade level), and only 32 percent attained a proficient reading achievement level. Moreover, in 2005, about 27 percent of eighth-grade students were below a basic level of reading achievement and only 29 percent achieved proficient reading standards. In addition, Rampey, Dion, and Donahue (2009) report that the 2008 reading score for twelfth-grade students was not significantly different when compared to the score in 1971. Because instruction after elementary school primarily focuses on subject content rather than on teaching basic skills, the needs of adolescents with reading problems are frequently overlooked. Approximately 75 percent of poor readers in third grade continue to be poor readers in ninth grade (Lyon, 1995), and, unfortunately, reading disabilities persist into adulthood (Lyon, Alexander, & Yaffe, 1997).

In a testimony provided to the subcommittee on Education Reform of the U.S. House of Representatives, Lyon (2001) indicates that over 75 percent of students who drop out of school report having difficulties learning to read and only 2 percent of students who receive special or compensatory education for difficulties learning to read complete a four-year college degree program. In addition, at least half of all adolescents and young adults with criminal records have reading difficulties, and approximately half of children and adolescents with a history of substance abuse have reading problems. Thus, the personal and societal costs of reading problems are substantial. Illiteracy is positively correlated with unemployment, low wages, poverty, crime, and low self-esteem (Brunner, 1993; Kirsch, Jungeblut, Jenkins, & Kolstad, 1993; National Institute for Literacy, 1997).

Concerns about high rates of illiteracy and demands for increased accountability led to federal legislation. As part of the No Child Left Behind Act of 2001, signed by President Bush on January 8, 2002, the federal government made money available to states and local educational agencies for Reading First and Early Reading First programs. These programs for children in kindergarten through third grade, and for children ages 3 through 5 years, offered grant money for 6 years (i.e., 2002 through 2007) to support assessment, intervention, and teacher training programs.

The goal of this initiative was to provide early identification and early reading interventions to prevent reading failure and to ensure reading success for all students by the end of third grade. It is encouraging to note that in a report of the long-term trend assessments in reading, Rampey et al. (2009) report that the average score in reading for 9-year-olds (i.e., fourth-grade students) increased between 2004 and 2008, and the average score for this age group was 12 points higher than in 1971.

It is clear that reading experiences have a significant impact on students' lives. Reading ability strongly influences a student's self-image and feelings of competency; furthermore, reading failure can lead to misbehavior, anxiety, and a lack of motivation. Learning to read is important in maintaining self-respect and obtaining the respect of others. Fortunately, research provides a wealth of information on how to teach reading effectively. Teachers can use these research-based assessment and teaching techniques to improve reading outcomes for all students.

THE READING PROCESS

To assess or teach reading skills effectively, it is helpful to understand the theoretical underpinnings of how the reading process works. Knowledge of Adams's (1990) parallel distributed processing reading model, Chall's (1996) stages of reading development, and Ehri's (1995) phases of sight word development provides the teacher with a wealth of information to use in the assessment of youngsters' reading development and skills. Moreover, this knowledge is essential for making instructional recommendations for students with reading difficulties. In essence, the reading processes described by Adams, Chall, and Ehri provide a rich context for assessing reading skills and making instructional recommendations in the areas of concepts about print, phonological awareness, phonics, fluency, comprehension, vocabulary development, and spelling. The reading assessment tests and instruments discussed in this chapter become more useful when examined within the context of how individuals learn to read.

Adams's Model of the Reading Process

Adams (1990) developed a parallel distributed processing model to describe the reading process. The model includes four processing units that must work together for the system to work properly. The four processing units are the orthographic processor, the phonological processor, the meaning processor, and the context processor. Each processor is responsible for its unique function, and the four processors must work simultaneously for the system to work effectively. The processors are connected (i.e., they send and receive information from each other), and these collective connections and interactions enable the processors to create and maintain the act of reading. Thus, in fluent reading, all four processors are performing their independent functions and receiving and sending messages to each other.

Because gaining meaning from print is the central purpose to reading, the meaning processor is central to the system, and the other three processors surround it (see Figure 7.1). The system begins with the orthographic processor, which receives visual input from print and sends the information to the meaning processor. When a reader sees a familiar word, the letters are strongly interconnected or "hang together" within the learner's orthographic memory. This causes the word to be recognized instantaneously. If the word encountered by the orthographic processor is not stored in the reader's memory, then the phonological processor attaches a pronunciation to the printed word and the meaning processor then attaches meaning. The phonological processor is the auditory processor, and it receives information from speech. Whereas the orthographic processor deals with an image or string of letters, the phonological processor interacts to determine whether the letters are pronounceable. Thus, the two processors work together to decipher sound-symbol relationships. Actually, the connectivity between the phonological, orthographic, and meaning processors is circular. After a word is perceived through the orthographic processor, the meaning processor arouses a pronunciation in the phonological processor; likewise, the pronunciation elicited from the phonological processor arouses meaning. A strong circular connectivity is crucial to the reading process. The context processor facilitates the ongoing coherent interpretation of text and speeds the work of the other processing units. The context processor also functions to confirm the work of the other processors, select between alternate word meanings, and emphasize word meanings that assist in the overall comprehension of the text. Together, the meaning and context processors work in parallel with the phonological processor to make sense of the orthographic information received from the written words. For fluent reading to occur, each processor must be prepared to send and receive information, and all four processors must be working together simultaneously.

The four processors (i.e., knowledge of common spelling patterns, spoken forms of words, word meanings, and context) work together to produce

FIGURE 7.1
Adams's model of the reading process

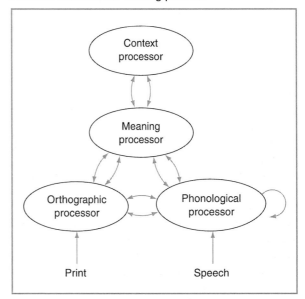

Source: From *Beginning to Read: Thinking and Learning About Print* (p. 158), by M. J. Adams, 1990, Cambridge, MA: The MIT Press. Copyright 1990 by Massachusetts Institute of Technology. Reprinted by permission.

reading. When information from one processor is weak, information from the other processors compensates. Given that the capacity or development of the four processors varies among learners and that reading approaches stress different processors, teachers must use a variety of reading approaches to meet the needs of diverse learners.

Adams's model of reading processes provides much insight into the assessment process. From this model, a diagnostician can note readily that it is important to assess reading skills associated with these processors. Weakness in one or more of these processors inhibits the ability to read fluently. Thus, an assessment of each of the four processors may be important in determining a reader's specific weakness or weaknesses. For example, phonological awareness testing relates to the skill of matching correct sounds to letters or words; orthographic testing relates to how well a student recognizes print (e.g., rapid letter recognition); the meaning processor relates to how well a student develops sight word vocabulary or decoding; and the context processor relates to how well a student uses thinking strategies to comprehend text. Moreover, the model provides a framework for making intervention recommendations. For example, it is well established that most youngsters who struggle with reading have difficulty with phonological awareness (Lyon, 1999). Thus, these students need phonological awareness training in order for the orthographic processor and meaning processor to receive the sounds that correspond to letters and letter combinations. Also, students with poor sight word vocabularies could have limited phonological processing, weak orthographic processing, or poor memory for sounds, letters, or words.

Chall's Reading Stages

Chall and Stahl (1982) discuss three reading models that differ in the importance they attach to text and meaning. The *bottom-up* model emphasizes that readers proceed from text to meaning; that is, letters and words are perceived and decoded and then the text's meaning is comprehended. In contrast, the *top-down* model emphasizes that readers rely on prior knowledge and comprehension of the textual material's meaning rather than on word recognition and decoding of individual text elements. In essence, the bottom-up model focuses primarily on the reader's skill in sound–symbol association and word recognition, whereas the top-down model focuses on the reader's ability to question, hypothesize, and comprehend rather than on decoding individual text elements. The *interactive* model emphasizes both text and meaning by proposing that readers shift between attending to the text (i.e., specific letters and words) and what is in their mind (i.e., predicting or hypothesizing). For example, a reader may use a top-down approach when the material is familiar but change to a bottom-up approach when confronted with unfamiliar text.

Reading content has a structure in which the student first constructs simple relationships (such as grapheme–phoneme) and then progresses to more complex tasks (such as critical reading). Thus, the interactive model may describe the reading process most adequately, especially in the early stages of learning to read. As the reader becomes more proficient, attention to comprehension is increased and less attention is given to scrutinizing individual letters and words. Chall (1996) believes that growth in reading skills occurs in several stages. Knowing the stages helps the teacher select assessment tasks, develop instructional goals, and choose instructional approaches. In addition, carefully monitoring student progress helps to determine when the student moves from one level to the next. Chall divides reading development into six stages, from 0 to 5, covering prereading to highly skilled reading: stage 0: prereading; stage 1: initial reading or decoding; stage 2: confirmation, fluency, and ungluing from print; stage 3: reading for learning the new; stage 4: multiple viewpoints; and stage 5: construction and reconstruction.

Stage 0: Prereading During the prereading stage, from birth to about age 6, children gradually accumulate understandings about reading. Most children learn the parts of a book (e.g., top, bottom, front, back, and page) and recognize letters, common signs, and a few words. Children gain insights into reading. They achieve some phonological awareness and begin to realize that print represents language and includes a message. Many children can print their own names and pretend they can read a story that has been read to them frequently. Prereading activities should include parents reading to children (i.e., especially reading that involves the child in discussions about books, pictures, words, letters, and stories). Other appropriate activities include experiences with environmental print (e.g., food labels, menus, store names, traffic signs, and print associated with toys and play activities).

The distinction between prereading and reading activities becomes less apparent during the latter period of this stage. Reading readiness activities (e.g., oral demonstrations of phonological awareness of words and syllables) that begin in some kindergarten classes are viewed as the teaching of specific concepts and skills that merge into reading.

Stage 1: Initial Reading or Decoding The initial reading stage (i.e., first to second grade) involves learning to use letter–sound relationships to decode printed words not recognized immediately. Children learn to recognize words and understand material in their books; however, what they can read at this stage is considerably below what they can understand in speech. Often the student reads slowly, word-by-word, trying to break a detailed, complicated code. Some students experience difficulty acquiring beginning decoding skills because they have problems with the phonological aspects of language. A basic phonological problem of poor readers is lack of awareness that words have parts (i.e., phonemes, syllables, and morphemes). Lyon (1995a) notes that the best predictor of reading ability from kindergarten and first-grade performance is phoneme segmentation ability, which is part of phonological awareness. For many students, adequate phonics instruction involving the sequencing and blending of sounds to form words is necessary for the acquisition of basic decoding skills; however, students who have difficulty with phonics analysis may use context analysis, syllabication, or structural analysis to aid in word identification. Kuhn and Stahl (2000) report that instruction in this stage focuses on helping students recognize basic sound–symbol correspondences by providing them with opportunities to establish decoding abilities.

Stage 2: Confirmation, Fluency, and Ungluing from Print

In second and third grades, what students previously have learned is consolidated in the recognition of words and the use of decoding skills to help them comprehend easy and familiar texts. At this stage, students confirm what they already know about word recognition (Kuhn & Stahl, 2000). They attain fluent reading and are able to read grade-level material in the range of 100 to 140 words per minute with two or fewer errors. By using their decoding skills along with repetitions inherent in the language and stories read, students gain competence in using context and, consequently, improve in fluency and reading rate. When the decoding process becomes automatic (i.e., accurate and rapid), attention is freed for higher level reading comprehension skills. Most students develop rapid word recognition as a result of the familiarity that develops from extended practice; however, students with reading problems require additional practice and repetition to reach automaticity. The transition from the initial stage to the fluency stage is similar to the transition experience of a baby who at first must concentrate intensely on learning to walk and then can walk automatically without thinking about it. Students at the initial stage read automatically until an unknown word is encountered and then they try a variety of word-attack approaches. By the end of this stage, students have developed fluency and can recognize familiar words quickly, sound out words they do not recognize, and predict other words according to context. Moreover, they begin to read with prosody (i.e., read with appropriate phrasing, stress, and intonation). Measures of reading speed and reading accuracy should be included in reading assessment to determine which students are ready to move to the next stage of reading instruction.

Stage 3: Reading for Learning the New

This stage, which begins in fourth grade and continues through eighth grade, marks the beginning of reading to learn, as opposed to learning to read in earlier stages. Reading is used to gain new knowledge, experience new feelings, and learn new ideas and attitudes. Thus, students acquire a rich base of information and vocabulary concepts by reading a wide variety of materials. At this stage, silent reading is done in large units (e.g., a complete story or selection), and word study is concerned more with meanings than with recognition or decoding because the reading materials contain more unfamiliar abstract, technical, and literary words. Students who read with slow and inaccurate decoding skills may fail to learn many of the concepts that are acquired typically during this stage by inference from the context and by analogical reasoning from prior knowledge. In other words, students with reading problems may be limited in learning from usual reading experiences because poor decoding skills present a barrier to the acquisition of knowledge. The resulting impoverished knowledge base may not allow students to comprehend more complex reading material. Thus, because of the cumulative effects of deficiencies at earlier stages, students with reading problems particularly need effective and efficient instruction at this stage.

Stage 4: Multiple Viewpoints

Reading at the secondary school level requires students to deal with a variety of viewpoints and to compare and evaluate information from a variety of sources. Secondary students are expected to read complex texts in advanced content areas. Through reading and studying materials that vary widely in type, content, and style, students practice acquiring difficult concepts and learning new concepts and points of view. At this level, metacognitive processes play an important role, monitoring and evaluating one's understanding of the text while reading. Instruction in comprehension monitoring should be followed by instruction in study skills and use of reference materials. The failure of a student to monitor understanding of the text may be due to an inability to decode rapidly and efficiently or to a lack of necessary information to understand the topic. To facilitate the use of textbooks with students who have difficulty reading them, it is important to help students increase vocabulary and sight words. Also, supplemental materials emphasizing vocabulary and background information should be developed to accompany content-area textbooks to help students with learning problems profit from reading in the content areas.

Stage 5: Construction and Reconstruction

At the college level, students read books and articles in the detail and depth that they need for their own purposes. From reading the writings of others, students construct knowledge for their own use. At this stage, the reader synthesizes information and forms hypotheses that usually are restricted to a specific area of study at an advanced level. Thus, reading at this stage requires extensive background knowledge in highly specialized content areas. The reader begins to synthesize numerous viewpoints in texts in order to ascertain his or her own perspective. This skill is fundamental to becoming a critical reader (Kuhn & Stahl, 2000). The acquisition of highly specialized knowledge in this stage depends upon the rich base of information acquired in stages 3 and 4, which, in turn, depends upon the accurate decoding and fluency skills developed in stages 1 and 2.

Ehri's Phases of Sight Word Development

During Chall's (1996) confirmation, fluency, and ungluing from print stage, the reader begins to develop automaticity in sight word vocabulary. Ehri (1995) defines *sight words* as words the reader recognizes accurately and instantly across reading occasions. Thus, sight words are words that the reader has in long-term memory that are quickly recognized and read.

Ehri (1995) notes that words become sight words through an analysis of the word's orthographic structure. From this analysis of print, the learner forms a mental representation of the word. This mental representation allows the reader to access the word quickly and automatically. Further, she reports that each encounter with the word triggers memory of the word. This identification of the word involves information about the word's spelling, meaning, and pronunciation. Ehri maintains that the process of building a sight word vocabulary involves going through four phases: prealphabetic, partial alphabetic, full alphabetic, and consolidated alphabetic.

Prealphabetic Phase Ehri's (1995) prealphabetic phase is similar to Chall's (1996) prereading phase. Youngsters at this stage remember sight words from the visual attributes of the letters. For example, they may remember the word *dog* because the *g* in dog has a tail, or they may see the golden arches of McDonald's and say "McDonald's." In essence, students at this stage focus on the shape, size, or color of letters to identify words. Moats (2000) states that young learners know that print represents spoken messages, and at this stage students use rote memory of visual patterns or they recognize a word in a physical or meaning context to read it. These visual strategies work with a small vocabulary but become ineffective as vocabulary increases. Learners at this stage do not know that letters represent sounds in words; thus, they do not know sound–symbol correspondences. They may string letters together and assign different meanings to them on different occasions. The words *ice cream* may be "yum yum" on one occasion and "cold" on another occasion. Selected activities appropriate for assessment and instruction during this phase include phonological awareness activities, alphabet matching, letter naming, activities involving concepts about print, and practice interacting with and reading grade-level books. Also, the teacher can encourage the student to follow print with a finger during read-aloud activities and can read stories to the student and discuss vocabulary and content.

Partial Alphabetic Phase In Ehri's (1995) partial alphabetic phase, youngsters make a qualitative shift in their approach to reading words because they discover the critical fact that letters correspond to the sounds in spoken words. In essence, they discover the alphabetic principle that letters and sounds are related. Readers begin to read sight words because they recognize some connections between letters and sounds in words. In this phase, the reader primarily focuses on initial and final letter–sound correspondences. Kuhn and Stahl (2000) note that, in this phase, for the first time the alphabetic system becomes available to the reader to assist in word recognition. The reader knows some letter names and has some phonological awareness. Moats (2000) states that youngsters begin to read and spell by sounding out parts of words using their knowledge of a few consonants (e.g., *kr* means *car*). Students in the partial alphabetic phase have limited knowledge of sound–symbol correspondences. They still lack knowledge of the spelling system (e.g., *ILTP* could mean *I like to play*), and they continue to lack ways to segment and match phonemes and graphemes; thus, their sight word recognition remains incomplete. Phonological awareness training at the word level, syllable level, onset-rime level, and phoneme level is appropriate during this phase. Other activities include the development of fluent recognition of uppercase and lowercase letters as well as common sight words (e.g., *the, I, am, you, is,* and *are*) and names of classmates. In addition, students should practice converting spoken word parts into written words parts and continue to read and interact with grade-level books.

Full Alphabetic Phase The full alphabetic phase parallels Chall's (1996) initial reading or decoding stage. Kuhn and Stall (2000) state that in this phase the reader recognizes how most graphemes represent phonemes in conventional spelling. Moats (2000) notes that the process of sounding out words and spelling them phonetically emerges. Thus, youngsters begin to identify all of the speech sounds in a word that need to be matched with letters. The unfolding skill of sounding out words during this stage is disfluent because so much conscious energy is needed to match symbols with sounds in a sequence (Moats, 2000). The reader begins to quickly recognize different words with similar spellings. Sight word vocabulary develops rapidly for regular and irregular words that are practiced. The student should practice breaking up and combining word parts as well as phonemic segmentation and blending phonemes into words. The teacher can help the student recognize "chunks" or "letter units" (e.g., *ing, est, ed, all, old,* and *pre*) and their appearance across words. Also, the student can practice writing sentences and using letter–sound correspondence knowledge to sound out unknown words. The student should continue to build sight word vocabulary, and material a little above grade level can be read to the student.

Consolidated Alphabetic Phase Ehri's (1995) consolidated alphabetic phase is similar to Chall's (1996) confirmation, fluency, and ungluing from print stage. During this phase, youngsters make extensive progress in learning the sound–symbol relationships of many words. Their knowledge of similar letter patterns across many different words continues to expand. The memory load of the orthographic system is lessened because of the learner's awareness of the ways letters co-occur within spellings of various words. Students become more aware of word parts at the phoneme, syllable, and morpheme levels; thus, they begin to recognize meaningful "chunks" of words (i.e., morphemes such as *s, ed, ing, pre, ab,* and *ad*) that occur frequently in spelling patterns. In essence, readers in this phase begin to generalize spelling patterns across words. They also use analogies to decode a new word (i.e., if *ball* is /b/a/l/, then *tall* must be /t/a/l/). Finally, students in this phase attain accurate and automatic word recognition, and sight vocabulary starts to expand rapidly. In this phase, the student should practice oral rereadings of stories to achieve a fluency rate, and have opportunities to read and comprehend books and materials at his or her reading level. The teacher can highlight new vocabulary words and point out their distinguishing graphemic and phonetic characteristics. Also, the teacher should expose the student to some expository text to prepare the student to read to learn new information, and the teacher can introduce a couple of comprehension strategies.

EMERGENT LITERACY

Extensive research exists indicating that children's early experiences with print and language strongly relate to later success in learning to read. For example, letter knowledge, phoneme discrimination, and the understanding that words consist of discrete units are strong predictors of later success in learning to read (Adams, 1990; Lyon, 1995a; Snow, Burns, & Griffin, 1998). During the past 15 years, the concept of phonological awareness has emerged to describe oral language components that develop early and are germane to later reading and spelling success. *Phonological awareness* is

defined as the ability to perceive that spoken words include a series of individual sounds. In essence, phonological awareness is the ability to notice, think about, and work with the individual sounds in spoken words (*Put Reading First,* 2001). Before assessing phonological awareness skills, a child's basic concepts about print (i.e., an understanding that the marks and squiggles on a page represent words and convey meaning) must be evaluated. Also, the child must know what a word is and be able to distinguish it from its referent (e.g., recognize that the word *lion* does not growl or roar). Emergent literacy assessment includes assessment of concepts about print and phonological awareness. If children fail to learn these emergent literacy skills prior to beginning formal reading instruction in kindergarten, the likelihood of reading failure is very high (Moats, 2000).

Uhry (2005) states that students with dyslexia or reading problems experience difficulty in understanding the alphabetic principle. Due to deficits in phonological awareness, many of these struggling readers fail to generalize sounds from one word to another. For example, a youngster who reads the word *hat* may fail to recognize that the /h/ sound in *hat* is the same as the /h/ sound in *hop*, or the child may not recognize that /c/ in *cat* is the same as /c/ in *cup*. A second reason why many struggling readers have difficulty learning the alphabetic principle is because they experience problems going from decoding to encoding (Wagner & Torgesen, 1987). Decoding involves seeing a word and determining the sounds for the letters in the word. Encoding involves hearing a word and producing the letters that represent the word. Thus, decoding primarily involves word recognition, whereas encoding involves spelling. A third reason learners struggle with the alphabetic principle is that they have limited short-term memories. They experience problems accessing letter–sound connections from their short-term or working memory (Levin, 2002). A fourth reason learners struggle is because they process print and sound too slowly. Each of these four phonological processing deficits can be improved with effective treatments (Torgesen & Wagner, 1998). Thus, it is important for these areas to be identified as early as possible so that treatments can be initiated. Tests of phonological awareness skills and tests of speed of letter, word, and sound processing are featured throughout this chapter.

In a nationwide longitudinal study of 3,959 secondary school seniors, Hanson and Farrell (1995) found that those who received a formal reading program in kindergarten outperformed comparable groups who did not participate in such a program. They conclude the following (p. 929):

> The major finding of this study, briefly stated, is: Students who learned to read in kindergarten were found to be superior in reading skills [current reading competency and reading attitude and behavior] and all other educational indicators [remediation, grades and attendance, and academic track] measured as seniors in high school. Further, this finding held up across districts and schools, as well as ethnic, gender, and social class groups. Also, there was absolutely no evidence of any negative effects from learning to read in kindergarten. Collectively, the results provide full support for the policy of teaching reading in kindergarten.

Waiting to begin formal reading instruction has many negative implications. Research indicates that 74 percent of children who do not learn to read by third grade will be poor readers as adults (Lyon, 1995a). Similarly, Juel (1988) notes that 88 percent of children who are poor readers at the end of first grade will remain poor readers at the end of fourth grade. Moreover, neurological studies suggest that the deficiency in word recognition skills of some children is associated with below-normal brain activity in the left temporal region (Lyon, 1995a). These children may become successful readers when they receive early phonological awareness training.

An examination of emergent literacy skill development prior to 3 years of age highlights the fact that language-reading skills are developing long before formal reading instruction. Dickinson and McCabe (2001) report that research indicates that these early developing skills have remarkable stability as key factors in children's language and literacy. McCardle, Cooper, Houle, Karp, and Paul-Brown (2001) further highlight the importance of early literacy development: "We know that developmental experiences, especially those that enhance vocabulary, language, and communication skills in general, help to establish a firm foundation on which to build literacy, as do book reading and experience with writing and fine-motor activities such as drawing and coloring" (p. 253). Educators, parents, and caregivers must focus on these important skills in order to improve the reading ability of all students. Snow et al. (1998) note that these skills include recognizing books by their cover, pretending to read books, sharing books with caregivers, interacting appropriately with books, labeling objects in books, and listening to stories.

To promote emergent literacy, Pullen and Justice (2003) provide activities in the areas of phonological awareness (e.g., rhyming, alliteration, blending, and segmenting), print awareness (e.g., adult–child shared storybook reading and print-enriched play), and oral language (e.g., focused simulation and interactive reading). In addition, Allor and McCathren (2003) present purposeful and developmentally appropriate storybook reading activities to facilitate the development of emergent literacy skills.

Concepts About Print

Because of different abilities and experiences with print, similar-age children can vary significantly in their knowledge of print-related concepts. An age-appropriate book for the child can be used to assess the child's knowledge of concepts about print. The child can perform the following tasks.

- Point out the front and back of the book
- Demonstrate awareness that print contains a message
- Indicate where to start reading on a page
- Point to a single word and to two words
- Indicate the direction to read words (i.e., left to right)
- Indicate that at the end of a line you sweep left to the next lower line
- Demonstrate an understanding of the concepts of *first* and *last*
- Indicate that you read the left page before the right page
- Indicate that you stop at a period
- Indicate that you pause at a comma
- Count words in a line to indicate the concept of *word*
- Point to one letter to indicate the concept of *letter*
- Point to an uppercase letter
- Point to a lowercase letter
- Point to the top and the bottom of a page
- Point to the top and the bottom of a picture

Phonological Awareness

Language Components To read, children need to know that the speech stream can be broken into smaller units of sound. This understanding of the sound structure of language is the foundation of phonological awareness. Phonological awareness includes four hierarchical language components: word, syllable, onset and rime, and phoneme. Word awareness is the least difficult and phoneme awareness is the most difficult. Ultimately, children must recognize and have an understanding that words are made up of individual sounds (i.e., phonemes), and that the sounds are blended together to make whole words.

1. *Word*—The awareness that speech flow consists of words occurs at a very young age. When a child

says a single word that has only been heard in combination with other words, the child is demonstrating the word level of phonological awareness. Counting or tapping out the number of spoken words in a sentence is an activity to assess or improve word awareness.

2. *Syllable*—Syllables are the easiest distinguishable units within words. Most children acquire the ability to segment words with minimal instruction. Tapping out the number of syllables in a spoken word is an activity used to assess and teach syllable awareness.

3. *Onset and rime*—This component represents an intrasyllable level and is useful as an intermediate level of analysis between the syllable and the phoneme. It involves splitting syllables into onsets and rimes. An onset is the part of the syllable that precedes the vowel (e.g., *p* in *pink* and *spl* in *split*). The rime is the rest of the syllable (e.g., *up* in *cup* and *own* in *brown*). All syllables must have a rime but not all syllables have an onset (e.g., *and, off,* and *up*). Requiring the student to split syllables into onset and rime is an activity for assessing and teaching this component.

4. *Phoneme*—Phonemes are the smallest unit of sound. Phonemic awareness differs from phonological awareness in that it applies to the relationship between phonemes (i.e., sound) and graphemes (i.e., print); that is, letters have specific sounds. Phonemic awareness skills include the ability to detect, segment, and blend phonemes and to manipulate their order in words (Adams, 1990). Phonemes are impossible to segment in a pure manner because in speech flow phonemes affect the pronunciation of adjacent phonemes. Phonemic awareness is much more sophisticated and difficult than syllable or intrasyllabic analysis. Requiring the student to identify the phonemes in a syllable or word is a task for assessing and teaching this component of phonemic awareness.

Phonological Awareness Tasks Once an evaluator realizes that the phonological awareness language components of word, syllable, onset and rime, and phoneme develop in a hierarchical manner, the level of tasks used to assess phonological awareness must be considered. Phonological awareness assessment tasks primarily are administered to 3- to 7-year-olds. These tasks are discussed next in ascending order of difficulty.

The first four tasks are used mostly with preschoolers and beginning kindergartners and include word oddity, sentence segmentation by words, word segmentation by syllables, and sound matching by initial and final sounds of words.

1. **Word oddity** requires the child to recognize words as a unit of language and compare similarities and differences among three to four spoken words. For example, the child can be given three to four spoken words and must tell which one does not belong. The words may differ on initial sounds (e.g., *pig, hill,* and *pal*), medial sounds (e.g., *pin, gun,* and *bun*), or final sounds (e.g., *doll, hop,* and *rap*). Oddity tasks usually consist of alliteration when based on initial sound, and rhyme detection when based on medial and final sounds. These tasks do not require the ability to fractionate a syllable.

2. **Sentence segmentation by words** requires the child to listen to a sentence and count (e.g., by tapping, clapping, or marching) the number of words heard. For example, when listening to the sentence, *Jiggles jumped over the hole,* the child would tap five times, or the child would repeat the sentence while clapping once for each word. This task simply requires the child to recognize a word and count how many words are heard.

3. **Word segmentation by syllables** requires the child to recognize the syllables in a spoken word. The task involves counting (i.e., by tapping, clapping, or marching) the syllables in a spoken word. For example, when given the word *cat,* the child must tap once; when given the word *candy,* the child must tap twice. This task is more complex than word oddity tasks because it involves intraword analysis. About 50 percent of kindergartners and 90 percent of first graders can segment words into syllables (Smith, 2004).

4. **Sound matching** requires the child to detect sound similarities in spoken words: The child may hear four words and be asked to match one of the last three words to the first word on the basis of beginning, middle, or ending sound. For example, in a beginning sound matching task, the teacher may say "card—farm, had, cake" and the child must match *cake* with *card.* This task also may be designed to have the child match pictures on the basis of sounds. About 50 percent of kindergartners can tell whether two words begin or end with the same sound (Smith, 2004).

The next three phonological awareness tasks are appropriate for children in kindergarten. The tasks include blending, word manipulation, and syllable splitting.

5. **Blending** requires the child to combine two to four spoken word segments. For example, the teacher may say "/l/. . ./a/. . . /m/. . . /p/," and the child must combine the segments and say "lamp." This task requires knowledge that strange little sounds can be smashed together to form a word (Adams, 1990). Although a child may know the individual sounds in the word, blending them requires more abstraction than simply saying them quickly.

6. **Word manipulation** requires the ability to delete a word segment and say what is left. This task is appropriate for kindergartners and beginning first graders when the task difficulty is controlled. The use of compound words, short words, or words with sound segments that easily are isolated is appropriate for 5- and 6-year-olds. For example, the teacher may say, "Say *football*. Now say *football* without saying *ball*" (i.e., foot) or "Say *tall*. Now say *tall* without saying /t/" (i.e., all). A task that is too difficult for most kindergartners would be "Say *driver*. Now say *driver* without saying the /v/ sound" (i.e., drier).

7. **Syllable splitting** requires the child to break off or isolate the first phoneme of a word or syllable and say the first phoneme or the remainder. For example, the teacher may ask for the first phoneme and say "Bear" and the child must say "/b/," or the teacher may ask for what is left and say "Feel" and the child must say "eel." This task does not require the child to think of a word as a string of phonemes; it only requires the child to attend carefully to the sounds of the syllable and break away the initial sound. Thus, the child thinks in terms of onsets and rimes rather than phonemes.

   The final two tasks, phoneme segmentation and phoneme manipulation, require some formal reading instruction before most children are able to do them. Thus, children in the latter part of first grade usually are able to do these tasks. Both phoneme segmentation and phoneme manipulation are strong predictors of beginning reading acquisition (Adams, 1990).

8. **Phoneme segmentation** requires the child to hear a syllable and break it into its component phonemes. For example, the teacher may say "mat" and the child must tap, clap, or step (i.e., march) three times—once for each phoneme (/m/, /a/, /t/). This task is difficult because individual phonemes are not distinguishable in many words. The attributes of each phoneme spill over to adjacent sound segments. In general, whereas no 4-year-olds and only a low percentage of 5-year-olds succeed at this task, a high percentage of 6-year-olds succeed.

9. **Phoneme manipulation** requires the child to add, delete, or move any designated phoneme and re-generate a word or nonword. For example, the child must pronounce a word without the first, middle, or last phoneme (e.g., *hill* without saying /h/, *monkey* without saying /k/, or *pink* without saying /k/). Also, the child may be asked to reorder the phonemes of a syllable (e.g., say "tap" backwards—"pat").

The development of phonological awareness prepares the youngster to succeed in both reading and spelling. Moreover, it complements the learning of letter names and sounds, as well as phonics instruction. A good way to assess letter skills is to have the child say each letter, pronounce its sound, and give a word that begins with the letter.

ASSESSMENT OF READING SKILLS

In addition to indicating the student's current reading ability, assessment can point to specific strengths and weaknesses and aid in planning instructional objectives. Both commercially prepared instruments and informal measures are useful. To obtain a valid assessment of the student's reading abilities, the teacher should use a variety of assessment procedures—standardized tests, observations, and informal inventories. The information the teacher wants to obtain should help determine the type of assessment device used. For example, a group-administered reading achievement test yields information on the level of reading of the entire class, whereas more specific information about one student's certain skills can be obtained from an individually administered diagnostic reading test or through informal assessment. The remainder of this chapter presents various formal and informal reading assessment techniques and devices.

myeducationlab

To enhance your understanding of reading assessment, go to the IRIS Center Resources section of the Topic Assessing and Teaching Literacy and Language in the MyEducationLab for your course and complete the Module entitled Classroom Assessment (Part 2): Evaluating Reading Progress.

Formal Reading Assessment

Many commercial tests have been standardized on large groups of students. Such norm-referenced tests enable the teacher to compare each student's performance with the population upon which the test was standardized. Scores from standardized reading tests are reported in several ways (such as reading grade level, reading age score, percentile, and stanine score). However, norm-referenced tests require strict administration, scoring, and interpretation procedures. In addition to norm-referenced tests, some published reading measures are criterion referenced. These tests describe performance, rather than compare it, and can be used to determine whether the student has mastered specific instructional objectives. This section presents achievement and diagnostic tests as well as criterion-referenced tests.

Achievement and Diagnostic Tests General achievement tests assess a student's ability in various academic areas. Achievement tests with reading subtests often are used to obtain an overall measure of reading achievement. These tests are norm referenced and thus yield objective results that can be compared with the norms of the standardization sample. Reading survey tests measure reading skills only and, like achievement tests, are used frequently to indicate a student's general range of reading abilities. Achievement and reading survey tests are basically screening measures and can help determine which students are experiencing reading difficulties and need further assessment. Reading survey tests and achievement tests with reading subtests include the following:

- *Gates-MacGinitie Reading Tests—Fourth Edition* (MacGinitie, MacGinitie, Maria, Dreyer, & Hughes, 2000); assesses word decoding, vocabulary, and comprehension
- *Iowa Tests of Basic Skills* (Hoover, Dunbar, & Frisbie, 2006); assesses word analysis, vocabulary, and reading comprehension
- *Kaufman Test of Educational Achievement—II* (Kaufman & Kaufman, 2004); assesses reading decoding and comprehension
- *Metropolitan Achievement Tests—Eighth Edition* (2000a); assesses emergent literacy, reading vocabulary, and reading comprehension
- *Woodcock-Johnson III Normative Update Tests of Achievement* (Woodcock, McGrew, & Mather, 2007); assesses letter–word identification, word attack, reading fluency, reading vocabulary, and passage comprehension

In contrast to achievement and general reading survey tests, which yield broad information, diagnostic reading tests provide a more precise, comprehensive analysis of specific reading abilities and disabilities. Diagnostic tests differ from achievement tests in that they generally have more subtests and test items related to specific reading skills. The teacher finds out *how* the student attempts to

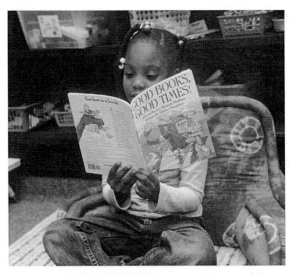

Listening to a student read provides information for planning instruction. T. Lindfors/Lindfors Photography

read. By identifying the student's specific strengths and weaknesses in various subskills of reading, diagnostic tests yield detailed, useful information for planning appropriate individualized educational programs.

Diagnostic reading test batteries are designed to measure many reading subskills. They often include multiple subtests that sample performance in word analysis, word recognition, comprehension, and various reading-related skills. In contrast to test batteries, some diagnostic reading tests measure the student's ability in a specific skill area. Table 7.1 lists selected standardized diagnostic reading test batteries and tests of specific skills.

Criterion-Referenced Tests Whereas norm-referenced tests compare a student's performance with the scores of others, criterion-referenced tests describe performance according to fixed criteria. The teacher discovers which skills the student has learned, which are being learned now, and which still must be taught. The teacher uses criterion-referenced reading tests to determine whether the student has mastered specific objectives, such as recognition of *-ed* endings or use of the *ch* consonant digraph. Test items are presented in a hierarchy to assess a sequence of reading skills. If performance on each skill does not reach the established criterion of success (e.g., 95 percent level of proficiency), the teacher provides instruction specifically for that skill. A student who demonstrates skill mastery according to the determined criterion progresses to the next skill in the sequence. Thus, criterion-referenced tests focus on the student's ability to master specific skills, and the assessment relates to curriculum content and instructional objectives. The student's progress is

TABLE 7.1

Selected standardized diagnostic reading tests

Test	Grade Levels	Areas Assessed
Test Batteries		
Stanford Diagnostic Reading Test— Fourth Edition (Karlsen & Gardner, 1995)	K–13	Emerging literacy skills, phonetic analysis, vocabulary comprehension, scanning

This group-administered test is both norm and criterion referenced. There are eight levels, identified by color, and two forms are available for the last three levels. In addition to yielding percentile ranks, stanines, grade equivalents, and scaled scores, the test results can be used to identify strengths and weaknesses in specific reading skills.

Woodcock-Johnson III Diagnostic Reading Battery (Woodcock, Mather, & Schrank, 2004)	K–college and adult	Phonemic awareness, phonics, fluency, vocabulary, reading comprehension

This individually administered comprehensive measure of reading achievement and ability can be used to screen students to determine the presence of reading difficulties, diagnose specific reading difficulties, monitor progress in reading achievement, or measure outcomes following interventions in instructional programs. The battery includes tests in the following areas: letter–word identification, passage comprehension, word attack, reading vocabulary, reading fluency, spelling of sounds, sound awareness, sound blending, oral vocabulary, and oral comprehension. A scoring and reporting program is included that automates scoring and provides several types of interpretive reports.

Woodcock Reading Mastery Tests—Revised (Woodcock, 1998)	K–college and adult	Visual auditory learning, letter identification, word identification, word attack, word comprehension, passage comprehension

This battery of tests provides thorough coverage of reading readiness, basic skills, and comprehension, and it yields a total reading score as well as derived scores (i.e., age- and grade-based percentile ranks and standard scores, and age and grade equivalents). The test contains two forms; one form omits visual-auditory learning and letter identification. Reading vocabulary, measured on the Word Comprehension subtest may be evaluated in four areas: general reading, science-mathematics, social studies, and humanities. A computer scoring program can be used to assist the examiner in computing scores and providing score printouts.

Tests of Specific Skills		
Comprehensive Test of Phonological Processing (Wagner, Torgesen, & Rashotte, 1999)	K–college	Phonological awareness, phonological memory, rapid naming

This test identifies individuals who are significantly below their peers in phonological abilities and determines their strengths and weaknesses in phonological processing. Two levels are available, one for ages 5 and 6, which includes seven core subtests and one supplemental test, and the other for ages 7 and above, which contains six core subtests and eight supplemental subtests. Core subtests assess phonological processing ability, and supplemental subtests provide additional information on specific phonological strengths and weaknesses. Subtests are grouped according to the areas of phonological awareness (i.e., elision, blending words, sound matching, blending nonwords, and segmenting nonwords), phonological memory (i.e., memory for digits and nonword repetition), rapid naming (i.e., rapid color naming, rapid object naming, rapid digit naming, and rapid letter naming), and additional diagnostic subtests (i.e., phoneme reversal and segmenting words). The core subtests of each version are individually administered in about 30 minutes, and percentiles, standard scores, and age and grade equivalents are provided.

DIBELS: Dynamic Indicators of Basic Early Literacy Skills (Good & Kaminski, 2003)	K–6	Phonological awareness, alphabetic principle, oral reading fluency

DIBELS is a set of standardized, individually administered measures of early literacy development. These 1-minute fluency measures are designed to regularly monitor the development of prereading and early reading skills and also can be used as a screening instrument to identify students with problems. The *DIBELS* measures assess areas of early literacy that are predictive of later reading proficiency: letter recognition (i.e., letter naming fluency), phonological awareness (i.e., initial sound fluency and phonemic segmentation fluency), alphabetic principle (i.e., nonsense word fluency), fluency with connected text (i.e., oral reading fluency), comprehension (i.e., retell fluency), and vocabulary (i.e., word use fluency). Multiple forms facilitate repeated measurement during the school year.

(continued)

TABLE 7.1
(continued)

Test	Grade Levels	Areas Assessed
Gray Oral Reading Tests—Fourth Edition (Wiederholt & Bryant, 2001)	1–12	Reading miscues, reading rate, comprehension

This test includes two forms, each of which contains 14 developmentally sequenced passages with five comprehension questions. As the student reads aloud, the teacher notes reading characteristics, errors, and time elapsed in reading each paragraph. Comprehension questions are asked after each paragraph is read. A system for performing a miscue analysis of reader performance yields information in four areas: meaning similarity, function similarity, graphic/phonemic similarity, and self-correction. Standard scores, percentile ranks, and grade equivalents are provided. The *Gray Diagnostic Reading Tests—Second Edition* (Bryant, Wiederholt, & Bryant, 2004) and the *Gray Silent Reading Tests* (Wiederholt & Blalock, 2000) can be used along with the *GORT—4* to form the Gray reading test battery. The *Gray Diagnostic Reading Tests—Second Edition* assesses students who have difficulty reading continuous print. The four core subtests assess the areas of letter–word identification, phonetic analysis, reading vocabulary, and meaningful reading, and the three supplemental subtests measure skills in listening vocabulary, rapid naming, and phonological awareness. The *Gray Silent Reading Tests* measures an individual's silent reading comprehension ability. The test consists of two parallel forms, and each form contains 13 developmentally sequenced reading passages with five multiple-choice questions.

Test	Grade Levels	Areas Assessed
Lindamood Auditory Conceptualization Test— Third Edition (Lindamood & Lindamood, 2004)	K–12	Phonemic awareness

This test measures an individual's ability to perceive and conceptualize speech sounds using a visual medium as well as the ability to distinguish and manipulate sounds. The student manipulates small colored blocks and colored felt squares to indicate conceptualization of speech sounds and single-syllable and multisyllable items. For example, red-red-blue could represent the phoneme sequence /d/-/d/-/j/ and yellow-blue-red could represent sounds in the nonword *vop*. The Tracking Phonemes subtest includes monosyllables of up to five phonemes. Multisyllable subtests include Counting Syllables, Tracking Syllables, and Tracking Syllables and Phonemes. The test can be administered to individuals in 20 to 30 minutes, and the results yield standard scores, percentile ranks, and age and grade equivalents.

Test	Grade Levels	Areas Assessed
Test of Early Reading Ability—3 (Reid, Hresko, & Hammill, 2001)	Preschool–3	Alphabet, conventions, and meaning

This test assesses children's mastery of early developing reading skills. Three subtests are included: Alphabet measures knowledge of the alphabet and its uses (e.g., letter naming), Conventions measures knowledge of conventions of print (e.g., book reading), and Meaning measures the construction of meaning from print (e.g., print in the environment). Two alternative forms are available, and testing time is approximately 30 minutes.

Test	Grade Levels	Areas Assessed
Test of Phonological Awareness—2 Plus (Torgesen & Bryant, 2004)	K–2	Phonological awareness, letter–sound correspondence

This test measures young children's ability to isolate individual sounds in spoken words and the ability to understand the relationships between letters and phonemes. On the kindergarten version, the child must (a) mark which of three words begins with the same sound as the target word, (b) mark which of four words begins with a different sound than the other three, and (c) mark which of four letters corresponds to a specific phoneme. On the elementary version, the child must (a) identify which of three words ends with the same sound as the target word, (b) mark which of four words ends in a different sound from the others, and (c) spell simple pseudowords that vary from two to five phonemes in length. Both versions can be administered either individually or to groups, and test results are reported in terms of percentile ranks or standard scores.

Test	Grade Levels	Areas Assessed
Test of Phonological Awareness Skills (Newcomer & Barenbaum, 2003)	K–5	Phonological awareness

This individually administered test is helpful in identifying students who have problems in phonological awareness. Four subtests (i.e., Rhyming, Incomplete Words, Sound Sequencing, and Sound Deletion) measure three areas of phonological awareness: sound comparison, phoneme blending, and phoneme segmentation. The test can be administered in 15 to 30 minutes and yields percentile ranks, age equivalents, and standard scores.

TABLE 7.1
(continued)

Test	Grade Levels	Areas Assessed
Test of Reading Comprehension—4 (Brown, Wiederholt, & Hammill, 2009)	2–12	Word identification, contextual meaning

This test of silent reading comprehension includes five subtests that measure word identification and contextual meaning. In Relational Vocabulary, the student must choose two of four words that are related to an initial set of three related words. In Sentence Completion, the student must choose a word pair that best completes a sentence that is missing two words. The student rearranges sentences to form a coherent paragraph in Paragraph Construction, and in Text Comprehension the student answers five multiple-choice questions after reading a short passage. Contextual Fluency measures how many individual words the student can recognize in 3 minutes in a series of passages printed in uppercase letters without punctuation or spaces between words. The test can be administered to an individual in 45 minutes or less and yields a Reading Comprehension Index, which represents the student's ability to understand contextual printed material.

Test	Grade Levels	Areas Assessed
Test of Silent Contextual Reading Fluency (Hammill, Wiederholt, & Allen, 2006)	1–12	Silent contextual reading fluency

This test includes short passages of contextually related words printed in uppercase letters with no spaces or punctuation between the words. The student must draw a line between as many recognizable words as possible within 3 minutes. The passages gradually become more complex in content, vocabulary, and grammar. The test has four equivalent forms and can be administered to individuals or to groups in about 10 minutes.

Test	Grade Levels	Areas Assessed
Test of Silent Word Reading Fluency (Mather, Hammill, Allen, & Roberts, 2004)	1–12	Silent word reading fluency

This test, which has two equivalent forms, measures a student's ability to recognize printed words accurately and efficiently. When presented with rows of words, ordered by reading difficulty, that have no spaces between the words, the student is given 3 minutes to draw a line between the boundaries of as many words as possible. A student's current reading skill level is measured by counting the number of printed words a student can identify within 3 minutes. The test, which can be administered in an individual or group format, yields standard scores, percentiles, and age and grade equivalents.

Test	Grade Levels	Areas Assessed
Test of Word Reading Efficiency (Torgesen, Wagner, & Rashotte, 1999)	1–college	Word reading accuracy, fluency

This test includes two subtests that can be administered quickly to monitor the growth of two word reading skills that are critical in the development of overall reading ability: the ability to accurately recognize familiar words as whole units and the ability to sound out words quickly. The Sight Word Efficiency subtest assesses the number of real printed words (i.e., sight words) that can be accurately identified within 45 seconds, and the Phonetic Decoding Efficiency subtest measures the number of pronounceable printed nonwords that can be accurately decoded within 45 seconds. Each subtest has two forms of equivalent difficulty.

determined by comparing current performance with previous performance. Table 7.2 includes two criterion-referenced reading assessment measures.

Informal Reading Assessment

Informal assessment involves examining the student's daily work or administering teacher-constructed tests by which the teacher can assess any measurable reading skill. The teacher also can determine specific strengths and weaknesses by analyzing reading errors. Informal procedures usually offer two advantages: They require less time to administer than formal tests, and they can be used with classroom materials during regular instruction periods.

An experienced teacher can obtain diagnostic information through careful, day-to-day observations. The teacher has many opportunities to observe and informally assess the student's reading skills and can obtain information about the student's reading interests and attitudes, as well as word analysis and comprehension skills, by observing the student during oral reading, seat-work assignments, instructional sessions, testing sessions, and recreational reading periods. Several informal observations during a period of time also can confirm or supplement the results of formal assessment tests.

When observing the student's performance on various reading tasks, the teacher should consider the following questions.

TABLE 7.2
Selected criterion-referenced reading tests

Test	Grade Levels	Areas Assessed
Brigance Comprehensive Inventory of Basic Skills—II (Brigance, 2010a)	K–9	Word recognition, oral reading, word analysis, reading comprehension
This inventory is used primarily to establish educational objectives and monitor progress toward these objectives. Grade placement tests are included for selected skills. Some of the reading tests (i.e., Word Recognition Grade Placement Test, Reading Vocabulary Comprehension Grade Placement Test, and Word Analysis Survey) have been normed and yield standard scores, percentile ranks, and grade equivalents. A reading comprehension section with larger passages at each grade level is included to assess fluency. Each passage is followed by questions on higher level thinking strategies including facts/details, compare/contrast, cause/effect, sequence, drawing conclusions/making inferences, fact/opinion, and figurative language. Student record books show at each testing the point of competence to which the student has progressed. Also, an online management system can be used to track student progress and generate reports.		
Standardized Reading Inventory—2 (Newcomer, 1999)	K–8	Oral and silent reading, word recognition, reading comprehension
This instrument is designed like an informal reading inventory, with each of its two forms consisting of ten graded reading passages, ranging from preprimer to eighth-grade level. The passages include typical words found in five popular basal reading series. The student reads passages aloud while the examiner records errors in oral reading. Then the student reads the same passages silently and responds to comprehension questions. The scoring of the inventory indicates whether the student's word recognition skills and reading comprehension are at an independent, instructional, or frustration level. In addition to being criterion referenced, this instrument is also norm referenced.		

myeducationlab

Go to the Building Teaching Skills and Dispositions section for the Topic Assessing and Teaching Literacy and Language in the MyEducationLab for your course and complete the activity entitled Assessing Students' Written Work.

- What is the student's attitude toward reading?
- What specific reading interest does the student have?
- Is the student making progress in reading?
- What strengths and weaknesses in reading does the student exhibit?
- During oral reading, does the student read word-by-word or with fluency?
- What kinds of errors does the student make consistently?
- What word analysis skills does the student use?
- Does the student use context clues to recognize words?
- Does the student have a good sight vocabulary?
- Does the student appear to pay attention to the meaning of the material when reading?

The *Reading Observation Scale* (Wiederholt, Hammill, & Brown, 2009) is a norm-referenced 25-item rating scale that can be used to assess the daily classroom reading behaviors of students ages 7 through 17. It consists of statements that relate to specific reading behaviors (e.g.,

"Enjoys reading" and "Retells read material correctly"), and the teacher rates each statement on a 5-point scale. The student's observed reading behaviors usually can be rated in 5 to 10 minutes, and the total score is reported as standard scores and percentile ranks. Moreover, teacher observations also can be recorded on a checklist of reading skills and behaviors. Figure 7.2 presents a reading diagnosis checklist of reading or related abilities in four areas: foundational skills, decoding and word recognition, fluency, and comprehension. The teacher observes the student reading and determines whether each skill has been mastered, is developing as expected, or if intervention is needed. Specific strengths and weaknesses are noted, and progress is charted.

Teacher observation is continuous and permeates all types of informal assessment. This section presents the following informal assessment techniques: graded word lists, informal reading inventory, curriculum-based measurement, portfolio assessment, cloze procedure, and teacher-made tests.

Graded Word Lists Graded word lists examine the student's word recognition skills. Word lists can be useful in informal diagnosis to indicate the student's sight vocabulary, to estimate the level at which the student can read with fluency and has little difficulty with word attack, and to reveal basic weaknesses in word-attack skills as the student confronts unknown words.

FIGURE 7.2
Reading diagnosis checklist

For each observation period, circle **M** if the student has *mastered* the skill, **D** if the student is still *developing* the skill, and **I** if *intervention* is needed in the skill.

	Date	Date	Date
Foundational Skills			
Blends phonemes	M D I	M D I	M D I
Segments phonemes	M D I	M D I	M D I
Identifies uppercase and lowercase letter names	M D I	M D I	M D I
Identifies letter sounds	M D I	M D I	M D I
Decoding and Word Recognition Skills			
Decodes consonant-vowel-consonant words	M D I	M D I	M D I
Decodes regular words beyond consonant-vowel-consonant words	M D I	M D I	M D I
Recognizes common phonograms	M D I	M D I	M D I
Decodes irregular words	M D I	M D I	M D I
Decodes multisyllable words	M D I	M D I	M D I
Uses multiple sources of information to decode and confirm (e.g., grapho-phonemic, syntactic, semantic)	M D I	M D I	M D I
Has basic sight word knowledge	M D I	M D I	M D I
Fluency			
Reads at an appropriate rate	M D I	M D I	M D I
Reads with appropriate phrasing	M D I	M D I	M D I
Reads with appropriate intonation and expression	M D I	M D I	M D I
Reads words accurately (i.e., 95% on grade appropriate passage)	M D I	M D I	M D I
Reads with few or no omissions, insertions, or reversals	M D I	M D I	M D I
Comprehension			
Retells narrative stories with accuracy	M D I	M D I	M D I
Answers literal comprehension questions correctly	M D I	M D I	M D I
Answers inferential comprehension questions correctly	M D I	M D I	M D I
Monitors reading for meaning and self-corrects	M D I	M D I	M D I
Applies fix-up strategies (e.g., rereads difficult material, reads aloud to aid comprehension) when comprehension breaks down	M D I	M D I	M D I
Uses context to learn new vocabulary	M D I	M D I	M D I

Notes for Observation 1

Notes for Observation 2

Notes for Observation 3

TABLE 7.3
Graded word lists

Preprimer	Primer	First	Second	Third	Fourth	Fifth	Sixth
am	went	after	also	beginning	amused	representative	apparatus
an	want	again	always	curious	frightened	glimmer	association
are	with	always	around	exclaimed	certainly	construction	complicated
be	your	begin	before	sixteen	decided	international	economical
big	children	book	yourself	believe	direction	necessary	submerge
came	come	could	everyone	several	eighty	exhaustion	explorer
go	have	does	carefully	through	environment	establish	memorial
had	here	find	eight	wear	government	disapproved	navigation
him	jump	friend	early	thoughtful	mystery	considerable	possession
in	know	from	light	straight	guard	develop	technical
is	little	give	made	worry	ocean	terrific	rehearse
like	play	how	people	important	island	scanty	temperate
me	said	live	please	information	memorize	registration	comment
my	that	night	should	museum	precious	touch	elementary
on	there	please	things	remove	whether	transportation	despite
run	this	our	those	laugh	couldn't	thistle	crucial
see	who	thought	where	questioned	reliability	relation	bridge
she	will	thank	which	drew	protect	vehicle	deliberate
the	help	which	yesterday	moment	science	acquainted	classification
you	book	three	quietly	prepare	favorite	biography	observation

The teacher can develop word lists by randomly selecting 20 to 25 words for each level from the glossaries of graded basal readers. To obtain a random sample of 25 words for each level, the teacher would divide the total number of words for each level by 25. For example, 250 total words divided by 25 would mean that every tenth word is included. The teacher should check to ensure that the words represent various phonics skills (such as consonant and vowel sounds in different positions, consonant blends, and digraphs). The words also should include prefixes, suffixes, and compound words. Sample graded word lists for preprimer through sixth-grade level are presented in Table 7.3. The words for each grade level can be typed on separate cards for the student to read, but the teacher should have a list of all the words. Another method would be to have the student's word list on a sheet of paper and present each word through a window with the use of a tachistoscope made from oaktag or strips cut from manila folders.

Word lists can be presented in two ways. First, a timed flash exposure (e.g., 1 second) can be given to assess the student's instant recognition or sight word vocabulary. Second, words the student initially is unable to recognize can be presented untimed to test ability to apply word-attack skills to unknown words. The teacher also can obtain additional information by giving prompts, such as providing an initial sound or covering part of the word. If prompts are provided, the teacher should make notes on the test protocol. Such notes will provide valuable information when analyzing all the data to make instructional decisions.

The teacher can determine a word recognition grade-level score—indicating the student's ability to identify words—by an untimed presentation of graded word lists. In general, the level at which the student misses none or only one word is the *independent level*. At the *instructional level* the student identifies two words incorrectly; when three or more words are missed, the student has reached the *frustration level*. As well as using word lists to determine grade-level placement in word recognition, the teacher also should note specific errors in word attack. When the student mispronounces a word, the teacher should write down the mispronunciation to analyze the method of word attack and look for error patterns. For example, the student may recognize only initial consonant sounds and guess at the remainder of the word, or may not be able to blend individual sounds into whole words. The student who reads *month* as *mouth* or *long* as *large* may be responding to configuration cues, whereas a response of a completely dissimilar word, such as *after* for *field,* may indicate a lack of phonetic word-attack skills. The teacher also should note the student's skill in structural analysis (i.e., knowledge of prefixes, roots, and endings).

TABLE 7.4

A list of 140 basic sight words

1. the	29. from	57. many	85. like	113. way
2. of	30. or	58. before	86. made	114. could
3. and	31. have	59. must	87. did	115. out
4. to	32. an	60. out	88. many	116. how
5. a	33. they	61. so	89. your	117. use
6. in	34. which	62. said	90. may	118. word
7. that	35. one	63. what	91. down	119. only
8. is	36. you	64. up	92. each	120. new
9. was	37. were	65. its	93. people	121. little
10. he	38. her	66. about	94. would	122. year
11. for	39. all	67. into	95. see	123. me
12. it	40. she	68. than	96. get	124. most
13. with	41. there	69. them	97. day	125. good
14. as	42. would	70. can	98. come	126. man
15. his	43. their	71. other	99. go	127. very
16. on	44. we	72. some	100. part	128. our
17. be	45. him	73. could	101. water	129. any
18. at	46. been	74. time	102. find	130. over
19. by	47. has	75. these	103. look	131. even
20. I	48. when	76. two	104. more	132. after
21. this	49. who	77. then	105. write	133. also
22. had	50. will	78. do	106. some	134. before
23. not	51. more	79. first	107. make	135. must
24. are	52. no	80. my	108. long	136. back
25. but	53. if	81. now	109. am	137. much
26. well	54. work	82. old	110. three	138. say
27. just	55. us	83. came	111. place	139. thing
28. too	56. great	84. take	112. around	140. me

In addition to graded word lists devised by the teacher, published word lists are available. For example, the widely used Dolch (1955) list includes 200 sight words (i.e., high-frequency words) that make up 50 to 65 percent of the words the student encounters in elementary school basal readers. Also, Fry and Kress (2006) provide lists of the most common words in English, and they indicate that the first 300 words make up about 65 percent of all written material. Table 7.4 presents a list of 140 basic sight words, which occur frequently in most reading material. Using graded word lists to determine word recognition skills is often the first step in administering an informal reading inventory.

Informal Reading Inventory An informal reading inventory provides information about the student's general reading level. It uses reading passages of increasing difficulty from various graded materials, such as selections from a basal reading series with which the student is unfamiliar. In general, the passages should consist of about 50 words (i.e., at preprimer level) to 200 words (i.e., at secondary level). The student begins reading passages aloud at a level at which word-attack and comprehension tasks are handled easily. The student continues reading passages of increasing difficulty until the passages become too difficult for him or her to read. As the student reads aloud, the teacher records errors and asks three to five questions about each passage. Many kinds of questions should be used: recall of facts (i.e., who, what, and where), inference (i.e., why), and vocabulary (i.e., general or specific meanings). To assess literal comprehension, the student can be asked to state the main idea of the passage, propose a title, recall details, present a series of events or ideas, or explain the meaning of vocabulary words. Inferential comprehension can be evaluated by asking questions that force the student to go beyond the information provided in the passage. For example, the student can be asked to draw conclusions, make predictions, evaluate ideas or actions, or suggest alternative endings. The student should be allowed to reread or inspect the passage before answering comprehension questions. Otherwise, it is possible that *memory* rather than comprehension is being tested. The percentage of words read correctly for each passage is computed by dividing the number of correctly read words by the number of words in the selection. The percentage of comprehension questions answered correctly is determined by dividing the number of correct answers by the number of questions asked.

Through this method the teacher can estimate ability at three levels: independent, instructional, and frustration (Johnson, Kress, & Pikulski, 1987). At the *independent level,* the student can read the graded passage with high accuracy, recognizing 98 to 100 percent of the words and answering the comprehension questions with 90 to 100 percent accuracy. The reading is fluent and natural, and there is no finger pointing or hesitation. At this level, the teacher can hand out supplementary materials for independent or enjoyment reading. The level at which the student needs some help is the *instructional level.* The student can recognize 95 percent of the words and comprehends about 75 percent of the material. The material is challenging but not too difficult, and the student reads in a generally relaxed manner. The teacher should provide reading instruction at this level. At the *frustration level,* the student reads with considerable difficulty. Word recognition is 90 percent or less, and comprehension is less than 70 percent. The student is tense and makes many errors or reversals. Reading material at this level cannot be used for instruction.

In addition to using an inventory to record oral reading word recognition and comprehension, the teacher should note various types of reading errors such as omitting words or parts of words, inserting or substituting words, reversing a word or its letters, and repeating words. It helps to develop a system for marking oral reading errors. Table 7.5 presents oral reading errors and a corresponding set of appropriate marks. Types of reading errors can have particular meanings. Omissions may indicate that the student is skipping unknown words or is reading quickly without attention. Insertions of words that do not appear in the passage may suggest a superficial reading, a reliance on context for assistance, or a lack of interest in accuracy. Whereas omissions and insertions are more characteristic of older students, reversals are common at the primary age level or with students for whom English is a second language. Repetitions may indicate that the reader is tense and nervous or is delaying to gain time to attack the next unknown word. Mispronunciations are common among students who attempt to sound out words without knowing exceptions to phonetic rules; they also may occur in students

who have low levels of listening vocabulary and are unable to use context clues. Self-corrections indicate that the reader is attempting to read more accurately and to rely upon information from the context of the sentence, whereas a dependent reader tends to make no attempt at decoding and needs the teacher to supply the unknown word.

An informal reading inventory also can be used to assess silent reading. Whereas oral reading focuses on word-attack skills, silent reading emphasizes comprehension. The student silently reads each passage and then answers comprehension questions. The percentage of correct responses indicates the student's silent reading level: independent (i.e., 90 to 100 percent), instructional (i.e., 75 percent), or frustration (i.e., 50 percent). While the student reads silently, the teacher can note whispering, lip movements, finger pointing, facial grimaces, and fidgeting. The student also may have difficulties such as low rate, high rate at the expense of understanding, poorly organized recall, and inaccurate recall. Comprehension errors can be classified according to an analysis of skills, including recall of factual details, comprehension and summary of main ideas, understanding of sequence, making inferences, and critical reading and evaluation. The teacher can compare the student's oral and silent reading performances to determine whether there is a great difference.

In addition, the material in an informal reading inventory can be read to the student to determine listening or hearing capacity level, which is the highest level at which the student can comprehend 75 percent of the material. This provides an estimate of the student's reading potential or what the level would be if the student had no problems with the mechanics of reading.

Although it is time-consuming to use informal reading inventories because they are individually administered, they are used widely. Walpole and McKenna (2006) caution teachers in the use of informal reading inventories and state that the information should be used along with more specific assessments. Word recognition, for example, may be helped by context; thus an informal reading inventory may not provide an effective assessment of decoding skills (McKenna & Picard, 2006/2007). Another concern is that the reliability of some informal reading inventories is less than adequate (Spector, 2005). However, when informal reading inventories are implemented along with other diagnostic assessments, they help the teacher to plan needed corrective instruction and to provide reading materials suited to the student's abilities. The teacher should realize that informal reading

TABLE 7.5
Oral reading errors and marking system

Type of Error	Marking System	Example
Omissions	Circle the word or parts of word omitted.	The boy went in ⌀ the ⟨burning⟩ building.
Insertions	Use a caret to mark the place of insertion and write the added word or letter(s).	down The children sat ∧ at the table to eat lunch. ^es
Substitutions	Cross out the word and write the substituted word above it.	realize Now I ~~recognize~~ your name.
Reversals	For letter reversals within a word, cross out the word and write the reversal word above it.	pot The ~~top~~ is lost.
	For reversals of words, draw a curved line going over, between, and under the reversed words.	Mary looked ⌒ often at the clock.
Repetitions	Draw a wavy line under the words which are repeated.	Everyone was cheering for me because I was a baseball hero.
Mispronunciations	Write the mispronounced word (indicating the student's pronunciation) over the correct word.	oc-top-us It was an octopus.
Hesitations	Use a slash to indicate improper hesitation.	The / judge asked the jury / to leave the courtroom.
Aided Words	Underline the word pronounced for the student.	The scared cat began to tremble.
Unobserved punctuation marks	Cross out the punctuation mark the student continued to read through.	Puppy saw the man He barked and barked. ✗
Self-corrected errors	Write **sc** over the error notation.	sc mouth This ~~month~~ is November.

Example of a Marked Passage

The three boys were ⟨very⟩ tired from their long journey. Now they had to swim across a river. John plunged
cold   swimming   may-naged   wet
into the icy ∧ water and started ⟨to swim⟩. He swam slowly but managed to reach the other side of the ~~wide~~ river.

---

inventories may be used at the classroom level as a component of comprehensive assessment but should not be used for decisions such as referral for placement in special education.

An informal reading inventory can be administered from time to time to check the student's reading progress. Several published informal reading inventories that contain graded word lists and graded passages are available. Four widely used inventories are the *Qualitative Reading Inventory—4* (Leslie & Caldwell, 2006), the *Analytical Reading Inventory* (Woods & Moe, 2007), the *Informal Reading Inventory* (Roe & Burns, 2007), and the *Classroom Reading Inventory* (Wheelock, Campbell, & Silvaroli, 2009).

Curriculum-Based Measurement Curriculum-based assessment includes any approach that uses direct observation and recording of a student's performance in the school curriculum as a basis for obtaining information to make instructional decisions. Within this model, *curriculum-based measurement (CBM)* refers to a specific set of standardized procedures in which rate samples are used to assess a student's achievement in academic skills (Deno, 1987, 1989). The assessment procedures involved in CBM are used primarily to establish district or classroom performance standards and to monitor individual student progress toward long-range goals; however, they also can be used to monitor progress toward short-range goals. Basically, in curriculum-based measurement of reading skills, basal reading passages are used to measure oral reading fluency. The student reads passages under timed conditions, the examiner counts the number of words read correctly and the number of words read incorrectly, and student performance is summarized as the rate correct. Some of the reasons that CBM is recommended for monitoring reading progress include the following:

1. CBM reading procedures have excellent reliability and validity (Fewster & MacMillan, 2002; Fuchs & Fuchs, 1986; Rasinski, 1990; Shinn, Good, Knutson, Tilly, & Collins, 1992; Tindal & Marston, 1990; Wayman, Wallace, Wiley, Ticha, & Espin, 2007).

2. CBM measures have been used extensively in research studies involving students with disabilities (Fewster & MacMillan, 2002; Fuchs, Fuchs, Hamlett, Walz, & Germann, 1993; Weinstein & Cooke, 1992).

3. CBM has high correlations with standardized tests of global reading, comprehension, and word identification (Deno, Mirkin, & Chiang, 1982; Fuchs, Fuchs, & Maxwell, 1988; Shinn et al., 1992; Wayman et al., 2007).

When CBM is used to establish performance standards in reading, measures are developed from the school reading curriculum and are administered to all the students in a target group (such as all fourth graders in a school or district). The results provide data to determine standards of performance. Using CBM to establish standards involves four components: material selection, test administration, performance display and interpretation, and decision-making framework (Tindal & Marston, 1990). Selecting the appropriate material from the school curriculum begins the assessment process; an appropriate difficulty level is that which the teacher expects the student to master by the end of the semester or school year. Passages of about 200 words—excluding poetry, exercises, and excessive dialogue—from the school's reading curriculum are selected and administered to targeted students (e.g., fourth graders). A comparison of all students on the same measure provides a norm-referenced database for making instructional decisions. Four to six sample passages should be selected to provide the teacher with enough material for several administrations. All passages should reflect similar difficulty, which can be based on their readability. Once materials are selected, they can be prepared by creating a student copy retyped to eliminate picture distractions and a teacher copy that has the cumulative number of words on successive lines printed along the right margin. When administering a reading passage, the teacher uses the following steps.

1. Select two or three brief (50- to 200-word) grade-level passages.
2. Have the student read each passage aloud for 1 minute.
3. For each passage, count the total number of words read, count the total number of errors, and subtract the total number of errors from the total number of words read. Errors include omitted words, mispronounced words, and words not read within 3 seconds. Correct words are those pronounced correctly, including self-corrections.
4. Compute the average number of correct words read per minute for all passages by dividing the total number of correct words read per minute by the number of passages (*Put Reading First,* 2001).

When all students in the grade or class are tested and the average score for each student is computed, the teacher can develop a plot of the entire group. These data enable teachers to identify low performers who need special instruction, divide students into instructional groups, plan instructional programs, and establish long-range goals. Thus, rather than placing students into a reading material according to a percentage of correct responses, as is done with informal reading inventories, a placement validated through research can be made by placing the student in the level where her or his reading ability is most comparable to others.

A second primary use of CBM is to monitor individual student progress toward long-range goals. Figure 7.3 includes the administration and scoring procedures of reading passages as well as procedures for determining long-range goals and graphing data. Figure 7.4 presents a graph of CBM data and illustrates a long-range goal or aim line and appropriate intervention changes. *Put Reading First* (2001) suggests the following words-correct-per-minute rates for fluency standards: end of first grade—60 words correct per minute; end of second grade—90–110 words correct per minute; end of third grade—114 words correct per minute. Moreover, Hasbrouck and Tindal (2006) provide the following oral reading fluency end-of-year norms: grade 1—53 words correct per minute; grade 2—89 words correct per minute; grade 3—107 words correct per minute; grade 4—123 words correct per minute; grade 5—139 words correct words per minute; grades 6 and 7—150 words correct per minute; grade 8—151 words correct per minute.

When monitoring progress toward a long-range instructional goal, patterns of errors may indicate areas for remediation. These areas become the focus of short-term goals (e.g., identification of sight words, letter sounds, or facts in a story). To monitor progress on short-term goals, mastery monitoring charts that are similar to those in precision teaching are used. When the student reaches mastery on a short-term goal, a new goal is established. Monitoring continues through a series of short-term goals, and the measurement items change each time the student masters a goal. Probes or task sheets frequently are used for evaluation of student progress in timings given two or three times a week. The teacher graphs the correct responses and analyzes the data to make instructional decisions.

FIGURE 7.3

Procedures for administering and scoring reading passages, determining long-range goals, and graphing data

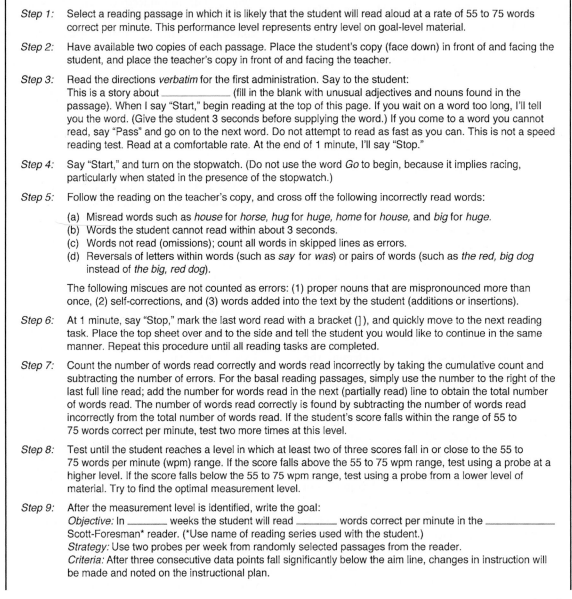

Step 1: Select a reading passage in which it is likely that the student will read aloud at a rate of 55 to 75 words correct per minute. This performance level represents entry level on goal-level material.

Step 2: Have available two copies of each passage. Place the student's copy (face down) in front of and facing the student, and place the teacher's copy in front of and facing the teacher.

Step 3: Read the directions *verbatim* for the first administration. Say to the student:
This is a story about _____ (fill in the blank with unusual adjectives and nouns found in the passage). When I say "Start," begin reading at the top of this page. If you wait on a word too long, I'll tell you the word. (Give the student 3 seconds before supplying the word.) If you come to a word you cannot read, say "Pass" and go on to the next word. Do not attempt to read as fast as you can. This is not a speed reading test. Read at a comfortable rate. At the end of 1 minute, I'll say "Stop."

Step 4: Say "Start," and turn on the stopwatch. (Do not use the word *Go* to begin, because it implies racing, particularly when stated in the presence of the stopwatch.)

Step 5: Follow the reading on the teacher's copy, and cross off the following incorrectly read words:

(a) Misread words such as *house* for *horse*, *hug* for *huge*, *home* for *house*, and *big* for *huge*.
(b) Words the student cannot read within about 3 seconds.
(c) Words not read (omissions); count all words in skipped lines as errors.
(d) Reversals of letters within words (such as *say* for *was*) or pairs of words (such as *the red, big dog* instead of *the big, red dog*).

The following miscues are not counted as errors: (1) proper nouns that are mispronounced more than once, (2) self-corrections, and (3) words added into the text by the student (additions or insertions).

Step 6: At 1 minute, say "Stop," mark the last word read with a bracket (]), and quickly move to the next reading task. Place the top sheet over and to the side and tell the student you would like to continue in the same manner. Repeat this procedure until all reading tasks are completed.

Step 7: Count the number of words read correctly and words read incorrectly by taking the cumulative count and subtracting the number of errors. For the basal reading passages, simply use the number to the right of the last full line read; add the number for words read in the next (partially read) line to obtain the total number of words read. The number of words read correctly is found by subtracting the number of words read incorrectly from the total number of words read. If the student's score falls within the range of 55 to 75 words correct per minute, test two more times at this level.

Step 8: Test until the student reaches a level in which at least two of three scores fall in or close to the 55 to 75 words per minute (wpm) range. If the score falls above the 55 to 75 wpm range, test using a probe at a higher level. If the score falls below the 55 to 75 wpm range, test using a probe from a lower level of material. Try to find the optimal measurement level.

Step 9: After the measurement level is identified, write the goal:
Objective: In _____ weeks the student will read _____ words correct per minute in the _____ Scott-Foresman* reader. (*Use name of reading series used with the student.)
Strategy: Use two probes per week from randomly selected passages from the reader.
Criteria: After three consecutive data points fall significantly below the aim line, changes in instruction will be made and noted on the instructional plan.

(continued)

FIGURE 7.3
(continued)

Use a calendar to count the number of weeks remaining in the school year or semester. Write that number in the first blank. To calculate the number for the second blank, refer to the baseline data, the three probes scores at or near the 55 to 75 wpm range. Determine which of the three scores is the median (i.e., in rank order, the middle score).

(a) If the student is being measured at or above the third-grade reader level, multiply the number of weeks (i.e., weeks in the instructional period) times 2 (rate of growth) and add this to the baseline score.

(weeks × 2) + baseline median = goal
For example: (30 × 2) + 66 = 126 wpm

(b) If the student is being measured below the third-grade reader level, multiply the number of weeks (i.e., weeks in instructional period) times 1.5 (rate of growth) and add this to the baseline median score.

(weeks × 1.5) + baseline median = goal
For example: (30 × 1.5) + 66 = 111 wpm

Step 10: Draw the aim line on the graph by connecting the baseline point and the goal point (see Figure 7.6).

Step 11: Write an instructional plan on the reverse side of the CBM graph.

Step 12: Implement the plan and collect CBM data twice a week. To collect CBM data, use the prepared probes from the respective reading series. Because these probes are already in a random sequence, use them in order. Try to measure the student in the same setting, at about the same time, and under the same general circumstances whenever possible. Read the directions each time so that the student consistently gets clues about the unusual words in the story. After scoring the performance, write the score in the appropriate box at the side of the graph page.

Step 13: Graph the median of the current score and the two previous scores instead of graphing every data point. This graphing system is called the moving median and is used to reduce the variability in the graphed data because these data are used for decision making. For example, if today's score is 66, last Thursday's was 70, and the previous Tuesday's was 59, graph the 66 because this is the median. Do not graph until three data points are collected after the baseline. Plot the moving median on the administration day even if the median score was from a previous day. In the given example, if the fourth probe (on Thursday) is 71, the last three probes would be 70, 66 and 71, and the median is 70. Thus, on the Thursday date, 70 is graphed as the median of the last three probes.

Step 14: To evaluate the effects of instruction, carefully examine the data. If the student has three consecutive scores graphed significantly below the aim line, make a change in instruction. (Significant is defined as ten or more points below the aim line.) Every time the student's data points fall significantly below the aim line three consecutive times, draw a vertical line on the graph after the third point (see Figure 7.6). Record the change in the reading instructional plan. If the student has six consecutive scores significantly above the aim line (six or more points above), probe with the next higher reading level book to see whether the student scores within the 55 to 75 wpm range on two of the three probes. This may mean establishing a new aim line for the student. This is done on the existing graph.

FIGURE 7.3
(continued)

Step 15: Change instruction. For ideas on what to change, consider using some of the following strategies: talk to another teacher; review suggestions in books, journals, and magazines; ask the student for ideas; or use the student's performance on the passages for error analysis.

Step 16: Use other measures for students who are word callers (i.e., can read aloud fluently but do not understand what they have read). These students can be asked to retell a story read silently, and the number of words used in the retelling can be scored and graphed. Also, these students can be asked to answer three to five comprehension questions, and the correct number of responses can be scored and graphed. The correct number of responses can be graphed between the 0 to 10 unit on the bottom of the graph chart. Examples of comprehension questions that can be asked after each assessment probe include the following: What are the main characters in the story? Where does the story take place? and What do you think will happen next?

Step 17: If the student reads more than 100 words correct per minute at or above the sixth-grade reader level on three consecutive probes, discontinue CBM. Note documentation of performance on the student's graph.

FIGURE 7.4

A curriculum-based measurement graph illustrating an aim line and intervention changes

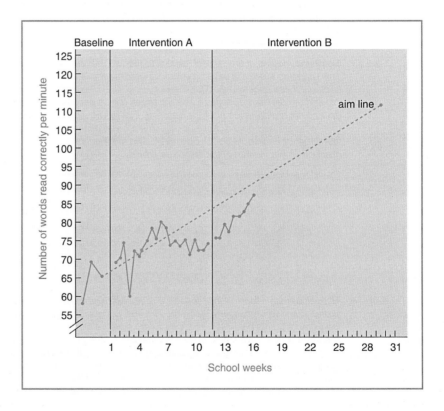

Potter and Wamre (1990) note that the use of oral reading rate measures in curriculum-based measurement is a viable measure of general reading skill and is consistent with developmental reading models such as Chall's (1996) stages of reading development. Moreover, Fewster and MacMillan (2002) indicate that measures of oral reading fluency are appropriate for screening and placement decisions. *DIBELS: Dynamic Indicators of Basic Early Literacy Skills* (Good & Kaminski, 2003), included in Table 7.1, is a set of standardized, 1-minute oral reading fluency measures for students in kindergarten through sixth grade that can be used as a screening instrument. Finally, to facilitate implementation of CBM, Salend (2009) notes that teachers can use technology by recording data on handheld devices and then using internet resources to create CBM assessment probes and to record, graph, analyze, and share the CBM data.

Portfolio Assessment A reading portfolio consists of a collection of materials that reflect the student's personal reading history and accomplishments as a reader. The student should participate in the selection and evaluation of the materials chosen for the portfolio. The materials can vary widely depending on the function of the portfolio assessment, which may include providing information for the teacher to use in assessing student achievement and making instructional decisions, documenting a record of student progress, and demonstrating student accomplishments to parents. Reading logs that indicate the number and variety of books read can be included, as well as checklists made from student observations and questionnaires completed by the student on reading interests and attitudes toward reading. Audiotapes of the student's best oral reading also can be collected at regular intervals. Reviews of the student's portfolio can provide information for teacher assessment as well as self-assessment by the student to evaluate reading progress and plan future activities to enhance reading achievement.

Cloze Procedure The cloze procedure can be used to measure reading levels and comprehension informally. It allows the teacher to estimate the difficulty the student will have with a specific reading material and thus helps determine whether a book is appropriate. The teacher presents an unfamiliar reading passage of about 250 words to the student. The first sentence is typed completely, but in subsequent sentences every fifth word is replaced with a blank. The blanks should be of uniform length. The remainder of the selection is typed as it appears in text. The student reads the passage and fills in the missing words or synonyms. Thus, the student must rely on context clues within the passage to make meaningful responses.

A variation of the cloze procedure is the maze procedure, in which the student is presented with a vertical array of choices for each omitted word. This changes the task from completion to multiple-choice or recognition. Another modification includes having the student select words from an answer key. The teacher also may choose to delete only every tenth word, or other appropriate words can be omitted to avoid the inadvertent continuous omission of articles or proper names.

A reading passage using the cloze procedure can be administered either individually or in groups. Reading levels are determined by changing the number of correct responses to percentages. Bormuth (1968) suggests the following scoring of cloze passages: *independent reading level,* above 57 percent correct responses; *instructional reading level,* 44 to 57 percent correct responses; and *frustration reading level,* below 44 percent correct responses. Because identification of a correct word is easier than production of a correct word, the criterion is higher when the maze procedure is used (e.g., about 60 to 85 percent correct for instructional level). For additional information, the teacher should attempt to analyze why the student makes certain errors. Cloze errors can be examined according to linguistic components and reasoning skills.

Teacher-Made Tests The teacher can devise an informal test to obtain a quick estimate of a specific skill. Probe sheets can be developed to assess a particular reading objective, such as consonant sounds, vowel sounds, blends, or compound words. A sample probe sheet to assess the student's ability to blend consonant-vowel-consonant sounds is presented in Figure 7.5. The probe is administered for 1 minute; then the correct and incorrect responses are tallied. Although the range of suggested proficiency reading rates varies in the literature, the median number of correct words per minute for saying isolated sounds is 70, and the median number of correct words per minute for saying words in a list is 80. Howell and Nolet (2000) suggest the following proficiency reading rates for saying words in text: early first grade—35 words per minute; late first grade—50 words per minute; early second grade—70 words per minute; late second grade—100 words per minute; early third grade—120 words per minute; late third grade and above—140 words per minute. Figure 7.6 presents a sample record sheet for probe assessment of various reading skills.

Teacher-made tests can be constructed by using items in standardized tests and workbook exercises as guides. A variety of items that measure a specific skill can be used (e.g., multiple choice, true–false, completion, or matching). The teacher should be careful to include enough items to sample the skill adequately. Figure 7.7 presents an informal assessment of word recognition and phonics sounds. In addition, short-form word analysis tests can be devised to measure specific skills. Items also can be developed to assess specific comprehension skills, such as stating the main idea, noting details, and understanding

FIGURE 7.5

Probe sheet for blending consonant-vowel-consonant sounds

luv	had	mok	hob	cuz
lit	def	cak	met	roc
nom	vig	pit	tik	fam
cum	zot	wet	bag	pod
fif	lid	hat	get	won
pik	soc	jox	vic	sut
sas	far	kah	par	gan
teg	tem	mez	zix	zec
pub	hun	nod	wol	wap
sel	top	nip	ris	dit

Name: _____

Time: _____

Number Correct: _____

Number Incorrect: _____

Comments: _____

_____

_____

FIGURE 7.6

Sample record sheet for probe assessments

Name ____ Greg ____				Grade ____ 4 ____	
Reading Areas	Session 1	Session 2	Session 3	Session 4	Suggested Rates for Proficiency
	correct/ error	correct/ error	correct/ error	correct/ error	correct error
Consonant Sounds (1 minute)	18/0	25/0	18/0	35/0	60–80 2 or fewer
Vowel Sounds (1 minute)	28/0	24/4	28/1	30/3	60–80 2 or fewer
Sight Words (1 minute)	28/3	35/3	41/3	44/9	70–90 2 or fewer
Grade 4 Word List (1 minute)	32/8	38/4	41/5	43/4	70–90 2 or fewer
Oral Reading (1 minute)	59/7	68/4	76/6	78/11	100–140 2 or fewer

From *Students with Learning Disabilities* (p. 191), 5th ed., C. D. Mercer, © 1997. Adapted by permission of Pearson Education, Inc., Upper Saddle River, NJ.

cause-and-effect relationships. Selected items for assessing the short *a* vowel sound are presented in Figure 7.8. When the student passes the informal test, the teacher can assume that he or she has mastered the objective and is ready to progress to another skill. Moreover, teacher-made tests often deal with reading skills the student must use daily, and they provide a measure of student progress over a specific period of time. Reading scope and sequence skills lists can help determine the order of skill as-

sessment and instruction. The scope and sequence skills list for reading presented in the Appendix is organized into word-attack skills and comprehension skills. Authorities disagree about the sequence for teaching reading skills, and research results about the sequence are inconclusive. Thus, a teacher should use a reading scope and sequence skills list in a flexible way and should tailor the sequence for assessing and teaching reading skills according to logic and experience.

FIGURE 7.7
Informal assessment of word recognition and phonics sounds

Phonograms in Isolation

Phonogram	Fall	Winter	Spring
ay			
ch			
ir			
ar			
kn			
eigh			
th			

Phonogram	Fall	Winter	Spring
oy			
al			
gn			
ph			
sh			
er			
ing			

Consonant-Vowel-Consonant Combinations

CVC Word	Fall	Winter	Spring
fan			
sun			
tin			
pet			
mom			
did			
big			
red			

CVC Word	Fall	Winter	Spring
gum			
hid			
cap			
kid			
lad			
nip			
pan			
van			

Consonant Blends with Long and Short Vowels

Word	Fall	Winter	Spring
string			
throne			
plant			
try			
please			
dust			
sweet			
tray			

Word	Fall	Winter	Spring
spill			
throw			
scratch			
clam			
grill			
freeze			
scribe			
snake			

Consonant Digraphs with Long and Short Vowels (*ch, sh,* voiced and unvoiced *th, wh, qu, ck, ng*)

Word	Fall	Winter	Spring
church			
splash			
spring			
chime			
thank			
shine			
flash			
smooth			

Word	Fall	Winter	Spring
trick			
these			
chore			
which			
quick			
where			
swing			
cloth			

FIGURE 7.7
(continued)

Words with Inflectional Endings (*-s, -es, -ed, -ing, -y, -ly, -er, -est*)

Word	Fall	Winter	Spring
plays			
dresses			
quickly			
helping			
wanted			
happiest			
singing			
boxes			
faster			
cleared			

Word	Fall	Winter	Spring
stops			
quietly			
sunny			
wished			
folded			
cooked			
lighter			
sweetest			
wishes			
trying			

Common Phonically Irregular Words

Word	Fall	Winter	Spring
have			
been			
said			
again			
come			
people			
Island			
does			

Word	Fall	Winter	Spring
answer			
listen			
what			
kind			
sure			
their			
often			
friend			

FIGURE 7.8

Teacher-made test items for assessing short *a* vowel sound

I. The student reads the words with short *a* in initial position.

am	ant	at
an	as	act
and	ask	add

Criterion: 7/9

II. The student reads the words with short *a* in medial position.

ham	pant	bat
can	gas	fact
hand	task	mad

Criterion: 7/9

III. The student selects the word of the pair that contains the short *a* sound.

hat—hate	plan—plane
say—sad	past—pay
ran—ray	stay—sand
tale—land	dad—pale

Criterion: 7/8

IV. The student chooses the word with the short *a* sound to complete the sentence.

The boy had a _____ on his head. (cap, cape)

The _____ was blowing. (sail, flag)

His mother was looking at the _____. (mail, map)

There was a _____ in the sidewalk. (crack, nail)

The father did not _____ his son. (blame, spank)

Criterion 4/5

Assessing and Teaching Spelling

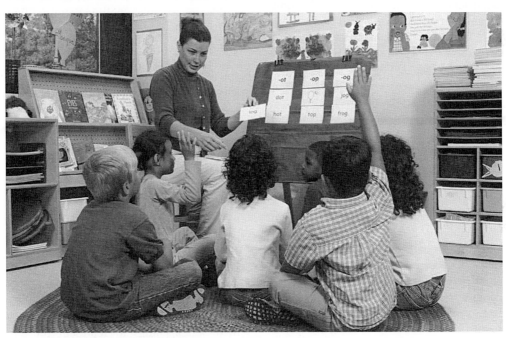

David Mager/Pearson Learning Photo Studio

From Chapter 9 of *Teaching Students with Learning Problems*, 8/e. Cecil D. Mercer. Ann R. Mercer. Paige C. Pullen.

Spelling is the forming of words through the conventional arrangement of letters. Young children use different types of spelling strategies as they developmentally move through stages of invented spelling to conventional spelling. According to Gentry (1982, 2004, 2006), students move through two distinct phases of spelling development. Phase 1, *Learning to Spell*, includes the following characteristics.

Level 1: *Precommunicative spelling.* The child uses scribbles, letters, and letterlike forms and shows a preference for uppercase letters. There is no understanding of phoneme-grapheme correspondence, and the child's writing shows a lack of understanding of conventions of print such as spaces between words and the left-to-right progression of writing. This level is typical of preschoolers, ages 3 through 5.

Level 2: *Semiphonetic spelling.* The child has some awareness that letters are used to represent sounds and may use abbreviated one-, two-, or three-letter spellings to represent an entire word (e.g., *DA* for *day,* *LF* for *laugh*). Thus, the child uses incomplete but reasonable phonetic representations of words. Also, the child demonstrates awareness of left-to-right progression but tends to run letters together with little or no sense of separate words (e.g., *RUDF* for *Are you deaf?*). Semiphonetic spellers include 5- and 6-year-olds.

Level 3: *Phonetic spelling.* The child represents all essential sound features in spelling a word and chooses letters on the basis of sound (e.g., *PEKT* for *peeked,* *KOM* for *come*). The child is aware not only of sounds but also of mouth positions used to make sounds (e.g., *y* may be used to spell /w/ because the mouth position to say the letter name *y* is the same as to say /w/). Typically, 6-year-old children are phonetic spellers.

Level 4: *Transitional spelling.* The child begins to use conventional alternatives for representing sounds and includes a vowel in every syllable (e.g., *AFTERNEWN* for *afternoon,* *TRUBAL* for *trouble*). Thus, the child becomes more aware of letter patterns in words. Many words are spelled correctly, but words with irregular spellings continue to be misspelled. The child's spelling may become a mixture of phonetic components and salient visual features in words. Transitional spellers generally are around 7 or 8 years old.

In phase 2, *Correct and Automatic Spelling,* the child spells many words correctly and applies the basic rules of the English orthographic system. The child recognizes when words look incorrect and can consider alternative spellings. Youngsters typically reach this phase by age 8 or 9 and develop this phase over several years.

Focusing on where a student is within the developmental sequence may help the teacher understand the logic of misspelled words from the perspective of the student. Formal spelling instruction typically is introduced at the beginning of the second grade, and each year the student learns progressively more difficult high-frequency words, patterns, and principles. The student extends knowledge of word structure and learns irregular spelling patterns. Typically, 9- to 11-year-olds learn to break words into syllables, add inflectional endings (e.g., *-es, -ed,* and *-ing*), and differentiate between homophones (e.g., *your* and *you're*), and 11- to 14-year-olds focus on morphemes, learn Greek and Latin root words and affixes, and learn that words with related meanings often are related in spelling despite changes in vowel and consonant sounds (e.g., *sign/signal* and *nation/national*) (Bear, Invernizzi, Templeton, & Johnston, 2008; Tompkins, 2009). The ability to spell is essential because it allows one to read written words correctly. In addition, incorrect spelling often results in an unfavorable impression, and the poor speller may be considered uneducated or careless.

The English language presents inconsistent relationships between phonemes (i.e., speech sounds) and graphemes (i.e., written symbols). There are 26 letters in the alphabet; however, about 44 phonemes are used in English speech. Moreover, there are more than 500 spellings to represent the 44 phonemes (Polloway, Patton, & Serna, 2008). Carreker (2005) notes that 24 speech sounds have only one spelling (e.g., /a/—*apple,* /b/—*bat,* and /p/—*pig*) or have one spelling that is far more frequent than any other spelling (e.g., /e/ is spelled *e*—*echo*—much more often than *ea*—*head,* and /f/ is spelled *f*—*feel*—much more often than *gh*—*cough*—or *ph*—*photo*), whereas spelling options for the 20 other phonemes depend not only on frequency but also on the position of the sound in a word, the length of the word, the accent or stress on the syllable, or the influence of surrounding sounds (e.g., /z/—*zoo, present* and /t/—*teacher, jumped*). Thus, differences exist between the spelling of various words and the way the words are pronounced. Many students with learning problems have difficulty mastering the regular spelling system, and inconsistent spelling patterns make learning to spell even more complex.

Students who have trouble recognizing words in reading usually have poor spelling skills as well (Carreker, 2005; Shanker & Cockrum, 2009). However, some students are able to read words but not spell them. Poor readers who are poor spellers have a deficit in phonological processing that interferes with their mastery of spelling, whereas good readers who are poor spellers have problems with the exact recall of letter sequences and subtle difficulties with complex spelling patterns and aspects of language structure (Moats, 1995). Thus, it appears that spelling a word may be more difficult than reading a word. Reading is a *decoding* process in which the reader receives clues (such as context) for word recognition. Spelling is an *encoding* process in which the learner must respond without the benefit of a complete visual stimulus; thus, there are fewer clues. Spelling requires concentration on each letter of every word, while in reading it is not necessary to know the exact spelling of words or to attend to every letter. Some students make the same types of errors in both reading and spelling. For example, a phonetic speller may mispronounce phonetically irregular words when reading. In addition, a student who lacks phonetic word-attack skills in reading may not be able to spell because of poor phonetic skills. In general, normal students spell with an accuracy from 70 to 100 percent at grade level and normal readers tend to make spelling errors that are readable, good phonetic equivalents of the dictated word.

To spell a word correctly, the student must apply various abilities including being able to read the word, apply knowledge of certain relationships of phonics and structural analysis, apply phonics generalizations, visualize the appearance of the word, retrieve the word from memory, and use the motor capability to write the word. Spelling errors may result from confused recall of spelling rules (e.g., *takeing* for *taking*) or be related to insertion of unneeded letters (e.g., *umberella* for *umbrella*), omission of needed letters (e.g., *famly* for *family*), substitution of letters (e.g., *kome* for *come*), phonetic spelling of irregular words (e.g., *laf* for *laugh*), directional confusion (e.g., *was* for *saw*), vowels in unaccented syllables (e.g., *cottin* for *cotton*), r-controlled vowels (e.g., *dert* for *dirt*), letter orientation confusion (e.g., *doy* for *boy*), and reversed letter sequences (e.g., *aminals* for

animals) (Poteet, 1980). Thus, spelling difficulties may stem from problems in visual memory, auditory memory, auditory and visual discrimination, attention deficits, or motor skills.

ASSESSMENT OF SPELLING SKILLS

A variety of techniques assess the student's spelling performance. Also, specific patterns of spelling errors may be determined. Spelling assessment can include the use of standardized and criterion-referenced tests as well as informal assessment techniques. In choosing spelling assessment techniques, the teacher should know what the test measures and its limitations, supplement the test where possible with other measures, and use informal evaluation techniques to gain specific information for planning a remedial program.

Formal Spelling Assessment

Standardized spelling tests (i.e., achievement and diagnostic tests) are norm referenced, whereas other published measures of spelling are criterion referenced. This section presents achievement tests, diagnostic tests, and criterion-referenced tests that can be used to assess spelling skills.

Achievement and Diagnostic Tests Achievement tests that contain spelling subtests provide an estimate of the student's general spelling ability. Achievement tests assess spelling by two procedures: recall and recognition. On tests using recall, the student must write words presented orally and used in sentences. On tests using recognition, the student selects the correctly spelled word from several choices. Recall items are related to the writing stage of the writing process, whereas recognition items are essentially proofreading and are related to the editing stage (McLoughlin & Lewis, 2008). Achievement tests yield a single score that is compared with the standardized norms and converted to a grade-equivalent score. Thus, achievement tests provide a general survey measure and can identify students who need corrective instruction and further diagnosis. These tests also are appropriate for documenting student outcomes. Some commonly used achievement tests that include spelling subtests include the following:

- *Iowa Tests of Basic Skills* (Hoover, Dunbar, & Frisbie, 2006)—assesses ability to choose the correctly spelled word from four words or to indicate "no mistakes"

TABLE 9.1

Diagnostic and criterion-referenced spelling tests

Test	Grade Levels
Diagnostic Tests	
Test of Orthographic Competence (Mather, Roberts, Hammill, & Allen, 2008)	1–12
This comprehensive norm-referenced measure of orthographic skills includes nine subtests, which vary by age level. Five subtests are related to spelling skills: Homophone Choice, Letter Choice, Word Scramble, Sight Spelling, and Word Choice. Additional subtests are Signs and Symbols, Grapheme Matching, Punctuation, and Abbreviations. The test, which yields standard scores and percentiles, has three age-related forms (i.e., 6–7 years, 8–12 years, and 13–17 years) and can be administered to individuals or groups in 30 to 45 minutes.	
Test of Written Spelling—4 (Larsen, Hammill, & Moats, 1999)	1–12
This dictated word test consists of 100 words chosen from ten basal spelling series. The test assesses the student's ability to spell words that have readily predictable spellings in sound–letter patterns as well as words whose spellings are less predictable (i.e., spelling demons). The test can be administered to individuals or small groups in about 20 minutes and yields standard scores, percentiles, spelling ages, and grade equivalents. Two equivalent forms are available.	
Word Identification and Spelling Test (Wilson & Felton, 2005)	2–12
The Spelling subtest assesses the student's ability to spell words correctly from dictation. It specifically measures (a) the student's recall of correct letter sequences for familiar words or the ability to apply sound–symbol relationships and spelling rules in order to spell unfamiliar words, and (b) the student's recall of letter order in high-frequency words with one or more irregularities. The Sound-Symbol Knowledge subtest assesses the student's ability to associate sounds (i.e., phonemes) with specific letters. The test also includes a Word Identification subtest. This individually administered diagnostic test includes both norm-referenced and informal assessments.	
Criterion-Referenced Test	
Brigance Comprehensive Inventory of Basic Skills—II (Brigance, 2010a)	K–9
The test contains a section that assesses spelling skills arranged in a developmental and sequential hierarchy. Tests include spelling-dictation grade placement, initial consonants, initial clusters, suffixes, and prefixes. The instructional objectives related to each test are defined clearly. In addition to determining the student's level of achievement, the results can help the teacher develop individualized programs.	

- *Kaufman Test of Educational Achievement—II* (Kaufman & Kaufman, 2004)—assesses ability to spell 50 increasingly difficult words, each of which is said by the examiner and used in a sentence
- *Peabody Individual Achievement Test—Revised* (Markwardt, 1998)—assesses ability to identify the correct spelling of a word after hearing the word pronounced
- *Wide Range Achievement Test—4* (Wilkinson & Robertson, 2006)—assesses skill in writing one's name and writing letters and single words from dictation

Diagnostic tests provide detailed information about the student's performance in various spelling skills. These tests are aimed at determining the student's strengths and weaknesses. Three diagnostic spelling tests are presented in Table 9.1.

Criterion-Referenced Tests Whereas standardized norm-referenced tests (i.e., achievement and diagnostic tests) *compare* a student's performance with the scores of those in the norm population, criterion-referenced tests *describe* performance in terms of fixed criteria. Thus, criterion-referenced tests mainly aid in specific instructional planning, rather than determining grade-level scores or percentile ranks. The teacher can use criterion-referenced spelling tests to determine whether a student has mastered specific spelling instructional objectives (e.g., *wh* spelling, contractions, or vocational words). The teacher determines what skills the student has learned and what skills still must be taught. Also, an objective measure of progress is provided as the student moves from task to task and current performance is compared with previous performance. A criterion-referenced spelling test is presented in Table 9.1.

Informal Spelling Assessment

The teacher can obtain diagnostic information through structured observation and evaluation of the student's attitudes, written work, and oral responses. Attitudes toward spelling and willingness to use a dictionary may be noted, as well as the student's work habits and ability to handle frustration. Analysis of written work can provide information about handwriting problems that are causing errors (such as letter forms or spacing), specific types of errors, range of the student's vocabulary, and knowledge of spelling rules. In addition, the teacher should observe the student's oral responses and note problems in pronunciation, articulation, and dialect. Oral spelling responses also can indicate phonics ability and method of spelling words orally (e.g., as units, by letter, by digraphs, or by syllables).

The spelling scope and sequence skills list presented in the Appendix can be used to devise informal assessment measures and to determine appropriate instructional objectives as the student progresses in spelling.

The following informal assessment techniques are discussed: dictated spelling test, informal spelling inventory, curriculum-based measurement, spelling error analysis, cloze procedure, and probes.

Dictated Spelling Test   The dictated spelling test is a commonly used procedure for assessing various skills in spelling and determining spelling grade level. Words can be selected from any graded word list; the student's performance indicates the spelling grade level. On dictated word lists of increasing difficulty, the instructional level is determined when the student achieves 70 to 90 percent accuracy. Dictated word lists also can assess skills in areas such as phoneme-grapheme association (e.g., *like, bike, hike*), spelling generalizations (e.g., *stories, cries, tries*), homonyms (e.g., *pain, pane; pear, pair*), and functional words (e.g., *menu, restaurant, cashier*). The dictated test presented in Table 9.2 assesses selected spelling objectives for students in second and third grades. Through error analysis the teacher readily can determine areas of weakness.

The student's proficiency in spelling frequently used words and words that often are misspelled also can be determined. Shanker and Cockrum (2009) note that the 100 top high-frequency words account for 60 percent of the words used in early writing. They also report that the following eight words represent 18 percent of all the words used in writing: *the, of, and, a, to, is, in,* and *you*. Moreover, Kuska, Webster, and Elford (1964) present a list of commonly misspelled words that are linguistically irregular and do not follow spelling rules (e.g., *ache, fasten, nickel, scratch,* and *double*).

Informal Spelling Inventory   An informal spelling inventory (ISI) can be used to determine the student's approximate grade level in spelling achievement. An ISI can be constructed by selecting a sample of words from spelling books in a basal spelling series (Mann, Suiter, & McClung, 1992). About 15 words should be chosen from the first-grade book and 20 words from each book for second through eighth grade. Random selection is obtained by dividing the total number of words at each level by 20. For example, 300 words at each level divided by 20 equals 15; therefore, every fifteenth word should be included in the ISI. For students in fourth grade and below, testing should begin with the first-level words. For students in fifth grade and above, assessment should start with words at the third level. The test is administered in a dictated-word format. The teacher says the word, uses it in a sentence, and repeats the word. Some students prefer for only the word to be given (i.e., without a sentence), and a 7-second interval between words usually is sufficient. Testing ends when the student responds incorrectly to six consecutive words. The achievement level is the highest level at which the student responds correctly to 90 to 100 percent of the items, and the instructional level is the highest level at which the student scores 75 to 89 percent correct. Various errors made on the ISI can be analyzed to provide additional diagnostic information.

Curriculum-Based Measurement   In curriculum-based measurement of spelling skills, rate samples on words from a given spelling curriculum are used to measure the student's spelling skills. The assessment process begins with the selection of appropriate word lists. Tindal and Marston (1990) note that the word lists can reflect a phonic-regularity base (i.e., words with consistency or generalizability of the grapheme-phoneme relationships) or a frequency base (i.e., words that appear frequently in writing). Also, the words can be from a given spelling curriculum level or from a new-words list for a particular reading series. The words can be selected randomly by printing all words in the test item pool on index cards, shuffling the cards before each measurement, and randomly picking ones to present during the measurement task.

The type of response to the spelling task can be either a selection response or a production response (Tindal & Marston, 1990). In word or sentence editing, an incorrectly spelled word is underlined or a blank space representing a specific word is presented in a phrase, and the student must select the correct word from several options to replace the underlined word or to fill in the blank. For example:

1. Her dress had a <u>stane</u> on it.

   a. staen   b. stain   c. stan   d. stene

2. The wind _____ his hat away.

   a. bled   b. blew   c. bliew   d. blued

TABLE 9.2

A dictated spelling test and objectives

Spelling Words	Spelling Objectives	Spelling Words Used in Sentences
1. man	short vowels and selected consonants	*The man* is big.
2. pit		The *pit* in the fruit was hard.
3. dug		We *dug* a hole.
4. web		She saw the spider's *web*.
5. dot		Don't forget to *dot* the i.
6. mask	words beginning or ending with consonant blends	On Halloween the child wore a *mask*.
7. drum		He beat the *drum* in the parade.
8. line	consonant-vowel-consonant-silent *e*	Get in *line* for lunch.
9. cake		We had a birthday *cake*.
10. coat	two vowels together	Put on your winter *coat*.
11. rain		Take an umbrella in the *rain*.
12. ice	variant consonant sounds for *c* and *g*	*Ice* is frozen water.
13. large		This is a *large* room.
14. mouth	words containing vowel diphthongs	Open your *mouth* to brush your teeth.
15. town		We went to *town* to shop.
16. boy		The *boy* and girl went to school.
17. bikes	plurals	The children got new *bikes* for their birthdays.
18. glasses		Get some *glasses* for the drinks.
19. happy	short *i* sounds of *y*	John is very *happy* now.
20. monkey		We saw a *monkey* at the zoo.
21. war	words with r-controlled vowels	Bombs were used in the *war*.
22. dirt		The pigs were in the *dirt*.
23. foot	two sounds of *oo*	Put the shoe on your *foot*.
24. moon		Three men walked on the *moon*.
25. light	words with silent letters	Turn on the *light* so we can see.
26. knife		Get a fork and *knife*.
27. pill	final consonant doubled	The doctor gave me a *pill*.
28. bat	consonant-vowel-consonant pattern in which final consonant is doubled before adding ending	The baseball player got a new *bat*.
29. batter		The *batter* hit a home run.
30. didn't	contractions	They *didn't* want to come.
31. isn't		It *isn't* raining today.
32. take	final *e* dropped before adding suffix	Please *take* off your coat.
33. taking		He is *taking* me to the show.
34. any	nonphonetic spellings	I did not have *any* lunch.
35. could		Maybe you *could* go on a trip.
36. ate	homonyms	Mary *ate* breakfast at home.
37. eight		There are *eight* children in the family.
38. blue		The sky is *blue*.
39. blew		The wind *blew* away the hat.
40. baseball	compound words	They played *baseball* outside.

When the teacher orally presents words from a list, the student must produce the spelling of the word during the dictation task. The teacher dictates words for 2 minutes by saying each word twice and using homonyms in a sentence. There should be a 7-second interval between words for students in fourth through eighth grade and 10-second intervals for younger students and those with fine motor difficulties. When a production response is required, scoring can be in terms of number of words spelled correctly or number of letters in correct sequence. The latter strategy focuses on successive pairs of letters, and the blank spaces preceding the first letter and following the last letter are included in counting the pairs of letter sequences. Thus, for a word spelled correctly, the number of correct letter sequences will be one more than there are letters in the word. For example:

1. Correct spelling: l a z y (five correct letter sequences)
2. Misspelling: l a s y (three correct and two incorrect letter sequences)

Deno, Mirkin, and Wesson (1984) suggest that the instructional level is 20 to 39 correct letter sequences for students in first and second grades and 40 to 59 correct letter sequences for students in third through sixth grade. They note that the long-range goal should be 60 to 80 correct letter sequences for students in first and second grades and 80 to 140 correct letter sequences for students in third through sixth grade. An individualized error analysis can help establish appropriate instruction.

The teacher can test all students in a grade or class and develop a box plot of the entire group. Table 9.3 presents curriculum-based measurement procedures for administering and scoring spelling word lists. Poor spellers (i.e., more than one standard deviation below the mean for the group) can be identified, and instructional planning decisions can be made. A graph of a student's weekly performance in spelling can be used to evaluate instruction (see Figure 9.1).

Spelling Error Analysis A spelling error analysis chart can be used to provide a profile of spelling strengths and weaknesses. Each time the student makes a specific error, it is recorded on the chart. Spelling errors can be analyzed in written compositions as well as on dictated tests. Selected spelling errors include spelling the word as it sounds (e.g., *doter* for *daughter*), omitting a letter that is pronounced (e.g., *aross* for *across*), using the wrong vowel digraph (e.g., *speach* for *speech*), reversing letters in words (e.g., *croner* for *corner*), using an incorrect vowel (e.g., *jab* for *job; anemals* for *animals*), using the wrong homonym for the meaning intended (e.g., *peace* for *piece*), inserting an unneeded letter (e.g., *ulgly* for *ugly*), doubling a consonant when not needed (e.g., *untill* for *until*), omitting a silent letter (e.g., *bome* for *bomb*), and ignoring spelling rules (e.g., *babys* for *babies; stoping* for *stopping; comeing* for *coming*). Thus, the following specific types of errors can be noted on a spelling error analysis chart: addition of extra letters; omission of needed letters; reversals of whole words, consonant order, or syllables; errors resulting from a student's mispronunciation or dialect; and phonetic spelling of nonphonetic words. Misspellings also can be categorized as phonetic and nonphonetic. Phonetic misspellings occur when the

TABLE 9.3

Curriculum-based measurement procedures for administering and scoring spelling word lists

Step 1:	Randomly select 20 words from the goal-level spelling curriculum material.
Step 2:	Present each student with lined, numbered paper.
Step 3:	Provide directions and administer the spelling test by pronouncing each word on the list in isolation, in a sentence or phrase, and again in isolation. Dictate words at a pace of one every 7 to 10 seconds, or sooner if all students finish. Do not acknowledge questions and ignore requests (such as "slow down"). Terminate testing after 2 minutes.
Step 4:	Score performance in terms of words and letter sequences correct.
Step 5:	Develop box plots of the entire group according to words spelled correctly and letters spelled correctly (see Chapter 3).
Step 6:	Analyze the individual protocols scored according to correct letter sequences. Place students in appropriate instructional groups.
Step 7:	Begin instruction based on student error patterns.
Step 8:	Introduce new words each week in accordance with the curriculum sequence. Vary the number of new words presented depending on the mastery of previous words. Graph the results of continuous assessment to evaluate instruction (see Figure 9.1). Because grouping is based on the rate of words learned, move students among groups as a function of their progress.

FIGURE 9.1
Graph of a student's weekly performance in spelling

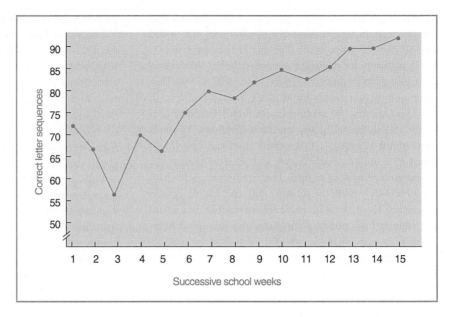

student attempts to use phonics rules to spell a word but applies the rule incorrectly or the word does not adhere to those rules, whereas nonphonetic spellings do not appear to be based on the application of phonics rules (McLoughlin & Lewis, 2008). Kelman and Apel (2004) recommend analyzing spelling errors according to linguistic factors: phonological, orthographic, or morphological. Phonological errors occur when a student does not represent the phonemes in a word with an appropriate grapheme (e.g., *stap* for *stamp*). An orthographic error may be phonologically accurate, but does not follow conventional orthographic patterns (e.g., *paynt* for *paint*). Morphological errors contain misspelled affixes or inaccurate alterations of the root word when affixes are added (e.g., *skipt* for *skipped; organizashun* for *organization*). Through a careful analysis of spelling errors, the teacher can focus on consistent patterns of errors and plan appropriate instruction.

Cloze Procedure The cloze procedure is a visual means of testing spelling. The student may be required to complete a sentence by writing the correct response in the blank; for example, "The opposite of down is _____" (*up*). In addition, the student may be asked to complete a word or supply missing letters: "The clouds are in the s_____ " (*sky*), or "Please give me a glass of w_t_r" (*water*). The cloze procedure can be especially useful in evaluating the student's knowledge of spelling generalizations. In this case, the student is required to fill in blanks pertaining to a rule, such as doubling the final consonant before adding -*ing*; for example, "The man was run_____ to catch the bus" (-*ning*). A multiple-choice format also may be

used; for example, "Mary needed _____ to pay for her lunch" (*munny, mony, money, monie*). The cloze procedure, which is visual, can be used effectively along with the auditory dictated spelling test.

Probes Spelling skills can be assessed through the use of probe sheets. The student works on the probe sheet for 1 minute, and the teacher records the rate of correct and incorrect responses and notes any error patterns. The probe task (e.g., see picture—write word, see words—write contractions, hear word—write word, or see partial word—write missing letter) may be administered several times to give the teacher a reliable index of how well the student can perform. Starlin and Starlin (1973b) suggest a proficiency rate for students in kindergarten through second grade of 30 to 50 correct letters per minute with two or fewer errors at the independent level, and 15 to 29 correct letters with three to seven errors at the instructional level. For third grade through adult, the independent level is 50 to 70 correct letters per minute with two or fewer errors, and the instructional level is 25 to 49 correct letters with three to seven errors. In addition, the teacher can collect data from students who are achieving satisfactorily and use their rates for comparison when assessing a student with spelling difficulties. A sample probe sheet for spelling contractions is presented in Figure 9.2.

TEACHING SPELLING SKILLS

Nine spelling competencies enable the student to be an effective speller. These nine skills and corresponding subareas are presented in Table 9.4. Carreker (2005) indicates that the teacher must assume an active role in spelling instruction, and students must be explicitly taught about language structure for spelling (e.g., sounds of the language, the most frequent and reliable letter patterns, and rules relating to how spoken words are represented in written language). Moreover, in a research summary of best practices in spelling instruction, Simonsen and Gunter (2001) note that highly effective spelling programs teach spelling through phonemic, whole-word, and morphemic approaches that include direct instruction research-validated components, such as sequenced lessons, cumulative review and distributed practice (i.e., spaced, frequent periods of study), and systematic error correction. In addition, Hauerwas and Walker (2003) found that some students with spelling deficits have more difficulty spelling words in dictated sentences than they do when spelling words in list form. They suggest that instructional programs for students with spelling deficits in inflectional morphology should not only include direct instruction that links oral morphology and written morphology, but also should provide opportunities for students to generalize what they have learned to sentence and paragraph contexts.

To select spelling words to be studied, Graham (1999) discusses four approaches: allowing students to choose the words from their writing, reading, or content subjects; teaching words that students commonly misspell when writing; teaching words that students are most likely to use in their writing; and identifying words that fit different but related patterns (e.g., *ee* and *ea* for the long *e* sound) that can be compared and contrasted as students learn the words. Shanker and Cockrum (2009) note that the words most frequently misspelled by nearly all students are exceptions to phonics rules. They suggest that it may be most helpful to teach students to spell correctly those words that appear most frequently in writing. Moreover, spelling should be emphasized in all subject matter and viewed as a skill that will enable students to be more effective writers.

In a research review of spelling instruction for students with learning problems, McNaughton, Hughes,

FIGURE 9.2

Probe sheet for spelling contractions

Task: See words–Write contractions	
do not	_____
I will	_____
can not	_____
have not	_____
we are	_____
I am	_____
could not	_____
is not	_____
it is	_____
you are	_____
she is	_____
are not	_____
would not	_____
I have	_____
did not	_____
they would	_____
has not	_____
was not	_____
they are	_____
he will	_____
Name: _____	
Time: 1 minute	
Number of correct letters written: _____	
Number of incorrect letters written: _____	

TABLE 9.4

Spelling competencies

Competency	Subareas
Auditory discrimination	Ability to discriminate consonant sounds and vowel sounds and use correct word pronunciation
Consonants	Knowledge of consonants in initial, final, and medial positions in words and knowledge of consonant blends
Phonograms	Ability to identify phonograms in initial, medial, and final positions in words and ability to identify word phonograms
Plurals	Ability to form a plural by adding *s*, adding *es*, changing *f* to *v*, making medial changes, and knowledge of exceptions
Syllabication	Ability to divide words into syllables
Structural elements	Knowledge of root words, prefixes, and suffixes
Ending changes	Ability to change ending of words that end in final *e*, final *y*, and final consonants
Vowel digraphs and diphthongs	Ability to spell words in which a vowel digraph forms one sound (e.g., *ai, ea, ay, ei, ie*) or a diphthong forms a blend (e.g., *oe, ou, ow*)
Silent *e*	Knowledge of single-syllable words that end in silent *e*

and Clark (1994) suggest that the following strategies may enhance learning of spelling skills: limiting the number of new vocabulary words introduced each day, providing opportunities for self-directed and peer-assisted instruction, directing students to name letters aloud as they are practiced, including instruction in morphemic analysis, providing immediate error imitation and correction, using motivating reinforcers, and providing periodic retesting and review. Likewise, Graham (1999) discusses various validated methods for teaching spelling words, including the test-study-test technique; the corrected-test method (i.e., students correct their errors immediately after taking a spelling test); systematic study strategies (e.g., simultaneous oral spelling); distributed practice (e.g., add-a-word program); decreasing the number of words to be mastered; cooperative practice (e.g., peer tutoring); self-monitoring of on-task behavior or productivity; and goal setting, reinforcement, and public posting of performance. Moreover, in a review and meta-analysis of spelling intervention studies, Wanzek et al. (2006) found that explicit instruction combined with multiple practice opportunities and error correction resulted in improved spelling outcomes for students. The following teaching methods and strategies provide alternatives for teaching spelling skills to students with spelling difficulties.

Rule-Based Instruction

Spelling instruction can be based on teaching rules and generalizations. After learning a general spelling rule, the student is able to use it with unfamiliar words. These rules can apply to instruction using both linguistics and phonics. Darch, Kim, and Johnson (2000) examined the effects of a rule-based approach compared to traditional spelling instruction and found that students receiving rule-based instruction outperformed students who received traditional spelling instruction.

The linguistic approach to teaching spelling is based on the idea that there is regularity in phoneme-grapheme correspondence. This method stresses the systematic nature of spelling patterns. Spelling rules, generalizations, and patterns that apply to whole words are taught. Spelling words are selected according to their particular linguistic pattern (e.g., *cool, fool, pool; hitting, running, batting*).

The phonics approach to teaching spelling stresses phoneme-grapheme relationships within parts of words. The student learns to associate a sound with a particular letter or combination of letters. Thus, phonetic rules can help the student determine how sounds should be spelled. Through phonics instruction, the student can learn to spell words according to syllables.

The student breaks the word into recognizable sound elements, pronounces each syllable, and then writes the letter or letters that represent each sound.

In rule-based instruction in both linguistics and phonics, only spelling rules and generalizations that apply to a large number of words and have few exceptions should be taught. The general rule should be applicable more than 75 percent of the time. Carreker (2005) notes that rules should be taught that aid the student in the memory of words by drawing attention to visual features (e.g., doubling, dropping, or changing a letter in a base word). Spelling rules can be taught by guiding the student to discover rules and generalizations independently. After analyzing several words that share a common linguistic property, the student is asked to apply the rule to unfamiliar words. After the student can generalize, exceptions to the rules can be discussed. The student should be taught that rules are not steadfast and that some words do not conform to spelling rules.

Although phonetic approaches to teaching spelling are used frequently, research indicates that only about 50 percent of spellings follow regular phonetic rules (Moats, 2000). Dixon (1991) suggests that incorporating morphological analysis into spelling instruction potentially may reduce misspellings due to phonetic irregularities and, thus, facilitate students' problem-solving behavior through focusing on both phonetic and morphemic generalization. For example, morphemic knowledge would indicate to the student that /jumpt/ contains two morphemes (i.e., the base word /jump/ and the suffix /t/, which makes the word past tense). Thus, the student would know that /t/ is spelled *ed* (rather than *t*) and would write *jumped* (rather than *jumpt*).

Multilinguistic Approach

Spelling instruction can utilize a multilinguistic approach that focuses on phonemic, orthographic, and morphological knowledge (Berninger et al., 2008; Kelman & Apel, 2004). This strategy is based on the theory that spelling skills develop across these three linguistic areas. The multilinguistic approach utilizes prescriptive assessment and matches the instruction to the specific weaknesses of the student. For example, if the misspellings of a student are primarily phonological, which is often the case for students with learning disabilities (Berninger et al., 2008), the spelling intervention would focus heavily on phonological aspects of language (i.e., phonemic awareness combined with the alphabetic principle). Likewise, for students whose errors are orthographic, orthographic rules and patterns would be addressed. In recent studies that evaluated the effectiveness of multilinguistic approaches (Apel &

Masterson, 2001; Berninger et al., 2008; Kelman & Apel, 2004), students improved their spelling abilities with relatively short interventions. Unlike traditional spelling instruction and memorizing the spellings of particular words on a spelling list, multilinguistic instruction is likely to generalize to new words.

Multisensory Approach

Spelling involves skills in the visual, auditory, and motor sensory modalities. The student must be able to exhibit visual and auditory recognition and discrimination of the letters of the alphabet and must have motor control to write the word. Thus, a child who has learned to spell a word by the use of the senses of hearing, sight, and touch may be in a good position to recall the spelling of that word when needed in writing because any or all the sensory modes can elicit memory of it.

Fernald's (1988) multisensory approach involves four sensory modalities: visual, auditory, kinesthetic, and tactile (VAKT). In this approach, Fernald focuses on the following areas as being important in learning to spell: clear perception of word form, development of a distinct visual image of the word, and habit formation through repetition of writing until the motor pattern is automatic. The following steps are included in learning to spell a new word.

1. The teacher writes and says a word while the student watches and listens.
2. The student traces the word with a finger while simultaneously saying the word. Then the student copies or writes the word while saying it. Careful pronunciation is emphasized, with each syllable of the word dragged out slowly as it is traced or written.
3. Next, the word is written from memory. If it is incorrect, the second step is repeated. If the word is correct, it is put in a file box. Later the words in the file box are used in stories.
4. At later stages the tracing method for learning is not always needed. The student may learn the word by observing the teacher write and say it and then by writing and saying it alone. As progress is made, the student may learn the word by looking at it in print and writing it and, finally, merely by looking at it.

The Gillingham method (Gillingham & Stillman, 1997) uses an alphabetic system with repetition and drill. Letter–sound correspondences are taught using a multisensory approach—visual, auditory, and kinesthetic. Words introduced initially include only those with consistent sound–symbol correspondences. The student is given experience reading and spelling one-syllable words as well as detached, regularly spelled syllables. Words of more than one syllable are learned syllable by syllable (e.g., *Sep tem ber*). Words whose spellings are not entirely consistent are sequenced carefully according to structural characteristics, and words following a pattern are grouped. The technique used in studying spelling words is called *simultaneous oral spelling*. When the teacher says a spelling word, the student repeats the word, names the letters, writes the letters while saying them aloud, and reads the written word. Letter names rather than sounds are used in this practice so that the technique can be applied to nonphonetic words. Sentence and story writing are introduced after the student is able to write any three-letter, phonetically pure word. Nonphonetic words are taught through drill. Thus, the Gillingham method differs from the Fernald (1988) approach in two major respects: words to be taught are selected carefully and sequenced or selected as needed for writing, rather than being of the student's own choosing, and instruction focuses on individual letters and sounds rather than on whole words. *How to Teach Spelling* (available from Educators Publishing Service) is a comprehensive resource manual based on the Gillingham approach to reading and spelling.

Kearney and Drabman (1993) used a modified write-say spelling intervention designed to provide immediate feedback to the visual and auditory modalities of students with learning problems. The students' spelling accuracy significantly increased through the use of the following procedure.

Day 1: Students receive the spelling word list and are asked to study on their own.

Day 2: Following taking a test on the spelling word list and receiving verbal teacher feedback on performance, students simultaneously say aloud and write the correct spelling (i.e., letter by letter) of any incorrectly spelled word five times.

Day 3: The procedure is repeated, except students simultaneously correctly rewrite and restate incorrectly spelled words ten consecutive times.

Day 4: The procedure is repeated, except students simultaneously correctly rewrite and restate incorrectly spelled words 15 consecutive times.

Day 5: To assess spelling accuracy, students write words from the list verbally presented by the teacher.

Another multisensory approach that features repetition is the cover-and-write method. The student is taught to spell words through the following steps.

1. The student looks at the word and says it.
2. The student writes the word twice while looking at it.

3. The student covers the word and writes it again.
4. The student checks the spelling by looking at it.

The steps are repeated, with the student writing the word as many as three times while looking at it, covering the word, writing it, and checking the spelling.

Test-Study-Test Technique

The test-study-test approach to teaching spelling is used frequently. The student is given a pretest at the beginning of each unit of study. The words the student misspells on the pretest become the study list. After instruction, another test determines the degree of mastery. A progress chart is kept, and words misspelled on the second test are added to the list of words for the following unit of study.

The study-test plan is similar to the test-study-test approach, except that it does not include a pretest. The student's study list consists of all of the words in the unit of study. The student is tested after completing various spelling activities. The test-study-test method may yield better spelling results than the study-test approach because the pretest identifies words that the student already knows how to spell and the elimination of these words allows the student to focus on the unknown words.

In addition, some studies indicate that added reinforcement procedures can encourage students to study harder to obtain higher test scores. For example, Lovitt, Guppy, and Blattner (1969) noted a substantial increase in the number of perfect spelling papers when students were given the test four days a week (Tuesday through Friday) and, after receiving 100 percent on that week's word list, were excused from spelling for the rest of the week and given free time. Also, Sidman (1979) used group and individual reinforcement contingencies with middle school students. Accuracy increased when free time was provided as a reward for improved test scores. The increase was greater during group contingency conditions.

Graham and Voth (1990) recommend daily testing on new and previously introduced words from a spelling unit, as well as periodic maintenance checks to ensure mastery or to identify words that need to be reincorporated into the instructional sequence. In addition, they suggest that the tests should be corrected, with supervision, by the students themselves. Thus, the students receive immediate feedback about their efforts to learn to spell. Because some students spell the words correctly on the test but misspell them in their writing, the teacher periodically should collect samples of student writing to determine whether the students are applying in their writing what they have learned through spelling instruction. To improve accuracy and fluency, practice on misspelled words

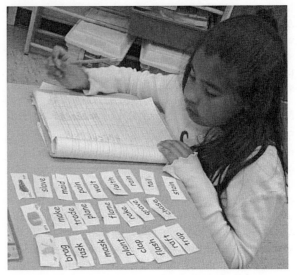

Effective spelling programs teach spelling through phonemic, whole word, and morphemic approaches.
Hope Madden/Merrill

should include a variety of high-interest activities and games. In addition, peer tutoring or cooperative learning arrangements can improve spelling performance.

Study Strategies Study techniques provide a structured format for the independent study of spelling words and help students with learning problems to organize their spelling study. Graham and Freeman (1986) found that students with learning problems who were trained to use an efficient study strategy were able to recall immediately the correct spelling of more words than were students who were allowed to choose their own methods for studying unknown spelling words. The study strategy included the following steps.

1. Say the word.
2. Write and say the word.
3. Check the word by comparing it with a model.
4. Trace and say the word.
5. Write the word from memory and check.
6. Repeat the first five steps.

The cover, copy, compare strategy also is effective in improving the spelling performance of students with learning problems (Nies & Belfiore, 2006). In this spelling study strategy, the student performs the following steps.

1. Say the word.
2. Point to the word.
3. Repeat the word.
4. Cover the word.
5. Print the word.
6. Compare the word to the correct model.
7. Correct errors if necessary.

In a study of the effectiveness of two spelling study strategies, Nies and Belfioe report that when students used the cover, copy, compare strategy, they spelled a higher percentage of words accurately than when they used a more conventional copy-only study method that did not include a self-evaluation/self-correction component.

Self-correction can have positive effects on student spelling performance. Wirtz, Gardner, Weber, and Bullara (1996) used a self-correction strategy in which students heard each spelling word presented on audiotape, wrote each spelling word, compared each word with a model on an answer key, corrected any misspellings by using proofreading marks, wrote the word correctly, and repeated the task. The effects of using this self-correction method were compared with the traditional method of having students write spelling words three times, arrange the words in alphabetical order, and use the words in a sentence or in stories. In addition to improved performances on weekly spelling tests, the self-correction strategy was more effective than the traditional method in helping students maintain their ability to correctly spell previously learned words.

In addition, visual mnemonics can help students with learning problems remember spelling words. Greene (1994) suggests that visual mnemonic stimuli can be incorporated into the student's spelling list or put on flash cards with the mnemonic word on one side and the nonmnemonic form of the word on the other side. For example, the word *look* is presented with two eyes drawn (L 👁👁 K) and *great* has the *e* circled and slashed to indicate it is silent (g r ⊘ a t). With eyes closed, the student visualizes the word, attempts to see the mnemonic aid presented in the word, and then writes the word from memory. Moreover, the student can generate associations to facilitate recall of correct spellings (e.g., princi*pal* is your *pal,* dessert is something sweet).

When structural word analysis, syllable rules, and spelling patterns are taught, Wong (1986) suggests that the student use the following self-questioning strategy.

1. Do I know this word?
2. How many syllables do I hear in this word? (Write down the number of syllables.)
3. I will write the word the way I think it is spelled.
4. Do I have the right number of syllables?
5. Is there any part of the word that I am not sure how to spell? (If so, underline that part and try spelling the word again.)
6. Does the word look right to me? (If not, underline the questionable part of the word and write it again. Listen to the word to find any missing syllables.)
7. When I finish spelling, I will tell myself that I have worked hard.

Finally, individual and classwide peer tutoring can be a viable instructional alternative to provide intensive one-to-one practice with spelling words. When the tutoring sessions include structured lessons, peers can provide direct, individual instruction. For example, Keller (2002) suggests incorporating a spelling mnemonic strategy called SPELLER into a classwide peer tutoring procedure. The seven-step strategy in SPELLER uses visual imagery, systematic testing, and auditory reinforcement.

S—*Spot* the word and say it.

P—*Picture* the word.

E—*Eyes* closed.

L—*Look* to see if the visual picture is correct.

L—*Look* away and write the word.

E—*Examine* the spelling of the word by checking it.

R—*Repeat* the procedure if the word is spelled incorrectly or reward if the word is spelled correctly.

During each 20-minute tutoring session, one student is the tutor and one is the tutee for 10 minutes, and then the students switch roles for another 10 minutes.

Fixed and Flow Word Lists

Spelling words frequently are presented and taught in fixed word lists. Generally, a new list of words is assigned each week. The words may be either somewhat unfamiliar or completely unknown to the students. Usually a test on each list is given on Friday. This method seldom results in spelling mastery for all students because misspelled words on the test usually are ignored or left for the students to practice independently. Another procedure using fixed word lists is to have students practice the words at their own rate until they are able to spell all of them correctly on a certain number of tests.

On a flow list of spelling words, words are dropped from each student's list when mastered (e.g., spelled correctly on two or three consecutive days), and then a new, unpracticed word is added. Thus, the list is individualized, and the student does not spend time practicing known words. McGuigan (1975) developed a teaching procedure, the Add-a-Word Program, which uses flow word lists. McGuigan found that students ages 7 to 13 and adults learned words more quickly with add-a-word lists than with fixed lists, and showed similar or superior retention of learned words.

Graham and Voth (1990) emphasize that the spelling words taught to students with learning problems initially should be limited to high-frequency words and misspelled words from their writing. They recommend that weekly spelling lists be limited to 6 to 12 words, all of which emphasize a common structural element, if possible; 2 or 3 words from the list should be introduced daily and practiced until the entire set of words is mastered. Likewise, Burns and Broman (1983) recommend presentation of only 5 to 10 words per week to poor spellers, whereas 20 words per week may be presented to adequate spellers. In a study of spelling performance of students with learning problems, Bryant, Drabin, and Gettinger (1981) found that a higher failure rate and greater variance in performance may occur when 3 or more new words are presented each day. They suggest that 7 to 8 new spelling words per week may be an appropriate number for these students. In general, these rough guidelines for the number of new words on weekly spelling lists should be adapted according to the capability and the motivation of the individual student.

MacArthur and Graham (1987) note that students with learning problems incorrectly spell 10 to 20 percent of the words they write. Thus, Graham, Harris, and Loynachan (1994) developed the Spelling for Writing list of 335 words, ordered from first- through third-grade level. The list includes words students use most often when writing, many of which are "spelling demons" and commonly misspelled words.

Additional Considerations

Different types of correctional procedures should be used with various kinds of spelling errors. Visual image should be emphasized with a student who omits silent letters or misspells phonologically irregular words, whereas incorrect spelling of homonyms indicates a need to stress word meanings. Also, words the student misspells in written compositions may be included in his or her spelling program. This can be motivating because the need to learn to spell those words is apparent.

Spelling also may be taught and reinforced throughout the language arts curriculum. One way to improve spelling is through word study in reading. In oral reading the student gives close attention to the sounds of the entire word. In addition, reading gives the student the meanings of words and thus increases interest in them. The student learns the correct usage of words in sentences and can determine whether the word is written correctly. Thus, learning to spell can accompany learning to read, and a program that stresses both skills may be both effective and motivating. The language experience approach and the whole language approach incorporate reading and spelling. When a student is forced to learn to spell words that he or she cannot read and understand, the student really is memorizing a nonmeaningful series of letters that will not be retained. Thus, spelling lists should be produced from the student's reading vocabulary. Moreover, to facilitate maintenance and generalization, the student should be encouraged to use learned spelling words frequently in writing.

Training in dictionary usage also should be included in the spelling program. Dictionaries help the student become more independent in locating spellings and provide such information as syllabication, meaning, pronunciation, synonyms, and homonyms. Picture dictionaries can be used in the primary grades. Beginning in the fourth grade, special practice in using the dictionary often is included in the curriculum, and the use of dictionaries may be encouraged during writing tasks. When the correct spelling of a word is not known, the student should predict possible spellings for the word by identifying root words and affixes, considering related words, and determining the sounds in the word. Then the student can check the predicted spelling by consulting a dictionary. *The Dictionary of Basic English* (available from AGS/Pearson) contains more than 5,000 frequently used and essential words and provides short, clearly written definitions as well as sample phrases and sentences showing proper word usage.

In teaching spelling skills at the secondary level, the teacher should help the adolescent understand the social and practical significance of correct spelling. For example, employers place value on accurate spelling on job applications. The student's own interests and various areas of study provide new words. Vocational words also can be emphasized. At the secondary level it may be best to teach spelling in conjunction with other activities rather than to use class time solely for spelling instruction. Practice in reading and other learning activities can help the adolescent learn to spell. Success in spelling increases in importance with the finding that students' beliefs about their efficacy as spellers may affect not only their spelling performance but their writing performance as well (Rankin, Bruning, Timme, & Katkanant, 1993). Finally, strategies to compensate for poor spelling should be taught to students whose spelling problems may affect their grades in content areas. For example, the teacher can provide such students with a spelling checker, which contains frequently used words and words they often misspell. The *Children's Talking Dictionary and Spell Corrector* (produced by Franklin Electronic Publishers) provides an automatic phonetic spell corrector and speaks over 40,000 easy-to-understand definitions.

SPELLING ACTIVITIES

Many activities and materials can be used to supplement a spelling program. Games and activities stimulate interest, provide practice, and add variety in teaching techniques. In addition, spelling instruction may be individualized by developing games and activities for particular individuals or small groups. The activities presented in this section and the instructional games and self-correcting materials presented in the following sections promote the development of spelling skills.

- Ask the student to complete words in sentences by filling in omitted letters. Lists of words from stories in basal readers or spelling textbooks can be used to develop reusable worksheets or dittos. For example:

The bo_ and _irl were bak__ a cak_.

- Provide a worksheet showing various words and their configurations. Ask the student to match each word with its configuration. Worksheets of specific words (e.g., reading selections or weekly spelling lists) can be made and reused for this seatwork activity.

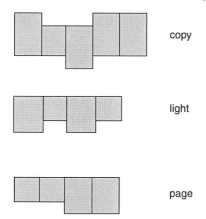

copy

light

page

- Use a hidden-word format to provide practice in letter sequence of spelling words. Provide a list of spelling words and a puzzle. Ask the student to

curve

held

ranch

young

locate the hidden spelling words and to draw a circle around them.

- Have the student keep a file box of spelling words that have caused some difficulty. The words should be arranged in alphabetical order, and the cards also may contain definitions or pictures. Encourage the student to study the cards and to practice writing the words from memory. New words can be included and others deleted as the student progresses.

- In compiling the weekly spelling word list, ask class members to volunteer words, such as those they have misspelled in writing or have encountered in independent reading. The teacher may want to include on the spelling list those words the students will use frequently in their writing. Give a pretest on the words on Monday and a second test on Friday. Keep a scoreboard graph for the entire class, scaled to 10. Have each student try to move "up 10" each week on the graph by spelling more words correctly on Friday than were spelled correctly on the pretest. Thus, the student is competing against a previous score. The advanced student who gets a perfect score and the less able student who improves by ten words both receive the "up 10" mark on the graph.

- Describe a current spelling word phonetically. For example, the word *move* may be described as "a one-syllable word beginning with a consonant and ending with a vowel." Call on a student to find the word in the spelling list; then give her or him a turn to describe a word and to call on another classmate.

- To focus on particular spelling patterns, have students sort a pack of word cards or the words on their weekly spelling list into two or more categories (e.g., according to vowel patterns, affixes, or root words). The teacher can design each weekly spelling list so that words correspond to two or three common spelling patterns and then ask students to sort the words into their respective categories and add other words that fit these patterns. Moreover, Carreker (2005) suggests that students can analyze and sort words into categories of regular words, rule words, and irregular words. Regular words can be sounded out and are spelled the way they sound; rule words can be sounded out but a letter must be doubled, dropped, or changed when written; and irregular words cannot be sounded out and must be memorized. Encourage the students to practice the words in each category by determining the best way to learn them (e.g., applying a rule when a suffix beginning with a vowel is added, or using a mnemonic association to remember the spelling of an irregular word).

- Have the student count the phonemes in a spelling word and write the word in Elkonin boxes, which also are called word boxes. To make Elkonin boxes, the student draws one box for each phoneme in the word. Then the student writes in each box the correct grapheme that represents the phoneme. The student also can cut apart the Elkonin boxes and rebuild the spelling word (see Figure 9.3)

- Have the student work with anagram activities, in which the student is given a word and must rearrange all the letters to make a new word. For example, *smile* is an anagram for *miles,* and *sister* is an anagram for *resist.* For students having particular difficulty, Scrabble letter tiles may be used,

FIGURE 9.3
Elkonin spelling boxes

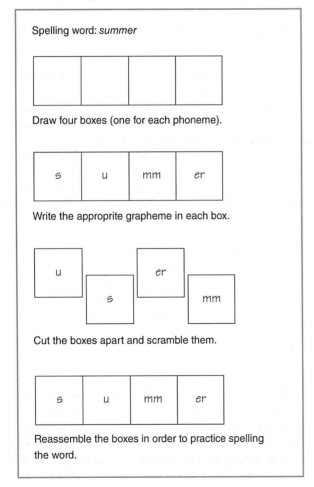

Spelling word: *summer*

Draw four boxes (one for each phoneme).

| s | u | mm | er |

Write the approprite grapheme in each box.

Cut the boxes apart and scramble them.

| s | u | mm | er |

Reassemble the boxes in order to practice spelling the word.

or the student can copy the word, cut it apart, and rearrange the letters. Also, have the student work anagram puzzles, in which one letter is changed each time until the top word is changed into the bottom word. Definitions or clues may be provided. For example:

POND   small lake

_____   young horse (*pony*)

_____   nickname for Anthony (*Tony*)

_____   dial (*tone*)

BONE   dog's treat

- Have a spelling bee in which the students stand in a line, and each time a student spells a word correctly the student "jumps" two persons toward the end of the line. When a student reaches the end, she or he sits down. Thus, students who need practice remain in line, and those who know the words have time for independent work.

- Begin an add-a-letter activity with a one- to two-letter word (e.g., *to*). Call on a student to make a different word by adding one letter (e.g., *top*). The letters may be rearranged, but one letter must be added each turn (e.g., *spot*). When no one can continue the process, start a new word. This can become a seatwork activity, in which each student works independently on a worksheet to add letters and make new words.

- Provide the student with a jar containing about 40 wooden cubes with letters on them (i.e., similar to alphabet blocks or Spill and Spell cubes). Spill the letters from the jar and see how many words the student can make in 5 minutes with the given letters. Link letters (i.e., letters that fit together to form words) also can be used for this activity.

- Provide two word cards for each spelling word and have the student play a concentration game. The cards are mixed up and placed face down in rows. The student turns over two cards at a time and tries to remember their location so that spelling matches can be made. When the student turns up two cards that match (i.e., the same spelling word), the cards are removed. Two students may play together by taking turns to see who can make the most matches.

- Encourage class members to choose words to write on word charts or large sheets of paper hanging in the classroom. The charts can list the correct spelling of words that the students are presently misspelling or difficult words that they are likely to use in current writing assignments. Have the students refer to the word charts for word-study activities and when they are writing.

- Have the student write a story or theme using the spelling list words. The theme may be on any subject and as long or as short as the student wishes to make it; however, every one of the spelling words must be included in what is written. Encourage the student to proofread the composition and to pay attention to spelling and using the words correctly.

- Encourage the student to develop memory devices to facilitate the spelling of difficult words or words that are not spelled as they sound. For example:

Station*ery* is writing pap*er*.

The princi*pal* is your *pal*.

- Present crossword puzzles that contain spelling words to give practice in writing the words and learning their meanings. Also, the student can be asked to make up a crossword puzzle that includes new and review spelling words and everyday words.

Across
1. small cat
3. not wild
6. what you hear with
7. a small clue
8. a father's boy
10. not old

Down
1. room you cook in
2. short periods of sleep
4. more than one man
5. puts in mouth and chews
9. opposite of yes

- For dictionary practice, provide a list of words (e.g., *overcoat, tongue-tied,* and *well-known*). Ask the student to locate the words in the dictionary and write *yes* or *no* to indicate whether each word is hyphenated. Also, provide sentences containing some unfamiliar words and ask the student to supply synonyms for four words in each sentence. For example:

The *clandestine* meeting was interrupted by *incorrigible bandits* who came *incognito.*

- Have a student describe a word from the spelling list by giving rhyming, meaning, or descriptive clues. The other class members are given 1 minute to guess the word. The first person to say the correct word goes to the chalkboard and writes it. If the word is spelled correctly, that student gets to describe a word.

- For motivation, allow the student to practice spelling words on a typewriter or computer keyboard. The student can say the letters when typing them, thus combining sight, sound, and touch.

- Select a student to pick a word from the dictionary and write on the chalkboard the exact pronunciation for the word as found in the dictionary. It should be written letter for letter with all diacritical marks and accents. The student can ask a class member to pronounce and spell the word the correct way.

INSTRUCTIONAL GAMES IN SPELLING

Find-a-Word

Materials: Two words containing the same number of letters written on the chalkboard.

Directions: The teacher divides the class into two teams. The first student from each team goes to the chalkboard and writes any word that can be made from the letters in the given word. Then the student gives the chalk to the next student on the team and goes to the end of the line. Each student must write a new word or correct a misspelled one. The game continues until the teacher calls time. The team with the most correctly spelled words at the end of the time limit is the winner. For example:

The given words are:	*place*	*dream*
The student may write:	pace	read
	cap	mad
	leap	dear
	pal	me

Detective

Materials: Spelling words with various letters omitted written on the chalkboard.

Directions: The teacher gives the definition of each word and calls on a student to fill in the missing letters. The student goes to the chalkboard and writes in the missing letters. One point is given for each correct word or letter.

The student with the most points at the end of the game is the winner. For example:

n__ghb__   person who lives next door

stor___s   short reading selections

ni___t   opposite of day

Jaws

Materials: Twenty-one (21) index cards with one consonant printed on each card; 21 index cards with pictures corresponding to the sound of each consonant; 1 index card with a shark named "Jaws" drawn on it.

Directions: The cards are dealt to three or more players. The players check for pairs (i.e., one consonant card and a picture card that has the same beginning consonant sound) and place them on the table. The first player turns to the left and picks a card from that player. If it matches a card already held, the player places the pair on the table. The game continues until all the cards have been matched and one student is left holding "Jaws."

Modification: The players can be asked to write the names of the pictures in the pairs. The player who spells the most pairs correctly wins the game.

Spell It—Keep It Card Game

Materials: Cards with spelling words printed on them placed on the chalkboard ledge with backs to the class.

Directions: The teacher divides the class into two teams. A student from the first team selects a card and reads the word. A student from the other team spells the word. If the word is spelled correctly, the student who spelled it gets to keep the card. If the word is spelled incorrectly, a student from the first team has a chance to spell it and get the card. Then a student from the second team selects a card, and the process is repeated until all cards are gone from the ledge. The winner is the team having the most cards at the end of the game.

Spelling Bingo

Materials: Cards divided into 24 squares (i.e., 4 squares across and 6 squares down), with a different spelling word printed in each space and words in different order on each card; numerous discs or markers.

Directions: Each student receives a card and several discs. As the teacher calls out and spells a word, each student covers the given word on the card with a disc. The first student to complete a column going across, down, or diagonally calls "Bingo" and wins the game.

Modifications: The students can make their own cards by dividing their paper into 24 squares. The spelling words are written on the chalkboard, and each student writes the words in any squares on the paper. One student is selected to stand facing away from the chalkboard, and the teacher calls out words for the student to spell. For each word the student spells correctly, the other students place a disc on the corresponding square on their card. The game continues until someone calls "Bingo." The teacher keeps a list of the words and checks the winning card. Also, for young students, the Bingo cards can consist of rows of selected consonants, short vowels, and long vowels. When the teacher calls a word, each student puts discs on the appropriate letters on the card.

Golf Game Board

Materials: Large game board on tagboard or laminated poster board; different-color golf tees for markers; cards with spelling words printed on them, with stars on the cards of the most difficult words (see Figure 9.4).

Directions: Two players each choose a golf tee and place it on the "tee off" square. The first player takes the top card and reads the word to the other player, who tries to spell the word. If the word is spelled correctly, the student moves ahead one space. If the word is spelled incorrectly, the student moves

FIGURE 9.4
Golf game board

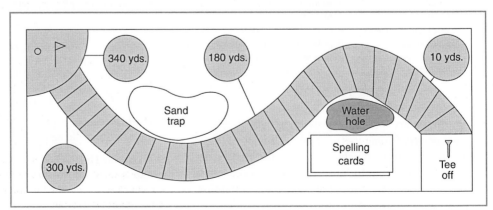

back one space. When a player correctly spells a word that has a star on the card, the student moves ahead two spaces. The first player to reach the golf hole wins the game.

Modifications:

- Game boards can be made on poster board to depict various themes, such as a racetrack, rocket path, mountain path, safari, or any other start-to-finish sequence.
- The spelling cards can consist of some words spelled correctly and some words spelled incorrectly. The player draws a card and must decide whether the word is spelled correctly. If it is misspelled, the player must spell it correctly. Each player moves one space for a correct answer. A third student can use an answer key to check responses.
- Stacks of index cards containing spelling words can be color coded or numbered according to difficulty level. Students may play with two different stacks of cards according to their ability levels. The players roll dice to determine the number of spaces they can move on the game board if they spell the word on the spelling card correctly.
- Chance dice that have one number covered with a sticker can be used. When one sticker is rolled, the player loses a turn; when two stickers are rolled (i.e., one on each die), the player goes back to the beginning square.
- For older students, the words on the spelling cards can be assigned a number of yards in multiples of 10, according to the difficulty level of the word. Each space on the board is worth 10 yards. When a word is spelled correctly, the player moves the number of yards indicated on the card. If a word is misspelled, the player does not advance.

Connect the Dots

Materials: Twenty-five (25) dots (i.e., rows of 5 dots across and 5 dots down) drawn on the chalkboard; cards with spelling words printed on them.

Directions: The students are divided into two teams. A member of the first team draws the top spelling card and reads the word to a member of the opposite team, who tries to spell it, either in writing or aloud. If the word is spelled correctly, the student draws a line connecting two dots, and that team gets another turn to try to spell a word. If the word is spelled incorrectly, the other team gets a turn. When a square is closed in by four lines, the number of the team is written in the square. The team that obtains the most squares is the winner.

Modification: Two players may play the game with a game board of dots made of tagboard covered with acetate so that marks made with a grease pencil can be erased. When a square is made, the player can write an initial in it.

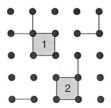

Checkers

Materials: A checker game board made of tagboard; 24 tagboard checkers (i.e., 12 of one color and 12 of another), each of which has a spelling word printed on the bottom.

Directions: Two players place their checkers on the board, and they take turns moving their checkers. If one player can "jump" the opponent's checker, the opponent looks on the bottom of the checker to be jumped and reads the word aloud. If the jumping player correctly spells the word, that player is allowed to jump and pick up the opponent's checker. If the word is misspelled, the player is not allowed to make the move. The game continues until one player has obtained all of the opponent's checkers through jumping.

Modifications: Additional checkers can be made so that different spelling words are used each time the game is played. Also, regular checkers can be used when spelling word cards are provided. To make a jump, the player must spell the word on the top card correctly to the opponent.

TV Talent

Material: Three decorated shoe boxes; spelling words of varying difficulty printed on index cards.

Directions: The game is presented as a television show with one student acting as master of ceremonies (MC). The words are placed in the three boxes, and two players are chosen from the "audience." The first player picks a card from one of the boxes and hands it to the MC without looking at it. The MC pronounces the word, and the player writes the word on the chalkboard. If the word is spelled correctly, the player gets 5 points. The players take turns until one player earns 50 points.

Modification: The spelling words can be divided into three levels of difficulty. The easiest words are placed in the box marked 1 point; the next level, in the box marked 3 points; and the most difficult words, in the box marked 5 points. The student chooses a card from a box according to the number of points the student will attempt to earn on that turn.

Dictionary Store Hunt

Materials: One dictionary per player; a stack of cards with nouns that are unlikely to be familiar to the players (e.g., *cockatiel, metronome,* and *colander*) written on them.

Directions: Each player randomly picks five word cards. At the same starting time, each player begins to find the words in a dictionary, reads the definitions silently, and writes down the kind of store to shop in for each item. The winner is the first person to complete the hunt. Other players can check responses by looking in the dictionary as the player names the stores.

Baseball Spelling Game

Materials: Baseball diamond with three bases and home plate drawn on the chalkboard; cards with spelling words written on them.

Directions: The class is divided into two teams, and the top speller in each group can act as pitcher. The pitcher draws a card and reads the word to the first batter of the other team. If the word is spelled correctly, the first player is given a "single" and stands in front of first base on the chalkboard. If the second batter correctly spells the next word, that batter goes to first base and the player on first base moves to second base. If a word is misspelled, that player is "out"; there are three outs for each team in each inning. Before hearing a word, any batter may declare "home run"; if the word is spelled correctly, that batter clears the bases and the number of runs is added to the score. However, if the batter misspells the word, it automatically counts as the third out for the team, regardless of the actual number of outs in the inning. The team with the most runs at the end of a set number of innings wins.

Modifications: The word cards can be labeled "single," "double," "triple," and "home run" according to the difficulty level of the spelling word. After the batter spells the word correctly, the pitcher tells what the "hit" was worth according to the card. The batter moves to the appropriate base, and batters already on base advance. Also, a baseball diamond can be arranged in the room by using chairs for the bases, and the "runners" can sit in the appropriate chair when they get "hits."

Football Spelling Game

Materials: A football field, including yard lines, drawn on the chalkboard; index cards with spelling words written on them.

Directions: The class is divided into two teams, and the ball is placed (i.e., drawn) on the 50-yard line by the "referee." The referee reads a word to a member of the first team. If the player spells the word correctly, the ball is moved 10 yards toward the opponent's goal line. If the word is misspelled, the offensive team loses 10 yards. Each team gets four words in one turn; then the other team takes a turn. A team is given 6 points each time it crosses the opponent's goal line. The winner is the team with the most points at the end of a specified time period.

Modifications:

- The football field may be made on tagboard, and two players can play using small tagboard footballs for their markers. One player draws a card and reads the word for the opponent to spell. If the word is spelled correctly, the opponent's marker is advanced 5 yards closer to the goal; if the word is misspelled, the opponent's marker is moved back 5 yards. The players take turns (i.e., one word a turn), and the first one to reach the goal line scores a touchdown and wins the game.

- The word cards can include the number of yards each spelling word is worth (e.g., 1 to 10 yards), and the ball is moved accordingly.

- In addition to spelling word cards, there can be "gain" cards and "loss" cards. When the word on the spelling card is spelled correctly, the player picks a gain card; when a word is misspelled, the player draws a loss card. The gain cards denote the number of yards gained (e.g., *completed 30-yard pass; 20-yard run*). The loss cards denote the number of yards lost (e.g., *quarterback sack, lose 10 yards; tackled, 5-yard loss*). The player moves the football accordingly.

- Rather than drawing, erasing, and redrawing the ball throughout the game, a chalkboard eraser can be used as the ball. The eraser is easy to see and move if set vertically on the chalkboard tray.

Nym Game

Materials: Two sets of three decorated coffee cans, with one labeled *antonyms,* one labeled *homonyms,* and one labeled *synonyms;* cards with pairs of words written on them, which are antonyms, homonyms, or synonyms, with all appropriate and acceptable antonyms, homonyms, or synonyms given for each initial word in the word pair.

Directions: The first player draws the top card and reads and spells the first word on the card to the opponent. The opponent must spell the word that completes the word pair, use the words in sentences, and identify the word pair as antonyms, homonyms, or synonyms. If correct, the word card is placed in the appropriate can of the opponent's set. If incorrect, the card is placed in the appropriate can of the first player's set. The players take turns, and when all the cards are gone, they count their score. Each card in the homonym can is worth 3 points; each antonym card is worth 2 points; and each synonym card is worth 1 point. The player with the highest total score wins the game.

Bottle Top Scrabble

Materials: One hundred and fifty (150) bottle tops with letters of the alphabet written inside them with a marking pen and point values written on the outside (e.g., letters most often used should appear most; point values may be the same as those in Scrabble).

Directions: Each student selects ten tops without looking. The first player spells a word using as many of the letters as possible and adds the point values of the letters used. Then the player picks more tops to have ten again. The players take turns spelling words that connect with previously spelled words, as in Scrabble. After all possible bottle tops have been used, the player with the highest score is the winner.

Modification: For older students, there can be a minimum number of letters for each word (e.g., four or more). Also, the number of tops may be increased.

SELF-CORRECTING SPELLING MATERIALS

Spelling Word Puzzles

Feedback device: The pieces of the puzzle fit together to indicate a correct choice.

Materials: Spelling words printed on heavy cardboard and then cut into two or more puzzle pieces.

Directions: The student looks at the puzzle pieces and fits together the pieces that correctly spell a word.

Flip-Sider Spelling Cards

Feedback device: Picture completion or the matching of objects, numbers, or colors provides feedback.

Materials: Sets of index cards with a spelling word on one card and the definition or a picture representing the word on another card; the reverse sides of the two cards that go together have the same object, number, or color, or the two cards complete a picture.

Directions: The student looks at the spelling word on a card and selects the card with the definition of that word or a picture representing it. Then the student flips over the two cards. If the student has chosen the correct definition or picture, the backs of the two cards will have the same object, number, or color, or they will complete a picture.

Modification: The front of the card can have a sentence in which the spelling word is omitted. The sentence may be a definition of the missing word, or there may be a picture illustrating the word in the blank. The spelling word that goes in the blank is written on the back of the card. The student reads the sentence, writes down the missing word, and then flips the card over to check the response.

Front

Back

Spelling Spinner

Feedback device: A flap is located on the poster board. When the flap is raised, the answer is revealed.

Materials: A round disc of poster board divided into several sections, each of which has a word written at the top and a picture or definition written in the lower portion of the section; a square piece of poster board that has the round disc attached to the back with a brass fastener, with a small window cut out at the top to reveal the top portion of the disc and a larger window below it to reveal the lower portion of the disc; a flexible flap (such as vinyl wallpaper) placed over the top window.

Directions: The student turns the spinner to reveal a picture or definition in the window. The student writes the spelling word for the picture or definition and then lifts the flap to check the answer.

Modification: Discs of spelling words selected from reading selections or spelling lists may be numbered and stored so that the teacher can select a disc appropriate for an individual student.

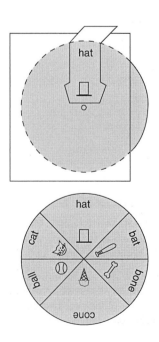

Tape Recorder Spelling

Feedback device: Following the spelling activity presented on the tape, the correct answers are given on the tape.

Materials: A tape recorder and a tape cassette that contains a spelling activity (e.g., a dictated spelling test or directions instructing the student to draw a house and label objects, such as "Add a chimney to your house and write the word *chimney.*").

Directions: The student follows the instructions given on the tape recorder and writes the specified words. Following the activity, the student continues to listen to the tape to hear the correct responses and thus checks the answers.

Answer Box

Feedback device: A flap is placed over the window; when lifted, the window reveals the answer.

Materials: An Answer Box (described in Chapter 2) and a set of index cards that present a spelling exercise.

Directions: The student writes an answer to the presented spelling problem and then lifts the flap to see the answer.

Modification: Change the two "eyes" to one long opening so that activities such as definitions or sentences with missing words can be presented.

Contraction cards to use in the Answer Box:

Definition cards to use in the modified Answer Box:

Fill in the Letters

Feedback device: When the correct letters are filled in, the message at the bottom of the page is completed. Deciphering the code thus provides feedback.

Materials: Worksheets on which the student either must cross out or add a letter so that the word is spelled correctly; blanks at the bottom of the page that give a message when the crossed-out or added letters are written in them.

Directions: The student completes the worksheet by crossing out or adding letters as indicated. Then each letter is written in the appropriate blank at the bottom of the page. If the correct letters are chosen, the student reads a message.

Color Spelling Sheet

1. rsed
2. bl e
3. orpange
4. belack
5. whirte
6. yeljlow
7. br wn
8. greben

(super job)

Spelling Crossword Puzzles

Feedback device: Only a correct response will fit in the squares and complete additional words.

Materials: A crossword puzzle in which spelling words are used (e.g., the crossword puzzle presented in the section on spelling activities).

Directions: The student completes the crossword puzzle and receives feedback by filling in the squares.

Scrambled Letters

Feedback device: The backs of the letters are numbered in the correct sequence of the spelling word.

Materials: Envelopes with pictures illustrating a word or definitions written on the front; square cards placed inside the envelopes, with each card giving a letter needed to spell the word; numbers written on the backs of the cards to represent the word's correct letter sequence.

Directions: The student reads the definition or looks at the picture on the envelope, takes the letters out of the envelope, and places them face up. The student unscrambles the letters, arranges them to spell the word, and then turns over the letters. The number order on the back of the cards indicates whether the word is spelled correctly.

Poke Box

Feedback device: The student places a stylus in the hole to indicate a response. If the correct answer is selected, the card can be pulled out of the Poke Box easily.

Materials: A Poke Box (described in Chapter 2) and a set of index cards that present a spelling exercise (e.g., a word and three abbreviations, or a definition or picture and three words).

Directions: The student selects an answer to the presented spelling problem by inserting the stylus in the hole below the answer. The student then pulls the card, which can be removed if the answer is correct.

Abbreviation and picture cards to use in a Poke Box:

Color Magic

Feedback device: The student receives feedback by opening the folder to see the answers written in color pencil.

Materials: A color plastic folder (such as the type typically used to hold term papers), inside of which is a spelling worksheet; answers written on the worksheet in the same color as the plastic folder (i.e., if the plastic folder is red, the answers are written with a red pencil so that they will not show through the folder).

Directions: The student follows the instructions on the worksheet by reading through the color plastic folder. After writing all the answers on a sheet of paper and finishing the activity, the student opens the folder to check the responses.

COMMERCIAL SPELLING PROGRAMS

The following selected basic developmental programs and corrective materials for spelling instruction may be helpful for students with spelling difficulties. Additional commercial materials include spelling calculators (e.g., Spelling Ace Pro and Puzzle Solver, produced by Franklin Electronic Publishers), spelling games (e.g., Scrabble, produced by Milton Bradley), and spelling reference books (e.g., Spellex Word Finder, published by Curriculum Associates).

Instant Spelling Words for Writing

Instant Spelling Words for Writing, developed by R. G. Forest and R. A. Sitton (published by Curriculum Associates), is an eight-level series designed for writers of all ages (i.e., first grade through adult) who have difficulty spelling and proofreading. The series focuses on 1,500 high-frequency words, which cover 90 percent of all words used in writing. All spelling words are introduced as whole words in list form, and students practice writing each word at least ten times in a variety of high-interest exercises. Visual imagery is emphasized through activities involving configuration of word shapes and visual discrimination. The program teaches a multimodality word-study procedure and uses the self-corrected test-study-test method. The last exercise in every lesson is a structured writing activity. Using a total language approach, the review lessons and optional extension activities provide language arts exercises that integrate spelling with listening, speaking, reading, writing, and thinking.

Spelling Mastery

Spelling Mastery (Dixon, Engelmann, Bauer, Steely, & Wells, 2007) is a six-level basal spelling series designed to teach spelling strategies to students in first through sixth grade. The series begins with phonemic (i.e., sound–symbol) and whole-word strategies and then shifts to morphemic (i.e., meaning–symbol) strategies. The program emphasizes learning to spell by generalization rather than memorization, and the 20-minute daily lessons can be used with an entire class or with small groups. Instructional software is included to track student progress and build individualized lessons.

Spelling Through Morphographs

Spelling Through Morphographs (Dixon & Engelmann, 2002) is an intensive remedial program for fourth-grade through adult students. The program includes fast-paced lessons that cover more than 500 morphographs (i.e., prefixes, suffixes, and base words) and a set of rules for combining them so that students can spell over 12,000 words, including problem words, by the end of the program. Because the lessons focus on basic units of meaning in written language (i.e., morphographs) that always are spelled according to specific rules, the student learns analytic techniques and generalizable rules that can be applied to words not in the program. The teacher presentation books provide step-by-step activities for each lesson and include mastery tests and crossword puzzles correlated with the words in the lessons of the program. Instructional software tracks known words so that study can be tailored to the student's individual needs.

Spellography

Spellography (Moats & Rosow, 2003) is designed for students in fourth through seventh grade and includes 27 lessons, divided into three books, that are filled with humorous games and entertaining activities. This structured program utilizes spelling research for effective spelling instruction, teaches vocabulary using root words, reinforces multisyllabic decoding, develops reading fluency, and strengthens spelling retention. Spelling concepts are taught explicitly, systematically, and cumulatively, and students learn phoneme-grapheme correspondence; common irregular words; syllable spelling patterns and combinations; prefix, root, and suffix constructions; contractions; sentence structure; parts of speech; and idioms and figures of speech. Most of the lessons, which may take a week or more to teach, include a set of 24 study words divided into groups of four by level of difficulty, phonemic awareness exercises, an introduction to the main spelling pattern, exercises on word usage and meaning, exercises to review syllable structure, practice with alphabetical order, exercises to study morphology, dictation exercises, and a timed exercise for reading fluency. Activities also include pretests, self-checks, partner pair-offs, and spelling journals. The program is effective for full-class as well as small-group instruction, and the exercises can be modified to match the instructional needs of the students.

Stetson Spelling Program

The *Stetson Spelling Program* (Stetson & Stetson, 2001) introduces the 3,000 words most frequently used in writing, which account for 97 percent of the total words written by the average child and adult. The program uses effective teaching and learning strategies including pretesting, immediate feedback and self-correction, visual imagery of the whole word, spelling clusters, mnemonics, and visual memory. The 30 units each contain ten lessons of ten words, and guidelines are provided for using the program for whole-class instruction as well as peer teaching.

Target Spelling

This series of six consumable books (published by Steck-Vaughn) is designed to teach spelling to students with learning problems in second through tenth grade. A systematic, highly ordered multimodality instructional approach is used in which 1,260 words are presented sequentially and with constant reinforcement throughout the six books. Students are asked to learn only six to eight new words per week, and learning experiences to ensure mastery include activities such as word shapes, word search, visual discrimination, recognition in context, matching words with pictures, sound blending, rhyming, and supplying missing letters.

COMPUTER SOFTWARE PROGRAMS IN SPELLING

Computer software can be used effectively to give students additional learning opportunities to improve or enrich their spelling skills. Many students with learning problems prefer to practice spelling words at a computer, and appropriate software can provide systematic support to students studying the spelling of new words. For example, MacArthur, Haynes, Malouf, Harris, and Owings (1990) found that a computer program that provided immediate corrective feedback during practice, required the correct spelling of a word before continuing, and recycled misspelled words for later review improved the weekly spelling performance of students with learning disabilities. Mayfield, Glenn, and Vollmer (2008) used computer-based instruction to teach spelling words to sixth-grade students. The computer-based instruction combined with a training procedure to correct errors resulted in improved spelling accuracy for students with learning problems. Moreover, Gordon, Vaughn, and Schumm (1993) report that computer-assisted instruction can develop positive attitudes toward spelling drill and practice, decrease spelling errors, promote individualized study strategies, and enhance spelling performance when used with time-delay procedures. In a meta-analysis of studies that examined the effects of several spelling interventions that included the use of computer software programs, Wanzek et al. (2006) found that the programs yielded small but positive effects in spelling accuracy and error correction.

Software programs can emphasize awareness of word structure and spelling strategies as well as use time-delay, voice simulation, and sound effects. Four techniques commonly are used in spelling software: (1) A word is flashed quickly on the screen and then erased, and the student must spell the word from memory; (2) a word is presented with the letters scrambled, and the student must unscramble the letters; (3) a word is missing within a presented sentence, and the student must use context clues to determine the word and then spell it; and (4) three or four versions of a word are shown, and the student must select the one that is spelled correctly. In addition, to aid in writing activities, some software programs offer a built-in spelling scanner that checks for misspelled words or typographical errors according to a predetermined file of common words. Hasselbring and Goin (1989) recommend that instructional computer programs in spelling should require the use of long-term memory, be limited in the size of the practice set of words, require practice spread over several different times, and emphasize speed as well as accuracy. The following computer programs are described to give examples of the types of software that are available to reinforce spelling skills.

Spelling Blaster Ages 6–9

Spelling Blaster Ages 6–9 (produced by Knowledge Adventure) features phonics-based activities that introduce spelling rules and patterns for over 1,700 words. The student learns to build words using phonics rules, recognize spelling patterns and word families, use phonics and rhyming words, and edit and complete misspelled words. Seven spelling activities with multiple levels of difficulty encourage the student to use various word-attack strategies to master basic spelling skills while reinforcing reading skills. The teacher can customize spelling lists with a word editor and monitor misspelling trends with a Spell Track feature. Printable word searches, crossword puzzles, and 25 story-books encourage learning away from the computer.

Spelling Rules

Spelling Rules (produced by Optimum Resource) includes progressive learning levels and hundreds of graded questions for students in third through ninth grade. This curriculum-based program covers 21 rules, including forming plurals and compound words, capitalization, and the "i before e" rule. After each rule is presented with examples, type-in questions are given for that rule, and a help screen offers additional examples. The degree of difficulty can be set to advance automatically or to remain at the chosen level for extended study and practice. The program can be customized to include new exercises, and progress reports and exercises can be printed.

Stickybear Spelling

In *Stickybear Spelling* (produced by Optimum Resource), students in second grade and up work on three action-packed activities. In *Stickybear Bee,* a true spelling bee, up to four players compete for the highest score in spelling words. In *Stickybear Bash,* each player takes turns clicking on a moving fish to select the correct order of letters for spoken words. Students use unscrambling skills in *Stickybear Jumble,* which is a solve-the-word activity. *Stickybear Spelling* contains more than 2,000 recorded words, but the program is open-ended and the teacher can customize the word lists for each student. Also, each activity has four levels of difficulty

and levels of play can be set to allow students of different ages or abilities to compete effectively.

Word Zapper

Word Zapper (produced by Micrograms Software) is designed to help students in second through sixth grade identify misspelled words and improve their own spelling. Over 1,000 grade-level appropriate words are provided within each grade level. As words move along a conveyor belt, the student uses the lively word-zapping machine to zap misspelled words and allow correctly spelled words to pass. The student can select a word list of appropriate challenge and control the speed at which the conveyor belt moves words across the screen. If the student gets 50 words completed with fewer than 10 errors, a bonus round begins, which draws words from higher levels or from the challenge list of over 400 commonly misspelled words. After each game, the student practices the missed words, which also are added to the student's individual focus list so that the words can be included in future games until the student demonstrates recognition of each word's correct spelling. The teacher or student can create, edit, and add to individualized word lists, and a recordkeeping system is provided.

Assessing and Teaching Handwriting and Written Expression

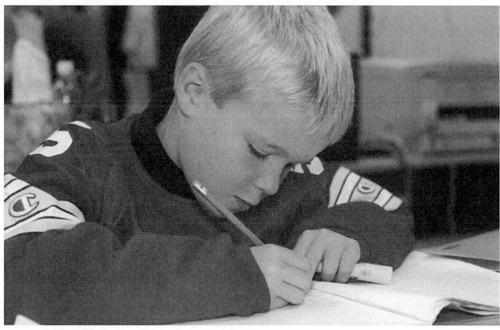

Cynthia Cassidy/Merrill

From Chapter 10 of *Teaching Students with Learning Problems*, 8/e. Cecil D. Mercer. Ann R. Mercer. Paige C. Pullen.

Writing is a highly complex form of communication. It is both a skill and a means of self-expression. The process of writing integrates visual, motor, and conceptual abilities and is a primary means through which students demonstrate their knowledge of advanced academic subjects.

Classroom instruction in handwriting usually begins in kindergarten or first grade. Readiness activities such as tracing, coloring, and copying are emphasized at first. The formation of letters, numbers, and words is stressed until about the third grade. After the third grade, more emphasis is placed on writing as a form of meaningful self-expression, and instruction focuses on using grammar and developing the quality of ideas expressed.

Handwriting and written expression tasks require sustained attention and concentration; thus, some students with learning problems have difficulty learning to write and producing written products. These students need direct, concentrated instruction to become proficient in written communication. This chapter presents the assessment and teaching of writing skills in two major problem areas: handwriting and written expression.

HANDWRITING PROBLEMS

The major objectives of instruction in handwriting are legibility and fluency, and the ability to write letters accurately and quickly is a predictor of success in written expression. To communicate thoughts effectively through writing, the student first must be taught to write legibly and fluently. Thus, instruction begins by focusing on holding the writing instrument, forming manuscript and cursive letters correctly, and maintaining proper spacing and proportion. Numerous factors contribute to handwriting difficulties: motor problems, faulty visual perception of letters and words, poor visual memory, poor instruction, and lack of motivation.

Fine motor problems also can interfere with handwriting and thus with schoolwork. For example, a student may know how to spell a word but be unable to write legibly or fast enough to keep up with the teacher; thus, the spelling may be poor. This same situation may exist in copying material from the chalkboard and working on seatwork. Unfortunately, many parents and teachers view students as academically slow when, in fact, the real problem is handwriting.

Students show a variety of handwriting problems: slowness, incorrect directionality of letters and numbers, too much or too little slant, spacing difficulty, messiness, inability to stay on a horizontal line, illegible letters, too much or too little pencil pressure, and mirror writing. In a study of the handwriting of first, second, and third graders, six lowercase letters (i.e., *q,*

j, z, u, n, and *k*) accounted for 48 percent of the omissions, miscues, and illegibilities, and, when only illegible responses were considered, five letters (i.e., *q, z, u, a,* and *j*) accounted for 54 percent of the miscues (Graham, 1999). Moreover, Newland (1932) examined the cursive handwriting of 2,381 people and found that about 50 percent of the illegibilities involved the letters *a, e, r,* and *t.* Most commonly, people failed to close letters (such as *a* and *b*), closed top loops (such as writing *e* like *i*), looped strokes that should be nonlooped (such as writing *i* like *e*), used straight-up rather than rounded strokes (such as writing *n* like *u*), and exhibited problems with end strokes (i.e., not brought up, not brought down, or not left as horizontal). In a study of illegibilities in cursive handwriting of sixth graders, Horton (1970) reports that 12 percent of all errors were incorrect formations of the letter *r.* Thus, the majority of handwriting errors involve the incorrect writing of a few letters. Common number malformations include writing 5 like 3 (**5**), 6 like 0 (**6**), 7 like 9 (**9**), and 9 like 4 (**4**).

ASSESSMENT OF HANDWRITING SKILLS

In assessing the young student (i.e., 8 or 9 years old and younger), the teacher should remember that occasional reversals, omissions, and poor spacing are normal. However, a writing problem exists if such errors continue for a long time and if the student does not improve in simple handwriting tasks. Unlike other academic skills, few standardized tests measure handwriting, and informal procedures are used widely. Minimum standards are difficult to set because activities differ in emphasis placed on speed, legibility, and character of handwriting.

Formal Handwriting Assessment

Because only a few norm-referenced measures of handwriting are available, rating scales and inventories frequently are used to assess a student's current proficiency in handwriting. Table 10.1 presents published handwriting assessment devices and includes two standardized measures and one criterion-referenced inventory. Published legibility examples of student handwriting, such as the evaluation guides produced by Zaner-Bloser, provide a subjective evaluation of general handwriting competence. However, these guides do not highlight specific errors and illegible forms of handwriting; thus, they may be used best to aid the teacher in rating a writing specimen for screening purposes. To obtain information for instructional purposes, various informal assessment techniques may be helpful.

TABLE 10.1
Published handwriting assessment devices

Test	Age/Grade Level
Basic School Skills Inventory–Third Edition (Hammill, Leigh, Pearson, & Maddox, 1998)	4–6 years
The writing section of this inventory assesses a student's handwriting ability in various tasks: writing from left to right, grasping a pencil, writing first name, maintaining proper writing position, writing letters upon request, copying words, copying from chalkboard to paper, staying on the line, and writing last name. This norm-referenced instrument can be used to identify students who are low in handwriting readiness compared with other students their age. The rating scale also can be used as a criterion-referenced test to determine what skills need to be taught.	
Brigance Comprehensive Inventory of Basic Skills—II (Brigance, 2010a)	K–ninth grade
This criterion-referenced test offers several tests of handwriting. Manuscript and cursive writing are assessed in the writing section of the test. To assess manuscript writing, the student is asked to print uppercase letters in sequence, print lowercase letters in sequence, print dictated uppercase letters, print dictated lowercase letters, print personal data, and write numerals in sequence. To assess cursive writing, the student is asked to write cursive lowercase letters in sequence, write cursive uppercase letters in sequence, and write personal data. Also, quality of writing is assessed, and manuscript and cursive criteria and samples are provided.	
Test of Handwriting Skills—Revised (Milone, 2007)	6–18 years
This standardized test assesses a student's handwriting skills in writing both uppercase and lowercase letter forms in either manuscript writing for students ages 6 through 8 or cursive writing for students ages 8 through 18. Ten subtests focus on abilities such as writing uppercase and lowercase letters in sequence from memory, writing letters out of sequence from dictation, writing eight numbers out of numerical order from dictation, copying 12 uppercase letters out of sequence, copying ten lowercase letters out of sequence, copying six words (i.e., 21 letters), copying two sentences (i.e., six words, 29 letters), and writing six words (i.e., 21 letters) from dictation. The student's handwriting speed can be assessed separately from the other skill areas. The test can be administered individually or in groups in 25 minutes, and, in addition to an overall standard score, subtest scores are reported as scaled scores and percentile ranks.	

Informal Handwriting Assessment

The teacher can obtain diagnostic information informally by visually examining the student's handwriting. Writing samples can be used to determine problem areas in legibility. Mann, Suiter, and McClung (1992) suggest obtaining three samples: the student's usual, best, and fastest handwriting. The usual writing sample shows the student's work under normal, non-fatiguing conditions. For the best sample, the student is told to take time and write the sentence with best effort. Then a 3-minute timing is given to see how many times the student can write a given sentence. Sometimes a student can write legibly only when specifically asked to do so. Also, some students write well but at an extremely slow rate. By comparing the three writing samples, the teacher can determine the student's ability with regard to speed and legibility.

While observing the student during handwriting activities, the teacher should note possible problem areas by answering the following questions.

- Does the student grip the pencil correctly and in a comfortable and flexible manner?
- Is the student's paper in the proper position on the writing surface?
- Does the student sit correctly when writing, or is the head too close or too far away from the paper?
- Does the student consistently write with the same hand?
- Does the student appear extremely frustrated, nervous, or emotional when writing?
- Does the student have a negative attitude toward handwriting and appear bored and disruptive?

Additional instructional information can be obtained by analyzing the student's writing samples for error patterns in the following various aspects of handwriting.

- *Letter formation.* Letter formation involves the strokes that make up each letter. In manuscript writing, letters are composed of vertical, horizontal, and slanted lines plus circles or parts of circles, whereas cursive letters are composed of slanted lines, loops, and curved lines. To check for legibility, the teacher can use a piece of cardboard with a hole cut in the center that is slightly larger than a single letter. By exposing one letter at a time, the teacher can see more easily which letters are illegible or poorly formed.

- *Letter size, proportion, and alignment.* The size and proportion of letters are indicated by their height relationship to one another; alignment refers to the evenness of letters along the baseline, with letters of the same size being the same height. These legibility elements can be measured by using a ruler to draw lines that touch the base and tops of as many letters as possible.

- *Spacing.* Spacing should be consistent between letters within words, as well as between words and between sentences.

- *Line quality.* Thickness and steadiness of the lines used to form letters should be consistent. The teacher should mark lines that waver or are too thick or too fine. Incorrect hand or body position or cramped fingers can result in inconsistent line quality.

- *Slant.* The slant of letters should be uniform. In general, manuscript letters are perpendicular to the baseline and have a straight up-and-down appearance. In cursive writing the paper is slanted, and strokes are pulled toward the body. Straight lines or lines with a uniform slant can be drawn through the letters to indicate which letters are off slant.

- *Rate.* Handwriting speed can be determined on a writing sample by asking the student to write as well and as rapidly as possible. The rate of handwriting—letters per minute (lpm)—is determined by divid-

ing the total number of letters written by the number of writing minutes allowed. Graham, Berninger, Weintraub, and Shafer (1998) suggest the following mean handwriting speeds.

	for girls	*for boys*
Grade 1	21 lpm	17 lpm
Grade 2	36 lpm	32 lpm
Grade 3	50 lpm	45 lpm
Grade 4	66 lpm	61 lpm
Grade 5	75 lpm	71 lpm
Grade 6	91 lpm	78 lpm
Grade 7	109 lpm	91 lpm
Grade 8	118 lpm	112 lpm
Grade 9	121 lpm	114 lpm

Table 10.2 displays a diagnostic chart for manuscript and cursive writing that highlights errors, likely causes, and remediation procedures.

Probes can be used to assess a specific handwriting skill and determine instructional targets. Handwriting probe sheets can include tasks such as repeatedly writing the same letter, writing first name, writing uppercase letters, writing lowercase letters, and writing words. The student is timed for 1 minute, and daily performance on each probe sheet is charted to monitor progress. Figure 10.1 presents a probe sheet on writing uppercase manuscript letters.

In assessing handwriting difficulties, the teacher also can encourage students to use self-evaluation. Diagnostic charts and evaluation guides can help students identify their own handwriting inaccuracies. Young students can check their manuscript writing to see if they have formed a particular letter correctly, if the round parts of letters are joined neatly, and if slanted strokes are joined in sharp points. Older students can examine their cursive writing to see if letters are consistently parallel and if the letters touch the baseline consistently. When students monitor their own writing, they can change their writing performance quickly and easily. Also, positive attitudes may be increased as students assume some responsibility for learning and improving their handwriting.

TEACHING HANDWRITING SKILLS

After assessment, the teacher can establish instructional objectives based upon targeted errors and the student's overall development of handwriting skills. Skills should be taught through meaningful and motivating real-life writing activities. Repetitious drills and mass practice without supervision should be avoided, and the student should receive immediate feedback.

TABLE 10.2
Diagnostic chart for manuscript and cursive writing

Factor	Problem	Possible Cause	Remediation
		Manuscript Writing	
Shape	Letters slanted	Paper slanted	Place paper straight and pull straight-line strokes toward center of body.
	Varies from standard	Improper mental image of letter	Have student write problem letters on chalkboard.
Size	Too large	Poor understanding of writing lines	Reteach size concept by pointing out purpose of each line on writing paper.
		Exaggerated arm movement	Reduce arm movement, especially on circle and part-circle letters.
		Improper mental image of letter	Have student write problem letters on chalkboard.
	Too small	Poor understanding of writing lines	Reteach size concept by pointing out purpose of each line on writing paper.
		Overemphasis on finger movement	Stress arm movement; check hand–pencil and arm–desk positions to be sure arm movement is possible.
		Improper mental image of letter	Have student write problem letters on chalkboard.
	Not uniform	Adjusting writing hand after each letter	Stress arm movement; move paper with nonwriting hand so writing hand can remain in proper writing position.
		Overemphasis on finger movement	Stress arm movement; check arm–desk and hand–pencil positions.
Space	Crowded letters in words	Poor understanding of space concepts	Reteach uniform spacing between letters (i.e., finger or pencil width).
	Too much space between letters	Improper lowercase letter size and shape	Review concepts of size and shape; provide appropriate corrections under size and shape.
Alignment	Letters not sitting on baseline	Improper letter formation	Evaluate work for letter shape; stress bringing straight-line strokes all the way down to baseline.
		Poor understanding of baseline concept	Review purpose of baseline on writing paper.
		Improper hand–pencil and paper–desk positions	Check positions to make sure student is able to reach baseline easily.
	Letters not of consistent height	Poor understanding of size concept	Review concept of letter size in relationship to lines provided on writing paper.
Line quality	Too heavy or too light	Improper writing pressure	Review hand–pencil position; place wadded paper tissue on palm of writing hand to relax writing grip; demonstrate desired line quality.

TABLE 10.2
(continued)

Factor	Problem	Possible Cause	Remediation
		Cursive Writing	
Shape	Letters too oval	Overemphasis of arm movement and poor image of letter	Check arm–desk position; review letter size and shape.
	Letters too narrow	Finger writing	Check positions to allow for arm movement.
		Overemphasis of straight-line stroke	Make sure straight-line stroke does not come all the way down to baseline in letters such as *l, b,* and *t*.
		Poor mental image of letter shape	Use transparent overlay for student's personal evaluation of shape.
			In all problems of letter shape, review letters in terms of the basic strokes.
Size	Letters too large	Exaggerated arm movement	Check arm–desk position for over-movement of forearm.
		Poor mental image of letter size	Review base and top line concepts in relation to $1/4$ space, $1/2$ space, and $3/4$ space; use transparent overlay for student's personal evaluation of letter size.
	Letters too small or letters not uniform	Finger movement	Check arm–desk and hand–pencil positions; stress arm movement.
		Poor mental image of letter size	Review concept of letter size (i.e., $1/4$ space, $1/2$ space, and $3/4$ space) in relation to base and top lines; use transparent overlay for student's personal evaluation of letter size.
Space	Letters in words crowded or uneven spacing between letters	Finger movement	Check arm–desk, hand–pencil positions; stress arm movement.
		Poor understanding of joining strokes	Review how letters are joined; show ending stroke of one letter joined to beginning stroke of following letter; practice writing letters in groups of five.
	Too much space provided between letters and words	Exaggerated arm movement	Check arm–desk position for over-movement of forearm.
		Poor understanding of joining strokes	Review joining strokes; practice writing groups of letters by rhythmic count.
	Uneven space between words	Poor understanding of between-word spacing	Review concept of spacing between words; show beginning stroke in second word starting under ending stroke of preceding word.
Alignment	Poor letter alignment along baseline	Incorrect writing position; finger movement; exaggerated arm movement	Check all writing positions; stress even, rhythmic writing movement.

(continued)

TABLE 10.2
(continued)

Factor	Problem	Possible Cause	Remediation
		Incorrect use of joining strokes	Review joining strokes.
	Uneven letter alignment in words relative to size	Poor understanding of size concept	Show size relationships between lower- and uppercase, and $1/4$ space, $1/2$ space, and $3/4$ space lowercase letters; use repetitive exercise with emphasis on uniform height of smaller letters.
Speed and ease	Writing becomes illegible under stress and speed (e.g., in grades 4, 5, and 6)	Degree of handwriting skill is insufficient to meet speed requirements	Improve writing positions; develop more arm movement and less finger movement.
	Writing becomes illegible when writing activity is too long	Handwriting positions have not been perfected to allow handwriting ease	Improve all writing positions, especially hand–pencil position; stress arm movement.
Slant	Back slant	Left-handedness	Correct hand–pencil and paper–desk positions.
	Vertical	Poor positioning	Correct hand–pencil and paper–desk positions.
	Too far right	Overemphasis of finger movement	Make sure student pulls slant strokes toward center of body if right-handed and to left elbow if left-handed.
			Use slant line instruction sheets as aid to teaching slant.
			Use transparent overlay for student's personal evaluation.
			Review all lowercase letters that derive their shape from the slant line.
			Write lowercase alphabet on chalkboard; retrace all slant strokes in color chalk.

Models should be provided of both good and poor work so that the student eventually can make comparisons to determine necessary changes.

Tompkins (2009) notes that brief lessons of handwriting instruction and practice sessions several times a week are more effective than a single lengthy period weekly or monthly. Separate periods of direct instruction and teacher-supervised practice help students avoid developing bad habits and errors in letter formation that may cause problems when they need to develop greater writing speed. The teacher should demonstrate the correct way to form letters and should supervise students' handwriting efforts carefully. For some students, observing moving models (i.e., watching the teacher write) is more effective

than copying models already written; thus, the teacher should circulate around the classroom to assist individual students and demonstrate a skill while the student is performing the handwriting task. Moreover, the teacher should *avoid* the following handwriting instructional errors: unsupervised handwriting practice while skills are being formed, lack of immediate feedback to correct errors, lack of emphasis on student analysis of errors, failure to provide close-range models of correct letter formation, and repeated drill of both correct and incorrect letter production.

To increase handwriting fluency, Graham (1999) notes that the most common recommendation is to have students frequently write connected text. Additional

FIGURE 10.1

Probe sheet for writing uppercase manuscript letters

Name: _____ Date: _____

Time: _____

Rate (letters per minute): _____ Correct

_____ Error

Comments: _____

_____

B -

G -

K -

M -

R -

S -

Y -

methods for increasing handwriting speed include self-competition on timed exercises and the use of reinforcement to increase motivation. Also, the teacher should help students develop a positive attitude toward handwriting by encouraging progress and stressing the skill's importance. In upper elementary grades and in secondary classrooms, greater emphasis is placed on identifying and remediating specific deficits revealed in students' daily written work. Students need to diagnose and correct handwriting problems because handwriting difficulties may im-

pede efficient work production and influence teacher evaluation and grading. Many teachers consistently give higher grades on papers with better handwriting than on papers with poor handwriting, regardless of content quality (Graham, 1992). Also, legible, fluent handwriting facilitates taking notes in class, filling out forms, and success in a work environment.

A scope and sequence chart of handwriting skills by grade level is presented in the Appendix. The development of handwriting skills and teaching strategies are presented next in the areas of readiness skills, manuscript writing, transitional writing, and cursive writing. Typewriting and keyboarding also are considered as alternatives.

Readiness Skills

Readiness handwriting activities in kindergarten typically include stimulating children's interest in writing, developing their ability to hold writing instruments, and refining their fine motor control. Writing requires muscular control, eye–hand coordination, and visual discrimination. The teacher needs to help each student develop these skills before the student is ready to begin handwriting. Muscular coordination can be developed in the young child through manipulative experiences (e.g., cutting with scissors, finger painting, tracing, and coloring). Eye–hand coordination is involved in drawing circles and copying geometric forms. Also, developing visual discrimination of sizes, shapes, and details aids the student's visual awareness of letters and their formation. Chalkboard activities provide practice and give the student the opportunity to use muscle movement of the shoulders, arms, hands, and fingers. Before beginning handwriting instruction, the student should be able to do the following:

- Perform hand movements such as up-down, left-right, and forward-back.
- Trace geometric shapes and dotted lines.
- Connect dots on paper.
- Draw a horizontal line from left to right.
- Draw a vertical line from top to bottom and bottom to top.
- Draw a backward circle, a curved line, and a forward circle.
- Draw slanted lines vertically.
- Copy simple designs and shapes.
- Name letters and discern likenesses and differences in letter forms.

Determining the student's hand preference also is important. The teacher should determine which hand the student uses most often in natural situations, such as eating or throwing a ball. Also, the teacher can ask the student to use one hand to take a pencil out of a box, cover one eye, or make a mark on the chalkboard. A youngster who indicates a strong preference for using the left hand should be allowed to do so when writing. A student who uses both hands well should be encouraged to make a choice and consistently use one hand (i.e., preferably the right) for writing.

The proper position of paper and pencil also must be taught before extensive handwriting instruction.

During writing, the student should be sitting in a comfortable chair, with the lower back touching the back of the seat and both feet on the floor. The desk or table should be at a height that allows the student to place forearms on the writing surface without discomfort. The nonwriting hand holds the writing paper in place. To prevent elbow bumping, left-handers should be seated in a left-hand desk chair or along the outside at a work table. The pencil should be held lightly in the triangle formed by the thumb and the first two fingers, and the hand should rest lightly on its outer edge. The pencil should be held about an inch above its point by right-handers; the pencil end should point toward the right shoulder. Left-handers should hold the pencil about $1\frac{1}{4}$ inches from its writing point; the pencil end should point toward the left elbow. Commercial pencil grips (available from Zaner-Bloser) or masking tape can be placed on the pencil to make it easier to hold. Students should be encouraged to use a reasonably comfortable grip to avoid fatigue or discomfort when writing for an extended period of time. Graham and Weintraub (1996) note that, regardless of the type of grip initially taught, most students modify how they hold the writing instrument as they mature.

For manuscript writing, the paper should be placed straight on the desk directly in front of the eyes. Some left-handers may be helped by slanting the paper so that the lower right corner of the paper points to the left of the center of the body. For cursive writing, the paper should be rotated about 45 degrees. The right-handed student places the paper so that the lower left corner points toward the center of the body and the writing stroke is pulled toward the center of the body. For the left-handed student, the paper is slanted north-northeast; the lower right corner points to the center of the body, and the writing stroke is pulled toward the left elbow. As they write, right-handed students pull their arms toward their bodies, whereas left-handed writers push away. Some left-handers begin "hooking" their hand and wrist while writing to see what they have written and to avoid smudging their writing. This practice should be avoided and can be controlled by finding the right slant for the paper and by practicing handwriting on the chalkboard to develop a more natural style.

Manuscript Writing

Manuscript writing usually is taught in kindergarten and first grade and is based entirely on the basic shapes of circles and straight lines. The basic strokes in manuscript writing are the top-to-bottom line (⇂), left-to-right line (➞), backward circle (◙), forward

FIGURE 10.2
Formation of uppercase and lowercase manuscript letters and numbers

Source: From *Zaner-Bloser Handwriting*, 2003, Columbus, OH: Zaner-Bloser. Reprinted by permission.

circle( ), and slant lines ( ). Figure 10.2 presents the formation of uppercase and lowercase manuscript letters and numbers, with arrows and numbering to indicate stroke direction and sequence. Handwriting instruction in kindergarten usually focuses on teaching children to recognize and form uppercase and lowercase letters and to write their names and other common words; students in first grade focus on forming uppercase and lowercase letters, spacing between letters, and developing skills related to legibility.

While being careful not to block the students' vision, the teacher can demonstrate letter forms on the chalkboard. The students should observe the handwriting process as well as the finished product. When writing on the chalkboard, students should write at eye level and stand at arm's length directly in front of the writing.

A multisensory approach often is used in teaching letter forms. The student sees, hears, and traces the letter model. The following steps can be used.

1. The teacher shows the student the letter to be written.

2. The teacher says aloud the letter name and stroke directions (e.g., "First we go up; then we go down").
3. The student traces the model with a finger and may report the movements aloud while tracing.
4. The student traces the letter model with a pencil.
5. The student copies the letter on paper while looking at the model.
6. The student writes the letter from memory while saying the name of the letter.

A fading model also can be used to teach handwriting. The letter model is presented at first in heavy, dark lines, and the student traces over the model with a finger and the nonwriting end of a pencil. Portions of the model gradually are faded, and the student traces the

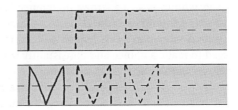

model with a pencil. The model eventually is removed, and the student writes the letter independent of the model.

As soon as possible, activities should be provided in which words are used and the writing says something. Copying meaningless letters may result in boredom and negative attitudes toward writing. Also, in copying exercises, the letter or word model should be presented at first on the kind of paper the student uses and be placed on the student's desk. It is more difficult for some students to copy far models (e.g., letters or words written on the chalkboard) than near models because the image of a far model must be transferred through space and from different planes.

Letters that consist entirely of vertical and horizontal strokes (such as *E, F, H, I, L, T, i, l,* and *t*) are learned more easily than letters in which straight and curved lines are combined (such as *b, f, h,* and *p*). Letters with easier strokes may be taught first. The teacher should give more attention to the formation of difficult letter forms. To provide a natural transition to cursive writing, Wolf (2005) recommends manuscript writing that uses a continuous stroke when possible. In continuous stroke letter formation, lines are retraced when possible and the pencil is lifted only when necessary (e.g., to cross a *t* or dot an *i*). In a study of first graders' errors in the formation of manuscript letters, Lewis and Lewis (1965) made the following observations.

* Incorrect size was the most common type of error and was seen more often in descender letters (*p, q, y, g,* and *j*).
* The most frequently reversed letters were *N, d, q,* and *y*.
* Incorrect relationship of parts occurred most frequently in the letters *k, R, M,* and *m*.
* Partial omission occurred most frequently in the letters *m, U,* and *I*.
* Additions often occurred in the letters *q, C, k, m,* and *y*.
* The most frequently misshaped letter forms were *j, G,* and *J*.

Numerous letters often are reversed, such as *b, d, p, q, s, y,* and *N*. In teaching these letters, the teacher should emphasize their correct beginning point and direction. Students who continue to reverse letters and numbers after the age of 7 or 8 may need direct intervention techniques. As well as receiving immediate corrective feedback followed by practice saying the letter name while tracing and writing the letter, the student can be instructed to associate the problem letter with another letter that does not cause confusion

(e.g., *c* within *d*). In addition to difficulties in formation, some students have problems spacing and aligning manuscript letters. In general, the widest space is left between straight-line letters, and the least amount of space is left between circle letters. Spacing between words equals about the size of one finger or a lowercase *o,* and twice as much space is left between sentences.

Poor formation and alignment should be pointed out to the student; however, if the student has extreme difficulty forming letters and staying on the lines of writing paper, the teacher may choose to facilitate instruction with commercial materials until the student improves. *The Perceptuomotor (Talking) Pen* (available from Stoelting Company) is an electronic pen with a small beam of infrared light in its tip. This infrared sensor picks up reflected light and triggers a buzzer. The battery-operated pen responds to any pattern of light and dark. When the tip of the pen is on a dark area, the pen is silent. If the pen is moved to a light area, it "squawks." This sound can be silenced only by placing the tip of the pen back on a dark area. Thus, by providing a dark pattern on a light background, the pen "talks" only when the pattern is traced incorrectly. Because the pen provides immediate auditory feedback, it is self-correcting and can be used without direct supervision. The pen can be used with standard headphones so that only the student knows when a mistake is made. Also, Right-Line Paper (available from PRO-ED) is produced in both wide rule and narrow rule and has a raised line superimposed on the printed line so that the writer can feel as well as see the baseline.

Graham and Harris (2005) recommend that young students with handwriting problems should be provided with supplemental instruction. In a study examining the effectiveness of extra handwriting instruction, students were randomly assigned to a handwriting intervention or to a phonological awareness intervention. The students receiving supplemental handwriting instruction performed significantly better on various literacy and writing measures, including accuracy in naming letters, writing letters of the alphabet, and copying connected text fluently. In addition, students in the handwriting instruction group improved their written expression performance. The intervention implemented by Graham and Harris includes a four-step sequence that focuses on writing lowercase letters accurately and fluently. In each lesson, students work on letters that use similar strokes; after the first lesson students use the letters to write words. The intervention includes the following lesson sequence.

1. *Alphabet warm-up*—The students practice naming, matching, and sequencing alphabet letters.
2. *Alphabet practice*—The students practice writing unit letters in isolation.
3. *Alphabet rockets*—The students repeatedly write a sentence containing unit letters during a 3-minute time frame, and the students record the number of letters written.
4. *Alphabet fun*—The teacher models how to make a unit letter in a funny way.

Transitional Writing

The transition from manuscript to cursive writing typically occurs during the second or third grade, after the student has mastered manuscript letters; however, because of individual differences in motor skills and levels of interest in cursive writing, some students are introduced to cursive writing in first or second grade, while other students are given additional time to refine their manuscript skills and learn cursive writing in third or fourth grade. Moreover, some controversy exists concerning whether to begin with manuscript or cursive writing. Those who favor manuscript writing (Anderson, 1966; Barbe, Milone, & Wasylyk, 1983; Herrick, 1960) claim that it requires less complex movements and reduces reading problems because most printed pages are in manuscript. In addition, manuscript writing tends to be more legible and has received acceptance in business and commercial contexts. Advocates of cursive writing (Early, 1973; Strauss & Lehtinen, 1947) believe that it results in fewer reversals because of its rhythmic flow and that it helps the student to perceive whole words. Also, transference problems are avoided if writing begins with cursive. However, some educators (Hildreth, 1963; Templin, 1960; Western, 1977) question the need for teaching cursive writing at all and believe that manuscript writing meets the adult needs of speed and legibility.

After reviewing research data concerning manuscript versus cursive writing, Graham and Weintraub (1996) note a lack of evidence clearly favoring one script over another. Moreover, Graham, Berninger, and Weintraub (1998) found no difference between the legibility or handwriting speed of students who used manuscript to write versus those who used cursive. However, for students with learning disabilities, Graham (1999) recommends that handwriting instruction should start with traditional manuscript letters for three reasons: (1) when most children come to kindergarten or first grade, they already know how to write some manuscript letters; (2) manuscript may be easier to learn than cursive writing; and (3) when manuscript has been mastered, it can be written as fast as and possibly even more legibly than cursive. Because good arguments are presented on all sides, the teacher should assess each individual situation. It may be best to teach students the form of writing used by their peers. Also, many young children want to learn cursive writing because older peers and adults use it. Regardless of the type of writing instruction, to increase handwriting efficiency, most students inevitably develop their own style (e.g., using more curved lines, combining letters from different scripts, and eliminating or modifying some connecting strokes). Thus, the student should be allowed to choose the preferred mode of writing for tests and expressive writing.

Mann et al. (1992) suggest the following method for transitional writing.

1. The word is printed in manuscript.
2. The letters are connected with a dotted line in color pencil.
3. The student traces over the manuscript letter and the connecting dotted line to form the cursive writing.

The teacher may begin teaching transitional writing with the easier letters and add more difficult letters one at a time. Certain letters must be taught specifically, such as *b, e, f, k, r, s,* and *z.* Also, when the letter *n* is in the middle or end of a word, enough space must be allowed in front of it for the additional hump needed in the cursive formation of the letter.

Hagin (1983) recommends a simplified handwriting method based on the vertical downstroke rather than the diagonal slant necessary for cursive writing. Manuscript letters are used as a bridge to a simplified writing style with connections between letters made by the natural movement to the next vertical downstroke. Thus, the simplicity of manuscript writing is combined with the speed of cursive writing. In this approach, letter forms are taught through four simple motifs (i.e., waves, pearls, wheels, and arrows) that serve as foundations for lowercase letters. After practice at the chalkboard, lessons at the desk include tracing letters on an acetate sheet placed over the printed model, trying to write the letter on the acetate without a model, matching the written letter with the model to determine whether more practice is needed, and providing a permanent record of the letters worked on in that lesson, which later can be compared with previous writing samples during self-evaluation. This approach may help students who have difficulty learning conventional cursive writing patterns.

In addition, the *D'Nealian Handwriting* program (Thurber, 1999) is designed to facilitate the transition from manuscript to cursive handwriting. In this program, manuscript letters are slanted and formed with a continuous stroke, and cursive letters are simplified. Additional information on the program is included in the section on commercial handwriting programs.

Cursive Writing

Cursive writing instruction usually begins in the second or third grade, depending upon the skill development of the individual student. In cursive writing the strokes are connected, and fine motor coordination is required to perform many precise movements. The basic strokes in cursive writing are the slant stroke (✓), understroke (✓), downstroke (✓), and overstroke (✓). Figure 10.3 presents the formation of uppercase and lowercase cursive letters and numbers, with arrows and numbering to indicate stroke direction and sequence. Usually letters are taught in isolation and then connecting strokes are introduced. Lowercase cursive letters are taught first; uppercase letters are taught later because they are used far less often in writing and are more difficult to form.

Many of the same techniques used to teach manuscript writing, such as the multisensory approach and fading model, also can be used in cursive writing instruction. For example, Wolf (2005) presents a sample lesson for teaching a cursive letter using a multisensory framework. The proper slant in cursive writing is achieved by slanting the paper and pulling strokes to the body, as described in the discussion of readiness skills.

Wolf (2005) recommends grouping cursive letters according to the four basic approach strokes, which always begin on the baseline and move from left to

FIGURE 10.3
Formation of uppercase and lowercase cursive letters and numbers

Source: From *Zaner-Bloser Handwriting,* 2003, Columbus, OH: Zaner-Bloser. Reprinted by permission.

right (i.e., "swing up, stop"—*i, p, w, r, t, u, j, s;* "push up and over"—*m, v, y, n, x, z;* "curve under, over, stop"—*a, d, o, c, g, q;* and "curve way up, loop left—*b, h, l, f, k, e*). Also, Hanover (1983) suggests teaching cursive writing by grouping letters into families based on similar strokes. The letter families include the following:

- The *e* family (taught first): *e, l, h, f, b, k*
- The family with a handle to which the next letter is attached: *b, o, v, w*
- The family that emphasizes the correct formation of hump-shaped letters: *n, s, y*
- The *c* family: *c, a, d, o, q, g*
- The hump family: *n, m, v, y, x*
- The family with tails in the back: *f, q*
- The family with tails in the front: *g, p, y, z*

Tompkins (2009) notes that the most troublesome cursive letter is the lowercase *r* and that other lowercase letters that students frequently form incorrectly are *k, p,* and *z.* Moreover, Newland (1932) notes that four specific letters—*a, e, r,* and *t*—contribute to a large number of errors in cursive writing. The teacher should give special attention to the proper formation of these letters and also should focus upon the types of errors that result in common illegibilities. Table 10.3 illustrates numerous common illegibilities in forming cursive letters. After students have learned how to form cursive letters accurately, they should be taught to connect letters and to write simple words.

Typewriting and Keyboarding

The typewriter or computer may be a viable alternative for students who have severe fine motor problems or who write very slowly. In addition to simplified motor movements, advantages of typing include faster speed, the highest degree of legibility, and inherent motivation. Also, the ability to type facilitates the use of computers and word processing programs, and keyboarding is becoming a basic literacy skill because word processing is a standard method of writing. However, it should be noted that for most youngsters, keyboarding is actually slower than handwriting, and the development of keyboarding skills occurs about 2 years later than handwriting skills (Connelly, Gee, & Walsh, 2007). Students need explicit instruction in keyboarding to make effective use of this accommodation.

In the primary grades, students can become familiar with the keyboard and learn basic hand positioning and proper posture. Formal instruction usually begins in the third or fourth grade, when students can learn touch-typing and begin to develop speed and accuracy

TABLE 10.3
Common illegibilities in handwriting

a	like u	*ce*	m	like n	*m*
a	like o	*a*	n	like u	*u*
a	like ce	*ce*	o	like a	*a*
b	like li	*li*	o	like v	*v*
be	like l	*bl*	p	like js	*fs*
b	like k	*k*	r	like n	*n*
c	like e	*e*	r	like v	*v*
c	like a	*a*	r	like l	*l*
d	like cl	*cl*	t	like l	*u*
e	like i	*i*	t	like l	*l*
g	like y	*y*	u	like ee	*ee*
g	like q	*g*	u	like ei	*ei*
l	like e	*e*	w	like n	*m*
h	like li	*li*	w	like ue	*ue*
h	like k	*k*	w	like eu	*eu*
k	like ls	*ls*	x	like v	*v*
m	like w	*w*	y	like ij	*y*

through practice. Selected computer programs available for teaching touch-typing and keyboarding include *JumpStart Typing* (Knowledge Adventure), *Mavis Beacon Teaches Typing* (Broderbund), *PAWS in Typing Town!* (SRA), *Stickybear Typing* (Optimum Resource), and *Type to Learn* (Sunburst). Moreover, NEO (produced by AlphaSmart) is a keyboard that weighs less than 2 pounds and is designed to let students take notes, practice keyboarding, and store reports, essays, or e-mails without having to use a computer. Later, students can transfer text into any application on a computer or directly into a printer.

HANDWRITING ACTIVITIES

Numerous activities and materials enhance the development of handwriting skills. This section presents handwriting activities in three areas: readiness skills, manuscript writing, and cursive writing.

Readiness Activities

- Use body exercises to practice movements such as up and down, left and right, and forward and backward. For example, give the student the following instructions: "Raise your writing hand *up* in the air"; "Make a long straight line with your hand going from *top to bottom*"; "Make a *circle* with your hand in front of your body"; "Make a long line from *left to right*."
- Have the student use scissors to cut out shapes or large letter forms. Coloring activities also can help the student develop muscle control and learn how to use a writing instrument and stay within lines. The student can be asked to color shapes or objects before cutting them out with scissors.
- In seatwork activities, have the student practice making circles by drawing balls, balloons, funny faces, coins, and apples.
- To help develop fine motor skills and strengthen hand and finger muscles, have the student participate in finger painting and clay modeling activities. Squeezing and molding clay is good exercise. Also, the student can be required to manipulate small objects such as nuts and bolts, cubes, buttons, and bottle caps.
- Have the student connect dots in dot-to-dot activities to form geometric shapes or pictures. To help the student draw straight lines, place dots in a straight line and gradually increase the distance between them. Also, circles and squares can be completed in dot-to-dot fashion. The figures eventually can include actual letters.
- Use chalkboard activities for exercises in copying, dot-to-dot, and completing incomplete figures. The large, free movements made at the chalkboard help develop muscles of the shoulders, arms, hands, and fingers. Academic skills also can be practiced through the use of a chalkboard. A student's lack of handwriting development should not be allowed to impede the completion of academic tasks.
- Have the student practice writing movements in a tray filled with a layer of sand, salt, or cornmeal.
- Provide tracing activities by making dark-line figures (such as shapes, letters, numbers, and objects) on white paper and covering the paper with a sheet of onionskin on which the student can trace. Also, the student can trace on sheets of acetate or plastic with a felt-tip pen or a grease pencil. Clipboards can be used to hold tracing paper in its place, or the paper can be taped to the student's desk.
- Make stencils and templates of shapes, numbers, and letters from plastic, styrofoam, or cardboard. Paper clip the stencil to a piece of paper so the student can write or trace the forms. When the stencil or template is removed, the student can view the figure. Lakeshore Learning Materials produces sets of see-through alphabet stencils to provide hands-on writing practice.
- To help develop visual discrimination, give the student pictures containing hidden uppercase and lowercase manuscript letters. Ask the student to locate the hidden letters. A variation of this activity is to have the student produce a picture from a letter (e.g., draw an umbrella from the letter *f*). Also, the student can be asked to think of things that different letters resemble.

Manuscript Writing Activities

- Give the student an individual copy of the alphabet and numbers 0 to 9 to use at a desk. Zaner-Bloser produces self-adhesive manuscript and cursive alphabet strips that have arrows showing correct stroke directions and sequence. Encourage the student to refer to the model during writing exercises.
- Have the student form manuscript letters and numbers by drawing between the double lines of outlined letters.

- Use paper with squares to help the student maintain correct letter size and proportion.

- Have the student form manuscript letters and numbers by completing slash-to-slash and dot-to-dot activities.

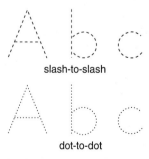

- On pieces of oaktag, print uppercase letters and their corresponding lowercase letters and cut the pair to

261

form puzzle pieces. Have the student match the uppercase and lowercase manuscript pairs. This activity is self-correcting, because the puzzle pieces will fit together only if the letters correspond to each other. A variation of this activity would be to match manuscript letters to corresponding cursive letters.

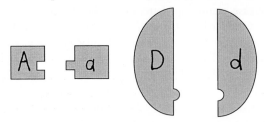

- Use arrows to provide the student with direction clues in forming specific letters.

- Use color dots to indicate the starting and stopping positions for each letter stroke.

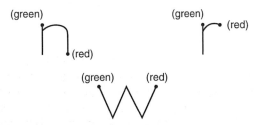

Also, letters can be color-coded to indicate their position with respect to the line on which the student is writing. Letters that stay on the line are written in green (i.e., grass letters), letters that extend above the line are written in blue (i.e., sky letters), and letters that extend below the line are written in brown (i.e., root letters). Eventually the color cueing is faded.

- Have the student who reverses letters (such as *b* and *d*) form an association to facilitate memory of the direction of the letters. For example, the student can learn to associate lowercase *b* with uppercase *B* or identify the stem of *b* with the left hand. Another method is to have the student raise the left arm in front of the body and grasp the left elbow with the right hand. When looking down, the student will see the letter *b*. For all reversal problems, encourage the student to refer to an alphabet taped to the desk before writing the letter.

- Have the student announce strokes while writing certain letters. For example:

  m—"short line down; back up, around, and down; back up, around, and down"

  h—"tall line down, back up halfway, around, and down"

  i—"short line down, dot"

- On balsa wood, print manuscript letters and numbers and use a razor-sharp knife to groove out the wood deep enough for a pencil to follow. Have the student practice forming letters by tracing the letters and numbers with a pencil in the grooves.

- For the student who has difficulty with letter size and staying on the baseline, make a cardboard frame with a rectangular piece cut out of the frame. The student writes within the window area and thus has a barrier that stops the downward movement. Frames can be made for words with one-line, two-line, and three-line letters.

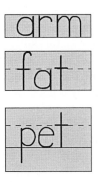

Masking tape also can be used on paper to represent baselines and margins.

- For the student who has difficulty with spacing between letters within a single word and between words themselves, make an underlay sheet. Trace over the lines on a piece of notebook paper with a felt-tip pen; then draw vertical lines on the paper one letter distance apart. This makes squares the appropriate size for letters. The student places notebook paper on top of the underlay sheet. The student can see the felt-tip pen lines and use them as cues for proper spacing. One letter is written in each square, and one square is skipped between words. An additional method for the student who has difficulty remembering to space between words involves giving the student a two-leaded pencil that has red on one end and blue on the other end. Have the student alternate colors each time a new word is written (e.g., first a blue word, then red, then blue, and so on). Changing the color serves as a cue to stop and space properly. Also, if words run together, have the student place the index finger of the nonwriting hand at the end of each word to allow space for the next word.

Cursive Writing Activities

- To help the student see the similarity of manuscript and cursive letters, make a chart that has manuscript and corresponding cursive letters written next to each other.
- Make dot-to-dot cursive letters and have the student form the letter by connecting the dots. The dots gradually can be faded so that the student is required to complete the letter.
- Have the student trace a cursive letter several times. Gradually reduce the cues to only the first stroke and have the student finish forming the letter.

- Use arrows and color-coded dots to show direction of the stroke and beginning and ending points.

- Have the student practice letters with similar movement patterns at the same time (e.g., the beginning stroke for the cursive lowercase letters *b, h, l, f, k,* and *e* is curve up and loop left). Also, the student can say the strokes of the letters while writing (e.g., *c*—"curve up and over, stop; trace back, down around; turn out").
- After the student has learned the correct letter formation of cursive writing, provide practice activities that involve meaningful writing. For example, on the chalkboard write an informative letter to parents and have the student copy it, giving special attention to good handwriting.

COMMERCIAL HANDWRITING PROGRAMS

Many commercial programs and materials are available to develop or improve handwriting skills. The following selected programs and materials may help students who have difficulty with handwriting.

Cursive Writing Program

The *Cursive Writing Program*, developed by S. Miller and S. Engelmann (published by SRA), consists of 140 developmentally sequenced lessons designed to teach cursive writing to students who have mastered manuscript writing. The program teaches how to form letters, create words, write sentences, and improve writing speed and accuracy. The 20-minute lessons feature a simplified orthography that reduces unnecessary frills, slant arrows to assist in slanting the paper correctly, slant bars to prompt proper spacing, exercises to correct errors, and an emphasis on high-frequency word and letter combinations. Points are awarded following the successful completion of a series of exercises. The materials include a teacher presentation book and a student workbook of practice exercises.

D'Nealian Handwriting

The *D'Nealian Handwriting* program (Thurber, 2008) is designed to simplify handwriting for students in kindergarten through sixth grade. The forms of most lowercase manuscript letters are the basic forms of the corresponding cursive letters (i.e., 87 percent of D'Nealian lowercase letters are the same as their cursive version). Each manuscript letter is made with a continuous stroke, except the dotted letters *i* and *j* and the crossed letters *f, t,* and *x*. The transition to cursive writing is simplified because the addition of simple joining strokes is all that is needed for all but five letters (i.e., *f, r, s, v,* and *z*). The program, which offers a multisensory approach to teaching handwriting, includes student workbooks and teacher editions for each grade level; alphabet teaching cards and self-sticking alphabet desk tapes are available.

Handwriting Without Tears

Handwriting Without Tears (available from PCI Education) is a multisensory handwriting program that features a developmentally based learning sequence. The program method uses unique, custom-designed materials designed to eliminate problems with letter formation, reversals, neatness, sentence spacing, and cursive connections. The readiness materials for students in kindergarten focus on fine and gross motor skill development and the recognition of shapes and letters. Students use a set of 26 word pieces to build uppercase letters on a foam mat before they practice writing the letters. A slate chalkboard also is used for practice. The program includes five student workbooks: *Letter and Numbers for Me*, used at the kindergarten level, focuses on correct letter and number formation; *My Printing Book*, which most often is used in first grade, features double lines and presents letters in groups by formation; *Printing Power*, which most often is used in second grade, uses smaller-size printing and students write words, sentences, and simple paragraphs; *Cursive Handwriting*, which most often is used in third grade, features a simple vertical style with easy connections for cursive writing and includes step-by-step illustrations; and *Cursive Success*, which most often is used in fourth grade and above, uses smaller-size letters, larger words, and more advanced sentences. Printing display cards and cursive display cards show uppercase and lowercase versions of all the letters. Notebooks also are available for student pictures, copying, or creative writing.

Zaner-Bloser Handwriting

Zaner-Bloser Handwriting (published by Zaner-Bloser) contains a series of eight workbooks for students in kindergarten through sixth grade. For seventh- and eighth-grade students there is an additional book that focuses on self-instruction in handwriting. Manuscript writing is introduced in kindergarten, and cursive writing is introduced in second or third grade. Letters are introduced systematically, and elements of legibility (i.e., shape, size, spacing, and slant) are emphasized. Each three-step lesson (i.e., present the letter, write and evaluate, and apply) takes about 15 minutes, and corrective strategies and coaching hints are provided to correct common problems. In addition to a teacher edition for each grade level, there are supportive materials available such as practice masters and wall charts of the manuscript and cursive alphabets and handwriting positions.

WRITTEN EXPRESSION SKILLS

Written expression, one of the highest forms of communication, reflects a person's level of comprehension, concept development, and abstraction. It is how an individual organizes ideas to convey a message. Whereas handwriting is primarily a visual-motor task that includes copying, tracing, and writing from dictation, written expression requires complex thought processes.

The skill of written expression usually is not acquired until an individual has had extensive experience with reading, spelling, and verbal expression. Problems in written expression may not be diagnosed until the upper elementary school years, when the student is required to use the various language components in written composition and emphasis is placed upon refining writing skills. However, difficulties in written expression may be as prevalent as reading disabilities, and efforts should be made to identify students earlier. In a recent epidemiological study on the prevalence of writing disabilities (Katusic, Colligan, Weaver, & Barbaresi, 2009), the presence of a written language disorder ranged from 6.9 percent to 14.7 percent depending on the formula applied. It is interesting to note that, regardless of the formula used, boys were two to three times more likely to be affected, and 25 percent of the students with a writing disability did not have a co-existing reading disability. Likewise, in a clinical study, Mayes and Calhoun (2007) found that a learning disability in written expression was the most common form of a learning disability identified.

Hochman (2005) notes that students with learning disabilities may not only have difficulties with spelling, word retrieval, and syntax, but also may have a limited vocabulary, weak organizational skills, and an inability to distinguish essential from nonessential information and to put ideas or facts in a logical order. Written expression is the most complex language arts skill and is based on listening, talking, handwriting, reading, and spelling. Thus, it generally is not stressed in instructional programs for learners with mild disabilities. Teachers tend instead to focus on the skills prerequisite to written expression. However, as the student acquires those prerequisite skills, instruction in written expression is warranted.

In a comparison of the written products of students with learning disabilities and their normally achieving peers in fourth, eighth, and eleventh grades, Houck and Billingsley (1989) found that students with learning disabilities write fewer words and sentences, write more words per sentence, produce fewer words with seven letters or more and fewer sentence fragments, and have a higher percentage of capitalization and spelling errors. Dockrell, Lindsay, Connelly, and Mackie (2007) found that students with specific language impairments also struggle with writing. Specifically, at ages 8 and 10 years, students with language impairments produce short texts with poor sentence structure and inadequate organization and presentation of ideas. Research indicates that the writing difficulties of students with learning disabilities result from problems with basic text production skills, scant knowledge about writing, and difficulties with planning and revising text (Graham, Harris, MacArthur, & Schwartz, 1991). Additional areas of difficulty may include idea generation, maturity of themes, organization, grammar, and theme development (Smith, 2004). Thus, the writing difficulties of students with learning disabilities range from the mechanical aspects of writing (i.e., spelling, grammar, punctuation, and capitalization) to the content aspects of writing (i.e., idea generation, organization, and coherence).

In general, written language instruction for students with mild disabilities can be improved by increasing the time allocated for instruction, teaching written language as an integrated process, and coordinating written language activities with different content areas. Students with learning problems experience a variety of writing problems, and the treatment of these difficulties in a systematic program requires that teachers at all levels allocate instructional time for writing and the review and editing of written products.

ASSESSMENT OF WRITTEN EXPRESSION SKILLS

Assessment of written expression yields information about a student's skill level and aids in instructional planning. The teacher can assess various components of written expression to determine deficiencies. A scope and sequence chart for written expression is provided in the Appendix according to the areas of capitalization and punctuation, written composition, and creative expression. It provides a skill hierarchy by grade level for assessing skills that need to be taught. Assessment techniques are presented in two broad categories: formal standardized and criterion-referenced tests and informal techniques specifically related to instructional planning. As noted by Bashir and Singer (2009), due to the complexity of writing and text production processes, no single test, informal technique, or writing sample can assess all the components of the writing process; thus, for an effective assessment of writing, it is essential to use various methods and sources of information.

Formal Written Expression Assessment

Many standardized survey tests of academic achievement contain some measure of written language. The most frequently assessed areas include word usage, mechanics, and grammar. However, with the shift in emphasis from the product to the process of writing, newer tests include measures of composition. Standardized achievement tests that evaluate written expression skills include the following:

- *Metropolitan Achievement Tests—Eighth Edition: Writing Test (2000b)*: assesses content and development, organizational strategies, word choice, sentence formation, usage, and writing mechanics
- *Peabody Individual Achievement Test—Revised (Markwardt, 1998)*: assesses prewriting skills for students in kindergarten through first grade and written language skills for students in second through twelfth grade
- *Stanford Writing Assessment Program—Third Edition (1996)*: assesses ideas and development; organization, unity, and coherence; word choice; sentences and paragraphs; grammar and usage; and mechanics in four modes of writing (i.e., descriptive, narrative, expository, and persuasive)
- *TerraNova, Third Edition (2007)*: assesses language skills including sentence structure, writing strategies, and editing skills

Standardized diagnostic tests of written expression and criterion-referenced tests of writing skills provide additional basic information useful in planning instruction. Measures of writing skills can focus on composition skills such as organization, vocabulary, style, and originality of ideas, as well as mechanical aspects including syntax, usage, capitalization, punctuation,

spelling, and handwriting. Table 10.4 describes diagnostic and criterion-referenced tests of written expression.

Informal Written Expression Assessment

The teacher begins informal assessment of written expression by obtaining representative writing samples from the student and analyzing them to determine specific weaknesses. Five major components of written expression that can be analyzed are fluency, syntax, vocabulary, structure, and content. Also, curriculum-based measurement is an informal assessment technique that uses a set of standardized procedures to assess written expression skills. Finally, portfolio assessment can give the teacher insight into student growth. In addition to these informal assessment techniques that focus on the content and form of the written product, the teacher can use observation and interviews to assess the process the student engages in to produce a written product.

Fluency *Fluency* is defined as quantity of verbal output and refers to the number of words written. Isaacson (2007) notes a significant correlation between fluency and other measures of writing skills. For example, a student who is able to write more words is likely to be more fluent in generating ideas as well. Fluency is related to age and includes sentence length and complexity. The average sentence length in a composition is determined by counting the number of words and the number of sentences in the composition and dividing the number of words by the number of sentences. In general, longer sentences indicate a more mature writing style. Cartwright (1968) found that the average sentence length of an 8-year-old is eight words and that this length increases one word per year through age 13. He suggests that any deviation of more than two words indicates a problem.

Syntax *Syntax* refers to construction of sentences or the way words are put together to form phrases, clauses, and sentences. Frequent written syntax errors of students with mild disabilities include word omissions, distorted word order, incorrect verb and pronoun usage, incorrect word endings, and lack of punctuation. Thomas, Englert, and Gregg (1987) found that a large proportion of the syntactic errors of older writers with learning disabilities is attributed to errors in which the student generates a phrase instead of a sentence.

One method for assessing syntactic maturity is counting the number of sentences that fall into several different categories: incomplete (i.e., fragment), simple, compound, and complex. The percentage of usage of the four sentence types in a writing sample can be computed to provide comparisons and a record of the student's

Test	Age/Grade Level

Diagnostic Tests

Oral and Written Language Scales: Written Expression (Carrow-Woolfolk, 1995b) — 5–21 years

This test measures writing skills including the use of conventions (i.e., handwriting, spelling, and punctuation), the use of syntactical forms (i.e., modifiers, phrases, and sentence structures), and the ability to communicate meaningfully (i.e., relevance, cohesiveness, and organization). The examiner presents a variety of developmentally appropriate writing prompts, either verbally, with pictures, or in print, and the student writes responses in a booklet. The scale can be administered individually or in small groups in about 15 to 25 minutes and yields standard scores, grade and age equivalents, and percentiles. Computer scoring with the ASSIST system provides a score profile, score narrative, suggested exercises, and a descriptive analysis.

Test of Early Written Language—2 (Hresko, Herron, & Peak, 1996) — 3–10 years

The test includes two forms, each with a Basic Writing and a Contextual Writing subtest. The Basic Writing subtest measures the student's ability in areas such as spelling, capitalization, punctuation, sentence construction, and metacognitive knowledge. The Contextual Writing subtest measures the student's ability to construct a story when provided with a picture prompt, and the subtest focuses on areas such as story format, cohesion, thematic maturity, ideation, and story structure. Administration time is 30 to 45 minutes; the test provides standard score quotient, percentiles, and age equivalents.

Test of Written Expression (McGhee, Bryant, Larsen, & Rivera, 1995) — 6–14 years

The test includes a series of items that assess different skills associated with writing. Also, the student reads or hears a prepared story starter and uses it as a stimulus for writing an essay. The essay is scored by evaluating performance across ideation, vocabulary, grammar, capitalization, punctuation, and spelling. The test can be administered to individuals or groups and yields standard scores and percentile ranks.

Test of Written Language—4 (Hammill & Larsen, 2009a) — 9–17 years

The test assesses conceptual, linguistic, and conventional components of written language by having the student look at pictures and write a complete story based on the pictures. Subtests with spontaneous formats (i.e., essay analysis) include contextual conventions—measures grammar, punctuation, and spelling; and story construction—measures plot, character development, and general composition. Subtests with contrived formats include vocabulary—measures word usage; spelling—measures ability to form letters into words; punctuation—measures punctuation and capitalization; logical sentences—measures ability to write conceptually sound sentences; and sentence combining—measures syntax. Two equivalent forms are available, and percentile ranks, scaled scores, and age and grade equivalents are provided for the subtests. The test can be administered to individuals or groups in 60 to 90 minutes.

Writing Process Test (Warden & Hutchinson, 1992) — 8–19 years

This direct measure of writing, which requires the student to plan, write, and revise an original composition, assesses both the written product and the writing process. The six development scales assess purpose and focus, audience, vocabulary, style and tone, support and development, and organization and coherence. The four fluency scales assess sentence structure and variety, grammar and usage, capitalization and punctuation, and spelling. The test can be administered individually or in groups in about 45 minutes, and analytic scoring provides diagnostic information.

Criterion-Referenced Test

Brigance Comprehensive Inventory of Basic Skills—II (Brigance, 2010a) — K–ninth grade

The writing section assesses the student's strengths and weaknesses in the following areas: writing manuscript and cursive lowercase and uppercase letters in sequence, quality of manuscript and cursive writing, writing personal data, capitalization, punctuation, addressing envelopes, writing a personal letter, writing a letter requesting information, and writing a customer-complaint letter. A student record book tracks assessments administered, correct and incorrect responses, progress since last testing, and instructional objectives. Also, an optional online management system tracks individual and group progress and generates reports.

progress. Compound and complex sentences are considered to be more advanced forms of expression than are simple sentences. Generally, the number of compound and complex sentences increases with age and the use of incomplete and simple sentences decreases.

Another common measure of syntax is T-unit length (i.e., words per terminable unit). A T-unit is the shortest grammatically correct segment that a passage can be divided into without creating fragments (Hunt, 1965). Thus, a sentence consisting of one T-unit may have subordinate clauses, phrases, or modifiers embedded within it, whereas a compound sentence is two T-units because it can be divided into two grammatically complete units without leaving fragments. The ratio of the average T-unit length is a total count of the number of words written divided by the number of T-units present. A general increase in the average T-unit length occurs throughout the school years.

Vocabulary *Vocabulary* refers to the originality or maturity in the student's choice of words and the variety of words used in the written task. The student's vocabulary should increase with age and experience; however, Scott and Windsor (2000) report that, compared with their chronologically aged peers, students with language learning disabilities use fewer different words in their writing. Some students with learning problems have adequate vocabularies for their age range but have assigned a small number of attributes to each word (Wiig & Secord, 1994).

The Type Token Ratio (TTR) (W. Johnson, 1944) is a measure of vocabulary that is the ratio of different words used (i.e., types) to the total number of words used (i.e., tokens). A high TTR represents few word repetitions. For example, the sentence *The two boys went fishing in Noonan's Lake early yesterday morning* has a high TTR (1.0)—11 total words are used, and all 11 words are different. In contrast, the sentence *The little girl saw the little boy in the little house* has a fairly low TTR (.63)—11 total words are used, but only 7 of these words are different. A low TTR may indicate inadequate vocabulary for the written expression task. This technique also can be used for measuring long compositions; however, the number of different vocabulary words decreases as the total number of words in the composition increases. When comparing several compositions produced by the same student or by different students, the same type of sample should be taken. For example, the first 50 words should be used from each composition instead of selecting the first 50 words from some compositions and the last 50 words from others.

Vocabulary variety also can be assessed by using the index of diversification. This refers to the average number of words between each occurrence of the most frequently used word in the writing sample. One assessment method is to divide the total number of words in the sample by the number of times *the* is used, or by the number of times the word used most often appears. The higher the value of the index, the more diverse is the vocabulary. In general, diversity of vocabulary is viewed as an indicator of mature writing.

Finally, vocabulary can be assessed by measuring the number of unusual words. For this assessment, a sample of the student's written expression should be compared with a list of words frequently used by other students—for example, the Dolch (1955, 1960) word list. The number of words the student uses that do not appear on the list indicates the extent of the student's vocabulary.

Structure *Structure* includes the mechanical aspects of writing, such as punctuation, capitalization, and rules of grammar. The Grammatical-Correctness Ratio (GCR) (Stuckless & Marks, 1966) can be used to assess structure. The GCR quickly analyzes the total number of the student's grammatical errors. To obtain the GCR, a sample of the student's writing (e.g., 50 words from a composition) is scored by counting the number of grammatical errors. The error count is subtracted from 50, and this difference is divided by 50. To obtain a percentage score, this last number is multiplied by 100. Because the final result can be displayed as a percentage, GCRs can be calculated for any number of words and still yield a score that can be compared with the student's previous scores. A GCR score also can be calculated for one specific type of grammatical error or for errors in punctuation or capitalization.

Structure also can be assessed by tabulating types of errors in the writing sample. The frequency of specific errors can be recorded to target individual weaknesses. An error analysis chart (presented in Figure 10.4) provides a profile of errors in writing structure. Errors in spelling (e.g., phonetic and nonphonetic misspellings) and handwriting (e.g., problems with letter formation, spacing, consistent slant, line quality, alignment, letter size, and fluency) also can be noted.

In addition to spontaneous writing samples, teacher-made test items also can be used to analyze specific elements of writing structure. Written compositions may not include enough opportunities for various errors to occur. For example, the student may write only sentences that contain grammatical forms or punctuation the student knows how to use. Thus, to assess punctuation, the teacher can devise several

FIGURE 10.4
Writing structure error analysis chart

Sample Elicitation Procedure: _____ _____ Date: _____ Students' Names	Verbs		Pro-nouns		Words					Sen-tences		Capitals			Punctuation						
	Agreement	Tense	Personal	Possessive	Additions	Substitutions	Modifiers	Negatives	Plurals	Incomplete	Run-on	Beginning sentences	Proper nouns	Inappropriate use	Period	Comma	Question mark	Apostrophe	Colon	Other	Total

short sentences in which punctuation rules are used. The sentences can be dictated for the student to write correctly or can be presented unpunctuated for the student to correct. For example:

- School starts at 8 30
- Twenty two boys are in the class
- Dr Goodman lives in Richmond Virginia
- His birthday is January 31 1943
- Blaze our Golden Retriever had four puppies

Content Content, the fifth component of written expression, can be divided into accuracy, ideas, and organization (Cartwright, 1968). Thus, aspects of content that should be considered in assessment include idea generation, coherence of all parts of the composition to the topic or theme, organization or logical sequence, and awareness of audience. The nature of the written assignment determines how the different factors should be weighed. For example, accuracy carries more weight when the written exercise is a presentation of historical facts. One assessment method involves rating each factor on a scale from 0 to 10. A 10 in ideas would indicate that the ideas were pertinent to the topic and represented a high degree of originality, and a 0 would indicate lack of originality or understanding of the task. Some youngsters with learning problems may have limited ideas

because of lack of experience, while others may have the ideas but not the ability to sequence them in logical order. Thomas et al. (1987) found that in expository writing (i.e., the ability to explain or provide information on a topic), students with learning disabilities frequently terminate their text prematurely, thus indicating difficulty in producing multiple factual statements about familiar topics. In addition, these students tend to repeat information and generate irrelevant items pertaining to the topic. Wallace, Larsen, and Elksnin (1992) note that evaluation of content is especially difficult because the ideas and levels of abstraction contained in the written product depend on the student's intelligence, language experiences, culture, background, and interests.

Profile of Components By examining a student's writing sample, such as an autobiography, the teacher can determine which skills need to be introduced or remediated and which have been acquired. Poteet (1980) developed the *Checklist of Written Expression Skills*, containing four areas: penmanship, spelling, grammar (i.e., capitalization, punctuation, and syntax), and ideation (i.e., type of writing, substance, productivity, comprehensibility, reality, and style). Likewise, Weiner (1980) devised the *Diagnostic Evaluation of Writing Skills*, consisting of the following areas: graphic (i.e., visual features), orthographic (i.e., spelling), phonologic (i.e., sound components), syntactic (i.e., grammatical), semantic (i.e., meaning), and self-monitoring.

A profile of the assessment of written expression components is presented in Figure 10.5. The profile can be used with an individual student or an entire class to record strengths and weaknesses and student progress. Although some interpretation is required, profiles standardize observations and thus yield a more reliable and valid informal assessment. Also, determining the error patterns associated with each writing component is essential for instructional planning.

Curriculum-Based Measurement Curriculum-based measurement allows the teacher to collect data routinely and monitor instructional progress. Writing skills are assessed through repeated 3-minute writing samples using stimulus story starters or topic sentences. The use of 3-minute writing samples represents a general assessment of writing skills rather than a diagnostic assessment of specific writing deficits; however, it allows the teacher to base instructional decisions on direct, repeated measurement.

In general, about 30 story starters are needed for a year of measurement. When the story starters are written on note cards, the teacher can write the students' initials on the back so that the story starter is not used

by the same student more than three times. The measures can be administered to a group of students rather than individually. Tindal and Marston (1990) present three evaluation strategies: (1) holistic scoring—raters review compositions within the same distribution to determine an overall impression and assign a value from a rating scale; (2) analytical scoring—writing samples are scored on specific qualities or traits (such as organization, ideas, wording, and punctuation) with operational definitions and criteria to aid the judgment process; and (3) primary-trait scoring—raters focus on the degree of consistency in the purpose of writing according to defined traits (such as creativity and persuasion). Parker, Tindal, and Hasbrouck (1991) indicate that holistic judgments appear to be reliable in a writing process approach when there is no judgment of improvement over time; however, in a subskill mastery instructional approach, the most useful indexes for monitoring writing progress are number of correct word sequences, mean length of correct word sequences, and percent of legible words written. Moreover, Espin et al. (2000) note that research at the elementary level supports the validity of three curriculum-based measurement scoring metrics as indicators of students' general performance in written expression: the number of words written, the number of words spelled correctly,

FIGURE 10.5
Profile of written expression components

Students' Names	Fluency	Syntax		Vocabulary			Structure		Content		
	Average Sentence Length	Sentence Type Variety	T-Unit Length	Type Token Ratio	Index of Diversi-fication	Number of Unusual Words	Gram-matical Correct-ness Ratio	Type of Errors	Accuracy Rating	Ideas Rating	Organi-zational Rating

and the number of correct word sequences written. At the middle school level, Espin et al. report that the most reliable and valid predictor of student writing proficiency is correct minus incorrect word sequences.

McMaster and Campbell (2008) evaluated the technical features of curriculum-based writing measures using various types of prompts or writing tasks, including passage copying, picture prompts, narrative prompts, and expository prompts with third, fifth, and seventh graders. They found that different tasks yield better reliability and validity based on grade level. For third-grade students, copying tasks are effective for screening, and narrative prompts with a 3- or 5-minute writing time are the most viable for monitoring progress across time. For fifth-grade students, both narrative and expository prompts with a 3- or 5-minute writing time result in acceptable reliability and validity. Finally, for seventh-grade students, the most viable prompt for monitoring progress is the use of expository prompts with a 5- or 7-minute writing time.

To implement curriculum-based measurement of written expression, the teacher can use the steps in Table 10.5, which includes the administration and scoring procedures of written expression measures as well as procedures for determining long-range goals and graphing data. These procedures may be modified for use with expository or picture prompts, which also are technically adequate for monitoring students' progress in written expression. Figure 10.6 presents a graph of curriculum-based measurement data and illustrates a long-range goal or aim line. Deno, Mirkin, and Wesson (1984) provide the following mean scores for average students: first grade—14.7 words in 3 minutes, second grade—27.8 words, third grade—36.6 words, fourth grade—40.9 words, fifth grade—49.1 words, and sixth grade—53.3 words.

In addition to increasing student motivation to write, monitoring written expression provides the teacher with information that encourages sensitive and relevant instructional modifications. For example, for a student who has great difficulty with written expression, the following modifications are useful.

- Allow the student to copy selected words during the 3-minute timing to help get the student started. Selected words may center around a theme (e.g., marine life), word family (e.g., *cat, fat, rat, bat*), or a special interest (e.g., sports).

TABLE 10.5

Procedures for administering and scoring written expression measures, determining long-range goals, and graphing data

Step 1:	To establish a baseline, provide each student with a lined sheet of paper and the same story starter or topic sentence on any 3 days of a given week. Discuss writing ideas, and then have the students write for a 3-minute period. Collect the papers after 3 minutes.
Step 2:	Count the number of words or letter sequences representing words written after the given story starter or topic sentence. Ignore misspellings, content, punctuation, and organization. Continue with this procedure for 2 more days, giving two new story starters or topic sentences during the week. Plot the student's scores on a graph (see Figure 10.6).
Step 3:	Find the median score from the three baseline scores. This is the middle number when ranked from lowest to highest.
Step 4:	Compute the long-range goal. Count the number of weeks left in the school year or semester. Multiply the number of weeks by 2.0 (i.e., rate of growth), and add the median score obtained from the baseline week (e.g., 21 weeks × 2.0 = 42; 42 + 14 [baseline median] = 56 [goal]).
Step 5:	Plot the goal data point on the graph on the line for the last week. Draw the aim line connecting the baseline median data point to the goal data point. This represents the line that the student's performance should follow as the student progresses through the school year.
Step 6:	Beginning with the first week after the baseline, measure student performance two times each week. On 2 different days in a given week, provide the students with a different story starter or topic sentence. Following a brief discussion of the story starter or topic, tell the students to write for 3 minutes and say "Begin writing."
Step 7:	After the 3-minute period, say "Stop." Collect the papers and count the number of words or letter sequences representing words written after the given story starter or topic sentence.
Step 8:	Plot each score on the graph in the space corresponding with the day and week. Connect the data points.
Step 9:	Continue with this procedure throughout the year. Analyze student error patterns for information regarding writing deficits of individual students. Use this information in planning instructional lessons. Graphs also can be made to monitor progress on specific skills (e.g., capitalization, punctuation, and subject-verb agreement).

FIGURE 10.6

A curriculum-based measurement graph illustrating an aim line

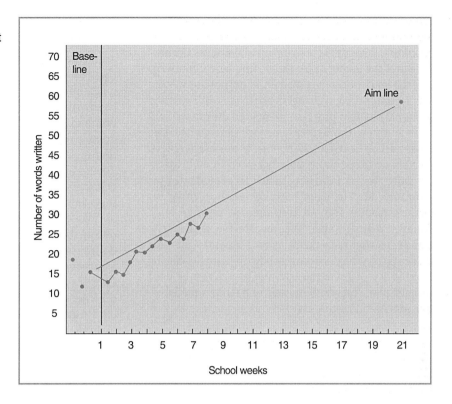

- Provide story starters that include sentences with missing words or letters. Have the student write words or letters for the blanks. Count the number of correct words that student input helped create.
- Periodically introduce specific written expression interventions (e.g., capitalization, punctuation, compound words, and contractions) and note whether student writings reflect content from instructional lessons.
- Use experiences (e.g., science project, class visitor, field trip, or movie) for story starters.
- If the student is unable to produce sentences, have the student generate words. Score the number of legible words.

Portfolio Assessment The student can compile a collection of self-produced written words to reflect efforts, progress, and achievements in written expression. Writing portfolios may include notes, diagrams, drafts, and the final version of a writing project, as well as diverse entries such as journal writings, letters, poems, or essays. The student's self-assessment of the writings as well as the teacher's notes about the writings and the student as a writer also may be included. Thus, the student is a participant in the assessment process and learns to set goals and evaluate learning in progress. In addition to drafts, revisions, and the final product of

writing samples, Olinghouse (2009) notes that other possible items that may be included in writing portfolios are planning, revising, and editing sheets; teacher and peer evaluations, curriculum-based measurement probes, and student goal-setting and monitoring forms.

For use as an assessment tool to chart student learning, performance, and growth, *Writing Portfolios* (published by Curriculum Associates) are available in two levels: primary for students in first through third grade and intermediate for students in fourth through eighth grade. These three-pocket student writing portfolios are divided into the areas of prewriting, drafting and revising, and publishing and editing, and they contain information and tips about writing as a process. The teacher's guide includes prewriting activities, writing conference forms, editing and proofreading checklists, and self-evaluations.

Observations and Interviews During classroom writing tasks, the teacher can observe the student's actions during various stages of the writing process. For example, the teacher can note whether the student spends time thinking and making notes during the prewriting stage as well as how much time is spent reviewing and rewriting during the revising stage. Also, interviews conducted before the student begins to write or after writing is completed can provide information on nonobservable aspects of writing. For example, before writing, the student can be asked to tell about the assignment and discuss the purpose and the audience for the writing task. After writing, the student can be asked if the purpose in writing was accomplished, if changes were made while writing, and what thought processes were used during writing.

In addition, the *Written Language Observation Scale* (Hammill & Larsen, 2009b) is a norm-referenced 25-item teachers' rating scale that can be used to assess the daily classroom writing behaviors of students ages 9 through 17. The items relate to specific writing behaviors readily seen in instructional settings (e.g., "Enjoys writing" and "Uses acceptable grammar"), and the teacher rates the items on a 5-point scale. The student's observed writing behaviors usually can be rated in 5 to 10 minutes, and the results can be used to help plan interventions and to monitor the effectiveness of interventions.

TEACHING WRITTEN EXPRESSION SKILLS

Written expression primarily is concerned with creative writing but also includes functional writing. *Creative writing* is the personal expression of thoughts and experiences in a unique manner, as in poetry, story writing, and personal narratives. Narrative compositions relate events in chronological order and can be written in either the first person (i.e., as a participant) or third person (i.e., as an observer). This form of writing is taught most frequently to young or less skilled writers. *Functional writing* focuses on conveying information in a structured form, such as writing answers to chapter questions, social and business letters, invitations, reports and essays, or minutes of a meeting. Usually in fourth grade and beyond, students are given assignments that require expository writing, which explains or informs (i.e., provides an example or describes a process). Three types of expository writing include persuasive writing, which presents a point of view to a specific audience; descriptive writing, which describes experiences about people, places, things, and thoughts; and compare-and-contrast compositions, which highlight similarities and differences among two or more people, places, things, ideas, or experiences. The writing program for students with learning problems should include a range of writing experiences in both creative and functional writing. The student must learn to organize thoughts logically and follow the proper mechanics of writing (such as punctuation and capitalization) to communicate clearly and accurately.

Process Approach to Writing

In teaching writing, the emphasis has shifted from the product of writing to the process involved in creating that product. The product approach focuses primarily on grammar, spelling, capitalization, punctuation, and handwriting. The process approach stresses meaning first and then skills in the context of meaning. Students work through five writing stages: prewriting, drafting, revising, editing, and publishing (Tompkins, 2009). The stages merge and interact as students develop and refine their compositions. For example, there can be interaction between prewriting and drafting (i.e., the writer can plan and draft simultaneously), between drafting and revising, and between drafting and editing. An overview of the writing stages is presented in Table 10.6. Moreover, Scott and Vitale (2003) present a writing process wheel that displays the five writing stages in a circular fashion and includes appropriate activities for each stage.

In the process approach, the student independently selects a writing topic and rehearses or brainstorms before writing. After drafting and redrafting for several days to get ideas in written form, the student discusses the work with the teacher or peers and then revises and edits. Revising refers to reworking the text in a way that alters its content or structure, whereas editing is the process of correcting errors in grammar, syntax, punctuation, and spelling. Finally, the product is published or shared with the audience for whom the student has written. For young children and for students with few successful writing experiences, the writing process can be shortened to the three stages of prewriting, drafting, and publishing, and the revising and editing stages can be added as the students become more fluent writers. Thus, in the process approach to writing, the teacher's role shifts from merely assigning and assessing a product to working with the student throughout the writing process. By working through the writing process, the student develops problem-solving skills, critical thinking skills, and a positive self-image.

Isaacson (2007) discusses four characteristics of the process approach in which the teacher introduces the student to the entire process of writing, from initial idea generation to editing of the final draft.

1. *The process should be modeled.* In a prewriting discussion, the teacher should model planning strategies by raising questions on the topic and demonstrate ways to organize information (e.g., charts or semantic maps). The teacher can model how to convert planning notes into written sentences by thinking aloud while performing the

TABLE 10.6
Overview of writing stages

Prewriting Stage

Select a topic for the written piece.

Consider the purpose for writing (e.g., to inform, describe, entertain, or persuade).

Identify the audience for whom the writing is intended (e.g., classmates, parents, businesspersons, or publishers).

Choose an appropriate form for the composition based on purpose and audience (e.g., story, report, poem, script, or letter).

Engage in rehearsal activities to gather and organize ideas for writing (e.g., drawing, talking, reading, interviewing, brainstorming ideas, and clustering main ideas and details).

Participate in writing a collaborative or group composition with the teacher so that the teacher can model or demonstrate the writing process and clarify questions and misconceptions.

Drafting Stage

Write a rough draft, skipping every other line and allowing adequate space for revising.

Emphasize content rather than mechanics, grammar, and spelling.

Revising Stage

Reread the rough draft and make changes by adding, substituting, deleting, and moving text.

Share the composition in writing groups in which listeners respond with compliments as well as comments and suggestions about how to improve the composition.

Make revisions based on feedback from the writing group by crossing out, drawing arrows, and writing in the space left between the writing lines.

Editing Stage

Focus on mechanics, including capitalization, punctuation, spelling, sentence structure, word usage, and formatting considerations.

Proofread the composition by reading word-by-word and hunting for errors (e.g., spelling, capitalization, and punctuation) rather than reading for meaning, and insert proofreading symbols to indicate needed changes.

Correct as many mechanical errors as possible and, if necessary, use a dictionary or have a conference with the teacher for instruction or a minilesson on a needed skill.

Publishing Stage

Publish the writing in an appropriate form (e.g., make a covered booklet or contribute to a newspaper or magazine).

Share the finished composition with classmates or appropriate audiences by reading it aloud in the class "author's chair" or displaying the writing on a bulletin board.

Source: From *Students with Learning Disabilities* (p. 318), 7th ed., by C. D. Mercer and P. C. Pullen, 2009, Upper Saddle River, NJ: Merrill/Pearson. Copyright 2009 by Pearson Education. Reprinted by permission.

task. Finally, the teacher should model reviewing and revising strategies and show that first drafts differ greatly from the finished copy.

2. *The process can be collaborative.* Collaboration can involve either the teacher or other students in activities such as brainstorming ideas, contributing and organizing information, giving constructive feedback, and editing for mechanical errors. Writing groups can be formed to share writing and develop ideas; a peer team is also a good arrangement for editing written work.

3. *The process can be prompted.* The teacher can assist by prompting the steps of the writing process or helping with writing decisions. For example, a prompt procedure in the prewriting stage can begin

with having students list isolated words related to a topic. In the editing stage the teacher can write a code in the margin for a type of error (e.g., *sp* for spelling, *v* for verb form, and *cap* for capitalization) to prompt the student to find and correct errors.

4. *The process should become self-initiated and self-monitored.* The teacher can show the student specific writing strategies and ideas for self-instructional statements, such as a sentence-writing strategy (e.g., PENS), a paragraph-writing strategy (e.g., PLEASE), an error-monitoring strategy (e.g., COPS), and acronyms for use in writing opinion papers (e.g., DARE), fictional narratives (e.g., SPACE), and themes (e.g., TOWER), which are presented later in this chapter.

Graham and Harris (1994) note three advantages of the process approach to writing: (1) student writing is frequent and meaningful, (2) environmental conditions are created that foster self-regulated learning, and (3) the integrative nature of learning in literacy development is emphasized. However, they note that these benefits may be weakened "by an overreliance on incidental learning and by a lack of emphasis on the mechanics of writing" (p. 275). Without careful instruction, many students with learning problems do not develop effective strategies and skills for writing. Thus, such students' writing may be improved by integrating the process approach to writing with skill-oriented instruction.

For students with academic learning problems, Kame'enui and Simmons (1990) recommend a skills-based approach to expressive writing instruction in which basic writing skills are developed systematically for advanced exercises and applications. In this approach, the instructional emphasis focuses first on the writing and editing phases, which are teacher-directed, and then on the process of planning, which is student-initiated. Thus, the student learns to rely on writing skills when planning more complex written products. Moreover, in a review of research on effective writing instruction, Stein and Dixon (2001) report that instructional programs for teaching writing are most likely to be effective if they incorporate the following features: big ideas (e.g., text structures, the writing process, and collaboration); explicit instruction on strategies that specify basic steps in a cognitive process and that can be applied to various examples; gradually diminished use of scaffolded instruction (e.g., providing written prompts, asking leading questions, and giving detailed feedback) to support students as they are learning; and review that is adequate, distributed, cumulative, and varied.

Graham and Harris (1988) offer ten instructional recommendations for developing an effective writing program for students with written expression difficulty.

1. *Allocate time for writing instruction.* A sufficient amount of time should be allocated to writing instruction (e.g., four times per week) because students can learn and develop as writers only by writing.
2. *Expose students to a broad range of writing tasks.* Students should participate in writing activities that present highly structured problem-solving situations as well as activities that involve self-selected and expressive writing.
3. *Create a social climate conducive to writing development.* The teacher needs to be encouraging in a nonthreatening environment and should try to develop a sense of community by promoting student sharing and collaboration.
4. *Integrate writing with other academic subjects.* Writing should be integrated with other language arts activities to increase writing and develop skills.
5. *Aid students in developing the processes central to effective writing.* The composition process can be divided into a series of discrete stages (e.g., prewrite, write, and rewrite), and students can be taught appropriate task-specific and metacognitive strategies (e.g., self-instructional strategy training).
6. *Automatize skills for getting language onto paper.* The teacher should provide direct instruction in mechanical skills and sentence and paragraph production, or the mechanical requirements of composing can be removed through the use of oral dictation.
7. *Help students develop explicit knowledge about the characteristics of good writing.* Students should be given exposure to the characteristics of various literary compositions either through reading or teacher presentation of written or live models that incorporate a specific skill or style, or students should receive direct instruction in the structured elements representative of a particular literary style.
8. *Help students develop the skills and abilities to carry out more sophisticated composing processes.* Three methods for the development of more mature composing processes include conferences during which teachers act as collaborators, procedural facilitation in which external support is provided, and self-instructional strategy training.
9. *Help students develop goals for improving their written products.* Goal setting and having students evaluate their own or others' written products according to specific criteria can help students accurately monitor and evaluate progress.
10. *Avoid instructional practices that do not improve students' writing performances.* Skills in grammar and usage should be developed within the context of real writing tasks, and the teacher should give specific, explanatory feedback on only one or two types of frequently occurring errors at any one time.

The following six principles are designed to prevent writing difficulties as well as to build writing skills (Graham, Harris, & Larsen, 2001).

1. *Provide effective writing instruction.* Selected features of exemplary writing instruction include

overt teacher modeling of the process of writing as well as positive attitudes toward writing; instruction covering a broad range of skills, knowledge, and strategies; daily writing with students working on a wide range of writing tasks for multiple audiences; regular teacher–student conferences concerning the current writing topic; cooperative arrangements where students help each other plan, draft, revise, edit, or publish their written work; group or individual sharing where students present written work to their peers for feedback; and integration of writing activities across the curriculum.

2. *Tailor writing instruction to meet the individual needs of students.* General adaptations include giving more attention to the development of critical skills, more explicit teaching of these skills, and more individually guided assistance. Teacher adaptations include giving additional one-to-one assistance, providing assistance with text production difficulties (e.g., allowing dictation or the use of a keyboard), and offering procedures for supporting the thinking and creative processes involved in writing (e.g., use of graphic organizers or checklists for revising). Also, tailoring writing instruction requires finding a balance between formal and informal instruction as well as between meaning, process, and form.

3. *Intervene early to provide a coherent and sustained effort to improve writing skills.* For example, instruction in handwriting or spelling can have a positive effect on compositional fluency.

4. *Expect that each student will learn to write.* The teacher should ignore negative expectations, set high but realistic expectations for each student's writing performance, and plan writing lessons so that all students can accomplish tasks successfully.

5. *Identify and address academic and nonacademic roadblocks to writing and school success.* The teacher needs to identify and address obstacles that might impede the writing development of students (e.g., difficulties with attention, low level of motivation, and maladaptive attributions).

6. *Employ technological tools that improve writing performance.* Technological tools can provide support for planning and revising through the use of outlining and semantic mapping software, multimedia applications, and prompting programs. Also, spell checkers, word prediction programs, grammar and style checkers, and speech synthesis facilitate text production.

In addition, through meta-analysis, Graham and Perin (2009) identify 11 research-supported elements of effective writing instruction for adolescent students. The identified elements include the following: teach explicit writing strategies for planning, composing, revising, and editing text; teach students how to summarize texts; use collaborative writing instructional arrangements in which students work together to plan, draft, revise, and edit their compositions; assign students specific product goals for their writing; use word processors and computers as instructional supports for writing assignments; use sentence combining to teach the use of more complex, sophisticated sentences; engage students in prewriting activities to help them generate or organize ideas for their compositions; engage students in inquiry activities in analyzing data to help them develop ideas and content for writing tasks; integrate a writing process approach into instruction, which stresses writing opportunities, writing for audiences, personalized instruction, and cycles of writing; provide students with opportunities to read, analyze, and emulate models of good writing; and use writing as a tool for learning content material.

myeducationlab

To enhance your understanding of writing instruction, go to the IRIS Center Resources section of the Topic Assessing and Teaching Literacy and Language in the MyEducationLab for your course and complete the Module entitled Improving Writing Performance: A Strategy for Writing Expository Essays.

Writing Instruction

The first step in writing instruction is to promote a positive attitude to motivate the student to write. The student must feel comfortable expressing thoughts and feelings. The teacher can promote discussion by encouraging the student to share ideas. Writing should be integrated into the entire curriculum, and the teacher should help the student understand that the purpose of writing is to communicate. Writing instruction thus begins with establishing a positive environment and then proceeds to skill development.

One of the most effective means of teaching writing skills to students with learning problems is through spontaneous written expression. Each student's writing samples can be used as a base from which to introduce instruction in various writing skills. In other words, the objective of the writing program may be for the student to express ideas and thoughts with ease. The written work then is used as the basis for skill development. Thus, spontaneous writing samples can be used to teach written expression within the context of various instructional programs such as whole language, language experience, or direct skill instruction. The teacher can provide events (e.g., discussions, field trips, and films) that stimulate topics. At first, the student may be most comfortable writing about personal material, such as family, trips, or holidays. Some students enjoy writing each day in journals about their experiences and reactions to events. Students also enjoy writing stories about pictures or intriguing titles and completing unfinished stories (i.e., story starters or story enders). Books in which the pictures are presented in sequence without text can provide stimuli for writing activities. In general, students should choose their own writing topics. When students produce their own stories, the material is meaningful to them, and they are motivated to study it. This may be especially important for adolescents, because the stories they compose are on their level of maturity. Also, writing tasks may become more meaningful when students

are allowed to work on the same writing project for an extended period of time. Students' involvement or interest in a given topic influences their ability to write about it.

To begin writing, brainstorming can generate ideas and words to be used. The student lists all words and phrases that come to mind in response to the topic. Clustering or mapping information also can help the student organize ideas for writing. The cluster or map can include main ideas, details, and examples. In these informal writing strategies and as the student begins tentatively to write ideas, content rather than mechanics is stressed.

As the student continues to be encouraged to express ideas well in writing, instruction on the more mechanical aspects of writing begins. The teacher can call attention to punctuation and capitalization errors in the student's written work, show the proper use of each skill, and point out how its use enhances meaning. Dowis and Schloss (1992) suggest using directed minilessons to teach specific skills during the writing process so that skills and content can develop concurrently. Thus, writing mechanics are explained as needed, and the student becomes aware of their importance.

The teacher should avoid excessive correction of the mechanical aspects of writing, which may discourage the student from trying to express ideas. The student may think that *how* thoughts are written is more important than *what* is written and, thus, may begin to limit vocabulary use, write only simple sentences, and avoid expressing complex and creative thoughts. Good writing models should be provided, as well as reinforcement combined with constructive criticism. The teacher should say something positive about the student's work prior to offering correction and give encouragement and praise for whatever amount the student has written. In general, more attention should be given to developing the written expression of ideas than to correcting mechanical errors. Mason (2009) notes that grammar, spelling, and handwriting skills should be focused on during the revision process rather than during prewriting, planning, or composing. Of course, students who learn to use the right punctuation, correct grammar, and good organization are likely to become better writers. Thus, balanced instruction targets both process and mechanics. Some teachers prefer to give two grades for some writing assignments—one for ideas and one for technical skills. Also, the teacher can provide selective feedback directly to a student through oral conferences.

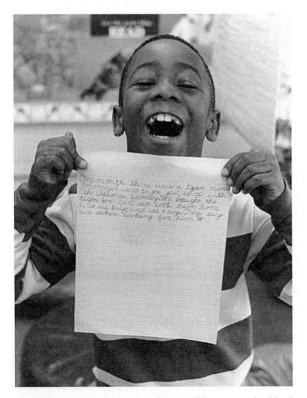

The student develops a positive self-image and critical thinking skills by working through the writing process.
Barbara Schwartz/Merrill

To help improve a student's writing, the teacher should emphasize sentence and paragraph development. The student should be helped to recognize the different syntactic patterns in which ideas can be expressed. Having the student read interesting material at his or her independent reading level will expose the student to good sentences in other people's writing and may help develop a sense of English sentence constructions. Also, through orally reading or recording stories, the student is likely to notice faulty sentence constructions. Learning to write unified, coherent paragraphs can be facilitated by activities in which the student categorizes or classifies ideas or organizes ideas in a logical sequence. An organizational framework can be provided through the use of content charts, semantic maps or webbings, and pyramid diagrams that present an overview of information and visually represent how items are related (Levy & Rosenberg, 1990). Suggesting the use of transition words (such as *finally* and *in addition to*) may help the student put compositions together.

Sentence combining (i.e., combining two simple sentences) is an effective intervention in which students learn and practice syntactic options and, thus, are prompted to write and rewrite sentences to better convey their intended meaning. Saddler (2009) provides the following possible sequence of sentence combining exercises: inserting adjectives and adverbs, producing compound subjects and objects, producing compound sentences with *and* and *but*, producing possessive nouns, producing sentences with adverbial clauses by using connecting words (e.g., *because*, *after*, *until*, and *when*), and producing sentences with relative clause. Practice exercises should include direct teacher modeling as well as support while students practice either alone or in pairs. In addition, students should have opportunities to apply sentence-combining options available in their own actual writing.

Moreover, a sentence-writing strategy designed by Schumaker and Sheldon (1998, 1999) can be used to teach the basic principles of sentence construction and expression. The student learns a set of steps and formulas that facilitates the recognition and writing of different kinds of sentences. The acronym PENS helps the student remember the steps to sentence writing.

P—*Pick* a sentence type and formula.

E—*Explore* words to fit the formula.

N—*Note* the words.

S—*Search* for verbs and subjects, and check.

PENS also is used in the paragraph-writing strategy developed at the University of Kansas Center for Research on Learning to help the student write a topic sentence, detail sentences, and a clincher sentence to form a paragraph (Schumaker & Lyerla, 1993). This learning strategy teaches the student to write various types of paragraphs: sequential (i.e., narrative or step by step), descriptive, expository, and comparison and contrast. Also, *Teaching Competence in Written Language* (Phelps-Terasaki & Phelps-Gunn, 2000) contains highly structured lessons in which the student progresses effectively in a step-by-step fashion from ideas to sentences to paragraphs.

Welch (1992) presents a metacognitive strategy to teach students to write paragraphs. The use of the following first-letter mnemonic cues the student how to complete the writing task independently.

P—*Pick* a topic, an audience, and the appropriate textual format (e.g., enumerative, comparison and contrast, or cause and effect).

L—*List* information about the topic to be used in sentence generation, ongoing evaluation, and organizational planning.

E—*Evaluate* whether the list is complete and plan how to organize the ideas that will be used to generate supporting sentences.

A—*Activate* the paragraph with a short and simple declarative topic sentence.

S—*Supply* supporting sentences based on items from the list.

E—*End* with a concluding sentence that rephrases the topic sentence, and *evaluate* the written work for errors in capitalization, punctuation, spelling, and appearance.

Welch notes that the intervention increases the student's metacognitive knowledge of the writing process involved in prewriting, planning, composing, and revising, as well as improves the student's attitude toward writing and writing instruction.

As basic writing skills are acquired, the student should learn to proofread and edit. In proofreading, the student reads the written work to identify and correct errors. To edit the work, the student can be guided to look for elements in the writing such as capitalization, sentence sense, punctuation, misspelled words, margins, and paragraph indention. At first it may be helpful for the student to proofread the work several times with a different purpose in mind each time. As the student reads the work aloud, errors such as omitted words, improper punctuation, or poor organization may be noticed. Also, peer critiquing can be used as a revision strategy, and individual conferences with the teacher in a supportive atmosphere can result in constructive editing.

To cue the student to detect four kinds of common errors, the teacher can introduce COPS questions to be used as an error-monitoring strategy (Schumaker, Nolan, & Deshler, 1985). The student is instructed to ask the following questions and look for specific errors.

C—Have I *capitalized* the first word and proper nouns?

O—How is the *overall* appearance? (i.e., look at spacing, legibility, indention of paragraphs, neatness, and complete sentences.)

P—Have I put in commas, semicolons, and end *punctuation*?

S—Have I *spelled* all the words correctly?

Periodically the teacher can review COPS and encourage each student to use it daily so that it will become a habit. The teacher can require all papers to be "COPSed" before being accepted.

Because the goal of writing is to communicate ideas, students should be encouraged to share their written work. Notebooks or books of stories the students want to share may be exchanged for reading material. Also, students can be given the opportunity to read their selections voluntarily in front of other students. Through sharing stories, students receive feedback and become more motivated to improve the quality of their work. Also, the students are provided with models to help them improve their writing.

After elementary school, greater written expression demands are placed on students. Monroe and Troia (2006) recommend two strategies for middle school students with writing difficulties. DARE is a strategy to help students compose appropriate opinion papers, while SPACE assists students in creating narratives. DARE is a first-letter mnemonic.

D—*Develop* a position statement.

A—*Add* supporting arguments.

R—*Report* and refute counter arguments.

E—*End* with a strong conclusion.

SPACE, which also is a first letter-mnemonic, prompts students to remember the elements necessary in a fictional narrative.

S—*Setting* elements

P—*Problems*

A—*Actions*

C—*Consequences*

E—*Emotions*

In a study of the effectiveness of these two first-letter mnemonics, students who received the strategy instruction improved their writing in the areas of content, organization, sentence fluency, word choice, and conventions.

At the secondary level, not only are students required to take notes during class lectures and express themselves on written tests, but they also frequently must write themes and reports. Teaching theme writing through the use of the acronym TOWER provides a structured approach (Schumaker, 2003).

T—*Think* (e.g., about content such as title, major subtopics, and details).

O—*Organize* it (i.e., topics and details).

W—*Write* a draft.

E—*Evaluate* it (i.e., look for errors by using COPS).

R—*Refine* it.

Before writing, the student can be encouraged to fill in a form with the topic at the top and ideas organized according to subtopics or paragraphs. After writing a rough draft, the student can ask COPS questions to edit the work and monitor errors.

Teachers expect written work to be reasonably neat and unconsciously may judge an assignment based on the paper's appearance. Archer and Gleason (2002) suggest a strategy using the acronym HOW to improve the appearance of written work and remind the student how the paper should look.

H—*Heading* (i.e., include name, date, subject, and page number if needed)

O—*Organized* (i.e., start on front side of paper, include a left and right margin, have at least one blank line at the top and at the bottom, and space well)

W—*Written neatly* (i.e., write words or numbers on the line, form words or numbers clearly, and neatly cross out or erase errors)

MacArthur, Schwartz, and Graham (1991) present a model for writing instruction that integrates word processing and strategy instruction into a process approach to writing. Strategy instruction in writing primarily has been used to help students learn to better internalize and regulate the cognitive activities involved in effective planning, production, and revision of text (Graham et al., 1991). To enhance the quality and quantity of writing, there should be increased focus on thinking as a critical aspect of the writing process, and writing should be practiced and applied in a variety of situations and contexts to foster generalization of these skills.

Self-Regulated Strategy Development (SRSD) instruction is an evidence-based practice that combines effective strategy instruction with effective instruction for teaching students to self-regulate learning (Baker, Chard, Ketterlin-Geller, Apichatabutra, & Doabler, 2009). Mason (2009) specifies the following stages in the development of strategy learning.

1. *Develop background knowledge.* The teacher assesses students' prior knowledge of the writing process, and remediates deficiencies prior to introducing the strategy.
2. *Discuss it.* After a discussion of what successful writers do when writing, the teacher introduces the strategy by discussing each writing step and using supporting materials (e.g., mnemonic charts with strategy steps) and writing samples to locate genre-specific elements and parts.
3. *Model it.* The teacher models each step of the writing process (i.e., generating ideas, planning, organizing, writing and saying more, and revising) by saying thoughts aloud and demonstrating how and when to use the strategy throughout the writing process.
4. *Memorize it.* Through daily individual, pair, or group practice, students memorize the strategy and demonstrate understanding of all mnemonics and each strategy step and part.
5. *Practice with guidance.* Guided practice begins with collaborative writing (i.e., teacher and students writing together), and the students practice applying the strategy to their own writing.
6. *Perform independently.* Students apply strategy steps without teacher or material support and practice writing with different formats in novel settings, and with different teachers.

In addition, throughout SRSD instruction, explicit instruction is given in four self-regulatory procedures. Students are taught to set individual and specific goals related to strategy use; students self-monitor strategy use by counting the number of strategy parts they have written; students list personal self-statements to be used before, during, and after writing; and students learn to recognize their successes in writing (i.e., self-reinforcement). In addition to the numerous strategies presented in this chapter, Harris, Graham, Mason, and Friedlander (2008) provide writing strategies validated for students with learning problems.

WRITTEN EXPRESSION ACTIVITIES

Writing skills improve through practice. Instructional activities should be chosen for each student according to particular skill deficits. This section presents numerous activities for developing skills in fluency and syntax, vocabulary, structure, and content.

Fluency and Syntax Development Activities

- Provide scrambled words from a sentence and ask the student to arrange the words to form a sentence. For example:

her quietly cat the food ate
friends yesterday Jane's left

Also, list several words and have the student write a sentence that contains all the words.

- Have the student complete partial sentences. Gradually decrease the number of words presented. For example:

Yesterday morning the dog barked at . . .
Yesterday morning the dog . . .
Yesterday morning . . .

- Provide a written paragraph that contains both incomplete and complete sentences. Ask the student to underline the subject and verb in each statement and determine which sentences are incomplete.
- Have the student practice connecting two simple sentences to make compound or complex sentences. Give a list of various words for the student to use when writing the compound or complex sentences (e.g., *but, because, or, and, after,* and *before*).
- Provide various noun and verb phrases and have the student expand each sentence by adding descriptive words. For example:

| man ate | The man in the blue shirt ate his dinner slowly. |
| dog barked | The big, black dog barked at the man with the stick. |

Also, have the student combine related sentences into one sentence. For example:

| The policeman is young. | The young policeman stopped the car. |
| The policeman stopped the car. | |

279

Yesterday the boys played a football game.	Yesterday the boys played a football game that lasted two hours.
The game lasted two hours.	

Vocabulary Development Activities

- Provide the student with a variety of experiences (e.g., taking structured field trips and listening to stories and poems) and include follow-up discussions of what was seen and heard. In addition, viewing films, listening to guest speakers, making a picture dictionary, and reading books, magazines, and newspapers may increase a person's vocabulary. Praise the student when a new vocabulary word is used appropriately.

- Discuss special interests (e.g., baseball, music, and cooking) with each student and make lists of words pertaining to the interests. New words and their definitions can be written on index cards and filed in a word box so that they can be considered for use in written compositions.

- Give the class a list of vocabulary words to learn. Write each word on a slip of paper, fold the paper slips, and place them in a decorated coffee can. The first student draws out a word and must begin a story by using the word in a sentence. Each student takes a turn drawing a word and then adds to the story by using the word. After all vocabulary words have been used, the teacher can develop an ending to the story.

- Read aloud to students daily. Choose books that have rich vocabulary and select two to four target vocabulary words to teach directly. Encourage students to use the words in their writing. For older students, use chapter books and select two to four words per chapter.

- Have each student discover new words by looking and listening for them outside the classroom (e.g., on signs, on television, and in reading material). One day each week the students can share newly found words and definitions with their classmates.

- Provide a written paragraph in which various words or phrases are underlined. Have the student substitute appropriate words or expressions in each underlined area.

- Divide the class into two teams and play a game involving synonyms and antonyms. Present a word and ask each team member, by alternating teams, to give a synonym. A point is awarded to each team for a correct response, and 5 points are taken away from the first team no longer able to give a synonym. Then the same word or a new word can be presented with the team members giving antonyms.

- Present a reading passage and ask the student to locate words or phrases according to specific questions (e.g., "Tell me the word in the second paragraph that describes Jim's car" and "Find the phrase in the last paragraph that indicates that Mary was mad at herself").

- Develop a crossword puzzle that includes words related to a single subject. Have the student complete the puzzle and then write a paragraph using all the puzzle words.

Structure Development Activities

- To help develop proper use of punctuation, cut large punctuation marks from black construction paper and pin them to students. After reviewing rules of punctuation usage, write an unpunctuated story on the chalkboard or present it on an overhead projector. As the story is read aloud, the student wearing the appropriate punctuation mark should call out its name when it is needed in the story.

- To increase awareness of the use of capital letters, have the student make a list of all capitalized words in a specific reading passage and give the reasons for their capitalization. Lists of capitalized words can be made according to various classifications, such as cities, people's names, states, and months.

- Provide a written paragraph that does not contain any capitalized words. Have the student correct the words that should be capitalized and give reasons for capitalizing them. Also, a reading selection can be dictated for the student to write, adding capitals where necessary.

- Provide written sentences that contain no capitals or punctuation and ask the student to write each sentence correctly. Also, the teacher can give a paragraph without punctuation and capitalization for the student to rewrite correctly. Tell the student the type and number of punctuation marks and capitals that must be added. To make the activity self-correcting, provide an answer key.

- Give a list of verbs or singular nouns and ask the student to write the past tense form of each verb or plural of each noun. For example:

do	*did*	child	*children*
ride	*rode*	boy	*boys*
eat	*ate*	deer	*deer*
sing	*sang*	hero	*heroes*
walk	*walked*	story	*stories*

In addition, the student can be asked to use each past tense verb or plural noun in a sentence. Sentences can be given with the verb omitted, and the student is required to choose the correct verb form from multiple-choice answers. For example:

I (*ride, rode, ridden*) the bus to school this morning.

Last Saturday we (*go, went, gone*) on a picnic.

When he (*fell, fall, fallen*), he hurt his leg.

- To work on grammatical skills, provide a paragraph with blanks that the student must complete. The blanks can require the use of different grammatical elements (e.g., plurals, verb tenses, possessive pronouns, and adverbs). A list of words for the student to use can be provided at the top of the worksheet.
- To practice editing skills, have students exchange papers and "COPS" each other's work. After the teacher reviews the material, each student can make a corrected copy of the work. The teacher also can provide a paragraph and ask the student to correct it according to the COPS questions.

Content Development Activities

- Read the beginning of an exciting story to the class and ask each student to write an ending. The students can share their work to see how others finished the story. Also, after watching a film or reading or listening to a story, the students can write a summary or abstract.
- To provide ideas for writing stories, cut three windows in a large piece of poster board. Make three circles, each of which is divided into eight sections. Write eight *Who* words on the first circle, eight

When words on the second circle, and eight *Where* words on the third circle. Attach the circles to the back of the poster board so that the writing shows through the windows (see Figure 10.7). To find a story starter, the student spins all three wheels. Also, to give the student story ideas, the poster board can contain two windows. Two circles can be made with one containing names of circus acts (or any subject) and the other containing phrases of things they might do (see Figure 10.8). The circles are attached to the poster board, and the student spins the wheels to find the subject for the composition.

- Encourage letter writing by establishing a post office in the classroom. Make mailboxes for each student out of cardboard or milk cartons. Have students write letters, invitations, birthday cards, poems, and so forth and send them through the class postal system. Also, the teacher can use the mailboxes to return papers, give feedback, or send notes to be taken home.
- On a large piece of poster board draw four circles, each divided into six sections. On each circle write characters, descriptors, settings, or actions. In the middle of each circle attach an arrow. Have the student spin all four arrows and then write a paragraph that includes the four designated elements in the story (see Figure 10.9).
- Provide a written paragraph in which the sentences are out of sequence. Have the student rewrite the paragraph by arranging the sentences in a meaningful order. Also, the student can be given a topic sentence and a closing sentence and be asked to write three detail sentences to form a paragraph.
- To provide practice in organization skills, give the student a set of cards, each containing a different

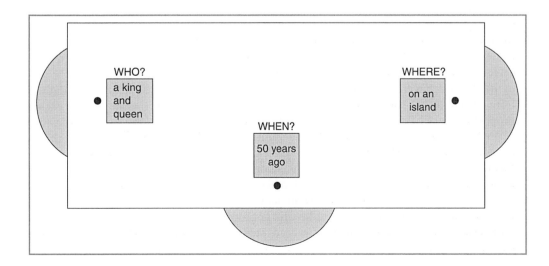

FIGURE 10.7
Who? When? Where? story board

FIGURE 10.8
Circus Acts story board

FIGURE 10.9
Write a Paragraph story board

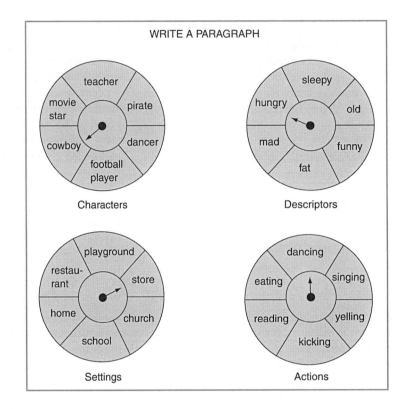

but related idea. Have the student arrange the cards in a logical sequence to form an outline and then write a composition from the outline.

- Reproduce several cartoons without captions or comic strips without the words spoken by the characters. Have the student write appropriate captions or fill in the conversations. Also, provide frames from a comic strip that the student must arrange in proper sequence before writing a comic strip story. These can be shared with the class, and the funniest or best ones can be included in a book.

- Prepare a worksheet on poems. Have the student arrange the lines in the proper order or fill in blanks with appropriate words. Then give the student an opportunity to select from various titles and compose a poem. To help the student get started, suggest a first line.

- Read a tall tale to the class and ask the students to identify parts of the story that are "tall" (i.e., exaggerated). Discuss the importance of accurate or truthful statements in compositions that are not tall tales. Have each student write a tall tale, which can be shared with the class.

- Have the student keep a daily diary in a spiral notebook. At the end of class each day, have the student write a diary entry that summarizes experiences, feelings, and activities of the day.

- Present letters like those that appear in a newspaper advice column such as *Dear Abby*. Have each student give advice by writing responses to the letters. The responses can be shared with classmates or compared with actual newspaper replies.

- Encourage students to develop a monthly class newspaper to which each student can contribute some form of writing. The newspaper can contain current events articles, interviews, short stories, poems, jokes, cartoons, comic strips, advertisements, sports articles, and want ads. Groups of students can take turns serving as editors, printers or typists, proofreaders, and distributors.

COMMERCIAL WRITTEN EXPRESSION PROGRAMS

Various published materials and programs are available for developing written expression skills. This section presents selected commercial written expression materials and programs that may be helpful to students with learning problems.

Expressive Writing 1; Expressive Writing 2

Expressive Writing 1 and *Expressive Writing 2*, developed by S. Engelmann and J. Silbert (published by SRA), present an effective writing program designed for students who read at or above the third-grade level. The program includes 50 daily 45-minute lessons that integrate sentence writing, paragraph construction, and editing skills. At the completion of the program, students are able to write, punctuate, and edit compound sentences, sentences with dependent clauses, direct quotations in dialogue form, and sentences that list items. The program, which is based on 5 years of field testing, includes a teacher presentation book and a student workbook, and students participate in self-evaluation activities. Walker, Shippen, Alberto, Houchins, and Cihak (2005) investigated the effectiveness of *Expressive Writing* for adolescent students. Curriculum-based writing measures indicated that participants improved their writing skills as a result of the program.

Language Roundup

Language Roundup (published by SRA) includes books at five levels designed to help students in second through sixth grade learn to apply specific grammar, usage, and mechanics rules in the context of writing. Instructional modeling with examples, abundant practice exercises, and formal and informal assessment are included. Self-tests allow students to assess their own understanding and identify skills that need additional practice.

Reasoning and Writing

Reasoning and Writing, developed by S. Engelmann, A. B. Arbogast, K. L. S. Davis, B. Grossen, and J. Silbert (published by SRA), is a real-life writing and thinking program that starts with templates to guide students in the process of writing and progresses to independent writing assignments. Six levels are available for students in kindergarten through twelfth grade. The beginning levels develop a foundation for reading comprehension and writing and expand thinking

skills. By the third level, students are fully engaged in the writing process, including drafting, revising, and editing for clarity. Knowledge of grammar and complex sentence structure is expanded, and students learn to vary word choice and sentence structure as well as to take notes, paraphrase, and evaluate evidence from various perspectives to form opinions. Editorial checklists allow the teacher to correct errors and provide precise instruction.

Step Up to Writing

Step Up to Writing, developed by M. E. Auman (published by Sopris West), uses multisensory strategies to teach students of all abilities to write clear, organized paragraphs, reports, and essays. Through the use of sequential steps to break down the writing process and color-coding to visualize writing organization, students learn to organize their thoughts, write topic sentences, connect key ideas with supporting details, write conclusions, and construct multiparagraph essays. Students also learn to transfer the organizational techniques taught in writing to oral presentations. Three classroom sets are available (i.e., primary for kindergarten to third grade, intermediate for third to sixth grade, and secondary for sixth to twelfth grade), and materials include reproducible student handouts and worksheets, overhead transparencies, reference guides to help students apply skills across the curriculum, and 15 posters per set. The manual also includes analytic scoring guides for expository paragraphs and narratives, writing prompts with creative topics, and a scope and sequence of skills for key strategies. Professional development training sessions for the program are available.

COMPUTER SOFTWARE PROGRAMS IN WRITTEN EXPRESSION

The use of the computer as a word processor can facilitate the teaching of writing. Word processing allows the student to correct, edit, revise, and manipulate text. Because words in a word processed document can be changed easily before the document is printed, older students may be motivated to proofread for spelling and mechanical errors as well as to make improvements in other aspects of composition writing. Moreover, the visibility of writing on a word processor can facilitate interaction between the student and teacher as well as collaborative writing activities among students and sharing of work in progress. The features of word processing programs also may help students with disabilities become more independent in their writing (Montgomery & Marks, 2006). In addition, the ability to revise without recopying, the availability of a spelling checker, and the ability to produce a neat, printed copy can be especially motivating to students with spelling or handwriting difficulties. Additional features of some computer-supported writing applications include speech synthesis, pronunciation editing, visually highlighted words, spell checking, spelling assistance, spelling modifications, insertion of correctly spelled words into document, word dictionaries, word prediction, organizational assistance, and grammar correction and tutoring (Hunt-Berg, Rankin, & Beukelman, 1994).

Outhred (1989) found that the use of a word processor with students with learning problems resulted in fewer spelling errors and the production of longer stories. Moreover, reviews of research studies indicate that the use of word processors has moderate positive effects on the quality of compositions for writing at all achievement levels but a larger effect for low achieving writers (Graham & Perin, 2007). A frequently mentioned advantage of the use of word processors is the ease of revision. However, research has not confirmed the advantages of word processors for all students with learning difficulties. For example, in a study involving fifth- and sixth-grade students with learning disabilities, MacArthur and Graham (1987) found no differences on several variables (e.g., length, quality, story structure, and mechanical errors) between handwritten stories and those composed on a word processor. Isaacson (2007) notes that before a word processor can contribute effectively to the development of writing skills, the teacher must teach the necessary subskills (such as keyboarding) and self-monitoring strategies for writing that take advantage of the computer's capabilities.

In a discussion of computer applications that have been developed to support writing, MacAuthur (2009) notes that word processing, spelling checkers, word prediction, and speech recognition offer support for transcription and revision, whereas outlining programs and concept mapping software help with the process of planning and organizing content. MacArthur also indicates that, due to the increasing importance of the internet in our society, students need to learn skills such as searching for information online, reading information critically, integrating multimedia in writing, networking, and writing online.

Internet applications also are available to support students in writing. One example is the TELE-Web software program (Technology-Enhanced Learning Environments on the Web). TELE-Web works within a web browser and provides teachers with various tools for helping students organize their writing as well as monitor their progress through archiving. Students work from a main menu that includes a writing room, a reading room, a library, and a publishing room. Within the various rooms are tools (e.g., note-taking tools and graphic organizers) for the students to plan, organize, write, and revise their products. Several studies provide evidence that the TELE-Web software is effective in improving the quality of writing for students with disabilities (Englert, Wu, & Zhao, 2005; Englert, Zhao, Dunsmore, Collings, & Wolbers, 2007).

Easy Book Deluxe (produced by Sunburst) provides students in third through eighth grade with a creative environment in which to write, design, illustrate, and print their stories in book format. Writing tools include a spell checker, a thesaurus, and editing and formatting help, and the text-to-speech feature allows students to hear their stories read aloud. Also, user-friendly desktop publishing programs such as *Print Shop* (produced by Broderbund) and *Student Writing Center* (produced by Riverdeep/Houghton Mifflin Harcourt Learning Technology) make it possible to publish in a wide range of professional-looking formats. Numerous other software programs focus on specific written expression skills. The following programs may facilitate instruction of students who have difficulty with written expression skills.

Grammar

Grammar (produced by Optimum Resource) is a multimedia, interactive program for students in third through ninth grade. The 48 lessons in six self-paced sections reinforce the parts of speech and build an awareness of sentence structure. Through the use of engaging sentences as examples, review exercises, and creative writing opportunities, activities focus on subjects and predicates (e.g., subject-verb agreement), singular and plural nouns, proper and common nouns, verbs (e.g., present, past, and future tense), direct objects, adjectives, adverbs, articles, prepositions, appositives, participles, infinitives, and gerunds. The program is open ended, and the teacher can add questions, answers, and activities. Lesson plans and supplementary materials are available.

Grammar for the Real World

In *Grammar for the Real World* (produced by Knowledge Adventure), students in fourth through twelfth grade improve their writing, grammar, and spelling skills and learn how mastering these skills is essential to everyday life. Six activities focus on the use of punctuation and capitalization, pronouns, parts of speech, verb usage, plurals, and possessives, and a variety of creative assignments at a Hollywood studio help students improve their creative writing, proofreading, and editing skills. Text-to-speech technology allows students to hear their scripts read back to them. The program also features automatic adjustment of difficulty level, and an online grammar book resource is available.

Punctuation Rules

Punctuation Rules (produced by Optimum Resource) is designed to help students in third through ninth grade improve their punctuation skills. The program features 20 common rules of punctuation in six levels with more than 350 graded multiple-choice questions. Material ranges from categories of sentences to forming possessives and covers the correct use of commas, apostrophes, question marks, colons, hyphens, quotation marks, and exclamation points. The teacher can customize the program to include additional rules and questions and can adjust the starting level and number of tries for each student. All rules and questions can be printed as practice tests or take-home sheets, and student progress can be tracked. A bilingual (i.e., English/Spanish) version also is available.

Write On! Plus

Write On! Plus (produced by Sunburst) integrates process writing, word processing, skill building, and literature with writing activities. Students use their word processors to write and illustrate letters, stories, poetry, journals, and essays while practicing grammar, sentence structure, and paragraph skills. The primary level for students in kindergarten to third grade includes *Beginning Writing Skills* (i.e., word families, cloze sentences, and sentence patterns) and *Writing with Picture Books*. The elementary titles for students in third to sixth grade are *Elementary Writing Skills* (i.e., editing skills, sentence combining techniques, and punctuation rules), *Steps to Better Writing* (i.e., prewriting, drafting, organizing, revising, and editing), and *Writing with Literature*. Students in sixth to ninth grade use *Middle School Writing Skills* (i.e., sentence development, structured paragraphs, essays, and revising), *Growing as a Writer* (i.e., writing essays, business letters, position statements, and persuasive arguments), and *Literature Studies I and II*. The high school level programs for students in ninth through twelfth grade include *High School Writing Skills* (i.e., word choice, grammar, punctuation, audience, sentence structure, and organization), *Essential Writing* (i.e., expository, descriptive, narrative, and persuasive writing; job skills; interviews; filling out forms; and follow-up), and *Responding to Great Literature*. All of the *Write On! Plus* titles can be used with the AlphaSmart keyboard and with a variety of word processors.

Assessing Math

Comstock Royalty Free Division

Mathematics affects the daily life of everyone. From a *practical* perspective, math knowledge influences many decisions, including the calculation of the effects of a salary increase, the comparison of interest rates on loans, and the figuring of unit prices. From a *civic* perspective, math concepts relate to public policies such as helping individuals understand taxation, debt, and statistics involving health, crime, ecology, and institutional budgets. In terms of *professional* parameters, math knowledge provides many individuals with the tools to succeed on the job. From a *recreational* perspective, math knowledge can be a source of relaxation and fun, including playing strategic games, keeping score in various card or sport games, or understanding probabilities in games. Finally, from a *cultural* viewpoint, math can be appreciated for its power to solve problems and predict outcomes.

Research indicates that the math deficiencies of students with learning problems emerge in the early years and continue throughout secondary school. Thus, math problems are common at all age levels. During the preschool and primary years, many young children cannot sort objects by size, match objects, understand the language of math, or grasp the concept of rational counting. During the elementary years, they have trouble with computational skills. In the middle and upper grades, students experience difficulty with fractions, decimals, percentages, and measurement. Secondary students may experience problems in these areas, but it is not uncommon for them to make errors similar to those of younger students (e.g., errors in place value and basic facts).

The mathematical knowledge of students with learning problems progresses about 1 year for every 2 years of school attendance, and the mean math scores of students with learning disabilities in the twelfth grade are at the high-5th-grade level (Cawley & Miller, 1989). Moreover, Cawley, Parmar, Yan, and Miller (1998) report that students with learning disabilities do not make systematic growth in arithmetic computation across ages (e.g., there is little evidence of growth in performance rate between the ages of 10 and 12) and they do not develop proficiency until near junior high school ages. The lack of systematic growth compared to that of their nondisabled peers is evident in scale score differences on measures such as the National Assessment of Educational Progress (NAEP). Meyen and Greer (2009) report that average scale scores on the NAEP are significantly lower for students with learning disabilities (e.g., a 21-point scale score difference at fourth grade and a 41-point scale score difference at eighth grade).

Students with learning problems in math obviously need quality instruction; however, the challenge intensifies when reforms in math education are examined. Woodward and Montague (2002) note that three forces have shaped mathematics reform: shifts in theoretical paradigms, students' disappointing levels of mathematical performance, and the impact of technological advances. *The Curriculum and Evaluation Standards for School Mathematics*, published in 1989 by the National Council of Teachers of Mathematics (NCTM), initiated reform efforts in math education, and the more recent set of standards, *Principles and Standards for School Mathematics* (NCTM, 2000), builds on the previous standards documents. Both sets of the standards reflect a high level of consensus regarding the efforts for educational reform. Spurred by poor performances of American youth on national math tests, these documents urge professionals to adopt the NCTM standards. Specifically, the NCTM calls for practitioners and researchers to embrace problem solving as the basis for math instruction and minimize meaningless rote drill and practice activities. The NCTM standards are grounded in cognitive and constructivist approaches to learning, and they emphasize developing the ability of students to think about mathematics. As noted by Maccini and Gagnon (2002), the focus of the standards is on conceptual understanding and problem solving rather than on procedural knowledge and rule-driven computation.

The National Council of Teachers of Mathematics (2000, p. 11) established six principles for mathematics instruction that address the following themes.

1. *Equity*. Excellence in mathematics education requires equity—high expectations and strong support for all students.
2. *Curriculum*. A curriculum is more than a collection of activities: It must be coherent, focused on important mathematics, and well articulated across the grades.
3. *Teaching*. Effective mathematics teaching requires understanding what students know and need to learn and then challenging and supporting them to learn it well.
4. *Learning*. Students must learn mathematics with understanding, actively building new knowledge from experience and prior knowledge.
5. *Assessment*. Assessment should support the learning of important mathematics and furnish useful information to both teachers and students.
6. *Technology*. Technology is essential in teaching and learning mathematics; it influences the mathematics that is taught and enhances students' learning.

These principles are to be applied in planning and instruction as related to the ten mathematics standards. There are five content standards (i.e., number and operations, algebra, geometry, measurement, and data analysis and probability), which represent the mathematics skills that should be taught in each grade from kindergarten to twelfth grade. In addition, there are five process standards (i.e., problem solving, reasoning and proof, communication, connections, and representation), which highlight the ways that students acquire and use content knowledge.

Upon initial inspection, the NCTM standards are appealing and their goals widely accepted. Closer inspection, however, reveals serious limitations regarding the education of students with learning problems. The following limitations center around the modest attention given to student diversity and the rigid adherence to select instructional paradigms.

- The standards make only modest reference to students with disabilities (Hofmeister, 1993; Hutchinson, 1993b; Rivera, 1993; Woodward & Montague, 2002).
- The standards are not based on replicable, validated instructional programs. Research-supported instructional programs for students with moderate to mild disabilities are especially lacking (Hofmeister, 1993; Hutchinson, 1993b; Rivera, 1993). For example, Hutchinson states that there is "no evidence to support the claim that exposure to the proposed content and experiences will result in mathematical power for students with disabilities" (p. 20).
- The standards promote a self-discovery approach for teaching math to all students. This position ignores the wealth of teaching practices generated from the process-product research (Englert, Tarrant, & Mariage, 1992) that have proven effective with students who have moderate to mild disabilities. Moreover, strict adherence to discovery learning does not recognize the promising findings being generated from educators who promote a directed discovery approach or educators who advocate a guided discovery approach.

Reforms that produce higher standards frustrate teachers and students who are struggling with current standards and traditional curricula. For example, some states have raised their secondary school diploma requirements to include the successful completion of Algebra I. Given that traditional mathematics instruction is failing many students (Carnine, 1991; Cawley, Miller, & School, 1987; Fuchs & Fuchs, 2001), not just those with learning problems, and that higher standards are being implemented, the reason for concern is apparent. Without better math instruction, these individuals will continue to face debilitating frustration, anxiety, and failure. Fortunately, the amount of research on teaching math has increased, and it is clear that appropriate curriculum and effective teaching behaviors can result in positive mathematical outcomes for students with learning problems. General and special educators must work together to ensure that students with learning problems receive adequate instruction and that the instructional reforms are sensitive to those students' unique learning and emotional needs.

DEVELOPMENT OF MATH SKILLS

Mathematics has a logical structure. The student first constructs simple relationships and then progresses to more complex tasks. As the student progresses in this ordering of math tasks, the learning of skills and content transfers from each step to the next. Hierarchies or lists of math concepts and skills that are useful in planning specific interventions are provided by Heddens and Speer (1997) and Stein, Kinder, Silbert, and Carnine (2006). The Appendix includes a scope and sequence skills list that shows a math hierarchy by skill area as well as a hierarchy of what commonly is stressed at each grade level. Although the hierarchy stops at sixth grade, these skills also apply to many adolescents with learning problems because their problems usually involve skills taught in the elementary grades. Basically, the hierarchy in the Appendix indicates the following skill introduction sequence: (1) addition and subtraction—first and second grades, (2) multiplication and division—third and fourth grades, (3) fractions—fourth and fifth grades, and (4) decimals and percentages—fifth and sixth grades.

Several cognitive factors are needed for a student to progress in mathematics. To begin formal math instruction, the student should be able to form and remember associations, understand basic relationships, and make simple generalizations. More complex cognitive factors are necessary as the student progresses from lower-level math skills to higher-order skills. Moreover, lower-level math skills must be mastered before higher-order skills can be learned; thus, the concept of *learning readiness* is important in math instruction. The National Council of Teachers of Mathematics (2000) highlights the need for students to understand basic facts and operations. Failure to acquire mastery of math facts and to understand basic concepts in beginning math instruction contributes heavily to later learning problems because fluent recall of basic math facts makes it easier to solve more complex problems in which these basic operations are embedded. Unfortunately, students with learning problems often fail to grasp basic math facts or to develop fluency in these initial skills.

Readiness for Number Instruction

Certain concepts are basic to understanding numbers: classification, ordering and seriation, one-to-one correspondence, and conservation. Mastering these concepts is necessary for learning higher-order math skills.

Classification involves a study of relationships, such as likenesses and differences. Activities include categorizing objects according to a specific property. For example, children may group buttons according to color, then size, then shape, and so on. Most children 5 to 7 years old can judge objects as being similar or dissimilar on the basis of properties such as color, shape, size, texture, and function.

Ordering is important for sequencing numbers. Many children do not understand order until they are 6 or 7 years of age. They first must understand the *topological* relation of order. When counting objects, students must order them so that each object is counted only once. The teacher can display objects in a certain order and ask students to arrange identical objects in the same order. Ordering activities include sequencing blocks in a certain pattern, lining up for lunch in a specific order, and completing "pattern" games—for example, students are given a series such as X-O-X-O-X-O-X _____ and then must determine what goes in the blank.

Topological ordering involves arranging a set of items without considering a quantity relationship between each successive item. The combination of *seriation* and *ordering*, however, involves ordering items on the basis of change in a property, such as length, size, or color. An example of a seriation task would be arranging items of various lengths in an order from shortest to longest, with each successive item being longer than the preceding item. Children 6 to 7 years old usually master ordering and seriation.

One-to-one correspondence is the basis for counting to determine how many, and is essential for mastering computation skills. It involves understanding that one object in a set is the same number as one object in a different set, whether or not characteristics are similar. If a teacher places small buttons in a glass one at a time and the students place the same number of large buttons in a glass one at a time, the glass containing the large buttons soon displays a higher stack. If students respond "Yes" to the question "Does each glass have the same number of buttons," they understand one-to-one correspondence. If they respond "No, because the buttons are higher in one glass," they are not applying one-to-one correspondence and instead are judging on the basis of sensory cues. Most children 5 to 7 years old master the one-to-one correspondence concept. Initial activities consist of matching identical objects, whereas later activities should involve different objects. Sample activities include giving one pencil to each child, matching each head with a hat, and matching a penny to each marble.

The concept of *conservation* is fundamental to later numerical reasoning. Conservation means that the quantity of an object or the number of objects in a set remains constant regardless of spatial arrangement. There are two types of conservation: quantity and number. Conservation of quantity is illustrated in the experiments of pouring identical amounts of water into a tall, thin glass and a low, wide glass and rolling a piece of clay into a ball and a long roll. Students who recognize that the amount of water or clay remains constant probably understand conservation of quantity. Conservation of number involves understanding that the number of objects in a set remains constant whether the objects are close together or spread apart. The teacher can ask students to select a spoon for each of seven plates and have them check their work by putting a spoon on each plate. The teacher then can remove the spoons, put them in a stack, and ask the students whether there is still the same number of spoons and plates. If they respond "Yes," they probably understand the concept of conservation of number. Most children master conservation between the ages of 5 and 7 years.

Several authorities consider an understanding of these concepts to be a prerequisite for formal math instruction. Many teachers in preschool through first grade directly teach to help students understand these concepts. Moreover, some authorities recommend that teachers in later grades should spot deficits in these concepts and provide remedial instruction.

Readiness for More Advanced Mathematics

Once formal math instruction begins, students must master operations and basic axioms to acquire skills in computation and problem solving. Operations are well known: addition, subtraction, multiplication, and division. Basic axioms are less familiar. Some axioms that are especially important for teaching math skills to students with learning problems are commutative property of addition, commutative property of multiplication, associative property of addition and multiplication, distributive property of multiplication over addition, and inverse operations for addition and multiplication.

Commutative Property of Addition No matter what order the same numbers are combined in, the sum remains constant:

$$a + b = b + a$$
$$3 + 4 = 4 + 3$$

Commutative Property of Multiplication Regardless of the order of the numbers being multiplied, the product remains constant:

$$a \times b = b \times a$$
$$9 \times 6 = 6 \times 9$$

Associative Property of Addition and Multiplication Regardless of grouping arrangements, the sum or product is unchanged:

Addition

$$(a + b) + c = a + (b + c)$$
$$(4 + 3) + 2 = 4 + (3 + 2)$$

Multiplication

$$(a \times b) \times c = a \times (b \times c)$$
$$(5 \times 4) \times 3 = 5 \times (4 \times 3)$$

Distributive Property of Multiplication over Addition This rule relates the two operations:

$$a(b + c) = (a \times b) + (a \times c)$$
$$5(4 + 3) = (5 \times 4) + (5 \times 3)$$

Inverse Operations These axioms relate operations that are opposite in their effects. The following equations demonstrate inverse operations:

Addition and Subtraction

$$a + b = c \quad 5 + 4 = 9$$
$$c - a = b \quad 9 - 5 = 4$$
$$c - b = a \quad 9 - 4 = 5$$

Multiplication and Division

$$a \times b = c \quad 9 \times 3 = 27$$
$$c \div a = b \quad 27 \div 9 = 3$$
$$c \div b = a \quad 27 \div 3 = 9$$

ASSESSMENT CONSIDERATIONS

The assessment of math concepts and skills follows a general-to-specific format. As presented in Figure 11.1, assessment begins with an evaluation of general math skills. At this level, a span of skills (e.g., operations, word problems, and measurement) is tested. Standardized or informal survey tests typically assess general math skills. The primary goal of assessment at this level is to identify the student's overall strengths and weaknesses. Also, standardized scores frequently are used to identify math disabilities and qualify students for special education services. Specific skill assessment usually involves standardized diagnostic tests or informal tests; however, informal tests are the preferred instruments for evaluating specific math skills. At this level, the purpose of assessment is to determine specific teaching objectives. The assessment of problem-solving skills involves examining the student's ability to solve word problems. This assessment tests the student's ability to apply mathematical concepts and operations to real-life problems and to determine problem-solving instructional objectives. Finally, diagnostic interviews and informal testing are used to evaluate the student's attitudes and feelings about learning math. These affective factors frequently provide essential insights into planning math instruction. Throughout the math assessment process (i.e., general skills to attitude assessment), types of errors, level of understanding, and mastery learning must be examined.

FIGURE 11.1
Math assessment progression

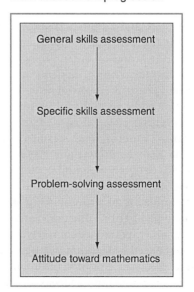

General skills assessment

Specific skills assessment

Problem-solving assessment

Attitude toward mathematics

Examining Math Errors

Although the specific error patterns of each student must be considered individually, it helps to examine some of the research regarding types of errors made by many students at different grades.

Computation   Errors in computation can be classified into four categories: random responses, basic fact error, wrong operation, and defective algorithm. Defective algorithm techniques account for most computation errors of many students. An algorithm includes the specific steps used to compute a math problem. An algorithm is defective if it does not deliver the correct answer. For example, the student who adds 24 + 16 by adding each number without regard for place value (i.e., 2 + 4 + 1 + 6 = 13) is using a defective algorithm.

In a study of multiplication and division errors made by 213 students with learning disabilities, Miller and Milam (1987) found that the majority were caused by a lack of prerequisite skills. Multiplication errors primarily resulted from a lack of knowledge of multiplication facts and inadequate addition skills. Division errors included many subtraction and multiplication errors. The most frequent error in division was failure to include the remainder in the quotient. According to Miller and Milam (p. 121),

> Many of the errors discovered in this study indicated a lack of student readiness for the type of task required. Students were evidently not being allowed to learn and practice the skills necessary for higher order operations. The implications are obvious: students *must* be allowed to learn in a stepwise fashion or they will not learn at all.

Kelly, Gersten, and Carnine (1990) examined the error patterns that secondary students with learning disabilities made in adding and multiplying fractions. They found that the errors of students instructed in a basal program primarily involved a confusion of the algorithms for addition and multiplication of fractions. However, an effective curriculum design decreased error patterns and resulted in better achievement. Kelly et al. conclude that a strong relationship exists between the number and types of errors and the curriculum.

The determination of a specific error is important because the type of error influences corrective intervention (e.g., whether the student receives place value instruction or specific algorithm instruction). Howell and Nolet (2000, p. 134) provide the following guidelines for conducting an error analysis.

1. Select an assessment or product that provides an opportunity for a variety of errors to occur.
2. Encourage the student to attempt everything and to show all work.
3. Try to get as many examples of meaningful errors as possible (by reviewing products on which the student was only partially correct or those that illustrate the student's best efforts).
4. Try to gain insight into the student's processes by noting patterns, or thought consistencies, in the errors.
5. Try to categorize errors or corrects by content, behavior, condition, or thought process (fact, concept, rule, strategy).
6. Note and categorize skills that were not displayed.
7. Ask yourself (or the student) "How did you arrive at this answer?"
8. Once you think you have found an error pattern, see if you can confirm it by predicting the sort of mistake a student will make and then giving a specific assessment to see if the pattern occurs.

Rivera and Bryant (1992) note the importance of conducting a *process assessment* to determine the strategies that students use to determine answers. Specifically, they suggest using passive and active process assessments. Passive process assessments involve examining a student's written work to determine error patterns and procedural strategies. Active process assessments involve a form of flexible student interviewing in which the student "thinks aloud" while solving an equation or word problem.

Ginsburg (1987) notes that student error patterns tend to fall into three categories: number facts, slips, and bugs. Number fact errors occur when the student has not mastered the basic facts. Slips consist of deficiencies in the execution of a readily available procedure (e.g., forgetting to add a regrouped number). Bugs are systematic procedural errors (e.g., always subtracting the smaller number from the larger number) that are made repeatedly during problem solving. To develop effective remedial programs, these error patterns must be identified.

The following common error patterns in addition, subtraction, multiplication, and division illustrate some of the computational difficulties of students with learning problems.

- The sums of the ones and tens are each recorded without regard for place value:

$$
\begin{array}{r} 83 \\ +\ 67 \\ \hline 1410 \end{array}
\qquad
\begin{array}{r} 66 \\ +\ 29 \\ \hline 815 \end{array}
$$

- All digits are added together. This pattern reflects a defective algorithm and no regard for place value:

$$
\begin{array}{r} 67 \\ +\ 31 \\ \hline 17 \end{array}
\qquad
\begin{array}{r} 58 \\ +\ 12 \\ \hline 16 \end{array}
$$

- Digits are added from left to right. When the sum is greater than 10, the unit is carried to the next column on the right. This pattern reflects no regard for place value:

$$
\begin{array}{r} {}^{21} \\ 476 \\ +\ 851 \\ \hline 148 \end{array}
\qquad
\begin{array}{r} {}^{37} \\ 753 \\ +\ 693 \\ \hline 1113 \end{array}
$$

- The smaller number is subtracted from the larger number without regard for placement of the number. The upper number (i.e., minuend) is subtracted from the lower number (i.e., subtrahend), or vice versa:

$$
\begin{array}{r} 627 \\ -\ 486 \\ \hline 261 \end{array}
\qquad
\begin{array}{r} 861 \\ -\ 489 \\ \hline 428 \end{array}
$$

- Regrouping is used when it is not required:

$$
\begin{array}{r} {}^{61} \\ 1\!\!\not{7}5 \\ -\ 54 \\ \hline 1111 \end{array}
\qquad
\begin{array}{r} {}^{71} \\ 1\!\!\not{8}5 \\ -\ 22 \\ \hline 1513 \end{array}
$$

- When regrouping is required more than once, the appropriate amount is not subtracted from the column borrowed from in the second regrouping:

$$
\begin{array}{r} {}^{511} \\ \not{6}32 \\ -\ 147 \\ \hline 495 \end{array}
\qquad
\begin{array}{r} {}^{411} \\ \not{5}23 \\ -\ 366 \\ \hline 167 \end{array}
\qquad
\begin{array}{r} {}^{411} \\ \not{5}63 \\ -\ 382 \\ \hline 181 \end{array}
$$

- The regrouped number is added to the multiplicand in the tens column prior to performing the multiplication operation:

$$
\begin{array}{r} {}^{2} \\ 17 \\ \times\ 4 \\ \hline 128 \end{array}
\qquad
\begin{array}{r} {}^{4} \\ 46 \\ \times\ 8 \\ \hline 648 \end{array}
$$

- The zero in the quotient is omitted:

$$
\begin{array}{r} 21 \\ 6\overline{)1206} \\ 1200 \\ \hline 6 \\ 6 \\ \hline \end{array}
$$

Many computational errors stem from an inadequate understanding of place value. Frequently, errors involve regrouping, a procedure that requires understanding place value. Place value is introduced in the primary grades; however, students of all ages continue to make mistakes because they do not comprehend that the same digit expresses different orders of magnitude depending on its *location* in a number. Many of the error patterns presented earlier reflect an inadequate understanding of place value.

Ashlock (2010) provides a thorough listing of computational error patterns. In addition to analyzing the student's work, one of the best ways to determine error patterns is to ask the student to show how the answer was computed. The response may offer immediate insight into the error pattern and its cause. Ashlock shares a story told by Dr. Geoffrey Matthews, organizer of the Nuffield Mathematics Teaching Project in England, about a youngster who computed correctly during one school year but missed more than half of the problems the following year. In a discussion with the student, Dr. Matthews found that the child used the rule, "Begin on the side by the piano." However, the following year the piano was on the other side of the room, and the student understandably was confused about where to start computing.

Problem Solving Recently, the problem-solving skills of students with learning problems have received much attention. Problem-solving skills primarily are assessed by means of word problems. Research indicates that many students with learning problems have trouble solving word problems, especially those categorized as more difficult (Andersson, 2008; Russell & Ginsburg, 1984; Swanson & Jerman, 2006). One way to vary the difficulty level of word problems is to vary what is unknown. For example, the following word problems increase in difficulty as a function of what is unknown.

1. Tom has 5 stickers. Pam gave him 3 more. How many stickers does Tom have now? (Result unknown)
2. Tom has 5 stickers. How many more does he need to have 7? (Change unknown)
3. Tom had some stickers. Pam gave him 3 more. Now he has 7. How many stickers did Tom have to start with? (Start unknown)

Cawley et al. (1987) found that students with math disabilities experienced difficulty with problems that include extraneous information. Montague and Bos (1990) report that students with math disabilities have difficulty predicting operations (such as multiplication or subtraction), choosing correct algorithms for multi-step problems, and correctly completing problems. Also, many students with learning problems experience difficulty in transforming word problems into mathematical representations (Hutchinson, 1993b). Fortunately, several researchers (Cawley et al., 1987; Hutchinson, 1993a; Montague, 1993) indicate that strategies exist to help such students become successful problem solvers. Moreover, researchers (Calhoon, Fuchs, & Hamlett, 2000; Fuchs, Fuchs, Eaton, Hamlett, & Karns, 2000) report that because reading deficits may lower problem-solving performance assessment scores for students with learning disabilities, the test accommodation of providing a reader, either human or computer, can yield positive effects.

Determining Level of Understanding

Students frequently memorize a fact or algorithm without understanding the concept or operation involved in the computation. This process leads to the rote memorization of information that is not comprehended. In reading, it is analogous to word calling without comprehension. An understanding of the information to be learned improves memorization and the manipulation of math concepts, operations, and axioms to solve computation and word problems. Thus, knowledge of the levels of understanding in mathematics is vital to math assessment and instruction. There are three basic levels of learning in mathematical learning experiences: *concrete, semiconcrete,* and *abstract.*

Concrete Level The concrete level involves the manipulation of objects. This level can be used to help the student relate manipulative and computational processes. At this level the learner concentrates on both the manipulated objects and the symbolic processes (e.g., 6×3) that describe the manipulations. For example, in assessing or teaching multiplication, the teacher presents the problem 5×3 and instructs the student to display the problem using objects. The student looks at the first number, 5, and forms five groups using paper plates. The student then looks at the second number, 3, and places three objects in each plate. The student counts or adds the number of objects on the plates and says "5 groups times 3 objects equals 15 objects." This procedure illustrates that the student understands at a concrete level that 5×3 means "5 groups of 3 objects equals 15 objects." Some students demonstrate their need for concrete-level activities by counting on their fingers when requested to complete simple computational problems. Concrete experiences are important for teaching and assessing skills at all levels in the math hierarchy.

Informal math assessment techniques can help the teacher determine the student's understanding of math concepts at the concrete, semiconcrete, and abstract levels. ZouZou/Shutterstock

Semiconcrete Level The semiconcrete level involves working with illustrations of items in performing math tasks. Items may include dots, lines, pictures of objects, or nonsense items. Some authorities divide this level into semiconcrete and semiabstract. *Semiconcrete* refers to using pictures of real objects; *semiabstract* involves the use of tallies. In this book, *semiconcrete* refers to both pictures and tallies. A worksheet that requires the learner to match sets of the same number of items is a semiconcrete-level task. One way to assess a student's understanding at this level is for the teacher to present a problem (such as 5×3) and ask the student to use drawings (i.e., lines and tallies) to solve the problem. The student looks at the first number, 5, and draws five horizontal lines. The student then looks at the second number, 3, and draws three tallies on each line. The student counts or adds the number of tallies on the lines and says "5 groups times 3 tallies equals 15 tallies." This procedure illustrates that the student knows at a semiconcrete level of understanding that

5 × 3 means "5 groups of 3 tallies equals 15 tallies." Many students with math learning problems need practice at this level to master a concept or fact. Often students demonstrate their reliance on this level by supplying their own graphic representations. For example, the problems 5 + 4 = ___ and 3 × 2 = ___ can be approached in the following manner:

$$\begin{array}{r} 5 \ \ ///// \\ + 4 \ \ //// \\ \hline 9 \end{array} \qquad \begin{array}{r} 3 \ \ // \\ \times 2 \ \ // \\ \hline 6 \ \ \underline{//} \end{array}$$

At the semiconcrete level, the emphasis is on developing associations between visual models and the numerical equations.

Abstract Level The abstract level involves the use of numerals. For example, in computation this level involves working only with numerals to solve math problems. Students who have difficulty in math usually need experience at the concrete and semiconcrete levels before they can use numerals meaningfully. Traditionally, assessment has focused on the abstract level; however, assessment should not be limited to this level. The goal of assessment involves determining the learner's ability to relate to math computation in a meaningful way. To do this, tasks are needed at each of the levels. Sample activities for assessing levels of understanding are presented later in this chapter.

Determining Mastery Learning

Many educators use percentage scores to determine a mastery level for a skill. In many cases these scores are a valid measure of a student's mastery learning. For some students, however, percentage scores are not sufficient for assessing mastery. Many students with learning problems produce accurate answers at a slow rate and use tedious procedures (such as counting on fingers and drawing tallies for large numbers) to compute answers without understanding the math concept or operation. Slow rates of computation are a primary problem of many students with math disabilities.

Rate is an excellent measure of mastery learning. In addition to helping with retention and higher math performance, high rates of correct responses help students complete tests on time, finish homework quickly, and keep score in games. Math rate assessment involves the use of probes (i.e., a sheet of selected math problems) that are administered under timed conditions (i.e., usually 1 minute). Scores are computed by counting the number of correct and incorrect digits written per minute. A sample probe is presented later in this chapter.

ASSESSMENT OF MATH SKILLS

Formal Math Assessment

Standardized math tests are norm referenced and provide many kinds of information (e.g., math grade level, math age score, percentile, and stanine score) based on a comparison of the student's performance with the population upon which the test was standardized. Standardized tests usually are classified into two categories: achievement (or survey) and diagnostic. Other published math measures are criterion referenced, and these tests describe performance, rather than compare it, to determine whether the student has mastered specific instructional objectives. This section presents achievement and diagnostic tests as well as criterion-referenced tests.

Achievement and Diagnostic Tests Most achievement tests include sections covering specific academic areas, such as reading, spelling, and math. Each of these specific academic areas is divided into skill areas. For example, a math section can be divided into numerical reasoning, computation, and word problems. Achievement or survey tests cover a broad range of math skills and are designed to provide an estimate of the student's general level of achievement. They yield a single score, which is compared with standardized norms and converted into standard scores or a grade- or age-equivalent score. These tests help identify students who need further assessment. Achievement tests with math subtests include the following:

- *Diagnostic Achievement Battery—3* (Newcomer, 2001): assesses mathematics reasoning and mathematics calculation
- *Kaufman Test of Educational Achievement—II* (Kaufman & Kaufman, 2004): assesses concepts, applications, numerical reasoning, and computation
- *Metropolitan Achievement Tests—Eighth Edition* (2000a): assesses mathematics computation, concepts, and problem solving
- *Peabody Individual Achievement Test—Revised* (Markwardt, 1998): assesses knowledge and application of math concepts and facts
- *Woodcock-Johnson III Normative Update Tests of Achievement* (Woodcock, McGrew, & Mather, 2007): assesses calculation, math fluency, and applied problems

In contrast to achievement tests, diagnostic tests usually cover a narrower range of content and are designed to assess the student's performance in math skill areas. Diagnostic tests aim to determine the student's strengths and weaknesses. No one diagnostic test assesses all mathematical difficulties. The examiner must decide on the purpose of the assessment and select the test that is most suited to the task. Table 11.1 presents several standardized diagnostic math tests.

Criterion-Referenced Tests Standardized tests compare one individual's score with norms, which generally does not help diagnose the student's math difficulties. However, criterion-referenced tests, which describe the student's performance in terms of criteria for specific skills, are more suited to assessing specific

TABLE 11.1
Selected diagnostic and criterion-referenced math tests

Test	Grade Levels	Areas Assessed
Diagnostic Tests		
Comprehensive Mathematical Abilities Test (Hresko, Schlieve, Herron, Swain, & Sherbenou, 2002)	2–12	Calculations, mathematical reasoning, practical applications
The test includes six core subtests that focus on addition; subtraction; multiplication; division; problem solving; and charts, tables, and graphs. There also are six supplemental subtests that provide information about higher-level mathematics ability in the areas of algebra, geometry, rational numbers, time, money, and measurement. All items represent real-world problems with current information and scenarios. The core subtests can be administered in about 40 minutes, and a computer scoring and report system is available.		
KeyMath–3: Diagnostic Assessment (Connolly, 2007)	K–12	Basic concepts, operations, applications
KeyMath–3 is a comprehensive norm-referenced measure of essential mathematical concepts and skills. It is composed of ten subtests in three areas: basic concepts (i.e., numeration, algebra, geometry, measurement, and data analysis and probability), operations (i.e., mental computation and estimation, written computation—addition and subtraction, and written computation—multiplication and division), and applications (i.e., foundations of problem solving and applied problem solving). Administration time is about 30 to 90 minutes, and two parallel forms are available. The test yields standard scores, grade and age equivalents, percentile ranks, and growth values. *KeyMath–3 ASSIST* software electronically generates normative scores and interpretive reports.		
Test of Early Mathematics Ability—3 (Ginsburg & Baroody, 2003)	Preschool–3	Concepts, counting skills, number facts, calculation
This test of early math functioning takes about 40 minutes to administer and measures informal as well as formal (i.e., school-taught) concepts and skills. Each of the two parallel forms contains 72 items that focus on numbering skills, number-comparison facility, numeral literacy, mastery of number facts, calculation skills, and understanding of concepts. Results are reported as standard scores, percentiles, or age and grade equilavents.		
Test of Mathematical Abilities—2 (Brown, Cronin, & McEntire, 1994)	3–12	Story problems, computation
In addition to information about a student's skills in two major areas (i.e., story problems and computation), the test provides related information regarding expressed attitudes toward mathematics, understanding of mathematical vocabulary used in a mathematical sense, and the application of mathematical content in real life. Administration time is 60 to 90 minutes, and results of the test can be reported in standard scores, percentiles, and grade or age equivalents.		
Criterion-Referenced Test		
Brigance Comprehensive Inventory of Basic Skills—II (Brigance, 2010a)	K–9	Numbers and operations, algebra, geometry, measurement, and data analysis and probability
This inventory provides instructional objectives and includes a recordkeeping system for monitoring progress of individual students. Also, grade placement tests in math computational skills and math problem solving are included. An option is offered that provides normed or standardized scoring.		

difficulties. Criterion-referenced survey or inventory tests usually cover several academic areas. Each of these areas is further subdivided into skill categories. Whereas survey tests locate general problem areas, diagnostic tests focus on more specific difficulties. Criterion-referenced diagnostic tests are the most suited for identifying specific math problems. Table 11.1 presents a criterion-referenced math test.

Informal Math Assessment

Informal assessment involves examining the student's daily work samples or administering teacher-constructed tests. Informal assessment is essential for the frequent monitoring of student progress and for making relevant teaching decisions regarding individual students. Such assessment enables teachers to sample specific skills through the use of numerous test items that are related directly to the math curriculum. Because the content of standardized math tests and the content of math curriculum texts have a low degree of overlap (Tindal & Marston, 1990), the practice of assessing each student's achievement within the curriculum becomes essential. With informal techniques, the teacher also can determine the student's understanding of math concepts at the concrete, semiconcrete, and abstract levels. By asking appropriate questions and listening to students' responses, teachers can assess not only whether a student can solve a particular problem but *how* the problem is solved. Informal assessment thus is the most efficient way of determining the instructional needs of individual students.

Curriculum-Based Measurement   When progress is assessed within the curriculum to measure achievement, the teacher is assured that what is being assessed is what is being taught. Curriculum-based measurement (CBM) offers the teacher a standardized set of informal assessment procedures for conducting a reliable and valid assessment of a student's achievement within the math curriculum. Two methods for developing curriculum-based measures exist, including curriculum sampling and the development of robust indicators (Foegen, Jiban, & Deno, 2007). Fuchs (2004) describes robust indicators as measures that provide information concerning a student's overall proficiency in mathematics (e.g., simple basic math facts probes). In early mathematics, the research focuses exclusively on robust indicators (Foegen et al., 2007). In elementary school and beyond, curriculum sampling is used along with robust indicators. The following description is based on a curriculum sampling model.

Curriculum-based measurement begins by assessing an entire class with a survey test of a span of appropriate skills. From the results of a survey test, a box plot (see Chapter 3) is developed for making instructional decisions. Five steps are required in developing and administering a survey test.

1. *Identify a sequence of successive skills included in the school curriculum.* Many curriculum unit tests or review tests provide a source of sequenced skills and corresponding test items. The scope and sequence list of math skills in the Appendix was developed from a review of numerous basal math programs, which indicated that there is much agreement (i.e., 90 to 95 percent) among the basal scope and sequence skills lists.

2. *Select a span of math skills to be assessed.* For a beginning fourth-grade class, it may be appropriate to administer a survey test of the computation skills covered in the third grade. This third-grade survey test would help identify students with math problems and provide some normative information to facilitate goal setting. Once a scope and sequence skills list across the grades has been identified, the teacher has a multitude of options for developing survey tests for different spans of skills. The options enable the teacher to identify instructional groups (such as high, average, and low achievers) or plan instruction for a new student.

3. *Construct or select items for each skill within the range selected.* A survey test may be used to assess computation and problem-solving skills. To maintain an adequate sample, it is a good practice to include a minimum of three items per specific skill. Table 11.2 presents a survey test of computation skills covered in a typical third-grade curriculum. This test could be used at the beginning of fourth grade to determine which students need additional teaching on third-grade skills and which are ready for fourth-grade computation skills.

4. *Administer and score the survey test.* The teacher instructs the students to solve successive problems during the 2-minute timing. In scoring, the teacher counts all correct digits. Figure 11.2 provides detailed CBM administration directions and scoring procedures.

5. *Display the results in a box plot, interpret the results, and plan instruction.* To increase the accuracy of the results, it helps to develop an alternate form of the survey test and administer both

TABLE 11.2
Survey test of third-grade computation skills

1. 476 + 200	2. 807 + 407	3. 9000 + 3010
4. 3168 + 5426	5. 4727 + 2761	6. 7964 + 385
7. 604 − 237	8. 704 − 369	9. 501 − 269
10. 7134 − 3487	11. 5094 − 4630	12. 8751 − 2683
13. 9 × 8	14. 9 × 6	15. 8 × 7
16. 7 × 8	17. 6 × 9	18. 9 × 0
19. 8 × 0	20. 6 × 1	21. 1 × 8
22. 34 × 2	23. 26 × 1	24. 31 × 8
25. 24 ÷ 3 = _____	26. 12 ÷ 2 = _____	27. 4)16̄
28. 5)16̄	29. 4)34̄	30. 7)58̄
31. 17 × 5	32. 49 × 2	33. 16 × 4
34. 82 + 4	35. 74 × 2	36. 81 × 5
37. 342 + 2	38. 637 × 1	39. 312 × 3
40. 436 + 3	41. 578 × 6	42. 638 × 7
43. 3)36̄	44. 4)44̄	45. 2)28̄
46. 3)51̄	47. 4)72̄	48. 7)84̄
49. $\frac{1}{3}$ of 6 = _____	50. $\frac{1}{4}$ of 8 = _____	51. $\frac{1}{2}$ of 12 = ____
52. $\frac{1}{2} = \frac{}{4}$	53. $\frac{2}{3} = \frac{}{6}$	54. $\frac{2}{5} = \frac{}{5}$

TABLE 11.2
(continued)

	Item Analysis of Survey Test
Problems 1–3:	Addition: With zero
Problems 3–6:	Addition: Multidigit plus multidigit
Problems 7–9:	Subtraction: Regrouping more than once with zero in minuend
Problems 10–12:	Subtraction: Four-digit numbers with regrouping
Problems 13–21:	Multiplication: Facts for 6 through 9 with 0 and 1 properties and order proportions
Problems 22–24:	Multiplication: Two-digit number times one-digit number
Problems 25–27:	Division: Facts
Problems 28–30:	Division: Two-digit number divided by one-digit number, with remainder
Problems 3–33:	Multiplication: Two-digit number times one-digit number, with tens regrouping
Problems 34–36:	Multiplication: Two-digit number times one-digit number, with hundreds regrouping
Problems 37–39:	Multiplication: Three-digit number times one-digit number, without regrouping
Problems 40–42:	Multiplication: Three-digit number times one-digit number, with regrouping
Problems 43–45:	Division: Two-digit number divided by one-digit number, without regrouping
Problems 46–48:	Division: Two-digit number divided by one-digit number, with regrouping
Problems 49–51:	Fractions: Of a whole number
Problems 52–54:	Fractions: Equivalent fractions

survey probes of the same skills. The results should be interpreted to help place students in instructional groups and to plan individual programs.

From an analysis of student performances on a span of skills, the teacher develops probes of specific skills for monitoring individual student progress. Specific skill monitoring usually involves a single skill until mastery is achieved. Although the range of proficiency rates on math skills varies in the literature, generally a rate of 40 to 60 correct digits per minute on math computation problems is appropriate for most third-grade and above students. Starlin and Starlin (1973a) suggest the following mastery rates according to specific math objectives and grade levels.

- Addition facts 0 to 9 and subtraction facts with top number 1 to 5 (grades 2 and 3): 20 to 30 correct digits per minute with two or fewer errors
- Addition facts and subtraction facts (grades 3 and 4): 40 to 60 correct digits per minute with two or fewer errors
- Two-column addition with regrouping (grades 4 and 5): 40 to 60 correct digits per minute with two or fewer errors

- Two-column subtraction with regrouping (grades 4 through 6): 40 to 60 correct digits per minute with two or fewer errors
- Multiplication facts (grades 5 and 6): 40 to 60 correct digits per minute with two or fewer errors
- Division facts (grade 6): 40 to 60 correct digits per minute with two or fewer errors

Figure 11.3 displays a student's progress on specific math skills during an 8-week period. The mastery or aim line in the chart is set at 50 correct digits per minute. The figure shows that the student has mastered two skills and has started working on a third skill.

Monitoring Basic Skills Progress: Basic Math (Fuchs, Hamlett, & Fuchs, 1999) provides a research-based standardized set of measurement and evaluation procedures so that the teacher can use curriculum-based measurement to monitor student progress in math. Reproducible tests are included for two major math areas: computation (for grades 1 through 6) and concepts and applications (for grades 2 through 6).

In addition to curriculum-based assessments that focus on math calculation and math reasoning, Jones (2001) notes that the teacher can create curriculum-based assessments to monitor student progress in

FIGURE 11.2
Curriculum-based measurement administration directions and scoring procedures for math

Administration Directions
The following steps are recommended for administering 2-minute timings to individuals or groups.
1. Select the appropriate measurement (i.e., survey test or specific skill probe) and pass it face down to students.
2. Give standardized directions at the beginning of the administration. Also, use specific instructions for different parts of some tests.
"The sheets I just passed out are math problems." If a single skill probe is used, tell the students the operation: "All problems are _____ (addition, subtraction, multiplication, or division)." If a multiple skill probe is used, say: "There are different types of problems on the sheet. There are some addition, subtraction, and multiplication problems. Look at each problem closely before you compute."
"When I say 'Begin,' turn the sheet over and answer the problems. Start with the first problem at the beginning of the first row. Touch the problem. Work across the sheet and then go to the beginning of the next row. If you are unable to do a problem, mark an X on it and go to the next problem. If you finish one page, go to the next page. Do you have any questions?
"Ready, start."
3. Monitor student work to ensure that students are following the directions (i.e., working in successive rows). Watch for students who want to skip around and do the easy problems.
4. When 2 minutes have elapsed, say: "Stop. Put your pencils down."

Scoring Procedures
1. Underline each correct digit.
2. Score numerals written in reverse form (e.g., ε for 3) as correct.
3. Score a correct digit in the proper place (column) as correct.
4. Award full points (number of digits used in solving a problem) when the student has a correct answer, even if the work is not shown.
5. If the student displays work and the answer is incorrect, give credit for each digit done correctly.
6. Do not count numerals written for regrouping purposes (i.e., carried numbers).
7. Do not count remainders of zero.
8. When an X or a zero is placed correctly as a place holder, count it as one digit correct.
9. Give credit for any correct digits, even if the problem has not been completed.
10. Total the number of correct digits and record it on the paper.

Sample Scoring of Student Copy

mathematics content reading. Graded mathematics word lists can include randomly selected new words that are introduced in each of the math grade-level textbooks, and mathematics vocabulary curriculum-based assessments can include all new mathematics words or terms introduced at each grade level in the math textbook series. Also, on mathematics comprehension curriculum-based assessments, which include four or five word problems that represent each of the basic math operations and other areas that require math reasoning abilities (e.g. money, fractions, and measurement), the student can answer

FIGURE 11.3

Chart showing a student's progress on specific math skills

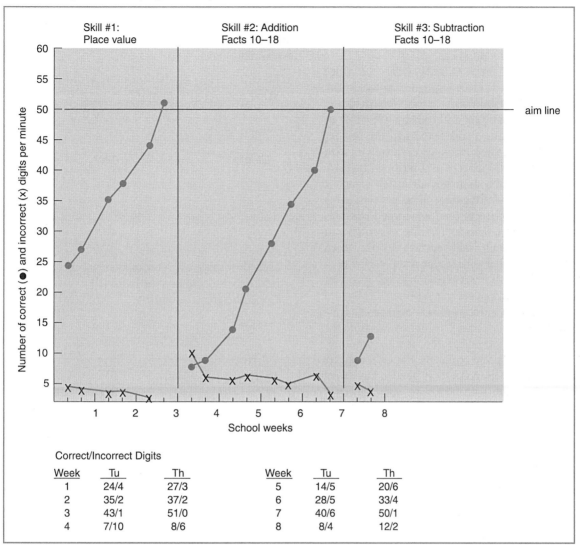

Correct/Incorrect Digits

Week	Tu	Th	Week	Tu	Th
1	24/4	27/3	5	14/5	20/6
2	35/2	37/2	6	28/5	33/4
3	43/1	51/0	7	40/6	50/1
4	7/10	8/6	8	8/4	12/2

questions about how to solve each problem, which information is relevant, and which operation(s) to use in solving the problem. Moreover, Helwig, Anderson, and Tindal (2002) report that curriculum-based measurement tasks that measure conceptual understanding of mathematics can be used to monitor student progress toward statewide math achievement standards.

Teacher-Constructed Tests Teacher-constructed tests are essential for individualizing math instruction. They enable the teacher to identify problems, determine level of understanding, and monitor progress.

The type of test the teacher selects depends, in part, on the purpose of the assessment. To identify specific problem areas, the teacher may construct a survey test with items at several levels of difficulty. There are four steps to developing and using this type of test.

1. *Select a hierarchy that includes the content area to be assessed.* This hierarchy may come from a math program series, a curriculum guide, or a textbook.
2. *Decide on the span of skills that needs to be evaluated.* Because a hierarchy includes a wide range of skills, the teacher must select which range of skills needs to be evaluated with an

individual student. This is done by examining the student's performance on published tests and by analyzing the math curriculum by grade level. In deciding on the span, the teacher should begin with items that are easy for the student and proceed to more difficult ones.

3. *Construct items for each skill within the range selected.* A survey test is designed to assess the student's computation performance within a hierarchy; thus, all items are at the abstract level. If an untimed criterion approach is used, the teacher should include three items for each skill and set 67 percent or 100 percent as a passing criterion. Most commercial tests do not adequately sample a specific skill. Including three items per skill helps to control the factor of carelessness and provides an adequate test sample. The use of probes can help assess specific skill mastery. To use timed probes, the teacher should construct one for each skill and establish the criterion in terms of correct and incorrect responses per minute. To obtain a valid performance, each probe should be administered at least three times. The highest rate from the three samples is used for determining the criterion. From analyzing proficiency rates, it appears that a useful criterion is a score of 40 to 60 correct digits per minute with no errors. Rate, however, can vary as a function of age, motor (i.e., handwriting) skills, and difficulty level of the task.

4. *Score the test and interpret the student's performance.* The teacher starts with the easiest skill items and applies the "two out of three" (i.e., 67 percent) criterion or the criterion of rate correct per minute. At the point where the criterion is not achieved, the teacher analyzes the student's performance (i.e., errors, basic fact deficit, and understanding) to determine what skill to teach. The test also can be used to monitor student progress.

In the division test presented in Figure 11.4, the skills become progressively more difficult, and three items are presented for each skill. The student is sometimes less intimidated if the items in each skill area are written on index cards. The teacher scores the student's responses under each skill and determines whether the 67 percent criterion has been obtained. Failure to reach the criterion on a skill alerts the teacher to a specific area of difficulty, which can become the target of instruction and further assessment. The type of survey test presented in Figure 11.4 is commonly used to determine what to teach. However, after becoming more

skillful in assessment and teaching, the teacher can construct other diagnostic tests to determine the student's level of understanding.

Teacher-constructed tests can include a number of formats. The following are sample skills and related assessment items.

- Identifies before or after for numbers to 10
  What numbers are missing?

  $$\_ \ 2 \ \_ \ \_ \ 5 \ \_ \ 7 \ \_ \ 9$$

  Fill in the spaces:

Before		After
—	9	—
—	7	—
—	3	—

- Identifies the greater or smaller number for numbers 0 to 100 and uses [gt] and [lt]
  Circle the greater number:

87	100		35	53		19	10

40	26		1	6		33	44

  Put > or < in the ◯:

  23 ◯ 32   8 ◯ 19   94 ◯ 76

  13 ◯ 43   43 ◯ 29   65 ◯ 59

- Identifies place value with ones and tens
  State the face value and the place value of the underlined digit:

46<u>3</u>	2<u>8</u>	48<u>4</u>3
face value —	face value —	face value —
place value —	place value —	place value —

  Complete the following:

  7 *ones*, 3 *tens* = _____

  5 *tens*, 4 *ones* = _____

  0 *tens*, 3 *ones* = _____

- Computes three two-digit numerals, sum of ones column greater than 20
  Add:

26	57	29
18	38	47
+ 47	+49	+ 36

FIGURE 11.4
Survey test: Division with whole numbers

Skill	*Criterion (score in %)*

1. Identify symbols for division by circling problems that require division.

$$\begin{array}{c}4\\+4\end{array} \qquad 6\times3 \qquad 6\times2 \qquad 7-4 \qquad \dfrac{6}{2}$$

$$4\overline{)16} \qquad 7\times4 \qquad 8\div2 \qquad \dfrac{9}{3} \qquad \begin{array}{c}13\\ \times7\end{array}$$

$$4\times1 \qquad \begin{array}{c}6\\ -2\end{array} \qquad 8\overline{)64} \qquad 6+2 \qquad 9=3$$

[ ]

2. Compute basic division facts involving 1.

$$1\overline{)8} \qquad 1\overline{)7} \qquad 1\overline{)1}$$

[ ]

3. Compute basic division facts.

$$4\overline{)36} \qquad 7\overline{)42} \qquad 8\overline{)56}$$

[ ]

4. Compute division of a nonzero number by itself.

$$7\overline{)7} \qquad 29\overline{)29} \qquad 1\overline{)1}$$

[ ]

5. Compute quotient of a one- or two-place dividend and a one-place divisor with a remainder.

$$3\overline{)7} \qquad 4\overline{)7} \qquad 2\overline{)9}$$
$$8\overline{)74} \qquad 6\overline{)39} \qquad 3\overline{)17}$$

[ ]

6. Compute quotient with expanding dividend.

$$3\overline{)9} \qquad 3\overline{)90} \qquad 3\overline{)900}$$
$$2\overline{)6} \qquad 2\overline{)60} \qquad 2\overline{)600}$$
$$4\overline{)8} \qquad 4\overline{)80} \qquad 4\overline{)800}$$

[ ]

7. Compute quotient of a three-place dividend with a one-place divisor.

$$8\overline{)638} \qquad 6\overline{)461} \qquad 3\overline{)262}$$

[ ]

8. Compute quotient of a many-place dividend with a one-place divisor.

$$7\overline{)47,864} \qquad 6\overline{)2783} \qquad 3\overline{)578,348}$$

[ ]

9. Compute quotient of a three-place dividend and a two-place divisor where divisor is a multiple of 10.

$$40\overline{)681} \qquad 30\overline{)570} \qquad 10\overline{)874}$$

[ ]

10. Compute quotient when divisors are 100, 1000, and so on.

$$100\overline{)685} \qquad 100\overline{)4360} \qquad 100\overline{)973}$$
$$1000\overline{)6487} \qquad 1000\overline{)99,490} \qquad 1000\overline{)7430}$$

[ ]
[ ]

11. Compute a quotient of a three-place dividend and a two-place divisor.

$$27\overline{)685} \qquad 39\overline{)871} \qquad 14\overline{)241}$$

[ ]

12. Compute quotient of a many-place dividend and a many-place divisor.

$$649\overline{)78,741} \qquad 3641\overline{)100,877} \qquad 247\overline{)8937}$$

[ ]

Note: When this test is administered, the directions for items 2–12 should simply state: Solve the following division problems.

- Identifies unit fraction inequalities
  Circle the numeral that represents the smaller number of each pair:

$$\frac{1}{2} \quad \frac{1}{3} \qquad \frac{1}{6} \quad \frac{1}{2} \qquad \frac{1}{4} \quad \frac{1}{3}$$

- Writes fractions in numeral form
  Write the fractional numerals for each of the shaded areas in numeral form:

_____ _____

- Identifies fraction names for 1

Fill in each ☐:

$$1 = \frac{\boxed{}}{8} \qquad 1 = \frac{\boxed{}}{77} \qquad 1 = \frac{\boxed{}}{689}$$

Teacher-made probes also can be used to identify problem areas. Mixed probes are used to locate areas that need further assessment or instruction. Figure 11.5 presents a mixed probe in addition. Each of the following categories has nine items: basic addition facts of sums-to-9 (i.e., first item and then every fourth item), two-digit number plus two-digit number with no regrouping (i.e., second item and then every fourth item), two-digit number plus one-digit number with no regrouping (i.e., third item and then every fourth item), and basic addition facts of sums-to-18 (i.e., fourth item and then every fourth item). On this probe, the student can obtain a maximum score of 63 correct digits with no errors. After three timings, a high score of 40 or more correct digits per minute with no errors is a reasonable criterion for diagnostic purposes. If the student fails to reach the criterion on a mixed probe, it is important to analyze the responses and locate the items being missed. This analysis provides the teacher with information for further assessment with specific skill probes (such as 0 to 9 facts). Also, specific skill probes can be used to monitor the student's daily progress.

Assessment at the Concrete, Semiconcrete, and Abstract Levels
As discussed earlier, learning math facts and concepts progresses through three

FIGURE 11.5
Mixed addition probe with no regrouping

4 + 3	22 +41	33 + 6	9 + 7	6 + 2	36 +62	41 + 3	6 + 5	8 + 0
53 +44	78 + 1	5 + 8	7 + 2	43 +36	82 + 5	7 + 4	5 + 3	61 +37
42 + 4	8 + 7	4 + 5	33 +52	31 + 8	9 + 9	6 + 0	24 +53	65 +24
7 + 6	5 + 2	82 +13	37 + 2	6 + 6	4 + 4	31 +18	57 +32	7 + 9

Name _____ Date _____

Correct Digits: _____

Incorrect Digits: _____

Patterns: 0–9 facts _____ /9

2D + 2D _____ /9

2D + 1D _____ /9

0–18 facts _____ /9

Comments: _____

_____

_____

levels of understanding: concrete, semiconcrete, and abstract. Most published tests consist of abstract-level items; therefore, they do not yield information on the student's understanding at the semiconcrete and concrete levels. The student's level of understanding determines whether manipulative, pictorial, or abstract experiences are appropriate. To obtain the type of information required for effective instructional planning, the teacher can construct analytical tests that focus on both identifying difficulties and determining level of understanding. Items at the concrete level involve real objects, items at the semiconcrete level use pictures or tallies, and items at the abstract level use numerals.

Assessment at the concrete level can begin either with a written problem (such as 5 + 3 = ___), with a display of objects, or with both numerals and objects. When assessment begins with a written problem, the student is instructed to read the problem and then solve it by using objects. When assessment begins with objects, the student is instructed to look at the display of objects (e.g., $\overset{\circ\circ}{\circ\circ}$ + $\overset{\circ}{\circ\circ}$ =_____) and then write the problem and solve it. When assessment begins with both numerals and objects (e.g., 5 $\overset{\circ\circ}{\circ\circ}$ + 3 $\overset{\circ}{\circ\circ}$ = ___), the student uses the objects (i.e., counts, removes, or groups) to solve the problem. The preferred sequence is to (1) use both numerals and objects, (2) use only objects and have the student write the problem, and (3) use only written problems and have the student arrange objects to solve them.

Assessment at the semiconcrete or representational level can begin with a written problem, with drawings (i.e., pictures or tallies), or with both numerals and drawings (e.g., 5 ///// + 3 /// = ___). When assessment begins with a written problem, the student is instructed to solve the problem by drawing tallies. When assessment begins with pictures or tallies, the student is instructed to write the problem and solve it. When assessment begins with both numerals and drawings, the student uses the pictures or drawings to solve the problem. The preferred sequence in assessing at the semiconcrete level is to (1) use both numerals and drawings, (2) use only drawings and have the student write the problem, and (3) use only written problems and have the student generate the drawings (i.e., tallies).

Sometimes it is not feasible to present the problem through the use of objects or drawings because the operation is not implied. For example, in arranging the objects for subtraction, only the objects or drawings for the minuend are used in beginning the problem. The subtrahend involves taking away objects from the minuend; thus, the subtrahend is not part of the original stimulus. At the abstract level, only numerals are used in presenting and solving problems. The examples that follow should help in developing analytical math tests in specific skill areas.

- Skill: Counting (1 to 5)
  Concrete level: Count the blocks.

  □ □ □ □ □

  Semiconcrete level: Circle five blocks.

  □ □ □ □ □ □ □ □

  Abstract level: Count to five and circle the number.

  1 2 3 4 5 6 7

- Skill: Addition facts (0 to 9)
  Concrete level: Write problem and sum.

  $$\overset{\square\ \square}{\underset{\square\ \square}{\square}} + \overset{\square}{\underset{\square}{\square}} =$$

  ____ + ____ = ____

  Semiconcrete level: Write problem and sum.

  $$\begin{array}{c} /\ /\ /\ /\ / \\ +\quad /\ /\ / \end{array} \qquad \begin{array}{c} \underline{\quad} \\ +\ \underline{\quad} \\ \hline \underline{\quad} \end{array}$$

  Abstract level: Write sum.

  $$\begin{array}{r} 5 \\ + 3 \\ \hline \end{array}$$

- Skill: Addition facts (0 to 18)
  Concrete level: Arrange blocks to show tens and ones, and then write sum.

  ___6___ + ___7___ = _____

  Student work:

  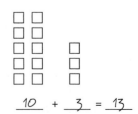

  ___10___ + ___3___ = ___13___

  Semiconcrete level: Circle tens and write sum.

Student work:

$$\underline{10} + \underline{3} = \underline{13}$$

Abstract level: Write sum.

$$\begin{array}{r} 6 \\ + 7 \\ \hline \end{array}$$

- Skill: Addition operation without regrouping
  Concrete level: Let ⬭ = 1 ten and □ = 1 one.
  Write problem and sum.

Semiconcrete level: Let ○ = 1 ten and ∘ = 1 one.
Write problem and sum.

○ ∘ ∘   _____
+ ○ ∘ ∘ ∘ ∘   + ____
                _____

Abstract level: Write sum.

$$\begin{array}{r} 12 \\ + 14 \\ \hline \end{array}$$

- Skill: Addition with regrouping ones and tens
  Concrete level: Use string to group units and
  write sum.
  Student work:

string for
regrouping
sets of 10

$$\begin{array}{r} 16 \\ + 27 \\ \hline 43 \end{array}$$

Semiconcrete level: Circle to group units and
write sum.
Student work:

$$\begin{array}{r} 16 \\ + 27 \\ \hline 43 \end{array}$$

Abstract level: Write sum.

$$\begin{array}{r} 16 \\ + 27 \\ \hline \end{array}$$

- Skill: Addition with regrouping ones, tens, and hundreds
  Concrete level: Let ▬ = 1 hundred ⬭ = 1 ten,
  and □ = 1 one. Use strings to show work. Write sum.

Student work:

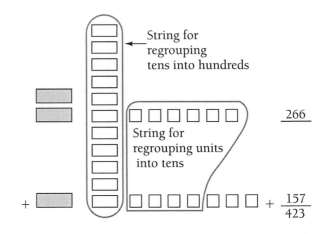

String for
regrouping
tens into hundreds

String for
regrouping units
into tens

266

$$+ \quad \frac{157}{423}$$

Semiconcrete level: Use the place value chart to show
work. Write sum.

100s	10s	1s
// /	//////	//////

= _____

Abstract level: Write sum.

$$\begin{array}{r} 266 \\ + 157 \\ \hline \end{array}$$

- Skill: Basic subtraction facts
  Concrete level: Write difference or missing addend.

■ ■ ■ ■ ■ ■ ■
$$\begin{array}{r} 7 \\ - 3 \\ \hline \end{array}$$

Student work:

$$\begin{array}{r} 7 \\ - 3 \\ \hline 4 \end{array}$$ ■ ■ ■ ■ (■ ■ ■)

moved away

Semiconcrete level: Write difference or missing
addend.

$$\begin{array}{r} 7 \\ - 3 \\ \hline \end{array}$$ ///////

Student work:

$$\begin{array}{r} 7 \\ -\ 3 \\ \hline 4 \end{array}$$ ////XXX cross out 3 to take away

Abstract level: Write difference or missing addend.

$$\begin{array}{r} 7 \\ -\ 3 \\ \hline \end{array}$$

- Skill: Subtraction operation with regrouping
  Concrete level: Rearrange blocks and use strings to show work. Write difference or missing addend.

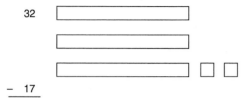

$$\begin{array}{r} -\ 17 \\ \hline \end{array}$$

Student work:

32

take ten away by moving

take ones away by moving

$$\begin{array}{r} -\ 17 \\ \hline 15 \end{array}$$ answer = 1 ten and 5 ones, or 15

Semiconcrete level: Show work with slashes. Write difference or missing addend.

Student work:

32   slash through number taken away after regrouping

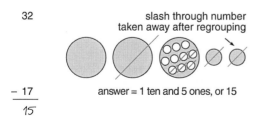

$$\begin{array}{r} -\ 17 \\ \hline 15 \end{array}$$ answer = 1 ten and 5 ones, or 15

Abstract level: Write difference or missing addend.

$$\begin{array}{r} 32 \\ -\ 17 \\ \hline \end{array}$$

- Skill: Basic multiplication facts
  Concrete level: Write product.

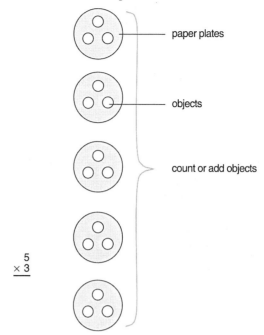

paper plates

objects

count or add objects

$$\begin{array}{r} 5 \\ \times\ 3 \\ \hline \end{array}$$

Semiconcrete level: Write product.

_____
_____
_____ groups
_____
_____

$$\begin{array}{r} 5 \\ \times\ 3 \\ \hline \end{array}$$

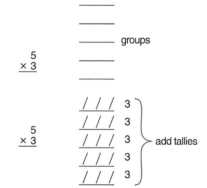

$$\begin{array}{r} 5 \\ \times\ 3 \\ \hline \end{array}$$ / / / 3
/ / / 3
/ / / 3   } add tallies
/ / / 3
/ / / 3

Abstract level: Write product.

$$\begin{array}{r} 5 \\ \times\ 3 \\ \hline \end{array}$$

- Skill: Basic division facts
  Concrete level: Use strings to show work. Write quotient.

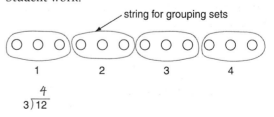

O O O O O O O O O O O O   3)12̄

Student work:

string for grouping sets

1   2   3   4

$$3\overline{)12}\ ^{4}$$

Semiconcrete level: Connect sets to show work. Write quotient.

Student work:

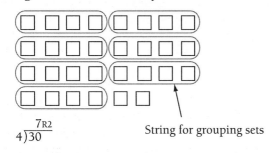

- Skill: Division with remainder
Concrete level: Given a large matrix of bloacks, figure out how many sets of 4 are in 30, or 30 ÷ 4. Use strings to show work. Write quotient.

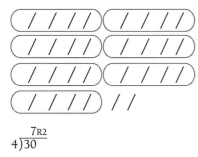

7R2
4)30   String for grouping sets

Semiconcrete level: Cicle sets to show work with tallies. Write quotient.

Student work:

7R2
4)30

Abstract level: Write quotient.
4)30

- Skill: Recognize simple fractions

Concrete level: Let ▭▭▭▭▭ = 1 or 5/5 and ▭ = 1/5. Stack the blocks to show 3/5.
Student work:

Semiconcrete level: Write a fraction for the shadowed part of the group.

○ ○ ○ ● ●

Abstract level: Write the fraction for three-fifths.

3/5

- Skill: Addition of fractions with like denominators

Concrete level: Let = 1/3. Show work with blocks. Write sum.
Student work:

1/3   +   1/3   =   2/3
_____

Semiconcrete level: Display the sum of 1/3 + 1/3 by shading in the circles.

● ○ ○ + ● ○ ○ = ○ ○ ○

Abstract level:

$$\frac{1}{3} + \frac{1}{3} = \underline{\quad}$$

- Skill: Money change for amounts up to $1.00
Concrete level: Given real money and items with marked prices, figure out correct change if a $.39 item is purchased with a dollar.
Semiconcrete level: Circle the coins given as change for a dollar when buying a $.39 item.

Abstract level: Answer this problem: How much change would you give when someone buys a $.39 item and gives you a dollar?

Periodic and continuous math assessments provide information for instruction. Periodic assessment includes an initial testing that generates instructional objectives; periodic evaluations include checkups of general progress and in-depth evaluations of students experiencing difficulty. Continuous assessment focuses on monitoring the student's progress. It involves daily, weekly, or biweekly assessments. Through frequent monitoring, the teacher quickly can detect a

FIGURE 11.6

Chart of a student's performance on basic multiplication facts

X	0	1	2	3	4	5	6	7	8	9
0	✓	—	—	—	—	—	—	—	—	—
1	—	✓	✓	✓	✓	✓	✓	✓	✓	✓
2	—	✓	✓	✓	✓	✓	✓	✓	✓	✓
3	—	✓	✓	✓	✓	✓	✓	✓	✓	✓
4	—	✓	✓	✓	✓	✓	✓	✓	✓	✓
5	—	✓	✓	✓	✓	✓	✓	✓	✓	✓
6	—	✓	✓	✓	✓	✓	✓	✓	✓	—
7	—	✓	✓	✓	✓	✓	✓	✓	—	✓
8	—	✓	✓	✓	✓	✓	✓	—	✓	✓
9	—	✓	✓	✓	✓	✓	—	✓	✓	✓

student's skill deficit and provide appropriate instruction so that the student does not practice doing the skill incorrectly for a long period of time.

Charts can be used to locate math facts that have not been memorized. The teacher gives the student a test of selected facts (e.g., sums 0 to 9 or 10 to 18, differences 0 to 9 or 10 to 18, or products 0 to 9). Then the teacher records the student's performance on the chart: ✓ = basic fact memorized; – = basic fact not memorized. The chart for multiplication facts presented in Figure 11.6 shows that the student is experiencing difficulty with facts involving 0. The chart for subtraction facts 0 to 18 presented in Figure 11.7 suggests that the student is

having difficulty with two-digit minus one-digit facts, except those involving 9 and those in which the subtrahend equals the difference.

Inspection of the sample items readily shows that the student's level of math understanding must be assessed individually. Developing and administering analytical math tests take time. Some teachers need several years to build an ample file of such tests, which then must be organized and stored in a functional system. Because of the time constraints, some teachers reserve this type of assessment for students who are not progressing with systematic math instruction and who appear to have serious math difficulties. Others include concrete experiences in their teaching and construct tests that include semiconcrete and abstract items. Instruction for students with math learning problems should include experiences at each of the three levels for teaching specific concepts and skills.

Diagnostic Math Interviews As a curriculum area, math is quite different from reading, language, or written communication. One major difference is that skill in math is not reflected in global tasks such as oral reading, language samples, or written passages. A student may know much about math but perform poorly on a math test that does not cover that specific material. Thus, to perform a functional math assessment, the teacher needs to know what the student has been taught and is expected to know. Moreover, basals vary dramatically in their sequences and coverages of math content, and grade-level scores from math tests are not comparable. Thus, placing students in math programs based on grade-level scores is strongly discouraged.

FIGURE 11.7

Chart of a student's performance on 0 to 18 subtraction facts

Because of growing dissatisfaction with math tests, a move toward "authentic" math assessment is evolving. This movement involves portfolio assessments typified by open-ended performance measures (California Mathematics Assessment Advisory Committee, 1990) and emphasizes that math is more than the language of numbers. Assessment procedures that ask students only to look at and write numbers are too limiting to reflect current views of math instruction. Given both the lack of consistency across programs and tests and the evolving portfolio approach, student interviews should be used when assessing math at specific levels. Interviews can provide insights into mathematical strategies, processes, products, and social-emotional reactions to math.

The diagnostic interview provides information to determine what math skills to teach the student and how to teach them. In this technique, the student expresses thought processes while solving math problems. This technique often is used in administering diagnostic math tests. Moreover, the diagnostic interview enables the teacher to identify specific problems, error patterns, or problem-solving strategies in math. The following sample interview illustrates how the procedure can yield important information:

> The teacher gave Mary three multiplication problems and said, "Please do these problems and tell me how you figure out the answer." Mary solved the problems in this way:

$$
\begin{array}{ccc}
2 & 4 & 3 \\
27 & 36 & 44 \\
\times\,4 & \times\,7 & \times\,8 \\
\hline
168 & 492 & 562 \\
\end{array}
$$

> For the first problem, Mary explained, "7 times 4 equals 28. So I put my 8 here and carry the 2. 2 plus 2 equals 4, and 4 times 4 equals 16. So I put 16 here." Her explanations for the other two problems followed the same logic.

By listening to Mary and watching her solve the problems, the teacher quickly determined Mary's error pattern: She adds the number associated with the crutch (i.e., the number carried to the tens column) *before* multiplying the tens digit. Mary explained that she had been taught to add the number being carried when regrouping in addition. After identifying Mary's error pattern and its origin, the teacher could plan instruction for teaching the correct algorithm and developing an understanding of the multiplication process. Without the interview, the teacher incorrectly may have planned instruction in the basic multiplication facts.

Clinical interviews also offer an excellent technique for identifying negative emotions and attitudes toward math. Knowledge of these feelings helps teachers adjust math instruction (e.g., using graphic cueing, prompts, reinforcement, and charts) to alter a student's feelings. The following activities can be used in an interview session to assess attitudes.

- Instruct the student to solve some math problems and observe the student's behavior (e.g., makes negative statements, becomes upset, or gives up quickly).
- Have the student respond to some oral sentence-completion tasks. The teacher starts a sentence and the student responds aloud. Sample starters include the following:

  Math is very . . .
  My best subject is . . .
  During math lessons I feel . . .

- Ask the student direct questions. The following are some sample questions:

  What is your favorite subject?
  Do you like to do math?
  What is your favorite thing about math?
  What do you not like about math?
  Do you use math outside school?
  What would you do to make math more interesting?

The validity of the diagnostic findings depends on the quality of the exchange between teacher and student. The teacher must establish rapport and ensure that the student feels free to respond honestly. General guidelines for conducting an interview include the following:

- Establish rapport and be alert to the student's attitudes toward math throughout the session. It often helps to start with items that are easy for the student to complete.
- Focus only on the student's problem area that is the lowest on the skill sequence. Limit each session to one area of difficulty (e.g., two-column addition with regrouping).
- Allow the student the freedom to solve the problem in his or her own way.
- Record the student's thinking processes and analyze for error patterns and problem-solving techniques.
- Once an error pattern or faulty problem-solving technique is discovered, introduce diagnostic activities for assessing the student's level of understanding. These activities should include tasks at the semiconcrete and concrete levels. (For a more detailed discussion of diagnostic math interviews, see Rivera and Bryant [1992].)

Teaching Math

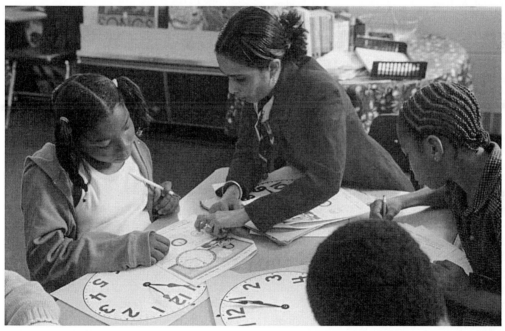

T. Lindfors/Lindfors Photography

From Chapter 12 of *Teaching Students with Learning Problems*, 8/e. Cecil D. Mercer. Ann R. Mercer. Paige C. Pullen.

The possible excitement about learning math is illustrated by the behavior of the students in the following story (Mercer & Pullen, 2009, p. 334).

> I had the opportunity to work on a math project with second-grade teachers and their students in a rural Florida school. During the last week of school I attended the end-of-the-school-year picnic. I was sitting at a table enjoying an ice cream cone when I heard a confident but quiet voice say, "I know 99 times 0." Standing beside the table was a second grader named Matt, with his hands in his pockets, waiting for my response. I decided to have some fun. I said, "How could you possibly know 99 times 0 and still be in the second grade? That must be at least a third-grade skill." Matt quickly replied, "99 times 0 is 0!" With a surprised expression, I said, "Lucky guess!" Matt looked directly at me and said, "I'll be back." Then he turned and walked away. A few minutes later, Matt approached me with several of his second-grade friends. Upon their arrival, one of Matt's friends said, "I know 1,000 times 1." I responded, "You're kidding. That problem is impossible for a second grader." The friend blurted out, "1,000!" More second graders joined our discussion. They continued to share with me their knowledge of multiplication—1,000,000 times 1, 6,000 times 0, 9 times 8, and so on. The group of eight to ten students consisted of normally achieving students and students with learning disabilities. They displayed their knowledge of rules, multiplication facts, and problem-solving skills. I praised them for their knowledge and smartness. I was surprised that the students continued to discuss math when they had the opportunity to be playing. That afternoon while driving home, I realized that I had learned a lesson about empowered students.

Unfortunately, this scenario of students excited about their math learning is uncommon. For many students, math problems often result in school failure and lead to much anxiety. Although deficiencies in reading are cited most often as a primary characteristic of students with learning disabilities, deficits in mathematics are as serious a problem for many of these students (Dirks, Spyer, van Lieshout, & de Sonneville, 2008). It is estimated that between 5 and 10 percent of school-age children have some form of math learning disabilities (Fuchs, Fuchs, & Hollenbeck, 2007; Geary, 2004).

In the 2009 National Assessment of Educational Progress in mathematics, students responded to questions designed to measure knowledge and abilities across five mathematics content areas: number properties and operations; measurement; geometry; data analysis, statistics, and probability; and algebra. According to the National Center for Education Statistics (2009), reports from these national assessments of mathematics progress indicate that gains in students' average scores seen in earlier years did not continue from 2007 to 2009

at the fourth-grade level but did continue at the eighth-grade level. In 2009, approximately 28 percent of fourth-grade students performed below a basic level of achievement (i.e., partial mastery of mathematics knowledge and skills necessary to perform work at grade level) and only 39 percent of fourth-grade students attained a proficient mathematics achievement level. Moreover, about 27 percent of eighth-grade students were below a basic level of mathematics achievement and only 34 percent achieved proficient mathematics standards. Whereas there was no significant change in the performance of the nation's fourth graders in mathematics from 2007 to 2009 (i.e., the overall average score in 2009 was unchanged from the score in 2007), the national average mathematics score for eighth graders was higher in 2009 than in any previous assessment year (i.e., a 2-point increase since 2007); however, for the lowest-performing eighth-grade students (i.e., those at the 10th percentile), there was no significant change in the score since 2007.

The inability to acquire and maintain math facts at fluency levels sufficient for acquiring higher-level math skills is common among students with learning problems, and unfamiliarity with basic number facts plays a major role in the math difficulties of students with math learning problems. It is apparent that many students with learning disabilities lack proficiency in basic number facts and are unable to retrieve answers to math facts efficiently.

Reforms in math education are increasing the overall complexity of the mathematics curriculum. General and special educators must work together to ensure that the instructional reforms are sensitive to the unique learning and emotional needs of students with learning problems. Although many students with math deficiencies exhibit characteristics (such as problems in memory, language, reading, reasoning, and metacognition) that predispose them to math disabilities, their learning difficulties often are compounded by ineffective instruction. Many authorities (Carnine, 1991; Cawley, Miller, & School, 1987; Kelly, Gersten, & Carnine, 1990) believe that poor or traditional instruction is the primary cause of the math difficulties of many students with learning problems. Numerous studies support the position that students with math disabilities can be taught to improve their mathematical performance (Maccini, Mulcahy, & Wilson, 2007; Mercer & Miller, 1992; Scheuermann, Deshler, & Schumaker, 2009; Xin & Zhang, 2009).

Given the poor math progress of students with learning problems and the reform in math education to increase standards, a need clearly exists to design an effective math curriculum for these students. Without better math instruction, these youngsters will continue to face much frustration and failure. Given the problems that students with learning problems exhibit with lower-level math skills (i.e., many students do not know the 390 basic math facts after 5 or more years of school) and the importance of these skills to overall math achievement, comprehensive programming to teach basic math facts obviously is needed.

This chapter is designed to help the teacher provide effective instruction to students with math problems. Included are basic terms and processes, research on effective math instruction, instructional practices for computation and problem solving (including math facts programs, concrete-semiconcrete-abstract activities, basic rules and algorithms, problem-solving interventions, life skills math, estimation, and calculators), math activities, instructional games, self-correcting materials, commercial programs, and computer software programs.

BASIC TERMS AND PROCESSES

Before beginning math instruction, the teacher needs to know basic terms used in math. Table 12.1 presents some major terms.

The teacher also should know basic information about the organization of math content. Five areas are essential to learning addition, subtraction, multiplication, and division: understanding, basic facts, place value, structures (i.e., laws), and regrouping. *Understanding*

TABLE 12.1
Math terms in basic computations

Operation	Terms
Addition	8 ←addend +4 ←addend 12 ←sum
Subtraction (take away)	9 ←minuend −4 ←subtrahend 5 ←difference
Subtraction (add on)	9 ←sum −4 ←known addend 5 ←difference
Multiplication	8 ←multiplicand or factor ×5 ←multiplier or factor 40 ←product
Division	8 ←quotient or factor 6)48 ←dividend or product ↑ divisor or factor

means comprehending the operation at the concrete, semiconcrete (i.e., representational), and abstract levels. *Basic facts* must be understood and memorized; these are the tools of computation. The basic facts are simple closed number sentences used in computation. Addition and subtraction facts involve two one-digit addends, and multiplication and division facts involve two one-digit factors (Ashlock, 2010). There are 390 basic facts— 100 addition, 100 subtraction, 100 multiplication, and 90 division facts. Once understanding and basic facts are mastered, the specific operation can be expanded readily by using *place value*. For example, if the student recognizes that 3×2 is 6, the place value concept can be applied to compute a series of problems such as the following:

$$
\begin{array}{ccc}
3 & 30 & 300 \\
\times 2 & \times 2 & \times 2 \\
\hline
6 & 60 & 600 \\
\\
3000 & 30 & 300 \\
\times 2 & \times 20 & \times 20 \\
\hline
6000 & 600 & 6000
\end{array}
$$

Structures are mathematical properties that help the student. A student who memorizes that 7×3 is 21 but sees 3×7 as a new problem to memorize needs to understand a basic structure (e.g., in this case, the commutative property of multiplication) to learn multiplication effectively. The last area is *regrouping*, which commonly is referred to as *carrying* or *borrowing*; this must be understood to solve more complex problems in each of the four operations.

Another important factor in teaching math is knowledge of algorithms. Algorithms are the steps used in solving a math problem. Numerous algorithms are presented later in this chapter.

RESEARCH ON EFFECTIVE MATH INSTRUCTION

The amount of research on teaching math has increased substantially in the last decade, and it is now clear that curriculum design, teacher behavior, and student engagement directly influence the mathematics achievement of students with learning problems (Bodovski & Farkas, 2007; Hutchinson, 1993a; Kame'enui & Simmons, 1990; Kelly et al., 1990; Mercer, Jordan, & Miller, 1994; Mercer & Miller, 1992). Although much remains to be learned about teaching math, educators need to examine existing research and literature to determine *what* should be taught in a math curriculum and the best practices for *how* to teach it. Only through the systematic examination and application of what is known about math instruction can educators ensure that the achievement levels of students with learning problems are commensurate with their potential. Fuchs and Fuchs (2001) present four principles of prevention of math difficulties: instruct at a quick pace with varied instructional activities and high levels of engagement, set challenging standards for achievement, incorporate self-verbalization methods, and present physical and visual representations of number concepts or problem-solving situations. Adaptations within the general education setting should be easily implemented within the normal classroom routine, be nondisruptive to the student, and be nonintrusive for classmates. When intervention is needed to enhance learning, Fuchs and Fuchs note that there should be a focus on the individual student as the unit for instructional decision making, intensive instructional delivery, and explicit conceptualization of skills-based instruction. Fuchs et al. (2007) present a response to intervention model in mathematics that provides a framework for preventing math difficulties and providing effective instruction that incorporates these four principles. The components of effective math instruction are presented next.

Selecting Appropriate Mathematics Content

Mathematics educators recommend reforms in the content of the mathematics curriculum. Although computation remains a vital component, experts agree that obtaining answers through the use of written work is not sufficient. Estimating answers and cross-checking with alternative methods are stressed in the current recommendations. Moreover, the ability to think critically and the understanding of concepts, operations, and real-life applications are important goals of a mathematics curriculum. The official 1988 statement of the National Council of Supervisors of Mathematics, *Twelve Components of Essential Mathematics,* has implications for planning math instruction for students with learning problems.

1. *Problem solving.* Learning to solve problems by applying previously acquired information to new and different situations is one of the primary reasons for studying math. Problem solving involves solving both verbal (i.e., text) and nonverbal problems. Skills involved include using trial and error, asking relevant questions, selecting an operation, illustrating results, analyzing situations, and translating results.

2. *Communication of mathematical ideas.* Students must learn the language and notation of math. They should present math ideas through the use of manipulative objects, drawings, written work, and speech.

3. *Mathematical reasoning.* Students must learn to conduct investigations of math concepts. These skills include making tentative conclusions, recognizing patterns, and using math knowledge to support conjecture.

4. *Application of mathematics to everyday situations.* Students should be encouraged to translate daily experiences into mathematical representations (i.e., graphs, tables, diagrams, or math expressions) and interpret the results.

5. *Alertness to the reasonableness of results.* Students must be able to examine results against viable conjecture. The use of calculators and computers makes this an essential skill.

6. *Estimation.* Students must be able to perform rapid mental approximations to establish the reasonableness of a math solution. In addition to approximating purchase costs, these estimations involve measurements such as length, area, volume, and weight.

7. *Appropriate computational skills.* Students must gain proficiency in using operations (i.e., addition, subtraction, multiplication, and division) with whole numbers and decimals. Knowledge of basic facts is essential, and mental arithmetic is important. Competence in using common fractions and decimals is necessary, and knowing when to use a calculator also is helpful.

8. *Algebraic thinking.* Students must learn to use letters to represent math quantities and expressions and to represent mathematical relationships and functions with graphs, tables, and equations. Students need to understand how one quantity changes as a function of another.

9. *Measurement.* Students must learn the basic concepts of measuring (i.e., distance, weight, time, capacity, temperature, and angles) through concrete experiences.

myeducationlab

To examine two challenging cases, go to the IRIS Center Resources section for the Topic Assessing and Teaching Math in the MyEducationLab for your course and complete the Cases entitled Algebra (Part 1): Applying Learning Strategies to Beginning Algebra, and Algebra (Part 2): Applying Learning Strategies to Intermediate Algebra.

10. *Geometry.* Students must learn geometric concepts to function in a three-dimensional world. Parallelism, perpendicularity, congruence, similarity, and symmetry are important concepts. These concepts should be explored in situations that involve measurement and problem solving.

11. *Statistics.* Students must learn to collect and organize data to answer daily questions. Measures of central tendency and variance are important, as well as interpreting tables, maps, graphs, and charts.

12. *Probability.* Students must understand the basic notions of probability to predict the likelihood of future events.

In recognition of the broad scope and the large number of objectives of the mathematics curriculum, the National Council of Teachers of Mathematics (2006) published *Curriculum Focal Points for Prekindergarten through Grade 8 Mathematics: A Quest for Coherence.* Three curriculum focal points are provided for each grade level (i.e., prekindergarten through eighth grade) to help teachers focus on specific goals according to the content standards published in 2000.

Moreover, a document by the National Research Council (2001) synthesizes the research on effective teaching of mathematics and provides an overview of the mathematical knowledge students should acquire. According to the report, mathematics proficiency includes conceptual understanding, procedural fluency, strategic competence, adaptive reasoning, and productive disposition.

1. *Conceptual understanding* refers to the comprehension of mathematical concepts, operations, and relations. In other words, the student's knowledge is deeper than rote memorization of facts or of procedural algorithms. Although students in the primary grades may not be able to verbalize their understanding of a concept, their ability to represent problems in various ways demonstrates their understanding. For example, when learning multiplication, rather than simply stating the rote fact that 6 times 3 equals 18, the student needs to demonstrate with manipulative materials pictorially what the problem represents.

2. *Procedural fluency* refers to the student's' understanding of the *what, why, when,* and *how* of mathematics procedures. Students must possess an understanding of procedures that allows for their efficient and flexible use (National Research Council, 2001). Procedural fluency is aided by the student's conceptual knowledge. For example, in order to perform basic and multidigit computations

efficiently, a solid understanding of place value is required. Procedural fluency means that students do not need to rely on one particular algorithm but possess multiple means of arriving at solutions quickly and accurately.

3. The student's skill in solving problems and accurately representing problems makes up *strategic competence.* Each day, adults encounter situations in which they are required to use their mathematical knowledge to solve problems. In real-life situations, problems are not presented in a number sentence. Students who have strategic competence are able to solve real-world problems by representing a problem and then solving it correctly.

4. *Adaptive reasoning* refers to the ability to think logically about the relationships among concepts and situations (National Research Council, 2001). One way students can demonstrate adaptive reasoning is by verbalizing how they determined a solution to a given problem. For example, after solving a problem with any combination of paper, pencil, manipulative materials, or calculator, the student can explain verbally how the problem was solved. This activity gives the teacher an insight into the student's adaptive reasoning and clarifies areas that need to be retaught when problems exist.

5. *Productive disposition* refers to the student's perception that mathematics is functional and valuable and the belief that the student can be successful at mathematics. Unfortunately, early failure with mathematics may lead students with learning problems to develop a negative mathematics disposition. It is critical during the primary grades that students experience many successes to increase the likelihood that they will develop a productive disposition.

Students with learning problems often perform poorly in these areas identified by the National Research Council as critical to success in mathematics.

Many experts recommend that math instruction focus on problem solving within an authentic context. One way to accomplish this is to introduce math concepts and operations within the context of a word problem. For example, solving division equations in algebra could be introduced with the following word problem: "Cindy plans to give 30 coupons for free pizza to 6 of her friends. How many coupons will each friend receive?" The teacher explains that this can be represented and solved through the use of simple division: 30 coupons ÷ 6 friends = _____ coupons per friend. Then the teacher demonstrates how the problem can be solved through the use of algebra by giving the unknown a letter name and moving it to the left side of the equation: 30 coupons ÷ 6 friends = ____ becomes 6 friends × *c* (coupons per friend) = 30 coupons. Furthermore, the teacher uses the students' prior knowledge about the multiplication and division relationship to solve the problem (i.e., What number multiplied by 6 equals 30?). As the lessons progress, the teacher guides and encourages the students to create their own word problems that can be solved through the use of division equations.

If mathematical content is to be authentic to learning, it must be presented in a real-world context. For example, if the instructional content fails to relate $6y + 2y + 6 = 48$ to a pragmatic word problem, then students are memorizing meaningless procedures for obtaining answers. In a study of technological math interventions with students with learning problems, Bottge and Hasselbring (1993) found that contextualized learning was a key factor.

Another consideration for determining what mathematics content to teach involves a student's prior learning. Mathematics is a logical interrelated system of concepts and operations that are hierarchically ordered. Numerous experts (Bley & Thornton, 2001; Kame'enui & Simmons, 1990; Stein, Kinder, Silbert, & Carnine, 2006) stress the importance of teaching students skills for which they have the necessary preskills. For example, students should know some addition facts before learning subtraction facts. Teaching students skills in which they lack the necessary preskills often leads to a limited amount of fragmented or rote learning and much frustration. A best teaching practice clearly involves teaching students the preskills that are germane to learning a new skill or beginning instruction with a skill in which students possess the essential preskills. Finally, educators must ensure that students with learning problems receive math instruction on relevant or practical math skills. For example, the teaching of Roman numerals appears to lack relevance.

Finally, to facilitate the ability of students to master a large number of instructional objectives and reach math standards, instruction can be organized around the big ideas of the content area. These big ideas represent foundational knowledge and are especially important for students to understand. According to Harniss, Carnine, Silbert, and Dixon (2007, p. 142), big ideas "represent major organizing principles, have rich explanatory and predictive power, help frame significant questions, and are applicable in many

situations and contexts." For example, the four operations of addition, subtraction, multiplication, and division are based on the big ideas of place value; the commutative, associative, and distributive properties; equivalence; and number sense. A significant amount of instructional time should be devoted to these major principles. When the teacher identifies the most critical knowledge, concepts, and skills for the student to learn and the curriculum is organized around these big ideas, the greatest amount of student learning can occur.

myeducationlab

Go to the Assignments and Activities section of the Topic Assessing and Teaching Math in the MyEducationLab for your course and complete the activity entitled Strategies in Mathematics Teaching.

Teaching the Acquisition of Math

Follow Teaching Steps A viable plan for teaching the acquisition of computation or problem-solving skills includes the following activities.

1. Assess the student's math skills and identify an appropriate instructional objective. To promote success, the objective should be relevant and one in which the student has the essential preskills.
2. Obtain a commitment from the student to learn the math skill and set goals. Discussions regarding the applications of the targeted skill help the student establish a desire to learn. Moreover, goal setting provides the student and teacher with instructional expectations and fosters motivation. Goal setting is enhanced by identifying the expected time period for reaching a mastery criterion. Good teachers are clear about instructional goals and communicate expectations and why the specific expectations exist. In presenting goals, effective teachers explain what the student needs to do to achieve the goal and what the student will learn in achieving the goal. There is growing support for the premise that teachers tend to make goals too easy for students with learning problems (Anderson & Pellicer, 1990; Clifford, 1990). Clifford reports that students need challenge rather than easy success and that tasks involving moderate risk taking provide the best level of difficulty in setting goals. She recommends that instructional environments should feature error tolerance and reward for error correction. A substantial research base (Locke & Latham, 1990)

verifies that difficult but attainable goals lead to higher effort and achievement than do easier goals. Elementary and secondary students with learning problems have responded well to goal setting in math. Goal setting helps the students become more proactive and involved in their own learning. Moreover, students perform better when the goals are self-set rather than assigned. Miller, Strawser, and Mercer (1996) provide the following guidelines in conducting a goal-setting conference.

- Allow adequate time for the goal-setting conference (e.g., 10 to 15 minutes).
- Arrange to confer with students in a place that does not permit others to overhear.
- Encourage students to do most of the talking (i.e., the teacher should listen).
- Begin the session by guiding students through a self-evaluation of their progress.
- Listen to students' ideas without interruptions or judgmental comments.
- If necessary, lead students to revise their goals realistically by asking open-ended questions.
- Encourage students to set goals in skills at the acquisition, proficiency, maintenance, and generalization levels of learning.
- Record the results of the conference and provide copies for students. A conference form can be developed that has space to record the time frame for the goals, self-evaluation of progress in skills, the amount of time spent working on each skill, prerequisite skills that the students did not have, and the amount of time the students plan to work on each skill.

3. Use effective teaching steps to teach the math skill (i.e., introduce the lesson, describe and model the skill or strategy, use scaffolding to guide practice and interactive discourse, conduct independent practice to mastery, provide feedback, and teach generalization and transfer). Numerous researchers have used these steps or variations of these steps to produce excellent math achievement in students with learning problems. Also, during the learning of new material, the student should review prior content and maintain a high success rate. Majsterek, Wilson, and Jones (2007) recommend four types of review: (1) review before beginning a math lesson, (2) review homework, (3) review within every lesson, and (4) review across lessons.

Use Teacher Modeling of Explicit Strategies

A promising feature from the mathematics problem-solving literature entails the *substance* of teacher modeling. Instead of the traditional teacher modeling of mathematical algorithms in a meaningless context, researchers are exploring the modeling of problem-solving strategies (i.e., cognitive and metacognitive) to solve meaningful problems and develop self-regulation processes. Woodward (1991) notes that cognitive task analyses enable teachers to model thinking processes involved in math problem solving. Explicit teacher modeling of cognitive and metacognitive strategies in solving word problems has yielded encouraging results, and these findings (Chung & Tam, 2005; Hutchinson, 1993a; Montague, 1992, 1993; Montague & Dietz, 2009) suggest that specific strategy instruction in math holds significant promise for students with learning problems. These findings support Zawaiza and Gerber's (1993) position that "successful strategy instruction . . . requires modeling of competent strategy use, sufficient and appropriate exemplar problems, ample opportunity to practice and receive correction on strategy use, and adequate opportunities for students to describe and evaluate how effectively they are employing newly learned strategies" (p. 67). Strategies that include explicit teacher modeling are presented in the section on problem-solving interventions.

Focus on Teacher–Student Interactions

A focus on teacher–student interactions provides a timely opportunity for educators to improve the quality of instructional discourse for teaching math. Earlier research mainly stressed the role of the teacher in providing instruction to cover content, whereas recent research focuses on the dynamic nature of the dialogue between the student and the teacher to develop conceptual understandings. In this dynamic process, the teacher constantly adapts the dialogue according to student needs. Teachers are encouraged to time their interactions prescriptively so that they know when it is appropriate to provide direct instruction, give guided instruction, ask questions, challenge, offer corrective feedback, encourage, let the student work independently, reflect with the student, set instructional goals, model a cognitive or metacognitive strategy, discuss rationales for learning new declarative or procedural knowledge, or discuss transfer. When teachers prescriptively interact (i.e., base interactions on student behavior) during instruction to ensure that students develop conceptual understandings, students are treated as active agents in their own learning.

Elmore (1992) notes that teachers need extensive help to learn and apply the ideas of current research on teaching. He claims that it is unrealistic to expect teachers to accomplish this by themselves. Apparently, teacher education and commercial materials have not helped teachers to teach conceptual understandings. Most materials present information that describes how to use algorithms to solve math problems. This algorithm-driven approach provides little or no help to teachers who desire to teach the conceptual underpinnings implicit in math.

To help teachers model strategies and teach understanding of math concepts, several researchers have provided scripts or sample dialogues (Hutchinson, 1993a; Mercer & Miller, 1992; Montague, 1993, 2003, 2007). These scripts or sample dialogues provide the teacher with an initial guide on how to model metacognitive strategies explicitly and how to lead the student to conceptual understandings of math concepts (i.e., declarative knowledge) and apply declarative and procedural knowledge to solve word problems and math equations. The scripts serve as a springboard for helping teachers engage in productive teacher–student discourse. As teachers gain confidence and experience with these interactions, the sample dialogues are not needed. Sample dialogues guide the teacher through the teaching steps. The describe-and-model step features explicit teacher modeling of strategies. The guided practice step parallels scaffolding as the teacher guides the students to conceptual understandings and independent work. The independent practice step incorporates working alone and with peers to gain mastery. The feedback step is used to recognize successes and relate them to learning goals and to use errors in math for teaching and learning opportunities. The generalization-and-transfer step encourages the students to reflect on strategy uses and create their own word problems.

Use the Concrete-Semiconcrete-Abstract Sequence

During the acquisition of a computational or problem-solving skill, the student must be instructed in such a way to ensure understanding. Many authorities believe that the concrete-semiconcrete-abstract (CSA) sequence is an excellent way to teach students with learning problems to understand math concepts, operations, and applications. Lambert (1996) notes that research supports the use of manipulative objects at all grade levels to teach math concepts. Several research studies (Harris, Miller, & Mercer, 1995; Mercer & Miller, 1992) reveal that the CSA sequence is an effective way to teach math facts to students with learning problems. Results indicate that such students do not need large numbers of formal experiences at the concrete and semiconcrete levels to understand the basic facts. In this research, within six 30-minute lessons (i.e., three concrete lessons and three semiconcrete lessons), students with learning problems demonstrated an understanding of the respective operation and generalized their learning to abstract-level (i.e., numbers only) problems. Moreover, the students retained the targeted skills during follow-up testing. The CSA sequence seems to be especially useful in helping students who have deficits in *representing* or *reformulating* math from word problems to equations, equations to objects, pictures or drawings to equations, and vice versa. In addition to the use of the CSA sequence to teach basic math facts, research supports the effective use of manipulative objects and pictorial representations to teach subtraction with regrouping (Flores, 2009), fractions (Butler, Miller, Crehan, Babbitt, & Pierce, 2003; Jordan, Miller, & Mercer, 1998; Witzel & Riccomini, 2009), area and perimeter problems (Cass, Cates, Smith, & Jackson, 2003), and algebra (Maccini & Hughes, 2000; Witzel, Mercer, & Miller, 2003). Because the CSA sequence requires students to represent math concepts and operations with objects and drawings, math concepts (such as addition, place value, multiplication, fractions, and equations) are understood. Examples of CSA teaching are presented later in this chapter.

Teach Concepts and Rules

The learning of concepts and rules also is germane to facilitating a student's understanding of math. A student who memorizes that 8 + 6 is 14 but sees 6 + 8 as a new problem to memorize needs to understand a basic concept (i.e., in this case, the commutative property of addition) to learn addition effectively. Likewise, the learning of subtraction is facilitated if a student understands the inverse relationship of addition and subtraction (i.e., $a + b = c$; $c - b = a$). Also, the concept of place value is difficult for many students and deserves much teacher attention. Finally, rules such as *any number times zero is zero* help students learn multiplication facts.

PEARSON myeducationlab

Go to the Building Teaching Skills and Dispositions section for the Topic Assessing and Teaching Math in the MyEducationLab for your course and complete the activity entitled Using Manipulatives as a Strategy in Teaching Math Concepts. As you watch the video and answer the accompanying questions, think about why it is beneficial to begin math instruction with concrete examples.

Concrete and semiconcrete experiences are excellent ways to demonstrate concepts and rules to students.

Monitor Progress and Provide Feedback

Monitoring the math progress of students with learning problems and giving feedback (e.g., through the use of charts) have yielded excellent results regarding student achievement. Gersten, Carnine, and Woodward (1987) report that teachers who provide immediate corrective feedback on errors produce higher student achievement. The implementation of curriculum-based measures in mathematics also allows teachers to identify students who are not progressing sufficiently and provide more intensive instruction (Clarke, Baker, Smolkowski, & Chard, 2008). Moreover, Robinson, DePascale, and Roberts (1989) found that feedback helped students with learning disabilities complete more problems and improved accuracy from 73 percent to 94 percent. They stress the importance of feedback (p. 28):

> Feedback is potentially even more important for learning disabled (LD) children, who may be less attentive, participate less in academic work, and make more errors than higher achieving learners. Academic environments that maximize LD students' opportunities to learn under direct teacher supervision with timely feedback are essential.

Kline, Schumaker, and Deshler (1991) developed and evaluated an elaborated feedback routine with students with learning problems. Their results indicate that this routine helps students achieve learning goals quickly and efficiently. A major factor in the routine stresses that errors represent learning opportunities for the students and teaching opportunities for the teacher. The essential features of elaborated feedback are included in the following mnemonic, FEEDBACK.

F—*Find* the score. Explain the grade.

E—*Enter* the score. Use a graph and goal setting and make it meaningful.

E—*Evaluate* the score in terms of the goal.

D—*Determine* errors by examining the pattern.

B—*Begin* error correction. The teacher models a similar problem.

A—*Ask* the student to apply the correction procedure.

C—*Close* out the session by giving positive feedback on correction.

K—*Kick* back and relax!

Clifford (1990) recommends that instructional environments feature error tolerance and reward for error correction. The letters *D*, *B*, *A*, and *C* in FEEDBACK stress error-correction procedures.

Maintain Flexibility

Given the heterogeneity of students with learning problems, the teacher must use some flexibility in teaching math. From the numerous learning characteristics that can affect math learning, it is apparent that a variety of teaching activities or procedures is needed. If a specific teaching activity does not result in student learning, it may help to try another. Low-stress algorithms, specific modality-oriented instruction, visual and auditory cueing, prompting, and reinforcement represent a few instructional alternatives that can be manipulated readily.

Teaching Mastery

In this discussion, *mastery learning* refers to teaching a skill to a level of automaticity. Individuals usually reach a level of automaticity when they continuously respond to math problems without hesitating to compute the answer. Most people operate at a level of automaticity when responding to questions such as What is your phone number? or What is 6 plus 2? Rate of responding is regarded as an effective measure of automaticity (Hasselbring, Goin, & Bransford, 1987). Reaching mastery on a skill provides numerous benefits, including improved retention and improved ability to compute or solve higher-level problems. Other benefits include finishing timed tests, completing homework faster, receiving higher grades, and developing positive feelings about math. In a study of 432 second-through fifth-grade students, VanDerHeyden and Burns (2009) found that students at all grade levels who failed to reach mastery on early math skills in a sequence were unable to meet criterion on future related skills. Likewise, reaching mastery on early skills in a hierarchy was positively related to future learning of more complex skills.

Before mastery instruction or techniques are used, the students must possess the preskills and understand the concept related to the targeted skill. Once they understand a skill, they can be instructed at mastery level. Understanding can be gained through the use of concrete and semiconcrete experiences, promoting relationship insights among operations (e.g., $4 + 3 = 7$, $7 - 4 = 3$; and $8 \times 3 = 24$, $24 \div 3 = 8$, $24 \div 8 = 3$), and fostering mature ways to determine missing numbers (e.g., using algorithms such as counting up in addition, or using rules such as *any number times zero equals zero*). Students with learning problems vary considerably on the number of trials they need before achieving automaticity. Independent practice is the primary instructional format used to acquire mastery. Because practice can become boring, the teacher must try to make practice interesting or fun. Instructional games, peer teaching, computer-assisted instruction, self-correcting materials, and reinforcement are helpful in planning practice-to-mastery activities.

The following techniques can improve speed in math computation.

- Reinforce high rates of correct responses.
- Set a rate goal.
- Chart performances and terminate daily practice once the goal is achieved.
- Tell students to work faster.
- Challenge students to beat their last rate score.
- Teach students to use rules (e.g., *any number times 2 is double that number*).
- Teach efficient algorithms (such as counting up in addition).
- Drill difficult problems with flash cards.
- Play instructional math games.
- Provide rate practice in small intervals (e.g., 10 to 20 seconds).
- Teach students the relationships between addition and subtraction or multiplication and division when they are learning the respective facts.

In establishing mastery rate levels for individuals, it is important to consider the learner's characteristics (such as age, academic skill, and motor ability). For example, oral responses may be more appropriate for a student who has handwriting difficulties. For most students, a rate of 40 to 60 correct digits written per minute with two or fewer errors is appropriate; however, for younger students (i.e., kindergarten through second grade), it often is necessary to lower the digits-per-minute criteria. Once a mastery level is achieved, the teacher and student are able to move to the next skill level with appropriate preskills and more confidence.

Teaching Problem Solving

Although problem solving has a high priority in math instruction and has received decades of attention from educators, its exact nature remains ambiguous. Problem solving relates to both word and computation

problems. It seems reasonable that a problem-solving activity is needed for any task the student finds difficult. Thus, word and computation problems both could require problem-solving procedures. For skills in which automaticity has been achieved, problem solving is probably not a necessary procedural process.

Most authorities (Cawley et al., 1987; Fleischner, Nuzum, & Marzola, 1987; Kame'enui & Simmons, 1990) interpret problem solving within the context of word problems. From an analysis of the problem-solving literature on students with learning problems, several components germane to problem solving are evident. These components include the idea that to problem solve, the student needs to have a mathematical knowledge base, apply acquired knowledge to new and unfamiliar situations, and actively engage in thinking processes. These thinking processes involve having the student recognize a problem, plan a procedural strategy, examine the math relationships in the problem, and determine the mathematical knowledge needed to solve the problem. Then the student needs to represent the problem graphically, generate the equation, estimate the answer, sequence the computation steps, compute the answer, and check the answer for reasonableness. The student self-monitors the entire process and explores alternative ways to solve the problem. Problem solving is a complex procedure, and these descriptors are offered as a frame of reference to promote understanding and appreciation of its numerous components.

Fortunately, in spite of the complexity of the concept, the problem-solving emphasis is generating research that provides insights into how to teach students with learning difficulties to solve word problems. Paralleling the emphasis on problem solving has been a focus on strategy instruction. In strategy instruction, students learn a strategy that helps them engage in the appropriate steps needed to recognize and successfully solve a word problem. Numerous learning strategies are being developed and evaluated to teach problem-solving skills to students with learning problems. For example, mnemonics help students with memory problems acquire, remember, and apply specific math content and procedures. The following are some guidelines for problem-solving instruction.

- Link instruction to students' prior knowledge and help them connect what they know in learning new information. For example, to help students learn division facts, point out the relationship of multiplication and division (i.e., $9 \times 7 = 63$, $63 \div 9 = 7$, $63 \div 7 = 9$).

- Teach students to understand concepts and operations.
- Give students problems that pertain to daily living.
- Teach word problems simultaneously with computation skills.
- Concentrate on helping students develop a positive attitude toward math.
- Teach students learning strategies that help them become independent learners.

Cawley et al. (1987, pp. 91–92) present the following list of do's and don'ts for teachers.

Do:

1. Begin problem solving the day a child enters school.
2. Make problem solving the reason for computation.
3. Develop long-term programs of problem solving.
4. Conduct problem solving as a multimodal activity.
5. Parcel out the effects of one variable on another. If the child cannot read the problem, rewrite it. If the computation is too complex, make it simpler.
6. Have children prepare or modify problems.
7. Differentiate between process and knowledge.
8. Prepare problems in such a way that children must act upon the information. Prepare a set of problems in which all problems have the same question.
9. Present problems dealing with familiar subject matter.
10. Constantly monitor progress and modify problems to fit the child's weaknesses and progress.

Don't:

1. Use cue words to signal an operation.
2. Teach children to use computational rules to solve problems. That is, do not tell children to add when they see three different numbers.
3. Use problem-solving activities as an occasional wrap-up to computation.
4. Mark a child wrong if he or she makes a computational error in problem solving if the operation is correct.
5. Train teachers to treat problem solving as secondary to computation.
6. Assume that because the child is able to perform an arithmetic operation that he or she can automatically solve problems that use that operation.
7. Conclude that an incorrect answer automatically indicates lack of facility in problem solving.
8. Fail to realize that problem solving is the most important aspect of mathematics for daily living.
9. Fail to seize the opportunities for training in problem solving in conjunction with other subject areas.
10. Present problem solving in a haphazard manner. Order and careful planning are essential.

Specific interventions for teaching problem-solving skills are presented later in this chapter.

Teaching Generalization

Generalization refers to the performance of the targeted behavior in different, nontraining conditions (i.e., across subjects, settings, people, behaviors, or time) without arranging the same events in the conditions that were present during training (Stokes & Baer, 1977). Students with learning problems typically have difficulty generalizing skills. A lack of instruction aimed at teaching students with learning problems to generalize math skills has contributed to their generalization problems. Ellis, Lenz, and Sabornie (1987a, 1987b) report that generalization must be taught prior to, during, and subsequent to instruction. Selected instructional practices to help students generalize math skills include the following:

1. Develop motivation to learn. It is believed that students who desire to learn a skill or strategy are most likely to generalize it. Motivation helps students feel responsible for their own learning and helps establish the independence needed to apply the new skill in settings without teacher support.
2. Throughout the instructional process, have periodic discussions with students about the rationale for learning the math skill and in which situations it is useful (e.g., homework, recreational activities, and shopping).
3. Throughout the instructional process, provide students with a variety of examples and experiences. For example, vary the manipulative objects (such as cubes, checkers, and buttons) in concrete activities, and use a variety of graphic representations (i.e., different pictures, drawings, and tallies) in semiconcrete activities. Likewise, vary the format in abstract computation or word-problem activities (e.g., present computation problems in vertical and horizontal formats). Also, vary the person doing the instruction (e.g., aide, peer, and parent).
4. Teach skills to a mastery level so that students can concentrate on using and not just remembering the skill.
5. Teach students strategies for solving multistep math problems. When students possess a strategy for solving difficult problems, they are more likely to develop independent behavior and to actively engage in the problem-solving process. Mnemonic devices frequently are used to help students retrieve appropriate strategies.
6. Teach students to solve problems pertinent to their daily lives. This connects the skill to functional

uses and promotes motivation and the need to generalize. Students also can be instructed to create their own word problems.

7. Use reinforcement contingencies that are likely to occur in the natural environment. In this way, students do not depend on artificial contingencies (i.e., reinforcers only available in the classroom) to maintain and use the learned skill.

8. Once the skill is established, move the teaching situation from a highly controlled format (i.e., teacher led) to a more loosely controlled format (such as independent work).

9. Encourage students to generalize.

Using Explicit–Implicit Math Instruction

A sampling of the math literature and research on constructivistic teaching and strategy instruction for students with moderate to mild disabilities provides perspectives on how constructivism is being interpreted and applied within the context of explicit and implicit instruction (Mercer, Jordan, & Miller, 1994, 1996). Moshman (1982) notes that constructivism can be interpreted on a continuum from explicit instruction (i.e., exogenous constructivism) to endogenous implicit instruction. Constructivism has been interpreted and applied in many ways, and the following instructional components are recommended in the constructivism and learning strategy literature.

1. Model target strategy
2. Engage in interactive dialogue (i.e., scaffolding, Socratic teaching, and collaborative discussion)
3. Encourage metacognition and self-regulation
4. Provide prompts and guidance
5. Focus on authentic learning and rationales for learning
6. Use graphs to monitor progress and provide feedback
7. Teach to mastery
8. Use goal setting
9. Teach for transfer
10. Focus on understanding and helping students link previous knowledge with new knowledge
11. Provide explicit instruction
12. Teach mnemonics
13. Encourage reflection and discussion
14. Use student "think alouds"
15. Use teacher scripts
16. Teach in zone of proximal development
17. Check preskill development prior to teaching
18. Use verbal rehearsal
19. Promote peer collaboration

Inspection of these instructional components indicates that constructivism has implications for teacher behaviors, instructional content, and learning factors.

Because teacher-directed instructional components (e.g., components 1, 4, 6, 11, and 15) are listed frequently, the majority of constructivists appear to use explicit instruction when students with moderate to mild disabilities are the target population. This position is understandable when the characteristics of these learners are considered. To expect students who have a history of problems with fluency, metacognitive strategies, memory, attention, generalization, and motivation to engage in efficient implicit learning (i.e., self-discovery learning) is not plausible. Thus, teacher-directed instruction or explicit instruction is a primary component for teaching math to students with disabilities. Cobb, Yackel, and Wood (1992) elaborate on the need for directed instruction in helping students to learn mathematical concepts and relationships. They question whether it is possible for students to recognize mathematical relationships that are developmentally more advanced than their current internal representations. Furthermore, they state that "it would seem necessary to consider the teacher's role in helping students construct replicas of the mathematical relationships presented to them in an easily apprehensible form" (p. 5). Finally, Cobb et al. maintain that much teacher assistance is necessary if learners are to have a conventional wisdom about math that took thousands of years to evolve.

In a meta-analysis of mathematics interventions for elementary students with special needs, Kroesbergen and Van Luit (2003) report that direct instruction and self-instruction (e.g., the use of strategies) were found to be more effective than mediated instruction. In general, direct instruction appears to be most effective for the learning of basic math facts, and self-instruction methods are also effective for the learning of problem-solving skills. Peer tutoring can be helpful and effective at times; however, it cannot replace or be as effective as instruction by an adult teacher.

Prescriptive instructional applications of explicit and implicit strategies have much appeal for helping students with moderate to mild disabilities acquire and use math fluently in their daily lives. To realize the potential of explicit–implicit instruction in our nation's schools, several obstacles must be overcome. Algorithm-driven instructional materials must be replaced with math materials that have been validated and replicated in various school settings prior to publishing; correspond to the academic school year (i.e., many materials have 40 to 60 more daily lessons than there are days in the school year); guide the teacher to use authentic content, model explicit metacognitive strategies, use instructionally prescriptive interactive dialogues, use elaborated feedback, and use transfer of learning techniques; and recognize the strengths of various paradigms.

The potential new knowledge that explicit–implicit instruction can provide is exciting if educators take the time and effort to apply and test it systematically with teachers and students. Given the heterogeneity of learners, deductive and inductive learning are probably *both* important for many individuals as they acquire, maintain, and generalize knowledge.

Promoting a Positive Attitude Toward Math

Many students with learning problems have a history of math failures. Consequently, they often develop negative attitudes toward math learning and feel insecure about their capabilities to succeed in math. Attitudes, beliefs, and motivation play an important role in the learning of math. Because students' feelings about their experiences with math can influence the level of their efforts, the teacher should promote a positive attitude toward math by providing an environment that is accepting, encouraging, stimulating, and enjoyable.

Clearly, math instruction must be designed to ensure success and promote positive attitudes. Selected guidelines for promoting positive attitudes toward math learning include the following:

* Involve students in setting challenging but attainable instructional goals. Goal setting has a powerful influence on student involvement and effort (Locke & Latham, 1990).
* Ensure success by building on prior skills and using task analysis to simplify the instructional sequence of a math skill or concept. Use charts to give students feedback on how well they are doing.
* Discuss the relevance of a math skill to real-life problems. Use word problems that are part of a student's daily life.
* Communicate positive expectancies of students' abilities to learn. Students need to sense that the teacher believes they will achieve in math.
* Help students understand the premise that their own efforts influence both success and failure. This premise helps students realize that their behavior directly affects what happens to them. In turn, they realize that they are in control of their own learning.

* Model an enthusiastic and positive attitude toward math and maintain a lively pace during math instruction.
* Reinforce students for effort on math work and stress that errors are learning opportunities.

myeducationlab

Go to the Assignments and Activities section of the Topic Assessing and Teaching Math in the MyEducationLab for your course and complete the activity entitled Computational Fluency.

INSTRUCTIONAL PRACTICES FOR COMPUTATION AND PROBLEM SOLVING

The instructional components for teaching computation presented in Figure 12.1 include teaching procedures and activities presented in the remainder of this chapter. Because many students with learning problems fail to master basic facts, two programs are discussed for teaching math facts. Following these programs, concrete-semiconcrete-abstract teaching activities, basic rules and algorithms, problem-solving interventions, life skills math, estimation, and calculators are presented.

Thornton and Toohey Math Facts Program

Thornton and Toohey (1985) report substantial literature that indicates that modifying the *sequence* and *presentation* of learning tasks can improve basic fact learning among students with learning problems. They offer ten guidelines that are supported by the literature for planning and implementing basic fact instruction for students with learning problems. These guidelines form the basis for *MATHFACT*, which was developed and used successfully in Queensland, Australia (Thornton & Toohey 1982–1985). Their guidelines include the following:

1. *Consider prerequisite learnings by looking ahead to review or reteach as necessary.* Mathematical concepts and operations are hierarchical. Concepts that are basic to learning a new skill or concept should be taught before introducing the new material. For example, ensure that sums-to-9 facts are mastered before introducing subtraction facts.
2. *Provide ongoing diagnosis and assessment.* Attention to the student's rate of progress, types of errors, understanding of concepts, and learning style is basic to successful math facts instruction.

FIGURE 12.1

Instructional components for teaching computation

1. Provide concrete experiences to promote understanding.
   Example:

      4   +   3   =   _____

2. Provide semiconcrete experiences to promote understanding.
   Example: *//// + ///*
   $$4 + 3 = \underline{\quad}$$

3. Provide abstract activities and practice to promote mastery.
   Example: $4 + 3 = \underline{\quad}$

4. Teach rules that show patterns and relationships.
   Example: *Zero rule:* Any number plus zero equals the number.
   $$4 + 0 = 4$$
   Order rule: Addends yield the same sum regardless of their order.
   $$4 + 3 = 7 \qquad 3 + 4 = 7$$

5. Teach algorithms for solving problems.
   Example: *Fact:* $7 + 2 = \underline{\quad}$ *Algorithm:* Start BIG and count on.

6. Use mnemonics to help students remember algorithms or problem-solving procedures.
   Example: DRAW
   D–*Discover* the sign (+, −, ×, ÷).
   R–*Read* the problem ("four plus three equals blank").
   A–*Answer,* or "DRAW" a conceptual representation of the problem, using lines
   //// ///
   and tallies, and check ($4 + 3 = \underline{\quad}$).
   //// ///
   W–*Write* the answer ($4 + 3 = \underline{\ 7\ }$).

7. Provide a variety of practice activities to promote mastery and generalization.
   Example: Provide vertical and horizontal problems.
   Use self-correcting materials, instructional games, peer tutoring, and computer-assisted instruction for seatwork.
   Provide activities to improve the rate of responses (e.g., 1-minute probes).

8. Teach problem solving.
   Example: Have students solve a variety of word problems.
   Have students create their own word problems.
   Provide students with strategies for solving problems.

3. *Modify the sequence in which facts are presented for learning.* Traditional fact instruction sequences addition facts by the size of the sum. Thornton and Toohey (1985) maintain that other sequences are more effective for various learners. For example, for immature students or those with serious deficits, they recommend beginning instruction with the 72 easiest addition facts: count-ons (i.e., +1, +2, +3) (45 facts), zeroes (19 facts), doubles (6 facts not previously encountered), and 10 sums (2 facts not previously encountered—6 + 4 and 4 + 6).

4. *Before drill, teach students strategies for computing answers to unknown facts.* Many students with learning problems need to be taught specific

strategies to help them solve problems independently. For example:

7	6	Start BIG and count on
+2	+3	
6	0	Plus zero stays the same
+0	+8	
8	6	Order of addends does not
+6	+8	affect sum

Overall, the following sequence is suggested: easy addition facts, easy subtraction facts, other addition facts, and other subtraction facts.

5. *Modify the presentation of activities to fit the learning style of each student.* Students with learning problems are a heterogeneous population with many different learning styles and preferences. Various procedures take advantage of different modality preferences. For example, for auditory learners, the teacher can (a) precede all actions and demonstrations with spoken instructions and (b) provide a verbal summary of each step. For visual learners, the teacher can (a) precede all oral instructions with concrete manipulations or mimed demonstrations and (b) provide a visual summary of each step. For kinesthetic/tactile learners, the teacher can (a) precede all instructions with guiding the student to physically manipulate the objects and (b) use textured material (e.g., pipe cleaners, sandpaper, and magnetic boards).

6. *Control the pacing.* Knowing when to move faster or slow down is critical to good fact instruction. Continuous monitoring of fact progress can facilitate pacing.

7. *Help students discriminate when to use a strategy, and integrate new learnings with old.* Some students with learning problems learn a strategy and apply it to all situations. For example, a student may learn a count-on strategy and apply it to all addition facts. A student's appropriate use of a strategy should be strengthened by activities that require identifying math facts to which it applies.

8. *Provide verbal prompts.* Repeatedly give students verbal prompts during instruction. This helps some students independently associate the prompts with the specific facts to which they apply.

9. *Help students develop self-monitoring skills.* Many students with learning problems need to acquire skills that focus on *how to learn*. Such techniques as cognitive behavior modification and academic strategy training enable the student to develop self-monitoring skills that are useful across tasks and situations.

10. *Ensure provisions for overlearning.* Once facts are mastered, emphasis shifts to activities that help students with learning problems store them in long-term memory. This usually requires a variety of drill activities and performances on tasks at a high criterion level. Instructional games, self-correcting materials, computer-assisted instruction, peer teaching, and periodic review are a few of the activities appropriate for developing overlearning.

Mercer and Miller Math Facts Program

The *Strategic Math Series* (Mercer & Miller, 1991–1993) features seven phases to teach basic math facts.

Phase 1: Pretest

Phase 2: Teach concrete application

Phase 3: Teach representational application

Phase 4: Introduce the "DRAW" strategy

Phase 5: Teach abstract application

Phase 6: Posttest

Phase 7: Provide practice to fluency and develop problem-solving strategies

To help teach basic facts, all lessons in the *Strategic Math Series* include a sequence of procedures developed from the effective teaching research. These steps have demonstrated effectiveness with students who have learning difficulties. These instructional procedures include the following:

1. *Give an advance organize.* The first component in each lesson is the advance organizer, which prepares the student for learning.

2. *Describe and model.* This component allows the teacher to describe and model the computation process, following two basic procedures. In Procedure 1, the teacher asks and answers questions aloud while demonstrating how to compute the answer for one or more problems on the learning sheet. In computing the problem, the teacher verbalizes thoughts so that students can better understand the thought processes involved. In Procedure 2, the teacher continues to demonstrate how to solve one or more problems by asking questions and soliciting student responses and using prompts and cues to facilitate correct responses. Thus, in Procedure 2, the teacher and the students work a problem together.

3. *Conduct guided practice.* Guided practice allows the teacher to instruct and support students as they move toward independently solving problems on their learning sheets. During this time, the teacher follows two basic procedures. In Procedure 1, the teacher's role is to prompt and facilitate students' thought processes. To facilitate correct responses, the teacher asks questions and solicits student responses, using prompts and cues, and, thus, guides students through each problem in a way that ensures success. In Procedure 2, the teacher instructs students to solve the next few problems on the learning sheet and offers assistance to individual learners only if needed.

4. *Conduct independent practice.* Independent practice of facts is an integral component of the lessons. It enables the teacher to determine whether students can solve facts independently. The sample dialogues for this component consist of simple directions, including a statement that reminds students to use previously learned skills and techniques to solve problems. To enhance generalization, students solve problems in horizontal and vertical formats; to promote mastery, the rules and relationships (i.e., structures) of each operation are covered. During this time, the teacher does not provide any assistance.

5. *Conduct problem-solving practice.* Like independent practice of computation facts, problem-solving practice constitutes an integral component of all lessons. To teach students the thought process involved in problem solving, the teacher uses a graduated sequence of word problems. For example, in early lessons, students solve problems involving three words; in later lessons, they write their own word problems. Along the way, students learn to extract any information that may be irrelevant to a problem. Thus, when students complete a facts program, they are able to solve word problems with and without extraneous information and to write their own word problems.

6. *Provide feedback.* Because proper feedback is critical to learning, a feedback component is found in all the lessons. This component follows the elaborated feedback routine developed by Kline et al. (1991) and allows the teacher to recognize and praise correct student responses and, thus, prevent future errors. Feedback is facilitated through the use of a facts progress chart on which the teacher and the student plot the student's scores for the last ten problems on a learning sheet.

The *Strategic Math Series* has yielded excellent results from field testing (Mercer & Miller, 1992; Miller, Mercer, & Dillon, 1992). The field-test results indicate that 109 students with learning problems were able to acquire computational skills across facts; solve word problems with and without extraneous information; create word problems involving facts; apply a mnemonic strategy to difficult problems; increase rate of computation; and generalize math skills across examiners, settings, and tasks.

Concrete-Semiconcrete-Abstract Activities

The concrete-semiconcrete-abstract (CSA) sequence is appropriate for teaching the understanding of math throughout the span of math concepts, skills, and word problems. The use of manipulative objects requires the following specific guidelines to ensure effective results.

- Before abstract experiences, instruction must proceed from concrete (i.e., manipulative) experiences to semiconcrete experiences.
- The main objective of manipulative aids is to help students understand and develop mental images of mathematical processes.
- The activity must accurately represent the actual process. For example, a direct correlation should exist between the manipulative activities and the paper-and-pencil activities.
- More than one manipulative object should be used in teaching a concept.
- The aids should be used individually by each student.
- The manipulative experience must involve the moving of objects. The learning occurs from the student's physical actions on the objects rather than from the object themselves.
- The teacher should continuously ask students questions about their actions as they manipulate objects and should encourage students to verbalize their thinking.
- The teacher should have students write the problem being solved through the use of objects and have students use objects to check answers.

Implicit in CSA instruction is an emphasis on enabling students to understand the concepts of math prior to memorizing facts, algorithms, and operations. According to the CSA sequence, instruction begins at the concrete level where the student uses three-dimensional objects to solve computation problems. After successfully solving problems at the concrete level, the student proceeds to the semiconcrete (or representational) level. At the semiconcrete level, students use two-dimensional drawings (i.e., pictures or lines and tallies) to solve computation problems. After successfully solving problems at this level, the student begins to work at the next level, the abstract level. At the abstract level, the student looks at the computation problem and tries to solve it without using objects or drawings. The student reads the problem, remembers the answer or thinks of a way to compute the answer, and writes the answer. No objects or drawings are used in the computation unless the student is unable to answer a problem. Because success in math requires the ability to solve problems at the abstract level, student mastery at this level is essential. The use of the CSA sequence to teach various computation skills is presented next.

Place Value   To begin place value instruction at the *concrete level,* gather two plastic cups, a bundle of straws, and a set of blocks. Set the two cups on poster board; label the right one *ones* and the left one *tens.* Tell the student to count the blocks. For each block the student counts, place a straw in the ones cup. Stop when nine blocks are counted and nine straws are in the ones cup. Before picking up the tenth straw, explain that one straw in the tens cup represents ten objects. The student then takes the nine straws out of the ones cup and places one straw in the tens cup. Next, the student continues to count the blocks and place the straws. Counting proceeds in the following manner: 1 ten and 1, 1 ten and 2, . . . 3 tens and 4, 3 tens and 5, and so on. Each time a ten is reached, empty the ones cup and place a straw in the tens cup. Although the student is told that 1 ten and 1 is another name for 11, and 3 tens and 5 is another name for 35, during place value instruction encourage the student to count using the 3 tens and 5 system. The student continues with the blocks and straws until able to do the task easily.

At the *semiconcrete level,* use illustrations instead of the blocks, straws, and cups. For example:

Task: Count the items and place the correct number in each cup.

The completed task would look like this:

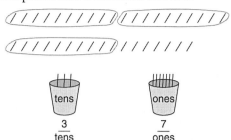

Gradually fade the pictures of the cups and replace them with:

$$\overline{\text{tens}} \quad \overline{\text{ones}}$$

The items may change to pictures of real objects.

At the **abstract level,** add numbers gradually in place of items. For example:

Task 1: Count the items and identify the number of tens and ones.

///////////////////////////
_____ tens ___ ones
× × × × × × × × × × × ×
_____ ten ____ ones

Task 2: Identify the number of tens and ones in each number.

24 _____ tens   87 _____ tens
_____ ones   _____ ones

These activities represent only one way of providing place value instruction at the concrete, semiconcrete, and abstract levels. The teacher can expand and use different activities across the three levels.

Addition: Sums-to-9   Learning sums-to-9 underlies later math functioning. These sums are the initial facts to be mastered.

Concrete level: 6 + 3 = _____

The student looks at the first number and counts that many objects. The student looks at the second number and counts that many objects. The student counts all objects for the sum.

Example:

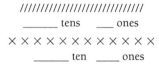

Semiconcrete level: 6 + 3 = _____

The student looks at the first number and draws that many tallies. The student looks at the second number and draws that many tallies. The student counts all tallies for the sum.

Example:

$$\begin{array}{r} 6 \\ + 3 \\ \hline 9 \end{array}$$

Abstract level: 6 + 3 = _____

The student looks at the problem and solves it without objects or drawings. The student uses an algorithm (such as start BIG and count up) or memory to solve the problem.

Example:

$$\begin{array}{r} 6 \\ + 3 \\ \hline 9 \end{array} \qquad \text{or} \qquad 6 + 3 = 9$$

Addition: Sums-to-18   After sums-to-9 and place value to two places are learned, the student is ready for instruction in addition facts of sums-to-18.

Concrete level: 7 + 5 = _____

The student looks at the first number and counts that many objects. The student looks at the second number and counts that many objects. The student manipulates the objects to form a group of ten and a group of two. The student writes and says the answer as 1 ten and 2 ones or 12.

Example:

7   +   5   =

○ ○ ○ ○ ○ ○ ○   ○ ○ ○ ○ ○

10   +   2   =   <u>12</u>

○ ○ ○ ○ ○ ○ ○ ○ ○ ○   ○ ○

Semiconcrete level: 7 + 5 = _____

The student looks at the first number and draws that many tallies. The student looks at the second number and draws that many tallies. The student circles a group of ten and computes the answer as 1 ten and 2 ones.

Example:

$$\begin{array}{r} 7 \\ + 5 \\ \hline \end{array} \qquad \text{/ / / / / / /} \\ \text{/ / / / /}$$

$$\begin{array}{r} 7 \\ + 5 \\ \hline 12 \end{array} \qquad \text{/ / / / / / /} \\ \text{/ / / / /} \qquad \begin{array}{r} 10 \\ + 2 \\ \hline 12 \end{array}$$

Abstract level: 7 + 5 = _____

The student answers the problem from memory or uses an algorithm.

Example:

$$\begin{array}{r} 7 \\ + 5 \\ \hline 12 \end{array} \qquad \text{or} \qquad 7 + 5 = 12$$

Addition with Regrouping   When going from the concrete to the semiconcrete level, the teacher simply replaces real objects with pictures of objects, dots, or tallies. The step from the semiconcrete to the abstract level involves replacing pictures and tallies with numbers. The following examples are provided to assist the teacher in developing instructional tasks for addition with regrouping.

Concrete level: 26 + 17 = _____

The student looks at the first number and counts the appropriate number of objects grouped into tens and ones. The student looks at the second number and counts the appropriate number of objects grouped into tens and ones. The student looks at the total number of ones and groups them into tens. The student counts the total groups of tens and ones and writes the answer.

Example:

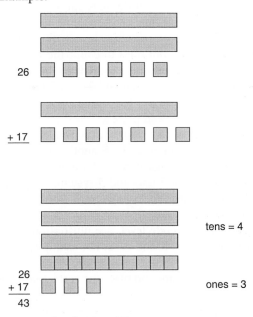

Semiconcrete level: 26 + 17 = _____

The student looks at the first number and draws tens and ones. The student looks at the second number and draws tens and ones. The student looks at the total number of ones and groups them into tens. The student counts the total groups of tens and ones and writes the answer.

Example:

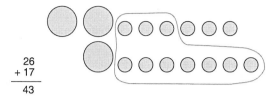

$$26$$
$$+\ 17$$
$$\overline{43}$$

= 4 tens, 3 ones

Abstract level: 26 + 17 = _____

The student uses an algorithm to solve the problem.

Example:

$$26 \quad \text{or} \quad 26 + 17 = 43$$
$$+\ 17$$
$$\overline{43}$$

Subtraction Facts (1 to 9)   After addition facts through 9 are learned, the teaching of subtraction facts (1 to 9) is simple. When the "add on" approach to subtraction is used, the student must find a missing addend instead of a difference. The missing addend approach involves the same logic used in addition; thus, the student can use knowledge of addition facts to solve subtraction problems. For example, an addition fact can be expressed as an addition *or* a subtraction equation, depending on which unknown the student is seeking to compute.

Addition: 4 + 3 = 7 (addend + addend = sum)

Subtraction: 7 − 3 = 4 (sum − addend = missing addend)

In the missing addend approach to subtraction, the student uses knowledge of addition facts to answer the subtraction question, "What number goes with 3 to make another name for (i.e., equal) 7?" Thus, when solving 7 − 3 = ___, the problem becomes 3 + ___ = 7. Although the missing addend approach is feasible mathematically, the "take away" approach is used more widely to teach students with learning problems. The "take away" approach appears more relevant to the real world of subtraction when solving word problems or demonstrating the subtraction process. Subtraction tasks at each of the three levels for the facts through 9 are presented next.

Concrete level: 7 − 3 = _____

The student looks at the first number and counts the appropriate number of objects grouped into tens and ones. The student looks at the second number and takes (or moves) away the appropriate number of objects. The student counts the remaining objects for the answer.

Example:

$$7$$
$$-\ 3$$
$$\overline{4}$$

objects taken away

Semiconcrete level: 7 − 3 = _____

The student looks at the first number and draws that many tallies. The student looks at the second number and crosses out that many tallies. The student counts the remaining tallies for the answer.

Example:

$$7 \quad ////XXX$$
$$-\ 3$$
$$\overline{4}$$

Abstract level: 7 − 3 = _____

The student answers the problem from memory or uses an algorithm.

Example:

$$7 \quad \text{or} \quad 7 - 3 = 4$$
$$-\ 3$$
$$\overline{4}$$

Subtraction Facts (10 to 18)   When solving subtraction facts 10 to 18, the student must recognize place value (i.e., recognize that a portion of the take-away number comes from the ten). It helps to teach the BBB rule: In subtraction, when the *bottom* number in the ones column is *bigger* than the tens number in the ones column, *break* down the ten in the next column and trade it for 10 ones.

Concrete level: 14 − 6 = _____

The student looks at the first number, counts that many objects, and groups them as the appropriate number of tens and ones. The student looks at the second number and takes away the appropriate number of objects from the ones and from a renamed group of ten ones. The student counts the remaining objects for the answer.

Example:

becomes

$$14$$
$$-\ 6$$
$$\overline{8}$$

take away

Semiconcrete level: 14 − 6 = _____

The student looks at the first number and draws a group of ten and the appropriate number of ones. The student uses the BBB rule to trade a ten for 10 ones. The student looks at the second number and crosses out the appropriate number of lines from the ones and from the 10 ones. The student counts the remaining lines for the answer.

Example:

$$
\begin{array}{r}
14 \\
- \ 6 \\
\hline
8
\end{array}
$$

Abstract level: 14 − 6 = _____

The student answers the problem from memory or uses an algorithm.

Example:

$$
\begin{array}{r}
14 \\
- \ 6 \\
\hline
8
\end{array}
\quad \text{or} \quad 14 - 6 = 8
$$

Subtraction with Regrouping   The following examples can help the teacher develop instructional tasks for subtraction with regrouping at all three levels.

Concrete level: 33 − 18 = _____

The student looks at the first number and counts that many objects and groups them as the appropriate number of tens and ones. The student looks at the second number, uses the BBB rule, and then takes away the appropriate number of objects from the ones and from a renamed group of 10 ones. The student counts the remaining objects for the answer.

Example:

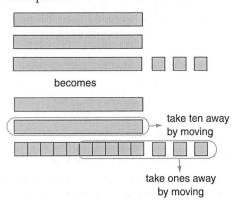

answer = 1 ten and 5 ones or 15

Semiconcrete level: 33 − 18 = _____

The student looks at the first number and draws tens and ones. The student looks at the second number, uses the BBB rule, and then crosses out the appropriate number from the ones and a renamed group of 10 ones. The student counts the remaining tens and ones for the answer.

Example:

becomes

slash through number taken away after regrouping

answer = 1 ten and 5 ones or 15

Abstract level: 33 − 18 = _____

The student uses an algorithm to solve the problem.

Example:

$$
\begin{array}{r}
33 \\
- \ 18 \\
\hline
15
\end{array}
\quad \text{or} \quad 33 - 18 = 15
$$

Multiplication   The 100 multiplication facts (×0 to ×9) are basic to more complex multiplication operations.

Concrete level: 3 × 4 = _____

The student looks at the first number and selects that many containers to represent groups. The student looks at the second number and puts that many objects in each container (i.e., group). The student counts or adds objects across the groups for the answer.

Example:

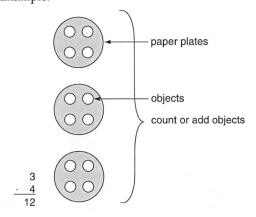

paper plates

objects

count or add objects

$$
\begin{array}{r}
3 \\
\cdot \ 4 \\
\hline
12
\end{array}
$$

Semiconcrete level: 3 × 4 = _____

The student looks at the first number and draws that many groups using horizontal lines. The student looks at the second number and draws that many tallies in each group (i.e., horizontal line). The student counts or adds the tallies across the groups for the answer.

Example:

```
  3  _____
× 4  _____  groups
     _____

  3  ////    4
× 4  ////    4    add tallies
 12  ////    4
```

Abstract level: 3 × 4 = _____

The student answers the problem from memory or uses an algorithm.

Example:

```
  3    or    3 × 4 = 12
× 4
 12
```

Division   Division is considered to be the most difficult of the four operations. For example, long division requires the use of division, multiplication, and subtraction in computing quotients. The following examples illustrate division problems involving solving for number of groups of objects.

Concrete level: 12 ÷ 4 = _____ or 4)‾12‾

The student looks at the first number, or the number within the lines, and counts that many objects. The student looks at the second number, or the number outside the lines, and groups objects according to that number. The student counts the number of groups for the answer.

Example:

```
● ● ● ● ● ● ● ● ● ● ● ●   objects
       becomes

●●●●   ●●●●   ●●●●   groups
  1      2      3
12 |4 = 3
```

Semiconcrete level: 12 ÷ 4 = _____ or 4)‾12‾

The student looks at the first number, or the number within the lines, and draws that many tallies. The student looks at the second number, or the number outside the lines, and circles (or groups) that many tallies until all the tallies are within circles (i.e., groups). The student

also can connect groups of tallies with lines. The student counts the number of circles (i.e., groups) for the answer.

Example:

```
/ / / / / / / / / / / /   tallies
       becomes
```

```
⟨///⟩ ⟨///⟩ ⟨///⟩   circled
  1      2      3     groups
```

```
//// //// ////   connected
  1     2     3    groups
```

12 | 4 = 3

Abstract level: 12 ÷ 4 = _____ or 4)‾12‾

The student answers the problem from memory or uses an algorithm.

Example:

```
                        3
12 ÷ 4 = 3   or    4)‾12‾
```

Division with Remainder   The following examples present division problems in which the answer contains a remainder.

Concrete level: 20 ÷ 3 = _____ or 3)‾20‾

The student looks at the first number, or the number within the lines, and counts that many objects. The student looks at the second number, or the number outside the lines, and groups objects (e.g., circles with string or rearranges groups) according to that number. The student counts the number of circles with string (or the rearranged groups) and the remaining number of ungrouped objects for the answer.

Example:

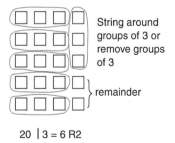

String around groups of 3 or remove groups of 3

remainder

20 | 3 = 6 R2

Semiconcrete level: 20 ÷ 3 = _____ or 3)‾20‾

The student looks at the first number, or the number within the lines, and draws that many tallies. The student looks at the second number, or the number outside the lines, and circles (or groups) objects according to that number. The student counts the number of circles (i.e., groups) and the remaining number of ungrouped tallies for the answer.

Example:

20 | 3 = 6 R2

At this level the student also may use a grid, which is covered with acetate and used with an overhead pen or grease pencil, to solve division problems (e.g., determine the number of 3s in 20). In performing the task, the student counts until the 20th block is identified. Then 1s are written in the first three blocks, 2s are written in the second three blocks, and so on until no more sets of 3 are left in the first 20 blocks. For example:

1	1	1	2	2	2	3	3	3	4
4	4	5	5	5	6	6	6	X	Ⓧ

student circles the 20th block
20 | 3 = 6 R2

Abstract level: 20 ÷ 3 = _____ or 3)‾20‾

The student answers the problem from memory or uses an algorithm.

Example:

$$\begin{array}{r} 6 \text{ R2} \\ 3\overline{)20} \\ \underline{-3} \\ 17 \\ \underline{-3} \\ 14 \\ \underline{-3} \\ 11 \\ \underline{-3} \\ 8 \\ \underline{-3} \\ 5 \\ \underline{-3} \\ \boxed{2} \end{array}$$

Recognition of Unit Fractions   The teacher can use the following instructional tasks to teach several skills in fractions.

Concrete level: Let [_____] be 1 and smaller size blocks represent fractional subregions of it.

[_____] may be a block or a container that holds fractional blocks. Use the blocks to display ¼, ⅓, ½ and so on.

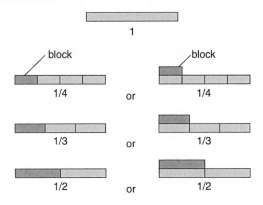

Numerous commercial materials are available for working with fractions at the concrete level (e.g., Cuisenaire rods and Unifix cubes).

Semiconcrete level: Write the unit fraction for the designs.

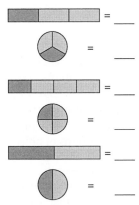

Abstract level: Use numbers to express the unit fractions for one-fourth, one-third, and one-half.

Addition of Fractions with the Same Denominators

Concrete level: (⅓ + ⅓)

Semiconcrete level: (¼ + ¾)

⊘ + ⊘ = ⊘

Abstract level:

1/3 + 1/3 = □/□

1/4 + 2/4 = □/□

Addition and Subtraction of Mixed Fractions

Concrete level:

Task 1: Use real blocks ($3\frac{2}{3} + 2\frac{2}{3}$)

Task 2: Use string ($5\frac{1}{4} - 2\frac{3}{4}$)

Semiconcrete level:

Task 1: Use drawings ($3\frac{2}{3} + 2\frac{2}{3}$)

$$5\ \ ^4/_3$$

Task 2: Use lines ($5\frac{1}{4} - 2\frac{3}{4}$)

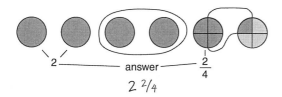

$$2\ ^2/4$$

Abstract level:

$$\begin{aligned}
3\tfrac{2}{3}&\\
+2\tfrac{2}{3}&\\
\hline
5\tfrac{4}{3}&=6\tfrac{1}{3}
\end{aligned}$$

$$\begin{aligned}
5\tfrac{1}{4}&=4\tfrac{5}{4}\\
-2\tfrac{3}{4}&=2\tfrac{3}{4}\\
\hline
2\tfrac{2}{4}&=2\tfrac{1}{2}
\end{aligned}$$

For activities on multiplying and dividing fractions at the various levels, see fraction activities presented later in this chapter.

Basic Rules and Algorithms

The teaching of basic rules and algorithms helps students compute math more efficiently. Moreover, many rules and algorithms are based on relationships that foster student understanding and computational problem solving.

Addition Rules The following five addition rules are basic for understanding math.

1. *Order rule.* The order of addends does not affect the answer (commutative property) (e.g., $6 + 3 = 9$; $3 + 6 = 9$).

2. *Zero rule.* Any number plus zero is the number (e.g., $3 + 0 = 3$; $0 + 7 = 7$).

3. *One rule.* Any number plus 1 is one more than the number (i.e., count up by 1) (e.g., $3 + 1 = 4$; $18 + 1 = 19$).

4. *Nine rule.* Any single-digit number greater than zero added to 9 results in the addend number minus 1 plus 10 (e.g., $9 + 7 = 6 + 10 = 16$).

5. *Tens rule.* Any single-digit number added to 10 results in the 0 in 10 being changed to the number being added to it (e.g., $10 + 6 = 16$).

Addition Algorithms After the student knows addition facts through sums-to-18, an adaptation of the *tens method* may be a useful algorithm. To illustrate:

$$\begin{array}{r}
\overset{2\;2\;2}{8}67\\
57\overset{5}{4}^1\\
\overset{1}{6}47\\
+78\overset{7}{6}\\
\hline
2874
\end{array}$$

Beginning at the top right in the example, $7 + 4 = 11$, which can be renamed as 1 ten and 1 one. A horizontal line is drawn through the 4 to represent the ten, and the ones number is written on the extension of the line. Because the line represents the ten, the student no longer needs to hold it in mind. The student uses the 1 (i.e., ones digit) that is left over to begin adding until another ten is obtained. In this example, $1 + 7 = 8$; then $8 + 6 = 14$. Thus, a line is drawn through the 6 to represent the ten, and the 4 ones are written on the line. Because all numbers in the ones column have been added, the 4 is recorded as the one's digit at the bottom of the column.

The two lines drawn in the ones column represent 2 tens; thus, addition in the tens column begins by carrying the 2 tens by writing 2 above the tens column. These 2 tens are added to the 6 tens, and this continues until there is a sum greater than or equal to 10 tens: 2 tens + 6 tens = 8 tens; 8 tens + 7 tens = 15 tens. A line is drawn across the 7 to represent 10 tens and the remaining 5 tens are written on the line. Then, 5 tens + 4 tens = 9 tens; 9 tens + 8 tens = 17 tens. A line is drawn across the 8, and the 7 is recorded on the line extension and as the tens digit at the bottom. In the tens column each line represents 10 tens or 1 hundred. Thus, the two lines in the tens column are carried by writing 2 at the top of the hundreds column to begin addition there. The 2 hundreds are added to 8 hundreds, and addition proceeds in a similar manner.

Another addition algorithm is referred to as *partial sums.* To illustrate:

$$\begin{array}{r} 47 \\ + \ 28 \\ \hline 15 \\ 60 \\ \hline 75 \end{array}$$

In this algorithm, when the sum of the ones column is greater than or equal to 10, it is written as a two-digit number at the bottom of the ones and tens columns. In the given example, $7 + 8 = 15$, so 15 is written at the bottom of the columns. Next, the tens column is added and the sum is written below the ones column sum. In this case, 4 tens + 2 tens = 6 tens, or 60. Then the two partial sums are added.

A left-to-right addition algorithm enables the student to regroup in the answer. This process offers some students a better understanding of the regrouping process. To illustrate:

$$\begin{array}{r} 898 \\ + \ 367 \\ \hline 11 \\ 15 \\ 15 \\ \hline 1265 \end{array}$$

Subtraction Rules   The following six subtraction rules are basic for understanding math.

1. *Zero rule.* Any number minus zero equals the number (e.g., $6 - 0 = 6$; $9 - 0 = 9$).
2. *One rule.* Any number minus 1 is one less (i.e., count backwards by one) (e.g., $6 - 1 = 5$; $19 - 1 = 18$).
3. *Same number rule.* Any number minus the same number is zero (e.g., $8 - 8 = 0$).
4. *One less rule.* Any number minus 1 is the next smaller number (e.g., $15 - 1 = 14$).
5. *BBB rule.* In subtraction, when the *bottom* number is *bigger* than the top number, it is necessary to *break* down the top number in the next column, trade it for 10 units, and then subtract.
6. *Addition/subtraction relationship rule.* In a subtraction problem, the answer (i.e., difference or missing addend) added to the number that is being subtracted (i.e., subtrahend or known addend) equals the top number (i.e., minuend or sum) (e.g., $13 - 5 = 8$; $8 + 5 = 13$). This rule enables the student to use knowledge of addition facts to solve subtraction facts. For example, to solve the problem $12 - 7$, the student asks, "What number added to 7 equals 12?"

Subtraction Algorithms   After the student has mastered subtraction facts with minuends to 18, selected algorithms are helpful. Several algorithms are based on the fact that adding or subtracting a constant number (i.e., the same number) to or from the minuend and the subtrahend does not change the answer (i.e., the difference or missing addend). To illustrate subtracting a constant to avoid regrouping:

$$\begin{array}{ccc} \begin{array}{r} 6000 \\ -3642 \\ \hline \end{array} & \text{Student work:} \quad \begin{array}{r} 6000 - 1 \\ -3642 - 1 \\ \hline \end{array} & \begin{array}{r} 5999 \\ -3641 \\ \hline 2358 \end{array} \end{array}$$

In the above problem, the zeros in 6000 are changed to 9s by subtracting 1. When the 1 is subtracted from both numbers, the problem is solved easily without regrouping. This algorithm is especially helpful because subtraction problems involving money frequently have zeros in the minuend (e.g., $\$5.00 - 2.38$; $\$10.00 - 6.74$).

To illustrate adding a constant to avoid regrouping:

$$\begin{array}{ccc} \begin{array}{r} 46 \\ -28 \\ \hline \end{array} & \text{Student work:} \quad \begin{array}{r} 46 + 2 \\ -28 + 2 \\ \hline \end{array} & \begin{array}{r} 48 \\ -30 \\ \hline 18 \end{array} \end{array}$$

In the above problem, when the bigger number is on the bottom in the ones column, a constant number that produces a zero in the ones column is added to both numbers. When the subtrahend becomes a zero, the problem is solved easily without regrouping.

Another example of adding a constant to the top and bottom numbers involves adding a ten in the top number of the ones column and a ten in the bottom number of the tens column. This helps simplify regrouping for some students. For example:

Student work:

$$\begin{array}{ccl} \begin{array}{r} 42 \\ - \ 27 \\ \hline \end{array} & \begin{array}{r} 4^{1}2 \\ -^{3}27 \\ \hline 15 \end{array} & \begin{array}{l} \text{add 10 to top number in} \\ \text{ones column} \\ \text{add 10 to bottom number} \\ \text{in tens column} \end{array} \end{array}$$

This procedure also can be used effectively to compute fractions. For example:

$$\begin{array}{ccl} \begin{array}{r} 5\,\tfrac{1}{4} \\ - \ 2\,\tfrac{3}{4} \\ \hline \end{array} & \begin{array}{r} 5\,\tfrac{5}{4} \\ -\ 3\,\tfrac{3}{4} \\ \hline 2\,\tfrac{2}{4} \end{array} & \begin{array}{l} \text{Student work: add one} \\ (\tfrac{4}{4}) \text{ to fraction in top number} \\ \text{add one (1) to whole number} \\ \text{in bottom number} \end{array} \end{array}$$

The following ***low-stress method of subtraction*** is an effective procedure in remedial instruction. It is based on notation for recording a minuend or sum in several ways. For example, 752 may be recorded as 6^152 or 6^14^12 or 74^12. When using this notation, the regrouped sum or minuend is recorded in the middle before the recalling of subtraction facts. For example:

(a) 8472
    − 6673

$$
\begin{array}{cccc}
8 & 4 & 7 & 2 \\
\hline
7 & {}^13 & {}^16 & {}^12 \\
\hline
- 6 & 6 & 7 & 3 \\
\hline
1 & 7 & 9 & 9
\end{array}
$$

(b) 65400062
    − 21450238

$$
\begin{array}{cccccccc}
6 & 5 & 4 & 0 & 0 & 0 & 6 & 2 \\
\hline
6 & 4 & {}^13 & 9 & 9 & {}^10 & 5 & {}^12 \\
\hline
- 2 & 1 & 4 & 5 & 0 & 2 & 3 & 8 \\
\hline
4 & 3 & 9 & 4 & 9 & 8 & 2 & 4
\end{array}
$$

In this algorithm, all renaming is completed before subtraction takes place. The student is reminded that renaming is necessary each time the subtrahend (or known addend) in each column is greater than the minuend (or sum).

A left-to-right subtraction algorithm requires the student to regroup in the answer. This process helps students understand regrouping. To illustrate:

$$
\begin{array}{cccc}
532 & 532 & 532 & 532 \\
-246 & -246 & -246 & -246 \\
\hline
3 & 3\!9 & 3\!9\!6 & 286 \\
 & 2 & 28 &
\end{array}
$$

Multiplication Rules The following six multiplication rules are basic for understanding math.

1. *Order rule.* The order of the numbers to be multiplied does not affect the answer (e.g., $6 \times 3 = 18$; $3 \times 6 = 18$).
2. *Zero rule.* Any number times zero is zero (e.g., $8 \times 0 = 0$; $647 \times 0 = 0$).
3. *One rule.* Any number times 1 is the number (e.g., $9 \times 1 = 9$; $78 \times 1 = 78$).
4. *Two rule.* Any number times 2 is double the number (e.g., $8 \times 2 = 8 + 8$ or 16; $12 \times 2 = 12 + 12$ or 24).
5. *Five rule.* Any number times 5 involves counting by 5s the number of times indicated by the multiplier (i.e., 5×6 means counting "5, 10, 15, 20, 25, 30") (e.g., $3 \times 5 = 5 + 5 + 5$ or counting "5, 10, 15").
6. *Nine rule.* When multiplying any number by 9, the answer can be obtained by subtracting 1 from the multiplier to obtain the tens digit and then adding enough to it to make 9 to obtain the ones digit (e.g., $9 \times 4 = 36$—3 is one less than 4 and $3 + 6 = 9$).

If these rules are used, there are only 15 facts left to be memorized:

$$
\begin{array}{ll}
3 \times 3 = 9 & 4 \times 8 = 32 \\
3 \times 4 = 12 & 6 \times 6 = 36 \\
3 \times 6 = 18 & 6 \times 7 = 42 \\
3 \times 7 = 21 & 6 \times 8 = 48 \\
3 \times 8 = 24 & 7 \times 7 = 49 \\
4 \times 4 = 16 & 7 \times 8 = 56 \\
4 \times 6 = 24 & 8 \times 8 = 64 \\
4 \times 7 = 28 &
\end{array}
$$

Some teachers report that these facts are learned faster by grouping the doubles (i.e., $3 \times 3 = 9$, $4 \times 4 = 16$, and so on), thus leaving only 10 facts.

Multiplication Algorithms The following *low-stress method of multiplication* reduces the amount of remembering required during computation. It is based on notation for recording the products of multiplication facts in a different manner. With *drop notation*, the product of

$$
\begin{array}{cc}
7 & \text{may be written} \\
\times 8 &
\end{array}
\qquad
\begin{array}{c}
7 \\
\times 8 \\
\hline
5 \\
6
\end{array}
$$

To illustrate:

Conventional notation:

$$
\begin{array}{ccc}
8 & 6 & 5 \\
\times 7 & \times 6 & \times 1 \\
\hline
56 & 36 & 5
\end{array}
$$

Drop notation:

$$
\begin{array}{ccc}
8 & 6 & 5 \\
\times 7 & \times 6 & \times 1 \\
\hline
5 & 3 & 0 \\
6 & 6 & 5
\end{array}
$$

Using the drop notation, multiplication problems can be computed in the following ways.

(a)

$$
\begin{array}{ccc}
\textit{Step 1} & \textit{Step 2} & \textit{Step 3} \\
476 & 476 & 476 \\
\times\ 8 & \times\ 8 & \times\ 8 \\
\hline
40 & 540 & 3540 \\
8 & 68 & 268 \\
 & & \hline \\
 & & 3808
\end{array}
$$

(b)

$$
\begin{array}{r}
57764 \\
\times \quad 7 \\
\hline
344420 \\
59928 \\
\hline
404348
\end{array}
$$

(c) Using two multidigit factors:

Step 1	Step 2	
476	476	
× 38	× 38	
3540	3540	} × 8
268	268	
	1210	} × 3
	218	
	18088	

This low-stress method of multiplication eliminates the regrouping requirement and allows the student to work only with multiplication facts in solving complex multiplication problems.

Another multiplication algorithm is the *partial products* algorithm. This algorithm reduces the regrouping requirement in multiplying multidigit numbers by one-digit numbers. For example:

$$
\begin{array}{ll}
27 & \\
\times\ 6 & \\
\hline
42 & (7 \times 6)\ \text{partial product} \\
120 & (20 \times 6)\ \text{partial product} \\
\hline
162 &
\end{array}
$$

$$
\begin{array}{ll}
362 & \\
\times\ 4 & \\
\hline
8 & (2 \times 4) \\
240 & (60 \times 4) \\
1200 & (300 \times 4) \\
\hline
1448 &
\end{array}
$$

Division Rules The following five division rules are basic for understanding math.

1. *Zero rule.* Zero divided by any number is zero (e.g., $9 \div 0 = 0$; $49 \div 0 = 0$).

2. *One rule.* Any number divided by 1 is the number (e.g., $8 \div 1 = 8$; $1\overline{)8}$; $67 \div 1 = 67$).

3. *Two rule.* Any number divided by 2 is half the number (e.g., $14 \div 2 = 7$; $2\overline{)66}$).

4. *Nines fact rule.* When 9 is divided into any of the 9s facts, the answer is one more than the number in the tens columns (e.g., $9\overline{)36}$—3 + 1 is 4; $9\overline{)45}$—4 + 1 is 5).

5. *Multiplication/division relationship rule.* The quotient multiplied by the divisor equals the dividend (e.g., $7 \times 5 = 35$; $35 \div 7 = 5$; $35 \div 7 = 5$). This

rule enables the student to use knowledge of multiplication facts to solve division facts. For example, to solve the problem $32 \div 8$, the student asks, "What number times 8 equals 32?"

Division Algorithms The following algorithms are less difficult than the traditional division algorithm. Using the algorithms is made simpler by knowing the shortcut for multiplying by multiples of 10. In the example of this algorithm, the student immediately pulls out the largest tens multiple of the divisor.

$$
\begin{array}{rr}
28\overline{)62372} & \\
56000 & 2000 \\
\hline
6372 & \\
5600 & 200 \\
\hline
772 & \\
560 & 20 \\
\hline
212 & \\
196 & 7 \\
\hline
16 & 2227
\end{array}
$$

The following algorithm helps the student identify or compute each number of the quotient when the first quotient number selected is too low.

Step 1	Step 2
	1
2	2
$23\overline{)8761}$	$23\overline{)8761}$
46	46
41	41
	23
	18

Steps 1 and 2 are repeated until no more multiplication is needed. The answer is computed by adding each column in the quotient computations.

$$
\text{(a)}\quad
\begin{array}{r}
2 \\
78 \\
8\overline{)784} \\
56 \\
\hline
22 \\
16 \\
\hline
64 \\
64
\end{array}
\qquad 98
$$

$$
\text{(b)}\quad
\begin{array}{r}
12 \\
260 \\
23\overline{)8761} \\
46 \\
\hline
41 \\
23 \\
\hline
186 \\
138 \\
\hline
48 \\
46 \\
\hline
21 \\
10 \\
21
\end{array}
$$

(answer is 380 R21—computed by adding each column in the quotient computations)

Fraction Algorithm A low-stress algorithm for teaching the addition and subtraction of fractions is called *ray multiplication* and consists of the following steps.

1. An overhead projection is used to drill the student on the location of geometric shapes and numbers. $\frac{\bigcirc}{\triangle}\,\frac{\square}{\diamond}$ are model items used to show the locations of bottom right, bottom left, top right, and top left.

2. The student is instructed to draw three rays: ╱ from bottom right to top left, from bottom left to top right, and from bottom left to bottom right. Thus, $\frac{\bigcirc}{\triangle}\,\frac{\square}{\diamond}$ would look like ⬭.

3. On a worksheet that has pairs of numerical fractions, the student is directed to draw the three rays and multiply along them. The student writes the answers to these multiplication tasks. After the rays are multiplied, the student writes the operation sign between the fractions in a pair. For example:

4. In this step the student writes a new fraction for each pair. The new numerator is formed by performing the correct operation on the products of the diagonal ray multiplications. The new denominator for both fractions is the product of the horizontal ray multiplication. For example:

$$\frac{3}{6} + \frac{2}{6}$$

5. Now the student computes the sum or difference of the numerators and writes the result over the denominator. For example:

$$\frac{3}{6} + \frac{2}{6} = \frac{(3+2)}{6} = \frac{5}{6}$$

or

$$\frac{3}{6} - \frac{2}{6} = \frac{(3-2)}{6} = \frac{1}{6}$$

This ray multiplication algorithm leads to reduced stress, reduced teaching time prior to mastery, and increased computation power.

Problem-Solving Interventions

In word problem solving, math problems are presented in the context of social situations, and information needed to solve each problem must be identified and then used. Some problems include extraneous information, and the number of operations may vary from one to several. The context of simple addition and subtraction problems varies significantly and students must understand mathematical concepts and develop strategies to solve these various problems. Table 12.2 presents four basic categories of addition and subtraction word problems.

Interventions That Use Sequential Steps
RIDE is a mnemonic strategy that identifies the steps needed to solve story problems successfully.

R—*Read* the problem correctly.

I—*Identify* the relevant information.

D—*Determine* the operations and unit for expressing the answer.

E—*Enter* the correct numbers and calculate and check the answer.

Also, Watanabe (1991) presents a five-step mnemonic strategy, SIGNS, which has been used successfully to teach students with learning difficulties to solve word problems.

S—*Survey* question.

I—*Identify* key words and labels.

G—*Graphically* draw problem.

N—*Note* operation(s) needed.

S—*Solve* and check problem.

Fleischner et al. (1987) discuss a study in which they used a strategy-based intervention with a cue card to help students with learning difficulties successfully solve addition and subtraction word problems. The cue card presents the following sequence.

1. *Read.* What is the question?
2. *Reread.* What is the necessary information?
3. *Think.* Putting together? = add; Taking apart? = subtract; Do I need all the information? Is it a multistep problem?
4. *Solve.* Write the equation.
5. *Check.* Recalculate, label, and compare.

In the study, during the *Read* step, students highlighted the question and wrote the metric pounds, inches, and so on. In the *Think* step, students were instructed to circle the largest number and write it. Then they were asked to see what happened to the number (i.e., did it get smaller or larger?). Finally, students used calculators to compute the answer so that they could focus on problem solving rather than on computation.

TABLE 12.2
Categories of addition and subtraction word problems

Problem Type	Sample Problems
Join (i.e., elements are added to a given set)	1. Jan had 7 cookies. Kevin gave her 4 more. How many does Jan have altogether? (result unknown) 2. Jan has 7 cookies. How many more cookies does she need to have 11 cookies altogether? (change unknown) 3. Jan had some cookies. Kevin gave her 4 more cookies. Now she has 11 cookies. How many cookies did Jan have to start with? (start unknown)
Separate (i.e., elements are removed from a given set)	1. Jan had 11 cookies. She gave 7 cookies to Kevin. How many cookies does she have left? (result unknown) 2. Jan had 11 cookies. She gave some to Kevin. Now she has 7 cookies. How many did Jan give to Kevin? (change unknown) 3. Jan had some cookies. She gave 7 to Kevin. Now she has 4 cookies left. How many cookies did Jan have to start with? (start unknown)
Part-Part-Whole (i.e., comparisons between two disjoint sets)	1. Jan has 7 oatmeal cookies and 4 chocolate cookies. How many cookies does she have? 2. Jan has 11 cookies. Seven are oatmeal and the rest are chocolate. How many chocolate cookies does Jan have?
Compare	1. Jan has 11 cookies. Kevin has 7 cookies. How many more cookies does Jan have than Kevin? 2. Kevin has 7 cookies. Jan has 4 more than Kevin. How many cookies does Jan have? 3. Jan has 11 cookies. She has 7 more cookies than Kevin. How many cookies does Kevin have?

To teach problem-solving strategies to middle school students with learning problems, Montague (1992) used explicit modeling of cognitive and metacognitive strategies. The intervention also included verbal rehearsal, corrective and positive feedback, guided practice, and mastery checks. The specific cognitive strategies included the following:

1. *Read* for understanding.
2. *Paraphrase* in your own words.
3. *Visualize* a picture or diagram.
4. *Hypothesize* a plan to solve the problem.
5. *Estimate* or predict the answer.
6. *Compute* or do the arithmetic.
7. *Check* to make sure everything is right.

Montague reports that students readily learned these strategies and applied them successfully in solving word problems. Because some students failed to maintain and generalize the strategies, she encourages the use of techniques to promote generalization. Specifically, she suggests mnemonics and verbal rehearsal as techniques to help students remember and gain access to procedural math knowledge. Finally, Montague concludes that strategy instruction holds much promise for helping students with learning problems achieve in math. This type of strategy instruction is included in *Solve It!*, a research-based instructional program for students who have difficulty solving mathematical word problems (Montague, 2003; Montague, Warger, & Morgan, 2000). The four major instructional techniques that help students actively acquire and effectively apply the cognitive processes and self-regulation strategies are problem-solving assessment, explicit instruction of problem-solving processes and strategies, process modeling (i.e., thinking aloud while demonstrating a cognitive activity), and performance feedback.

Hutchinson's (1993a) intervention for teaching adolescents with learning disabilities included explicit teacher modeling of strategies for solving algebra word problems. The strategies consisted of self-questions for representing and solving algebra word problems. The intervention also featured scripts to guide instruction, teacher prompts, encouragement, corrective feedback, student think alouds, guided practice, independent practice, and the use of graphs to monitor student progress. Selected self-questions for representing algebra word problems included the following: (1) Have I read and understood the sentence? (2) Do I have the whole picture, a representation, for this problem? and (3) Have I written the representation on the worksheet? The students displayed improved performance on algebra word problems, and maintenance and transfer of the problem-solving strategy were evident.

An intervention to help students solve equations in algebra involves use of the following mnemonic, CAP.

C—*Combine* like terms. Combine terms on each side of the equation that have the same variable (e.g., $3m + 2m$ combines to $5m$). Combine terms on each side of the equation that do not have a variable (e.g., $15 - 7$ combines to 8). Combine terms by doing the computations indicated by the signs (e.g., $6p - 4p$ combines to $2p$; $+7 - 13$ combines to -6).

A—*Ask* yourself, "How can I isolate the variable?" Remove nonvariable numbers (e.g., $+6$, -8) by changing them to zero by doing the opposite computation (e.g., -6 removes $+6$, $+8$ removes -8). Remove a variable number (e.g., $6s$) by changing it to 1 by doing the opposite computation (e.g., $6s$ becomes s when divided by 6).

P—*Put* the values of the variable in the initial equation, and check to see if the equation is balanced.

Interventions That Use the CSA Sequence

Howell and Barnhart (1992) developed a concrete-semiconcrete-abstract instructional sequence for teaching young students to solve word problems. The concrete stage features six steps and involves the systematic manipulation of objects to represent equations. The following activity is included in the sixth step. The student reads (or has someone read aloud) the problem, "There are three blue circles and two orange circles. How many circles are there?" The student places the correct numbers and colors of circles on the display boards. The student states, "I placed three blue circles on one side and two orange circles on the other side. To find out how many circles there are, I place the groups together, so three circles plus two circles equals five circles." If this activity is done correctly, the student goes to the next stage.

In the semiconcrete stage the student is guided through six steps in which manipulative objects are replaced with pictures or drawings. In the sixth step the student represents a story problem by drawing tallies, writing the equation, and calculating the answer.

In the abstract stage a series of five questions is presented to promote a thinking strategy for solving word problems.

1. What is the question?
2. What are the numbers in the problem?
3. What do I do to the numbers?
4. What is the answer?
5. Do I need to check the answer by drawing tallies?

The final step at the abstract stage involves having the student independently write a story problem. For example, the number sequence $7 - 4 = 3$ may be written as the following story problem: "My dog had 7 puppies. There are 4 male puppies and the rest are females. How many puppies are females?"

Mercer and Miller (1991–1993) present a learning strategy approach to teach students with learning problems math facts and word problems simultaneously. The multiplication word problems as presented in Figure 12.2 feature a graduated sequence of difficulty in which students learn to solve problems with extraneous information and create their own word problems. This CSA sequence guides the student to understand and apply multiplication to real-life word problems. Field-test results indicate excellent acquisition of math facts, generalization, and problem-solving skills.

Marsh and Cooke (1996) used manipulative objects to teach word problem solving to students with math learning difficulties. Their intervention uses the following procedures.

1. The student reads a word problem aloud and receives help with unknown words.
2. The teacher rereads each line of the problem and asks the student to set up the appropriate numerical values with manipulative objects.
3. The teacher uses prompts and cues to help the student create correct concrete representations of the word problem parts.
4. The student rereads the word problem while touching and counting the respective objects.
5. The student holds up a flash card showing the correct operation to use. An incorrect response results in correction procedures.

Marsh and Cooke report that this intervention helps students generalize problem-solving strategies to solve written problems.

For elementary and middle school students who struggle with learning fractions, Witzel and Riccomini (2009) use the CSA sequence of instruction in their intervention to teach seven areas involving fractions: division with fractional answers/mixed numbers, multiplication of fractions, division of fractions, finding equivalent fractions, reducing and comparing fractions, adding and subtracting fractions with like denominators, and adding and subtracting fractions with unlike denominators. Their intervention includes 30 sequenced teacher-directed lessons with accompanying scripts and problems.

Interventions that use the CSA sequence also are effective instructional approaches for teaching algebra to students with learning problems (Gagnon & Maccini, 2001; Maccini, McNaughton, & Ruhl, 1999; Witzel et al., 2003; Witzel, Smith, & Brownell, 2001).

FIGURE 12.2
Multiplication problem-solving sequence

Description	Example
A computation problem is presented with the word *groups* written to the right of the first number and blanks beside the second number and the answer space.	6 groups of 3 _____ _____
The student writes the name of the manipulative objects used in the lesson in the blanks, solves the problem, and reads the statement. "Six groups of 3 checkers is 18 checkers."	6 groups of 3 checkers 18 checkers
A computation problem is presented with the word *groups* written to the right of the first number and blanks beside the second number and the answer space.	6 groups of 3 _____ _____
The student writes the name of the drawings used in the respective lesson in the blanks, solves the problem, and reads the statement. "Six groups of 3 circles is 18 circles."	6 groups of 3 circles 18 circles
A computation problem is presented with the word *groups* written to the right of the first number and common words written to the right of the second number and the answer space.	6 groups × 3 apples apples
The student solves the problem and reads the statement. "Six groups of 3 apples is 18 apples."	6 groups × 3 apples 18 apples
A computation problem is presented with a noun or phrase (adjective-noun) written to the right of the first and second numbers and the answer space.	6 brown bags × 3 red apples red apples
The student solves the problem and reads the statement. "Six brown bags of 3 red apples is 18 red apples."	6 brown bags × 3 red apples 18 red apples
A computation problem is presented with words on both sides of the numbers and the answer space. The numbers remain lined up in a vertical format.	Susan had 6 bags of 3 apples She has ____ apples
The student solves the problem and reads the statement.	Susan had 6 bags of 3 apples She has 18 apples
A regular sentence-style word problem is presented in which the numbers are not aligned.	Susan had 6 bags. There are 3 apples in each bag. How may apples does Susan have?
The student solves the problem and writes the equation.	6 × 3 = 18
A sentence-style word problem including extraneous information is presented.	Susan had 6 bags. There are 3 apples in each bag. Bill has 2 pet turtles. How many apples does Susan have?
The student crosses out the extraneous information, solves the problem, and writes the equation.	Susan had 6 bags. There are 3 apples in each bag. ~~Bill has 2 pet turtles~~. How many apples does Susan have? 6 × 3 = 18

FIGURE 12.2
(continued)

The student is instructed to write or dictate his or her own multiplication word problem.

_____
_____
_____

The student writes or dictates a multiplication word problem, solves the problem, and writes the equation.

There are 3 puppies. Each puppy has 2 spots. How many spots are there altogether?
$3 \times 2 = 6$

Three types of word problems are presented:
1. One problem without extraneous information
2. One problem with extraneous information
3. One problem to be created by the student

The student writes or dictates the created problem, solves the problem, and writes the equation.

Witzel et al. (2003) used the CSA sequence of instruction for teaching students with learning difficulties to solve algebraic transformation equations. The students who learned how to solve the equations through the CSA sequence outperformed peers receiving traditional instruction and also had fewer procedural errors when solving for variables. Moreover, Maccini and Hughes (2000) used the CSA sequence to represent word problems involving integer numbers. Within the instructional sequence, they incorporated the use of the algebra problem-solving strategy STAR, which includes the following steps.

S—*Search* the word problem (i.e., read the problem carefully, regulate thinking through self-questions, and write down facts).

T—*Translate* the words into an equation in picture form (i.e., choose a variable, identify the operation, and represent the problem through manipulatives or picture form).

A—*Answer* the problem.

R—*Review* the solution (i.e., reread the problem and check the reasonableness of the answer).

The students' problem-solving skills involving integer numbers dramatically improved following instruction at the CSA levels, and the students' strategy use also increased.

Interventions That Use Graphic Representation

Schema-based instruction is a strategy that helps students represent mathematical problems graphically. Evidence supports the use of this strategy to improve the problem-solving skills of students with learning disabilities (Jitendra, 2002, 2007; Jitendra, Griffin, Deatline-Buchman, & Sczesniak, 2007). The following presents the steps for implementing schema-based instruction.

Problem: Gabriel had 6 toy airplanes. He gave an airplane to each of his 4 friends. How many airplanes does Gabriel have left?

Step 1: Problem schemata identification and representation. This step helps the student generate a conceptual understanding of the problem. The student reads the problem and identifies the type of problem. In the given word problem, the student identifies that it is a *change* problem. The quantity at the end of the problem is different than the quantity at the beginning. Next, the student selects a graphic organizer that represents the beginning amount and the amount of the change.

Step 2: Problem solution. The student then uses the graphic organizer to make a plan for solving the problem. The child in the story problem is giving airplanes away; therefore, the operation is subtraction. The student writes the subtraction problem using the graphic organizer and solves the problem (see Figure 12.3).

Life Skills Math

Math instruction for students with learning problems rarely equips them with skills essential for independent living. Yet, the primary goal of math instruction for these students should be to prepare them to use math in their daily adult lives. To do this, math curricula must include content that promotes this pragmatic outcome. Math in the real world involves such skills as budgeting, estimating, purchasing, hiring, playing games of chance, reading graphs and tables, and planning travel and transportation. Moreover, it

TABLE 12.3
Math demands for daily living

Consumer	Employment
Make change	Determine bring-home pay
Determine costs of sale items	Understand deductions
Compute tax amounts	Calculate sick leave and vacation time
Compare prices	Calculate hourly wage
Balance checkbooks	Understand bonus pay criteria
Understand warranties	Understand gross pay and net pay
Understand borrowing costs	Plan and understand work schedules
Shop for groceries	Operate a phone
Estimate costs and change	Operate a cash register or a calculator
	Understand minimum wage and fringe benefits
Homemaking	**Recreation**
Pay income taxes	Budget for a vacation
Pay real estate taxes	Compute costs of leisure activities
Buy home insurance	Schedule leisure activities
Determine measurements for carpets, room sizes, house	Operate a remote control
size, carpentry, furniture, and cooking	Play games involving math
Mix solution proportions (e.g., insecticide sprays)	Understand probabilities (e.g., lottery tickets and
Budget	card games)
Conduct banking	
Understand interest	**Travel**
Buy health insurance	Buy car insurance
Read thermometers and scales	Buy airline, train, and bus tickets
Count calories and fat grams	Rent or lease a motor vehicle
Schedule medication times and amounts	Buy a car
Understand clothing measurements	Understand costs of car repairs
Set timers	Determine tire pressure
Understand charitable contributions	Read car gauges
	Read maps and compute mileage and time
	Locate lodging and determine costs

FIGURE 12.3
Graphic representation of a subtraction problem

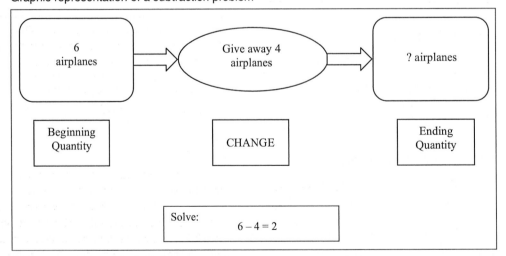

involves computing costs, change, taxes, interest, measurements, and profits and losses. Table 12.3 presents the math demands of daily living within five areas: consumer, employment, homemaking, recreation, and travel.

The systematic steps discussed in this chapter effectively teach students with moderate to severe learning problems to apply essential math skills in authentic contexts. Also, because real-life math events are oral, students need to practice mental math calculations.

Estimation

Estimation entails the forming of an approximate answer (e.g., approximating the cost of grocery items or the dimensions of a room or yard) and the ability to check the reasonableness of calculations (e.g., the reasonableness of a calculation total on a cash register). Estimation has applications to every aspect of mathematics and is an essential part of an effective mathematics program for students with learning problems (Bezuk & Cegelka, 1995; Bley & Thornton, 2010). Ashlock (2010) notes that the ability to estimate requires a robust number sense. Specifically, students need to be fluent in math facts, understand numeration concepts, and understand mathematical relationships and rules. For example, calculators do not tell whether an answer is reasonable. Determining reasonableness requires computational knowledge and skills. Thus, the combination of a strong number sense and instruction in estimation skills enables students with learning problems to learn and apply estimation. Also, students need to distinguish events for using estimation, mental computation, paper-and-pencil calculations, and calculators.

In initial estimation instruction, it helps to allow students time to guess, opportunities to test their guesses, and time to revise their guesses as needed. Moreover, it should be stressed that estimation does not result in only one correct answer but that numerous answers are acceptable; however, some estimations are more reasonable than others. Estimation involves a set of skills in which most students with learning problems require explicit instruction. Ashlock (2010, p. 192) reports that the following skills are important for estimation of whole numbers.

1. Adding a little bit more than one number to a little bit more than another; adding a little bit less than one number to a little bit less than another; and, in general, adding, subtracting, and so on, with a little bit more than or a little bit less than.
2. Rounding a whole number to the nearest ten, hundred, and so on.
3. Multiplying by ten and powers of ten—in one step.
4. Multiplying two numbers, each of which is a multiple of a power of ten (e.g., 20×300). This should be done as one step, without the use of a written algorithm.

With fractions, Ashlock notes that estimation often involves identifying a particular fraction as close to zero, one-half, or one.

Activities to promote estimation skills include the following:

- Present the student with a computation problem and several answers. Have the student select the answer that is most reasonable and verify it by computation.
- Provide a number and have the student determine which multiple of ten, hundred, or thousand is close to it on a number line. For example, have the student locate 42 on the number line and determine whether it is closer to 40 or to 50.
- Provide cards with two-digit numbers on them (e.g., 73, 58, 13, 27, 84, 39, 42, 87, 16, and 61). Instruct the student to spread the cards on a table, mentally round each number to the nearest ten, and then combine sets of numbers that sum to 100.
- Give a group of students a set of cards in which each card includes the name of a grocery item, a picture of the item, and its price. Advertisements from newspapers or magazines can be used. After one student turns over three cards, have all members of the group estimate the amount of money needed to buy the items indicated on the cards. The students can discuss their estimates, and record the number of times their estimates agree. If several groups are involved, they can compare the respective number of agreements. A variation of this activity involves giving the students several cards and asking them whether a specific amount of money (e.g., $20) is enough to buy the items. Finally, calculators can be used to compare the cost of the items with the student estimates (Bezuk & Cegelka, 1995).
- Color cue or underline the "thinking" digit (i.e., the digit to the right of the digit that changes when rounding) to help the student focus on the digit that influences the rounding process. This activity can help the student round money amounts to make estimates (e.g., to round $7.28 to the nearest whole number, the 2 would be colored or underlined, and to round $1.76 to the nearest dime, the 6 would be colored or underlined).

Calculators

Calculators are used widely in our society to make computation accurate and easy. Dessart, DeRidder, and Ellington (1999) note that research suggests that calculators should be an integral part of mathematics instruction. However, because effective math instruction stresses understanding, problem solving, and computation, the instructional role of calculators needs clarification. In general, calculators should be used primarily with problems that students are capable of doing by hand. Also, students should *understand* the math concept (e.g., multiplication) involved in the computation before using a calculator to solve problems. Paper and pencil may be most effective with simple computation problems, whereas calculators are better suited for complex or tedious problems (e.g., long division).

Initially, students need to learn the correct procedures for using a calculator. Proper early instruction helps promote positive experiences with calculators and prepares students for successful applications of the calculator as they advance in mathematics. Guidelines for early calculator instruction include the following:

- Encourage the student to press the *Clear* key twice prior to beginning each problem on the calculator.
- Point out the sequential number configuration on the calculator and the location of the initial function keys the student will use.
- Encourage the student to watch the display panel after each entry and check the results for reasonableness (Heddens & Speer, 1997).
- Stress that weak batteries or broken calculators can produce incorrect answers (Heddens & Speer, 1997).
- Encourage the student to operate the calculator with the hand not used for writing. This facilitates the ability to record the results with one hand and operate the calculator with the other hand (Heddens & Speer, 1997).

Hembree (1986) reviewed 79 studies on the use of calculators and reports the following findings.

- When used appropriately, calculators promote skill acquisition.
- Sustained calculator use in the fourth grade appears to interfere with skill development.
- The use of calculators when taking tests results in higher achievement scores.
- The use of calculators improves the attitudes of students toward mathematics.

Moreover, Fleischner et al. (1987) note that the use of calculators allows students to focus on problem solving rather than becoming bogged down in computations; thus, their use may be especially helpful with students who have difficulty solving problems.

Heddens and Speer (1997) note that calculators can help students develop understanding of place value, reversibility, relationships among numbers, operations, and mathematical estimates. Selected activities with calculators include the following:

- Instruct the young student to place interesting or personal numbers on the display screen (e.g., age,

age of best friend, today's calendar date, address number, and telephone number). Provide copies of the student's personal numbers if not known (Heddens & Speer, 1997).

- Present real-life problem situations for the student to solve on the calculator. For example, place three books on one student's desk and five books on another student's desk. State the problem situation and ask the student to use the calculator to show how many total books are on the two desks. Discuss the reasonableness of the answer.
- Instruct the student to enter *5748* into the calculator. Next, ask the student to use addition or subtraction to change *7* to *0*. Ask for the new number and discuss why *5048* is correct (i.e., subtracted 700). Repeat the task by changing *5* to *6, 4* to *2,* and *8* to *1*.
- Have the student round each addend in an addition problem to the nearest hundred and estimate a sum. Then have the student use a calculator to determine the actual sum of the addends and compare the answer with the estimate. Discuss reasonableness of estimates. For example:

	Student work:
329	300
289	300
474	500
+ 336	300
	1400 (estimated sum)

- Instruct the student to use the calculator to divide several numbers by 10. The student should generalize that every time the *Equals* (=) key is pressed, the decimal point of the number divided by 10 moves one space to the left (Heddens & Speer, 1997).
- Provide various math problems for the student to complete. Instruct the student to use the calculator as a self-correcting device to check answers to completed computations.

MATH ACTIVITIES

Various activities can be used for teaching or practicing math skills. Activities can be used to stimulate interest, individualize instruction, extend practice, and provide variety in teaching methods. Also, the teacher can incorporate the various cultures of students into the math curriculum by developing story problems that reflect events from diverse cultures, using data about individuals or events representing other cultures, and playing multicultural games, such as the two games presented by De la Cruz, Cage, and Lian (2000).

The activities presented in this section and the instructional games and self-correcting materials presented in the following sections promote the development of math skills.

Readiness

Classification

Give the student a collection of circles, squares, and triangles of various colors. Have the student classify the items according to shape and then according to color. Other useful objects in classification activities are buttons, wooden blocks, dominoes, spoons, nails, and golf tees.

Ordering

Provide the student with a set of different-size objects (e.g., wooden blocks, buttons, straws, nails, washers, shapes, and Cuisenaire rods). Have the student arrange them in order from the smallest to the largest or vice versa.

One-to-One Correspondence

Provide a pegboard design and instruct the student to duplicate it. Other helpful activities include putting screws on bolts, passing out papers, playing musical chairs, and adding the same part to several items (such as strings to kites, sails to boats, stems to flowers, or straws to cups).

Counting

Provide the student with Language Master cards with a number of objects to count and a taped message (such as "One, two, three—three cats").

Assign each student a secret number. Have a student knock on the door the number of times that matches his or her secret number. The class members can respond, "Come in Number Five (or Seven, Fourteen, . . .)."

Have the student circle the number that corresponds to the configuration.

••••	4	5	6	8
•	2	3	4	7
•••	7	6	9	8
••	3	5	6	4

Attach a number line to the top of the student's desk to provide a helpful reference.

Greater Than, Less Than

Use a number line to help students decide which numbers are greater than and less than in completing sentences with < or > symbols (Heddens & Speer, 1997). For example:

Fill each blank with < or >: 7___5   0___4   10___8

Provide a drawing of a "creature" with numbers written in the sections of the body. Instruct the student to mark an X on each body part that has a number greater than 15 and less than 39.

Place Value

Chip-Trading Games

Use chip-trading games to teach place value. These games stress the idea of exchanging many for one. The values of chips correspond to a numeration place value pattern. For example, white chips represent ones, blue chips represent tens, and red chips represent hundreds. The student rolls a die and receives the number of ones indicated on the die. Exchanges for higher valued chips are made according to the rules of the game (i.e., four for one if base 4; ten for one if base 10). The first player to get a chip of a certain high value wins.

Bank Game

Use a game board and a bank to help students understand place value. For example:

345

In computing the problem

$$527$$
$$+893$$

the student places 5 hundreds, 2 tens, and 7 ones blocks in the upper row. Then the student places the appropriate blocks for 893 in the second row. Starting with the ones (i.e., at the green dot), the student collects 10 ones if possible and moves all remaining ones below the wide line. The student trades to the bank each 10 ones collected for the correct number of tens. The tens collected from the bank are placed at the top of the tens column. In this problem (see example), 10 ones are traded to the bank for 1 ten, and zero blocks are placed below the wide line in the ones column. Next, 10 tens are traded for a hundreds block, and 2 tens blocks are placed below the wide line in the tens column. The student trades 10 hundreds for a thousands block and then places 4 hundreds blocks below the wide line in the hundreds column. Finally, the student moves the thousands block below the wide line in the thousands column. The student counts the blocks in each column and writes the answer, 1,420.

Making Columns

Present FIND as a mnemonic strategy to help the student understand and solve place value problems.

F—**Find** the columns.

I—**Insert** the ts.

N—**Name** the columns.

D—**Determine** the numbers of hundreds, tens, and ones.

For example:

Find the columns	Insert the ts		
643	6	4	3

Name the columns			Determine the numbers
100s	10s	1s	6 hundreds
6	4	3	4 tens
			3 ones

Labeling Columns

Insert the initial letters for ones, tens, hundreds, and so on over their respective coluns:

t th	th	h	t	o
	4	5	4	7
	1	7	5	6
+	3	3	1	1

Vertical lines can be in colors for additional cueing.

Pegboard

Use a pegboard to teach borrowing and carrying. For example:

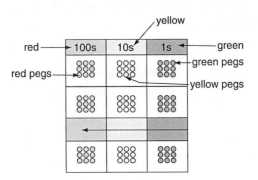

Use masking tape to divide the pegboard into three rows and three columns, with nine holes in each subdivision. An arrow is drawn from right to left on a piece of tape that separates the bottom third. This line serves as an equals sign; answers to problems always are shown by inserting pegs below this line. In addition to helping the student recall the different values for each column, color coding reminds the student to start with green (i.e., *go*). The top two rows hold the pegs representing the first two numbers in an addition or subtraction problem. To solve 5 + 6, the student starts to transfer all the pegs in the ones column to the ones section below the arrow. The student discovers that not all 11 pegs will fit in the bottom row of the ones column. Consequently, the student must exchange 10 green pegs for 1 yellow peg (i.e., 10 ones for 1 ten) and carry this yellow peg into the tens column. Borrowing consists of trading 1 yellow peg for 10 green pegs and putting the green pegs in the top row of the ones column.

Place Value Cards

Make cards with numbers on one side and tallies for the number of hundreds, tens, and so on in that number on the other side. For example:

Also, strings can be attached to the cards for stringing beads to represent the number in each column.

Place Value Table

Instruct the student to complete the missing spaces in the place value table (Heddens & Speer, 1997). For example:

100	10	1		1	10	100
Less	Less	Less		Greater	Greater	Greater
178			278	279		
		141	142		152	
	359		369			469
420			520			
		400	401	402		

General Computation

This section presents activities that easily are adapted for any of the four operations. Many of the games and self-correcting materials presented later in this chapter also are useful with all four operations.

Small Work Samples

Present assignments in small segments. Because of attention problems or lack of interest, some students cannot complete an entire worksheet of math problems. Presenting assignments in small segments may help these students complete as many problems as their classmates. Cut a worksheet into small parts (e.g., rows), or place problems on cards that the student picks up each time a problem is completed.

Mystery Math

Cut tagboard into 5" × 5" squares or draw a square on a ditto. Put a decorative drawing, decal, or picture in the middle. Draw seven or more evenly spaced lines on each side of the decorative square in the middle. Write numbers at random on the left side. If the concept being taught is ÷6 and the first number is 42, the first number on the right should be 7. All other lines on the right side remain blank. The process is repeated with the top and bottom lines. By looking at the top

	6						
42							7
24		Mystery Math					
48							
18							
6		(☺?)					
36							
54							
	54	72	36	27	81	90	18

lines on the left and right sides, the student tries to figure out the mathematical function involved. The student then fills in the remaining blanks using the same function. Next the process is repeated with the top and bottom lines.

Learning Ladders

Provide the student with math problems in a vertical order on strips of paper or cardboard. Have the student start at the bottom of the "ladder" (i.e., strip) and proceed upward as problems are answered correctly. A marker is placed at the last problem answered correctly. When the student gets three markers (e.g., star, tack, or pin) on the top problem, progress is recorded and the student is allowed to take the strip home. Learning ladders also can be used to practice number identification, telling time, and coin identification.

4 × 4	16 − 8	4)36	6 + 7	1/2 + 1/2
6 × 4	14 − 8	4)20	8 + 7	5/6 + 1/6
9 × 4	13 − 4	4)16	7 + 4	2/3 + 1/3
5 × 4	17 − 8	4)28	7 + 4	1/5 + 1/5
7 × 4	12 − 8	4)36	6 + 5	1/4 + 1/4
8 × 4		4)12	9 + 7	

Addition

Nail Abacus

Use a nail abacus for teaching counting, place value (or regrouping), and addition. Make the nail abacus by driving five finishing nails at 2-inch intervals into a wooden board 2″ by 10″ by ½.″ The abacus is used by placing washers or beads on the nails. To display the number 43,062 on the abacus, two beads are placed on the ones nail, six beads are placed on the tens nail, no beads on the hundreds nail, three beads on the thousands nail, and four beads on the ten-thousands nail:

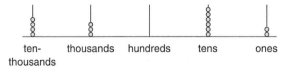

ten-thousands · thousands · hundreds · tens · ones

The student adds on the abacus by placing washers or beads on the appropriate nails and counting. For example, in solving the problem 43 + 32, the student first would place three beads on the ones nail and four beads on the tens nail. Next, 32 would be shown on the abacus by placing two beads on the ones nail and three beads on the tens nail. Now the student computes the sums of the ones (i.e., 5) and the tens (i.e., 7) by counting the beads on the respective nails.

Instruct the student to use the following rules about regrouping when using the abacus.

1. Ten discs on the ones nail are exchanged for one disc on the tens nail.
2. Ten discs on the tens nail are exchanged for one disc on the hundreds nail.
3. No nail can have more than nine discs remaining.

Thus, in solving 18 + 26, the following steps are used.

1. Display 18 on the abacus.
2. Leaving the 18, put 26 on the abacus.
3. Check to see whether any nails are overloaded (i.e., 10 or more discs).
4. Because the ones nail is overloaded with 14 discs, exchange 10 ones discs for one more disc on the tens nail.
5. Record the answer in a table. For example:

Tens	Ones	
1	8	
2	6	
3	14	sum
4	4	regrouped sum

Number Line

Provide a number line to help the student compute addition facts. Number lines for use in seatwork are made easily by cutting strips from a manila folder. Besides helping the student compute, they provide models for the correct form of numerals. In computing 2 + 4, the student is taught to start at 2 and move four spaces to the right to obtain the answer (i.e., 6) (see Figure 12.4). Later, the dot patterns can be eliminated and the numbers can be increased to 18.

Dot Addition

Place reference points on numerals to help students with math problems:

The system offers consistency in perception of the numbers and provides direct association between the number and its value. Actually, the dots provide a semiconcrete-level task for basic addition facts. Also, the dot cues can be faded as the student becomes proficient in learning the facts. For example:

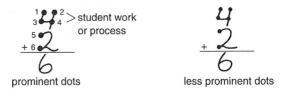

Computational Cues

Provide cues for helping the student remember to regroup or recall the steps in an algorithm. For example, the square reminds the student to carry:

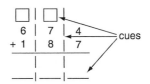

Direction Cue

For the student who adds from left to right rather than right to left, place a green dot over the ones column to serve as a reminder to begin computation there.

• — green dot

$$384$$
$$+\ 948$$

Addition Facts Family

Present the addition facts (i.e., sums 0 to 18) within a number family framework to help the student learn them (see Figure 12.5). By teaching that any number plus 0 equals the number, and any number plus 1 is counting by 1, only 64 facts out of 100 must be memorized. If the doubles are taught in terms of doubling the addend to compute the sum, only 56 facts remain to be memorized.

FIGURE 12.4
Number line showing computation of 2 + 4

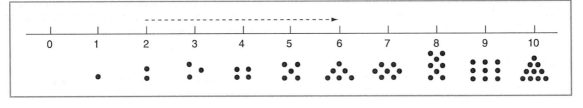

FIGURE 12.5
Addition facts family

```
   0         1         2         3         4         5         6         7         8         9
 0 | 0*    0 | 1*    0 | 2*    0 | 3*    0 | 4*    0 | 5*    0 | 6*    0 | 7*    0 | 8*    0 | 9*
         1 | 0*    2 | 0*    3 | 0*    4 | 0*    5 | 0*    6 | 0*    7 | 0*    8 | 0*    9 | 0*
                   1 | 1*    1 | 2*    1 | 3*    1 | 4*    1 | 5*    1 | 6*    1 | 7*    1 | 8*
                             2 | 1*    3 | 1*    4 | 1*    5 | 1*    6 | 1*    7 | 1*    8 | 1*
                                       2 | 2*    2 | 3     2 | 4     2 | 5     2 | 6     2 | 7
                                                 3 | 2     4 | 2     5 | 2     6 | 2     7 | 2
                                                           3 | 3*    3 | 4     3 | 5     3 | 6
                                                                     4 | 3     5 | 3     6 | 3
                                                                               4 | 4*    4 | 5
                                                                                         5 | 4


  10        11        12        13        14        15        16        17        18
 1 | 9*    2 | 9     3 | 9     4 | 9     5 | 9     6 | 9     7 | 9     8 | 9     9 | 9*
 9 | 1*    9 | 2     9 | 3     9 | 4     9 | 5     9 | 6     9 | 7     9 | 8
 2 | 8     3 | 8     4 | 8     5 | 8     6 | 8     7 | 8     8 | 8*
 8 | 2     8 | 3     8 | 4     8 | 5     8 | 6     8 | 7
 3 | 7     4 | 7     5 | 7     6 | 7     7 | 7*
 7 | 3     7 | 4     7 | 5     7 | 6
 4 | 6     5 | 6     6 | 6*
 6 | 4     6 | 5
 5 | 5*
```

Note: Facts marked with an asterisk do not need to be memorized

Subtraction

Nail Abacus

For solving the problem 57 − 34, have the student put 57 on the nail abacus: five washers on the tens nail and seven washers on the ones nail. The teacher can use the "take away" or the "find the missing addend" approach. With the take away approach, the student is instructed to take away 34 (i.e., 3 tens, 4 ones) from the abacus and count the remaining washers to find the difference. With the missing addend approach, the student is instructed to remove the known addend (i.e., 34) from the sum (i.e., 57) and count the remaining washers to determine the missing addend. For example:

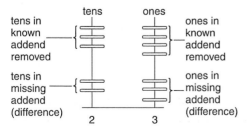

For solving 57 − 39, have the student put 57 on the abacus. Because the student cannot take 9 ones from 7 ones, 1 ten is taken off the tens nail and replaced with 10 washers on the ones nail. Now 9 washers are removed from the ones nail, and 3 washers are removed from the tens nail. The number left on the abacus is the answer.

Number Line

Provide a number line to help the student compute subtraction facts. In solving the problem 14 − 8, the student is taught to start at 14 and move eight spaces to the left to obtain the answer (i.e., 6) (see Figure 12.6).

Addition—Subtraction Pattern

Improve understanding of the relationship between addition and subtraction by having the student compute the sum of two addends and then subtract the two addends from the sum.

```
   47          70          70
 + 23        − 23        − 47
 ────        ────        ────
   70          47          23
```

349

FIGURE 12.6
Number line showing
computation of
$14 - 8$

Self-Monitoring Subtraction Strategy

Provide a modified worksheet format to help the student remember the strategies for regrouping in subtraction (Frank & Brown, 1992). Each problem on the worksheet has cue words above it to remind the student to follow the strategy steps.

1. Begin? In the 1s column.
2. Bigger? Which number is bigger?
3. Borrow? If the bottom number is bigger, I must borrow.
4. Basic Facts? Remember basic facts. Use drawings or touch math if needed.
   For example:

If the teacher develops a problem-solving sequence to other operations, this self-monitoring strategy can be modified for use in addition, multiplication, and division.

Multiplication

Array Multiplication

Have the student form arrays using tiles, pegboards, or other objects and determine the number of rows and columns. Explain that the number of rows and the number of columns represent the factors in a multiplication problem. Then instruct the student to write the multiplication facts represented by various arrays.

Next, present multiplication problems and have the student form the corresponding arrays.

Napier's Rods

Use Napier's rods to strengthen the student's recall of multiplication facts or to check seatwork. The rods can be constructed from heavy construction paper, tongue depressors,

or popsicle sticks. They consist of ten strips numbered according to the pattern presented in Figure 12.7. The numbers on top of the strips are the multiplicands, and the numbers on the index are the multipliers. The products are in the squares with the diagonal lines. By putting a strip next to the index, the student easily can determine the product of the respective factors. For example:

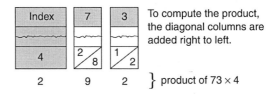

The rods can be used for multiplying more than one digit by a one-digit number. For example, to compute 73×4, the rods would be lined up accordingly:

To compute the product, the diagonal columns are added right to left.

} product of 73×4

Multiplication Chart

Provide a multiplication chart so that the student can check work and do seatwork. For example:

1	2	3	4	5	6	7	8	9
2	4	6	8	10	12	14	16	18
3	6	9	12	15	18	21	24	27
4	8	12	16	20	24	28	32	36
9	18	27	36	45	54	63	72	81

Addition–Multiplication Pattern

To facilitate understanding of the relationship between addition and multiplication, have the student first add the same number several times, then multiply that number by the times it was added. For example:

$$7 + 7 + 7 + 7 + 7 = 35$$
$$7 \times 5 = 35$$

Dot Cards

Make ten sets of cards representing numerals from 1 to 9. Set 1 contains nine cards with one dot on each card; Set 2 contains

FIGURE 12.7
Napier's rods

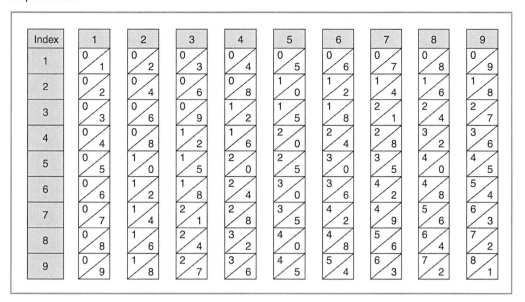

nine cards with two dots on each card; Set 3 contains nine cards with three dots on each card; and so on. Instruct the student to use the cards to compute multiplication problems.

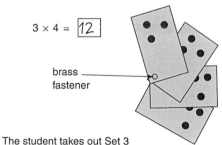

$3 \times 4 = \boxed{12}$

brass fastener

The student takes out Set 3 and turns out four cards with three dots. The student can count the dots to determine the product or can use the cards to check the answer.

Division

Number Line

To divide with the number line, have the student count backward from the dividend by the set determined by the divisor until 1 is reached. The quotient is the number of sets used in counting from the dividend to 1. In computing $18 \div 3$, for example, the student counts by threes because the divisor is 3, and then the student counts the loops for the answer. Thus, $18 \div 3 = 6$ (see Figure 12.8).

Dividing Numbers into Parts

To facilitate understanding of division, have the student divide numbers into equal parts. For example:

12 = ___3s	24 = ___6s
9 = ___3s	36 = ___6s
16 = ___4s	18 = ___6s

Dot Division

Use dots to present division problems and have the student write the numerical statement. For example:

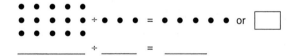

Long Division Steps

Present a face illustrating the four steps in long division problems to remind the student to follow the steps.

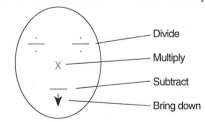

Divide
Multiply
Subtract
Bring down

FIGURE 12.8
Number line showing computation of $18 \div 3$

Also, the words Daddy, Mother, Sister, and Brother can be used to help the student remember the four steps in long division.

Fractions

Number Line

Use the fraction number line for illustrating the value of improper fractions (see Figure 12.9). Also, ask the student to indicate whether fractions are equal to one whole, greater than one whole, less than one whole, or equal to several wholes. Use the number line to illustrate simple division problems involving fractions. For example:

= 3 or 1½ ÷ ½ = 3

Fraction Chart

Use fraction charts to show the relationship of a fraction to 1 and to other fractions. Activities with the charts include determining greater-than and less-than values of fractions, finding the lowest common denominator, and determining equivalent fractions.

1							
1/2				1/2			
1/4		1/4		1/4		1/4	
1/8	1/8	1/8	1/8	1/8	1/8	1/8	1/8

Front

1					
1/3		1/3		1/3	
1/6	1/6	1/6	1/6	1/6	1/6
1/12	1/12	1/12	1/12	1/12	1/12	1/12	1/12	1/12	1/12	1/12	1/12

Back

Matching Graphic Form to Numerical Symbol

Have the student match fractions in word or graphic form to the numerical symbol for that fraction. To do this, provide the student with library pockets labeled 1/4, 1/8, and so forth and a stack of cards with graphic representations of a fraction.

Have the student match the cards with the correct pocket. For example:

Use discs (concrete level) or circles (semiconcrete level) to illustrate the division of fractions. For example:

Also, grids help illustrate division by fractions.

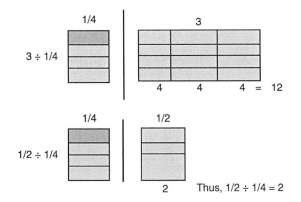

Fraction Bars

Make fraction bars out of tongue depressors, popsicle sticks, or construction paper. On each bar, the multiples of a single-digit number are written. For example:

FIGURE 12.9
Fraction number line

When one bar is placed over another bar, fractions are formed. The two numbers at the extreme left indicate the fraction formed (such as 3/4); the remaining fractions are a set in which each member of the set is equivalent (such as 3/4, 6/8, 9/12, and so on). The fraction and its equivalents are formed by putting the 3 bar over the 5 bar. For example:

Sample activities include reading the equivalent fractions, forming fractions with other bars, and making new bars.

To compute with fraction bars, instruct the student to use the bars to add two fractions, such as 2/3 + 2/5. The student should complete the following steps.

1. Form the fraction 2/3 by placing the 2 bar over the 3 bar.

2. Form the fraction 2/5.

3. Look at the denominators of each fraction and locate the lowest number that is the same on each denominator bar. In this example it is 15.
4. Slide the fraction 2/5 over until 6/15 lies directly under 10/15.

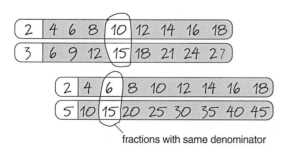

fractions with same denominator

5. To add, simply add the numbers on the numerator bars: 10 + 6 = 16; thus, the sum is 16/15.
6. To subtract, simply subtract one numerator from the other: 10 − 6 = 4; thus, the difference or missing addend is 4/15.

7. To divide 2/3 by 2/5, use the common denominator method:

$$2/3 \div 2/5 = {}^{10}/_{15} \div {}^{6}/_{15} =$$
$$(10 \div 6) \div (15 \div 15) =$$
$$(10 \div 6) \div 1 = 10 \div 6 = {}^{10}/_{6}$$

Multiplying Fractions with Grids

Have the student draw a grid and represent the two fractions that are being multiplied on it. The student should complete the following steps.

1. Make a rectangle and section it equally into the number of squares indicated by the product of the denominators. For example, 2/3 × 1/4 = 12 squares.

2. Represent 2/3 on the grid by shading in the correct number of rows.

3. Represent 1/4 by shading in the correct number of columns.

4. The number of squares that overlap represents the numerator of the product of 2/3 × 1/4; the total number of squares represents the denominator.

At the concrete level, the student can use tiles of different sizes.

Time

Number Line

Use a circular number line from 1 to 60 to help the student learn to tell time, as shown in Figure 12.10. The number line can be used to help the student construct a clock face, determine the minutes "after the hour," and note the relationship

FIGURE 12.10
Clock face with a circular number line

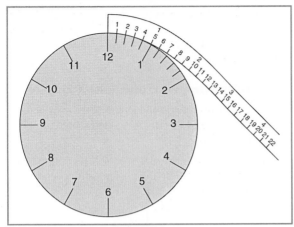

between the hour-hand movement (i.e., 5 increments per hour) and the minute-hand movement (i.e., 60 increments per hour).

Record Schedule

Mark the correct time on clocks for each school bell. Larger clocks can be used to record major events.

7:50
Opening bell

8:05
Tardy bell
1st period

8:55
End of
1st period

9:00
Tardy bell
2nd period

FIGURE 12.11
Decimal and fraction number lines

Examining Schedules

Provide the student with blank clock faces and a variety of schedules (such as those for television programs, a movie, or a bus). Have the student record schedule times on the clock faces.

Calendar Quiz

Provide the student with a calendar and a worksheet with numerous questions. Ask the student to respond to questions such as the following:

1. How many days are in a week?
2. On what day is the 27th of May?
3. List the dates of all the Wednesdays in January.
4. How many months are in a year?
5. List the months with 31 days.

Decimals/Money

Number Line

Use number lines to display decimals and their fractional equivalents (see Figure 12.11). In addition to using the lines as an aid in computing decimal–fraction problems, the student can be instructed to fill in blank sections of number lines.

Completion of Missing Parts

Instruct the student to fill in missing parts of various charts and figures as an activity in learning the relationship among fractions, decimals, and percentages.

Fraction	___	___	½	⅗	
Percent	___%	33%	___%	___%	___%
Decimal	.25	___	___	___	.67

Expanded Place Value Chart

Use an expanded place value chart to demonstrate the relationship among column values, column names, and decimals (see Figure 12.12). An activity consists of leaving parts unlabeled and instructing the student to fill in the missing labels.

Money Cards

Use money cards to help the student determine correct change. For example, the following $10 change card can be used to compute correct change when a $10 bill is received:

$10.00 Money Card

$	$	$	$	$	$	$	$	$
⑩	⑩	⑩	⑩	⑩	⑩	⑩	⑩	⑩
①	①	①	①	①	①	①	①	①

To solve the problem of how much change to give when a $10 bill is received and the purchase is for $6.77, the student simply marks out the amount of the purchase on the card. The remaining money is the correct change.

Real Money

Use real money as often as possible to teach money values. For example, provide combinations of coins and ask the student to total the amounts. Money stamps from commercial publishers also can be used.

Coupon Shopping

On a manila folder, draw a chart and label the columns *Grocery Items, Price, Coupon Value,* and *Actual Cost.* In the *Coupon Value* column, write the value of the coupon or use the real coupon. Ask the student to determine the actual cost of each item. For example:

Grocery Items	Price	Coupon Value	Actual Cost
1. coffee	$3.12	10% off	_____
2. pickles	$1.14	$ .15	_____
3. cereal	$1.39	15% off	_____
4. jelly	$ .79	$ .20	_____

Taking Orders

Have the student become a waiter and write down orders after listening to a prerecorded audio cassette. Using the menus provided, the student can look up the prices of the items ordered, compute the cost of the order, and write the total on the order pad.

Check the Charge

Make worksheets with instructions to check the cashier's slips and see whether they are added correctly. For example:

$1.19		$1.38
.99		2.64
.37		.26
1.03		.15
$3.38		$4.43

Measurement

Measure Box

Provide the student with a box of objects to measure (such as popsicle stick, comb, paper clip, and straw) and a worksheet with the objects listed on it. Have the student measure the objects and record their lengths in inches and centimeters on the worksheet. This activity can be repeated for weighing objects.

FIGURE 12.12
Expanded place value chart

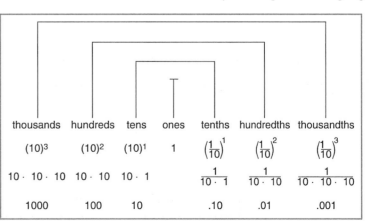

Measurement and You

Have the student complete the following worksheet:

> Your height:
> ____ feet ____ inches
>
> Your weight:
> ____ pounds
>
> Your speed:
> Number of seconds to run 40 yards:
> ____ seconds
>
> Your agility:
> Number of seconds to deal 52 cards:
> ____ seconds
>
> Your writing speed:
> Number of times you can write your first name in one minute: ____ times
>
> Number of times you can write 6s in one minute: ____ times
>
> Your reading speed:
> Number of words read in one minute:
> ____ words
>
> Circumference of your head: ____ inches
>
> Circumference of your waist: ____ inches

Word Problems

Story Problems

Initially, provide the student with simple, interesting word problems. This helps the student understand that sentences may request specific math computations. For example:

1. How much are 3 marbles and 4 marbles?
2. What number represents a triple?
3. How many points is a field goal in football?
4. To get a first down in football, how many yards must you gain?
5. How many points are 10 baskets in basketball?

Have the student write a number sentence after reading a story problem. For example:

Mary has 6 comic books. She has read 2 of them. How many books does she have left to read? 6 − 2 = _____

Table Problems

Provide problems that include computing answers from information on a table. An interesting activity that requires computing percentages and decimals from a table is to give the student baseball standings (or football or basketball standings, depending on the season) from the newspaper with only the won/lost record beside each team. Have the student do the following:

1. Compute the percentage for each team in the American League East and the National League East.
2. Place the American and National League teams in order based on their won/lost records.
3. Determine how many teams have records over .500.
4. Determine how many percentage points the team in the American League East with the most losses is behind the team with the most wins.

INSTRUCTIONAL GAMES IN MATH

Math War

Materials: Sets of index cards consisting of family patterns. (With sums-to-9, each of the numbers from 1 to 9 has a family of two one-digit addends. The entire set for sums-to-9 includes 54 cards. The family pattern for 7, for example, is 0 + 7, 7 + 0, 1 + 6, 6 + 1, 2 + 5, 5 + 2, 3 + 4, and 4 + 3.)

Directions: All players shuffle their 54-card decks. With cards face down, one card at a time is turned face up. The player who turns the card showing the number fact with the largest sum wins all the turned cards. The players then turn their next card. If cards of equal sums are turned up at the same time, players with the equivalent cards declare war. They place three cards face down and turn the fourth card face up. The player whose fourth card has the highest value wins all four cards of the other players (i.e., three face-down cards and one face-up card). Whoever has the most cards after 54 cards are played wins. Another way of winning is to play until the other players only have five or ten remaining cards.

Modifications: Any set of math facts or operations can be placed on the cards (such as multiplication facts; sums-to-18; and sets of fractions, decimals, and percents). Also, students who play the game during the school day may keep the cards they win and give up the cards they lose. For homework, each player can complete the missing cards in the deck and remove the extra cards. (Each player always comes to school with one complete deck, which has no extra or missing cards.)

Pig Game

Materials: Dice, scoring pad.

Directions: Pig Game usually is played by two students with one pair of dice. The object is to be the first player to score 100 points by adding the totals on the dice after each roll. The players take turns rolling the dice; however, a player may roll as many times as desired as long as the player does not roll a 1 on one or both of the dice. If a 1 is rolled on one die, the player gives up the turn and loses all points earned during that turn. If a 1 is rolled on both dice, the player gives up the turn, loses all points, and starts again at zero.

Modifications: Wooden blocks with numerals on all sides except one can be used. A drawing of a pig is placed on the empty side. When pig dice are used, each player can be given an appropriate worksheet for his or her math level. If no pigs are rolled, the player answers an item on the worksheet, and the answer is checked by a student with the answer key. If the answer is correct, the item number is checked; however, if the answer is incorrect, the item number is not checked and the player must attempt that item on another turn. If one pig is rolled on the dice, the player loses a turn. If two pigs are rolled (i.e., one on each die), the player is allowed to attempt to answer two items on the worksheet. This procedure is continued until one player correctly answers all the items on the worksheet and wins the game. Also, to minimize erratic dice throwing, the dice can be placed in a pill container. The student shakes the container and then opens the lid to see the numbers that are upright on the dice.

Make the Numbers Count

Materials: Dice or a spinner; score sheets.

Directions: Each player is provided with a score sheet that has five columns—one each for ones, tens, hundreds, thousands, and ten thousands. The left side of the score sheet is numbered from 1 to 10. A die, which shows 1 to 6, or a spinner, which shows 1 to 5 (e.g., a spinner from a commercial game) is rolled or spun 10 times by each player. On each turn the players must enter the number shown on the die or spinner in one of the columns. For a game of ten turns, only two numbers may be put in each column. After ten turns, the columns are totaled and the player with the highest number wins.

Spinner Number	10,000s	1000s	100s	10s	1s
1. 3			3		
2. 5	5				
3. 1					1
4. 3		3			
5. 2				2	
6. 2				2	
7. 1					1
8. 4	4				
9. 5		5			
10. 5			5		
Total	9	8	8	4	2

Note: The player in this example would have had a higher score if the 4 in spin #8 had not been used in the 10,000 column. The 5 in either turn 9 or 10 could have been used there.

Rook Math

Materials: A deck of Rook cards (i.e., four suits or colors of cards numbered 1 through 14); four dice.

Directions: The cards are shuffled, and five cards are dealt to each player. The remaining cards are placed on the table, and one card is turned up beside the deck. The player to the left of the dealer throws the four dice and attempts to match the sum on the dice with a card or cards in his or her hand. The player can lay down a single card or a combination of cards that equals the sum. The player can take the face-up card or draw from the deck. Whether the player lays down cards or not, he or she then discards on the face-up pile. The next player then takes a turn. When one player is out of cards, the players total the cards that have been played, and the player with the highest sum wins the game.

Math Concentration

Materials: Ten stimulus cards with math problems on one side and blank on the other side; 10 cards with the answers to the problems of the stimulus cards on one side and blank on the other side.

Directions: The cards are placed face down in a 5 × 4 array. Two or more students can play. The first player turns over a card and gives an answer. If the answer is correct, the player turns over a second card. If the second card shows the answer to the first card, the player gets to keep both cards. If an incorrect answer is given to the first card, the player does not turn over a second card. The next player then takes a turn. The winner is the player with the most cards when all cards are taken.

Fraction Game

Materials: One-inch cubes of wood with gummed stickers on each side marked $\frac{1}{2}$, $\frac{1}{4}$, $\frac{1}{6}$, $\frac{1}{12}$, $\frac{1}{3}$, and $\frac{1}{12}$; 1-inch cardboard squares marked as follows: 24 pieces with $\frac{1}{4}$ label, 31 pieces with $\frac{1}{6}$ label, 12 pieces with $\frac{1}{2}$ label, 18 pieces with $\frac{1}{3}$ label, and 60 pieces with $\frac{1}{12}$ label; six game boards marked into 12 sections.

Directions: Each player is given a game board. The player attempts to collect fractional parts that will cover $\frac{12}{12}$ of the board without overlapping pieces. The first player throws a cube and collects the fractional piece designated by the cube. This piece is placed on the playing board. The next player then takes a turn. Play continues until a player's board is covered. If a player throws the cube and all corresponding pieces have been taken, the player receives nothing. Likewise, if the cube indicates a fraction that is larger than needed, the player collects nothing.

Toss a Bean Bag

Materials: Six 1-gallon cans; bean bags; six discs with numerals written on them; masking tape; score cards.

Directions: The six cans are placed in bowling pin format and are taped together with masking tape. One disc is placed in the bottom of each can. A strip of masking tape is placed on the floor about 10 feet from the cans. Each player stands behind the strip, tosses two bean bags into the cans, and adds the numbers in the bottom of the cans in which the bean bags land. If a bag does not land in a can, a 1 is used in computation. The players take turns and record their scores on their score cards. After five tosses by each player, the player with the highest score wins.

Modifications: For column addition practice, each player can toss three or four bean bags and add the numerals. Also, discs with different numbers can be used for other computations (e.g., subtraction and multiplication of whole numbers, and addition of fractions).

Multiplication and Division Facts Rummy

Materials: Forty to 52 cards containing a family of multiplication/division facts (e.g., 9×6, 6×9, $54 \div 6$, $54 \div 9$).

Directions: Seven cards are dealt to each player. The player on the dealer's left draws a card from the remaining cards. If the card matches two others in the player's hand in the same family, the player lays down the book of cards and gives the answer to each fact. If an incorrect answer is given, the cards must remain in the player's hand until the next turn. After the player lays down cards or is unable to do so, the player discards by placing a card from his or her hand face up beside the deck so that all the other discards can be seen. The next player may choose from the stack or pick up the previous discard if the player can match it with two cards in his or her hand. If there are two cards in the discard pile that match one in a player's hand, the player may pick up both cards. The player does not have to take the whole pack, provided he or she can give the correct answers of the cards between the two desired cards. Also, during a turn a player may lay down one or more cards that match another player's books. When a player is out of cards, he or she says, "Rummy," and wins the game.

Modifications: Cards can be constructed to play Place Value Rummy. One-fourth of the 52 cards display groups of tens and ones, one-fourth display standard notation, one-fourth show expanded notation, and one-fourth name the tens and ones.

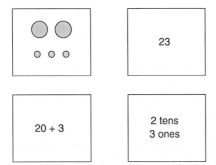

Travel Game

Materials: Large map of the United States; markers or pictures of vehicles; cards with math problems on them.

Directions: On a large map of the United States, a course across the nation is marked off into 50-mile segments. Each card presents a math problem and the number of miles it is worth (such as 50, 100, or 200 miles). Each player draws a card and responds to the problem. If correct, the player's marker is moved the number of miles indicated on the card. If incorrect, the player moves *back* the specified miles. The winner is the first player (or team) to reach the destination.

Modification: Players can be provided with cards of various difficulty levels. Each student can select cards from the desired difficulty level. The more difficult the problem, the more miles it is worth.

Basketball Math

Materials: A drawing of a basketball court on the chalkboard or on poster board; sets of cards presenting math problems labeled *lay-up*, *10-foot jump shot*, *15-foot jump shot*, and *3-point shot*.

Directions: The cards are divided into stacks. Each lay-up card has a problem to be answered for 2 points and two problems, which are slightly more difficult, that may be answered to block the lay-up. If the opposing player can answer either of the block problems, the lay-up is blocked. If the shooter answers the lay-up problem correctly and it is not blocked, the player receives 2 points. For the next most difficult stack (i.e., 10-foot jump shot), there is only one block question on the card. The 15-foot jump shot has the next most difficult problems and no block questions. The 3-point-shot stack has the most difficult problems and no block questions. A time limit (e.g., 5 seconds) is set for answering the questions.

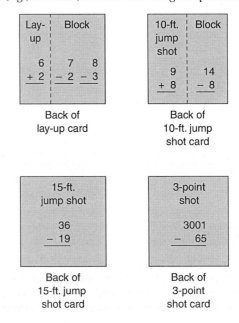

Counting Coins

Materials: Timer; paper and pencil.

Directions: The object of the game is to use the fewest coins to make a given sum. The leader calls out an amount (such as 65 cents). Each player must write down the coins that make the sum within a given time limit. All players who correctly sum the coins receive 1 point. The player or players who use the fewest coins receive 5 points. The first player to receive 25 points wins the game.

Rate Game

Materials: A start-to-finish game board; math worksheets and corresponding answer sheets; game markers; dice.

Directions: Each player is given an individual worksheet at the appropriate instructional level. The first player rolls one die and may elect to move his or her marker that number of spaces on the game board or to write the answers to problems on the worksheet for 10 seconds and move the marker according to the number of problems answered correctly. The opposing player uses the answer sheet to check the responses. If the choice is made to write answers on the worksheet, the player must take these results even if the number is less than the number rolled on the die. The first player to reach the finish space on the board wins the game.

Fraction Blackjack

Materials: Deck of playing cards.

Directions: All picture cards are given any value from 1 to 10. The cards are separated into two stacks: red cards (i.e., diamonds and hearts) and black cards (i.e., spades and clubs). The first player draws one card from each stack and forms a fraction using the value of the black card as the numerator and the value of the red card as the denominator. Thus, if the player draws a black 8 and a red 2, the fraction is $^8/_2$. The same player continues by drawing two more cards (i.e., one black and one red), forming the fraction, and adding the new fraction to the first fraction ($^8/_2$). This continues until the player makes a sum of 10 or as close to 10 as possible. The sum may be above or below 10, and the winner of each round is the player who gets closest to 10.

Modification: The game may be played more like traditional blackjack, in which the players take turns receiving their two cards and a player loses if the sum goes over 10.

Fraction Removal

Materials: Dice (i.e., one green and one white); paper and pencil.

Directions: Each player writes the following 22 numbers on a sheet of paper: 1.00, .50, .33, .25, .20, .26, 2.00, .66, .40, 3.00, 1.50, .75, .60, 4.00, 1.33, 1.20, 5.00, 2.50, 1.66, 1.25, .83, and 6.00. One green die and one white die are used. The green die determines the numerator, and the white die determines

the denominator. Thus, a dice roll of a green 4 and a white 2 is equivalent to $^4/_2$, or 2. The decimal equivalent of this is 2.00. A roll of a green 3 and a white 5 equals $^3/_5$, or .60. Each player rolls the dice, forms the fraction, computes the decimal form, and crosses it out on his or her paper. One point is scored for each decimal crossed out, and 5 bonus points are given for each fraction rolled that is equivalent to 1.00 (e.g., $^4/_4$). The winner is the player who scores 50 points first.

Decimal Shapes

Materials: A game board with sections containing numbers in decimal form; 10 markers (i.e., 5 each of two colors); a chip marked *L* on one side and *S* on the other; an answer sheet that has the numbers on the board listed in order from smallest to largest.

Directions: Both players place their markers on the starting spaces of the board (i.e., spaces enclosed with dark lines). The first player flips the chip. If the chip lands on the *L* side, the player must move one of his or her markers to an adjacent space having a number larger than the number the marker is on. If the chip lands on the *S* side, the player must move one of his or her markers to an adjacent space having a number smaller than the number the marker is on. If the player can move one of the markers to a space occupied by the opponent, the opponent's marker is moved back to a starting position. Only one marker may be on a space at one time. The player must move one of his or her markers, no matter what the direction, if able to do so. If unable to move, the player loses a turn. The two players take turns, and each move can be checked for correctness by using the answer sheet. The winner is the first player to get all of his or her markers to the starting spaces on the other side of the board.

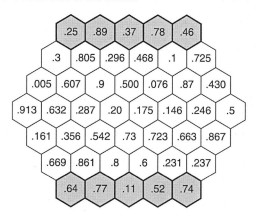

SELF-CORRECTING MATH MATERIALS

Flip-Sider Math Cards

Feedback device: The correct answer is written on the back of each stimulus card.

Materials: Stimulus cards with a math problem on one side and the correct answer on the other side.

Directions: The student looks at the math problem on the card and writes the answer on a worksheet. Then the student flips over the card to check the response.

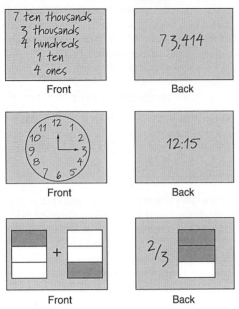

Front   Back

Front   Back

Front   Back

Clipping Answers

Feedback device: When the clothespin containing the correct answer is clipped to the problem on the board and the board is turned over, the symbol on the back of the clothespin matches the symbol on the back of the board.

Materials: Segmented stimulus board showing math problems on the front and symbols on the back; clothespins with answers on one side and symbols corresponding to those on the stimulus board on the other side.

Directions: The student matches the answer on the clothespin to a problem by clipping the clothespin to the problem on the board. Then the student turns over the board. If the symbol on the back of the clothespin matches the symbol on the back of the board, the answer is correct.

Modifications: For easy storage, the clothespins can be kept in a plastic bag with a zipper. Also, cardboard pizza wheels make good stimulus cards.

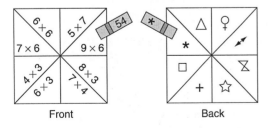

Front   Back

Math Squares

Feedback device: After completing the squares, the student can check the work by turning the squares over. If the squares are placed correctly, a message or picture appears on the back.

Materials: A set of poster board squares that include math problems and answers to problems on adjoining squares, and a message or picture is written on the back of the large piece of poster board before the squares are cut; a large box with a window in the bottom, which is made by placing a piece of acetate over an opening.

Directions: The student fits the squares together so that each fact adjoins its correct answer. The student puts the pieces, with the message or picture side down, inside the box and on top of the acetate. When the puzzle is completed, the student places the cover on the box and flips the box over. If the puzzle is completed correctly, the player can read the message or view the picture on the back of the puzzle.

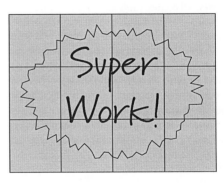

Front

Back

Color Code Folders

Feedback device: When the worksheet is in the red folder, the problems can be seen but the answers cannot. After completing the problems on a separate sheet of paper, the student removes the worksheet from its folder to check the answers.

Materials: Red transparent folder (such as a term-paper folder); worksheet with problems written in black felt-tip pen and answers written in yellow.

Directions: The student inserts the worksheet into the red folder. Then the student numbers a separate sheet of paper and records the answer for each problem. The worksheet is removed from the folder, and the student checks the answers with those written in yellow on the worksheet.

Modification: Different colors may be used, and answers can be written in the same color as the folder.

Worksheet

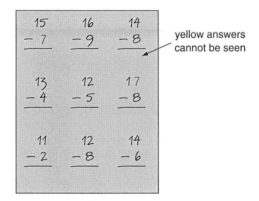

Red folder
with worksheet inside

Fast Facts

Feedback device: The correct answers are written inside the open folder.

Materials: Manila folder with math problems in a column on the right side inside the folder, the answers to the problems on the left side of the same flap inside the folder, and the outside flap of the folder cut so that only the problems are exposed when the folder is closed.

Directions: The student computes the problems presented in the closed folder and then opens the folder to check the work.

Closed folder

Open folder

Snoopy Math

Feedback device: When the student puts a pencil in the hole of the completed problem and turns over the cutout (i.e., Snoopy), the correct answer is written next to the hole where the pencil is.

Materials: Snoopy figure cut out of poster board with (1) holes punched around the cutout, (2) a number placed near each hole, (3) an operation and a number (such as +8) written in the middle of the cutout, and (4) answers written on the other side beside the holes; pencil.

Directions: The student computes problems according to the operation and number presented in the middle of the cutout. For example, if +8 is presented, the student is to add 8 to each number near each hole. The student places a pencil in the hole beside a problem, computes the answer, and turns over Snoopy to check the response by looking at the answer where the pencil is.

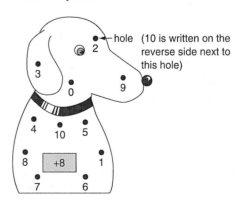

Modification: Each side can be used as the problem or the answer. For example, the problems on the other side of the example +8 become −8.

Equivalent Fractions, Decimals, and Percents

Feedback device: The correct answers are written in the bottom of each box section.

Materials: A box divided into six sections by partitions, with each section having correct answers written on the bottom of the box; a lid to the box that has six slits cut in it and a fraction, decimal, or percent written above each slit; index cards with values written on them that correspond to the slit labels.

Directions: The student places each index card in the slit named by an equivalent decimal, fraction, or percent on the card. For example, cards marked 2/6, .33, and 33% would be placed in the slit marked 1/3. When all the cards have been placed in a slit, the student removes the lid from the box and checks the answers by looking at the bottom of the box where the correct values for each section are listed.

COMMERCIAL MATH PROGRAMS

Numerous published programs and materials are available for teaching math concepts and skills. The following selected programs and materials are useful for teaching math skills to students with learning problems.

Connecting Math Concepts

The *Connecting Math Concepts* curriculum, developed by S. E. Engelmann, D. Carnine, B. Kelly, and O. Engelmann (published by SRA), establishes relationships among math concepts and their application. The basal program includes Levels A through F for students in kindergarten through eighth grade, and skills are organized in tracks for the ongoing development of a particular topic. This direct instruction program introduces ideas gradually, and each lesson is divided into 5- to 10-minute segments that address different topics. Following detailed explanations and guided practice, students move to independent work for skill mastery and maintenance. Suggestions are provided for problem-solving activities, games, cooperative learning activities, and the use of manipulative materials.

Corrective Mathematics

Corrective Mathematics, developed by S. E. Engelmann and D. Carnine (published by SRA), is an intervention program in basic math for students in third grade through adult age who have not mastered basic skills. Four modules focus on the basic facts in addition, subtraction, multiplication, and division. Content includes the concepts of carrying and borrowing as well as translating story problems into numerical statements. Three additional modules developed by S. E. Engelmann and D. Steely focus on basic fractions; fractions, decimals, percents; and ratios and equations. Each module

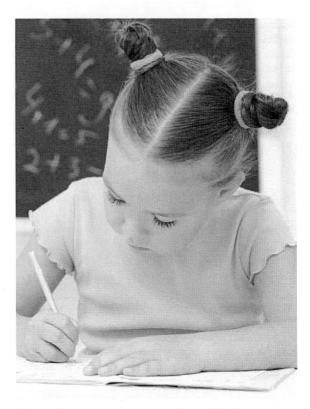

The student must master lower-level skills before higher-order skills can be learned.
Serhiy Kobyakov/Fotolia

provides 55 to 75 daily lessons and includes both teacher-directed instruction and independent review activities. Student workbooks include daily worksheets as well as print summary charts for recording student performance and awarding grades. The software program, *ExamView*, provides worksheets for each module and allows the teacher to create paper or computer-based tests and worksheets.

Great Leaps Math

Great Leaps Math (Mercer, Mercer, & Campbell, 2002) focuses on building fluency in the basic facts, including addition, subtraction, multiplication, and division. It features concrete lessons, which include the use of manipulative objects, and representational lessons, which include the use of student drawings, to help the student understand math operations. After the student demonstrates understanding through the concrete and representational lessons, fluency-building lessons begin through 1-minute timings of oral and written student responses to math facts. The student repeats the 1-minute timings until a standard practice rate on oral timings and a standard fluency rate on written timings are achieved. During the 5- to 7-minute daily session, the instructor follows the word GREAT as a mnemonic device to conduct a five-step lesson plan. The student moves from oral practice lessons to written fluency lessons to written generalization fluency lessons. Results of the timings are recorded on a math chart, and goals are provided according to the age of the student. The use of rules and relationships throughout the lessons enhances mastery of the math facts. The program consists of three instructor manuals and three student workbooks: *Addition and Subtraction Facts 0 to 9, Addition and Subtraction Facts 10 to 18,* and *Multiplication and Division Facts 0 to 81.* Placement tests and instructional math games are provided. The program has been field tested, and the data indicate excellent student progress and teacher acceptance.

KeyMath—3 Essential Resources

KeyMath—3 Essential Resources, developed by A. J. Connolly (published by Pearson), is a comprehensive math intervention program that contains hundreds of lessons, student practice sheets, and brief tests. When used as a companion to the *KeyMath—3: Diagnostic Assessment,* the program provides effective intervention materials tailored to the individual student's strengths and weaknesses. There are two levels of instruction (i.e., level 1 for kindergarten through second grade; level 2 for third grade through sixth grade), which cover ten instructional strands in the three content areas of foundational math concepts, operational skills, and problem solving. Each lesson is designed for a 30- to 40-minute class period and is appropriate for whole group, small group, or individual settings. An easy-to-use CD for each level includes reproducible guided and independent practice sheets, lesson displays, tests for monitoring progress, and supplementary materials.

Strategic Math Series

The *Strategic Math Series,* developed by C. D. Mercer and S. P. Miller (published by Edge Enterprises), is designed to enable students with math difficulties to understand, acquire, remember, and apply math concepts and skills. The program is based on research in effective teaching, learning strategies, memory, mastery learning, applied behavior analysis, generalization, and student motivation. Eight instructional stages are included: pretest, concrete, representational, DRAW (i.e., a mnemonic), abstract, posttest, practice to mastery, and periodic review. All lessons include scripts to guide the teacher through the instructional components of advance organizer, demonstrate/explain, guided practice, independent practice, problem solving (i.e., students learn to create their own story problems), and lesson feedback. Manuals are available for addition facts 0 to 9, subtraction facts 0 to 9, place value, addition facts 10 to 18, subtraction facts 10 to 18, multiplication facts 0 to 81, and division facts 0 to 81.

TransMath

TransMath, developed by J. Woodard and M. Stroh (published by Sopris West), is a comprehensive intervention designed for students in fifth through tenth grade who are performing 2 or more years below grade level. Students learn essential concepts, computational skills, and problem-solving strategies through the use of explicit, cumulative instruction and engaging visual representations. The 28-unit curriculum includes three levels: Developing Number Sense (e.g., place value, estimation, and multistep problems), Making Sense of Rational Numbers (e.g., geometry, fractions, decimals, percentages, and negative numbers), and Understanding Algebraic Expressions (e.g., exponents, ratios, square roots, and irrational numbers). Group-administered placement assessments are available as well as an online assessment system for individualized student placement. The teacher resource kit includes manipulatives and transparencies.

COMPUTER SOFTWARE PROGRAMS IN MATH

Computer software programs in math can be used to provide motivating drill-and-practice activities. Some programs present game-playing situations; others effectively use animation and sound effects to maintain student interest. The computer also can provide self-correcting feedback so that the student does not practice errors. For effective learning results, it is helpful to combine direct teacher instruction with tutorial and drill-and-practice software. Kroesbergen and Van Luit (2003) note that students can use the computer to practice and automatize math facts and receive direct feedback; however, the use of the computer as an aid to instruction cannot replace the teacher and the computer cannot remediate the basic difficulties that students encounter. In a meta-analysis of interventions for solving word problems, Xin and Jitendra (1999) report that computer-assisted instruction was found to be highly effective, especially in studies that combined principles of effective curriculum design with interactive videodisc programs. The following software programs present various math skills and can help the student understand and master these skills.

Fraction Attraction

Fraction Attraction (produced by Sunburst Communications) is designed to help students in third through eighth grade learn fundamental fraction concepts. Four animated carnival-style activities strengthen students' understanding of ordering, equivalencies, relative size, and multiple representations of fractions. Each multilevel activity features diagnostic help to assist students in correcting conceptual errors. The program is fully customizable and includes a teacher guide with activities.

Math Blaster

Math Blaster: Master the Basics (produced by Knowledge Adventure) covers various math curriculum skills. Students ages 6 through 12 participate in a fast-paced, action-packed futuristic adventure in which robots controlling the galaxy must be defeated. Through practice and play, students build math confidence and increase speed and accuracy in math areas such as addition, subtraction, multiplication, division, fact families, problem solving, equivalents, and mental math.

Math FACTMASTER

Math FACTMASTER (produced by Curriculum Associates) offers addition, subtraction, multiplication, and division facts games and activities tailored to each individual student's needs. The program remembers the facts each student has mastered from one session to the next and focuses on unmastered facts in each succeeding lesson. Facts are presented in horizontal/vertical, true–false, and open-sentence formats. Responses that are incorrect or exceed the mastery time limit set by the teacher reappear at random until the student masters them. Checkpoint activities provide word problems that use only mastered facts, and as students master facts in each session they move toward their ultimate goal of automatic recall of number facts. Individual student reports indicate mastered and unmastered facts, response times for each fact, and percentage of mastered facts in each operation. Test preparation activities are included, and printable homework sheets are available at the end of each session. *Math FACTMASTER* is online so that students can log in from school or home and the teacher can access data at any time. Also, this research-based program to build fluency in recall of math facts through the 12s is available on a CD for single-computer installation.

Math Munchers for the 21st Century

In *Math Munchers for the 21st Century* (produced by PCI Education), students travel through the Mata Matica system to explore planets and solve math problems. This quick-paced software focuses on three main math skill areas: numbers (i.e., number identification, number vocabulary, place value, decimals, and fractions), operations (i.e., addition, subtraction, multiplication, and division), and number functions (i.e., patterns, classification, fact families, multiples, and factors). Skills progress in difficulty from kindergarten to fifth grade, and students can select any category and level. Student progress is tracked throughout the game, and a tutorial is available for every skill in the program. Also, teacher options allow for individualized play and adaptation.

PERSPECTIVE

Many students with learning problems experience math difficulties. However, if educational researchers can scientifically tap the potential benefits of research-driven principles and if teacher educators and publishers of commercial materials can place the products of these findings in the hands of teachers, educators have an opportunity to improve significantly the math learning of students and the math instruction of teachers. Perhaps student beliefs about learning math will change, and more math teachers will experience the satisfaction and joy of having a student approach them and say, "I know how to solve $9x - 6x + 12 = 24$" . . . and the fun begins.

Teaching Learning Strategies, Content, and Study Skills

Arthur Tilley/Creatas–Jupiter Images

From Chapter 13 of *Teaching Students with Learning Problems*, 8/e. Cecil D. Mercer. Ann R. Mercer. Paige C. Pullen.

Chapters 1 through 12 of this text primarily focus on helping teachers create instructional environments that assist students with academic problems to learn to listen, speak, read, write, compute, problem solve, and socialize. These foundational skills are important for early school successes and provide a basis for the expanded school demands that students face in middle school, secondary school, and postsecondary school settings. Adolescents are faced with the complex task of using these academic and social skills to acquire knowledge about science, social studies, literature, and independent living in settings that are demanding for teachers and students.

The characteristics of students with learning problems combine with the complex academic demands and instructional realities to make it difficult for these adolescents to succeed in school. Figure 13.1, which contains information compiled from Bulgren and Lenz (1996) and Mercer and Pullen (2005), highlights the parameters of learning characteristics, academic demands, and setting realities that operate in the middle school and secondary school arenas. Inspection of these instructional conditions makes it apparent that adolescents with learning problems need intensive and explicit instruction to succeed.

Fortunately, there have been efforts in the field of learning disabilities to develop effective secondary programs. For example, the University of Kansas Center for Research on Learning was established in 1978 to study the needs of adolescents with learning disabilities and develop appropriate interventions. Under the leadership of Don Deshler and his colleagues, this center has a nationwide impact and produces research critical to the field of learning disabilities. Its learning strategy materials and content enhancement routines are used successfully to help adolescents with learning problems experience school success. Moreover, other authorities (Hoover, 2004; Meltzer et al., 1996; Therrien, Hughes, Kapelski, & Mokhtari, 2009; Wood, 2002) present study skills techniques that are effective. Figure 13.1 presents learning strategies, content enhancements, and study skills techniques as essential

FIGURE 13.1

Instructional conditions and essential services for students with learning problems

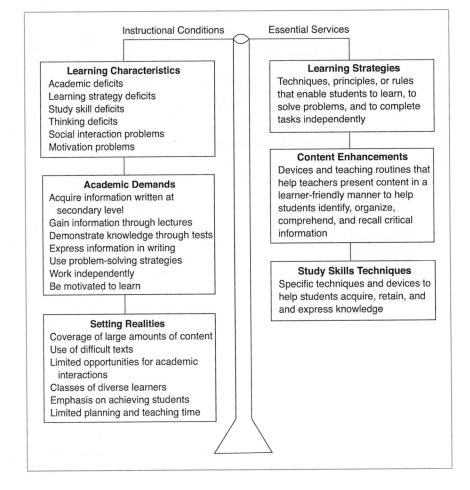

instructional options for students with learning problems. Following a discussion on motivation and the adolescent, this chapter presents information that assists teachers in teaching learning strategies, content, and study skills to adolescents with learning problems.

MOTIVATION

Motivation to learn or participate is essential to the success of any intervention approach. The adage, "You can lead a horse to water, but you can't make him drink," certainly applies to learning. For an intervention approach to be effective with a student who has learning problems, the individual must be motivated to participate. For the adolescent with learning problems, lack of motivation is often a roadblock to school success. Thus, regarding motivation, the adage may be altered to, "Although you can't make a horse drink the water, you can salt the hay."

Several motivation techniques are available to help low-achieving students in secondary school. These approaches are divided into two broad categories: those using extrinsic controls and those that focus on developing intrinsic motivation. Several extrinsic control techniques have been used successfully to improve the academic skills of adolescents with learning problems. Extrinsic reinforcers that appear to be effective with adolescents include the following:

- Time for listening to music on a CD or MP3 player
- Tokens for progress on academics
- Charting or self-recording of academic accomplishments
- Allowances at home tied to grades
- Time to play games or enjoy a recreational activity
- Opportunity to participate in scheduling academic activities
- Tangible reinforcers such as restaurant coupons, magazines, and movie tickets
- Exemption from some homework or assignments
- Extra time for a break or lunch

The most useful techniques include token economies, contingency contracting, and verbal feedback. Techniques aimed at facilitating intrinsic motivation also are receiving support.

Motivation strategies are one of the curriculum components of the Strategies Intervention Model developed at the University of Kansas Center for Research on Learning. Motivation strategies within this model are techniques and procedures that involve the learner in key aspects of the learning process and are used to increase a student's commitment to learn. Motivation strategies can be used to increase students' interest in their own learning and foster their ability to gain control over their own performances. *Possible Selves* (Hock, Schumaker, & Deshler, 2003) is a motivation strategies program in which students examine their strengths and interests as well as their hoped-for, expected, and feared possible selves. Students construct a visual depiction of these possible selves and their characteristics, identify areas they wish to nurture and write goals related to these areas, and work toward accomplishing their goals. In addition, to enhance student motivation and self-determination, this program can be followed by teaching the *Self-Advocacy Strategy for Enhancing Student Motivation and Self-Determination* (Van Reusen, Bos, Schumaker, & Deshsler, 2002), which focuses on the following education skill areas: reading, writing, math, study skills, classroom behavior skills, social skills, computer/technology skills, and career and employment skills. Also, the strategy features eight transition skill areas. The five steps of the strategy are included in I PLAN (i.e., *Inventory* your strengths, needs, goals, and choices; *Provide* your inventory information; *Listen* and respond; *Ask* questions; and *Name* your goals). Students can use the strategy when preparing for and participating in any type of conference, including individualized educational program and transition planning conferences.

To promote the development of active and independent learners, some motivation strategies attempt to teach self-control skills, including one or more of the following: goal setting, self-recording of progress, self-evaluation, and self-reinforcement. Self-control training can help students with learning problems complete their assignments, and the training procedures are easy to implement and do not depend on expensive extrinsic reinforcers. Moreover, the following tactics can enhance intrinsic motivation.

1. Provide choices in curriculum content and procedures to enhance the student's perception that learning is worthwhile, and discuss the relevance (i.e., real-life applications) of various content.
2. Through discussion, obtain a commitment to options that the student values and indicates a desire to pursue. Contractual agreements are helpful.
3. Schedule informal and formal conferences with the student to enhance her or his role in making choices and negotiating agreements.
4. Provide feedback that conveys student progress. The student must not perceive the feedback as an effort to entice and control. Self-correcting materials are useful.

Student involvement is a recurring theme in the literature on managing and motivating adolescents with learning problems. The secondary classroom teacher should encourage students to participate in all aspects of the curriculum. Students can be allowed to make choices among tasks, curriculum, materials, and instructional sequences, and they should be involved in selecting and prioritizing their own social goals, in making decisions about the classroom structure, and in setting consequences and contingencies.

Another dimension that may be included in efforts to promote student motivation relates to the beliefs that students have about themselves. Many students do not believe that they can learn or change. Ellis, Deshler, Lenz, Schumaker, and Clark (1991) present four techniques for teachers to use to help students alter their beliefs about their learning and performance.

1. Engineer instructional arrangements to promote and reinforce student independence.
2. Communicate high expectations for students through words and actions.
3. Help students identify and analyze beliefs that underlie their behavior as ineffective learners.
4. Help students discard unproductive beliefs through a variety of activities and interactions.

LEARNING STRATEGIES

A learning strategies approach helps students with learning problems cope with the complex demands of the secondary curriculum. Deshler and his colleagues at the University of Kansas Center for Research on Learning define *learning strategies* as techniques, principles, or rules that enable a student to learn, to solve problems, and to complete tasks independently. The goal of strategy development is to identify strategies that are optimally effective (i.e., help students meet the demands of both current and future tasks) and efficient (i.e., help students meet the demands of the task in appropriate, timely, resourceful, and judicious ways). The goal of strategies instruction is to teach the strategies effectively (i.e., the strategy is learned and generalized by the student) and efficiently (i.e., the strategy is learned to an optimal level with a minimum amount of effort by the teacher and the student). This approach attempts to help students learn course content (such as geography) through instruction in skills necessary to acquire, store, and express content. Basically, it focuses on teaching students how to learn and how to demonstrate command of their knowledge in performing academic tasks. For example, a reading strategy may be used by a student with fourth-grade reading skills to obtain relevant information from a textbook chapter written at the tenth-grade level. As one part of the Strategies Intervention Model, Deshler and his colleagues developed a learning strategies curriculum with components that have been specified, developed, and validated in classrooms. Because the strategies included in the Strategies Intervention Model have the longest history of comprehensive research and development for adolescents with learning problems, a detailed description of this approach is presented.

Learning Strategies Curriculum

The Learning Strategies Curriculum of the University of Kansas Center for Research on Learning includes intervention manuals and support materials. The manuals, available through training, advise teachers on how to provide intensive instruction to adolescents with learning problems and how to promote the acquisition, storage, and expression of information and demonstration of competence through instruction in learning strategies. The strategies included in the curriculum are listed and described in Table 13.1. The study skills section of this chapter also presents many skills that are organized within a strategic framework. Each teacher manual details how to teach the strategy and how to prompt the student to transfer it across settings. Teachers are trained in the basic concepts of the strategy that previously has been validated through research, and they are encouraged to tailor strategy instruction according to their personal teaching styles to meet the needs of students. Thus, while integrity in the basic features of the strategy and the instructional procedures must be retained to ensure student success, the teacher is given wide latitude to make the intervention meaningful in individual situations.

The learning strategy interventions respond to the specific needs of teachers who need instructional procedures and curricula for adolescents with learning problems. Because most special education teachers provide instruction in a support class setting rather than in the general classroom setting, the curriculum materials are used mainly to teach strategies in one setting and then prompt generalization of the strategies to additional settings (e.g., the general classroom). The student's general classroom materials are used in the process so that the student learns to associate the strategy with success in meeting naturally occurring learning demands. Changes in service delivery options permit general classroom teachers to infuse many dimensions of these strategy interventions into content-area instruction, which allows the student to see the

TABLE 13.1
The learning strategies curriculum of the University of Kansas Center for Research on Learning

---

Acquisition Strand

Strategic Math Series: Teaches students problem-solving procedures for acquiring and applying basic math facts. The strategies are designed to help students develop fluency in basic math facts and use strategies for solving word problems.

Word Identification Strategy: Teaches students a problem-solving procedure for quickly attacking and decoding unknown words in reading materials, which allows them to move on quickly for the purpose of comprehending the passage.

Paraphrasing Strategy: Directs students to read a limited section of material, ask themselves the main idea and the details of the section, and put that information in their own words. The strategy is designed to improve comprehension by focusing attention on the important information of a passage and by stimulating active involvement with the passage.

Self-Questioning Strategy: Aids reading comprehension by having students actively ask questions about key pieces of information in a passage and then read to find the answers for these questions.

Visual Imagery Strategy: Improves students' acquisition, storage, and recall of prose material. Students improve reading comprehension by reading short passages and visualizing the scene that is described (i.e., incorporating actors, action, and details).

Storage Strand

FIRST-Letter Mnemonic Strategy: Aids students in memorizing lists of information by teaching them to design mnemonics or memorization aids, and to find and make lists of crucial information.

Paired Associates Strategy: Aids students in memorizing pairs or small groups of information by using visual imagery, matching pertinent information with familiar objects, coding important dates, and using a first-syllable technique.

LINCS Vocabulary Strategy: Helps students learn the meaning of new vocabulary words using powerful memory-enhancement techniques. Strategy steps cue students to focus on the critical elements of the concept; to use visual imagery, associations with prior knowledge, and keyword mnemonic devices to create a study card; and to study the card to enhance comprehension and recall of the concept.

Expression and Demonstration of Competence Strand

SLANT: A Strategy for Class Participation: Helps students participate in class discussions. Students learn how to use appropriate posture, track the talker, activate their thinking, and contribute information.

Fundamentals in the Sentence Writing Strategy: Teaches the fundamental concepts and skills associated with writing simple sentences and how to identify subjects, verbs, prepositions, infinitives, and adjectives.

Proficiency in the Sentence Writing Strategy: Teaches students how to recognize and generate four types of sentences: simple, compound, complex, and compound-complex.

Paragraph Writing Strategy: Teaches students how to write well-organized, complete paragraphs by outlining ideas, selecting a point-of-view and tense for the paragraph, sequencing ideas, and checking their work.

Error Monitoring Strategy: Teaches students a process for detecting and correcting errors in their writing and for producing a neater written product. Students are taught to locate errors in paragraph organization, sentence structure, capitalization, overall editing and appearance, punctuation, and spelling by asking themselves a series of questions. Students correct their errors and rewrite the passage before submitting it to their teacher.

Fundamentals in the Theme Writing Strategy: Teaches students to generate ideas for themes, organize these ideas into a logical sequence, write the paragraphs, monitor errors, and rewrite the theme.

Assignment Completion Strategy: Teaches students to monitor their assignments from the time an assignment is given until it is completed and turned in to the teacher. Students write down assignments; analyze the assignments; schedule various subtasks; complete the subtasks and, ultimately, the entire task; and submit the completed assignment.

Test-Taking Strategy: Teaches students to allocate time during a test and read instructions and questions carefully. A question is either answered or put aside for later consideration. The obviously wrong answers are eliminated from the abandoned questions and a reasonable guess is made. The last step is to survey the entire test for unanswered questions.

InSPECT Strategy: Teaches students to detect and correct spelling errors in their documents by using a computerized spellchecker or a handheld spelling device.

TABLE 13.2
Parameters and features of effective learning strategies

Parameter	Features
Content	The strategy steps: • lead to a specific and successful outcome. • are sequenced to ensure an efficient approach for the task. • remind students to use specific cognitive and metacognitive processes. • remind students to choose and use appropriate procedures, rules, and skills. • cue the use of overt action. • are performed in a reasonable amount of time.
Design	The strategy steps: • include a remembering system. • include brief and simple wording in the remembering system. • begin with an action word. • use seven or fewer steps in the remembering system.
Usefulness	The strategy: • addresses important and common problems that students encounter. • addresses demands faced over time. • is applicable across settings and situations.

application of the strategy in natural settings. However, additional intensive instruction by the special education teacher in a support class setting usually is required because many secondary content teachers are unable to provide the explicit or intensive instruction needed to overcome the difficulties of students with learning problems.

Features of Effective Learning Strategies

Ellis and Lenz (1996) note that effective and efficient learning strategies share critical features in the parameters of content, design, and usefulness. These parameters and accompanying features are presented in Table 13.2. All strategies use a mnemonic (i.e., an acronym) to organize the strategy steps and assist the student to remember the content and order of the steps. Ellis and Lenz note that content features provide guidelines for "how to think and act when planning, executing, and evaluating performance on a task and its outcomes" (p. 30). Design features focus on how the strategy is packaged. Good designs organize the content for the student's optimal learning and application. Usefulness features relate to how applicable the strategy is across settings, situations, and people.

Instructional Procedures

Several instructional procedures are used to promote the acquisition of skills by adolescents. These approaches use activities involving guided practice, modeling, peer instruction, provision of feedback, and task

analysis. Since 1978, the University of Kansas Center for Research on Learning has studied how these instructional procedures are integrated and used to promote adolescent learning. The Center's research has culminated in a set of instructional procedures that integrate instructional methods into specific stages of instruction. A detailed description of instructional issues and the instructional stages is presented by Ellis and Lenz (1996) and Lenz, Ellis, and Scanlon (1996).

Table 13.3 depicts the instructional stages that are used successfully to teach adolescents with learning problems a variety of skills and strategies. These instructional stages are characterized by their intent to increase the adolescent's role in the instructional process so that the student learns to self-control learning and become empowered. Several important dimensions are built into these instructional stages. Though the term *strategy* is used, the same stages are applied to promote the acquisition of many other skills as well (e.g., applying for a job, accepting criticism, self-questioning, outlining, setting goals, identifying words, completing a word problem in math, and writing a paragraph).

The following instructional procedures relate to the acquisition and generalization of skills and strategies.

1. *The student should be committed to learning the strategy and fully understand the purpose and benefits.* The student's understanding of the potential effect of the strategy and the consequences of continued use of ineffective and inefficient strategies is the first step in the instructional process. The student must

TABLE 13.3
Stages of strategy acquisition and generalization developed by the University of Kansas Center for Research on Learning

---

Stage 1: Pretest and Make Commitments

Purpose: To motivate students to learn a new strategy and establish a baseline for instruction

Phase 1: Orientation and pretest
   Give rationales and overview
   Administer pretest
   Determine whether strategy is appropriate

Phase 2: Awareness and commitment
   Describe:
     the alternative strategy
     results others have achieved
   Ask for a commitment to learn the new strategy

Stage 2: Describe the Strategy

Purpose: To present a clear picture of the overt and covert processes and steps of the new strategy

Phase 1: Orientation and overview
   Give rationales for the strategy
   Describe situations in which the strategy can be used

Phase 2: Present the strategy and the remembering system

   Describe the overall strategic processes
   Explain the remembering system and its relationship to self-instruction
   Set goals for learning the strategy

Stage 3: Model the Strategy

Purpose: To demonstrate the cognitive behaviors and physical actions involved in using the strategy

Phase 1: Orientation
   Review previous learning
   State expectations

Phase 2: Presentation
   Think aloud
   Self-instruct
   Self-monitor
   Perform task

Phase 3: Student enlistment
   Prompt involvement
   Check understanding

Stage 4: Verbal Elaboration and Rehearsal

Purpose: To ensure comprehension of the strategy and facilitate student mediation

Phase 1: Verbal elaboration
   Have students describe the intent of the strategy and the process involved
   Have students describe what each step is designed to do

Phase 2: Verbal rehearsal
   Require students to name each of the steps at an automatic level

Stage 5: Controlled Practice and Feedback

Purpose: To provide practice in controlled materials, build confidence and fluency, and gradually shift the responsibility for strategy use to students

Phase 1: Orientation and overview
   Review the strategy steps
   Prompt reports of strategy use and errors

(*continued*)

TABLE 13.3
(*continued*)

Phase 2: Guided practice
    Prompt student completion of activities as teacher models
    Prompt increasing student responsibility
    Give clear instructions for peer-mediated practice

Stage 6: Advanced Practice and Feedback

Purpose: To provide practice in advanced materials (e.g., general class or work related) and situations and gradually shift the responsibility for strategy use and feedback to students

The instructional sequence for Advanced Practice and Feedback is the same as the instructional sequence used for Controlled Practice. However, this level of practice should:
    use grade-appropriate or situation-appropriate materials
    fade prompts and cues for use and evaluation

Stage 7: Confirm Acquisition and Make Generalization Commitments

Purpose: To document mastery and to build a rationale for self-regulated generalization

Phase 1: Confirm and celebrate
    Congratulate student on meeting mastery
    Discuss achievement and attribution for success

Phase 2: Forecast and commit to generalization
    Explain goals of generalization
    Explain phases of generalization
    Prompt commitment to generalize

Stage 8: Generalization

Purpose: To ensure the use of the strategy in other settings

Phase 1: Orientation
    Prompt students to:
        discuss rationales for strategy use
        identify settings in which the strategy may be used
        discuss how to remember to use the strategy
Evaluate appropriateness of the strategy in various settings and materials

Phase 2: Activation
    Prompt and monitor student application across settings
    Enlist assistance of other teachers
    Prompt students to:
        apply the strategy in a variety of settings, situations, materials, and assignments
        set goals for the use of the strategy
    Prompt general classroom teachers to:
        understand the strategy
        cue use of the strategy
        provide feedback on strategy use

Phase 3: Adaptation
    Prompt students to:
        identify where these processes and strategies are required across settings
        identify how the strategy can be modified
        repeat application with the modified strategy

Phase 4: Maintenance
    Prompt students to:
        discuss rationales related to long-term use of the strategy
        set goals related to monitoring long-term use
        identify self-reinforcers and self-rewards

Source: From *Students with Learning Disabilities* (pp. 507–509), 7th ed., by C. D. Mercer and P. C. Pullen, 2009, Upper Saddle River, NJ: Merrill/Pearson. Copyright 2009 by Pearson Education. Reprinted by permission.

understand that the goal is to learn the content or perform a certain task successfully, rather than simply to learn a strategy. Thus, the teacher must inform the student of the strategy's goals and obtain a commitment from him or her to learn the strategy.

2. *The physical and mental actions covered in the strategy should be fully described and explained.* The student must be taught what to do and how to think about each step of the strategy, and the full content of the strategy should be made apparent to the student. Examples and circumstances relevant to the student's experiences should be incorporated into the presentation, and the student should play an active role in exploring and commenting on the strategy and its uses.

3. *The student should be taught how to remember the strategy to facilitate the process of self-instruction.* After the content of the strategy is presented to the student, the teacher should demonstrate how the strategy can be remembered easily. If a mnemonic is used, the teacher explicitly should relate the mnemonic to the intended physical and mental associations and demonstrate how to use the mnemonic to guide the student in the self-instructional process.

4. *The student should understand the process of learning the strategy and participate in goal-setting activities to anticipate and monitor learning.* The student should be informed of the acquisition and generalization process, understand the goals and vocabulary associated with each step, and set goals for mastery of each step. As instruction proceeds, the student should evaluate each step as it is completed to determine whether specified learning goals have been met.

5. *Multiple models of the strategy should be provided, and an appropriate balance between the physical and mental activities involved in the strategy should be achieved.* The heart of strategic instruction is in the think-aloud model in which the teacher accurately and completely demonstrates the strategy's application. Though a complete and thorough initial model is critical, additional modeling episodes should be inserted throughout the instructional process. In each of these models, the physical activities must be demonstrated as the associated mental activities are made apparent in an overt think-aloud depiction of the strategy.

6. *The student should be enlisted in the model and become a full participant in guiding the strategy instructional process.* Although the modeling phase

of instruction begins with the teacher, it should end with student participation in and experience with the modeling process. The teacher gradually should include the student in the model. The student eventually should be able to perform the strategy while providing many of the key mental actions associated with each step.

7. *The strategy should be understood fully and memorized before practice in the strategy is initiated.* Sufficient rehearsal of the strategy steps should be provided before the student is asked to perform the strategy from memory. Before applied practice of the strategy begins, the student should know the remembering system and be able to demonstrate how to use it to guide the self-instructional process. During the forthcoming practice phase, the student must sufficiently understand the strategy and be able to concentrate on applying it rather than focus unnecessary mental effort on remembering its aspects.

8. *Practice should begin with controlled guided practice and conclude with advanced independent practice.* The goal of the initial practice stage should be mastering the strategy without having to struggle with content or situational demands. Thus, practice should occur under conditions in which the student feels comfortable or knowledgeable. As the strategy is learned, conditions that approximate actual setting and task demands should be introduced gradually until the student uses the strategy fully to meet actual learning demands.

9. *A measurement system should provide ongoing information that will demonstrate to the student and the teacher that the strategy is being learned and used and that the demands of the setting are being met.* Knowledge of progress and performance is a critical part of the learning process. The measurement system should tell the student whether the strategy is promoting success. However, the measurement system also should provide information related to the student's mastery of the strategy.

10. *Though generalization should be promoted throughout the strategy acquisition process, specific efforts to promote generalization should follow strategy acquisition.* After the strategy has been mastered, the student should attempt to generalize it. In the generalization stage, the teacher and student must work together to identify where the strategy can be used across settings and conditions, identify modifications in the strategy to make it more generalizable, and program use of the strategy across settings.

Additional information about the Strategies Intervention Model and the Learning Strategies Curriculum can be obtained by contacting the Coordinator of Training, University of Kansas Center for Research on Learning, 1122 West Campus Road, Room 521, Lawrence, KS 66045.

CONTENT INSTRUCTION

In developing programs for adolescents with learning difficulties, educators must determine how students can master the content of the secondary curriculum and, at the same time, develop important skills and strategies. In most educational programs, adolescents with learning problems spend the majority of their school day in general education classes.

In many cases, the general classroom teacher must individualize and modify instruction to accommodate the needs of students with learning problems. The accommodations requested from special educators may include altering either how content is delivered or evaluated or the nature or quantity of the content that the teacher expects students to master. Inclusion teachers use numerous instructional alternatives to help these students. These alternatives often are referred to as *accommodation techniques*, *compensatory techniques*, or *instructional adaptations*. Special and general educators can use the following steps in a problem-solving sequence in developing instructional alternatives for students with learning difficulties.

1. Determine the requirements for "making it" in the general class.
2. Specify the course requirements that the student is not satisfying.
3. Identify factors hindering the student's performance.
4. Brainstorm possible classroom modifications.
5. Select a plan of action.
6. Implement the plan.
7. Evaluate the plan.

Determining the types of modifications needed is critical in providing program alternatives. The alternatives

myeducationlab

Go to the Assignments and Activities section of the Topic Assessing and Teaching Other Content Areas in the MyEducationLab for your course and complete the activity entitled Assistive Technology for Instruction and Understanding. As you watch the video and answer the accompanying questions, consider the impact of AT on student learning in content areas.

listed in Table 13.4 provide an overview of some modification possibilities. This section presents instructional alternatives in the following areas: content enhancements, adapting materials, assignments, tutoring, testing, and administrative considerations.

Content Enhancements

Research on learning has led to an increase in studies on how content-area teachers can present information that is sensitive to the strategies used by students. When information is presented in a manner that helps students organize, understand, and remember important information, the effect of ineffective or inefficient strategies may be minimized. To accomplish this, the content-area teacher must select enhancements that can be used during a presentation to meet specific learning goals and then must teach students how to use each enhancement successfully. For example, to help students understand something unfamiliar and abstract, the teacher may use an analogy of something that is familiar and concrete. The teacher then must present the analogy so that students see the relationship between the two concepts, and the new concept becomes meaningful. Thus, content enhancements are techniques that enable the teacher to help students identify, organize, comprehend, and retain critical content information (Lenz, Bulgren, & Hudson, 1990).

Content enhancements can be used when a lesson's content appears to require more manipulation than the teacher predicts the student can handle effectively or efficiently. According to Schumaker, Deshler, and McKnight (2001), the enhancements can be used to make abstract information more concrete, connect new knowledge with familiar knowledge, highlight relationships and organizational structures within the information to be presented, and draw the unmotivated learner's attention to the information. However, simply using a content enhancement as part of a lesson cannot be viewed as an effective practice. Research indicates that the teacher must help the student see how the enhancement is working and enlist each student's active involvement and support in using the enhancement in the learning process.

Bulgren and Lenz (1996) discuss devices and routines as two components of content enhancements that make them effective for both general education students and students with learning problems. *Devices* are instructional tools that teachers use to promote learning. They help teachers foster explicit learning, focus on specific points, and make a concrete connection between ideas and relationships. Different types of devices are used to help students organize, understand, describe, demonstrate, and recall content. These devices include

TABLE 13.4
Instructional alternatives for an inclusion teacher

Classroom Organization	Classroom Management	Methods of Presentation	Methods of Practice	Methods of Testing
Examine Grouping Arrangements	**Examine Grading System**	**Examine Content**	**Examine General Structure**	**Examine Type**
Large-group instruction	Homework	Authentic context	Amount to practice	Oral short answer
Small-group instruction	Tests	Different instructional goals	Time to practice	Oral elaborated answer
Individual instruction	Class participation	Time for learning	Group/individual practice	Written objective items
Adult with student	Goals	Amount of content	Teacher-led practice	Written essay items
Peer-mediated learning	Group projects	Difficulty of content	Independent practice	Demonstration
Computer-assisted instruction	Individual projects	**Examine General Structure**	Peer-mediated practice	**Examine General Structure**
	Examine Rein-forcement System	Previews	Difficulty level	Group/individual
Examine Methods of Instruction	Tangibles	Organizers	Feedback	Timed/untimed
Explicit instruction	Points	Content enhancements		Amount tested
Guided instruction	Praise	Assignments	**Examine Response**	
Implicit instruction	Grades	Mnemonic devices	Written	**Examine Response**
	Special activity	Feedback	True–false	Objective— recognition
	Free time	Student involvement	Multiple choice	Objective—recall
	Goal setting		Matching	Essay—list
	Progress chart	**Examine Type**	Short answer	Essay—short answer
	Computer time	Review	Open book/ closed book	Essay—long answer
	Student involvement in planning	Advance organizers	Create	
		Guided practice	Oral	
	Examine Rules	Discussion	Long answer	
	Behavior expectations	Question/answer	Presentation	
	Rule rationales	Videotapes	Discussion	
	Student involvement	Audiotapes		
	Number of rules	Movies	**Examine Type of Materials**	
		Computers	Texts	
		Transparencies	Worksheets	
			Computer	
			Audiotape	
			Videotape	

verbal and visual modes of presentation. Deshler, Ellis, and Lenz (1996) present the following content enhancement devices according to function (i.e., use) and mode of presentation (i.e., verbal or visual).

1. To organize (i.e., arrange information in meaningful structures)
   Verbal mode: summarization, chunking, advance organizer, post organizer, and verbal cues about organization
   Visual mode: outline, web, hierarchical graphic organizer, table, grid, and flowchart
2. To promote understanding (i.e., clarify words or concepts)

Verbal mode: analogy, synonym, antonym, example, comparison, metaphor, and simile
Visual mode: symbol, concrete object, picture, model, diagram

3. To describe (i.e., tell a story)
   Verbal mode: current events, past events, fictional story, hypothetical scenario, and personal story
   Visual mode: film, filmstrip, and video
4. To demonstrate (i.e., show through action)
   Verbal mode: role play and dramatic portrayal
   Visual mode: physical gesture or movement, movable objects, and demonstration

5. To promote recall:
   Verbal mode: acronyms and keywords
   Visual mode: visual images and sketches

Routines are strategic instructional procedures that involve students in developing, acquiring, and applying the device. Bulgren and Lenz (1996) define a teaching routine as "a set of integrated instructional procedures revolving around a specific teaching device designed to promote broad learning goals associated with the full spectrum of information acquisition, storage, and expression/demonstration of content information" (p. 447). When devices are embedded in these instructional procedures, they become a routine. The University of Kansas Center for Research on Learning developed and published the following routines.

- The *Course Organizer Routine* (Lenz, Schumaker, Deshler, & Bulgren, 1998) includes a set of activities to help the teacher create a course around big ideas for diverse learners. It features a mnemonic device to help the teacher reflect on course concepts and outcomes and formulate questions.
- The *Unit Organizer Routine* (Lenz, Bulgren, Schumaker, Deshler, & Boudah, 1994) includes a set of steps that the teacher uses to create a unit of instruction for diverse learners. It involves reflecting on the content of a unit and important outcomes and the development of a graphic "road map."
- The *Lesson Organizer Routine* (Lenz, Marrs, Schumaker, & Deshler, 1993) includes a set of steps that the teacher uses to create a lesson for diverse learners. It involves reflecting on the content and important outcomes and the creation of a graphic device that serves as a "road map" for the lesson.
- The *Concept Mastery Routine* (Bulgren, Deshler, & Schumaker, 1993) features a concept diagram that allows the teacher to exhibit information related to a key concept. The teacher works with students to analyze and understand the concept.
- The *Concept Anchoring Routine* (Bulgren, Schumaker, & Deshler, 1994) features a visual device called the *anchoring table,* which allows the teacher to display information about a new concept by tying it to a familiar concept that shares critical characteristics with the target concept.
- The *Concept Comparison Routine* (Bulgren, Lenz, Deshler, & Schumaker, 1995) features a visual device called the *concept comparison table,* which enables the teacher to display information about two or more concepts or topics through analyzing the characteristics they share.

- The *Quality Assignment Routine* (Rademacher, Deshler, Schumaker, & Lenz, 1998) is a routine for planning high-quality assignments. It features a planning phase, an explanation phase, and an evaluation phase. Each interactive phase helps the teacher guide students to complete assigned tasks.
- The *Survey Routine* (Deshler, Schumaker, & McKnight, 1997) is a routine for providing an overview of a reading assignment.
- The *Clarifying Routine* (Ellis, 1997) features a set of procedures and a graphic device to enable the teacher to present information associated with new terms to students.
- The *Framing Routine* (Ellis, 1998) features several graphic devices for presenting complex sets of interrelated information to students.
- The *Recall Enhancement Routine* (Schumaker, Bulgren, Deshler, & Lenz, 1998) enables the teacher to show students how to create and use mnemonic devices.
- The *Question Exploration Routine* (Bulgren, Lenz, Deshler, & Schumaker, 2001) focuses on how teachers can help students explore important questions about content information being taught and how teachers can prepare assessment tools or other ways to measure students' understanding of specific content.

In a review of research on the use of content enhancements to improve the performance of adolescents with learning disabilities in content classes, Hudson, Lignugaris-Kraft, and Miller (1993) discuss the following seven types of content enhancements.

1. *Advance organizers.* These enhancements help orient and prepare the student for the upcoming lesson. An advance organizer is presented before the lesson presentation and can include an array of information about the lesson. Some of the most common features include linking the lesson content to prior lessons or information, introducing the targeted content, explaining tasks to be performed by the teacher and student, providing a rationale for the lesson, and introducing materials and new vocabulary. Ellis and Friend (1991) present a simple procedure to help teachers use advance organizers. The FORM device is used to introduce content-area lessons.

   F—*Focus.* What will be the focus of the lesson and the focus of students' questions?
   O—*Organization.* What organizational devices will be used to make the lesson easier to learn, and what sequence of activities will be used during the lesson?

R—*Relationship*. What have you learned before that will help you now? If you master the material, how will you benefit in the future?

M—*Most important goal*. What do you need to learn if you do not learn anything else?

The teacher can adapt the advance organizer and use the aspects that help him or her deliver the content and orient students to what is being taught. In addition to the advance organizer, the teacher can use lesson organizers that reinforce the critical structure and content of the lesson. To clarify the organization and focus of the content, the teacher can use words and statements such as "first . . ., second . . ., third . . .," and "the most important idea is . . ." Diagrams, tables, or charts also can help students see the content structure. Organizers can be used before an instructional sequence (i.e., advance organizer), throughout an instructional sequence (i.e., lesson organizer), or at the end of an instructional sequence (i.e., post organizer). For example, to help orient students to a learning task, the teacher can use a teaching routine on introducing a typical chapter. In this routine, the teacher leads students through an introductory and focused exploration of the chapter before they begin to read it. In the exploration process, the teacher guides students to discover how the chapter fits in with surrounding chapters, prompts them to discuss and rephrase the chapter title and subsections, and helps them identify the critical main ideas and vocabulary presented in the various sections of the text.

2. *Visual displays*. These enhancements feature several formats that graphically display the organization of the content. For example, Figure 13.2 illustrates three types of visual displays (e.g., representative, directional, and hierarchical/central). Visual displays can be combined to build powerful and sophisticated teaching routines. Concept diagramming (Bulgren et al., 1993), semantic feature analysis (Bos & Anders, 1987), and semantic webbing (Anders & Bos, 1984) are three routines that help students understand the various parts of concepts. The use of a graphic organizer is included in all of these routines. In the concept diagramming routine, the teacher helps students brainstorm information about an important concept, and these characteristics of the concept are organized into three separate lists (i.e., *always present, sometimes present*, and *never present*). Students construct a definition for the concept from the list of characteristics that are always present and then generate examples and nonexamples of the concept based on the definition. The semantic feature analysis routine involves the use of a table in which concept examples are listed in a vertical column and important concept characteristics or features are listed in a horizontal column. By reading across the table for a given example, students can identify which concept features the example contains. Also, students can construct a table by exploring information about an example of a concept and placing a plus or minus sign in the intersection to indicate a positive or negative relationship, a zero to indicate no relationship, or a question mark if the student is unsure of the relationship. The third routine, semantic webbing, involves writing the important term, idea, or concept on the chalkboard and encouraging students to generate information. The appropriate placement of the information about the concept in relation to the original stimulus concept is discussed, and lines are drawn to indicate coordinate and subordinate relationships, examples, or features. In a review of the research on vocabulary instruction, Jitendra, Edwards, Sacks, and Jacobson (2004) note that cognitive strategy instruction, including semantic feature analysis and semantic webbing, has large effects on student learning of vocabulary.

3. *Study guides*. These enhancements are used to highlight critical information. Study guides usually consist of statements or questions that stress important content, and formats include matching, short-answer questions, and framed outlines or fill in the blanks. Thus, guides can consist of outlines or lists of questions that the teacher can use to focus student attention, point out important information, and encourage the student to inspect the material more closely. In guides involving the use of graphics, the student is directed to complete missing parts of constructed diagrams of the content. Both question- and graphic-oriented study guides are more helpful to students than self-study alone; however, the use of graphics in study guides is perceived as the most effective (Bergerud, Lovitt, & Horton, 1988).

4. *Mnemonic devices*. These enhancements are designed to help students remember content. They feature pictorial or verbal techniques that promote recall of unfamiliar information. Studies on how teachers can help students consolidate information into meaningful chunks affirm the premise that students need to understand what

FIGURE 13.2
Types of visual displays

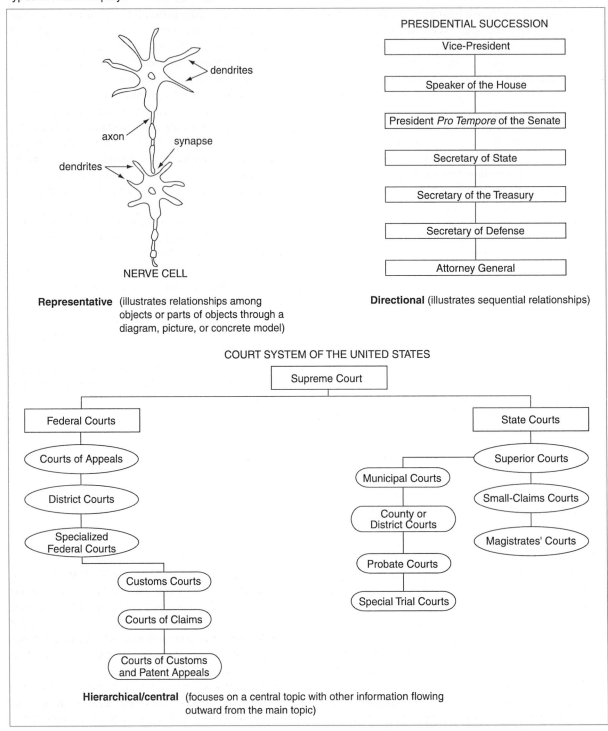

they must remember before reducing the memory load with the use of a mnemonic device (Nagel, Schumaker, & Deshler, 2003). Thus, the teacher and students should identify what is most important about the information presented and then label and organize it. The actual manipulations that can help students remember important information consist of a variety of tactics including creating mental images, making familiar associations, using first-letter mnemonics, or using keyword strategies. In a review of vocabulary instruction studies using keyword strategies and first-letter mnemonics, Jitendra et al. (2004) note that students benefit from these strategies in comparison to more traditional drill-and-practice activities. First-letter mnemonics is the primary verbal format used to help students who have learning problems remember information. In this technique, students learn the first letter of a word, phrase, or sentence to cue them to remember the targeted information. For example, the word EASY is a mnemonic for remembering the following study strategy (Ellis & Lenz, 1987).

E—*Elicit* "wh" questions to identify important information (i.e., who, what, when, where, and why).
A—*Ask* yourself which information is least troublesome.
S—*Study* easy parts first, hardest parts last.
Y—*Yes*—do use self-reinforcement.

Popular verbal formats include keyword, mimetic, and symbolic. The keyword format pairs a picture of a familiar object that is phonetically similar to the term to be learned. The mimetic format includes pictorial representations of the targeted information; for example, to remind students of a definition of a lighthouse, a picture of a lighthouse is used. Symbolic mnemonics use common symbols to represent critical information; for example, doves may be used to symbolize peace.

5. *Audio recordings.* These enhancements include verbatim audiotapes of written materials and key information audiotapes that are used along with other materials.
6. *Computer-assisted instruction.* This enhancement involves delivering instruction through computers. The primary formats include simulations and tutorials, which students usually complete independently. However, Hudson et al. (1993) note that few computer programs, to date, are designed well enough for students with learning problems to learn new content independently. In computer simulations, students review and apply facts and concepts previously learned.
7. *Peer-mediated instruction.* This enhancement involves the use of classmates to teach one another. It features peer tutoring, classwide peer tutoring, and cooperative learning.

The overall results from the content enhancement research are encouraging (Bulgren & Lenz, 1996; Hudson et al., 1993). Furthermore, the research indicates that various enhancements can be used effectively at different phases in the instructional cycle. For example, mnemonic devices can be used during presentation of new material and guided practice, whereas peer mediation can be integrated during independent practice and evaluation of student progress. In a study of evidence-based practices for content-area instruction, Mastropieri, Berkeley, Scruggs, and Marshak (2008) note that students with learning disabilities as well as English language learners benefit from the addition of various content enhancements to classwide peer tutoring.

Activities for Presenting Content   The following activities may help present content to students who have learning problems.

- Provide a list of simple questions before a lecture or reading assignment to serve as an effective advance organizer.
- Provide written backup to oral directions and lectures (e.g., use an outline on a handout or overhead transparency).
- Use the following activities for presenting information to the student who has difficulty with auditory input:
  - Provide pre-presentation questions.
  - Develop vocabulary before presentation.
  - Pace presentation and give frequent examples.
  - Cluster main points.
  - Summarize.
  - Provide opportunities for student questions and discussion.
  - Repeat important points.
  - Relate content to other topics.
- For the student who has difficulty following oral presentations, provide audios of the lectures or allow him or her to record the class presentation and discussions. In addition, good notetakers can use carbon paper to make copies of their notes for problem learners, or photocopies of notes can be given to problem learners.
- Instruct the student with learning problems to sit near the front of the class. This encourages attention to teacher-directed activities and reduces distractions.
- Match a problem learner with a peer helper who can assist by explaining directions and assignments, reviewing essential information from a lecture, sharing and correcting notes, and working on joint assignments or projects.

- Use the following suggestions to help the student maintain attention and learn:
  - Combine visual and auditory presentations.
  - Establish eye contact with students during oral directions and lectures.
  - Write assignments, directions, and lecture objectives on the chalkboard.
  - Pause after questions to provide thinking time.
  - Pause after each segment while giving directions and presenting content.
  - Give examples and demonstrations.
  - Briefly review information from previous lectures, and summarize information at the end of each lecture.
  - Provide the student with time after the lecture for reviewing and improving notes.
  - Talk distinctly and at a reasonable rate.
  - Give cues concerning what is important, and refer the student to textbook pages for more clarification or information.
- Use a pause procedure during lectures to improve the recall of adolescents with learning problems. Pause several times during a lecture (e.g., every 6 to 12 minutes) for students to discuss the content covered. To help groups of three to four students systematically discuss the content, instruct students to use the RAP mnemonic.

Adapting Materials

The difficulty level of texts and materials used in content-area classes may present a problem to a secondary student with learning difficulties because the reading level may be several grades above the student's reading level. To assist the student in learning, it often is necessary to modify or adapt the ways in which content is presented. These modifications aim to change the format and mode of presentation while maintaining the basic content. Alternatives for adapting materials include developing parallel curriculum, simplifying texts, and using audio texts.

Developing Parallel Curriculum   Parallel curriculum materials present essential content in ways that help the problem learner organize, practice, and master important information. Many school districts provide general and special educators with release time or summer employment to write curriculum guides for various courses designed for use with low achievers. Thus, a low achiever receives the standard text and a curriculum guide or booklet.

Moreover, some publishers offer adapted textbooks in which the content matches the grade-level textbook but is written at a lower readability level (e.g., *Wonders of Science* and *America's Story*, published by Steck-Vaughn). However, in inclusive settings, many students with learning problems prefer to use the same text that others are using; thus, it is helpful to provide the simplified materials as a supplement to help the students study the grade-level textbook.

Simplifying Texts   The simplification of textbooks assists low achievers to master essential information efficiently. The following activities and procedures can be used for simplifying texts.

- Provide the student with a highlighted text. Underlining or highlighting the main ideas, words, and concepts with a marker pen helps the student focus on relevant material. Also, deleting irrelevant or nonessential words with a dark pen identifies important content.
- Transform words into graphic aids by creating charts, graphs, drawings, or models. Also, real materials are helpful in presenting content.
- Use advance organizers to prepare the student for the reading material. These include outlines, diagrammatic overviews, study guides, questions, and directed previewing (e.g., drawing attention to selected headings or illustrations).
- Reduce the complexity and length of work units to the extent that the low achiever receives periodic and consistent closure.
- Provide self-correcting learning materials. Self-checking answer keys at frequent intervals are helpful checkpoints to guide the student through the material.
- When simplifying texts, concentrate on content, sentence structure, and vocabulary. In simplifying content, it helps to present generalizations first and follow with supporting details, sequence events in chronological order, and cluster related material.
- For the student with limited reading skills, consider using rewritten texts. In situations where rewriting is feasible, the following guidelines are helpful:
  - Keep sentences short; a five- to eight-word total is best.
  - Use basic words of few syllables.
  - Use present tense and avoid passive voice.
  - Use simple sentences and try to begin each sentence with a subject. Avoid appositives and parenthetical expressions. Simple sentences with the verb following the subject are easier to read than compound and complex sentences or sentences in inverted order.
  - Avoid figurative or symbolic language (e.g., change "thundering herd" to "The herd galloped

so hard the hoofs sounded like thunder when they hit the ground.").

- Use picture clues as much as possible.
- Be certain that every pronoun has an unmistakable antecedent.
- Use new words sparingly. Repeating key words rather than using synonyms results in simpler content.
- Eliminate unnecessary words.

Using Audio Texts An alternative to reading a textbook is to listen to it on audio. Use of an audio textbook can increase student independence and be an effective tool for increasing content acquisition of secondary-level academic content (Boyle et al., 2003). Audio texts can be acquired for the student in two ways. One is to qualify the student for the special recordings provided for individuals who are blind or have learning disabilities. Applications are available from Recording for the Blind and Dyslexic, 20 Roszel Road, Princeton, NJ 08540. In addition to making available its audio books and providing texts on audio files for MP3 players, this service records requested books at no charge. Another way to acquire audio texts is for teachers, students, or parents to prepare them. Guidelines for taping include the following:

- Tape in a quiet place where rugs, draperies, and upholstered furniture can absorb extraneous noises.
- Place the microphone on the table about 6 inches from the recorder's mouth. Turn the volume control about halfway and read a portion of the material. Listen to the tape and adjust the volume and microphone location until desirable recording is obtained.
- Eliminate clicks by turning the volume on low before starting the recorder. At the end of the recording, let the tape run for a few moments and then gradually turn the volume down and off.
- Avoid recording during the first 5 seconds and take a break every 15 minutes. Use alternating voices to reduce boredom.
- Monitor the tape before giving it to the student.
- At the beginning of the tape, identify the title of the text, author, and chapters or portions to be read.
- Include the following directions in the initial text information: "Please stop the tape any time you wish to answer questions, write notes for yourself, or look at a section of the book more carefully. You will hear this sound (e.g., ring a bell) at the end of each page to help you follow along in your textbook. Please turn to page ____ for the beginning of chapter ____."
- Include selected study questions at the beginning of the tape. This alerts the student to important content.

Assignments

Many special education teachers prefer to have students complete their work in the classroom so that they can observe performance and assist students who cannot complete assignments. Lenz, Ehren, and Smiley (1991) argue that students must be given the opportunity to complete work independently because assignment completion often signifies the independence of a learner in an academic setting. Lenz et al. organize assignment completion into completion knowledge and completion management. *Completion knowledge* involves the academic skills and background knowledge required to finish the assignment. *Completion management* involves the planning, integration, and organization of time, interests, and resources that facilitate the use of academic skills and knowledge. Lenz et al. also identify three basic types of assignments: study, daily work, and project. *Study assignments* require students to prepare for a test or some type of class activity, and the focus of the assignment usually is on the process rather than on a permanent product. *Daily work* consists of assignments (e.g., completion of chapter questions and worksheets) that follow up the content covered in class and are designed to promote practice and understanding of the content. *Project assignments* take more than 1 or 2 days to complete and often require students to extend or apply content by preparing a report, theme, visual product, or presentation. Depending on the teacher's expectations, all three assignment types can be completed in the classroom setting (i.e., seatwork) or out of the classroom setting (i.e., homework) and can be performed either individually or in a group.

Research in the area of homework indicates that the more time a student spends working on homework, the higher the student's achievement (Cooper, 2001; Jenson, Sheridan, Olympia, & Andrews, 1994). The effects of this positive relationship of homework to achievement are substantial for secondary students and good for middle school students. However, to ensure the positive benefits of homework, the assignments must be appropriate for the student's ability and achievement levels.

Research findings on different types of assignments and the assignment-completion process indicate that creating better-structured and better-organized assignments may not improve the assignment-completion process if students' interest or motivation is not addressed. Thus, the teacher must attend to the basic nature and quality of the assignments. Lenz and Bulgren (1988) propose the following suggestions regarding classroom assignments to improve the achievement of adolescents with learning difficulties.

- Assignment requirements must be explicit and clear.
- Requirements should relate to important learning outcomes.
- Choices must be provided that enable students to personalize learning.
- Over time, choices should include what to learn, how to learn, and how to demonstrate what has been learned.
- Assignment completion initially should be modeled and guided in class by the teacher with student involvement.
- Students should know the dimensions of assignments and be prompted to ask questions about assignment completion.
- The process of learning about assignment completion should be considered as important as learning the content.
- Discussions regarding the quality of assignments and the outcomes associated with assignment completion should be a regular part of classroom activities.
- Students should regularly set goals related to improving the completion process and what is being learned as a result of assignment completion.
- Fewer assignments should be given, and they should emphasize the most important learning outcomes.
- Assignments should be evaluated rather than graded, and students should revise their work to improve the quality rather than the grade.
- Peers should be used frequently to promote a variety of learning models.

Meese (1994) provides the following suggestions regarding assignments for students with learning problems.

- Divide assignments into chunks and have timelines for each chunk.
- Extend time for completing assignments.
- Encourage the use of computers and calculators in assignment completion.
- Allow groups to complete some written assignments.
- Reduce the amount of copying needed throughout the assignment (i.e., having to copy assignment material from the text or the chalkboard and having to copy problems from a text).
- Require students to paraphrase an assignment's tasks.

Tutoring

At the secondary level, earning academic credits is a major instructional concern. Some special education teachers teach and assign credit for course content or provide tutoring in subject areas required for graduation. Given the tutorial emphasis in secondary grades, Carlson (1985) suggests that guidelines or standards are needed for implementing and evaluating tutoring. He provides three principles for tutoring instruction.

1. *Instruction should be powerful.* To offer powerful instruction, the teacher must know the content well, provide enough time for intensive teaching, and follow the principles of effective instruction (e.g., reinforcement, engaged time, modeling, and feedback).
2. *Instruction should result in long-range benefits to the learner.* Effective instruction should diminish the effect that the learning difficulty may have on future learning or help the student function more adequately. In addition to immediate subject-matter content, the teacher should stress skills (e.g., study skills and test-taking skills) that increase the student's potential for later learning.
3. *Teacher expectations for learner performance should be high.* Success must be maintained, but expected levels of performance should not be reduced unless necessary.

Hammill and Bartel (2004) offer the following nonacademic guidelines for tutors.

- Be dependable. Missing a few sessions can negatively affect the tutor–tutee relationship and impede the student's progress.
- Be patient during instruction. Be willing to review or go over the material until the student learns it.
- Focus on understanding the student's concerns and feelings.
- Maintain integrity by giving the student accurate feedback concerning progress.
- Respect the interpersonal relationship and handle it with sensitivity.

Testing

Students with learning problems frequently have difficulty displaying their knowledge or skills on tests. Modifications in test formats often help them perform better. The following suggestions are provided for improving test performances.

- Give frequent, timed minitests so that testing is not such an isolated, anxiety-provoking situation. Give practice tests and have students test one another and review answers.
- Use alternative response forms when existing formats appear to hinder student expression. Variations between and within response formats (e.g., multiple choice, short answer, and essay) are possible.

- Multiple-choice alternatives include using yes-or-no questions, reducing the number of choices, providing more information from which to make a choice, and using matching items.
- Short-answer alternatives include providing a list of facts and information to use in the answer, allowing the student to list information or choose from several prepared short answers, using the cloze technique in prepared paragraphs, and scrambling information to be arranged.
- Essay alternatives include providing a partial outline for the student to complete, allowing the student to tape answers, noting important points to be included in the response, and using take-home tests.

- In addition to the written test, provide a tape of the test items. Tapes allow the student to hear instructions and items as well as read them. Also, tapes are convenient for test makeups.
- Leave ample white space between test questions, and underline key words in the directions and test items.
- Provide test-study guides that feature various answer formats (e.g., essay, multiple choice, and fill in the blank).
- Provide additional time for the student who writes slowly, or use test items that require minimal writing. Oral tests also may be given and the answers can be recorded on tape.

Administrative Considerations

Administrative support is critical to the development and maintenance of a viable program for low achievers. Principals need support from central office staff, and teachers and counselors definitely need the support of the school principal. The following supportive activities and procedures help facilitate quality programs for low-achieving students by administrative actions.

- Identify general class teachers who are the most sensitive to the needs of students with learning problems. Schedule the student with these "sensitive" teachers, and support the teachers through such activities as providing favorable scheduling—for example, including an extra planning period; assigning teacher aide(s) to their classes; releasing time to develop curriculum; placing volunteers in their classes; providing in-service training tailored to their needs; offering summer employment to develop curriculum; providing opportunities to attend conferences and workshops; offering support for university coursework; providing salary

supplements; recognizing the value of the program to the entire faculty; and providing a budget that allows the purchase of some useful materials.
- Support the development of a homework hotline.
- Help establish a parental involvement and training program.
- Work with guidance counselors to schedule students so that a balanced workload is maintained (e.g., a balance between demanding courses or teachers and less demanding courses or teachers).
- Encourage the development of parallel alternative curriculum for the content classes.
- Support the development of equitable diploma options for mainstreamed students.

STUDY SKILLS

The ability to acquire and use study skills is a key factor in school success. Applying efficient study skills involves learning how to learn and helps individuals acquire, retain, and use new information across a variety of learning situations. Although study skills are viewed as important to learning, systematic instruction in study skills is not provided with the curriculum. Unfortunately, many students with learning problems lack study skills and need instruction to learn them.

Hoover (1993) provides a framework for examining and assessing study skills. These 11 study skills and their respective subskills include the following:

1. *Reading rate.* Reads at different rates for scanning, skimming, normal reading, rapid reading, and careful reading.
2. *Listening.* Attends to listening tasks, applies meaning to verbal messages, and filters out auditory distractions.
3. *Notetaking/outlining.* Uses headings appropriately, takes brief and clear notes, records important information, uses notetaking and outlining for report writing and during lectures, constructs well-organized outlines, and has organized note card format.
4. *Report writing.* Organizes thoughts, uses proper punctuation, and uses proper spelling and grammar.
5. *Oral presentation.* Participates freely, organizes presentation, uses gestures, and speaks clearly.
6. *Graphic aids.* Attends to relevant elements, understands purposes, incorporates aids in presentations, and develops own visual aids.
7. *Test taking.* Organizes answers, proofreads, reads and understands directions, identifies clue words, properly records responses, answers difficult

questions last, narrows possible correct answers, and corrects previous test-taking errors.

8. *Library use.* Uses card or computerized catalog, can locate materials, understands organization of a library, understands role of media specialist.

9. *Reference/dictionary use.* Identifies components, uses guide words, understands uses of reference materials, uses reference materials for written assignments, and identifies different reference materials.

10. *Time management.* Organizes daily activities, organizes weekly and monthly schedules, understands time management, reorganizes time when necessary, and prioritizes activities.

11. *Self-management of behavior* Monitors own behavior, changes own behavior, thinks before acting, and takes responsibility for own behavior.

Preparatory Study Skills

Preparatory study skills involve skills and factors that are relevant precursors to efficient learning. The student's attitude and motivation are critical to student effort and consequent learning. The adolescent with learning problems needs to understand the relevance of assigned tasks and exhibit an attitude that facilitates effort. The discussion on motivation presented earlier in this chapter presents strategies and activities aimed at improving motivation. This section focuses on time management and self-management.

Activities for Developing Time Management

Considering the many demands placed on students to complete tasks at specific times and participate in a host of competing activities (such as being with peers, joining clubs, watching television, and listening to music), time management obviously is critical to surviving in school. The adolescent with learning problems usually needs instruction in time management. Activities for teaching time management include making schedules, making time estimates, and establishing priorities.

- Give the student a 5-day schedule of after-school time and ask him or her to record all activities during these time blocks. Next, have the student allocate time blocks for specific activities (see Table 13.5) and follow the schedule as much as possible. Initially it may help the student to plan only a day and then gradually build to a week.

- Provide the student with a calendar to assist in scheduling daily or weekly activities. Notations can be made on the calendar to remind the student of project due dates or test dates. The student also can keep a notebook with all academic assignments and due dates.

- Encourage the student to allow some flexibility in the daily schedule. Occasionally unexpected events will take precedence over the planned activity. Introduce new events in the daily schedule and explain how adjustments can be made (e.g., if friends invite the student to get a pizza during study time, the student can replace television time with study time). Finally, the student should show the teacher the schedule with written adjustments when applicable.

- Either provide assignments or have the student list at least four school assignments and estimate how long it will take to complete each task. Then have the student record the amount of time it actually takes to complete the assignments. These times can be written on the student's schedule. Have the student practice on tasks or subject areas in which her or his estimates are consistently inaccurate (i.e., off by more than 20 percent) until the estimates become realistic.

- Have the student list and prioritize school assignments. The student can rank the activities in the order they would be completed (i.e., place a 1 beside

TABLE 13.5
A student's after-school schedule

	Monday	Tuesday	Wednesday	Thursday	Friday
3:00–4:00	with friend eat snack	with friend eat snack	with friend eat snack	with friend eat snack	with friend eat snack
4:00–5:00	play ball	play ball	do chores	play ball	play ball
5:00–6:00	play ball	play ball	do chores	play ball	play ball
6:00–7:00	eat dinner	eat dinner	eat dinner	eat dinner	eat dinner
7:00–8:00	study	study	study	go to game	go to movie
8:00–9:00	study	watch TV	study	go to game	go to movie
9:00–10:00	listen to music	watch TV	play video games	watch TV	watch TV

the first activity, a 2 beside the next activity, and so on). For example:

_____ Work on social studies project due in 2 weeks.
_____ Write a lab report in science due in 2 days.
_____ Complete a math worksheet due tomorrow.
_____ Practice baseball for the game in 3 days.
_____ Read 20 pages in a book in preparation for an oral report due in 4 days.

Discuss the need to consider consequences and time factors in prioritizing lists of things to do. Review the rankings and point out the correct and incorrect rankings in terms of consequences, breaking large tasks into smaller amounts (e.g., subdividing reading material into a number of pages per day), and time factors. Also have the student practice using value steps in prioritizing activities and tasks by grouping the list into three areas: activities with high value, activities with medium value, and activities with low value.

- To enhance the efficient completion of academic tasks, encourage the student to work in an environment conducive to studying. Ideally, the study area should be relatively quiet and unstimulating. If noise (e.g., television or classmates) becomes too distracting, the student can consider using earplugs.

Activities for Developing Self-Management

Self-management helps students learn to be responsible for their own behavior. Effective self-management enables students to monitor their behavior and decrease behaviors that interfere with the completion of assigned tasks (Hoover, 2004). Effective activities to enhance self-management include the following:

- Ensure that the student understands specific behavioral expectations regarding assignments and class routines.
- Help the student478 set goals and timelines regarding schoolwork.
- Focus on "if-then" discussions in which the student explores the consequences of doing or not doing school assignments. Guide the student to realize that his or her actions influence consequences in life. Stress the positive possibilities of this proactive point of view.
- Provide the student with a self-monitoring chart to monitor a target behavior. Have the student record a check mark each time the behavior is displayed.

Acquisition Study Skills

To survive in the secondary setting, students must acquire and organize information from written and spoken input. Secondary teachers use the lecture/notetaking format extensively. Students also are required to obtain and organize information from textbooks. This section presents teaching activities and strategies aimed at developing information-gathering and organization skills. The skills are organized into the following areas: listening and notetaking, textbook usage, reading and study skills, reading and notetaking skills, using visual aids, and sequential study methods.

Activities for Listening and Notetaking

Notetaking is defined as an individualized process for recording and organizing information into a usable format and is dependent on active student participation. Although it is apparent that notetaking assists the student, no one approach is considered superior. Notetaking strategies can include either an outline format that stresses the identification of a main idea and supporting subordinate ideas or a columnar format that serves as a guide for organizing and classifying information. The importance and complexity of the notetaking process suggest the need for guidelines and activities, such as the following, to facilitate its development.

- To assist with listening and notetaking, teach the student to use the following strategies:
  - Physically prepare for listening and notetaking by sitting alertly (e.g., leaning forward) in a comfortable desk with the essential materials (e.g., notebook, two or more pencils or pens, and textbook). Remove all extraneous materials from the desk. To encourage listening and active class participation, students can be taught to use the SLANT mnemonic.
  - Review vocabulary (e.g., from text or handouts) related to the lecture topic before the lecture begins. It helps some students to have a list of difficult vocabulary words on their desks during the lecture/notetaking session.
  - Listen for organizational cues or signal words (e.g., statements referring to time spans or sequences—*first, second, phase, period, era, next,* and *finally*). Signal words include words that indicate a sequence or additional ideas (e.g., *first, second, also, furthermore, again, plus, next,* and *after that*); caution words, which point to concluding ideas (e.g., *consequently, thus, therefore, in conclusion, to summarize, finally,* and *as a result*); turn words, which indicate a change in ideas (e.g., *in contrast, opposed to, however, to the contrary, on the other hand, in spite of, although, yet,* and *despite*); stop words, which signal special significance (e.g., *significantly, absolutely, whenever, without doubt,*

and *without question*); and application words, which indicate concrete application of a thought (e.g., *because, for example, specifically,* and *for instance*).

- Listen for content importance by noticing such cues as change in voice, tone, pitch, pauses, and volume.
- Ask for elaboration on specific points or content when confusion exists.
- Request examples to illustrate specific concepts.
- Paraphrase certain points to check understanding.
- Ask for visual references (e.g., pages in the text).

- Use the following guided listening and notetaking activities to provide the student with opportunities to practice a variety of skills:
  - The teacher plays a 5- to 8-minute audio recording of a lecture on content appropriate to the student's needs. The teacher and student sit beside each other and simultaneously take notes.
  - At the end of the tape the teacher provides corrective feedback by sharing notes with the student and explaining listening and notetaking strategies. The teacher may elect to replay the tape and point out key factors (e.g., content organization and voice cues) in listening and notetaking.
  - The student listens to the tape again and takes a new set of notes. At the end of the tape the student compares the new notes to the teacher's model notes and makes corrections. The student practices this procedure to criterion with several different tapes.
  - Short tapes are made of selected general classroom teachers' lectures. The student practices listening and notetaking on these tapes with corrective feedback until criterion is achieved.
  - As the student progresses, the lecture tapes-feedback sequence is expanded to include more teachers in various content areas.
  - Eventually the student takes notes only from live lectures and uses a set of model notes (e.g., from the teacher or a classmate) to correct or complete the notes.

This activity can be used with an individual or group to assess and remediate listening and notetaking skills. Notes from proficient peers can be used as models. In addition, teacher aides can be trained to tape lectures and provide model notes.

- To improve legibility, have student pairs read each other's notes and circle illegible words. Have each student rewrite the circled words.

- Present directed listening activities according to the following three stages.
  1. The Readiness Stage
     a. Establish motivation for the lesson.
     b. Introduce any new or difficult concepts.
     c. Introduce any new or difficult words.
     d. Set purposes for listening.
  2. The Listening-Reciting Stage
     a. Students listen to satisfy the purposes for listening set during readiness.
     b. The teacher asks several literal and inferential questions that relate to the purposes set during readiness.
     c. The students volunteer interpretive and evaluative comments about the lesson. Some class discussion may ensue.
     d. If there are errors or gaps in the students' understanding of the lesson, the teacher directs the students to relisten to certain parts of the lesson.
  3. The Follow-Up Stage
     a. The teacher provides opportunities for and encourages students to engage in activities that build on and develop concepts acquired during the lesson. These may include writing, reading, small-group discussions, and art activities.

- To improve listening comprehension and retention, use the following sequence of activities:
  - The teacher asks the student to try to remember everything the student is about to hear.
  - The teacher lectures or plays a recorded selection. If the teacher lectures, the lecture is recorded.
  - The teacher reminds the student about the instructions that were given. The teacher then writes everything the student says on the chalkboard without making any corrections or asking specific questions.
  - The teacher reads everything listed on the chalkboard and asks the student to note incorrect information and think about missing information.
  - The student listens to the recording again, corrects inaccurate information, and obtains missing information.
  - The information on the chalkboard is amended and expanded.
  - The teacher asks which ideas on the chalkboard are the main and important ideas and which ones should be remembered for a long time. The teacher highlights these items.

- Now that the student has mastered the literal content of the selection, the teacher asks inferential questions that appear vital for understanding.
- The teacher erases the chalkboard and tests memory with items (e.g., oral multiple choice and true–false) that are not too dependent on reading or writing skills.
- The teacher tests long-term memory with a similar test several weeks later.

- Teach the student to recognize the main idea and the contributing points from which it is derived. In this way the student gains control of what to write by determining how much detail is needed in terms of expected outcome (i.e., main idea). Looking for the main and contributing ideas helps the student become a more active listener by encouraging thinking, comprehension, and questions. Also teach the student to look for the order and organization of the lecture. Stress that notes are a skeletal representation of the material.
- Teach the student to use abbreviations to reduce the writing demands of the task (e.g., w/ for with, U.S. for United States).
- Encourage the use of columned notetaking formats. One notetaking format contains a topic sentence at the top of the page and three columns (e.g., widths of 5 inches, 2 inches, and 1 inch) designed for recording three types of information. The first column, Basic Ideas, is for material (such as facts, figures, dates, people, and places) that will be needed for future tests. The second column, Background Information, includes pertinent related information plus ideas, facts, and topics that interest the student. This column may begin with key words or concepts from the preceding lecture. The third column, Questions, includes space for marking unclear information that needs clarification or elaboration.

Activities for Developing Skills in Textbook Usage   The textbook is a primary source of information for secondary students. Practice in correct textbook usage benefits students with learning problems and helps them complete assignments and review pertinent information. This section features a variety of activities to help students improve their textbook usage skills.

- To assist in developing instructional objectives and measuring competence in textbook usage, administer a pretest and posttest. A test format may include the following questions.

  What part of the book explains how the book is organized?
  The authors are listed in what part of the book?
  On what page(s) would you look for information on _____?
  What part of the book gives meanings of words?
  How many chapters are in the book?
  What part of the book provides page references for any given topic?
  Define _____.
  On what page would you find a chapter titled _____?
  In what part of the book would you find information on a topic in the form of visual aids?
  Who publishes the book?
  On what pages does chapter _____ begin and end?
  On what page would you find out about _____?
  What is the meaning of the term _____?
  What information is included in the appendix of this book?

- Instruct the student to locate specific parts of a textbook. Allow 15 seconds for each part (e.g., the index). The following format is useful.

  Name of textbook _____
  Give the page number of the following:

Table of contents	_____
Index	_____
Glossary	_____
Appendix	_____

- Instruct the student to use the table of contents to determine the beginning and ending page numbers of specific chapters.
- Instruct the student to use the table of contents to name the chapter in which a given topic is located. The following format is helpful.

  Directions: Place the chapter title listed on the right under the correct heading listed on the left.
  I. Weather   Reptiles
     A.   Precipitation
     B.   Nutrition—proteins and vitamins

II. Animals   Amphibians
  A.   High-pressure system
  B.   Medications
III. Health
  A.
  B.

- Discuss the purpose of a glossary and have the student look up several words in a textbook glossary.
- From a content reading assignment, instruct the student to identify key words and find their meanings in the glossary.
- Explain what an index is, how it is developed, and how it can be used. Provide a page from an index and instruct the student to locate a list of terms and write down corresponding page numbers.
- Give a question and have the student identify the key words and locate them in the index. Have the student write the page number(s) pertaining to the question topic. A suggested format is as follows:

Underline key words. Locate them in the index and write the page number on which the answer is found. What was the population of San Francisco in 1980?

_____

What causes a tidal wave? _____

- Instruct the student to use the following cognitive strategies to help learning (Ellis & Lenz, 1987).
CAN-DO: A strategy for learning content information

C—*Create* a list of items to be learned.
A—*Ask* yourself whether the list is complete.
N—*Note* the main ideas and details using a tree diagram.
D—*Describe* each component and how it relates to others.
O—*Overlearn* main parts, then supporting details.

RIDER: A visual imagery strategy for reading comprehension

R—*Read* the sentence.
I—Make an *image* or picture in your mind.
D—*Describe* how the new image is different from the last sentence.
E—*Evaluate* the image to make sure it contains everything necessary.
R—*Repeat* the steps to RIDE as you read the next sentence.

FIST: A self-questioning strategy for reading comprehension

F—*First* sentence in the paragraph is read.
I—*Indicate* a question based on information in the first sentence.

S—*Search* for the answer to the question.
T—*Tie* the answer to the question with a paraphrase.

Activities for Developing Reading and Study Skills An extensive demand for gaining information from reading material exists at the secondary level. Students with learning problems are faced with obtaining content from a variety of reading materials. Several reading styles and rates are needed for these students to acquire essential information. Thus, students with learning problems must be taught strategies to help them acquire information quickly from a variety of printed materials.

Skimming is a systematic and efficient reading strategy that helps students in dealing with the reading and study demands of secondary classes. In this strategy, students isolate and rapidly read key sentences, phrases, and words to determine the main ideas. The steps in skimming are as follows:

1. Read the title and headings (i.e., dark print) as they appear.
2. Read the introduction (i.e., a few paragraphs at the beginning of a chapter or article).
3. Read the first sentence of each subsequent paragraph. In textbooks, the first sentence usually contains the main idea of the paragraph.
4. Read the captions of pictures and study any illustrations in the chapter.
5. Read the conclusion or chapter summary.

The following activities involving skimming are helpful in developing this reading-study skill.

- Have the student skim the major headings of a classroom text and formulate several questions for each heading. As a group activity, the teacher can require each student to generate one question for each heading.
- Discuss the terms *chronological*, *sequential*, and *causal* and provide examples of each.

Chronological—topics or events in the order of their happening. Most history books are organized chronologically.
Sequential—a step-by-step procedure. This frequently occurs in a science lab experiment or in instructions for assembling a project.
Causal—an "if-then" presentation pattern. Some texts use a causal pattern to explain a phenomenon (e.g., conditions that lead to weather happenings such as rain, lightning, and hurricanes).

- Give the student a content reading selection and a list of comprehension questions covering several main themes. Instruct the student to skim the selection and answer the questions.

- Use the following skimming activity as a pretest/posttest or as practice. Provide the student with a four- to five-page passage and a list of 20 comprehension questions covering main ideas and key words. Instruct the student to use skimming techniques to read the passage quickly and gain the most important information. At the end of 5 minutes, have the student answer the comprehension questions. Set the criterion for mastery at 90 percent correct on the comprehension questions.

Scanning is another reading and study strategy that helps students with learning problems deal with the demands of acquiring information from printed material. It involves the quick reading of key sentences, phrases, and words to locate specific information. This information could be an important term, definition, or answer to a question. Scanning is a great help in reading and studying because it enables the reader to find specific items rapidly. The steps in scanning are as follows:

1. Remember the specific question to be answered.
2. Estimate in what form the answer will appear (i.e., word, name, number, graphic, or date).
3. Use the expected form of the answer as a clue for locating it.
4. Look for clues by moving the eyes quickly over the page. When a section that appears to contain the answer is found, read it more carefully.
5. Find the answer, record it, and stop reading.

The following activities involve scanning.

- Give the student a list of alphabetized items. Name an item on the list and instruct the student to circle the item within 15 seconds. Once the student becomes proficient, the activity can be repeated with an unalphabetized list.
- Give the student an unalphabetized list and related questions. Read a question and instruct the student to write the number of the question next to the appropriate word. Initially, the time limit for each question is 30 seconds. As the student progresses, the time limit can be shortened to 10 seconds. A sample format is as follows:

—— equator	—— green	—— sophomore
—— mammals	—— mare	—— ewe
—— sentence	—— blue	—— six
—— red	—— hog	—— bulls

1. What is the name for warm-blooded animals with fur or hair?
2. What do you call a female sheep?
3. What color is grass?
4. What do you call a group of words that expresses a complete thought?
5. The American flag is red, white, and _____.
6. In tenth grade you are called a _____.
7. How many class periods are in a day?
8. What do you call a female horse?
9. What do you call male cattle?
10. What color is an apple?
11. What do you call a male pig?
12. What is the imaginary line that runs around the Earth?

This activity can be adapted to independent seatwork by having the student complete the task (i.e., match questions to words) within a specified time (e.g., 2 to 6 minutes).

- Give some questions from a chapter the student is studying in a class. Indicate the page number where the answer to each question is found. Have the student answer each question using the following instructions and format.

    Directions: Answer each question in 60 seconds or less. Each question has four steps: (1) Find the page listed, (2) read the question, (3) scan the page to find the answer, and (4) write your answer.

    (page 118) How long did Nat Turner's rebellion last?
    (page 72) What states were included in the Northwest Territory?
    (page 164) Why did Dred Scott think he should be a free man?
    (page 210) What does the term "Jim Crow" mean?

- Give some questions from a chapter the student is studying in a content area. Vary the questions so that some key words are found in the index (e.g., names, places, and events) and others are found in the chapter (e.g., section headings, italicized words, and boldface print). Instruct the student to (1) identify key words for locating information in text, (2) locate the appropriate page number, (3) read the question, (4) scan the page to locate key words, and (5) answer the question.
- Use the following activity as a pretest/posttest or as a practice activity. Select ten pages from different textbooks and write ten questions on 3″ × 5″ cards (i.e., one question per card). Have two questions each to cover information contained in the heading; information contained in topic sentences; information contained in charts, graphs, or maps; information contained in the index; and information contained in

myeducationlab

Go to the Building Teaching Skills and Dispositions section for the Topic Study Skills in the MyEducationLab for your course and complete the activity entitled Reading for Content Information. As you work through the learning unit, consider the need to develop the skill to read for content.

key words and terms. Give the student one question along with the number of the page on which the question is answered in the text. Have the student read the question, locate the answer, and write the answer. Begin timing when the student starts to read the question and stop timing when the student finishes writing the answer. Record the time. Continue in this manner until all questions are answered. Criterion is achieved when the student answers all questions correctly in a 10-minute time period (i.e., one question per minute).

Activities for Developing Reading and Note-taking Skills Taking notes on material read for classes facilitates memory and often makes it unnecessary to reread the material at a later time. When taking notes on reading material, the student is forced to think about the material and thus enhance recall of the content at a later date (Roe, Stoodt-Hill, & Burns, 2004). Moreover, the act of writing ideas helps the student remember content. Notetaking from reading material usually follows either an outline or a paraphrasing format. This section presents activities designed to develop or improve reading and notetaking skills.

- Teach students how to use an outline format. The first step in making an outline is determining the main ideas. The next step involves locating the supportive ideas for each of the main ideas. The sequence continues by locating specific details that go with respective supportive ideas. A blank outline format helps demonstrate the proper form.

Title

I. Main concept
   A. Information supporting I
   B. Information supporting I
      1. Specific information supporting B
      2. Specific information supporting B
         a. Specific information supporting 2
         b. Specific information supporting 2
   C. Information supporting I
II. Main concept
   A. Information supporting II
   B. Information supporting II

   C. Information supporting II
      1. Specific information supporting C
      2. Specific information supporting C

- To demonstrate outlining, show the student how the headings in a textbook chapter indicate different levels of subordination. For example, in many textbooks the main headings would be Roman numerals in an outline, side headings would be uppercase letters in an outline, and italic or paragraph headings would be Arabic numerals in an outline.
- Provide partially completed outlines and instruct the student to complete them (Roe et al., 2004).

Title

I. (Given by teacher)
   A. (Given by teacher)
      1. (Completed by student)
      2. (Completed by student)
   B. (Given by teacher)
      1. (Given by teacher)
      2. (Completed by student)
II. (Completed by student)
   A. (Given by teacher)
   B. (Completed by student)

This technique gradually can increase in difficulty until the teacher provides only the structural arrangement (i.e., the Roman numerals, uppercase letters, and Arabic numerals). This task becomes more relevant if the teacher uses textbooks from the student's general content classes.

- To facilitate notetaking from printed material, teach the student to use a columned format. For example, in the following format, the 2″ column on the left side is used to record main ideas, the 6″ column is used to record supporting details of the main ideas, and the 2″ space at the bottom is used to summarize ideas, raise questions, and note areas of concern.

- Provide several paragraphs and several summaries. Instruct the student to select the best summary of the paragraphs. Point out the importance of locating the main idea (i.e., usually the topic sentence of a paragraph) and essential supporting details.

- Provide passages from a textbook the student is using and instruct him or her to write a summary by following these steps: (1) Locate the main idea, (2) locate essential supportive details, and (3) write information as concisely as possible by leaving out illustrative material and statements that merely elaborate on main ideas.

Activities for Developing Skills in Using Visual Aids

Secondary textbooks are replete with visual aids, and adolescents with learning problems need to be taught how to use and understand them. This section presents activities and techniques for developing skills in the use of various types of visual aids.

- Explain that a map represents a geographic area. Review the following map-reading steps (Roe et al., 2004): Locate and comprehend the title of the map; determine map directions; interpret the map legend; apply the map's scale; discuss common map terms (e.g., *latitude, longitude, equator, gulf, bay,* and *continent*); make inferences from map material (e.g., climate, population, and industry); and understand projections (e.g., flat map or globe).
- Give the student index cards with a map legend on one side and its use or definition on the other side. Instruct the student to define or describe the legend's use and turn over the card to check the answer.
- Present road maps and instruct the student to estimate miles between locations and write directions from one place to another.
- Provide the student with a table and explain that it includes information arranged in vertical columns and horizontal rows. Review the following table-reading steps: Locate and comprehend the title of the table; determine information located in columns; determine information located in rows; and locate specific information through pinpointing intersections.
- Instruct the student to make a table of respective cities and their average monthly temperatures or of the student's class periods and corresponding 6-week grades.
- Use sample graphs to explain the four basic types of graphs: picture, circle, bar, and line graphs. Roe et al. (2004) recommend that teachers help students interpret graphs by reviewing the following steps:

  - Purpose of the graph (i.e., usually indicated by the title but becomes more evident when the accompanying narrative is studied)

- Scale of measure on bar and line graphs
- Legend of picture graphs
- Items being compared
- Location of specific pieces of information within a graph (e.g., finding the intersection of the point of interest on the vertical axis with the point of interest on the horizontal axis)
- Trends indicated by a graph (e.g., whether an amount increases or decreases over a period of time)
- Application of graphic information to actual life situations (e.g., a graph showing the temperatures for each month in Sydney, Australia, could be used for planning what clothes to take for a particular time of the year)

- Instruct the student to make a line graph using the student's reading rate (i.e., words per minute) in textbooks for various content areas.
- Instruct the student to make a bar graph of the heights of the starting lineups for two basketball teams. A basketball program may be used to provide the data. This activity can be adapted to various sports and selected information (e.g., weights in football and batting averages in baseball).
- Have the student make a circle graph of how he or she spends time (e.g., attending school, sleeping, playing, eating, completing homework, and miscellaneous).
- Instruct the student to make a picture graph from the following information: Dallas scored 70 touchdowns; Washington scored 76; Miami scored 47; Pittsburgh, 64; San Francisco, 37; New York, 54; Denver, 62. Let the symbol $\overline{\#}$ = 10 touchdowns.
- Use a model to demonstrate how diagrams are used to picture events, processes, structures, relationships, or sequences described in a textbook. Highlight the use of arrows, labeling, and various degrees of shading in diagrams.
- Instruct the student to make a diagram of a basketball play and orally present it to the teacher or class.
- For practice or for a pretest/posttest format in assessing visual aids, provide the student with a map, table, graph, or diagram, and ask questions pertaining to purpose, legend, columns, and specific information from the visual aid.
- Instruct the student to use the following cognitive strategy for reading visual aids (Ellis & Lenz, 1987).

  R—*Read* the written material until you are referred to a visual aid or until the material is not making sense.

  V—*View* the visual aid using CLUE.

C—*Clarify* the stated facts in the written material.

L—*Locate* the main ideas (i.e., global information) and details (i.e., specific parts).

U—*Uncover* the signal words (i.e., look for captions or words in the visual aid).

E—*Examine* the logic. (i.e., Does what you "read" from the picture make sense in light of what you read in the material?)

A—*Ask* yourself about the relationship between the visual aid and the written material using FUR.

F—Ask how the visual aid and the written material *fit* together.

U—Ask how the visual aid can help you *understand* the written material.

R—Ask how the visual aid can help you *remember* the written material.

S—*Summarize* the most important information.

- To facilitate analysis of visual aids presented in textbook chapters or study guides, instruct the student to use the SNIPS procedure (Ellis & Friend, 1991).

S—*Start* with questions (e.g., why you are analyzing the visual aid and what is important to understand and remember about the visual aid).

N—*Note* what you can learn from the hints (such as lines, numbers, color, and title).

I—*Identify* what is important (i.e., facts).

P—*Plug* it into the chapter (i.e., note how the visual aid relates to the chapter's content).

S—*See* whether you can explain the visual aid to someone.

Sequential Study Methods

Several methods have been developed to help students obtain and organize information from textbooks. Robinson (1961) developed the SQ3R method (i.e., survey, question, read, recite, and review), which remains one of the most widely known study methods. Study methods clearly hold much promise for teaching secondary students with learning problems, but systematic applications are needed to determine the effectiveness of various methods with specific populations. This section presents three sequential study methods for students with learning problems.

Multipass is an adaptation of SQ3R designed to teach effective study skills to adolescents with learning problems (Schumaker, Deshler, Alley, Warner, & Denton, 1982). The Multipass steps include the following:

1. *Survey Pass* is designed for the student to determine the main ideas and organization of the chapter. In this step the student is instructed to do the following:

a. Read the chapter title.
b. Read the introductory paragraph.
c. Review the chapter's relationship to adjacent chapters by examining the table of contents.
d. Read primary subtitles of the chapter and determine the chapter organization.
e. Note illustrations and read their captions.
f. Read the chapter summary.
g. Paraphrase the information gained in the preceding steps.

2. *Size-Up Pass* is designed for the student to gain specific information and facts from the chapter without reading it from beginning to end. In this step the student's instructions are as follows:

a. Read each question at the end of the chapter and determine what information is important. If the student can answer a question, a check mark is placed next to the question.
b. Examine the entire chapter following these guidelines: Look for textual cues (e.g., italicized words, boldface print, and subtitles); transform the cue into a question (e.g., if the cue italicized word is *mitosis,* the student asks "What is mitosis?"); skim through surrounding text to locate the answer to the question; and orally paraphrase the answer without looking at the book.
c. Paraphrase all the ideas and facts obtained from applying Step b to all contextual cues in the chapter.

3. *Sort-Out Pass* is designed to have the student self-check understanding of the chapter material. In this step the student reads and answers each question at the end of the chapter. If the student can answer a question immediately, a check mark is placed next to it. If unable to answer the question, the student follows these instructions.

a. Think about the section that most likely contains the answer.
b. Skim through that section for the answer and place a check mark next to the question if the answer is found.
c. If the answer is not in that section, continue to think and skim until the answer is located and the question is marked with a check mark.

The S.O.S. strategy is an alternative version of Multipass for students with reading abilities 4 or more years below their grade level. It includes the same three passes over the textbook as specified in Multipass but, in addition, uses a visually marked version and an audiotaped version of the chapter. The teacher or a paraprofessional can modify the chapter (i.e., mark and tape the chapter). The marking system consists of highlighting important facts, main ideas, and key words. After the chapter is marked, it is read (i.e., according to markings rather than verbatim) into a tape recorder. Thus, the taped version stresses important content and reduces information that can be presented in a few sentences. Each chapter tape is limited to no more than 90 minutes. The students are taught to survey, obtain details, and test themselves (i.e., Multipass steps). During the use of the S.O.S. strategy, students complete an organizer outline. This process helps students become active learners while listening to the tape.

The PANORAMA study technique includes eight steps divided into the following three stages (Edwards, 1973).

Preparatory Stage

1. *Purpose.* The learner determines why the material is being read.
2. *Adapting rate to material.* The teacher decides at what rate the material should be read. This involves maintaining flexibility of rate within sections as a function of the type of content being covered (e.g., the rate is slow on an initial reading if the main idea is being presented, whereas elaboration and expansion content may be read more rapidly).
3. *Need to pose questions.* The student uses headings or cue words to develop questions.

Intermediate Stage

4. *Overview.* The student surveys the major parts of the chapter to determine the organization of the material.
5. *Read and relate.* The student reads the material in terms of a specified purpose and seeks specific answers to questions.
6. *Annotate.* The student makes written annotations (i.e., paraphrases and outlines) of main ideas, key words, and concepts.

Concluding Stage

7. *Memorize.* The student uses outlines and summaries to learn the important content. Acronyms and associations are used to facilitate recall of main points.
8. *Assess.* The student assesses efforts in relation to the purpose of the reading (e.g., answers questions).

Recall Study Skills

Secondary students are expected to retain much of the information they obtain through lectures and readings. The retention of material is facilitated by rehearsal strategies. Many students need a strategy for rehearsing organized content (e.g., notes, outlines, summaries, discussions, or demonstrations).

Activities for Developing Study-Rehearsal Skills Activities for rehearsal of material include the following:

- Have the student rehearse from various content formats. For example:
  - *Rehearsing notes:* Rework notes, create test questions, construct lists of important points, write summaries, and review with classmates.
  - *Rehearsing outlines:* Verbalize the content by giving a lecture from the outline, and construct graphic aids (e.g., diagrams, charts, and graphs) from the outline.
  - *Rehearsing discussion:* Write a summary, use supplementary materials, and give examples to support important points.
  - *Rehearsing demonstrations:* Role play, practice segments of behavior chains, and practice with peers and critique one another.
- Encourage the student to use verbal rehearsal in reviewing content. This basic step in the learning strategies teaching sequence can be used in the initial learning of material and in reviewing it. Verbal rehearsal basically involves self-instructional training.
- Instruct the student to use questioning strategies when reviewing content. For example, a questioning treatment can consist of the following steps:
  - Appropriate reading material is selected, and the teacher and student read two or three paragraphs following these steps: both read the first sentence silently; the student asks as many questions as possible pertaining to the sentence, and the teacher answers them; the teacher asks questions pertaining to the sentence, and the student answers them.
  - After several paragraphs are read using the previously discussed steps, the student is instructed to write a question or make a prediction about the outcome of the story. The student then reads and answers the question or checks the prediction.

- To help the student rehearse information for later recall, use the following activities and suggestions (Roe et al., 2004).

  - Have the student review material with a specific purpose (e.g., to answer a question).
  - Encourage the student to obtain an understanding of the organization of the material through outlining. This helps the student categorize information to be learned under main headings.
  - Instruct the student to visualize what the text or notes are trying to present.
  - Encourage the student to make notes during rehearsal. In addition to facilitating retention, writing keeps the learner actively involved.
  - Have the student paraphrase the main and supporting information. Rewording the content helps improve understanding.
  - Encourage the student to discuss the material with a classmate.
  - For long-term retention, encourage the student to use spaced practice (i.e., several short practice sessions extended over a period of time) rather than massed practice (i.e., one long practice session).
  - Instruct the student to recite the material as soon as possible after reading it and to check for accuracy and correct any errors immediately.

- Encourage the student to use the keyword method.

Activities for Developing Mnemonic Devices

Nagel et al. (2003) present the mnemonic FIRST as a strategy to create mnemonics to recall information.

F—*Form* a word. For example, the student can form the word PENS to remember the parts of an atom: **p**roton, **e**lectron, **n**eutron, and **s**hell.

I—*Insert* extra letters to form a mnemonic word. For example, to remember scientific objects that have never been seen (e.g., **b**lack holes, **a**ntimatter, **c**osmic rays, and **e**arth's core), the letter *r* can be added to the first letters of the words to form BrACE.

R—*Rearrange* the first letters to form a mnemonic word. Some lists need to be memorized in order. For example, the sequence of the RAP paraphrasing strategy (i.e., *Read* the paragraph, *Ask* yourself about the main idea and two details, and *Put* it in your own words) needs to be remembered in order. With other lists, order is not important. With these lists, the first letter of each word can be manipulated to form a mnemonic word. For example, to remember the parts of the eye (i.e., **e**yelid, **i**ris, **p**upil, and **s**clera) the word PIES can be formed as a mnemonic.

S—*Shape* a sentence to form a mnemonic. For example, to remember the Roman numerals and their ascending order, the student can form the sentence **I** vacuumed x-rays last Christmas Day morning.

T—*Try* combinations of the first four steps to create a mnemonic.

Expression Study Skills

To succeed in secondary school, students must be able to demonstrate knowledge on classroom tests, minimum competency tests, and written assignments. Moreover, the application of knowledge in real-life settings becomes important to successful independent living during and after secondary school.

Activities for Developing Test-Taking Skills

The following activities are suggested for helping students develop their test-taking skills.

- Instruct the student to determine what general information is relevant in preparing for a test. The following list can be used as a guide or reminder:

  Subject content _____
  Date of test _____
  Chapters covered _____
  Notes covered _____
  Type of questions _____
  Number of questions _____
  Timed or untimed test _____
  Information emphasized in class _____

  Also, to facilitate test preparation, give the student a test that has been used previously.

- Identify vocabulary terms that are used frequently in test directions. Instruct the student to define the terms and perform the specified behavior, for example:

  Compare means _____. *Contrast* means _____. Compare and contrast milk and water.
  Criticize means _____. Criticize some aspect of your school schedule.
  Illustrate means _____. Illustrate the difference between a triangle and a circle.
  Evaluate means _____. Evaluate the importance of reading.

  Other words that can be covered include discuss, list, justify, outline, diagram, trace, match, define, and elaborate.

- Present the SCORER system (Carman & Adams, 1972) as a strategy for helping students take tests. Each letter represents an important test-taking rule.

  S—*Schedule* your time. The student reviews the entire test and plans time according to the number of items, point value per item, and easy and difficult items.
  C—Look for *clue* words. The student searches for clue words on each item. For example, on

true–false items words such as *always* and *never* usually indicate that the statement is false. Words such as *usually* and *sometimes* frequently indicate that the statement is true.

O—*Omit* difficult questions. Postponing hard questions until later in the testing session can improve a student's score. Specifically, Carman and Adams (1972, p. 217) suggest that the student use the following procedure.

- Move rapidly through the test.
- When you find an easy question or one you are certain of, answer it.
- Omit the difficult ones on the first pass.
- When you skip a question, make a mark in the margin (− or √). (Do not use a red pencil or pen. Your marks could get confused with grader's marks.)
- Keep moving. Never erase. Don't dawdle. Jot brief notes in the margin for later use if you need to.
- When you have finished the easy ones, return to those with marks (− or √), and try again.
- Mark again those answers you are still not sure of. Change the − to + or √ to √ √.
- In your review (that's the last R in SCORER), you will go over all the questions that time permits, first the ÷ ÷, then the ÷, then the unmarked.

R—*Read* carefully. A careful reading of test directions and each item can improve test performance. Careless reading can lead to confusion on essay items and careless errors on objective items.

E—*Estimate* your answers. On test items requiring calculations or problem solving, the student should estimate the answer. This helps correct careless errors. Moreover, if guessing is not penalized, all questions should be answered. After eliminating alternatives that are obviously incorrect, the student should take a best guess.

R—*Review* your work. The student should be encouraged to use every minute available. After all items are answered, have the student review the test. Carman and Adams (1972, p. 222) suggest that the student use the following checklist.

- Return to the double-checked (√ √) difficult questions. Reread them. Look for clue words. Look for new hints. Then go to the √ questions, and finally to the unmarked ones if there is still time.
- Don't be too eager to change answers. Change only if you have a good reason.
- Be certain you have considered all questions.
- PRINT your name on the test. If there are separate sheets, print your name on each sheet.

- Present the following activities and guidelines to help the student with answering true–false test items:
- Note the following rule to remember with true–false items: A statement must be completely true to be true. If any part of the statement is false, the whole statement is false. Instruct the student to be careful about tricky words. Some of these words include *some*, *many*, *most*, *everyone*, *no one*, *never*, and *always*. Demonstrate how these words cue true and false statements.
- Instruct the student to notice that directions to true–false items may vary. Sample directions include the following:

  Next to each statement, print *T* for true or *F* for false.

The effective use of learning strategies can help adolescents master content at the secondary level. Corbis RF

Write the word *true* or the word *false* on the line next to each statement.

If a statement is true, do nothing to it. If a statement is false, cross out the part that makes it false. Rewrite the part you crossed out to make a true statement.

- In true–false and multiple-choice test items, instruct the student to look for reworded statements in which positive or negative words have been used to change the answer.
- Present the following activities and guidelines to help the student answer multiple-choice test items:
  - Explain to the student that in most multiple-choice questions several alternatives usually are easy to eliminate because they are obviously incorrect. Frequently two alternatives seem correct, but instructions require the selection of the *best* answer.
  - Provide the student with sample multiple-choice items that illustrate different ways of thinking. For example, use items that include such key words as *except*, *not*, and *all of the above*.
  - Encourage the student to use the following guidelines with multiple-choice items:

    Know how many answers to select.
    Be aware of the kind of answer you are seeking (e.g., for a negative question).
    Remember the question.
    Eliminate the obvious wrong answers.
    Choose the answer that fits best.
    Be careful in recording the answer.

- Present the following activities and guidelines to help the student answer essay questions:
  - Instruct the student to read the directions and questions carefully and underline key words. In directions, the student should underline such parts as *answer two of the following questions*. In questions, key words include *discuss*, *compare*, *list*, and so on.
  - Instruct the student to outline or organize the answer before attempting to write it. If time becomes a serious factor, the question can be finished in outline form.
  - Teach the student to use the SCORER system with essay questions.
- Instruct the student to use the following techniques when taking all tests:
  - Review the entire test.
  - Know the time allotted for taking the test.
  - Know the value of specific questions.

- Follow the directions carefully.
- Notice key words in instructions and questions.
- Reread directions and questions.
- Go through the test and answer questions you are sure of first.
- Place a check mark beside questions you need to return to later.
- Return to questions that have been checked.
- Mark an *X* at the bottom of each completed page.
- Review all questions.

- Use a test that the student has taken previously to review ways in which performance can be improved.
- Provide the student with a machine-scorable sheet and a set of multiple-choice questions. Instruct the student to answer each test question by filling in the appropriate space. Many students with learning problems have difficulty with standardized and minimum-competency tests. Practice in using different types of answer formats helps students develop skills with these formats.
- Instruct the student to use the PIRATES test-taking strategy (Hughes, Schumaker, Deshler, & Mercer, 1993).

  P—*Prepare* to succeed. Put your name and PIRATES on the test. Prioritize the test sections and allow time. Say something positive and start within 2 minutes.

  I—*Inspect* the instructions. Read the instructions, underline how and where to respond, and notice special requirements.

  R—*Read, Remember, Reduce.* Read the whole question, remember what you studied, and reduce the alternatives.

  A—*Answer or Abandon.* Answer the question or abandon it for the moment.

  T—*Turn* back. At the end of the test, go back to the abandoned items and answer them.

  E—*Estimate.* Estimate unknown answers using ACE:
  A—*Avoid* absolutes.
  C—*Choose* the longest or most detailed choice.
  E—*Eliminate* similar choices.

  S—*Survey.* Survey to be sure that all items are answered, and change an answer only if you are sure it is incorrect.

Activities for Developing Written Expression Skills To survive in the secondary curriculum, students with learning problems must be able to express their knowledge in writing. Projects, papers, and essay tests require a degree of writing skills. This section features strategies that pertain to teaching written expression strategies.

- Teach adolescents with learning problems an error-monitoring strategy that is designed to enable students to locate and correct errors in written material. The following steps can be used to teach the error-monitoring strategy.

  1. Provide the student with teacher-generated one-page passages, which include some at the student's ability level and some at the student's grade level. Capitalization errors, appearance errors, and spelling errors are included in each passage.
  2. Teach the student to detect and correct errors in the teacher-generated passages by following these procedures:

     - Read each sentence separately.
     - Ask the COPS questions.
     - When an error is detected, circle it and put the correct form above the error.
     - Ask for help if unsure of an item.

  3. Teach the student to monitor work by following these steps:

     - Use every other line as you write the rough draft.
     - As you read a sentence, ask the COPS questions.
     - When an error is located, write the correct form above it.
     - Ask for help if unsure about a correct form.
     - Copy the paragraph neatly before giving it to the teacher.
     - Reread the paragraph as a final check.

- Present DEFENDS as a cognitive strategy for developing written expression skills when presenting a written position (Ellis & Friend, 1991).

  D—*Decide* on goals and theme. Decide who will read the written work and what kind of information you need to communicate.

  E—*Estimate* main ideas and details. Think of at least two different main ideas that explain your theme, and note at least three details that can be used to explain each main idea.

  F—*Figure* best order of main ideas and details. Decide which main idea to write about first, and note the best order for presenting the details.

  E—*Express* the theme in the first sentence. State what the essay is about.

  N—*Note* each main idea and supporting points. Explain the first main idea using the details, and repeat this for each of the other main ideas.

  D—*Drive* home the message in the last sentence. Restate what the theme is about using different wording from the first sentence.

  S—*SEARCH* for errors and correct.

    S—*Set* editing goals.

    E—*Examine* your essay to see whether it makes sense. Read the paper aloud and make sure each sentence expresses a complete thought and makes sense.

    A—*Ask* yourself whether the message will be clear to others. Make sure the ideas are clear and that the order of the ideas is logical.

    R—*Reveal* picky errors. Correct all capitalization, punctuation, spelling, and grammar errors you can find, and have someone check your work.

    C—*Copy* over neatly.

    H—*Have* a last look for errors.

- Teach adolescents to write summaries of content-area information. A meta-analysis of writing intervention studies indicates that summary writing has positive effects on the quality of composition products of adolescent students (Graham & Perin, 2007). Explicit instruction in summary writing can be integrated with content-area learning (e.g., science and social studies) to enhance growth in reading comprehension as well as writing in the content areas. Troia (2009) presents tactics for improving students' summarization of content-area information. Specific tactics include the use of graphic organizers (e.g., the K-W-L procedure), jigsaw content learning groups (i.e., a form of cooperative learning), the story impressions method (i.e., a method similar to exchange-compare writing in a cooperative learning framework), and writing frames.

Activities for Developing Oral Presentation Skills

Some assignments in secondary classes require the student to present information orally. The following activities may develop the student's ability to give an oral presentation.

- Provide the student with practice in making oral presentations in one-to-one, small-group, and whole-class settings.
- Provide the student with opportunities to gain or share information orally (e.g., interviews, investigative reporting, and debates).

- Be flexible in structuring the conditions under which the student makes oral presentations (e.g., seated or standing, at desk, in the front of the room, member of a panel, or role play).
- Guide the student in preparing to speak by having the student (1) know the purpose of the presentation, (2) develop a presentation outline, (3) practice in a nonthreatening environment, and (4) maintain a proactive attitude.
- Encourage the student to practice good body basics when presenting by using TALKS.

  T—*Talk* with a pleasant voice tone.

  A—*Act* confident and make eye contact with individuals.

  L—*Look* at the audience.

  K—*Keep* a pleasant facial expression.

  S—*Stand* with a straight body posture.

COMMERCIAL LEARNING STRATEGIES AND STUDY SKILLS PROGRAMS

Commercial programs that focus on learning strategies and study skills may be helpful to adolescents with learning problems. This section presents programs that can be used to facilitate the learning of content in the secondary setting.

Advanced Skills for School Success

Advanced Skills for School Success, developed by A. Archer and M. Gleason (published by Curriculum Associates), is a teacher-directed program consisting of four modules for students in seventh through twelfth grade. Module 1, School Behaviors and Organization Skills, stresses appropriate school behaviors and organization and time management skills. The second module, Completing Daily Assignments, focuses on planning assignments, writing answers to factual and opinion questions, and proofreading. In Module 3, Effective Reading of Textbooks, students practice previewing for reading, active reading, indentation notetaking, mapping a visual display of content, and writing a summary paragraph. Module 4, Learning from Verbal Presentations and Participating in Discussions, presents strategies for notetaking, brainstorming, and effectively participating in class discussions. The Teacher Guides contain scripted lessons as well as review lessons and follow-up activities. Lesson books also are available for students in third through sixth grade.

The FIRST-Letter Mnemonic Strategy

The FIRST-Letter Mnemonic Strategy (Nagel et al., 2003) provides an organized way of independently approaching large bodies of information that need to be mastered. It is designed to help students identify lists of information that are important to learn, generate an appropriate title or label for each set of information, select a mnemonic device for each set of information, create study cards, and master and recall each set of information. While using this strategy, students actively manipulate information to put it into a form that is easy to remember. The manual is part of the Learning Strategies Curriculum, and Strategies Intervention Model training is required.

The Test-Taking Strategy

The Test-Taking Strategy (Hughes et al., 1993) offers a strategy for students to use while taking classroom tests. Students learn to allocate time and priority to each section of a test, carefully read and focus on important elements in test instruction, recall information by accessing mnemonic devices, systematically and quickly progress through a test by selectively answering or abandoning questions, make well-informed guesses, check their work, and take control of the testing situation through regular use of self-talk and the application of test-wiseness principles. The strategy can be used in a variety of test-taking situations. The manual is part of the Learning Strategies Curriculum, and Strategies Intervention Model training is required.

COMPUTER SOFTWARE PROGRAMS IN LEARNING STRATEGIES AND STUDY SKILLS

Practice in preparing for and taking tests can enhance the student's ability to express knowledge in content-area classes. In addition to computer software programs to provide practice, new technologies, such as smart pens which link audio to what a student writes, can be helpful to students in the classroom. For example, Livescribe's Pulse Smartpen (available from various retailers) has an infrared camera that records the student's written words or drawings, a microphone to record audio around the student, a speaker for playback, and a mini headphone jack for listening to the recordings. Using a Livescribe notebook or special paper available with the smart pen, the student takes notes while the pen records what is being said in the classroom. The student can write brief notes or main ideas and, thus, focus on what the teacher is saying rather than trying to take comprehensive notes on paper. When reviewing the notes, the student simply touches the pen to a word on the paper and the pen plays back the audio of what was being said at the moment the note was taken. Because difficulty taking notes is often a barrier to success in content areas for students with learning disabilities, the smart pen technology has the potential to impact the learning of adolescents with learning problems. The following software programs focus on teaching effective study and test-taking skills.

Learning Skills: The Basis of Academic Success

Learning Skills (produced by Cambridge Educational), designed for students in seventh through twelfth grade, features four informative modules that show how to apply proven learning strategies to language arts, math, and science. The modules include using graphic organizers (e.g., diagrams and concept maps), memorizing (e.g., mnemonics and imagery), notetaking (e.g., focused listening and writing for understanding), and reading (e.g., substitution and main ideas). The 12 strategy segments include step-by-step instructions, animated exercises, and incremental feedback as the student works on interactive exercises in core academic subjects, and a final assignment pulls each lesson together.

Multimedia Study Skills

Multimedia Study Skills (produced by Cambridge Educational) focuses on teaching students in seventh grade and above how to prepare for tests and improve their study habits. Subjects covered in the Learning Skills module include learning styles, prime study times, assignment notebooks or calendars, notetaking techniques, reading, listening, remembering, and getting to the point of an assignment. The Test Preparation module covers the four As to test taking, objective tests, and subjective tests. Through video clips and on-screen examples, students learn techniques to help them understand and retain information and be relaxed and prepared for different kinds of tests.

Promoting Transitions

Getty Images–Digital Vision

From Chapter 14 of *Teaching Students with Learning Problems*, 8/e. Cecil D. Mercer. Ann R. Mercer. Paige C. Pullen.

When students with disabilities graduate or drop out of school, they face enormous challenges as they make the transition from school to community life and employment or postsecondary education. Analyzing their interests and strengths and weaknesses, choosing a career, pursuing employment or postsecondary education, and becoming independent are a few of the challenges they encounter. Unfortunately, substantial research indicates that most adults with disabilities struggle to find an acceptable quality of life and employment (Lindstrom & Benz, 2002; U.S. Department of Education, 1994; Wagner, Newman, Cameto, Garza, & Levine, 2005). Goode (1990) states that "when an individual, with or without disabilities, is able to meet important needs in major life settings (work, school, home, community) while also satisfying the normative expectations that others hold for him or her in those settings, he or she is more likely to experience a high quality of life" (p. 46). The development of self-determination is being recognized as an important factor in achieving an acceptable quality of life. Self-determination involves the ability to make informed decisions and is germane to self-sufficiency and independence (Patton & Trainor, 2004). According to Sitlington, Neubert, and Clark (2010), as transition planning occurs, "the emphasis must remain not only on employment and postsecondary education but also on living in the community. Underlying all of these transitions must be the knowledge and skills needed to be a self-determined adult" (pp. 260–261).

Examining the results of follow-up studies of adults with learning disabilities provides some perspectives on their postschool circumstances. These studies include both successful and unsuccessful individuals and provide some important insights in planning programs to help individuals with disabilities achieve an acceptable quality of life.

ADULTS WITH LEARNING DISABILITIES

The negative effects of learning disabilities persist into adulthood (Spekman, Goldberg, & Herman, 1992; Vogel & Adelman, 2000; White 1992). Individuals with learning disabilities face the same adult issues as others; however, they encounter these issues with more risk because of their learning difficulties and fragile emotional status. The overall findings of studies of adults with learning disabilities affirm that many such adults have difficulties finding quality employment, living independently, feeling good about themselves, and having satisfaction with their lives (Lindstrom & Benz, 2002; Trainor, 2007;

White, 1992). Also, when compared to students without disabilities, high school graduates with learning disabilities are significantly less likely to attend any form of postsecondary school and are less likely to graduate from postsecondary programs (Murray, Goldstein, Nourse, & Edgar, 2000). Although these findings are discouraging, the studies also indicate that a substantial number of adults with learning disabilities are independent, have quality jobs, enjoy many leisure activities, and are satisfied with their lives (Spekman et al., 1992; Vogel & Adelman, 2000).

A study of adults with learning disabilities begins with an understanding of adult development across the life span. Just as characteristics change between childhood and adolescence, the characteristics of adults change as they move through their adult years. Keogh (1993) notes that, given time and intervention, many adults with learning disabilities move through the developmental stages successfully but do so more slowly than adults without learning disabilities. Biological, environmental, historical, and social forces affect who they are, how they function, and what they need. Spekman, Goldberg, and Herman (1993) highlight the need for a lifelong perspective: "It must be remembered that LD involves a lifelong process of change and adaptation. Individuals doing poorly at one stage can be helped to demonstrate resilience, competence, and success at another" (p. 16).

The years between 18 and 25 are difficult for most individuals. During this time, they are expected to exit the sheltered environment of home and secondary school and enter the "real world." This real-world setting demands more independence and requires the individual to make decisions regarding postschool education, vocational training, employment, and independent living arrangements. Moreover, the transition becomes increasingly difficult when the individual faces higher expectations regarding social maturity, independence, and self-direction.

Although some young adults with learning disabilities make successful postschool adjustments, many of them struggle. An examination of studies and research reviews (Fourqurean & LaCourt, 1990; Lindstrom & Benz, 2002; Reiff & deFur, 1992; Sitlington, Frank, & Carson, 1993; Wagner, 1990; White, 1992; Witte, Philips, & Kakela, 1998) on the postsecondary adjustments of individuals with learning disabilities reveals some of the difficulties they experience.

- *Underemployment.* Many young adults with learning disabilities obtain part-time rather than full-time jobs, mostly at the unskilled or semiskilled level. They receive low wages and generally work in jobs of low social status.

- *Job dissatisfaction.* Many young adults with learning disabilities report less job satisfaction than their peers without disabilities.
- *Dependent living arrangement.* About 60 to 70 percent of young adults with learning disabilities continue to live with their parents several years after leaving secondary school.
- *Social skills problems.* Many young adults with learning disabilities have problems with relationships in the work setting. These are manifested in disagreements, misunderstandings, poor communication, and inappropriate appearance.
- *Poor work habits.* Not working fast enough, difficulty coping with job pressures, possessing deficient academic skills, and having problems following directions all interfere with the job performance of many individuals with learning disabilities.
- *Job selection.* Many individuals with learning disabilities have jobs that accentuate their weaknesses. For example, they take jobs that require extensive organization when they have organizational skills deficits.

In an effort to understand what factors contribute to postschool adjustments of individuals with learning disabilities, many researchers study both individuals who have made successful adjustments and those who have not. These studies yield data on conditions or factors that appear common to most adults with learning disabilities, individuals with learning disabilities who have been successful, and individuals with learning disabilities who have been unsuccessful. Table 14.1 presents these findings summarized from the following sources: Adelman and Vogel (1993), Reiff and deFur (1992), Reiff, Ginsberg, and Gerber (1995); Sitlington et al. (1993); Spekman, Goldberg, and Herman (1993); and Spekman, Herman, and Vogel (1993). Moreover, results from a 20-year longitudinal study indicate that such attributes as self-awareness, proactivity, perseverance, emotional stability, goal setting, and the use of effective support systems are predictors of success in individuals with learning disabilities (Goldberg, Higgins, Raskind, & Herman, 2003; Raskind, Goldberg, Higgins, & Herman, 1999).

In most of these studies, a multidimensional view is used to determine success. Some common markers of success include age-appropriate activities in relation to employment, school attendance, involvement with peers, involvement with family, participation in leisure and social activities, reported satisfaction with life, and description of endeavors in a realistic manner (i.e., perception matches reality) (Sitlington et al., 1993; Spekman et al., 1992). Likewise, a multidimensional view is used to define unsuccessful postschool adjustments and typically includes difficulty with age-appropriate activities and thoughts in work, school, family, leisure, friendships, satisfaction with life, and aspirations (Spekman et al., 1992). The findings from the research on successful adults with learning disabilities compel educators to focus on interventions that help individuals with disabilities recognize and understand their strengths and weaknesses and learn self-determination (i.e., take control of their lives to achieve positive outcomes).

In several studies, social deficits are reported as the major area of concern for adults with learning disabilities. Many adults with learning disabilities need assistance in the following areas.

1. Social relationships and skills
2. Career counseling
3. Developing self-esteem and confidence
4. Overcoming dependence; survival
5. Vocational training
6. Getting and holding a job
7. Reading
8. Spelling
9. Managing personal finances
10. Organizational skills

In general, problems such as social relationships of individuals with learning disabilities appear to persist in adolescents, young adults, and general adulthood; these individuals must adapt to situations that change over time and often present new challenges and problems. Studies of adults with learning disabilities who have been out of school for several years yield some encouraging findings. For example, Lewandowski and Arcangelo (1994) examined the social adjustment and self-concept of adults with and without learning disabilities who graduated from secondary school over a 6-year period. They found that the adults with learning disabilities were similar to the adults without learning disabilities in terms of social adjustment and self-concept. They conclude, "It appears that any negative effects of a disability classification abate once individuals leave the public school environment, and that previous forecasts of the socioemotional status of adults with learning disabilities may be unnecessarily pessimistic" (p. 598). Likewise, Spekman et al. (1992) maintain that young adults with learning disabilities

TABLE 14.1
Common factors of adults with learning disabilities

All adults with learning disabilities tend to:
  have learning disabilities throughout adulthood
  face more stress
  be late bloomers
  need a continuing support system
  need help in understanding their disabilities
  need transition planning
  need to be included in developing their own transition plans
  need assistance with problem-solving strategies
Successful adults with learning disabilities tend to:
  understand and accept their learning disabilities
  maintain a proactive approach
  maintain perseverance in dealing with life events
  develop coping strategies and know how to reduce stress
  maintain emotional stability
  set appropriate goals and maintain goal-directedness
  have and use support systems (e.g., a history of tutoring and therapeutic and supportive relationships)
  maintain a sense of control in their lives (e.g., make decisions to take charge of their lives and make
    useful adaptations to move ahead)
  maintain a determination to "make it" (i.e., motivation)
  pursue careers that maximize their strengths and minimize their weaknesses
  develop creative ways to compensate and problem solve
  maintain a positive attitude toward learning
  participate in a family or community ethic that values work and independence
  graduate from secondary school
  exhibit high verbal skills
Unsuccessful adults with learning disabilities tend to:
  have higher rates of unemployment if female
  not understand or accept their learning disabilities
  fail to take control of their lives
  maintain a sense of learned helplessness and fail to assume responsibility
  seek and promote dependent relationships
  pursue careers that accentuate their weaknesses
  have a severe math disability
  have an absence of protective factors (e.g., nurturing home environments) or factors associated with
    successful adults (e.g., support systems, proactivity, and motivation)
  drop out of secondary school

Source: From *Students with Learning Disabilities* (p. 518), 7th ed., by C. D. Mercer and P. C. Pullen, 2009, Upper Saddle River, NJ: Merrill/ Pearson. Copyright 2009 by Pearson Education. Reprinted by permission.

who are highly dependent on their support systems (i.e., family) tend to become more independent over time. Better jobs, improved wages, and ability to use community services facilitate independence.

Patton and Polloway (1992) report that as individuals with learning disabilities become older, their problems often become more complex. Likewise, Gerber et al. (1990) note that the complexity and interaction of variables associated with disabilities are magnified in adulthood. Cronin and Patton (1993) indicate that these mediating variables need to be considered within the contexts of the following adult domains: employment and education, home and family, leisure pursuits, community involvement, physical/emotional health, personal responsibility, and relationships. Gerber (1994) notes that consideration of the mediating variables within these contexts holds promise for more meaningful research on adults with learning disabilities.

Because many adults with disabilities do not enjoy an acceptable quality of life (U.S. Department of Education, 1994; Wagner et al., 2005) despite their apparent potential to do so, educators should develop and implement viable transition programs for these individuals. In an article titled "Transition: Old Wine in New Bottles," Halpern (1992) notes that educators have been trying for over 30 years to prepare adolescents with disabilities to make successful transitions to adult life. The 1960s featured cooperative/work study programs, the 1970s introduced career education, and the 1980s and 1990s focused on transition. According to Halpern, "In the area of curriculum and instruction, we are still frequently deficient in what we teach, how we teach, and where we teach. Curriculum content still tends to focus too much on remedial academics and not enough on functional skills" (p. 206). To achieve the goal of relevance, Sitlington et al. (2010) recommend integration of the focus on improved adult outcomes (i.e., life skills competencies) with the focus on improved academic outcomes (i.e., higher achievement in academic competencies). They indicate that many educators "are advocating for functional, generalizable skills for responsible citizenship as the ends and academic skills as a means to those ends" (p. 257). In transition planning, there always should be an emphasis on the skills and support needed for successful transition to the next environment and, ultimately, to the environment of life as an adult.

TRANSITIONS FROM SECONDARY SETTINGS

Because of the continuing failure of many students with disabilities to make positive adjustments to adult life, transition services remain a national priority (Halpern, 1992). In 1990, a transition mandate was included in the Amendments to the Individuals with Disabilities Education Act (IDEA) (Public Law 101-476). This law (Section 602[a][19]) defines *transition services* as

> a coordinated set of activities for a student, designed within an outcome-oriented process, which promotes movement from school to post-school activities, including post-secondary education, vocational training, integrated employment (including supported employment), continuing and adult education, adult services, independent living, and community participation. The coordinated set of activities shall be based upon the individual student's needs, taking into account the student's preferences and interests, and shall include: instruction, community experiences, the development of employment and other post-school adult living objectives, and when appropriate, acquisition.

In addition, the 1997 reauthorization of IDEA (Public Law 105-17) integrates transition planning within the process of educational planning starting at age 14 years. For all students who qualify for special education, the law requires a statement of transition needs beginning at age 14 and updated annually. A statement of needed transition services is required beginning at age 16 years. Moreover, the Individuals with Disabilities Education Improvement Act of 2004 (Public Law 108-446) reaffirmed the mandate for conducting transitional assessment and developing transition plans to assist students in planning for life after high school. These mandates ensure that the development and delivery of transition services for students with disabilities receive serious and overdue consideration.

Transition Program Components

To be successful, transition programs need to include (1) academic programs that prepare respective students to function independently and enter work or postsecondary education, (2) career education, (3) vocational education, (4) self-advocacy training, and (5) collaboration among a multitude of professionals, parents, and employers. Rojewski (1992) reviewed nine prototype transition projects and identified seven essential components.

1. Individualized planning
2. Systematic vocational assessment, job exploration, vocational counseling, and vocational skills training
3. Academic remediation
4. Academic and vocational counseling and intervention in advocacy training, social skills, and social support
5. The identification and coordination of support systems such as vocational rehabilitation, employers, and vocational educators
6. A systematic job-seeking curriculum that features activities such as writing a resume, finding job openings, filling out applications, and interviewing for employment
7. An evaluation plan to monitor the short-term and long-term effectiveness of the program

Transition Program Participants and Transition Plans

Participants in the transition program include a variety of individuals. The primary participants and their roles include the following:

- *Special educators:* Act as transition case managers, teach job-related academic strategies, social skills, and job-finding and job-keeping program prerequisites; collaborate with the transition team to coordinate the plan; teach self-advocacy.

- *Guidance counselors:* Provide career, individual, and small-group counseling; provide career awareness and exploration information.
- *Vocational evaluator or school psychologist:* Conducts vocationally relevant evaluations.
- *Employers:* Provide information about job needs and requirements; provide job training sites and permanent jobs; evaluate students before and after graduation.
- *Vocational educators:* Provide vocational training both in and out of school; make instructional modifications when appropriate; obtain information regarding job needs and job requirements.
- *Parents:* Help adolescents develop realistic career goals; promote and support independence; help adolescents explore career options.
- *Students:* Acquire strategies and skills needed to be vocationally successful; work toward achieving independence; acquire strategies and skills needed for postsecondary educational settings.
- *College and university personnel:* Advise students regarding admission procedures; plan support services such as scheduling, accommodations, and advisement.
- *Vocational rehabilitation counselors:* Obtain funding for job-related services; provide vocational evaluation information; assist with job placement and provide support services; act as primary postsecondary receiving agency.

These participants are the key planners at the secondary school level; however, a school-based career development and transition program begins in elementary school and continues into adulthood. Clark and Kolstoe (1990) present a school-based career development and transition education model that covers preschool through lifelong learning opportunities. The model comprises four content elements.

1. Job-acquisition and daily living skills appropriate for current and future needs
2. Occupational information, including various occupational roles, occupational vocabulary, occupational alternatives, and basic realities about the world of work
3. Human relationships on the job, in the family, and in the community
4. Values, attitudes, and habits essential for work

Public Law 105-17 requires the development of an individualized transition plan for students with disabilities (i.e., a transition needs statement beginning at age 14 and a transition services statement beginning at age 16). Whereas some states require an individualized transition plan that is a separate document from the individualized educational program (IEP), other states include transition goals within the existing IEP. Instructional goals (i.e., knowledge and skills development) and linkage goals (i.e., connection with needed supports and services) are developed for transition areas where needs have been identified. Because students' needs vary, the plans reflect many different types of services and providers. The *Transition Planning Inventory—Updated Version* (Clark & Patton, 2006) is an instrument designed to provide a systematic way to identify and plan for an individual student's transition needs (i.e., knowledge, skills, support, or services). Areas covered in the inventory include employment, further education/training, daily living, living arrangements, leisure activities, community participation, health, self-determination, communication, and personal relationships.

PROGRAM AREAS IN TRANSITION EDUCATION

Effective transition programs must prepare the student with disabilities to function successfully in many adult roles to attain an acceptable quality of life. Some of the primary curriculum areas are academic, vocational, domestic living, mobility, leisure and recreation, and accessing community services. Students planning to make the transition to postsecondary educational institutions receive their preparatory training in a curriculum that features career education and academic instruction that promotes success in higher education. The vocational aspects of the curriculum are provided through career education, vocational education, and academic programs. Domestic living, mobility, leisure and recreation, and accessing community services are covered within the independent living skills academic curriculum. Finally, an academic program that includes self-advocacy training helps the student succeed in all adult roles. This section presents the major components of a transition program: academic interventions, life skills instruction, career and vocational education, and self-advocacy and self-determination instruction.

Academic Interventions

Academic interventions within transition programs consist of skill-oriented instruction or content-oriented instruction.

Skill-Oriented Instruction Skill-oriented instruction teaches students skills that relate to the academic areas they find difficult. Skills are broken down and taught to the students over time. Zigmond (1990) maintains that intensive and efficient instruction in basic academic skills is essential for helping students succeed in employment and in independent living situations. Academic interventions seem especially appropriate for ninth and tenth graders who are achieving below fourth-grade level in one of the basic skill areas. Basic skills remediation is the foundation of special education programs in the elementary school setting. The academic chapters of this text provide a wealth of information to help teachers develop academic skills with students who have learning problems.

In a review of secondary curriculum content for students with learning disabilities, Rieth and Polsgrove (1994) report several noteworthy findings. In the area of teaching reading to adolescents, they report that phonics instruction appears to be a weak intervention. In the area of spelling, they found that spelling ability appears to improve when spelling instruction is integrated with other meaning-based language arts instruction. In the area of teaching mathematics to adolescents, the use of videodisc technology has yielded impressive achievement gains and has been well received by teachers (Woodward & Gersten, 1992).

Because secondary students face numerous curriculum demands and have little time to ameliorate deficits, educators are seeking ways to increase the intensity of instruction (e.g., learning labs and high-intensity learning centers). For example, *Corrective Reading* (published by SRA) can be used with adolescents with learning problems to increase the level of instructional intensity of academic remediation. Summer school programs also can provide an opportunity for high-intensity instruction without delaying graduation.

Content-Oriented Instruction Content-oriented instruction promotes the direct acquisition of content by students. Skill or strategy instruction also is designed ultimately to lead to content-area learning, but the relationship is indirect. Content acquisition is promoted through designing content enhancements; planning courses in which the content is organized into levels of content that all students learn, most students learn, and some students learn; tutoring in the content areas; and providing equivalent-content instruction. Chapter 4 presents leveled content planning, and Chapter 13 features the use of content enhancements and equivalent-content instruction through accommodations and modifications.

Moreover, Chapter 13 presents learning strategies and study skills techniques, both of which help students learn content.

In a survey of state departments of education, McKenzie (1991) found that content instruction by special educators is used extensively throughout the nation. In the tutorial approach, the general education teacher delivers content, but the special education teacher provides short-term assistance in mastering key aspects of the content in which the student is experiencing difficulty or failure. With the increase in inclusion, general education and special education teachers are collaborating more to deliver content in learner-friendly ways.

In a multistate study of teachers' and supervisors' perceptions of secondary learning disabilities programs, Cline and Billingsley (1991) found that the primary program components have remained consistent over the past decade but the relative importance of these areas is changing. The four highest-rated program components of teachers and supervisors include direct teaching of content subjects, basic skills remediation, learning and study strategies, and tutorial assistance. The respondents, however, indicate that special education teachers should decrease content-area instruction and increase learning strategies instruction. Also, the results highlight a need to provide more consultation to general education teachers.

Life Skills Instruction

An appropriate education for students with disabilities must be implemented according to individual needs as related to the life skills demands of adulthood. *Life skills* are those skills an adult needs to perform successfully in a variety of community settings. A life skills curriculum includes instructional content that focuses on the concepts and skills needed by students in the areas of personal-social, daily living, and occupational adjustment.

A functional or essential life skills program typically is designed for secondary students whose academic skills are very low (i.e., below fourth-grade level). Functional life skills must be taught directly and systematically to some students with learning problems, or otherwise the students may never acquire these essential skills or may learn them through trial and error, which is both costly and time consuming. Brolin and Lloyd (2004) present a comprehensive functional life skills curriculum model and framework. Within the context of this Life-Centered Career Education Curriculum, Brolin (1997) provides the following competencies and subcompetencies in daily living skills.

1. *Manages personal finance:* Counts money and makes correct change; makes responsible expenditures; keeps basic financial records; calculates and pays taxes; uses credit responsibly; uses banking services.

2. *Selects and manages a household:* Maintains home exterior and interior; uses basic appliances and tools; selects adequate housing; sets up household; maintains home grounds.

3. *Cares for personal needs:* Demonstrates knowledge of physical fitness, nutrition, and weight; exhibits proper grooming and hygiene; dresses appropriately; demonstrates knowledge of common illness prevention and treatment; practices personal safety.

4. *Raises children and meets marriage responsibilities:* Demonstrates physical care by raising children; knows psychological aspects of raising children; demonstrates marriage responsibilities.

5. *Buys, prepares, and consumes food:* Purchases food; clears food preparation areas; stores food; prepares meals; demonstrates appropriate eating habits; plans and eats balanced meals.

6. *Buys and cares for clothing:* Washes and cleans clothing; purchases clothing; irons, mends, and stores clothing.

7. *Exhibits responsible citizenship:* Demonstrates knowledge of civic rights and responsibilities; knows nature of local, state, and federal governments; demonstrates knowledge of the law and ability to follow the law; demonstrates knowledge of citizen rights and responsibilities.

8. *Utilizes recreational facilities and engages in leisure:* Demonstrates knowledge of available community resources; chooses and plans activities; demonstrates knowledge of the value of recreation; engages in group and individual activities; plans vacation time.

9. *Gets around the community:* Demonstrates knowledge of traffic rules and safety; demonstrates knowledge and use of various means of transportation; finds way around the community; drives a car.

These competencies are an excellent framework for a functional life skills curriculum and, when combined with personal-social and occupational guidance and preparation competencies, they form the foundation of a strong career-centered education. Many of these skills can be taught within the traditional curriculum. For example, Area 1 can be included in math; Areas 3 and 5 in science; Areas 4, 7, and 9 in social studies; Areas 2 and 6 in home economics and shop; and Area 8 in music, art, and physical education.

Polloway, Patton, and Serna (2008) suggest several options for covering life skills topics within the curriculum. One option is the development of a series of specific life skills courses (e.g., personal finance, practical math, health and hygiene, and everyday science). A second option is the creation of a single life skills course that covers a range of general topics (e.g., functional living skills) or that focuses on one area (e.g., real-life math). Another option involves the integration of life skills topics into the content of existing coursework. Dedicating a portion of the course to life skills topics can augment a course, or real-life topics that relate to information being covered can be infused into existing content.

The *Brigance Transition Skills Inventory* (Brigance, 2010b) assesses basic skills and functional life skills in the context of real-world situations. Nine skill areas are included: speaking and listening, functional writing, words on common signs and warning labels, telephone, money and finance, food, clothing, health, and travel and transportation.

Activities for Developing Life Skills Cronin (1988) presents functional or life skills curriculum tasks in the areas of consumer economics, occupational knowledge, health, community resources, and government and law. These tasks are presented across academic areas (e.g., reading and writing) at the elementary, junior high, and senior high school levels. Table 14.2 displays this information in a manner that enables the teacher to integrate these tasks and skills across academic areas and grade levels. Moreover, the following specific activities may be helpful in developing students' life skills.

• To focus on managing family finances, have students keep a record of expenses for a certain period of time. The budget should include areas such as food, clothing, transportation, savings, medical expenses, and recreation. Student also may itemize their families' purchases during a period of time. To encourage students to spend money wisely, provide a shopping list of products available at different stores, and require students to compare prices or to select items based on a fixed amount of money.

• Take a field trip to a bank and a credit union facility or arrange classroom demonstrations by representatives from these establishments. A classroom bank and individual accounts can be set up to acquaint students with checks, deposits, withdrawals, and passbooks. Activities can provide extensive practice in writing checks, filling out deposit slips, and balancing a checkbook. To learn about other banking services, students also can be required to fill out forms for obtaining a loan or opening a charge account.

TABLE 14.2
Life skills curriculum tasks across academic areas

Elementary School

	Consumer Economics	Occupational Knowledge	Health	Community Resources	Government and Law
Reading	Look for ads in the newspaper for toys.	Read books from a library on various occupations.	Read the school lunch menu.	Find a television listing in the *TV Guide*.	Read road signs and understand what they mean.
Writing	Write prices of items to be purchased.	Write the specific tasks involved in performing one of the classroom jobs.	Keep a diary of food you eat in each food group each day.	Complete an application to play on a little league team.	Write a letter to the mayor inviting him or her to visit your school.
Speaking, Listening, Viewing	Listen to a bank official talk about savings accounts.	Call a newspaper in town to inquire about delivering papers in your neighborhood.	View a film on brushing teeth.	Practice using 911 emergency number.	Discuss park playground improvements with the mayor.
Problem Solving	Decide whether you have enough coins to make a purchase from a vending machine.	Decide which job in the classroom you do best.	Role play what you should do if you have a stomachache.	Role play the times you would use a 911 emergency number.	Find the city hall on the map. Decide whether you will walk or drive.
Interpersonal Relations	Ask for help finding items in a grocery store.	Ask a student in the class to assist you with a classroom job.	Ask the school nurse how to take care of mosquito bites.	Call the movie theater and ask the performance times of a movie.	Role play asking a policeman for help if lost.
Computation	Compute the cost of a box of cereal using a coupon.	Calculate how much you would make on a paper route at $3 per hour for 5 hours per week.	Compute the price of one tube of toothpaste if they are on sale—3 for 1.	Compute the complete cost of going to the movie (admission, food, transportation).	Compute tax on a candy bar.

Junior High School

	Consumer Economics	Occupational Knowledge	Health	Community Resources	Government and Law
Reading	Read an ad for a sale locating name of store, location, phone number, and price of item.	Read a job description.	Locate poison-control numbers in phone book.	Use phone book to locate recreational program in community.	Locate and read a list of state and U.S. representatives.
Writing	Fill out a magazine order form completely.	Practice writing abbreviations for words.	Write a menu for a balanced diet.	Write a letter to a TV station about a program they just canceled.	Fill out a voter registration form.

	Consumer Economics	Occupational Knowledge	Health	Community Resources	Government and Law
Speaking, Listening, Viewing	Discuss saving vs. spending money.	Discuss reasons why we work.	Listen to positive and negative feedback on personal appearance.	Call a library to find out whether they have a certain book.	Discuss why we need to vote.
Problem Solving	Given $10 for the evening, choose an activity: movies, bowling, or pizza.	Decide on job environment: inside, outside, desk, travel, etc.	Role play appropriate behavior for various places (movies, church, restaurant).	Locate the skating rink on a city map and decide the best way to get there.	Decide what items have state and/or local tax.
Interpersonal Relations	Ask salesperson for help in purchasing jeans.	List questions to ask in job interview.	Discuss honesty, trust, and promise. Define each.	Call a skating rink to inquire about hours.	Call to find out what precinct you live in.
Computation	Compute the sales tax on a pair of jeans.	Compute net income.	Calculate and compare the prices of hair shampoo.	Calculate bus fare to and from the teen center.	Calculate the cost of getting a driver's license (fee, gas).

Senior High School

	Consumer Economics	Occupational Knowledge	Health	Community Resources	Government and Law
Reading	Read and compare prices of grocery store ads.	Read a job description and qualifications.	Read directions on a cough-syrup bottle.	Read a movie schedule.	Obtain and read a sales tax sheet for your county/state.
Writing	Write a check for amount of purchase.	Complete a job application.	Write a grocery list for the week, including all the food groups.	List government and community employment agencies from a phone book.	Apply for a work permit.
Speaking, Listening, Viewing	Explain the difference between charge, check, and cash purchases.	Role play calling your boss when ill.	Practice calling a doctor's office for an appointment.	Listen to a state patrolman talk about highway driving.	Describe an accident.
Problem Solving	Decide what amount you can afford to rent an apartment.	Decide what to wear to a job interview.	Decide whether you should go to a community clinic or a hospital for an injury.	Role play what you would do if your car broke down.	Decide which candidate to vote for.
Interpersonal Relations	Ask a salesperson if the store offers layaway and the costs involved.	Role play a mock interview.	Ask a pharmacist about a prescription.	Ask directions to a video store.	Call legal aid and ask what services are available.
Computation	Calculate and compare savings on items from different stores.	Calculate pay-check deductions.	Decide how many times a day to take a pill.	Compute cost of doing laundry in a laundromat vs. home.	Calculate the cost of a speeding ticket.

Source: From "Applying Curriculum for the Instruction of Life Skills" by M. E. Cronin. In *Best Practices in Mental Disabilities* (pp. 44–46), Vol. 2, by G. A. Robinson, J. R. Patton, E. A. Polloway, and L. R. Sargent (Eds.), 1988, Des Moines: Iowa Department of Education, Bureau of Special Education. Copyright 1988 by Iowa Department of Education, Bureau of Special Education. Reprinted by permission.

- Have small-group discussions in which students examine various kinds of taxes (such as sales, gas, property, and income). Have them identify items that are taxed and determine the amount, how the tax is collected, and how it is used. The procedure for filing income tax forms can be presented by requiring each student to fill out a 1040 short form. Cut instructions from a tax guide according to numbered sections (e.g., 1—name and address, 2—Social Security number, and so on). Fasten each instruction and the corresponding section of the 1040A form to a card. Provide one sample form filled out as well as blank 1040A forms that are laminated for reuse. Instruct each student to fill out a 1040A form number by number, referring if necessary to the completed form and the individual instruction cards.

- Discuss various types of housing available in the community. Have students explore the advantages and disadvantages of each according to factors such as cost, space, utilities, and location. In discussing renting a home or apartment, include such factors as deposits, leases, and tenant rights and responsibilities. Cut out newspaper ads that list rentals and tape them to the inside of a manila folder. On index cards write questions related to the rental ads and place the cards in a pocket pasted to the folder. Have students pick a card, look for the answer in the classified ads mounted on the inside of the folder, and write a response. An answer key can be provided by numbering the questions and assigning letters to the ads.

- Have students role play potential problems in marriage and child raising and discuss solutions. Encourage students to refer to their own life experiences when suggesting appropriate practices in raising children. Also have students identify community agencies and sources that assist in family planning and marriage problems.

- Identify emergency situations that can occur in the home (such as fire or storm damage) or with a family member (such as accident or injury). Have each student look up emergency phone numbers and make a booklet containing information on how to get help for emergencies. First-aid procedures for injury situations should be demonstrated in the classroom and listed in the student's booklet. Also, safety procedures for hazardous situations can be discussed.

- Have each student determine recreational activities in which he or she can participate, and list resources and facilities available in the community. If the student is interested in music, the teacher can make a recording of five different types of music and have the student select a favorite. Then the student can explore places where that type of music is available, or the student can study favorite composers. To develop an interest in art as a leisure activity, the teacher can present prints of various types of art. The student can determine places or events in which to enjoy art during recreational time. Also, the student can participate in clubs or hobbies to explore using leisure time effectively.

myeducationlab

Go to the Assignments and Activities section of the Topic Transitions in the MyEducationLab for your course and complete the activity entitled Vocational Training. As you watch the video and complete the accompanying questions, note the value of helping students transition with the aid of vocational training.

Career and Vocational Education

The emphasis on career education began in the early 1970s and evolved from dissatisfaction with the educational system's ability to prepare students adequately for the future. Career education focuses on experiences through which students learn to live a meaningful, satisfying work life, and it provides the opportunity for students to learn academic, daily living, personal-social, and occupational skills for economic, personal, and social fulfillment.

Students with learning problems often need attractive options in career training. Career-related instruction enables an individual to explore the occupational world, identify with it, and make job decisions that increase self-fulfillment. Moreover, the content places value on all work, regardless of its current social status. Cegelka and Greene (1993, pp. 142–143) state the following:

> By emphasizing the relationship of subject matter to various careers and occupations and by developing needed work skills, career education sought to make education more relevant to the economic and employment realities of the day . . . Career education has been seen as the sum of all experiences through which one learns to live a meaningful, satisfying, and productive work life.

Meers (1992) reports that career education spans kindergarten through twelfth grade and features three components: (1) instruction to help individuals live independently at home, (2) instruction to help individuals live independently in the community, and (3) vocational instruction to prepare individuals for successful employment. Thus, career education involves a comprehensive educational program, focusing on careers, that begins in early childhood and continues throughout adulthood. At the elementary level, the

FIGURE 14.1
Career development stages

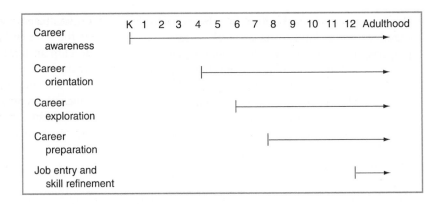

major objective is to introduce the student to various occupations. The primary objective at the secondary level is to shape the student's awareness of occupations into preparation for a career.

Figure 14.1 presents the stages of career development and approximate grade levels for each stage. Beginning in kindergarten and continuing through high school, the career awareness stage establishes a foundation for career education and provides an understanding of various occupations and jobs, the importance of work, and an initial self-awareness of career interests. Career orientation, which begins in the elementary grades in conjunction with awareness activities, focuses on the identification of career interests through practical experience and exposure to a variety of occupations. In middle school and high school, career exploration activities give students simulated and direct experiences with many occupations to help them determine their career goals and interests. Through vocational education, on-the-job training, or college preparation during the career preparation stage, students receive the training necessary for eventual employment. Finally, in the final stage of job entry and skill refinement, students effectively function in jobs or other postsecondary settings.

Wiederholt and Wolffe (1990) offer a normal sequence of independent living-related developments that provide a complement to the career development stages. These independent living-related developments provide a framework of how students develop attitudes, values, interest, and information about work.

1. *Preschool age:* Learns to listen, cooperate, do for self, show initiative, be honest; differentiates work from other activities; understands different types of work and associated roles; develops feelings toward work.

2. *Elementary age:* Fantasizes different roles; understands parents' work; has continued and more complex career fantasies; is exposed to and develops understanding of a wide variety of work roles; develops understanding of good work qualities; continues to develop and implement communication skills; learns to interact appropriately with peers and authority.

3. *Junior high school age:* Has part-time or summer job; does chores at home; develops hobbies or special interests; begins to understand personal strengths and weaknesses; understands relative rewards, demands, and requirements of major categories of work; accepts responsibility for career decisions; begins to crystallize personal values and self-concept.

4. *Senior high school age and older:* Continues exploration of various career possibilities; prepares for career or initial employment; crystallizes interests; changes plans or jobs; understands and acts upon personal strengths and weaknesses; develops skills; crystallizes personal values and self-concept; handles independent living; establishes intimate relationships; refines hobbies or special interests; learns how to get jobs and holds several different jobs; learns and displays appropriate work behavior.

Career education enables an individual to explore the occupational world, to identify with it, and to make job decisions that increase self-fulfillment. Brolin (1997) recommends that career education be a major part of the curriculum for students with disabilities and that it focus on the total life plan of an individual. The total life plan facilitates growth and development in all life roles and settings. In addition to the competencies in daily living skills presented earlier, Brolin includes the following competencies in personal-social skills and occupational guidance and preparation.

- *Personal-social skills:* Achieves self-awareness; acquires self-confidence; achieves socially responsible behavior; maintains good interpersonal skills; achieves independence; makes adequate decisions; communicates with others.
- *Occupational guidance and preparation:* Knows and explores occupational possibilities; selects and plans occupational choices; exhibits appropriate work habits and behavior; seeks, secures, and maintains employment; exhibits sufficient physical-manual skills; obtains specific occupational skills.

Career education has a broad emphasis and includes vocational training. Vocational education, which usually is provided at the secondary or postsecondary level, is designed to develop skills, abilities, understanding, attitudes, work habits, and appreciations needed by individuals to enter and make useful and productive progress in employment. The goal of vocational education is to prepare the individual for gainful employment. Both career and vocational education are needed if students with learning problems are to make successful transitions from secondary school to adult lives. In general, to progress from secondary school to employment, some students with disabilities require vocational and supportive life-skills instruction as ongoing services or on a time-limited basis, whereas other students require no special support services.

Vocational training specifically focuses on developing vocational skills essential to entering the world of work. Historically, it has been difficult to obtain vocational training for students with mild disabilities. A variety of options and services are needed to provide low achievers with the programs they need. Such students can learn specialized skills in a career area in a vocational-technical school, a special vocational school, work-study off campus, and work-study on campus. Postschool alternatives include entry-level jobs, trade school, community college, college or university, and referral to the Bureau of Vocational Rehabilitation or other appropriate community or government agencies.

A variety of measures and procedures can be used to assess students in terms of appropriate decisions on career direction. Information can be obtained informally through student–teacher interaction and a consultative process. Also, the *Brigance Transition Skills Inventory* (Brigance, 2010b) is a criterion-referenced instrument that assesses the basic skills and employability skills needed to gain employment and succeed in the workplace (e.g., preemployment writing,

math skills and concepts, career awareness and self-understanding, and job-seeking skills and knowledge). In addition, a number of standardized tests assess vocational interest or aptitude. The following instruments can be used to help secondary students choose appropriate careers based on their particular abilities and interests: *Career Decision-Making System—Revised* (Harrington & O'Shea, 2000), *Occupational Aptitude Survey and Interest Schedule—3* (Parker, 2001), and *Wide Range Interest and Occupation Test—Second Edition* (Glutting & Wilkinson, 2003). In addition to standardized testing procedures, the work-sample method provides a means of prevocational evaluation. The work sample is a simulated task or occupational activity that is representative of tasks and activities in various employment settings. As the individual attempts different work samples, personality characteristics and skill aptitudes can be observed to indicate vocational potential.

Curriculum-based vocational assessment offers an alternative approach to commercial tests. Schloss, Schloss, and Schloss (2007) note that curriculum-based vocational assessment is based on each student's learning needs and includes four primary characteristics.

1. It provides relevant information in the beginning stages of planning an individual's vocational program.
2. Assessment is an integral and ongoing part of a student's vocational program.
3. The person conducting curriculum-based vocational assessment is the same person responsible for the student's vocational instruction.
4. Informal and direct assessment measures are used to evaluate a student's progress throughout the vocational program.

When curriculum-based vocational assessment is used, information is available during all phases of the program (i.e., making placement decisions, working in vocational classes and jobs, and exiting the program). Also the assessment provides information for helping teachers collaborate with other professionals and make instructional or program modifications and for planning future job placements.

PEARSON
myeducationlab)

To enhance your understanding of post-school transitioning, go to the IRIS Center Resources section of the Topic Transitions in the MyEducationLab for your course and complete the Module entitled School Counselors: Facilitating Transitions for Students with Disabilities from High School to Post-School Settings.

Activities for Developing Career-Related Skills

The following activities may help develop students' career-related skills.

- Invite students who have graduated recently to return to the school to discuss their jobs or problems in leaving secondary school for college, work, or military service. Selected students can be responsible for inviting alumni and for developing appropriate questions. The graduates' discussions should include positive aspects about their careers and how they handle problems encountered on the job. If possible, interested members of the class should have the opportunity to observe the individuals actually working.

- Plan field trips to visit businesses and industries and request personnel to speak with the students. A person from the business can be invited to speak to the class before or after the visit to answer questions or distribute information. During the trip, students should have enough time to observe persons performing various jobs and to record pertinent information about the job (such as job requirements, working conditions, and good and bad features of the job). Students can share their observations in class discussions after the visit.

- Divide the class into small groups and have each obtain information on one particular job per week. During group discussion, students can determine job responsibilities, identify personal and social values met through the work, and compile a list of words used on the job.

- Have each student write a want ad for what he or she considers to be the perfect job. The ad should include information such as hours, salary, qualifications, and responsibilities. Then have students check the want-ad section of the newspaper to locate ads for jobs in their interest areas and compare these ads with their ideal ads. If appropriate, students can contact personnel directors of various businesses to find out the number of people recently hired, their salaries, and their qualifications. Also, visits may be arranged or volunteer or observation work can be set up with the business in which each student is most interested.

- Cut out several newspaper ads for available jobs. Have each student choose a job from the given ads and state why he or she would want that particular job and what preparation and qualifications are needed. Then have the student complete an application form for that job. The completed application can be reviewed for improvement.

- Role play interviews for various jobs. Discuss punctuality, appropriate dress, and questions to ask during the interview and acceptable responses. Role playing can build a student's self-confidence in an actual interview situation.

Self-Advocacy and Self-Determination Instruction

The development of self-advocacy skills can empower students to seek employment and independent living opportunities. In a literature review of self-advocacy components in transition programs for students with learning disabilities, Merchant and Gajar (1997) found that self-advocacy is most often taught through the use of role play, strategies such as I PLAN (i.e., *Inventory* your strengths, needs, goals, and choices; *Provide* your inventory information; *Listen* and respond; *Ask* questions; and *Name* your goals), and direct instruction (i.e., description of target behavior, demonstration, rehearsal, practice, feedback, and practice in a natural environment). Van Reusen, Bos, Schumaker, and Deshler (2002) provide *The Self-Advocacy Strategy for Enhancing Student Motivation and Self-Determination* for teaching adolescents to identify their strengths, develop transition goals, and advocate for themselves. Specifically, students examine and plan in the following eight transition skill areas: independent living skills, financial and consumer skills, citizenship and legal skills, community involvement skills, career and employment skills, social and family-living skills, health and wellness skills, and leisure and recreation skills. Also, to help students become self-advocates, communication skills are taught through SHARE behaviors (i.e., *Sit* up straight, *Have* a pleasant tone of voice, *Activate* your thinking, *Relax*, and *Engage* in eye communication).

Moreover, Durlak, Rose, and Bursuck (1994) note that several affective factors appear positively related to the successful postschool adjustments of adults with learning disabilities. Specifically, Durlak et al. identify self-determination skills as being important, and they examined the efficacy of directly teaching such skills to secondary students with learning disabilities. Their results indicate that these students were able to acquire, maintain, and generalize self-advocacy and self-awareness skills when the skills were taught using explicit instruction, opportunities to practice skills in the training setting and natural environment, and specific feedback. These findings have encouraging implications for developing secondary transition curricula for teaching affective skills.

One process by which teachers can promote self-regulated problem solving and enhance self-determination is through the Self-Determined Learning Model of Instruction (Wehmeyer, Palmer, Agran,

Mithaug, & Martin, 2000). The model includes three instructional phases in which students regulate their problem solving by setting goals to meet needs (i.e., What is my goal?), constructing plans to meet goals (i.e., What is my plan?), and adjusting actions to complete plans (i.e., What have I learned?). The students solve the problem in each instructional phase by answering a series of student questions that focus on identifying the problem, potential solutions to the problem, barriers to solving the problem, and consequences of each solution. In addition to enabling adolescents to attain educationally valued goals, Palmer and Wehmeyer (2003) note that the model can be used to teach students in early elementary grades to set goals and begin the process of being self-determined.

COLLEGE STUDENTS WITH SPECIAL NEEDS

Because many students with learning disabilities possess average or above intelligence and significant academic strengths in select areas, a significant number make the transition from secondary school to colleges and universities. This section presents information regarding the adjustments of college students with learning disabilities.

An increasing number of students with learning disabilities are being admitted into colleges and universities (Henderson, 2001). In a survey of 66 state universities and colleges, Spillane, McGuire, and Norlander (1992) found that the academic (e.g., grades, recommendations, and admission tests) and nonacademic

(e.g., intelligence, motivation, and independence) criteria used to admit individuals with learning disabilities to colleges are similar to the criteria used for applicants without disabilities. Section 504 of the Rehabilitation Act of 1973 and the Americans with Disabilities Act of 1990 state that no individual should be excluded on the basis of a disability. Moreover, the Individuals with Disabilities Education Act (IDEA) states that a "qualified" college person with a disability is someone who with reasonable program modifications can meet the academic requirements. Some reasonable modifications include extended time to finish the program; course substitution, modification, or waiver of a foreign language requirement; part-time study; and extended time for tests. Scott (1994) reviews guidelines for weighing accommodation requests and presents recommendations for determining appropriate academic adjustments for college students with learning disabilities.

Section 504 also states that students must identify or refer themselves and that the university must provide full program accessibility to ensure a fair chance for success. Unfortunately, many college students with learning disabilities do not reveal their learning disability until they are in an academic crisis. Suggestions for college students with learning disabilities include the following:

- Talk to your instructors before the semester begins.
- If you think that you may have a specific learning disability, contact the disabled student services office on campus.
- Maintain realistic goals and priorities for course work.

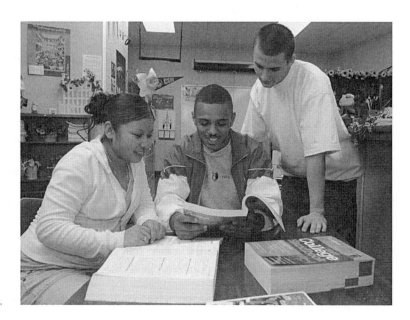

Many students with learning problems successfully make the transition from secondary school to colleges and universities. Bob Daemmrich Photography, Inc.

- Keep only one calendar with all appointments and relevant dates (i.e., assignments, tests, and project due dates) clearly marked.
- Use an audio recorder during lectures and listen to the recording as soon after class as possible to reorganize your notes.
- Seek help for any questions you may have so that they can be answered before the next test.
- Sit near the front of the classroom.
- Estimate how long a given class assignment will take to complete. Build in study breaks because fatigue is a time waster.
- Obtain a course syllabus and make sure that course expectations are clear.
- Ask for reading assignments in advance if you are using books on tape or audio files for an MP3 player.
- Use campus support services (e.g., preregistration, assistance in ordering audio books, alternative testing arrangements, specialized study aids, peer support groups, diagnostic consultation, study skills, and academic tutorial assistance).

In addition, the following selected services may help college students with learning disabilities: tutors, note-takers, audio books, proctored testing with alternative modes, audio recording, peer pairing, academic remediation, organizational skill remediation, modification in time span of program, course analysis and prescriptive scheduling, early registration, counseling (i.e., academic, vocational, and personal), lecture-pause procedure, learning strategies, social skills training, advocacy program, testing and evaluation modifications, support groups, coaching with students and faculty, and self-monitoring training.

Many studies focus on the status of college students with learning disabilities in terms of identification and intervention. Based on a review of more than 100 studies on college learning disabilities programs, Hughes and Smith (1990) provide the following conclusions and information.

- The intellectual functioning of college students with learning disabilities can be described as comparable to college students without learning disabilities.
- College students with learning disabilities score in the average or above-average range on intelligence tests.
- The reported reading levels vary widely with word-attack skills ranging from the second-grade level to college level. The average reading level for college students with learning disabilities is tenth grade.
- In studies using self-report measures, college students with learning disabilities most frequently report problems in reading comprehension, reading rate, and retaining information.
- Empirical evidence indicates that most college students with learning disabilities can identify their own skill problems accurately when compared with measured skill levels on achievement tests.
- There is a lack of consensus on which measures should be used to evaluate the skill levels of college students with learning disabilities. This presents problems in interpreting data and findings across studies.
- Many college students with learning disabilities have problems with math computation and application, as well as with more abstract areas of math such as algebra and geometry.
- Many college students with learning disabilities have severe deficits in written expression areas such as spelling, punctuation, and sentence structure.
- Learning a foreign language presents a particularly formidable task to many college students with learning disabilities.
- Few empirical studies focus on the effectiveness of particular interventions or instructional approaches for college students with learning disabilities.

Although the development of college programs for individuals with learning disabilities is receiving much attention, few efforts have been made to validate specific interventions. In an intervention study, Ruhl, Hughes, and Gajar (1990) investigated a pause procedure for enhancing the recall of facts presented through lectures with students both with and without learning disabilities. The pause procedure consisted of providing three 2-minute periods for student discussions and notetaking during a standard lecture. Results indicate that the procedure is effective for promoting short-term recall on objective tests for all the students. Ruhl et al. hypothesize that the pausing provides structure and time for extra processing of information presented in a class, and they note that this procedure is simple to implement in the college setting. In another study, Ruhl and Suritsky (1995) found that the pause procedure is more effective than a lecture outline for enhancing the immediate recall of lecture ideas and completeness of recorded notes of college students with learning disabilities.

It is hoped that higher education will respond to the needs of adults with learning disabilities. The Learning Disabilities Association of America (4156

Library Road, Pittsburgh, PA 15234) provides resources related to postsecondary education for students with learning disabilities programs. Also, *The Complete Learning Disabilities Directory* (available from Grey House Publishing) includes entries about schools, colleges, learning centers, vocational and transitional skills, and associations and organizations involved in learning disabilities.

COMMERCIAL TRANSITION EDUCATION PROGRAMS

Numerous commercial programs and materials are designed to help students make successful transitions from school to work and daily living. The following commercial programs as well as the computer software programs presented in the next section may help students develop life skills and career-related skills.

Next S.T.E.P

Next S.T.E.P—Second Edition, developed by A. S. Halpern, C. M. Herr, B. Doren, and N. K. Wolf (published by PRO-ED), is a student transition and educational planning curriculum designed to help secondary students take charge of their own transition planning process. The curriculum contains 16 lessons through which students select and implement a variety of goals that relate to jobs, education and training, personal life, and living on their own. Students develop their own individualized transition plans, and the ultimate goal of the curriculum is to help students assume responsibility for important life decisions with support from teachers and parents. An instructional videotape is included as well as a manual with useful suggestions on using the curriculum successfully.

Steps to Self-Determination

Steps to Self-Determination—Second Edition, developed by A. Hoffman and S. Field (published by PRO-ED), is a 16-session curriculum designed to help secondary students learn to define and achieve important goals. The curriculum addresses five main elements of self-determination: know yourself, value yourself, plan, act and experience outcomes, and learn. Areas included are identifying strengths, weaknesses, needs and preferences; developing decision-making skills; identifying rights and responsibilities; goal setting; anticipating consequences; enhancing creativity; developing communication skills; accessing resources and support; developing negotiation skills; and experiencing and learning from outcomes. The curriculum emphasizes actively setting and working toward goals. In addition to an instructor guide with detailed lesson plans, a CD-ROM contains a student activity book and the *Self-Determination Knowledge Scale,* which provides a pretest and posttest for the curriculum.

COMPUTER SOFTWARE PROGRAMS IN TRANSITION EDUCATION

Computer software programs can facilitate the transition from school to employment or community life by helping students develop career-related skills and functional living skills. In addition, students who use computers in transition programs increase their technological skills and are better prepared for technologically advanced workplaces. The National Center on Education and the Economy (2007) reports that technology in the workplace is changing rapidly and, thus, employees must possess advanced skills to maintain employment. Dettmar (2007) suggests that technology can be embedded into academics so that students exit high school with the technology skills necessary in the workplace. Technologies such as interactive white boards, smart pens, text messaging, and general computer use enhance transition programs. Computer programs also can provide helpful information on career options.

Independent Living Learning Package

The *Independent Living Learning Package* (produced by Impact Publications) is designed to help students in high school through adult age learn important independent living skills. Eight programs are included: *Banking: Credit and Loans* (e.g., establishing credit and applying for loans), *Banking: Checking and Savings* (e.g., terms and procedures of opening accounts), *Skills for Buying a Car* (e.g., negotiating techniques, insurance, and responsibilities), *This Apartment's for You* (e.g., terms, leases, options, costs, and price), *On Your Own* (e.g., paying bills on time, cleaning, and budgeting), *Life Skills for the Telephone* (e.g., using the phonebook, types of calls, and area codes), *Getting Around in Today's World* (e.g., maps, time management, and mass transportation), and *Consumer Shopping* (e.g., making decisions by reading labels and comparison shopping). Also included are competency requirements, a video, student activity worksheets, and assessment checklists.

Job Readiness Skills Series

The *Job Readiness Skills Series* (produced by Impact Publications) provides high school students and adults with interactive lessons on job readiness and employability skills in the areas of *Career Goals, Job Applications, Good Appearance, Finding a Job, Interviews, Communication, Resumes, Positive Attitudes,* and *Written Communication.* Each CD-ROM provides individualized instruction as well as internet links to expand learning experiences. Student activities can be printed or completed on the screen, and the program includes management capabilities for the teacher.

Scope and Sequence Skills Lists

READING SCOPE AND SEQUENCE SKILLS LIST

KINDERGARTEN

Emergent Literacy

Participates and listens during reading situations.

Joins in to read refrains in predictable pattern books.

Develops a repertoire of favorite books, poems, rhymes, and songs.

Chooses books as a free-time activity.

Engages in talk about books and stories.

Uses book language while pretending to read.

Demonstrates awareness that print conveys meaning by trying to read.

Understands concepts about books such as knowing the front and back of a book, turning pages correctly, and using pictures as cues to meaning.

Understands concepts about print such as knowing left-to-right and top-to-bottom directionality and pointing to words one-to-one as teacher reads.

Understands difference between a letter and a word.

Knows where to begin reading.

Knows letters of own name and some letters in environment.

Recognizes own name in print.

Discusses meaning of stories.

Responds to texts in a variety of ways (orally, artistically, and dramatically).

Recounts through retelling details, events, and ideas and concepts from familiar stories, other literary materials, and informational texts.

Reads own dictated stories, pretends to read predictable pattern books, and reads some environmental print.

GRADE 1

Word Attack

Relates spoken sounds to written symbols.

Recognizes all initial and final consonant sounds (single sounds and blends up to first vowel in word).

Identifies likenesses and differences in sounds and structure of words.

Names the letter of the alphabet for single sounds heard.

Recognizes short vowels in one-syllable words and substitutes different vowels to form new words (*bad*: substitute *e* = *bed*).

Substitutes initial consonant to form new words.

Substitutes final consonant to form new words.

Recognizes long vowels in words ending in silent *e*.

Identifies rhyming words; decodes words with same phonogram/phonemic pattern (*at, cat, bat*).

Recognizes endings: *-s, -es, -ed, -ing.*

Identifies compound words (*football*).

Predicts and self-corrects using initial letter, final letter, and letter clusters.

Uses context clues to read words within own experience.

Comprehension

Relates printed words to objects or actions.

Follows printed directions (*Find the boy's house.*).

Reads to find information.

Relates reading to personal experiences before, during, and after reading.

Draws conclusions from given facts (*What do you think happened then?*).

Recalls main ideas of what has been read aloud.

Recalls details in story.

Arranges increasing numbers of events in sequence.

Uses pictures and context clues for meaning.

Uses commas, end punctuation, and quotation marks as clues to meaning.

Identifies main characters and settings.

Makes comments and asks questions that indicate involvement with characters and story line.

Predicts events in a story.

Relates causes and effects.

Describes characters' feelings.

Discusses feelings evoked by stories.

Tells whether story is factual or fanciful (true to life or make-believe).

GRADE 2

Word Attack

Produces the consonant blends in isolation: *bl, br, cl, cr, dr, dw, fr, fl, gl, gr, mp, nd, pl, pr, qu, sc, sl, st, str, sw, scr, sm, sn, sp, spl, squ, sk, spr, tr, tw, thr, -nt, -nk, -st.*

Decodes words with consonant blends.

Substitutes initial consonant blends to form other words.

Identifies forms and sounds of consonant digraphs in initial position: *sh-, ch-, ph-, th-, wh-.*

Identifies forms and sounds of consonant digraphs in final position: -sh, -ch, -gh, -ng, -ph, -th, -sh.

Decodes four- and five-letter words that have regular short-vowel sounds.

Decodes words in which the vowels are long.

Decodes words with final consonant blends.

Decodes words ending in vowel-consonant plus silent e (make, smoke, bone).

Decodes consonant variants (s—has, see; g—garden, large; c—music, ice).

Decodes long e and i sound of y.

Decodes vowel diphthongs: oi, oy, ou, ow, ew.

Decodes words in which vowel is controlled by r (far, fur, bar, more).

Forms compound word with two known words (baseball).

Identifies root/base words in inflected forms of known words (helpful, help; darkness, dark; unhappy, happy; recall, call).

Decodes words in which final silent e is dropped before adding ending (smoke, smoking).

Identifies sounds and forms of consonant digraphs in medial position (wishing).

Decodes vowel digraphs/vowel teams: oa, ai, ay, ee, ea, ie, ei.

Identifies sounds of a followed by l, w, or u.

Decode suffixes (-less, -ful, -ness, -er, -est, -ly).

Decodes prefixes (un-, re-, dis-, pre-, pro-, ex-, en-).

Identifies multiple sounds of long a (ei, weigh; ai, straight; ay, day; ey, they).

Decodes words with vowel digraph/vowel team irregularities (bread, heart).

Recognizes and knows meaning of contractions with one-letter omission.

Identifies plural endings, irregular plurals, and 's possessives.

Searches, predicts, monitors, and cross-checks using semantic, syntactic, pragmatic, and graphophonic cues independently.

Experiments to see what makes sense and makes a second attempt if words or phrases do not sound right or make sense.

Comprehension

Skims for information.

Reads to answer questions who, when, where, how, and what.

Makes judgments from given facts.

Draws conclusions, answering such questions as "What do you think happened next?"

Begins to use contextual clues to determine meaning of a new word.

Interprets simple figurative expressions.

Interprets feelings of characters in stories.

Recognizes the stereotyping of people in stories.

Retells characters, events, setting, problem, and solution.

Uses pragmatics to construct meaning (prior knowledge and context of situation).

GRADE 3

Word Attack

Uses phonetic clues to recognize words.

Identifies the beginning, middle, and ending sounds of each word given orally.

Recognizes silent vowels in words.

Uses consonant digraphs as an aid to word attack.

Identifies diphthongs (ou, ow, oi, oy) and pronounces words containing diphthongs.

Knows when to double the final consonant before adding -ing.

Uses vowel digraphs correctly.

Reads unfamiliar words that contain r-controlled vowels.

Reads root words and recognizes prefixes and suffixes (er, est, ing, ed, es, ly, un, re, less).

Decodes silent k in kn (know).

Decodes silent gh (through).

Decodes words ending in -ed (ed, crooked; t, looked).

Decodes dg (edge).

Divides two-syllable words.

Recognizes contractions.

Recognizes the use of the apostrophe to show ownership.

Hyphenates words using syllable rules.

Recognizes the meanings of words used in different contexts.

Selects the meaning that fits best according to the context in which the word is used.

Perseveres and problem solves when the reading task becomes difficult.

Focuses on details of print only when meaning is lost.

Comprehension

Finds main idea.

Selects facts to support main idea, lesson, theme, or moral in a variety of prose (fairy tales, tall tales, fables, legends, and myths).

Draws logical conclusions.

Reads literacy, informational, and practical materials for a variety of purposes.

Reads for a definite purpose: to enjoy, to obtain answers, and to obtain a general idea of content.

Recognizes shifts of meaning caused by using words in different contexts.

Answers specific questions about material read.

Follows written directions.

Interprets descriptive words and phrases.

Selects an appropriate title after reading an untitled selection.

Composes own questions about material read.

Makes inferences about material read.

Distinguishes between fact and opinion.

Recognizes structure of plot (summarizes sequence of events).

Recognizes that characters change as a story develops.

Identifies relationships among characters in a story.

Compares similar elements in different stories.

GRADE 4

Word Attack

Uses phonetic clues to accent unfamiliar words correctly.

Uses dictionary as an aid to attacking and pronouncing new words.

Identifies and defines prefixes and suffixes.

Reads synonyms, antonyms, and homonyms correctly at independent reading level.

Recognizes and uses words that signal relationships (*and, or, except, still, but, furthermore, especially, in this way, such as, on the other hand*).

Comprehension

Summarizes main ideas and selects facts to support main ideas.

Identifies the subtopics of a selection.

Finds factual and inferential information in answer to questions.

Compares or contrasts selections.

Compares information from different sources.

Interprets literal and figurative language.

Selects the meaning of a specific word when the meaning is implied but not stated.

Predicts possible endings based on previous events in an unfinished selection.

Recognizes theme of story.

Describes times, places, characters, and sequence of action in a story.

GRADE 5

Word Attack

Applies phonetic principles and structural analysis skills in combination with context clues to read unfamiliar words.

Uses context clues to derive meaning from unfamiliar words.

Uses phonetic clues to accent unfamiliar words correctly.

Comprehension

Investigates facts.

Identifies and recalls story facts and significant details.

Infers a character's appearance, moods, feelings, traits, and motives.

Recognizes large thought divisions within an expository work including parts, chapters, sections, acts, and scenes.

Distinguishes between good and poor summaries.

Identifies the point of view in a selection.

Analyzes a story in terms of who acted, what action was taken, and what resulted from the action.

Cites examples of one good and one bad quality of a character treated in a biography.

Recognizes structure of plot and identifies conflict or problems.

Identifies influence of setting on characters and events.

GRADE 6

Word Attack

Uses a repertoire of word-attack skills.

Uses root words, prefixes, and suffixes to derive the meaning of words.

Comprehension

Compares reading selections as to suitability for a given purpose (dramatization, reading to others, or inclusion in a bibliography).

Recognizes elements of characterization (presentation of the characters, completeness of characters, function of the characters, and relationships with other characters).

Recognizes transitional paragraphs that connect chapters, sections, and episodes.

Proves a point with factual information from the reading selections.

Interprets colloquial and figurative expressions.

Describes the rising action, climax, and falling action in a story.

Summarizes the main conflict in a story, giving the underlying causes of the conflict and the events that contributed to the conflict.

Identifies the mood of a selection and the words or phrases that establish the mood.

Identifies the basic elements of a news story (who, what, where, when, why, and how).

Analyzes and describes the point of view in an editorial.

SPELLING SCOPE AND SEQUENCE SKILLS LIST

Many spelling skills are repeated at each grade level. However, the difficulty level of the words that the spelling skill applies to increases with grade level. **Boldface type denotes** the initial introduction of a specific skill.

GRADE 1

Uses temporary spelling that generally can be read by others.
Spells two- and three-letter words.
Spells own first and last name correctly.

GRADE 2

Spells Consonant Sounds Correctly:

regular consonants (*bed, hat, sun, yes*)
sh, ch, ng, wh, and *th* (*fish, much, sing, which, this, with*)
x spelling of *ks* (*box, fox*)
c spelling of *k* (*cold*)
c and k (*cat, kept*)
ck (*duck, black*)
s spelling of *s* and *z* (*sun, as*)
consonant blends (*flag*)
silent consonants (*doll, hill, who, know, would*)

Spells Vowel Sounds Correctly:

short vowel in initial or medial position (*am, did*)
long vowel spelled by a single vowel (*go, be*)
two vowels together (*meat, rain*)
vowel-consonant-silent *e* (*home, ride*)
ow spelling of long *o* (*snow, grow*)
ay spelling of long *a* (*day, play*)
final *y* spelling of long *e* (*baby, very*)
final *y* spelling of long *i* (*my, why*)
oo spelling of *u* and *ŭ* (*good, soon*)
ow and *ou* spellings of the *ou* sound in *owl* and *mouse* (*down, house*)
oy spelling of the *oi* sound (*boy, toy*)
vowel sounds before *r*
the *er* spelling of *r* at the end (*over, teacher*)
er, ir, or, and *ur* spellings of *er* (*her, bird, work, hurt*)
the *or* and *ar* spelling of *ôr* (*for*)
the *ar* spelling of *är* (*car*)
unexpected single-vowel spellings (*from, off, cold*)
unexpected vowel-consonant-silent *e* (*give, done*)
unexpected spellings with two vowels together (*been, said*)
other unexpected vowel spellings (*they, are*)

Uses Morphemes to Make Structural Changes:

s plural (*cats, cows*)
s or *es* for third-person singular (*live, lives*)
s to show possession (*yours, ours*)
d or *ed* ending for past tense (*played*)
ing ending (*blowing*)
er noun agent ending (*singer, player*)
er and *est* endings (*old, older, oldest*)

Uses Devices to Aid Spelling Recall:

syllabication (*yel low, go ing*)
recognizing compounds (*today*)
recognizing rhyming words (*pet, get*)

Spells Selected Words Correctly:

simple homonyms (*to, two, too*)

GRADE 3

Spells Consonant Sounds Correctly:

regular consonants (*must, trip, ask, zoo*)
sh, ch, ng, wh, and *th* (*shoe, child, sang, while, those, thank*)
nk (*drunk, drank*)
x (*next*)
c spelling of *k* (*cup*)
c and *k* (*ask, cake*)
ck (*chicken, clock*)
s spelling of *s* and *z* (*gas, has*)
gh spelling of *f* (*laugh*)
consonant blends (*twin*)
silent consonants (*bell, grass, walk, catch, wrote, night*)

Spells Vowel Sounds Correctly:

short vowel in initial or medial position (*bad, send, stop*)

long vowel
   single vowel in open syllables (*paper, table*)
   two vowels together (*soap, cream, train*)
   vowel-consonant-silent *e* (*game, side, snake*)
   ow spelling of long *o* (*window*)
   ay spelling of long *a* (*always, yesterday*)
   final *y* spelling of long *e* (*city, study, sorry*)
   final *y* spelling of long *i* (*cry, try*)
oo spelling of *u* and *ŭ* (*cook, shoot*)
ow and *ou* spellings of the *ou* sound in *owl* and *mouse* (*flower, ground*)
vowel sounds before *r*
   the *er* spelling of *r* at the end (*ever, another*)
   the *or* spelling of *r* at the end (*color*)
   er, ir, or, and *ur* spellings of *er* (*person, third, word, turning*)
   the *or* and *ar* spelling of *ôr* (*horse, warm*)
   the *ar* spelling of *är* (*star, party*)
unexpected single vowels (*kind, full, cost*)
unexpected vowel-consonant-silent *e* (*whose, sure*)
unexpected spellings with two vowels together (*bread, great, friend*)
other unexpected vowel spellings (*aunt, says, could*)
le spelling of the *el* sound (*people, table*)

Uses Morphemes to Make Structural Changes:

s or *es* plural (*cups, buses, dishes*)
changing *y* to *i* before *es* (*cry, cries*)
s or *es* for third-person singular (*jumps, races, misses*)
d or *ed* ending for past tense (*asked, laughed*)
ing ending (*reading, thinking*)
ing ending with doubled consonant (*clapping, beginning*)
ing ending with dropped silent *e* (*skating, moving*)
er noun agent ending (*painter, builder*)
er and *est* endings (*high, higher, highest*)

Uses Devices to Aid Spelling Recall:

syllabication (*bas ket, ta ble*)
recognizing compounds (*airplane, something*)
recognizing rhyming words (*hand, land*)

Spells Selected Words Correctly:

homonyms (*its—it's; eight—ate*)

Uses Dictionary Skills:

alphabetizing—sequencing of words in alphabetical order

GRADE 4

Spells Consonant Phonemes Correctly:

sh, ch, and *ng* (*ship, rich, hang*)
voiced and unvoiced *th* (*bath, those*)
ch spelling of *k* (*schoolhouse*)
wh spelling of *hw* (*wheel*)
g spelling of *g* or *j* (*frog, bridge*)
c spelling of *k* or *s* (*cage, circus*)
ck spelling of *k* (*luck*)
x spelling of *ks* (*fix*)

qu spelling of *kw* (*queen*)
nk spelling of *ngk* (*monkey*)
ph spelling of *f* (*elephant*)
consonant blends (*brain*)
silent consonants (*answer*)

Spells Vowel Phonemes Correctly:

short medial vowel (*cap*)
long sound spelled with vowel-consonant-silent *e* (*bone*)
long sound spelled with two vowels (*tie*)
long sound spelled in open syllables (*hotel*)
vowels before *r* (*fur, born*)
ou and *ow* spellings of *ou* (*count, cowboy*)
ow spelling of the ŏ sound (*unknown*)
oo spelling of the *u* and *ŭ* sounds (*hook, stood*)
oi and *oy* spellings of *oi* (*noise, enjoy*)
o, al, au, and *aw* spellings of *ô* (*north, tall*)
əl and *l* (*castle, jungle*)
y spelling of long *e* (*busy*)

Uses Morphemes to Make Structural Changes:

d and *ed* ending (*recalled, untied*)
s and *es* ending (*socks, chimneys, churches*)
irregular plurals (*feet*)
doubling a final consonant before *ing* (*stepping*)
dropping final silent *e* before *ing* (*trading*)
er and *est* endings (*paler, palest*)
ly ending (*finally*)
changing *y* to *i* before *es* (*bodies*)
ing ending (*interesting*)
number suffixes (*fifteen, fifty*)
suffixes to change part of speech (*kindness, playful, friendly*)
prefixes to change meaning (*unlock, exchange, replace, promote*)

Uses Devices to Aid Spelling Recall:

syllable divisions (*bot tom, ho tel, cab in*)
unexpected spellings (*minute*)
compounds (*upstairs, watermelon*)

Spells Selected Words:

homonyms (*whole—hole; hymn—him*)
contractions (*aren't*)
months (*February*)

Uses Dictionary Skills:

using guide words—recognition of words grouped by alphabetical similarities

GRADE 5

Spells Consonant Phonemes Correctly:

sh, ch, and *ng* (*shade, chest, among*)
voiced and unvoiced *th* (*sixth, either*)
ch spelling of *k* (*echo*)
wh spelling of *hw* (*whistle*)
g spelling of *g* or *j* (*gate, damage*)
c spelling of *k* or *s* (*cook, princess*)

ck spelling of *k* (*attack*)
x spelling of *ks* (*expect*)
qu spelling of *kw* (*quarter*)
nk spelling of *ngk* (*trunk*)
silent consonants (*ghost*)

Spells Vowel Phonemes Correctly:

short medial vowels (*bunch*)
vowel-consonant-silent *e* (*prize*)
various spellings before *r* (*term, artist*)
ou and *ow* spellings of *ou* (*outfit, shower*)
ow spelling of long *o* (*crow*)
oo spelling of the *u* and *ŭ* sounds (*loose, choosing*)
oi and *oy* spellings of *oi* (*join, voice*)
o, al, au, and *aw* spellings of *o* (*crawl, chalk*)
spellings of el and l (*model, central*)
y spelling of long *e* (*worry, crazy*)

Uses Morphemes to Make Structural Changes:

d or *ed* ending (*excited, earned*)
s or *es* ending (*beads, beaches*)
doubling final consonant before *ing* (*chopping, snapping*)
dropping final silent *e* before *ing* (*ruling, shaking*)
number suffixes (*thirteen, sixty*)

Spells Selected Words:

contractions (*they're*)

Uses Dictionary Skills:

locating words in a dictionary—ability to find words of uncertain spelling in a dictionary

GRADE 6

Spells Consonant Phonemes Correctly:

sh, ch, and *ng* consonants (*shelf, chain, gang*)
voiced and unvoiced *th* (*thread, leather*)
ch spelling of *k* (*orchestra*)
wh spelling of *hw* (*whale*)
g spelling of *g* or *j* (*cigar, pledge*)
c spelling of *k* or *s* (*cabbage, voice*)
ck spelling of *k* (*ticket*)
x spelling of *ks* (*expedition*)
qu spelling of *kw* (*acquaint*)
nk spelling of *ngk* (*plank*)
ph spelling of *f* (*alphabet*)

Spells Vowel Phonemes Correctly:

long sound with two vowels (*coach*)
long sound in open syllables (*soda*)
various spellings before *r* (*stairs, skirt*)
ou and *ow* spellings of *ou* (*growl, surround*)
ow spelling of long *o* (*narrow*)
oo spelling of *u* and *ŭ* (*bloom, shook*)
oi and *oy* spellings of *oi* (*spoil, voyage*)
o, al, au, and *aw* spelling of *ô* (*author, naughty*)
əl and l sounds (*carnival, barrel*)

Uses Morphemes to Make Structural Changes:

changing *y* to *i* before *es* (*pantries, colonies*)
forming plurals of nouns that end in *o* (*pianos, potatoes*)
ing ending (*stretching*)
er and *est* endings (*tinier, tiniest*)
ly ending (*dreadfully, especially*)
suffixes and prefixes (*harmless, attractive, dishonest, incorrect*)
d or *ed* ending (*continued, contracted*)
s or *es* ending (*insects, sandwiches*)
irregular plurals (*calves, geese*)

Uses Dictionary Skills:

locating appropriate word meaning—awareness and selection of multiple word meanings and appropriate word usage

GRADE 7 AND ABOVE

Spells Selected Words:

hyphenated words (*tongue-tied*)
silent letters—*b, h, m, g, p* (*pneumonia*)
letter combinations: *-ient, -ian, -ium, -iasm, -iable, -ure* (*transient, enthusiasm*)
word endings: *-ance, -ence, -ense, -ogy, -cede, -ceed* (*biology, ignorance*)

Uses Dictionary Skills:

understanding pronunciation marks—ability to interpret diacritical markings

HANDWRITING SCOPE AND SEQUENCE SKILLS LIST

Many handwriting skills are emphasized at more than one grade level. **Boldface type denotes a skill that has not been emphasized at a previous grade level.**

KINDERGARTEN

Begins to establish a preference for either left- or right-handedness.
Voluntarily draws, paints, and scribbles.
Develops small-muscle control through the use of materials such as finger painting, clay, weaving, and puzzles.
Uses tools of writing in making letters, writing names, or attempting to write words.
Understands and applies writing readiness vocabulary given orally, such as left/right, top/bottom, beginning/end, large/small, circle, space, around, across, curve, top line, dotted line, and bottom line.
Begins to establish correct writing position of body, arms, hand, paper, and pencil.
Draws familiar objects using the basic strokes of manuscript writing.
Recognizes and legibly writes own name in manuscript letters using uppercase and lowercase letters appropriately.
Uses writing paper that is standard for manuscript writing.

GRADE 1

Establishes a preference for either left- or right-handedness.
Understands and applies writing readiness vocabulary given orally, such as left/right, top/bottom, beginning/end, large/small, circle, space, around, across, curve, top line, dotted line, and bottom line.
Draws familiar objects using the basic strokes of manuscript writing.
Begins manuscript writing using both lowercase and uppercase letters introduced to correlate with the child's reading program.
Writes at a desk with correct posture, pencil grip, and paper position; works from left to right; and forms letters in the correct direction.
Uses writing paper that is standard for manuscript writing.
Copies words neatly from near position.
Writes with firm strokes and demonstrates good spacing between letters, words, and sentences.
Writes manuscript letters independently and with firm strokes.
Writes clear, legible manuscript letters at a rate appropriate for ability.
Arranges work neatly and pleasingly on a page (i.e., uses margins and paragraph indentions and makes clean erasures).

GRADE 2

Establishes a preference for either left- or right-handedness.
Uses correct writing position of body, arm, hand, paper, and pencil.
Writes with firm strokes and demonstrates good spacing between letters, words, and sentences.
Writes clear, legible manuscript letters at a rate appropriate for ability.
Arranges work neatly and pleasingly on a page (i.e., uses margins and paragraph indentions and makes clean erasures).
Evaluates writing using a plastic overlay and identifies strengths and weaknesses.
Writes all letters of the alphabet in manuscript from memory.
Recognizes the differences in using manuscript and cursive writing.
Reads simple sentences written in cursive writing on the chalkboard.
Demonstrates physical coordination to proceed to simple cursive writing.

GRADE 3

Uses correct writing position of body, arm, hand, paper, and pencil.
Uses writing paper that is standard for manuscript writing.
Evaluates writing using a plastic overlay and identifies strengths and weaknesses.
Writes with firm strokes and demonstrates good spacing between letters, words, and sentences.

Arranges work neatly and pleasingly on a page (i.e., uses margins and paragraph indentions and makes clean erasures).

Demonstrates ability to decode cursive writing by reading paragraphs of cursive writing both from the chalkboard and from paper.

Identifies cursive lowercase and uppercase letters by matching cursive letters to manuscript letters.

Begins cursive writing with lowercase letters and progresses to uppercase letters as needed.

Uses writing paper that is standard for cursive writing.

Writes all letters of the cursive alphabet using proper techniques in making each letter.

Recognizes the proper joining of letters to form words.

Writes from memory all letters of the alphabet in cursive form.

GRADE 4

Uses correct writing position of body, arm, hand, paper, and pencil.

Evaluates writing using a plastic overlay and identifies strengths and weaknesses.

Writes with firm strokes and demonstrates good spacing between letters, words, and sentences.

Arranges work neatly and pleasingly on a page (i.e., uses margins and paragraph indentions and makes clean erasures).

Uses writing paper that is standard for cursive writing.

Slants and joins the letters in a word and controls spacing between letters.

Uses cursive writing for day-to-day use.

Begins to write with a pen if pencil writing is smooth, fluent, and neat.

Maintains and uses manuscript writing for special needs, such as preparing charts, maps, and labels.

Writes clear, legible cursive letters at a rate appropriate for ability.

GRADE 5

Uses correct writing position of body, arm, hand, paper, and pencil.

Evaluates writing using a plastic overlay and identifies strengths and weaknesses.

Writes with firm strokes and demonstrates good spacing between letters, words, and sentences.

Arranges work neatly and pleasingly on a page (i.e., uses margins and paragraph indentions and makes clean erasures).

Uses cursive writing for day-to-day use.

Begins to write with a pen if pencil writing is smooth, fluent, and neat.

Writes clear, legible cursive letters at a rate appropriate for ability.

Maintains and uses manuscript writing for special needs, such as preparing charts, maps, and labels.

Reduces size of writing to "adult" proportions of letters (i.e., one-quarter space for minimum letters, one-half space for intermediate letters, and three-quarters space for tall lowercase and uppercase letters).

Takes pride in presenting neat work.

GRADE 6

Uses correct writing position of body, arm, hand, paper, and pencil.

Evaluates writing using a plastic overlay and identifies strengths and weaknesses.

Writes with firm strokes and demonstrates good spacing between letters, words, and sentences.

Arranges work neatly and pleasingly on a page (i.e., uses margins and paragraph indentions and makes clean erasures).

Uses cursive writing for day-to-day use.

Begins to write with a pen if pencil writing is smooth, fluent, and neat.

Maintains and uses manuscript writing for special needs, such as preparing charts, maps, and labels.

Reduces size of writing to "adult" proportions of letters (i.e., one-quarter space for minimum letters, one-half space for intermediate letters, and three-quarters space for tall lowercase and uppercase letters).

Writes clear, legible cursive letters at a rate appropriate for ability.

Customarily presents neat work.

Evaluates own progress in the basic handwriting skills pertaining to size, slant, shape, spacing, and alignment.

WRITTEN EXPRESSION SCOPE AND SEQUENCE SKILLS LIST

KINDERGARTEN

Understands that writing conveys meaning.

Retells story or experience using pictures or letter strings.

Dictates experience stories.

Creates pictures for own dictated stories.

Draws a picture and then adds words (using invented spelling) about the picture.

GRADE 1

Capitalization and Punctuation

Copies sentences correctly.

Capitalizes first word of a sentence.

Capitalizes first letter of a proper name.

Uses period at the end of a sentence.

Uses question mark after a written question.

Uses period after numbers in a list.

Written Composition

Arranges scrambled words in correct sentence order.

Writes answers to simple questions.

Dictates thoughts to scribe and does copy work.

Suggests titles for dictated stories.

Forms sentences in dictating and in writing.

Writes own name and address without using a model.
Writes from both personal experience and imagination.
Writes given sentences from dictation.
Writes phrases that describe location.

Creative Expression

Uses prewriting strategies such as drawing, brainstorming, or storyboarding with support.
Dictates and begins to write captions and comments about pictures.
Writes group poems.
Writes riddles, songs, or poems.
Creates make-believe stories.
Shows increasing selectivity in choice of words to convey meanings effectively.

GRADE 2

Capitalization and Punctuation

Capitalizes titles of compositions.
Capitalizes proper names used in written compositions.
Uses comma after salutation and after closing of a friendly letter.
Uses comma between day of the month and the year.
Uses comma between names of city and state.

Written Composition

Recognizes kinds of sentences—statement and question.
Writes a paragraph of three to five sentences in accordance with specified criteria: relate to topic, capitalize first word of each sentence, use correct end punctuation, and indent first line.
Supplies titles for sentence groups.
Writes given sentences from dictation.
Copies sentences correctly.

Creative Expression

Can retell a story.
Continues and expands prewriting strategies such as drawing, brainstorming, or storyboarding.
Responds to sensory stimuli with descriptive words.
Uses a variety of descriptive words or phrases.
Writes imaginative stories in which ideas and feelings are expressed.
Draws pictures to express a theme, to inform, or to persuade.
Writes in a logical sequence including beginning, middle, and end.

GRADE 3

Capitalization and Punctuation

Capitalizes correctly the names of months, days, and holidays; first word in a line of verse; titles of books, stories, and poems; salutation and closing of letters and notes; and names of special places.
Begins to apply correct punctuation for abbreviations, initials, contractions, items in a list, quotations, questions, and exclamations.
Uses proper indention for paragraphs.

Written Composition

Gives written explanations using careful selection, relevant details, and sequential order.
Begins to proofread for accuracy and to do occasional revising.
Writes simple thank-you notes using correct form.
Builds ideas into paragraphs.
Uses a variety of sentences.
Combines short, choppy sentences into longer ones.
Avoids run-on sentences.
Keeps to one idea.
Correctly sequences ideas in sentences.
Finds and deletes sentences that do not belong in a paragraph.

Creative Expression

Demonstrates and uses prewriting strategies (drawing, brainstorming, webbing, and storyboarding).
Writes imaginative stories—imagines how others feel or how he or she might feel in another situation.
Uses a variety of words to express action, mood, sound, and feeling.
Writes original poetry.
Writes interesting dialogue.

GRADE 4

Capitalization and Punctuation

Capitalizes correctly in the following areas: proper nouns, first word of poetry line, principal words in titles, common and proper nouns, and seasons as common nouns.
Uses commas correctly in the following areas: after introductory adverbial clause, to set off interjections, to separate items in a series, to separate coordinate clauses, to set off words in direct address, and after salutation.
Uses periods correctly after declarative sentences.
Uses apostrophes correctly to show possession.

Written Composition

Makes simple outline with main ideas.
Proofreads for accuracy in writing.
Uses correct form and mechanics in writing invitations and business letters.
Compiles a list of books read, including the title and author of the books and their subjects.
Writes a paragraph defining a term, using an example.

Creative Expression

Writes descriptions of people, places, and events.
Writes narrative paragraphs in which events are presented chronologically.
Writes a story including characters, setting, and plot.
Distinguishes between imaginative and factual description.
Writes a brief story in response to a picture.

GRADE 5

Capitalization and Punctuation

Capitalizes correctly in the following areas: first word of poetry line, first word of direct quotation, seasons as common nouns, and ordinary position titles (not capitalized).

Uses commas correctly in the following areas: after introductory phrases, to set off nonrestrictive clauses, in addresses, in dates, to separate subordinate clause from main clause, to set off appositives, to set off parenthetical elements, and to separate quotations from rest of sentence.

Uses periods correctly.

Uses colons after introductory lines.

Uses apostrophes correctly in contractions and to show possession, and not in possessive pronouns.

Uses quotation marks correctly in direct quotations.

Uses hyphens in compound numbers.

Uses semicolons correctly with coordinate clauses.

Written Composition

Uses a variety of sentences—declarative, interrogative, exclamatory, and imperative.

Uses compound subjects and compound predicates.

Consistently uses transitions (e.g., *as a result of* and *in addition*).

Writes a paragraph from an outline.

Begins to organize writing by sticking to one subject and striving for a continuous thought flow.

Produces a factual report from notes and an outline.

Outlines main ideas (I, II, III) and subordinate ideas (A, B, C).

Edits writing for errors in spelling, capitalization, punctuation, and usage.

Writes a paragraph that contains a topic sentence based upon a fact and supports that fact with at least three additional facts.

Creative Expression

Records and expands sensory images, observations, memories, opinions, and individual impressions.

Writes patterned and free verse.

Develops a story plot including at least two characters, a challenge or a struggle, and a climax that results from events that prepare the reader.

Writes short scripts based on stories read by the group.

GRADE 6

Capitalization and Punctuation

Capitalizes names of outline divisions.

Writes correctly punctuated dialogue.

Correctly punctuates dictated paragraphs.

Uses underlining and quotation marks correctly for titles.

Edits own writing for correct spelling, punctuation, capitalization, and usage.

Written Composition

Develops concise statements by avoiding wordiness.

Uses complex sentences.

Checks paragraphs for accurate statements.

Uses transition words to connect ideas.

Shows improvement in complete composition—introduction, development, and conclusion.

Writes from point of view that is consistent with the intention.

Plans carefully before beginning to write and revises periodically.

Edits all writing to be read by another person and revises it in accordance with accepted mechanics of writing.

Writes a well-constructed paragraph (topic sentence, supporting details, and conclusion).

Writes a newspaper story from given facts.

Narrows topics for reports.

Writes a paragraph of comparison and contrast.

Uses correct form for business letters.

Creative Expression

Uses figurative language—similes and metaphors.

Writes descriptions and narratives.

Writes a variety of prose and verse based on personal experience.

Writes a variety of short fiction—tall tales, fables, mysteries, and adventure stories.

Describes a character by including details (the way the character looks, behaves, dresses, or speaks).

Writes original scripts to be produced by groups in the class.

MATH SCOPE AND SEQUENCE SKILLS LIST BY SKILL AREA[1]

ADDITION HIERARCHY

Recognizes inequalities of numbers less than 10.

Understands seriation of numbers less than 10.

Recognizes the words *addend* and *sum*.

Understands the "+" sign.

Computes sums less than 10 (memorize).

Understands place value of ones and tens.

Computes sums 10 to 18, both addends less than 10 (memorize).

Computes 2D + 1D without regrouping.

Computes 2D + 2D without regrouping.

Understands place value concerning regrouping tens and ones.

Computes 2D + 1D with regrouping.

Computes 2D + 2D with regrouping.

Computes 2D + 2D + 2D with sums of ones greater than 20.

Understands place value of hundreds, tens, and ones.

Computes 3D + 3D without regrouping.

Understands place value concerning regrouping hundreds and tens.

Computes 3D + 3D with regrouping.

Estimates sums.

SUBTRACTION HIERARCHY

Finds missing addends (e.g., 4 + ___ = 9).

Understands the "−" sign.

Uses set separation as model for subtraction.

[1]Key:

1D = one-digit number	< = less than
2D = two-digit number	> = more than
3D = three-digit number	≤ = less than or equal to

Expresses a related addition statement in subtraction form (e.g., addend + addend = sum ⟷ sum − addend = addend).

Relates the words *minuend, subtrahend,* and *difference* to *sum, given addend,* and *missing addend.*

Memorizes basic subtraction facts 0 to 9.

Understands place value of ones and tens.

Memorizes basic subtraction facts 0 to 18.

Names the difference between a two-place whole number (2D) and a one-place whole number (1D) (not a basic fact and no regrouping).

Names the difference between 2D and 2D with no regrouping.

Names the difference between 3D and 2D with no regrouping.

Names the difference between 3D and 3D with no regrouping.

Names the difference between two many-digit whole numbers with no regrouping.

Names the difference between 2D and 1D (not a basic fact) with regrouping.

Names the difference between 2D and 2D with regrouping from tens to ones.

Names the difference between 3D and 2D with regrouping from tens to ones.

Names the difference between 3D and 2D with double regrouping.

Names the difference between 3D and 3D with single regrouping.

Names the difference between 3D and 3D with double regrouping.

Names the difference between two many-place whole numbers with several regroupings.

Names the difference when a zero appears in a single place in the minuend.

Names the difference when zeros appear in the tens and ones place of the minuend.

Estimates differences.

MULTIPLICATION HIERARCHY

Recognizes sets as a model for multiplication (number of sets and number of objects in each set).

Recognizes and uses arrays as a model for multiplication; for example,

$$2$$

$$\times \qquad \times$$

$$\times \qquad \times \qquad 3$$

$$\times \qquad \times$$

Understands the words *factor* and *product.*

Understands the "×" sign.

Understands the commutative property of multiplication; for example, $a \times (b + c) = (a \times b) + (a \times c)$ [$a \le 5$, $b \le 5$].

Memorizes basic multiplication facts for $a \times b$ ($a \le 5$, $b \le 5$).

Memorizes basic multiplication facts for $a \times b$ ($5 < a < 10$, $b < 10$).

Names the product if one factor is 10, 100, etc.

Expands the basic multiplication facts (e.g., 4×3 to 4×30).

Computes 2D × 1D without regrouping.

Understands place value of tens, ones, regrouping.

Computes $a \times (b + c) = (a \times b) + (a \times c)$ [$a < 10$, $a \times (b + c) < 100$ with regrouping] (e.g., $6 \times (10 + 3) = \underline{\quad} + \underline{\quad} = \underline{\quad}$).

Computes 2D × 1D with regrouping, product < 100.

Understands place value of hundreds, tens, ones.

Computes 2D × 1D with regrouping, product < 100.

Computes 2D × 2D with regrouping.

Computes 3D × 1D with regrouping.

Computes 3D × 2D with regrouping.

DIVISION HIERARCHY

Finds missing factor (e.g., $6 \times \underline{\quad} = 36$).

Uses symbols that indicate division ($2\overline{)6}$, $6 \div 2$, $6/2$).

Expresses a related multiplication sentence as a division sentence (product ÷ factor = factor).

Computes division facts with 1 as divisor (e.g., $1\overline{)6}$).

Computes basic division facts ($a \div b$ where $a \le 81$, $b \le 9$).

Computes division of a nonzero number by itself (e.g., $12\overline{)12}$).

Computes 1D ÷ 1D with a remainder.

Estimates 2D ÷ 1D and computes 2D ÷ 1D with a remainder.

Computes quotients with expanding dividend (e.g., $3\overline{)9}$, $3\overline{)90}$, $3\overline{)900}$).

Estimates 3D ÷ 1D and computes 3D ÷ 1D (e.g., $6\overline{)747}$).

Computes quotient of many-place dividend with a one-place divisor (e.g., $4\overline{)78,743}$).

Estimates 3D ÷ 2D and computes 3D ÷ 2D where divisor is multiple of 10 (e.g., $20\overline{)684}$).

Computes quotient with divisors of 100, 1,000, etc. (e.g., $1,000\overline{)6,897}$

Estimates 3D ÷ 2D and computes 3D ÷ 2D (e.g., $17\overline{)789}$).

Computes quotient of many-place dividend and many-place divisor (e.g., $3,897\overline{)487,876}$).

FRACTION HIERARCHY

Readiness Areas

Separates regions into subregions that are equivalent.

Expresses 1 in many different ways.

Uses the terms *fraction, fraction bar, numerator,* and *denominator.*

Models equivalent fractions on the number line.

Generates sets of equivalent fractions.

Renames fractions in simplest form.

Rewrites improper fractions as mixed numerals.

Rewrites mixed numerals as improper fractions.

Develops concept of least common denominator using the concept of least common multiple.

Compares fractional numbers.

Develops concept of least common denominator using the concept of greatest common factor.

Addition

Computes sums less than 1, same denominator.

Computes sums of mixed numerals, no regrouping, same denominator.

Computes sums between 1 and 2, same denominator, regrouping.

Computes sums of mixed numeral and nonunit fraction, regrouping, same denominator (e.g., $3\frac{2}{5} + \frac{4}{5}$).

Computes sums of mixed numerals with regrouping, same denominator (e.g., $8\frac{3}{5} + 2\frac{4}{5}$).

Computes sums less than 1, different denominators.

Computes sums of mixed numerals, no regrouping, different denominators.

Computes sums of mixed numerals, regrouping, different denominators.

Computes sums of three nonunit fractions, different denominators.

Solves word problems requiring addition of fractions.

Subtraction

Computes differences between two fractions with like denominators without regrouping, then with regrouping.

Computes differences between two fractions with unlike but related denominators without regrouping, then with regrouping.

Computes differences between two fractions with unlike and unrelated denominators without regrouping, then with regrouping.

Solves word problems requiring subtraction of fractions.

Multiplication

Computes product of whole number $\times$ unit fraction, product < 1 (e.g., $3 \times \frac{1}{4} =$ ___).

Computes product of whole number $\times$ nonunit fraction, product < 1 (e.g., $2 \times \frac{2}{5} =$ ___).

Gives fraction names for one (e.g., $1 = \frac{?}{7}$).

Solves regrouping problem by writing fraction as mixed numeral, $1 < a < 2$ (e.g., $\frac{7}{5} =$ ___).

Computes product of whole number $\times$ nonunit fraction, $1 < $ product < 2 (e.g., $3 \times \frac{3}{5} =$ ___).

Computes product of unit fraction $\times$ unit fraction (e.g., $\frac{1}{3} \times \frac{1}{4} =$ ___).

Computes product of nonunit fraction $\times$ nonunit fraction (e.g., $\frac{2}{3} \times \frac{4}{5} =$ ___).

Computes $a \times (b + c) = (a \times b) + (a \times c)$, a and b are whole numbers, c is a unit fraction, no regrouping (e.g., $3 \times (2 + \frac{1}{4}) =$ ___ $+$ ___).

Computes $a \times (b + c) = (a \times b) + (a \times c)$, a and b are whole numbers, c is a nonunit fraction, regrouping (e.g., $4 \times 3\frac{2}{5} = 4 \times (3 + \frac{2}{5}) =$ ___ $+$ ___ $=$ ___).

Computes product of nonunit fraction $\times$ mixed numeral using improper fractions—e.g., $\frac{5}{6} \times 2\frac{1}{3}$ (change to improper fractions).

Computes product of mixed numeral $\times$ mixed numeral using improper fractions—e.g., $3\frac{3}{4} \times 1\frac{7}{8}$ (use improper fractions).

Division

Computes quotient of $1 \div$ unit fraction (e.g., $1 \div \frac{1}{5}$).

Computes quotient of whole number $\div$ nonunit fraction: $1 <$ whole number < 10—e.g., $2 \div \frac{3}{5}$ (use repeated subtraction and remainder as fractional part).

Computes $\frac{1}{a} \div \frac{1}{b}$ where $a < b$ (common denominator approach) (e.g., $\frac{1}{2} \div \frac{1}{3}$).

Computes $\frac{a}{b} \div \frac{c}{d}$ (common denominator approach) (e.g., $\frac{3}{5} \div \frac{3}{4}$).

Computes quotient of two mixed numerals (common denominator approach) (e.g., $2\frac{1}{5} \div 1\frac{2}{3}$).

DECIMAL HIERARCHY

Readiness Areas

Generates decimal place value by rewriting fractions with denominators of powers of 10.

Recognizes decimal place value to millionths place.

Reads and writes rational numbers expressed as decimals.

Rewrites fractions as decimals.

Models rational numbers expressed as decimals using the number line.

Generates equivalent decimals by appending zeroes.

Addition

Names the sum of two rational numbers expressed as decimals having the same place value.

Names the sum of two rational numbers expressed as decimals having different place values.

Names the sum of more than two rational numbers expressed as decimals having different place values.

Solves word problems requiring addition of rational numbers expressed as decimals.

Subtraction

Names the difference between two rational numbers expressed as decimals having the same place value (without regrouping and with regrouping).

Names the difference between two rational numbers expressed as decimals having different place values (without regrouping and with regrouping).

Solves word problems requiring subtraction of rational numbers expressed as decimals.

Multiplication

Names the product of two rational numbers expressed as decimals when it is necessary to append zeroes to the left of a nonzero digit as decimal holders.

Names the product of more than two rational numbers expressed as decimals.

Solves word problems requiring multiplication of rational numbers expressed as decimals.

Division

Names the quotient of rational numbers expressed as decimals when the divisor is a whole number.

Names the quotient of any two rational numbers expressed as decimals by using the division algorithm.

Solves word problems requiring division of rational numbers expressed as decimals.

Percents

Interprets the symbol for percent (%) as a fraction and as a decimal.

Rewrites percents as decimals and fractions for percents less than 100% and then for percents equal to or greater than 100%.

Rewrites fractions or decimals as percents.

Solves word problems requiring percents.

MONEY HIERARCHY

Identifies coins.

Recognizes relative value of coins.

Makes change for amounts up to $1.00. Recognizes and uses money notation.

Recognizes currency and makes change for currency.

Solves examples and word problems involving money.

TIME HIERARCHY

Relates the face of the clock with the number line through 12 for hours.

Relates the face of the clock with the number line through 60 for minutes.

Tells time by the hour.

Tells time by the minute.

Understands the difference between A.M. and P.M.

Solves examples and word problems involving time.

MEASUREMENT HIERARCHY

Linear

Uses a straightedge of arbitrary length to measure an object.

Makes a ruler of at least 12 inches with 1-inch markings.

Uses an inch-marked ruler to measure items.

Recognizes that 12 inches measure the same length as 1 foot.

Identifies measurements of objects that are less than, greater than, or equal to 1 foot.

Introduces the symbols for inches and feet.

Makes a ruler with ½-inch and ¼-inch markings to measure objects.

Uses a ruler with ½-inch and ¼-inch markings to measure objects.

Estimates heights and lengths in feet and inches.

Recognizes and relates inch, foot, yard, and mile.

Solves examples involving denominate numbers related to linear measurement.

Solves word problems applying the concepts of linear measurement.

Recognizes metric units and relates them to one another.

Liquid and Dry

Recognizes relationships between and relative values of cup, pint, quart, half-gallon, and gallon.

Recognizes metric units and relates them to one another.

Solves examples involving denominate numbers related to liquid or dry measurements.

Solves word problems involving liquid measurement.

Weight

Compares relative weights of objects using a balance.

Recognizes relationships between and relative values of ounce, pound, and ton.

Weighs objects to nearest pound and ounce.

Uses the abbreviations *oz*, *lb*, and *T* in recording weights.

Recognizes metric units and relates them to one another.

Solves examples involving denominate numbers related to weight measurement.

Solves word problems involving weight measurements.

MATH SCOPE AND SEQUENCE SKILLS LIST BY GRADE LEVEL

KINDERGARTEN

Position concepts: *above, below, in, out, on, off, left, right, top, bottom, middle, front, back.*

Classification: identity, color, size, shape, pattern.

One-to-one: as many as, using tallies to count events or objects.

Comparing: more than, less than, same.

Counting: 0 to 5.

Ordinal numbers: first, second, third.

Geometry: box, ball, square, circle, triangle, rectangle, inside, outside.

Measurement: comparing larger, smaller, taller, shorter, longer, same length.

Time: daytime, nighttime, sequence, duration, clock, calendar.

Money: value of penny, identifying nickel and dime, reading price tags, determining whether enough money.

Writing numerals: 0 to 10.

Combining sets: picture addition stories.

Sums to 5: picture addition stories.

Separating sets: picture subtraction stories.

GRADE 1

Numeration: numbers and values 1 to 10.

Matching and joining sets.

Sums to 6.

Addition properties: commutative property of addition, zero property.

Ordinal numbers: first to fifth.

Sums 7 to 10.

Families of facts: sum of 1, 2, 3, 4, 5, 6, 7, 8, 9 families (e.g., sum of 7 family is 0 + 7, 7 + 0, 6 + 1, 1 + 6, 5 + 2, 2 + 5, 3 + 4, 4 + 3).

Addition sentences: completing, writing, and choosing.

Finding missing addends (e.g., 4 + ___ = 7).

Subtracting from sums or minuends to 6.

Subtracting from sums or minuends to 10.

Subtraction sentences: completing, writing, and choosing.

Money: subtracting prices, determining how much money (pennies, nickels, dimes).

Numeration/place value: counting and writing tens and ones, recognizing numbers 10 to 90, order of numbers to 100.

Counting: one more than, less than, counting by 2s, 3s, 5s, and 10s, skip-counting.

Time: calendar, hour, half hour, quarter hour.

Sums 11 to 18.

Subtracting from sums or minuends 11 to 18.

Families of facts: sum of 11 to 18 families.

Adding three addends.

Money: adding and subtracting with money.

Geometry: rectangle, square, circle, triangle.

Measurement: linear—comparing lengths, arbitrary units, metric units (centimeter, meter), customary units (inch, foot, yard); capacity—metric units (liter), customary units (cup, pint, quart); weight— kilogram; temperature—thermometer scales.

Addition of 2D + 1D without regrouping.

Addition of 2D + 2D without regrouping.

Subtraction of 2D − 1D without regrouping.

Subtraction of 2D − 2D without regrouping.

Fractions: recognizing equal parts or shapes, $\frac{1}{2}$s, $\frac{1}{3}$s, $\frac{1}{4}$s, finding $\frac{1}{2}$ of set.

Story problems: involving addition and subtraction.

GRADE 2

Numeration/place value: grouping tens and ones, order to 100, hundreds, tens, and ones.

Equations with missing numbers (e.g., 7 + ___ = 14, ___ + 3 = 13, 6 + 5 = ___).

Three or more addends: sums to 18.

Addition of 2D numbers with regrouping.

Subtraction of 2D numbers with regrouping.

Story problems: using addition and subtraction.

Fractions: identifying and writing fractional parts, dividing shapes in half.

Time: writing times, 15-minute intervals, 5-minute intervals, telling time, calendar—earlier or later.

Geometry: solid shapes, polygons, congruent figures, symmetry.

Measurement: linear—nearest inch, perimeter in centimeters; area—square units, by counting; capacity—milliliter; volume—by counting; weight— customary units (pound, ounce); temperature—Celsius, Fahrenheit.

Multiples facts: multiples of 2, 3, 4, 5: factors 2, 3, 4, 5, 0, 1; commutative property of multiplication.

Numeration: order of numbers to 1,000, 100 more than, 100 less than.

Subtraction of 3D − 2D with regrouping.

Subtraction of 3D − 3D with regrouping.

Story problems: using 3D numbers and two-step problems.

Money: half dollar, using ¢ and $, adding and subtracting money, writing amounts (e.g., $6.75).

GRADE 3

Adding zero property.

Rounding to nearest 10 or 100.

Estimating sums: to three digits.

Adding larger numbers: multidigit + multidigit.

Addition as a check for subtraction.

Subtraction with regrouping more than once and with zero in minuend.

Estimating differences: to three digits.

Subtraction of 4D numbers with regrouping.

Story problems: using addition and subtraction.

Multiplication facts: 6 to 9, zero and one properties, order property.

Multiplication of 2D × 1D without regrouping.

Division facts: 2D ÷ 1D, division equation, division and sets.

Story problems: using multiplication and division.

Division in vertical format.

Multiplication and division related: division by finding the missing factor.

Division with remainders.

Fractions of a number.

Equivalent fractions.

Measurement: linear—kilometer, mile, perimeter of polygons by adding inches; area—square centimeters by counting, square inches by counting; capacity—gallon; volume—cubic centimeters, cubic inches; mass weight—gram, kilogram; temperature—below zero.

Comparing fractions using < and >.

Geometry: areas, rectangular solid, segments, end points, sides, diagonals, symmetry, points on a grid.

Multiplication of 2D × 1D with tens regrouping.

Multiplication of 2D × 1D with hundreds regrouping.

Multiplication of 3D × 1D without regrouping.

Multiplication of 3D × 1D with regrouping.

Division of 2D numbers without regrouping (e.g., 36 ÷ 3).

Division of 2D numbers with regrouping (e.g., 51 ÷ 3).

Multiplication with addition, subtraction, and division using symbols (e.g., 8 × 4 ÷ 2 − 2 =).

GRADE 4

Rounding to nearest 100.

Numbers to millions.

Addition of numbers to six digits.

Place value of decimals.

Order and grouping properties of multiplication: (3 × 2) × 4 = 24, 3 × (2 × 4) = 24.

Multiples and common multiples: 36 is a multiple of 6, 36 is a common multiple of 6 and 4.

Finding missing factor: 4 × ___ = 36.

Zero as divisor.

Story problems: using addition, subtraction, multiplication, and division.

Fractions: fractions and sets, equivalent fractions, fractions of a number, numerator of 1 and more than 1.

Reducing fractions.

Adding fractions with like denominators.

Adding fractions with unlike denominators.

Subtracting fractions with like and unlike denominators.

Writing mixed numbers as fractions.

Changing fractions to mixed numbers.

Adding and subtracting mixed numbers.

Story problems: using addition and subtraction of fractions.

Measurement: linear—decimal measures, perimeter formulas, area formulas; volume—by counting, by multiplying; estimating temperature.

Multiplication of 3D × 1D with regrouping.

Multiplication of 4D × 1D with regrouping.

Estimating products.

Division of 3D number by 1D number with regrouping: including estimation.

Division of 4D number by 1D number with regrouping: including estimation.

Multiplication as a check for division.

Geometry: segments, lines, rays, angles, parallel lines.

Multiplication by 10 and multiples of 10.

Multiplication by a 2D number (e.g., 24 × 13).

Division by a 2D number with regrouping (e.g., 12$\overline{)53}$, 15$\overline{)328}$).

Decimals: writing and reading decimals to hundredths, place value of decimal numbers, adding and subtracting decimals with regrouping.

Applications: catalogs and order forms, computing averages.

GRADE 5

Values to billions.

Rounding to nearest millions and billions.

Roman numerals: I to X.

Story problems: using addition and subtraction with fractions and mixed numbers.

Least common multiples.

Multiplying by 100 and multiples of 10 and 100.

Distributive property: (9 × 4) × 3 = ___, 9 × (4 × 3) = ___.

Multiplication of 3D × 2D with regrouping.

Story problems: using multiplication and division with fractions.

Factors and common factors.

Geometry: vertex, perpendicular lines, corresponding parts, naming angles, protractor, diagonals, measuring angles.

Least common denominators.

Multiplication and division of fractions.

Decimals to thousandths.

Rounding to the nearest whole number.

Measurement: linear—millimeter, decimeter, nearest $\frac{1}{16}$ of an inch, perimeter formulas, curved figures, circumference, area formulas by multiplying, area of triangles; capacity—fluid ounce; volume—rectangular prisms, by counting, by multiplying.

Multiplying decimals.

Dividing decimals.

Story problems: using multiplication and division with decimals.

Applications: discounts, sales tax, profits.

GRADE 6

Base two numerals.

Place value in metric system.

Multiplication: exponents.

Prime factorization.

Division with 3D numbers.

Rounding divisors.

Geometry: intersecting lines; acute, right, obtuse angles; parallelogram, rhombus, decagon, trapezoid, kite.

Decimals: finding decimal between two numbers, decimals and money, rounding decimals, multiplying dollars, changing decimals to fractions, multiplying and dividing decimals, repeating decimals.

Measurement: linear—relation of metric units to decimal system, adding metric units, adding customary units, area formulas, parallelograms, surface areas of rectangular prisms, cylinders, circle; capacity—metric cup, kiloliter, half-gallon, comparing measures, adding measures; mass weight—milligram.

Estimating: time, volume, weight, bar graph.

Decimals and percents: converting dollars and cents, multiplying dollars

Story problems: using percent.

Applications: stocks, unit pricing, installment buying, checking account.

References

Abruscato, J. (1993). Early results and tentative implications from the Vermont Portfolio Project. *Phi Delta Kappan, 74,* 474–477.

Ackerman, P. T., Dykman, R. A., & Gardner, M. Y. (1990). Counting rate, naming rate, phonological sensitivity, and memory span: Major factors in dyslexia. *Journal of Learning Disabilities, 23,* 325–327.

Adams, G. L., & Englemann, S. (1996). *Research on direct instruction: 25 years beyond DISTAR.* Seattle, WA: Educational Achievement Systems.

Adams, M. J. (1990). *Beginning to read: Thinking and learning about print.* Cambridge, MA: MIT Press.

Adams, M. J., & Bruck, M. (1995). Resolving the "great debate." *American Educator, 19*(7), 10–20.

Adelman, P. B., & Vogel, S. A. (1993). Issues in the employment of adults with learning disabilities. *Learning Disability Quarterly, 16,* 219–232.

Adler, S. (1988). A new job description and a new task for the public school clinician: Relating effectively to the nonstandard dialect speaker. *Language, Speech, and Hearing Services in Schools, 19,* 28–33.

Alberto, P. A., & Troutman, A. C. (2009). *Applied behavior analysis for teachers* (8th ed.). Upper Saddle River, NJ: Merrill/Pearson.

Alderman, M. K. (1990). Motivation for at-risk students. *Educational Leadership, 48*(1), 27–30.

Allinder, R. M., Bolling, R. M., Oats, R. G., & Gagnon, W. A. (2000). Effects of teacher self-monitoring on implementation of curriculum-based measurement and mathematics computation achievement of students with disabilities. *Remedial and Special Education, 21,* 219–226.

Allor, J. H., & McCathren, R. B. (2003). Developing emergent literacy skills through storybook reading. *Intervention in School and Clinic, 39,* 72–79.

Alter, P. J., Wyrick, A., Brown, E. T., & Lingo, A. (2008). Improving mathematics problem solving skills for students with challenging behavior. *Beyond Behavior, 17,* 2–7.

Altieri, J. L. (2008). Fictional characters with dyslexia: What are we seeing in books? *Teaching Exceptional Children, 41*(1), 48–54.

Al-Yagon, M. (2007). Socioemotional and behavioral adjustment among school-age children with learning disabilities: The moderating role of maternal personal resources. *The Journal of Special Education, 40,* 205–217.

American Psychiatric Association. (1980). *Diagnostic and statistical manual of mental disorders* (3rd ed.). Washington, DC: Author.

American Psychiatric Association. (2000). *Diagnostic and statistical manual of mental disorders* (4th ed., text revision). Washington, DC: Author.

American Speech-Language-Hearing Association. (1991). A model for collaborative service delivery for students with language-learning disorders in the public schools. *Asha, 33*(Suppl. 5), 44–50.

American Speech-Language-Hearing Association. (1992). Definitions for communicative disorders and differences. *Asha, 24,* 949–950.

Anders, P. L., & Bos, C. S. (1984). In the beginning: Vocabulary instruction in content classrooms. *Topics in Learning and Learning Disabilities, 3*(4), 53–65.

Anderson, D. W. (1966). Handwriting research: Movement and quality. In T. D. Horn (Ed.), *Research on handwriting and spelling.* Champaign, IL: National Council of Teachers of English.

Anderson, L. W., & Pellicer, L. O. (1990). Synthesis of research on compensatory and remedial education. *Educational Leadership, 48*(1), 10–16.

Andersson, U. (2008). Mathematical competencies in children with different types of learning difficulties. *Journal of Educational Psychology, 100,* 48–66.

Apel, K., & Masterson, J. J. (2001). Theory guided spelling assessment and intervention: A case study. *Language, Speech, and Hearing Services in Schools, 32,* 182–195.

Archer, A. L., & Gleason, M. M. (2002). *Skills for school success.* North Billerica, MA: Curriculum Associates.

Archer, A. L., Gleason, M. M., & Isaacson, S. (1995). Effective instructional delivery. In P. T. Cegelka & W. H. Berdine, *Effective instruction for students with learning difficulties* (pp. 161–194). Boston: Allyn & Bacon.

Ashlock, R. B. (2010). *Error patterns in computation: Using error patterns to help each student learn* (10th ed.). Boston: Allyn & Bacon/Pearson.

Baechle, C. L., & Lian, M. J. (1990). The effects of direct feedback and practice on metaphor performances in children with learning disabilities. *Journal of Learning Disabilities, 23,* 451–455.

Bahr, M. W., & Kovaleski, J. F. (2006). The need for problem-solving teams: Introduction to the special issue. *Remedial and Special Education, 27,* 2–5.

Baker, E. T., Wang, M. C., & Walberg, H. J. (1994/1995). The effects of inclusion on learning. *Educational Leadership, 52*(4), 33–35.

Baker, S. K., Chard, D. J., Ketterlin-Geller, L. R., Apichatabutra, C., & Doabler, C. (2009). Teaching writing to at-risk students: The quality of evidence for self-regulated strategy development. *Exceptional Children, 75,* 303–318.

Baker, S. K., Simmons, D. C., & Kame'enui, E. J. (1994). Making information more memorable for students with learning disabilities through the design of instructional tools. *LD Forum, 19*(3), 14–18.

Bankson, N. W. (1990). *Bankson Language Test—2.* Austin, TX: PRO-ED.

Barbe, W., Milone, M., & Wasylyk, T. (1983). Manuscript is the "write" start. *Academic Therapy, 18,* 397–406.

Bashir, A. S., & Singer, B. D. (2009). Theme editors' introduction: Assessment, instruction, and intervention for the struggling writer. *Perspectives on Language and Literacy, 35*(3), 7–10.

Battle, J. (2002). *Culture-Free Self-Esteem Inventories—3.* Austin, TX: PRO-ED.

Bauwens, J., & Hourcade, J. J. (1995). *Cooperative teaching: Rebuilding the schoolhouse for all students.* Austin, TX: PRO-ED.

Bear, D. R., Invernizzi, M., Templeton, S., & Johnston, F. (2008). *Words their way: Word study for phonics, vocabulary, and spelling instruction* (4th ed.). Upper Saddle River, NJ: Merrill/Prentice Hall/Pearson.

Beck, I. L., & Juel, C. (1995). The role of decoding in learning to read. *American Educator, 19,* 8, 21–25, 39–42.

Beck, I. L., McKeown, M. G., & Kucan, L. (2002). *Bringing words to life: Robust vocabulary instruction.* New York: Guilford Press.

Belson, S. I. (2003). *Technology for exceptional learners: Choosing instructional tools to meet students' needs.* Boston: Houghton Mifflin.

Bender, W. N. (2008). *Learning disabilities: Characteristics, identification, and teaching strategies* (6th ed.). Boston: Allyn & Bacon/Pearson.

Bender, W. N., Vail, C. O., & Scott, K. (1995). Teachers' attitudes toward increased mainstreaming: Implementing effective instruction for students with learning disabilities. *Journal of Learning Disabilities, 28,* 87–94, 120.

Bender, W. N., & Wall, M. E. (1994). Social-emotional development of students with learning disabilities. *Learning Disability Quarterly, 17,* 323–341.

Benner, G. J., Trout, A., Nordness, P. D., Nelson, J. R., Knobel, M., Epstein, A., Maguire, K., Birdsell, R., & Epstein, M. H. (2002). The effects of the Language for Learning program on the receptive language skills of kindergarten children. *Journal of Direct Instruction, 2*(2), 75–86.

Bergerud, D., Lovitt, T. C., & Horton, S. (1988). The effectiveness of textbook adaptations in life science for high school students with learning disabilities. *Journal of Learning Disabilities, 21,* 70–76.

Berninger, V. W., Winn, W. D., Stock, P., Abbott, R. D., Eschen, K., Lin, S., Garcia, N., Anderson-Youngstrom, M., Murphy, H., Lovitt, D., Trivedi, P., Jones, J., Amtmann, D., & Nagy, W. (2008). Tier 3 specialized writing instruction for students with dyslexia. *Reading and Writing, 21,* 95–129.

Bernstein, D. K. (1993). Language development: The preschool years. In D. K. Bernstein & E. Tiegerrman (Eds.), *Language and communication disorders in children* (3rd ed., pp. 97–122). Boston: Allyn & Bacon.

Bezuk, N. S., & Cegelka, P. T. (1995). Effective mathematics instruction for all students. In P. T. Cegelka & W. H. Berdine, *Effective instruction for students with learning difficulties* (pp. 345–383). Boston: Allyn & Bacon.

Bhat, P., Griffin, C. C., & Sindelar, P. T. (2003). Phonological awareness instruction for middle school students with learning disabilities. *Learning Disability Quarterly, 26,* 73–87.

Binder, C. V. (1988). Precision teaching: Measuring and attaining academic excellence. *Youth Policy, 10,* 12–15.

Blackham, G. J., & Silberman, A. (1980). *Modification of child and adolescent behavior* (3rd ed.). Belmont, CA: Wadsworth.

Blackhurst, A. E. (2005). Perspectives on applications of technology in the field of learning disabilities. *Learning Disability Quarterly, 28,* 175–178.

Bley, N. S., & Thornton, C. A. (2001). *Teaching mathematics to students with learning disabilities* (4th ed.). Austin, TX: PRO-ED.

Bloomfield, L., & Barnhart, C. L. (1961). *Let's read—A linguistic approach.* Detroit, MI: Wayne State University Press.

Boehm, A. E. (2000). *Boehm Test of Basic Concepts—3.* San Antonio, TX: Psychological Corporation.

Boone, R., Higgins, K., Falba, C., & Langley, W. (1993). Cooperative text: Reading and writing in a hypermedia environment. *LD Forum, 18*(3), 29–37.

Borich, G. D. (2007). *Effective teaching methods: Research-based practice* (6th ed.). Upper Saddle River, NJ: Merrill/Prentice Hall/Pearson.

Borkowski, J. G., Estrada, M. T., Milstead, M., & Hale, C. A. (1989). General problem-solving skills: Relations between metacognition and strategic processing. *Learning Disability Quarterly, 12,* 57–70.

Borkowski, J. G., Weyhing, R. S., & Carr, M. (1988). Effects of attributional retraining on strategy-based reading comprehension in learning-disabled students. *Journal of Educational Psychology, 80*(1), 46–53.

Borman, G. D., & Hewes, G. M. (2002). The long-term effects and cost-effectiveness of Success for All. *Educational Evaluation and Policy Analysis, 24,* 243–266.

Bormuth, J. R. (1968). The cloze readability procedure. *Elementary English, 45,* 429–436.

Bos, C. S., & Anders, P. L. (1987). Semantic feature analysis: An interactive teaching strategy for facilitating learning from text. *Learning Disability Focus, 3*(1), 55–59.

Botsas, G., & Padeliadu, S. (2003). Goal orientation and reading comprehension strategy use among students with and without reading difficulties. *International Journal of Educational Research, 39,* 477–495.

Bottge, B. A., & Hasselbring, T. S. (1993). A comparison of two approaches for teaching complex, authentic mathematics problems to adolescents in remedial math classes. *Exceptional Children, 59,* 556–566.

Boyle, E. A., Rosenberg, M. S., Connelly, V. J., Washburn, S. C., Brinckerhoff, L. C., & Banerjee, M. (2003). Effects of audio texts on the acquisition of secondary-level content by students with mild disabilities. *Learning Disability Quarterly, 26,* 203–214.

Bracken, B. A. (1992). *Multidimensional Self-Concept Scale.* Austin, TX: PRO-ED.

Braine, M. (1971). *On two types of models of the internalization of grammar.* New York: Academic Press.

Brandt, R. (1991). Overview: Time for reflection. *Educational Leadership, 48*(6), 3.

Brandt, R. (1994/1995). Overview: What is best? *Educational Leadership, 52*(4), 3.

Brendtro, L., & Long, N. (1995). Breaking the cycle of conflict. *Educational Foundation Leadership, 15*(5), 52–56.

Brigance, A. H. (2010a). *Brigance Comprehensive Inventory of Basic Skills—II.* North Billerica, MA: Curriculum Associates.

Brigance, A. H. (2010b). *Brigance Transition Skills Inventory.* North Billerica, MA: Curriculum Associates.

Brigham, F. J., Scruggs, T. E., & Mastropieri, M. A. (1992). Teaching enthusiasm in learning disabilities classrooms: Effects on learning and behavior. *Learning Disabilities Research & Practice, 7,* 68–73.

Brolin, D. E. (1997). *Life-centered career education: A competency-based approach* (5th ed.). Reston, VA: Council for Exceptional Children.

Brolin, D. E., & Lloyd, R. J. (2004). *Career development and transition services: A functional life skills approach* (4th ed.). Upper Saddle River, NJ: Merrill/Prentice Hall/Pearson.

Brophy, J. (1987). Synthesis of research on strategies for motivating students to learn. *Educational Leadership, 45*(2), 40–48.

Browder, D. M., & Snell, M. E. (1993). Functional academics. In M. E. Snell (Ed.), *Instruction of students with severe disabilities* (4th ed., pp. 442–479). Upper Saddle River, NJ: Merrill/Prentice Hall.

Brown, K. J., Morris, D., & Fields, M. (2005). Intervention after grade 1: Serving increased numbers of struggling readers effectively. *Journal of Literacy Research, 37,* 61–94.

Brown, L. L., & Alexander, J. (1991). *Self-Esteem Index.* Austin, TX: PRO-ED.

Brown, L. L., & Hammill, D. D. (1990). *Behavior Rating Profile—2.* Austin, TX: PRO-ED.

Brown, R. (1973). *A first language: The early stages.* Cambridge, MA: Harvard University Press.

Brown, R., & Berko, J. (1960). Word associations and acquisition of grammar. *Child Development, 31,* 1–14.

Brown, V. L., Cronin, M. E., & McEntire, E. (1994). *Test of Mathematical Abilities—2.* Austin, TX: PRO-ED.

Brown, V. L., Wiederholt, J. L., & Hammill, D. D. (2009). *Test of Reading Comprehension—4.* Austin, TX: PRO-ED.

Bruininks, R. H., Woodcock, R. W., Weatherman, R. F., & Hill, B. K. (1996). *Scales of Independent Behavior—Revised.* Rolling Meadows, IL: Riverside.

Brunner, M. S. (1993). *Reduced recidivism and increased employment opportunity through research-based reading instruction.* Washington, DC: Office of Juvenile Justice and Delinquency Prevention, Juvenile Justice Clearinghouse.

Bryan, J. (1988, April). *Perspectives on the regular education initiative.* Paper presented at the meeting of the Council for Exceptional Children, Washington, DC.

Bryan, T. H. (1986). Self-concept and attributions of the learning disabled. *Learning Disabilities Focus, 1,* 82–89.

Bryan, T. H., & Sullivan-Burstein, K. (1998). Teacher-selected strategies for improving homework completion. *Remedial and Special Education, 19,* 263–275.

Bryant, B. R., Wiederholt, J. L., & Bryant, D. P. (2004). *Gray Diagnostic Reading Tests—Second Edition.* Austin, TX: PRO-ED.

Bryant, D. P., Goodwin, M., Bryant, B. R., & Higgins, K. (2003). Vocabulary instruction for students with learning disabilities: A review of the research. *Learning Disability Quarterly, 26,* 117–128.

Bryant, D. P., Smith, D. D., & Bryant, B. R. (2008). *Teaching students with special needs in inclusive classrooms.* Boston: Allyn & Bacon/Pearson.

Bryant, N. D., Drabin, I. R., & Gettinger, M. (1981). Effects of varying unit size on spelling achievement in learning disabled children. *Journal of Learning Disabilities, 14,* 200–203.

Bulgren, J. A., Deshler, D. D., & Schumaker, J. B. (1993). *The content enhancement series: The concept mastery routine.* Lawrence, KS: Edge Enterprises.

Bulgren, J. A., & Lenz, B. K. (1996). Strategic instruction in the content areas. In D. D. Deshler, E. S. Ellis, & B. K. Lenz, *Teaching adolescents with learning disabilities: Strategies and methods* (2nd ed., pp. 409–473). Denver, CO: Love.

Bulgren, J. A., Lenz, B. K., Deshler, D. D., & Schumaker, J. B. (1995). *The content enhancement series: The concept comparison routine.* Lawrence, KS: Edge Enterprises.

Bulgren, J. A., Lenz, B. K., Deshler, D. D., & Schumaker, J. B. (2001). *The content enhancement series: The question exploration routine.* Lawrence, KS: Edge Enterprises.

Bulgren, J. A., Schumaker, J. B., & Deshler, D. D. (1988). The effectiveness of a concept teaching routine in enhancing the performance of students with learning disabilities in mainstream classes. *Learning Disability Quarterly, 11,* 3–17.

Bulgren, J. A., Schumaker, J. B., & Deshler, D. D. (1994). *The content enhancement series: The concept anchoring routine.* Lawrence, KS: Edge Enterprises.

Burns, P. C., & Broman, B. L. (1983). *The language arts in childhood education* (5th ed.). Chicago: Rand McNally.

Bursuck, W. D., Harniss, M. K., Epstein, M. H., Polloway, E. A., Jayanthi, M., & Wissinger, L. M. (1999). Solving communication problems about homework: Recommendations of special education teachers. *Learning Disabilities Research & Practice, 14*, 149–158.

Bursuck, W. D., Polloway, E. A., Plante, L., Epstein, M. H., Jayanthi, M., & McConeghy, J. (1996). Report card grading and adaptations: A national survey of classroom practices. *Exceptional Children, 62*, 301–318.

Butler, F. M., Miller, S. P., Crehan, K., Babbitt, B., & Pierce, T. (2003). Fraction instruction for students with mathematics disabilities: Comparing two teaching sequences. *Learning Disabilities Research & Practice, 18*, 99–111.

Caesar, L. G., & Kohler, P. D. (2007). The state of school-based bilingual assessment: Actual practice versus recommended guidelines. *Language, Speech, and Hearing Services in Schools, 38*, 190–200.

Calhoon, M. B., Fuchs, L. S., & Hamlett, C. L. (2000). Effects of computer-based test accommodations on mathematics performance assessments for secondary students with learning disabilities. *Learning Disability Quarterly, 23*, 271–282.

California Department of Education. (1994). *I can learn: A handbook for parents, teachers, and students.* Sacramento, CA: Author.

California Mathematics Assessment Advisory Committee. (1990). *Guidelines for the mathematics portfolio: Working paper.* Sacramento: California Assessment Program, California State Department of Education.

Canady, R. L., & Rettig, M. D. (1995). The power of innovative scheduling. *Educational Leadership, 53*(3), 4–10.

Carbo, M. L. (1987). Matching reading styles: Correcting ineffective instruction. *Educational Leadership, 45*(2), 55–62.

Carlson, S. A. (1985). The ethical appropriateness of subject-matter tutoring for learning disabled adolescents. *Learning Disability Quarterly, 8*, 310–314.

Carman, R. A., & Adams, W. R. (1972). *Study skills: A student's guide for survival.* New York: Wiley.

Carnine, D. (1989). Teaching complex content to learning disabled students: The role of technology. *Exceptional Children, 55*, 524–533.

Carnine, D. (1991). Curricular interventions for teaching higher order thinking to all students: Introduction to the special series. *Journal of Learning Disabilities, 24*, 261–269.

Carnine, D. W., Silbert, J., Kame'enui, E. J., & Tarver, S. G. (2010). *Direct instruction reading* (5th ed.). Boston: Merrill/Pearson.

Carreker, S. (2002). Fluency: No longer a forgotten goal in reading instruction. *Perspectives* (The International Dyslexia Association), *28*(1), 1, 4.

Carreker, S. (2005). Teaching spelling. In J. R. Birsh (Ed.), *Multisensory teaching of basic language skills* (2nd ed., pp. 257–295). Baltimore, MD: Paul H. Brookes.

Carrow-Woolfolk, E. (1995a). *Oral and Written Language Scales: Listening Comprehension and Oral Expression.* Minneapolis, MN: Pearson.

Carrow-Woolfolk, E. (1995b). *Oral and Written Language Scales: Written Expression.* Minneapolis, MN: Pearson.

Carrow-Woolfolk, E. (1999a). *Comprehensive Assessment of Spoken Language.* Minneapolis, MN: Pearson.

Carrow-Woolfolk, E. (1999b). *Test for Auditory Comprehension of Language—3.* Austin, TX: PRO-ED.

Cartwright, G. P. (1968). Written language abilities of normal and educable mentally retarded children. *American Journal of Mental Deficiency, 72*, 499–508.

Cartwright, G. P. (1969). Written expression and spelling. In R. M. Smith (Ed.), *Teacher diagnosis of educational difficulties* (pp. 95–117). Upper Saddle River, NJ: Merrill/Prentice Hall.

Cass, M., Cates, D., Smith, M., & Jackson, C. (2003). Effects of manipulative instruction on solving area and perimeter problems by students with learning disabilities. *Learning Disabilities Research & Practice, 18*, 112–120.

Cawley, J. F., & Miller, J. H. (1989). Cross-sectional comparisons of the mathematical performance of children with learning disabilities: Are we on the right track toward comprehensive programming? *Journal of Learning Disabilities, 23*, 250–254, 259.

Cawley, J. F., Miller, J. H., & School, B. A. (1987). A brief inquiry of arithmetic word-problem solving among learning disabled secondary students. *Learning Disabilities Focus, 2*, 87–93.

Cawley, J. F., Parmar, R. S., Yan, W., & Miller, J. H. (1998). Arithmetic computation performance of students with learning disabilities: Implications for curriculum. *Learning Disabilities Research & Practice, 13*, 68–74.

Cegelka, P. T., & Berdine, W. H. (1995). *Effective instruction for students with learning difficulties.* Boston: Allyn & Bacon.

Cegelka, P. T., & Greene, G. (1993). Transition to adulthood. In A. E. Blackhurst & W. H. Berdine (Eds.), *An introduction to special education* (3rd ed., pp. 137–175). New York: Harper-Collins.

Chalfant, J. C., & Pysh, M. V. (1989). Teacher assistance teams: Five descriptive studies of 96 teams. *Remedial and Special Education, 19*(6), 49–58.

Chall, J. S. (1987). Reading and early childhood education: The critical issues. *Principal, 66*(5), 6–9.

Chall, J. S. (1989). Learning to read: The great debate 20 years later—A response to "Debunking the great phonics myth." *Phi Delta Kappan, 70*, 521–538.

Chall, J. S. (1996). *Stages of reading development* (2nd ed.). Fort Worth, TX: Harcourt Brace.

Chall, J. S., & Stahl, S. A. (1982). Reading. In H. E. Mitzel (Ed.), *Encyclopedia of educational research* (5th ed., pp. 1535–1559). New York: Free Press.

Chapman, J. W., & Boersma, F. J. (1979). Learning disabilities, locus of control, and mother attitudes. *Journal of Educational Psychology, 1*, 250–258.

Chard, D. J., Simmons, D. C., & Kame'enui, E. J. (1995). *Understanding the primary role of word recognition in the reading process: Synthesis of research on beginning reading* (Tech. Rep.). Eugene: University of Oregon, National Center to Improve the Tools of Educators.

Chera, P., & Wood, C. (2003). Animated multimedia 'talking books' can promote phonological awareness in children beginning to read. *Learning & Instruction, 13,* 33–52.

Chiang, B., & Ford, M. (1990). Whole language alternatives for students with learning disabilities. *LD Forum, 16*(1), 31–34.

Chomsky, N. A. (1965). *Aspects of the theory of syntax.* Cambridge, MA: MIT Press.

Christenson, S. L., Ysseldyke, J. E., & Thurlow, M. L. (1989). Critical instructional factors for students with mild handicaps: An integrative review. *Remedial and Special Education, 10*(5), 21–31.

Cianciolo, P. J. (1965). Children's literature can affect coping behavior. *Personnel and Guidance Journal, 43*(9), 897–903.

Clark, C. M. (1989, October). *The good teacher.* Paper presented at the Norwegian Research Council for Science and the Humanities Conference: "Education from Cradle to Doctorate," Trondheim, Norway.

Clark, G. M., & Kolstoe, O. P. (1990). *Career development and transition education for adolescents with disabilities.* Boston: Allyn & Bacon.

Clark, G. M., & Patton, J. R. (2006). *Transition Planning Inventory—Updated Version.* Austin, TX: PRO-ED.

Clay, M. M. (1985). *The early detection of reading difficulties* (3rd ed.). Auckland, New Zealand: Heinemann Educational Books.

Clements, D. H. (1987). Computers and young children: A review of research. *Young Children, 42*(1), 34–44.

Clifford, M. M. (1990). Students need challenge, not easy success. *Educational Leadership, 48*(1), 22–26.

Cline, B. V., & Billingsley, B. S. (1991). Teachers' and supervisors' perceptions of secondary learning disabilities programs: A multi-state survey. *Learning Disabilities Research & Practice, 6,* 158–165.

Cobb, P., Yackel, E., & Wood, T. (1992). A constructivist alternative to the representational view of mind in mathematics education. *Journal of Research in Mathematics Education, 23,* 2–33.

Cohen, P. A., Kulik, J. A., & Kulik, C. C. (1982). Educational outcomes of tutoring: A meta-analysis of findings. *American Educational Research Journal, 19*(2), 237–248.

Coie, J., Dodge, K., & Coppotelli, H. (1982). Dimensions and types of social status: A cross-age perspective. *Developmental Psychology, 18,* 557–570.

Coiro, J., & Dobler, E. (2007). Exploring the online comprehension strategies used by sixth grade skilled readers to search for and locate information on the internet. *Reading Research Quarterly, 42,* 214–257.

Collins, M., Carnine, D., & Gersten, R. (1987). Elaborated corrective feedback and the acquisition of reading skills: A study of computer-assisted instruction. *Exceptional Children, 54,* 254–262.

Colvin, G., Sugai, G., & Patching, B. (1993). Precorrection: An instructional approach for managing predictable problem behaviors. *Intervention in School and Clinic, 28,* 143–150.

Conderman, G., & Koroghlanian, C. (2002). Writing test questions like a pro. *Intervention in School and Clinic, 38,* 83–87.

Connelly, V., Gee, D., & Walsh, E. (2007). A comparison of keyboarded and handwritten compositions and the relationship with transcription speed. *British Journal of Educational Psychology, 77,* 479–492.

Conners, C. K. (2008a). *Conners Comprehensive Behavior Rating Scales.* San Antonio, TX: Pearson.

Conners, C. K. (2008b). *Conners—Third Edition.* San Antonio, TX: Pearson.

Connolly, A. J. (2007). *KeyMath—3: Diagnostic Assessment.* Minneapolis, MN: Pearson.

Cook, B. G., Cameron, D. L., & Tankersley, M. (2007). Inclusive teachers' attitudinal ratings of their students with disabilities. *The Journal of Special Education, 40,* 230–238.

Cook, B. G., Tankersley, M., Cook, L., & Landrum, T. J. (2000). Teachers' attitudes toward their included students with disabilities. *Exceptional Children, 67,* 115–135.

Cooper, H. (2001). *The battle over homework. Common ground for administrators, teachers, and parents* (2nd ed.). Thousand Oaks, CA: Corwin Press.

Cooper, H., & Nye, B. (1994). Homework for students with learning disabilities: The implications of research for policy and practice. *Journal of Learning Disabilities, 27,* 470–479.

Cooper, H., Robinson, J. C., & Patall, E. A. (2006). Does homework improve academic achievement? A synthesis of research. *Review of Educational Research, 76,* 1–62.

Coopersmith, S. (1981). *Coopersmith Self-Esteem Inventories.* Palo Alto, CA: Consulting Psychologists Press.

Covey, S. R. (1989). *The seven habits of highly effective people.* New York: Simon & Schuster.

Covey, S. R., Merrill, A. R., & Merrill, R. R. (1994). *First things first.* New York: Simon & Schuster.

Coyne, M. D., Simmons, D. C., Kame'enui, E. J., & Stoolmiller, M. (2004). Teaching vocabulary during shared storybook readings: An examination of differential effects. *Exceptionality, 12,* 145–162.

Cronin, M. E. (1988). Applying curriculum for the instruction of life skills. In G. A. Robinson, J. R. Patton, E. A. Polloway, & L. R. Sargent (Eds.), *Best practices in mental disabilities* (Vol. 2, pp. 41–52). Des Moines: Iowa Department of Education, Bureau of Special Education.

Cronin, M. E., & Patton, J. R. (1993). *Life skills instruction for all students with special needs: A practical guide for integrating real-life content into the curriculum.* Austin, TX: PRO-ED.

Cummings, R. E., & Maddux, C. D. (1985). *Parenting the learning disabled: A realistic approach.* Springfield, IL: Charles C. Thomas.

Cunningham, A. E., & Stanovich, K. E. (1998). What reading does for the mind. *American Educator, 22*(Spring/Summer), 8–15.

D'Agostino, J. V., & Murphy, J. A. (2004). A meta-analysis of Reading Recovery in United States schools. *Educational Evaluation and Policy Analysis, 26,* 23–38.

Darch, C., Kim, S., & Johnson, J. H. (2000). The strategic spelling skills of students with learning disabilities: The results of two studies. *Journal of Instructional Psychology, 27,* 15–26.

DeBoer, A. (1994). *Grading alternatives.* Presentation conducted at Project TIDE Training, Myrtle Beach, SC.

DeFord, D. E., Pinnell, G. S., Lyons, C. A., & Young P. (1988). *Reading Recovery: Volume IX, report of the follow-up studies.* Columbus, OH: Ohio State University.

De la Cruz, R. E., Cage, C. E., & Lian, M. J. (2000). Learning math and social skills through ancient multicultural games. *Teaching Exceptional Children, 32*(3), 38–42.

Delquadri, J., Greenwood, C. R., Whorton, D., Carta, J. J., & Hall, R. V. (1986). Classwide peer tutoring. *Exceptional Children, 52,* 535–542.

Dempster, F. N. (1991). Synthesis of research on reviews and tests. *Educational Leadership, 48*(7), 71–76.

Denckla, M. B., & Rudel, R. (1974). Rapid "automatized" naming of pictured objects, colors, and letters, and numbers by normal children. *Cortex, 10,* 186–202.

Denham, C., & Lieberman, A. (Eds.). (1980). *Time to learn.* Washington, DC: National Institute of Education.

Deno, S. L. (1987). Curriculum-based measurement. *Teaching Exceptional Children, 20*(1), 41–42.

Deno, S. L. (1989). Curriculum-based measurement and special education services: A fundamental and direct relationship. In M. R. Shinn (Ed.), *Curriculum-based measurement: Assessing special children* (pp. 1–17). New York: Guilford Press.

Deno, S. L., Mirkin, P. K., & Chiang, B. (1982). Identifying valid measures of reading. *Exceptional Children, 49,* 36–45.

Deno, S. L., Mirkin, P. K., & Wesson, C. (1984). How to write effective data-based IEPs. *Teaching Exceptional Children, 16,* 99–104.

Denton, C. A., Swanson, E. A., & Mathes, P. G. (2007). Assessment-based instructional coaching provided to reading intervention teachers. *Reading and Writing, 20,* 569–590.

Deshler, D. D., Ellis, E. S., & Lenz, B. K. (1996). *Teaching adolescents with learning disabilities: Strategies and methods* (2nd ed.). Denver, CO: Love.

Deshler, D. D., & Lenz, B. K. (1989). The strategies instructional approach. *International Journal of Disability, Development, and Education, 36*(3), 203–224.

Deshler, D. D., & Schumaker, J. B. (1986). Learning strategies: An instructional alternative of low achieving adolescents. *Exceptional Children, 52,* 583–590.

Deshler, D. D., Schumaker, J. B., & McKnight, P. C. (1997). *The content enhancement series: The survey routine.* Lawrence: University of Kansas Center for Research on Learning.

Dessart, D. J., DeRidder, C. M., & Ellington, A. J. (1999). The research backs calculators. *Mathematics Education Dialogues, 2*(3), 6.

Dettmar, R. (2007). Transition, technology, and employment for the 21st century: A review of the literature. *Special Education Technology Practice, 9,* 21–28.

DeVries, D. L., & Slavin, R. E. (1978). Teams-games-tournament (TGT): Review of ten classroom experiments. *Journal of Research and Development in Education, 12,* 28–38.

Dickinson, D. K., & McCabe, A. (2001). Bringing it all together: The multiple origins, skills, and environmental supports of early literacy. *Learning Disabilities Research & Practice, 16,* 186–202.

Dixon, R. C. (1991). The application of sameness analysis to spelling. *Journal of Learning Disabilities, 24,* 285–291, 310.

Dixon, R. C., & Carnine, D. (1994). Ideologies, practices, and their implications for special education. *The Journal of Special Education, 28,* 356–367.

Dixon, R. C., Carnine, D., & Kame'enui, E. J. (1992). *Curriculum guidelines for diverse learners* (Monograph for National Center to Improve the Tools of Educators). Eugene: University of Oregon.

Dixon, R. C., & Engelmann, S. (2002). *Spelling through morphographs.* DeSoto, TX: SRA.

Dixon, R. C., Engelmann, S., Bauer, M. M., Steely, D., & Wells, T. (2007). *Spelling mastery.* DeSoto, TX: SRA.

Dockrell, J. E., Lindsay, G., Connelly, V., & Mackie, C. (2007). Constraints in the production of written texts in children with specific language impairments. *Exceptional Children, 73,* 147–164.

Dodge, K. A. (1983). Behavioral antecedents of peer status. *Child Development, 54,* 1400–1416.

Dodge, K. A., Pettit, G. S., McClaskey, C. L., & Brown, M. M. (1986). Social competence in children. *Monograph of the Society for Research in Child Development, 51*(2, Serial No. 213).

Dolch, E. W. (1955). *Methods in reading.* Champaign, IL: Garrard.

Dolch, E. W. (1960). *Better spelling.* Champaign, IL: Garrard.

Dowhower, S. L. (1987). Effects of repeated reading on second-grade transitional readers' fluency and comprehension. *Reading Research Quarterly, 22,* 389–406.

Dowhower, S. L. (1994). Repeated reading revisited: Research into practice. *Reading and Writing Quarterly, 10,* 343–358.

Dowis, C. L., & Schloss, P. (1992). The impact of mini-lessons on writing skills. *Remedial and Special Education, 13*(5), 34–42.

Driscoll, M. J. (2008). Embracing coaching as professional development. *Principal Leadership, 9,* 40–44.

Duling, W. P. (1999). Literacy development of second language learners with technology and LEA. In O. G. Nelson & W. M. Linek (Eds.), *Practical classroom applications of language experience: Looking back, looking forward* (pp. 248–256). Boston: Allyn & Bacon.

Dunn, L. M., & Dunn, D. M. (2007). *Peabody Picture Vocabulary Test—Fourth Edition.* Minneapolis, MN: Pearson.

Dunn, R., Beaudry, J. S., & Klavas, A. (1989). Survey of research on learning styles. *Educational Leadership, 46*(6), 50–58.

Durlak, C. M., Rose, E., & Bursuck, W. D. (1994). Preparing high school students with learning disabilities for the transition to postsecondary education: Teaching the skills of self-determination. *Journal of Learning Disabilities, 27,* 51–59.

Early, G. (1973). The case for cursive writing. *Academic Therapy, 9,* 105–108.

Ecalle, J., Magnan, A., & Calmus, C. (2009). Lasting effects on literacy skills with a computer-assisted learning using syllabic units in low-progress readers. *Computers and Education, 52,* 554–561.

Edwards, P. (1973). Panorama: A study technique. *Journal of Reading, 17,* 132–135.

Ehren, B. J. (2006). Partnerships to support reading comprehension for students with language impairment. *Topics in Language Disorders, 26,* 42–54.

Ehri, L. C. (1995). Phases of development in learning to read words by sight. *Journal of Research in Reading, 18,* 116–125.

Ehri, L. C. (1998). Grapheme-phoneme knowledge is essential for learning to read words in English. In J. Methsala & L. Ehri (Eds.), *Word recognition in beginning literacy* (pp. 3–40). Mahwah, NJ: Erlbaum Associates.

Ekwall, E. E., & Shanker, J. L. (1988). *Diagnosis and remediation of the disabled reader* (3rd ed.). Boston: Allyn & Bacon.

Elbaum, B., Vaughn, S., Hughes, M., & Moody, S. W. (1999). Grouping practices and reading outcomes for students with disabilities. *Exceptional Children, 65,* 399–415.

Elksnin, L. K., & Elksnin, N. (1998). Teaching social skills to students with learning and behavior problems. *Intervention in School and Clinic, 33,* 131–140.

Ellett, L. (1993). Instructional practices in mainstreamed secondary classrooms. *Journal of Learning Disabilities, 26,* 57–64.

Elliott, S. N. (1998). Performance assessment of students' achievement: Research and practice. *Learning Disabilities Research and Practice, 13,* 233–241.

Elliott, S. N., Gresham, F. M., Beddow, P. A., & Frank, J. L. (2008). Intervention validity of social behavior rating scales: Features of assessments that link results to treatment plans. *Assessment for Effective Intervention, 34,* 15–24.

Elliott, S. N., Gresham, F. M., & Heffer, R. W. (1987). Social-skill interventions: Research findings and training techniques. In C. A. Maher & J. E. Zins (Eds.), *Psychoeducational interventions in the schools* (pp. 141–159). New York: Pergamon.

Ellis, E. S. (1986). The role of motivation and pedagogy on the generalization of cognitive strategy training. *Journal of Learning Disabilities, 19,* 66–70.

Ellis, E. S. (1997). *The content enhancement series: The clarifying routine.* Lawrence, KS: Edge Enterprises.

Ellis, E. S. (1998). *The content enhancement series: The framing routine.* Lawrence, KS: Edge Enterprises.

Ellis, E. S., Deshler, D. D., Lenz, B. K., Schumaker, J. B., & Clark, F. L. (1991). An instructional model for teaching learning strategies. *Focus on Exceptional Children, 24*(1), 1–14.

Ellis, E. S., & Friend, P. (1991). Adolescents with learning disabilities. In B. Y. L. Wong (Ed.), *Learning about learning disabilities* (pp. 505–561). San Diego, CA: Academic Press.

Ellis, E. S., & Lenz, B. K. (1987). A component analysis of effective learning strategies for LD students. *Learning Disabilities Focus, 2*(2), 94–107.

Ellis, E. S., & Lenz, B. K. (1996). Perspectives on instruction in learning strategies. In D. D. Deshler, E. S. Ellis, & B. K. Lenz, *Teaching adolescents with learning disabilities: Strategies and methods* (2nd ed., pp. 9–60). Denver, CO: Love.

Ellis, E. S., Lenz, B. K., & Sabornie, E. J. (1987a). Generalization and adaptation of learning strategies to natural environments: Part I: Critical agents. *Remedial and Special Education, 8*(1), 6–20.

Ellis, E. S., Lenz, B. K., & Sabornie, E. J. (1987b). Generalization and adaptation of learning strategies to natural environments: Part II: Research into practice. *Remedial and Special Education, 8*(2), 6–23.

Elmore, R. F. (1992). Why restructuring alone won't improve teaching. *Educational Leadership, 49*(7), 44–48.

Emmer, E. T., & Evertson, C. M. (2009). *Classroom management for middle and high school teachers* (8th ed.). Upper Saddle River, NJ: Merrill/Pearson.

Engelmann, S. (1988). The Direct Instruction Follow Through model: Design and outcomes. *Education and Treatment of Children, 11,* 303–317.

Engelmann, S., & Bruner, E. C. (2002). *Reading mastery* (Classic ed.). DeSoto, TX: SRA.

Engelmann, S., Bruner, E. C., Hanner, S., Osborn, J., Osborn, S., & Zoref, L. (2001). *Reading mastery plus.* DeSoto, TX: SRA.

Engelmann, S., Bruner, E. C., Hanner, S., Osborn, J., Osborn, S., Zoref, L., Engelmann, O., & Davis, K. (2008). *Reading mastery signature edition.* DeSoto, TX: SRA.

Engelmann, S., Carnine, L., Johnson, G., Meyer, L., Becker, W., Eisele, J., Haddox, P., Hanner, S., & Osborn, S. (2008). *Corrective reading.* DeSoto, TX: SRA.

Englehart, J. (2006). Teacher perceptions of student behavior as a function of class size. *Social Psychology of Education, 9,* 245–272.

Englert, C. S., & Mariage, T. V. (1991). Making students partners in the comprehension process: Organizing the reading "POSSE." *Learning Disability Quarterly, 14,* 123–138.

Englert, C. S., Tarrant, K. L., & Mariage, T. V. (1992). Defining and redefining instructional practice in special education: Perspectives on good teaching. *Teacher Education and Special Education, 15,* 62–86.

Englert, C. S., Tarrant, K. L., Mariage, T. V., & Oxer, T. (1994). Lesson talk as the work of reading groups: The effectiveness of two interventions. *Journal of Learning Disabilities, 27,* 165–185.

Englert, C. S., Wu, X., & Zhao, Y. (2005). Cognitive tools for writing: Scaffolding the performance of students through technology. *Learning Disabilities Research & Practice, 20,* 184–198.

Englert, C. S., Zhao, Y., Dunsmore, K., Collings, N. Y., & Wolbers, K. (2007). Scaffolding the writing of students with disabilities through procedural facilitation: Using an internet-based technology to improve performance. *Learning Disabilities Quarterly, 30,* 9–30.

Epstein, M. H., & Cullinan, D. (1998). *Scale for Assessing Emotional Disturbance.* Austin, TX: PRO-ED.

Epstein, M. H., Munk, D. D., Bursuck, W. D., Polloway, E. A., & Jayanthi, M. (1999). Strategies for improving home-school communication about homework for students with disabilities. *The Journal of Special Education, 33,* 166–176.

Ervin-Tripp, S., & Mitchell-Kernan, C. (Eds.). (1977). *Child discourse.* New York: Academic Press.

Espin, C., Shin, J., Deno, S. L., Skare, S., Robinson, S., & Benner, B. (2000). Identifying indicators of written expression proficiency for middle school students. *The Journal of Special Education, 34,* 140–153.

Fernald, G. (1988). *Remedial techniques in basic school subjects.* Austin, TX: PRO-ED.

Fewster, S., & MacMillan, P. D. (2002). School-based evidence for the validity of curriculum-based measurement of reading and writing. *Remedial and Special Education, 23,* 149–156.

Fisher, C. W., Berliner, D. C., Filby, N. N., Marliave, R., Cahen, L. S., & Dishaw, M. M. (1980). Teaching behaviors, academic learning time, and student achievement: An overview. In C. Denham & A. Lieberman (Eds.), *Time to learn.* Washington, DC: National Institute of Education.

Fisher, C. W., Berliner, D. C., Filby, N. N., Marliave, R., Cahen, L. S., Dishaw, M. M., & Moore, J. E. (1978). *Teaching and learning in the elementary school: A summary of the Beginning Teacher Evaluation Study.* San Francisco: Far West Laboratory for Educational Research and Development.

Fister, S. L., & Kemp, K. A. (1995). *TGIF: But what will I do on Monday?* Longmont, CO: Sopris West.

Fitts, W. H., & Warren, W. L. (1996). *Tennessee Self-Concept Scale: Second Edition.* Los Angeles: Western Psychological Services.

Flanders, N. (1970). *Analyzing teacher behavior.* Menlo Park, CA: Addison-Wesley.

Fleischner, J. E., Nuzum, M. B., & Marzola, E. S. (1987). Devising an instructional program to teach arithmetic problem-solving skills to students with learning disabilities. *Journal of Learning Disabilities, 20,* 214–217.

Foegen, A., Jiban, C. L., & Deno, S. L. (2007). Progress monitoring measures in mathematics: A review of the literature. *The Journal of Special Education, 41,* 121–139.

Folk, M. C., & Campbell, J. (1978). Teaching functional reading to the TMR. *Education and Training of the Mentally Retarded, 13,* 322–326.

Fontana, J. L., Scruggs, T., & Mastropieri, M. A. (2007). Mnemonic strategy instruction in inclusive secondary social studies classes. *Remedial and Special Education, 28,* 345–355.

Foorman, B. R., & Torgesen, J. (2001). Critical elements of classroom and small-group instruction promote reading success in all children. *Learning Disabilities Research & Practice, 16,* 203–212.

Forgan, J. W. (2002). Using bibliotherapy to teach problem solving. *Intervention in School and Clinic, 38,* 75–82.

Forness, S. R., & Kavale, K. A. (1985). Effects of class size on attention, communication, and disruption of mildly mentally retarded children. *American Educational Research Journal, 22*(3), 403–412.

Forness, S. R., & Kavale, K. A. (1996). Treating social skill deficits in children with learning disabilities: A meta-analysis of the research. *Learning Disability Quarterly, 19,* 2–13.

Fourqurean, J. M., & LaCourt, T. (1990). A follow-up study of former special education students: A model for program evaluation. *Remedial and Special Education, 12*(1), 16–23.

Fowler, J. W., & Peterson, P. L. (1981). Increasing reading persistence and altering attributional style of learned helpless children. *Journal of Educational Psychology, 73,* 251–260.

Frank, A. R., & Brown, D. (1992). Self-monitoring strategies in arithmetic. *Teaching Exceptional Children, 24*(2), 52–53.

Frith, G. (1991). Facilitating homework through effective support systems. *Teaching Exceptional Children, 24*(1), 48–49.

Fry, E. (1977). Fry's readability graph: Clarifications, validity, and extension to level 17. *Journal of Reading, 21,* 242–252.

Fry, E. B., & Kress, J. E. (2006). *The reading teacher's book of lists* (5th ed.). San Francisco: Jossey-Bass.

Fuchs, D., & Fuchs, L. S. (1988). Evaluation of the adaptive learning environments model. *Exceptional Children, 55,* 115–217.

Fuchs, D., & Fuchs, L. S. (1994). Inclusive schools movement and the radicalization of special education reform. *Exceptional Children, 60,* 294–309.

Fuchs, D., Fuchs, L. S., & Burish, P. (2000). Peer-assisted learning strategies: An evidence-based practice to promote reading achievement. *Learning Disabilities Research & Practice, 15,* 85–91.

Fuchs, D., Fuchs, L. S., Mathes, P. G., & Simmons, D. C. (1997). Peer-assisted learning strategies: Making classrooms more responsive to diversity. *American Educational Research Journal, 34,* 174–206.

Fuchs, D., Fuchs, L. S., Thompson, A., Svenson, E., Yen, L., Otaiba, S. A., Yang, N., McMaster, K. N., Prentice, K., Kazden, S., & Saenz, L. (2001). Peer-assisted learning strategies in reading. *Remedial and Special Education, 22,* 15–21.

Fuchs, D., Mathes, P. G., & Fuchs, L. S. (1996). *Peabody peer-assisted learning strategies reading methods.* Nashville, TX: Peabody College.

Fuchs, L. S. (1986). Monitoring progress of mildly handicapped pupils: Review of current practice and research. *Remedial and Special Education, 7*(5), 5–12.

Fuchs, L. S. (2004). The past, present, and future of curriculum-based measurement research. *School Psychology Review, 33,* 188–192.

Fuchs, L. S., Bahr, C. M., & Rieth, H. J. (1989). Effects of goal structures and performance contingencies on the math performance of adolescents with learning disabilities. *Journal of Learning Disabilities, 22*, 554–560.

Fuchs, L. S., & Fuchs, D. (1986). Effects of systematic formative evaluation: A meta-analysis. *Exceptional Children, 53*, 199–208.

Fuchs, L. S., & Fuchs, D. (2001). Principles for the prevention and intervention of mathematics difficulties. *Learning Disabilities Research & Practice, 16*, 85–95.

Fuchs, L. S., & Fuchs, D. (2007). A model for implementing responsiveness to intervention. *Teaching Exceptional Children, 35*(5), 14–23.

Fuchs, L. S., Fuchs, D., Craddock, C., Hollenbeck, K. N., Hamlett, C. L., & Schatschneider, C. (2008). Effects of small-group tutoring with and without validated classroom instruction on at-risk students' math problem-solving: Are two tiers of prevention better than one? *Journal of Educational Psychology, 100*, 491–509.

Fuchs, L. S., Fuchs, D., & Deno, S. L. (1985). The importance of goal ambitiousness and goal mastery to student achievement. *Exceptional Children, 52*, 63–71.

Fuchs, L. S., Fuchs, D., Eaton, S., Hamlett, C. L., & Karns, K. (2000). Supplementing teacher judgments of mathematics test accommodations with objective data sources. *School Psychology Review, 29*, 65–85.

Fuchs, L. S., Fuchs, D., & Hamlett, C. L. (1989). Effects of instrumental use of curriculum-based measurement to enhance instructional programs. *Remedial and Special Education, 10*(2), 43–52.

Fuchs, L. S., Fuchs, D., Hamlett, C. L., Hope, S. K., Hollenbeck, K. N., Capizzi, A. M., Craddock, C. F., & Brothers, R. L. (2006). Extending responsiveness-to-intervention to math problem-solving at third grade. *Teaching Exceptional Children, 38*(4), 59–63.

Fuchs, L. S., Fuchs, D., Hamlett, C. L., Walz, L., & Germann, G. (1993). Formative evaluation of academic progress: How much growth can we expect? *School Psychology Review, 22*(1), 27–48.

Fuchs, L. S., Fuchs, D., Karns, K., & Phillips, N. (1996). *Peabody peer-assisted learning strategies in math.* Nashville, TX: Peabody College.

Fuchs, L. S., Fuchs, D., & Kazdan, S. (1999). Effects of peer-assisted learning strategies on high school students with serious reading problems. *Remedial and Special Education, 20*, 309–318.

Fuchs, L. S., Fuchs, D., & Maxwell, L. (1988). The validity of informal reading comprehension measures. *Remedial and Special Education, 9*(2), 20–28.

Fuchs, L. S., Fuchs, D., Phillips, N. B., Hamlett, C. L., & Karns, K. (1995). Acquisition and transfer effects of classwide peer-assisted learning strategies in mathematics for students with varying learning histories. *School Psychology Review, 24*, 604–620.

Fuchs, L. S., Hamlett, C., & Fuchs, D. (1999). *Monitoring Basic Skills Progress: Basic Math.* Austin, TX: PRO-ED.

Fulghum, R. (1988). *All I really need to know I learned in kindergarten.* New York: Ballantine Books.

Gagnon, J. C., & Maccini, P. (2001). Preparing students with disabilities for algebra. *Teaching Exceptional Children, 34*(1), 8–15.

Gajria, M., Salend, S. J., & Hemrick, M. A. (1994). Teacher acceptability of testing modifications for mainstreamed students. *Learning Disabilities Research & Practice, 9,* 236–243.

Garcia, E., Jensen, B. T., & Scribner, K. P. (2009). The demographic. *Association for Supervision and Curriculum Development, 66*(7), 8–13.

Garden, J. L., Casey, A., & Christenson, S. L. (1985). Implementing a prereferral intervention system. Part I. The model. *Exceptional Children, 51*, 377–384.

Gartland, D. (2007). Reading instruction. In P. J. Schloss, M. A. Schloss, & C. N. Schloss, *Instructional methods for secondary students with learning and behavior problems* (4th ed., pp. 233–256). Boston: Allyn & Bacon/Pearson.

Geary, D. C. (2004). Mathematics and learning disabilities. *Journal of Learning Disabilities, 37*, 4–15.

Gentry, J. R. (1982). An analysis of developmental spellings in Gnys at wrk. *The Reading Teacher, 36*, 192–200.

Gentry, J. R. (2004). *The science of spelling: The explicit specifics that make great readers and writers (and spellers!).* Portsmouth, NH: Heinemann.

Gentry, J. R. (2006). *Breaking the code: The new science of beginning reading and writing.* Portsmouth, NH: Heinemann.

Gerber, P. J. (1994). Researching adults with learning disabilities from an adult-development perspective. *Journal of Learning Disabilities, 27*, 6–9.

Gerber, P. J., & Popp, P. A. (1999). Consumer perspectives on the collaborative teaching model: Views of students with and without LD and their parents. *Remedial and Special Education, 20*, 288–296.

Gerber, P. J., & Popp, P. A. (2000). Making collaborative teaching more effective for academically able students: Recommendations for implementation and training. *Learning Disabilities Quarterly, 23*, 229–236.

Gerber, P. J., Schneiders, C. A., Paradise, L. V., Reiff, H. B., Ginsberg, R., & Popp, P. A. (1990). Persisting problems of adults with learning disabilities: Self-reported comparisons from their school-age and adult years. *Journal of Learning Disabilities, 23*, 570–573.

German, D. J. (1984). Diagnosis of word-finding disorders in children with learning disabilities. *Journal of Learning Disabilities, 17*, 353–359.

German, D. J. (1990). *Test of Adolescent/Adult Word Finding.* Austin, TX: PRO-ED.

German, D. J. (2000). *Test of Word Finding—2.* Austin, TX: PRO-ED.

Gersten, R., & Baker, S. (2001). Teaching expressive writing to students with learning disabilities: A meta-analysis. *Elementary School Journal, 101*, 251–272.

Gersten, R., Camine, D., & Woodward, J. (1987). Direct instruction research: The third decade. *Remedial and Special Education, 8*(6), 48–56.

Gersten, R., & Dimino, J. (1993). Visions and revisions: A special education perspective on the whole language controversy. *Remedial and Special Education, 14*(4), 5–13.

Gersten, R., Fuchs, L. S., Compton, D., Coyne, M., Greenwood, C., & Innocenti. M. S. (2005). Quality indicators for group experimental and quasi-experimental research in special education. *Exceptional Children, 71*, 149–164.

Gersten, R., Fuchs, L. S., Williams, J. P., & Baker, S. (2001). Teaching reading comprehension strategies to students with learning disabilities: A review of research. *Review of Educational Research, 71*, 279–320.

Gersten, R., & Woodward, J. (1994). The language-minority student and special education: Issues, trends, and paradoxes. *Exceptional Children, 60*, 310–322.

Gettinger, M. (1991). Learning time and retention differences between nondisabled students and students with learning disabilities. *Learning Disability Quarterly, 14*, 179–189.

Gillingham, A., & Stillman, B. W. (1997). *The Gillingham manual: Remedial training for children with specific disability in reading, spelling, and penmanship* (8th ed.). Cambridge, MA: Educators Publishing Service.

Ginsburg, H. P. (1987). How to assess number facts, calculation, and understanding. In D. D. Hammill (Ed.), *Assessing the abilities and instructional needs of students* (pp. 483–503). Austin, TX: PRO-ED.

Ginsburg, H. P., & Baroody, A. J. (2003). *Test of Early Mathematics Ability—3.* Austin, TX: PRO-ED.

Glasser, W. (1965). *Reality therapy: A new approach to psychiatry.* New York: Harper & Row.

Glutting, J. J., & Wilkinson, G. S. (2003). *Wide Range Interest and Occupation Test—Second Edition.* Austin, TX: PRO-ED.

Goldberg, M. F. (1990). Portrait of Madeline Hunter. *Educational Leadership, 47*(5), 41–43.

Goldberg, R. J., Higgins, E. L., Raskind, M. H., & Herman, K. L. (2003). Predictors of success in individuals with learning disabilities: A qualitative analysis of a 20-year longitudinal study. *Learning Disabilities Research & Practice, 18*, 222–236.

Goldiamond, I. (1984). Training parent trainers and ethecists in nonlinear analysis of behavior. In R. F. Dangle & A. Polster (Eds.), *Foundations of research and practice* (pp. 504–545). New York: Gilford Press.

Goldman, R., & Fristoe, M. (2000). *Goldman-Fristoe Test of Articulation—2.* Austin, TX: PRO-ED.

Goldstein, A. P., & McGinnis, E. (1997). *Skillstreaming the adolescent* (Rev. ed.). Champaign, IL: Research Press.

Good, R. H., III, & Kaminski, R. (2003). *DIBELS: Dynamic Indicators of Basic Early Literacy Skills* (6th ed.). Frederick, CO: Sopris West.

Goode, D. (1990). Thinking about and discussing quality of life. In R. Schalock & M. Begab (Eds.), *Quality of life: Perspectives and issues* (pp. 41–58). Washington, DC: American Association on Mental Retardation.

Goodlad, J. I. (1984). *A place called school.* New York: McGraw-Hill.

Goodman, K. S. (1986). *What's whole in whole language?* Portsmouth, NH: Heinemann.

Gordon, J., Vaughn, S., & Schumm, J. S. (1993). Spelling interventions: A review of literature and implications for instruction for students with learning disabilities. *Learning Disabilities Research & Practice, 8*, 175–181.

Goswami, U. (1998). Rime-based coding in early reading development in English: Orthographic analogies and rime neighborhoods. In D. Hulme & R. M. Joshi (Eds.), *Reading and spelling: Development and disorders* (pp. 69–86). Mahwah, NJ: Erlbaum Associates.

Graden, J. L., Casey, A., & Christenson, S. L. (1985). Implementing a prereferral intervention system. Part I. The model. *Exceptional Children, 51*, 377–384.

Graham, S. (1990). The role of production factors in learning disabled students' compositions. *Journal of Educational Psychology, 82*, 781–791.

Graham, S. (1992). Issues in handwriting instruction. *Focus on Exceptional Children, 25*, 1–14.

Graham, S. (1999). Handwriting and spelling instruction for students with learning disabilities: A review. *Learning Disability Quarterly, 22*, 78–98.

Graham, S. (2006). Writing. In P. Alexander & P. Winne (Eds.), *Handbook of educational psychology* (pp. 457–478). Mahwah, NJ: Erlbaum.

Graham, S., Berninger, V., & Weintraub, N. (1998). The relationship between handwriting style and speed and legibility. *Journal of Educational Research, 91*, 290–297.

Graham, S., Berninger, V., Weintraub, N., & Shafer, W. (1998). The development of handwriting fluency and legibility in grades 1 through 9. *Journal of Educational Research, 92*, 42–52.

Graham, S., & Freeman, S. (1986). Strategy training and teacher vs. student-controlled study conditions: Effects on LD students' spelling performance. *Learning Disability Quarterly, 9*, 15–22.

Graham, S., & Harris, K. R. (1988). Instructional recommendations for teaching writing to exceptional students. *Exceptional Children, 54*, 506–512.

Graham, S., & Harris, K. R. (1994). Implications of constructivism for teaching writing to students with special needs. *The Journal of Special Education, 28*, 275–289.

Graham, S., & Harris, K. R. (2005). Improving writing performance of young struggling writers: Theoretical and programmatic research from the Center on Accelerating Student Learning. *The Journal of Special Education, 39*, 19–33.

Graham, S., Harris, K. R., & Larsen, L. (2001). Prevention and intervention of writing difficulties for students with learning disabilities. *Learning Disabilities Research & Practice, 16*, 74–84.

Graham, S., Harris, K. R., & Loynachan, C. (1994). The Spelling for Writing list. *Journal of Learning Disabilities, 27*, 210–214.

Graham, S., Harris, K. R., MacArthur, C. A., & Schwartz, S. (1991). Writing and writing instruction for students with learning disabilities: Review of a research program. *Learning Disability Quarterly, 14,* 89–114.

Graham, S., & Perin, D. (2007). *Writing next: Effective strategies to improve writing of adolescents in middle and high schools* (A report to Carnegie Corporation of New York). Washington, DC: Alliance of Excellent Education.

Graham, S., & Voth, V. P. (1990). Spelling instruction: Making modifications for students with learning disabilities. *Academic Therapy, 25,* 447–457.

Graham, S., & Weintraub, N. (1996). A review of handwriting research: Progress and prospects from 1980 to 1994. *Educational Psychology Review, 8,* 7–87.

Grant, R. (1993). Strategic training for using text headings to improve students' processing of content. *Journal of Reading, 36,* 482–488.

Gravois, T. A., & Rosenfield, S. A. (2006). Impact of instructional consultation teams on the disproportionate referral and placement of minority students in special education. *Remedial and Special Education, 27,* 42–52.

Greene, G. (1994). The magic of mnemonics. *LD Forum, 19*(3), 34–37.

Greenwood, C. R. (1991). Longitudinal analysis of time, engagement, and achievement in at-risk versus non-risk students. *Exceptional Children, 57,* 521–534.

Greenwood, C. R., Arreaga-Mayer, C., & Carta, J. J. (1994). Identification and translation of effective teacher-developed instructional procedures for general practice. *Remedial and Special Education, 15,* 140–151.

Greenwood, C. R., Carta, J. J., & Hall, R. V. (1988). The use of peer tutoring strategies in classroom management and educational instruction. *School Psychology Review, 17*(2), 258–275.

Greenwood, C. R., Delquadri, J. C., & Carta, J. J. (1997). *Together we can! ClassWide Peer Tutoring to improve basic academic skills.* Longmont, CA: Sopris West.

Gresham, F. M., & Elliott, S. N. (1989). Social skills assessment technology for LD students. *Learning Disability Quarterly, 12,* 141–152.

Gresham, F. M., & Elliott, S. N. (2008). *Social Skills Improvement System Rating Scales.* Minneapolis, MN: Pearson.

Gresham, F. M., & Reschly, D. J. (1988). Issues in the conceptualization, classification, and assessment of social skills in the mildly handicapped. In T. Kratochwill (Ed.), *Advances in school psychology* (pp. 203–247). Hillsdale, NJ: Erlbaum.

Gresham, F. M., Sugai, G., & Horner, R. H. (2001). Interpreting outcomes of social skills training for students with high-incidence disabilities. *Exceptional Children, 67,* 331–344.

Griggs, S. A., & Dunn, R. (1988). High school dropouts: Do they learn differently from those who remain in school? *The Principal, 35*(1), 1–8.

Grossen, B. (1999). *The research base for corrective reading.* Columbus, OH: SRA/McGraw-Hill.

Gunter, P. L., Coutinho, M. J., & Cade, T. (2002). Classroom factors linked with academic gains among students with emotional and behavioral problems. *Preventing School Failure, 46,* 126–132.

Gunter, P. L., Miller, K. A., Venn, M. L., Thomas, K., & House, S. (2002). Self-graphing to success: Computerized data management. *Teaching Exceptional Children, 35*(2), 30–34.

Hagin, R. A. (1983). Write right—or left: A practical approach to handwriting. *Journal of Learning Disabilities, 16,* 266–271.

Hallahan, D. P., & Kauffman, J. M. (1994). Toward a culture of disability in the aftermath of Deno and Dunn. *The Journal of Special Education, 27,* 496–508.

Hallahan, D. P., Kauffman, J. M., & Pullen, P. C. (2009). *Exceptional learners: An introduction to special education.* Boston: Allyn & Bacon/Pearson.

Halpern, A. S. (1992). Transition: Old wine in new bottles. *Exceptional Children, 58,* 202–211.

Hammill, D. D., & Bartel, N. R. (2004). General teaching strategies and final thoughts. In D. D. Hammill & N. R. Bartel, *Teaching students with learning and behavior problems* (7th ed., pp. 403–417). Austin, TX: PRO-ED.

Hammill, D. D., Brown, V. L., Larsen, S. C., & Wiederholt, J. L. (2007). *Test of Adolescent and Adult Language—4.* Austin, TX: PRO-ED.

Hammill, D. D., & Larsen, S. C. (2009a). *Test of Written Language—4.* Austin, TX: PRO-ED.

Hammill, D. D., & Larsen, S. C. (2009b). *Written Language Observation Scale.* Austin, TX: PRO-ED.

Hammill, D. D., Leigh, J. E., Pearson, N. A., & Maddox, T. (1998). *Basic School Skills Inventory—Third Edition.* Austin, TX: PRO-ED.

Hammill, D. D., & Newcomer, P. L. (2008). *Test of Language Development—Intermediate: 4.* Austin, TX: PRO-ED.

Hammill, D. D., Wiederholt, J. L., & Allen, E. A. (2006). *Test of Silent Contextual Reading Fluency.* Austin, TX: PRO-ED.

Hancock, V., & Betts, F. (1994). From the lagging to the leading edge. *Educational Leadership, 51*(7), 24–29.

Hanover, S. (1983). Handwriting comes naturally? *Academic Therapy, 18,* 407–412.

Hanson, R. A., & Farrell, D. (1995). The long-term effects on high school seniors of learning to read in kindergarten. *Reading Research Quarterly, 30,* 908–933.

Harniss, M. K., Carnine, D. W., Silbert, J., & Dixon, R. C. (2007). Effective strategies for teaching mathematics. In M. D. Coyne, E. J. Kame'enui, & D. W. Carnine, *Effective teaching strategies that accommodate diverse learners* (pp. 129–170). Upper Saddle River, NJ: Merrill/Prentice Hall/Pearson.

Harniss, M. K., Epstein, M. H., Bursuck, W. D., Nelson, J., & Jayanthi, M. (2001). Resolving homework-related communication problems: Recommendations of parents of children with and without disabilities. *Reading and Writing Quarterly, 17*(3), 205–225.

Harper, G. F., & Maheady, L. (2007). Peer-mediated teaching and students with learning disabilities. *Intervention in School and Clinic, 43,* 101–107.

Harrington, T. F., & O'Shea, A. J. (2000). *Career Decision-Making System—Revised.* San Antonio, TX: Pearson.

Harris, C. A., Miller, S. P., & Mercer, C. D. (1995). Teaching initial multiplication skills to students with disabilities in general education classrooms. *Learning Disabilities Research & Practice, 10,* 180–195.

Harris, K. R., & Graham, S. (1996). Making the writing process work: Strategies for composition and self-regulation. Cambridge, MA: Brookline Books.

Harris, K. R., & Graham, S. (1999). Programmatic intervention research: Illustrations from the evolution of self-regulated strategy development. *Learning Disability Quarterly, 22,* 251–262.

Harris, K. R., Graham, S., & Mason, L. H. (2003). Self-regulated strategy development in the classroom: Part of a balanced approach to writing instruction for students with disabilities. *Focus on Exceptional Children, 35,* 1–16.

Harris, K. R., Graham, S., Mason, L. H., & Friedlander, B. (2008). *Powerful writing strategies for all students.* Baltimore, MD: Brookes.

Harrison, P. L., & Oakland, T. (2003). *Adaptive Behavior Assessment System—Second Edition.* San Antonio, TX: Pearson.

Hasbrouck, J., & Tindal, G. A. (2006). Oral reading fluency norms: A valuable assessment tool for reading teachers. *The Reading Teacher, 59*(7), 636–644.

Hasselbring, T. S., & Goin, L. I. (1989). Use of computers. In G. A. Robinson, J. R. Patton, E. A. Polloway, & L. R. Sargent (Eds.), *Best practices in mild mental disabilities.* Reston, VA: Division on Mental Retardation, Council for Exceptional Children.

Hasselbring, T. S., Goin, L. I., & Bransford, J. D. (1987). Developing automaticity. *Teaching Exceptional Children, 19*(3), 30–33.

Hasselbring, T. S., Goin, L. I., & Bransford, J. D. (1988). Developing math automaticity in learning handicapped children: The role of computerized drill and practice. *Focus on Exceptional Children, 20*(6), 1–7.

Hauerwas, L. B., & Walker, J. (2003). Spelling of inflected verb morphology in children with spelling deficits. *Learning Disabilities Research & Practice, 18,* 25–35.

Haynes, M. C., & Jenkins, J. R. (1986). Reading instruction in special education resource rooms. *American Educational Research Journal, 23,* 161–190.

Hazel, J. S., & Schumaker, J. B. (1988). Social skills and learning disabilities: Current issues and recommendations for future research. In J. F. Kavanagh & T. J. Truss (Eds.), *Learning disabilities: Proceedings of the national conference* (pp. 293–344). Parkton, MD: York Press.

Heath, N. L., & Ross, S. (2000). Prevalence and expression of depressive symptomology in students with and without learning disabilities. *Learning Disability Quarterly, 23,* 24–36.

Heckelman, R. G. (1969). The neurological impress method of remedial reading instruction. *Academic Therapy, 4,* 277–282.

Heddens, J. W., & Speer, W. R. (1997). *Today's mathematics. Part 2: Activities and instructional ideas* (9th ed.). Upper Saddle River, NJ: Merrill/Prentice Hall.

Heiman, T., & Margalit, M. (1998). Loneliness, depression, and social skills among students with mild mental retardation in different educational settings. *The Journal of Special Education, 32,* 154–163.

Hellman, A. W., Blair, T. R., & Rupley, W. H. (1998). *Principles and practices of teaching reading* (9th ed.). Upper Saddle River, NJ: Merrill/Prentice Hall.

Helwig, R., Anderson, L., & Tindal, G. (2002). Using a concept-grounded, curriculum-based measure in mathematics to predict statewide test scores for middle school students with LD. *The Journal of Special Education, 36,* 102–112.

Hembree, R. (1986). Research gives calculators a green light. *The Arithmetic Teacher, 34,* 18–21.

Henderson, C. (2001). *College freshmen with disabilities: A biennial statistical profile.* Washington, DC: American Council on Education, HEATH Resource Center.

Henry, M. K., & Rome, S. O'C. (1995). Results of Orton-Gillingham tutoring on students with reading disabilities: A retrospective study. In C. W. McIntyre & J. S. Pickering (Eds.), *Clinical studies of multisensory structured language education for students with dyslexia and related disorders* (pp. 138–143). Salem, OR: International Multisensory Structured Language Education Council.

Herman, R., & Stringfield, S. (1997). *Ten promising programs for educating all children: Evidence of impact.* Arlington, VA: Educational Research Service.

Heron, T. E., & Kimball, W. H. (1988). Gaining perspective with the educational consultation research base: Ecological considerations and further recommendations. *Remedial and Special Education, 9*(6), 21–28, 47.

Herrick, V. E. (1960). Handwriting and children's writing. *Elementary English, 37,* 248–258.

Heshusius, L. (1989). The Newtonian-mechanistic paradigm, special education, and contours of alternatives: An overview. *Journal of Learning Disabilities, 22,* 403–415.

Heshusius, L. (1991). Curriculum-based assessment and direct instruction: Critical reflections on fundamental assumptions. *Exceptional Children, 57,* 315–329.

Hildreth, G. (1963). Simplified handwriting for today. *Journal of Educational Research, 56,* 330–333.

Hirschman, A. O. (1986). *Rival views of market society and other recent essays.* New York: Viking.

Hoagland, J. (1972, March). Bibliotherapy: Aiding children in personality development. *Elementary English,* 390–394.

Hochman, J. C. (2005). Composition: Expressive language and writing. In J. R. Birsh (Ed.), *Multisensory teaching of basic language skills* (2nd ed., pp. 439–456). Baltimore, MD: Paul H. Brookes.

Hock, M. F., Schumaker, J. B., & Deshler, D. D. (2003). *Possible selves.* Lawrence, KS: Edge Enterprises.

Hofmeister, A. M. (1993). Elitism and reform in school mathematics. *Remedial and Special Education, 14*(6), 8–13.

Hogan, T. P., Catts, H. W., & Little, T. D. (2005). The relationship between phonological awareness and reading: Implications for the assessment of phonological awareness. *Language, Speech, & Hearing Services in Schools, 36,* 285–293.

Hook, P. E., & Jones, S. D. (2002). The importance of automaticity and fluency for efficient reading comprehension. *Perspectives* (The International Dyslexia Association), 28(1), 9–14.

Hoover, H. D., Dunbar, S. B., & Frisbie, D. A. (2006). *Iowa Tests of Basic Skills.* Rolling Meadows, IL: Riverside.

Hoover, J. J. (1993). *Teaching study skills to students with learning problems.* Boulder, CO: Hamilton.

Hoover, J. J. (2004). Teaching study skills to students. In D. D. Hammill & N. R. Bartel, *Teaching students with learning and behavior problems* (7th ed., pp. 291–324). Austin, TX: PRO-ED.

Horner, R. H., Carr, E. G., Halle, J., McGee, G., Odom, S., & Wolery, M. (2005). The use of single-subject research to identify evidence-based practice in special education. *Exceptional Children, 71,* 165–180.

Horton, L. W. (1970). Illegibilities in the cursive handwriting of sixth graders. *Elementary School Journal, 70,* 446–450.

Houck, C. K., & Billingsley, B. S. (1989). Written expression of students with and without learning disabilities: Differences across the grades. *Journal of Learning Disabilities, 22,* 561–567, 572.

Howell, K. W., & Lorson-Howell, K. A. (1990). What's the hurry: Fluency in the classroom. *Teaching Exceptional Children, 22*(3), 20–23.

Howell, K. W., & Nolet, V. (2000). *Curriculum-based evaluation: Teaching and decision making* (3rd ed.). Belmont, CA: Wadsworth/Thomson Learning.

Howell, S. C., & Barnhart, R. S. (1992). Teaching word problem solving at the primary level. *Teaching Exceptional Children, 24*(2), 44–46.

Hresko, W. P., Herron, S. R., & Peak, P. K. (1996). *Test of Early Written Language—2.* Austin, TX: PRO-ED.

Hresko, W. P., Reid, D. K., & Hammill, D. D. (1999). *Test of Early Language Development—3.* Austin, TX: PRO-ED.

Hresko, W. P., Schlieve, P. L., Herron, S. R., Swain, C., & Sherbenou, R. J. (2002). *Comprehensive Mathematical Abilities Test.* Austin, TX: PRO-ED.

Hudson, P., Lignugaris-Kraft, B., & Miller, T. (1993). Using content enhancements to improve the performance of adolescents with learning disabilities in content classes. *Learning Disabilities Research & Practice, 8,* 106–126.

Hudson, R. F., Pullen, P. C., Lane, H. B., & Torgesen, J. K. (2009). The complex nature of reading fluency: A multidimensional view. *Reading and Writing Quarterly, 25,* 4–32.

Hughes, C. A., Ruhl, K. L., & Peterson, S. K. (1988). Teaching self-management skills. *Teaching Exceptional Children, 20*(2), 70–72.

Hughes, C. A., Ruhl, K. L., Schumaker, J. B., & Deshler, D. D. (2002). Effects of instruction in an assignment completion strategy on the homework performance of students with learning disabilities in general education classes. *Learning Disabilities Research & Practice, 17,* 1–18.

Hughes, C. A., Schumaker, J. B., Deshler, D. D., & Mercer, C. D. (1993). *Learning strategies curriculum: The test-taking strategy* (Rev. ed.). Lawrence, KS: Edge Enterprises.

Hughes, C. A., & Smith, J. O. (1990). Cognitive and academic performance of college students with learning disabilities: A synthesis of literature. *Learning Disability Quarterly, 13,* 66–79.

Hunt, K. W. (1965). *Grammatical structures written at three grade levels* (NCTE Research Report No. 3). Champaign, IL: National Council of Teachers of English.

Hunt-Berg, M., Rankin, J. L., & Beukelman, D. R. (1994). Ponder the possibilities: Computer-supported writing for struggling writers. *Learning Disabilities Research & Practice, 9,* 169–178.

Hutchinson, N. L. (1993a). Effects of cognitive strategy instruction on algebra problem solving of adolescents with learning disabilities. *Learning Disability Quarterly, 16,* 34–63.

Hutchinson, N. L. (1993b). Second invited response: Students with disabilities and mathematics education reform—Let the dialogue begin. *Remedial and Special Education, 14*(6), 20–23.

Hutton, J. B., & Roberts, T. G. (2004). *Social-Emotional Dimension Scale—Second Edition.* Austin, TX: PRO-ED.

Hyson, M. C. (1985). Emotions and the microcomputer. An exploratory study of young children's responses. *Computers in Human Behavior, 1,* 143–152.

Idol, L. (1987). A critical thinking map to improve content area comprehension of poor readers. *Remedial and Special Education, 8*(4), 28–40.

Idol, L. (1988). A rationale and guidelines for establishing special education consultation programs. *Remedial and Special Education, 9*(6), 48–58.

Idol, L. (1993). *Special educator's consultation handbook* (2nd ed.). Austin, TX: PRO-ED.

Idol, L., & Croll, V. J. (1987). Story-mapping training as a means of improving reading comprehension. *Learning Disability Quarterly, 10,* 214–229.

Idol, L., Paolucci-Whitcomb, P., & Nevin, A. (1986). *Collaborative consultation.* Austin, TX: PRO-ED.

Idol, L., & West, J. F. (1991). Educational collaboration: A catalyst for effective schooling. *Intervention in School and Clinic, 27,* 70–78.

Institute of Education Sciences. (2007a, February 15). *What Works Clearinghouse intervention report: Bilingual cooperative integrated reading and composition.* Washington, DC: U.S. Department of Education.

Institute of Education Sciences. (2007b, July 16). *What Works Clearinghouse intervention report: Cooperative integrated reading and composition.* Washington, DC: U.S. Department of Education.

Institute of Education Sciences.(2008, December 2). *What Works Clearinghouse intervention report: Reading Recovery.* Washington, DC: U.S. Department of Education.

Isaacson, S. (2007). Written language. In P. J. Schloss, M. A. Schloss, & C. N. Schloss, *Instructional methods for secondary students with learning and behavior problems* (4nd ed., pp. 213–232). Boston: Allyn & Bacon/Pearson.

Jacobson, R., & Halle, M. (1956). *Fundamentals of language.* The Hague: Mouton.

Jayanthi, M., Nelson, J. S., Sawyer, V., Bursuck, W. D., & Epstein, M. H. (1995). Homework-communication problems among parents, classroom teachers, and special education teachers: An exploratory study. *Remedial and Special Education, 16*(2), 102–116.

Jenkins, J. J., & Palermo, D. S. (1964). Mediation processes and the acquisition of linguistic structure. In U. Bellugi & R. Brown (Eds.), *The acquisition of language. Monographs of the Society for Research in Child Development, 29*(1, Whole No. 92).

Jenkins, J. R., Graff, J. J., & Miglioretti, D. L. (2009). Estimating reading growth using intermittent CBM progress monitoring. *Exceptional Children, 75,* 151–163.

Jenson, W. R., Sheridan, S. M., Olympia, D. E., & Andrews, D. (1994). Homework and students with learning disabilities and behavior disorders: A practical, parent-based approach. *Journal of Learning Disabilities, 27,* 538–548.

Jitendra, A. K., Edwards, L. L., Sacks, G., & Jacobson, L. A. (2004). What research says about vocabulary instruction for students with learning disabilities. *Exceptional Children, 70,* 299–322.

Johnson, D. W., & Johnson, R. T. (1994). *Learning together and alone: Cooperative, competitive, and individualistic learning* (4th ed.). Boston: Allyn & Bacon.

Johnson, K. R., & Layng, T. V. J. (1992). Breaking the structuralist barrier: Literacy and numeracy with fluency. *American Psychologist, 47,* 1475–1490.

Johnson, M. S., Kress, R. A., & Pikulski, J. J. (1987). *Informal reading inventories.* Newark, DE: International Reading Association.

Johnson, W. (1944). Studies in language behavior. A program of research. *Psychological Monographs, 56*(2).

Joint Committee on Teacher Planning for Students with Disabilities. (1995). Planning for academic diversity in America's classrooms: Windows on reality, research, change, and practice. *Effective School Practices, 14*(2), 1–53.

Jones, C. J. (2001). CBAs that work: Assessing students' math content-reading levels. *Teaching Exceptional Children, 34*(1), 24–28.

Jones, V. F., & Jones, L. S. (1995). *Comprehensive classroom management: Creating positive learning environments for all students* (4th ed.). Boston: Allyn & Bacon.

Jordan, L., Miller, D. M., & Mercer, C. D. (1998). The effects of concrete to semiconcrete to abstract instruction in the acquisition and retention of fraction concepts and skills. *Learning Disabilities: A Multidisciplinary Journal, 9*(3), 115–122.

Jordan, L., Reyes-Blanes, M. E., Peel, B. B., Peel, H. A., & Lane, H. B. (1998). Developing teacher-parent partnerships across cultures: Effective parent conferences. *Intervention in School and Clinic, 33,* 141–147.

Jorissen, K. T., Salazar, P., Morrison, H., & Foster, L. (2008). Instructional coaches: Lessons from the field. *Principal Leadership: Middle School Edition, 9,* 17–19.

Juel, C. (1988). Learning to read and write: A longitudinal study of 54 children from first through fourth grades. *Journal of Educational Psychology, 80,* 437–447.

Juel, C., & Minden-Cupp, C. (2000). Learning to read words: Linguistic units and instructional strategies. *Reading Research Quarterly, 35,* 458–492.

Just Read, Florida! Final Report of the Department of Education. (February 15, 2002). Tallahassee, FL: Department of Education.

Kagan, S. (1989/1990). The structural approach to cooperative learning. *Educational Leadership, 47*(4), 12–15.

Kame'enui, E. J. (April, 2000). Reading presentation at Council for Exceptional Children International Conference, Vancouver, B.C.

Kame'enui, E. J., Darch, C. B., & Colvin, G. (1995, April). *Instructional classroom management.* Paper presented at the meeting of the Council for Exceptional Children, Orlando, FL.

Kame'enui, E. J., & Simmons, D. C. (1990). *Designing instructional strategies: The prevention of academic learning problems.* Upper Saddle River, NJ: Merrill/Prentice Hall.

Kaminski, R., & Good, R. H., III. (1996). Toward a technology for assessing basic early literacy skills. *School Psychology Review, 25*(2), 215–227.

Kamphaus, R. W., & Reynolds, C. R. (2007). *BASC-2 Behavioral and Emotional Screening System.* Minneapolis, MN: Pearson.

Kamps, D. M., Greenwood, C., Arreaga-Mayer, C., Veerkamp, M. B., Utley, C., Tapia, Y., Bowman-Perrott, L., & Bannister, H. (2008). The efficacy of classwide peer tutoring in middle schools. *Education & Treatment of Children, 31,* 119–153.

Karemaker, A. M., Pitchford, N. J., & O'Malley, C. (2008). Using whole-word multi-media software to support literacy acquisition: A comparison to traditional books. *Educational and Child Psychology, 25*(3), 101–122.

Karlsen, B., & Gardner, E. F. (1995). *Stanford Diagnostic Reading Test—Fourth Edition.* San Antonio, TX: Pearson.

Katsiyannis, A., Zhang, D., & Conroy, M. (2003). Availability of special education teachers: Trends and issues. *Remedial and Special Education, 24,* 246–253.

Katusic, S. K., Colligan, R. C., Weaver, A. L., & Barbaresi, W. J. (2009). The forgotten learning disability: Epidemiology of written-language disorder in a population-based birth cohort (1976–1982), Rochester, Minnesota. *Pediatrics, 123,* 1306–1313.

Kauffman, J. M. (1994). Places of change: Special education's power and identity in an era of educational reform. *Journal of Learning Disabilities, 27,* 610–618.

Kauffman, J. M., & Hallahan, D. P. (1993). Toward a comprehensive delivery system for special education. In

J. I. Goodlad & T. C. Lovitt (Eds.), *Integrating general and special education* (pp. 73–102). Upper Saddle River, NJ: Merrill/Prentice Hall.

Kauffman, J. M., & Hallahan, D. P. (Eds.). (1995). *The illusion of full inclusion: A comprehensive critique of a current special education bandwagon.* Austin, TX: PRO-ED.

Kaufman, A. S., & Kaufman, N. L. (2004). *Kaufman Test of Educational Achievement—II.* Minneapolis, MN: Pearson.

Kaufman, M., Agard, J., & Semmel, M. (1985). *Mainstreaming: Learners and their environment.* Cambridge, MA: Brookline Books.

Kay, P. J., Fitzgerald, M., Paradee, C., & Mellencamp, A. (1994). Making homework work at home: The parent's perspective. *Journal of Learning Disabilities, 27,* 550–561.

Kayser, H. (1989). Speech and language assessment of Spanish-English speaking children. *Language, Speech, and Hearing Services in Schools, 20,* 226–241.

Kearney, C. A., & Drabman, R. S. (1993). The write–say method for improving spelling accuracy in children with learning disabilities. *Journal of Learning Disabilities, 26,* 52–56.

Keller, C. (2002). A new twist on spelling instruction for elementary school teachers. *Intervention in School and Clinic, 38,* 3–7.

Kelly, B., Gersten, R., & Carnine, D. (1990). Student error patterns as a function of curriculum design: Teaching fractions to remedial high school students and high school students with learning disabilities. *Journal of Learning Disabilities, 23,* 23–29.

Kelman, M. E., & Apel, K. (2004). Effects of a multiple linguistic and prescriptive approach to spelling instruction: A case study. *Communication Disorders Quarterly, 25,* 56–66.

Keogh, B. (1993, December). *Viewing learning disabilities through a developmental lens: The importance of time and context.* Paper presented at The Cove School and Cove Foundation meeting, Educational and Psychological Needs of Students with Learning Disabilities, Winnetka, IL.

Keogh, B. K. (1994). What the special education research agenda should look like in the year 2000. *Learning Disabilities Research & Practice, 9,* 62–69.

Kerr, M. M., & Nelson, C. M. (2010). *Strategies for addressing behavior problems in the classroom* (6th ed.). Boston: Pearson.

King-Sears, M. E. (2001). Three steps for gaining access to the general education curriculum of learners with disabilities. *Intervention in School and Clinic, 37,* 67–76.

King-Sears, M. E., & Evmenova, A. S. (2007). Premises, principles, and processes for integrating TECHnology into instruction. *Teaching Exceptional Children, 40*(1), 6–14.

Kirk, S. A., Kirk, W. D., Minskoff, E., Mather, N., & Roberts, R. (2007). *Phonic reading lessons.* Novato, CA: Academic Therapy.

Kirsch, I. S., Jungeblut, A., Jenkins, L., & Kolstad, A. (1993). *Executive summary from adult literacy in America: A first look at the results of the National Adult Literacy Survey.* Washington, DC: U.S. Department of Education.

Kleinert, H. L., Green, P., Hurte, M., Clayton, J., & Oetinger, C. (2002). Creating and using meaningful alternate assessments. *Teaching Exceptional Children, 34*(4), 40–47.

Kleinert, H. L., Kennedy, S., & Kearns, J. F. (1999). The impact of alternate assessments: A statewide teacher survey. *The Journal of Special Education, 33,* 93–102.

Kline, F. M., Schumaker, J. B., & Deshler, D. D. (1991). Development and validation of feedback routines for instructing students with learning disabilities. *Learning Disability Quarterly, 14,* 191–207.

Klingner, J. K., Vaughn, S., Hughes, M. T., Schumm, J. S., & Elbaum, B. (1998). Outcomes for students with and without learning disabilities in inclusive classrooms. *Learning Disabilities Research & Practice, 13,* 153–161.

Knapp, M. S., Turnbull, B. J., & Shields, P. M. (1990). New directions for educating the children of poverty. *Educational Leadership, 48*(1), 4–8.

Koorland, M. A., Keel, M. C., & Ueberhorst, P. (1990). Setting aims for precision learning. *Teaching Exceptional Children, 22*(3), 64–68.

Kovaleski, J. F., & Glew, M. C. (2006). Bringing instructional support teams to scale: Implications of the Pennsylvania experience. *Remedial and Special Education, 27,* 16.

Kroesbergen, E. H., & Van Luit, J. E. H. (2003). Mathematics interventions for children with special needs: A meta-analysis. *Remedial and Special Education, 24,* 97–114.

Kroth, R. L., & Edge, D. (1997). *Strategies for communicating with parents and families of exceptional children* (3rd ed.). Denver, CO: Love.

Kuhn, M. R., & Stahl, S. A. (2000). *Fluency: A review of developmental and remedial practices* (CIERA Report No. 2-008). Ann Arbor: Center for the Improvement of Early Reading Achievement, University of Michigan.

Kuska, A., Webster, E. J. D., & Elford, G. (1964). *Spelling in language arts 6.* Don Mills, Ontario, Canada: Thomas Nelson & Sons.

Laberge, D., & Samuels, J. (1974). Toward a theory of automatic information processing in reading. *Cognitive Psychology, 6,* 293–323.

Lahey, M. (1988). *Language disorders and language development.* Boston: Allyn & Bacon.

Lalley, J. P., & Gentile, J. R. (2009). Classroom assessment and grading to assure mastery. *Theory into Practice, 48,* 28–35.

Lambert, M. A. (1996). Mathematics textbooks, materials, and manipulatives. *LD Forum, 21*(2), 33, 41–45.

Lambert, N., Nihira, K., & Leland, H. (1993). *AAMR Adaptive Behavior Scale—School* (2nd ed.). Austin, TX: PRO-ED.

Landrum, T. J., Tankersley, M., & Kauffman, J. M. (2003). What is special about special education for students with emotional or behavioral disorders? *The Journal of Special Education, 37,* 148–156.

Lane, K. L., Graham, S., Harris, K. R., & Weisenbach, J. L. (2006). Teaching writing strategies to young students struggling with writing and at risk for behavior disorders: Self-regulated strategy development. *Teaching Exceptional Children, 39*(1), 60–64.

Langford, K., Slade, K., & Barnett, A. (1974). An explanation of impress techniques in remedial reading. *Academic Therapy, 9,* 309–319.

Langone, J. (1990). *Teaching students with mild and moderate learning problems.* Boston: Allyn & Bacon.

Larsen, S. C., Hammill, D. D., & Moats, L. (1999). *Test of Written Spelling—4.* Austin, TX: PRO-ED.

Larson, V. L., & McKinley, N. (1995). *Language disorders in older students.* Eau Claire, WI: Thinking Publications.

Lazar, R. T., Warr-Leeper, G. A., Nicholson, C. B., & Johnson, S. (1989). Elementary school teachers' use of multiple meaning expressions. *Language, Speech, and Hearing Services in Schools, 20,* 420–429.

Ledford, J. R., Gast, D. L., Luscre, D., & Ayres, K. M. (2008). Observational and incidental learning by children with autism during small group instruction. *Journal of Autism and Developmental Disorders, 38,* 86–103.

Lee, D. M., & Allen, R. V. (1963). *Learning to read through experiences* (2nd ed.). New York: Appleton-Century-Crofts.

Lenneberg, E. H. (1967). *Biological foundations of language.* New York: Wiley.

Lenz, B. K., & Bulgren, J. A. (1988). *Issues related to enhancing content acquisition for students with learning disabilities.* Lawrence: University of Kansas Center for Research on Learning.

Lenz, B. K., Bulgren, J. A., & Hudson, P. (1990). Content enhancement: A model for promoting the acquisition of content by individuals with learning disabilities. In T. Scruggs & B. Wong (Eds.), *Intervention research in learning disabilities* (pp. 122–165). New York: Springer-Verlag.

Lenz, B. K., Bulgren, J. A., Schumaker, J. B., Deshler, D. D., & Boudah, D. J. (1994). *The content enhancement series: The unit organizer routine.* Lawrence, KS: Edge Enterprises.

Lenz, B. K., Deshler, D. D., & Schumaker, J. B. (1990). *The development and validation of planning routines to enhance the delivery of content to students with handicaps in general education settings* (Progress report). Lawrence: University of Kansas Center for Research on Learning.

Lenz, B. K., Ehren, B. J., & Smiley, L. R. (1991). A goal attainment approach to improve completion of project-type assignments by learning disabled adolescents. *Focus on Learning Disabilities, 6,* 166–176.

Lenz, B. K., Ellis, E. S., & Scanlon, D. (1996). *Teaching learning strategies to adolescents and adults with learning disabilities.* Austin, TX: PRO-ED.

Lenz, B. K., Marrs, R. W., Schumaker, J. B., & Deshler, D. D. (1993). *The content enhancement series: The lesson organizer routine.* Lawrence, KS: Edge Enterprises.

Lenz, B. K., Schumaker, J. B., Deshler, D. D., & Beals, V. L. (2007). *The word identification strategy.* Lawrence: University of Kansas Center for Research on Learning.

Lenz, B. K., Schumaker, J. B., Deshler, D. D., & Bulgren, J. A. (1998). *The content enhancement series: The course organizer routine.* Lawrence, KS: Edge Enterprises.

Leonard, L. B., Wilcox, M. J., Fulmer, K. C., & Davis, G. A. (1978). Understanding indirect requests: An investigation of children's comprehension of pragmatic meanings. *Journal of Speech and Hearing Research, 21,* 528–537.

Leslie, L., & Caldwell, J. (2006). *Qualitative Reading Inventory—4* (4th ed). Boston: Allyn & Bacon/Pearson.

Levin, H., Glass, G., & Meister, C. (1984). *Cost-effectiveness of four educational interventions.* Stanford, CA: Institute for Research on Educational Finance and Governance, Stanford University.

Levin, M. (2002). *A mind at a time.* New York: Simon & Schuster.

Levy, N. R., & Rosenberg, M. S. (1990). Strategies for improving the written expression of students with learning disabilities. *LD Forum, 16,* 23–30.

Lewandowski, L., & Arcangelo, K. (1994). The social adjustment and self-concept of adults with learning disabilities. *Journal of Learning Disabilities, 27,* 598–605.

Lewis, E. R., & Lewis, H. P. (1965). An analysis of errors in the formation of manuscript letters by first grade children. *American Educational Research Journal, 2,* 25–35.

Lewis, R. B., & Doorlag, D. H. (2006). *Teaching special students in general education classrooms* (7th ed.). Upper Saddle River, NJ: Merrill/Prentice Hall/Pearson.

Liberman, I. Y., & Liberman, A. M. (1990). Whole language vs. code-emphasis: Underlying assumptions and their implications for reading instruction. *Annals of Dyslexia, 40,* 51–77.

Licht, B. G. (1984). Cognitive-motivational factors that contribute to the achievement of learning-disabled children. *Annual Review of Learning Disabilities, 2,* 119–126.

Lieberman, L. M. (1983). The homework solution. *Journal of Learning Disabilities, 16,* 435.

Lindamood, P. C., & Lindamood, P. D. (1998). *Lindamood phoneme sequencing program for reading, spelling, and speech* (3rd ed.). Austin, TX: PRO-ED.

Lindamood, P. C., & Lindamood, P. D. (2004). *Lindamood Auditory Conceptualization Test—Third Edition.* Austin, TX: PRO-ED.

Lindsley, O. R. (1971). Precision teaching in perspective: An interview with Ogden R. Lindsley. *Teaching Exceptional Children, 3*(3), 114–119.

Lindstrom, L. E., & Benz, M. R. (2002). Phases of career development: Case studies of young women with learning disabilities. *Exceptional Children, 69,* 67–83.

Lipinski, J. M., Nida, R. E., Shade, D. D., & Watson, J. A. (1986). The effects of microcomputers on young children: An examination of free-play choices, sex differences, and social interactions. *Journal of Educational Computing Research, 2,* 147–168.

Locke, E. A., & Latham, G. P. (1990). *A theory of goal setting and task performance.* Upper Saddle River, NJ: Merrill/Prentice Hall.

Long, N. J., Wood, M. M., & Fecser, F. A. (2001). *Life space crisis intervention: Talking with students in conflict* (2nd ed.). Austin, TX: PRO-ED.

Lovitt, T. C. (1977). *In spite of my resistance: I've learned from children.* Upper Saddle River, NJ: Merrill/Prentice Hall.

Lovitt, T. C. (1995). *Tactics for teaching* (2nd ed.). Upper Saddle River, NJ: Merrill/Prentice Hall.

Lovitt, T. C., Guppy, T. E., & Blattner, J. E. (1969). The use of free-time contingency with fourth graders to increase spelling accuracy. *Behavior Research Therapy, 7,* 151–156.

Lyon, G. R. (1995a). Research initiatives in learning disabilities: Contributions from scientists supported by the National Institute of Child Health and Human Development. *Journal of Child Neurology, 10*(Suppl. 1), 120–126.

Lyon, G. R. (1995b). Towards a definition of dyslexia. *Annals of Dyslexia, 45,* 3–27.

Lyon, G. R. (1998). Overview of reading and literacy initiatives (Report to Committee on Labor and Human Resources, U.S. Senate). Bethesda, MD: National Institute of Child Health and Human Development, National Institutes of Health.

Lyon, G. R. (1999). *Education research: Is what we don't know hurting our children?* (Report to House Science Committee, Subcommittee on Basic Research, U.S. House of Representatives). Bethesda, MD: National Institute of Child Health and Human Development, National Institutes of Health.

Lyon, G. R. (2001, March 8). *Measuring success: Using assessments and accountability to raise student achievement.* Testimony provided to the Subcommittee on Education Reform, Committee on Education and the Workforce, U.S. House of Representatives, Washington, DC.

Lyon, G. R., Alexander, D., & Yaffe, S. (1997). Progress and promise in research in learning disabilities. *Learning Disabilities: A Multidisciplinary Journal, 8*(1), 1–6.

Maag, J. W. (2001). Management of surface behavior: A new look at an old approach. *Counseling and Human Development, 33*(9), 110.

Maag, J. W. (2002). A contextually based approach for treating depression in school-age children. *Intervention in School and Clinic, 37,* 149–155.

Maag, J. W., & Reid, R. (2006). Depression among students with learning disabilities: Assessing the risk. *Journal of Learning Disabilities, 39,* 3–10.

MacArthur, C. A. (2009). Assistive technology for struggling writers. *Perspectives on Language and Literacy, 35*(3), 31–33.

MacArthur, C. A., & Graham, S. (1987). Learning disabled students' composing under three methods of text production: Handwriting, word processing, and dictation. *The Journal of Special Education, 21,* 22–42.

MacArthur, C. A., & Haynes, J. B. (1995). Student assistant for learning from text (SALT): A hypermedia reading aid. *Journal of Learning Disabilities, 28,* 150–159.

MacArthur, C. A., Haynes, J. B., Malouf, D., Harris, K., & Owings, M. (1990). Computer-assisted instruction with learning disabled students: Achievement, engagement, and other factors that influence achievement. *Journal of Educational Computing Research, 6,* 311–328.

MacArthur, C. A., Schwartz, S. S., & Graham, S. (1991). A model for writing instruction: Integrating word processing and strategy instruction into a process approach to writing. *Learning Disabilities Research & Practice, 6,* 230–236.

Maccini, P., & Gagnon, J. C. (2002). Perceptions and application of NCTM Standards by special and general education teachers. *Exceptional Children, 68,* 325–344.

Maccini, P., & Hughes, C. A. (2000). Effects of a problem-solving strategy on the introductory algebra performance of secondary students with learning disabilities. *Learning Disabilities Research & Practice, 15,* 10–21.

Maccini, P., McNaughton, D., & Ruhl, K. L. (1999). Algebra instruction for students with learning disabilities: Implications from a research review. *Learning Disability Quarterly, 22,* 113–126.

MacGinitie, W. H., MacGinitie, R. K., Maria, K., Dreyer, L. G., & Hughes, K. E. (2000). *Gates-MacGinitie Reading Tests—Fourth Edition.* Rolling Meadows, IL: Riverside.

Madden, N. A., Slavin, R. E., Karweit, N. L., Dolan, L. J., & Wasik, B. A. (1993). Success for All: Longitudinal effects of a restructuring program for inner-city elementary schools. *American Educational Research Journal, 30,* 123–148.

Maheady, L., Harper, G. F., & Mallette, B. (1991). Peer-mediated instruction: A review of potential applications for special education. *Reading, Writing, and Learning Disabilities International, 7,* 75–103.

Maheady, L., Harper, G. F., & Mallette, B. (2001). Peer-mediated instruction and interventions and students with mild disabilities. *Remedial and Special Education, 22,* 4–14.

Mainzer, R. W., Jr., Mainzer, K. L., Slavin, R. E., & Lowry, E. (1993). What special education teachers should know about cooperative learning. *Teacher Education and Special Education, 16,* 42–50.

Majsterek, D., & Wilson, R. (1993). Computer-assisted instruction (CAI): An update on applications for students with learning disabilities. *LD Forum, 19*(1), 19–21.

Majsterek, D., Wilson, R., & Jones, E. D. (2007). Mathematics instruction. In P. J. Schloss, M. A. Schloss, & C. N. Schloss, *Instructional methods for secondary students with learning and behavior problems* (4th ed., pp. 257–276). Boston: Allyn & Bacon/Pearson.

Mann, P. H., Suiter, P. A., & McClung, R. M. (1992). *A guide to evaluating mainstreamed students* (4th ed.). Boston: Allyn & Bacon.

Margalit, M. (2006). Loneliness, the salutogenic paradigm and learning disabilities: Current research, future directions, and interventional implications. *Thalamus, 24,* 38–48.

Markwardt, F. C., Jr. (1998). *Peabody Individual Achievement Test—Revised.* Minneapolis, MN: Pearson.

Marsh, L. G., & Cooke, N. L. (1996). The effects of using manipulatives in teaching math problem solving to students with learning disabilities. *Learning Disabilities Research & Practice, 11,* 58–65.

Martinussen, R., & Tannock R. (2006). Working memory impairments in children with attention-deficit hyperactivity disorder with and without comorbid language learning disorders. *Journal of Clinical Experimental Neuropsychology, 28,* 1073–1094.

Maskel, S., & Felton, R. (1995). Analysis of achievement at the Hill Learning Development Center: 1990–1994. In C. W. McIntyre & J. S. Pickering (Eds.), *Clinical studies of multisensory structured language education for students with dyslexia and related disorders* (pp. 129–137). Salem, OR: International Multisensory Structured Language Education Council.

Mason, L. H. (2009). Effective instruction for written expression. *Perspectives on Language and Literacy, 35*(3), 21–24.

Mastropieri, M. A. (1988). Using the keyword method. *Teaching Exceptional Children, 20*(2), 4–8.

Mastropieri, M. A., Berkeley, S., Scruggs, T. E., & Marshak, L. (2008). Improving content-area instruction using evidence-based practices. *Insights on Learning Disabilities, 5,* 73–88.

Mastropieri, M. A., Leinart, A., & Scruggs, T. E. (1999). Strategies to increase reading fluency. *Intervention in School and Clinic, 34,* 278–283.

Mastropieri, M. A., & Scruggs, T. E. (1997). Best practices in promoting reading comprehension in students with learning disabilities: 1976 to 1996. *Remedial and Special Education, 18,* 197–213.

Mastropieri, M. A., Scruggs, T. E., & Fulk, B. J. M. (1990). Teaching abstract vocabulary with the keyword method: Effects on recall and comprehension. *Journal of Learning Disabilities, 23,* 92–96, 107.

Mastropieri, M. A., Scruggs, T. E., Mohler, L., Beranek, M., Spencer, V., Boon, R. T., & Talbot, E. (2001). Can middle school students with serious reading difficulties help each other learn anything? *Learning Disabilities Research & Practice, 16,* 18–27.

Mather, N. (1992). Whole language reading instruction for students with learning disabilities: Caught in the cross fire. *Learning Disabilities Research & Practice, 7,* 87–95.

Mather, N., Hammill, D. D., Allen, E. A., & Roberts, R. (2004). *Test of Silent Word Reading Fluency.* Austin, TX: PRO-ED.

Mather, N., & Roberts, R. (1994). Learning disabilities: A field in danger of extinction? *Learning Disabilities Research & Practice, 9,* 49–58.

Mather, N., Roberts, R., Hammill, D. D., & Allen, E. A. (2008). *Test of Orthographic Competence.* Austin, TX: PRO-ED.

Mathes, P. G., & Babyak, A. E. (2001). The effects of peer-assisted literacy strategies for first-grade readers with and without additional mini-skills lessons. *Learning Disabilities Research & Practice, 16,* 28–44.

Mathes, P. G., Clancy-Menchetti, J., & Torgesen, J. K. (2001). *Kindergarten peer-assisted literacy strategies.* Longmont, CO: Sopris West.

Mathes, P. G., & Torgesen J. K. (2005). *SRA early interventions in reading.* DeSoto, TX: SRA.

Mathes, P. G., Torgesen, J. K., Allen, S. H., & Allor, J. H. (2001). *First grade peer-assisted literacy strategies.* Longmont, CO: Sopris West.

Mayes, S. D., & Calhoun, S. L. (2007). Challenging the assumptions about the frequency and coexistence of learning disability types. *School Psychology International, 28,* 437–448.

Mayfield, K. H., Glenn, I. M., & Vollmer, T. R. (2008). Teaching spelling through prompting and review procedures using computer-based instruction. *Journal of Behavioral Education, 17,* 303–312.

Maynard, K., Pullen, P., & Coyne, M. (2010). Teaching vocabulary to first grade students at risk of reading difficulties through repeated shared storybook reading: A comparison of rich and basic instruction to incidental exposure. *Literacy Research and Instruction, 49.*

McCardle, P., Cooper, J. A., Houle, G. R., Karp, N., & Paul-Brown, D. (2001). Next steps in research and practice. *Learning Disabilities Research & Practice, 16,* 250–254.

McCarney, S. B., & Arthaud, T. J. (2005). *Behavior Evaluation Scale—3.* Columbia, MO: Hawthorne Educational Services.

McCarty, H., & Chalmers, L. (1997). Bibliotherapy: Intervention and prevention. *Teaching Exceptional Children, 29*(6), 12–13, 16–17.

McConnell, S., & Odom, S. (1986). Sociometrics: Peer-referenced measures and the assessment of social competence. In P. Strain, M. Guralnick, & H. Walker (Eds.), *Children's social behavior: Development, assessment, and modification* (pp. 215–284). Orlando, FL: Academic Press.

McDougall, D. (1998). Research on self-management techniques used by students with disabilities in general education settings: A descriptive review. *Remedial and Special Education, 19,* 310–320.

McGhee, R., Bryant, B. R., Larsen, S. C., & Rivera, D. M. (1995). *Test of Written Expression.* Austin, TX: PRO-ED.

McGillivray, J., & McCabe, M. (2007). Early detection of depression and associated risk factors in adults with mild/moderate intellectual disability. *Research in Developmental Disabilities, 28,* 59–70.

McGillivray, J., McCabe, M., & Kershaw, M. (2008). Depression in people with intellectual disability: An evaluation of a staff-administered treatment program. *Research in Developmental Disabilities, 29,* 524–536.

McGinnis, E., & Goldstein, A. P. (1997). *Skillstreaming the elementary school child* (Rev. ed.). Champaign, IL: Research Press.

McGuigan, C. A. (1975). *The effects of a flowing words list vs. fixed words lists and the implementation of procedures in the add-a-word spelling program* (Working Paper No. 52). Seattle: University of Washington, Experimental Education Unit.

McIntyre, C. W., & Pickering, J. S. (1995). *Clinical studies of multisensory structured language education for students with dyslexia and related disorders.* Salem, OR: International Multisensory Structured Language Education Council.

McKenna, M. C., & Picard, M. (2006/2007). Does miscue analysis have a role in effective practice? *The Reading Teacher, 60,* 378–380.

McKenzie, R. G. (1991). Content area instruction delivered by secondary learning disabilities teachers: A national survey. *Learning Disability Quarterly, 14,* 115–122.

McLoughlin, J. A., & Lewis, R. B. (2008). *Assessing students with special needs* (7th ed.). Upper Saddle River, NJ: Merrill/Prentice Hall/Pearson.

McMaster, K. L., & Campbell, H. (2008). New and existing curriculum-based writing measures: Technical features within and across grades. *School Psychology Review, 37,* 550–566.

McMaster, K. L., & Fuchs, D. (2002). Effects of cooperative learning on the academic achievement of students with learning disabilities: An update of Tateyama-Sniezek's review. *Learning Disabilities Research & Practice, 17,* 107–117.

McMaster, K. L., Fuchs, D., & Fuchs, L. S. (2006). Research on peer-assisted learning strategies: The promise and limitations of peer-mediated instruction. *Reading and Writing Quarterly: Overcoming Learning Difficulties, 22,* 5–25.

McMaster, K. L., Kung, S. H., Han, I., & Cao, M. (2008). Peer-assisted learning strategies: A "Tier 1" approach to promoting English learners' response to intervention. *Exceptional Children, 74,* 194–214.

McNaughton, D., Hughes, C. A., & Clark, K. (1994). Spelling instruction for students with learning disabilities: Implications for research and practice. *Learning Disability Quarterly, 17,* 169–185.

McNeil, D. (1970). The development of language. In P. H. Mussen (Ed.), *Carmichael's manual of child psychology* (Vol. 2, 3rd ed., pp. 1061–1161). New York: Wiley.

Meers, G. D. (1992). Getting ready for the next century. *Teaching Exceptional Children, 24*(4), 36–39.

Meese, R. L. (1994). *Teaching learners with mild disabilities: Integrating research and practice.* Pacific Grove, CA: Brooks/Cole.

Meichenbaum, D. (1977). *Cognitive-behavior modification: An integrative approach.* New York: Plenum Press.

Mellard, D. F., & Hazel, J. S. (1992). Social competencies as a pathway to successful life transitions. *Learning Disability Quarterly, 15,* 251–271.

Meltzer, L. J., Roditi, B. N., Haynes, D. P., Biddle, K. R., Paster, M., & Taber, S. E. (1996). *Strategies for success: Classroom teaching techniques for students with learning problems.* Austin, TX: PRO-ED.

Mercer, C. D., & Campbell, K. U. (1997). *Great leaps reading program: Grades K–2.* Gainesville, FL: Diarmuid.

Mercer, C. D., Campbell, K. U., Miller, M. D., Mercer, K. D., & Lane, H. B. (2000). Effects of a reading fluency intervention for middle schoolers with specific learning disabilities. *Learning Disabilities Research & Practice, 15,* 179–189.

Mercer, C. D., & Corbett, N. L. (1991). Enhancing assessment for students at risk for school failure. *Contemporary Education, 62,* 259–265.

Mercer, C. D., Jordan, L., & Miller, S. P. (1994). Implications of constructivism for teaching math to students with mild to moderate disabilities. *The Journal of Special Education, 28,* 290–306.

Mercer, C. D., Jordan, L., & Miller, S. P. (1996). Constructivistic math instruction for diverse learners. *Learning Disabilities Research & Practice, 11,* 147–156.

Mercer, C. D., Lane, H. B., Jordan, L., Allsopp, D. H., & Eisele, M. R. (1996). Empowering teachers and students with instructional choices in inclusive settings. *Remedial and Special Education, 17,* 226–236.

Mercer, C. D., Mercer, A. R., & Evans, S. (1982). The use of frequency in establishing instructional aims. *Journal of Precision Teaching, 3*(3), 57–63.

Mercer, C. D., Mercer, K. D., & Campbell, K. U. (2002). *Great leaps math* (A series of three manuals: *Addition and Subtraction Facts 0 to 9; Addition and Subtraction Facts 10 to 18; Multiplication and Division Facts 0 to 81*). Gainesville, FL: Diarmuid.

Mercer, C. D., & Miller, S. P. (1991–1993). *Strategic math series* (A series of seven manuals: *Addition Facts 0 to 9; Subtraction Facts 0 to 9; Place Value: Discovering Tens and Ones; Addition Facts 10 to 18; Subtraction Facts 10 to 18; Multiplication Facts 0 to 81; Division Facts 0 to 81*). Lawrence, KS: Edge Enterprises.

Mercer, C. D., & Miller, S. P. (1992). Teaching students with learning problems in math to acquire, understand, and apply basic math facts. *Remedial and Special Education, 13*(3), 19–35, 61.

Mercer, C. D., & Pullen, P. C. (2009). *Students with learning disabilities* (7th ed.). Upper Saddle River, NJ: Merrill/Pearson.

Merchant, D. J., & Gajar, A. (1997). A review of literature on self-advocacy components in transition programs for students with learning disabilities. *Journal of Vocational Rehabilitation, 8,* 223–231.

Merritt, D. D., & Liles, B. Z. (1987). Story grammar ability in children with and without language disorder: Story generation, story retelling, and story comprehension. *Journal of Speech and Hearing Research, 30,* 539–552.

Metropolitan Achievement Tests—Eighth Edition. (2000a). San Antonio, TX: Pearson.

Metropolitan Achievement Tests—Eighth Edition: Writing Test. (2000b). San Antonio, TX: Pearson.

Meyen, E. L., & Greer, D. L. (2009). The role of instructional planning in math instruction for students with learning disabilities. *Focus on Exceptional Children, 41*(5), 1–12.

Meyer, M. S., & Felton, R. H. (1999). Repeated reading to enhance fluency: Old approaches and new directions. *Annals of Dyslexia, 49,* 283–306.

Meyer, M. S., Wood, F. B., Hart, L. A., & Felton, R. H. (1998). Selective predictive value of rapid automatized naming in peer readers. *Journal of Learning Disabilities, 31,* 106–117.

Miller, J. H., & Milam, C. P. (1987). Multiplication and division errors committed by learning disabled students. *Learning Disabilities Research, 2*(2), 119–122.

Miller, S. P., Mercer, C. D., & Dillon, A. S. (1992). CSA: Acquiring and retaining math skills. *Intervention in School and Clinic, 28,* 105–110.

Miller, S. P., Strawser, S., & Mercer, C. D. (1996). Promoting strategic math performance among students with learning disabilities. *LD Forum, 21*(2), 34–40.

Mills, H., O'Keefe, T., & Stephens, D. (1992). *Looking closely: Exploring the role of phonics in one whole language classroom.* Urbana, IL: National Council of Teachers of English.

Milone, M. (2007). *Test of Handwriting Skills—Revised.* Novato, CA: Academic Therapy.

Milwaukee Public Schools. (1990). *One at a time together! Best practices: Integrated programming and therapy.* Milwaukee, WI: Milwaukee Public Schools, Department of Exceptional Education and Supportive Services.

Mims, A., Harper, C., Armstrong, S. W., & Savage, S. (1991). Effective instruction in homework for students with disabilities. *Teaching Exceptional Children, 24*(1), 42–44.

Miramontes, O. B. (1991). Organizing for effective paraprofessional services in special education: A multilingual/multiethnic instructional service team model. *Remedial and Special Education, 12*(1), 29–36.

Moats, L. C. (1995). *Spelling: Development, disabilities, and instruction.* Timonium, MD: York Press.

Moats, L. C. (2000). *Speech to print: Language essentials for teachers.* Baltimore, MD: Paul H. Brookes.

Moats, L. C., & Rosow, B. (2003). *Spellography: A student road map to better spelling.* Longmont, CO: Sopris West.

Mohlman, G., Sparks-Langer, S., & Colton, A. B. (1991). Synthesis of research on teachers' reflective thinking. *Educational Leadership, 48*(6), 37–44.

Monroe, B. W., & Troia, G. A. (2006). Teaching writing strategies to middle school students with disabilities. *The Journal of Educational Research, 100,* 21–33.

Montague, M. (1992). The effects of cognitive and metacognitive strategy instruction on the mathematical problem solving of middle school students with learning disabilities. *Journal of Learning Disabilities, 25,* 230–248.

Montague, M. (1993). Student-centered or strategy-centered instruction: What is our purpose? *Journal of Learning Disabilities, 26,* 433–437, 481.

Montague, M., & Bos, C. S. (1990). Cognitive and metacognitive characteristics of eighth grade students' mathematical problem solving. *Learning and Individual Differences, 2,* 371–388.

Montague, M., & Rinaldi, C. (2001). Classroom dynamics and children at-risk: A follow-up. *Learning Disability Quarterly, 24,* 73–84.

Montague, M., Warger, C., & Morgan, T. H. (2000). Solve it! strategy instruction to improve mathematical problem solving. *Learning Disabilities Research & Practice, 15,* 110–116.

Montgomery, D. J., & Marks, L. J. (2006). Using technology to build independence in writing for students with disabilities. *Preventing School Failure, 50,* 33–38.

Montgomery, M. S. (1994). Self-concept and children with learning disabilities: Observer-child concordance across six context-dependent domains. *Journal of Learning Disabilities, 27,* 254–262.

Mooney, P., Ryan, J., Uhing, B., Reid, R., & Epstein, M. (2005). A review of self-management interventions targeting academic outcomes for students with emotional and behavioral disorders. *Journal of Behavioral Education, 14,* 203–221.

Morgan, D. L., & Guilford, A. M. (1984). *Adolescent Language Screening Test.* Austin, TX: PRO-ED.

Morgan, P. L., Fuchs, D., Compton, D. L., Cordray, D. S., & Fuchs, L. S. (2008). Does early reading failure decrease children's reading motivation? *Journal of Learning Disabilities, 41,* 387–404.

Morrow, L. M. (1992). The impact of a literature-based program on literacy achievement, use of literature, and attitudes of children from minority backgrounds. *Reading Research Quarterly, 25,* 251–275.

Morse, W. C. (1971). Worksheet on life space interviewing for teachers. In N. J. Long, W. C. Morse, & R. G. Newman (Eds.), *Conflict in the classroom: The education of emotionally disturbed children* (2nd ed.). Belmont, CA: Wadsworth.

Morse, W. C. (1994). Comments from a biased viewpoint. *The Journal of Special Education, 27,* 531–542.

Moses, N., Klein, H. B., & Altman, E. (1990). An approach to assessing and facilitating casual language in adults with learning disabilities based on Piagetian theory. *Journal of Learning Disabilities, 23,* 220–228.

Moshman, D. (1982). Exogenous, endogenous, and dialectical constructivism. *Developmental Review, 2,* 371–384.

Moss, M., Jacob, R., Boulay, B., Horst, M., & Poulos, J. (2006). *Reading First implementation evaluation: Interim report.* Cambridge, MA: Abt.

Mueller, D. J., Chase, C. I., & Walden, J. D. (1988). Effects of reduced class size in primary classes. *Educational Leadership, 45*(5), 48–50.

Mueller, P. H. (2002). The pareducator paradox. *Exceptional Parent, 32,* 64–67.

Muhlstein, E. A., & Croft, D. J. (1986). *Using the microcomputer to enhance language experiences and the development of cooperative play among preschool children* (ERIC Document Reproduction Service No. ED 269 004). Cupertino, CA: De Anza College.

Munk, D. D., & Bursuck, W. D. (1998). Report card grading adaptations for students with disabilities: Types and acceptability. *Intervention in School and Clinic, 33,* 306–308.

Munk, D. D., & Bursuck, W. D. (2001). What report card grades should and do communicate: Perceptions of parents of secondary students with and without disabilities. *Remedial and Special Education, 22,* 280–287.

Murray, C., Goldstein, D. E., Nourse, S., & Edgar, E. (2000). The postsecondary school attendance and completion rates of high school graduates with learning disabilities. *Learning Disabilities Research & Practice, 15*, 119–127.

Nagel, D. R., Schumaker, J. B., & Deshler, D. D. (2003). *The learning strategies curriculum: The FIRST-letter mnemonic strategy* (Rev. ed.). Lawrence, KS: Edge Enterprises.

Naglieri, J. A., LeBuffe, P. A., & Pfeiffer, S. I. (1993). *Devereux Behavior Rating Scale—School Form.* San Antonio, TX: Psychological Corporation.

Nagy, W., & Anderson, R. C. (1984). How many words are there in printed school English? *Reading Research Quarterly, 19*, 304–330.

National Center for Education Statistics. (2007a). *National assessment of educational progress 2007 report card for the nation* (Publication No. NCES 2007–496). Washington, DC: U.S. Department of Education, Office of Educational Research and Improvement.

National Center for Education Statistics. (2007b). *Reading report card for the nation and the states* (NAEP 2005 and 2007 reading assessments). Washington, DC: U.S. Department of Education.

National Center for Education Statistics. (2009). *The nation's report card: Mathematics 2009* (NCES 2010–451). Washington, DC: Institute of Education Sciences, U.S. Department of Education.

National Center on Education and the Economy. (2007). *Tough choices or tough times: The report of the new Commission on the Skills of the American Workforce.* San Francisco: Jossey-Bass.

National Council of Supervisors of Mathematics. (1988). *Twelve components of essential mathematics.* Minneapolis, MN: Author.

National Council of Teachers of Mathematics. (1989). *Curriculum and evaluation standards for school mathematics.* Reston, VA: Author.

National Council of Teachers of Mathematics. (2000). *Principles and standards for school mathematics.* Reston, VA: Author.

National Council of Teachers of Mathematics. (2006). *Curriculum focal points for prekindergarten through grade 8 mathematics: A quest for coherence.* Reston, VA: Author.

National Institute for Literacy. (1997). *Literacy: It's a whole new world.* Washington, DC: Author.

National Reading Panel. (2000). *Teaching children to read: An evidence-based assessment of the scientific research literature on reading and its implications for reading instruction* (NIH Pub. No. 00-4754). Washington, DC: National Institute of Child Health and Human Development, National Institutes of Health.

National Research Council. (2001). *Adding it up: Helping children learn mathematics.* Washington, DC: Author.

Nelson, N. W. (1994). Curriculum-based assessment and intervention across the grades. In G. P. Wallach & K. G. Butler (Eds.), *Language learning disabilities in school-age children and adolescents* (pp. 104–131). Boston: Allyn & Bacon.

Neuhaus, G. F., & Swank, P. R. (2002). Understanding the relations between RAN letters subtest components and word reading in first-grade students. *Journal of Learning Disabilities, 35*, 158–174.

Newcomer, P. L. (1999). *Standardized Reading Inventory—2.* Austin, TX: PRO-ED.

Newcomer, P. L. (2001). *Diagnostic Achievement Battery—3.* Austin, TX: PRO-ED.

Newcomer, P. L., & Barenbaum, E. (2003). *Test of Phonological Awareness Skills.* Austin, TX: PRO-ED.

Newcomer, P. L., & Hammill, D. D. (2008). *Test of Language Development—Primary: 4.* Austin, TX: PRO-ED.

Newcomer, P. L., & Hammill, D. D. (2009). *Pragmatic Language Observation Scale.* Austin, TX: PRO-ED.

Newland, T. E. (1932). An analytical study of the development of illegibilities in handwriting from the lower grades to adulthood. *Journal of Educational Research, 26*, 249–258.

Newmann, F. M., & Wehlage, G. G. (1993). Five standards of authentic instruction. *Educational Leadership, 50*(7), 8–12.

Nicholls, J. G., McKenzie, M., & Shufro, J. (1994). Schoolwork, homework, life's work: The experience of students with and without learning disabilities. *Journal of Learning Disabilities, 27*, 562–569.

Nies, K. A., & Belfiore, P. J. (2006). Enhancing spelling performance in students with learning disabilities. *Journal of Behavioral Education, 15*, 163–170.

Niesyn, M. E. (2009). Strategies for success: Evidence-based instructional practices for students with emotional and behavioral disorders. *Preventing School Failure, 53*, 227–233.

Nowicki, E. A. (2003). A meta-analysis of the social competence of children with learning disabilities in inclusive classrooms: Comparisons with average to high and low achieving classmates. *Learning Disability Quarterly, 26*, 171–188.

Ogle, D. (1986). K-W-L: A teaching model that develops active reading of expository text. *The Reading Teacher, 39*, 564–570.

Okolo, C. M., Bahr, C. M., & Rieth, H. J. (1993). A retrospective view of computer-based instruction. *Journal of Special Education Technology, 12*, 1–27.

Okolo, C. M., Cavalier, A. R., Ferretti, R. P., & MacArthur, C. A. (2000). Technology, literacy, and disabilities: A review of the research. In R. Gersten, E. P. Schiller, & S. Vaughn (Eds.), *Contemporary special education research: Synthesis of the knowledge base on critical instructional issues* (pp. 179–250). Mahwah, NJ: Erlbaum.

Olinghouse, N. G. (2009). Writing assessment for struggling learners. *Perspectives on Language and Literacy, 35*(3), 15–18.

Olson, J. L., Platt, J. C., & Dieker, L. A. (2008). *Teaching children and adolescents with special needs* (5th ed.). Upper Saddle River, NJ: Merrill/Prentice Hall/Pearson.

Olympia, D. E., Sheridan, S. M., & Jenson, W. R. (1994). Homework: A natural means of home-school collaboration. *School Psychology Quarterly, 9*, 60–80.

O'Melia, M. C., & Rosenberg, M. S. (1994). Effects of cooperative homework teams on the acquisition of mathematics skills by secondary students with mild disabilities. *Exceptional Children, 60,* 538–548.

O'Neil, J. (1994/1995). Can inclusion work? A conversation with Jim Kauffman and Mara Sapon-Shevin. *Educational Leadership, 52*(4), 7–11.

Ortiz, A. A., Wilkinson, C. Y., Robertson-Courtney, P., & Kushner, M. I. (2006). Considerations in implementing intervention assistance teams to support English language learners. *Remedial and Special Education, 27,* 53–63.

Orton, J. L. (1976). *A guide to teaching phonics.* Cambridge, MA: Educators Publishing Service.

Orton, S. T. (1937). *Reading, writing, and speech problems in children.* New York: W. W. Norton.

Osguthorpe, R. T., & Scruggs, T. E. (1986). Special education students as tutors: A review and analysis. *Remedial and Special Education, 7*(4), 15–26.

Outhred, L. (1989). Word processing: Its impact on children's writing. *Journal of Learning Disabilities, 22,* 262–264.

Owens, R. E., Jr. (2006). Development of communication, language, and speech. In N. B. Anderson & G. H. Shames, *Human communication disorders: An introduction* (7th ed., pp. 22–58). Boston: Allyn & Bacon/Pearson.

Owens, R. E., Jr. (2008). *Language development: An introduction* (7th ed.). Boston: Allyn & Bacon/Pearson.

Paine, S. C., Radicchi, J., Rosellini, L. C., Deutchman, L., & Darch, C. B. (1983). *Structuring your classroom for academic success.* Champaign, IL: Research Press.

Palinscar, A. S., & Brown, A. L. (1986). Interactive teaching to promote independent learning from text. *The Reading Teacher, 39*(8), 771–777.

Palinscar, A. S., & Brown, A. L. (1988). Teaching and practicing thinking skills to promote comprehension in the context of group problem solving. *Remedial and Special Education, 9*(1), 53–59.

Palincsar, A. S., Magnusson, S. J., Collins, K. M., & Cutter, J. (2001). Making science accessible to all: Results of a design experiment in inclusive classrooms. *Learning Disability Quarterly, 24,* 15–32.

Palmer, S. B., & Wehmeyer, M. L. (2003). Promoting self-determination in early elementary school. *Remedial and Special Education, 24,* 115–126.

Parette, H. P., Hourcade, J. J., Dinelli, J. M., & Boeckmann, N. M. (2009). Using Clicker 5 to enhance emergent literacy skills in young learners. *Early Childhood Education Journal, 36,* 355–363.

Parker, R. I., Tindal, G., & Hasbrouck, J. (1991). Progress monitoring with objective measures of writing performance for students with mild disabilities. *Exceptional Children, 58,* 61–73.

Parker, R. M. (2001). *Occupational Aptitude Survey and Interest Schedule—3.* Austin, TX: PRO-ED.

Parnell, M. M., Amerman, J. D., & Harting, R. D. (1986). Responses of language-disordered children to *wh*-questions.

Language, Speech, and Hearing Services in Schools, 17, 95–106.

Patton, J. R. (1994). Practical recommendations for using homework with students with learning disabilities. *Journal of Learning Disabilities, 27,* 570–578.

Patton, J. R., & Polloway, E. A. (1992). Learning disabilities: The challenges of adulthood. *Journal of Learning Disabilities, 25,* 410–416.

Patton, J. R., & Trainor, A. (2004). Transition from school to independent living. In D. D. Hammill & N. R. Bartel, *Teaching students with learning and behavior problems* (7th ed., pp. 325–368). Austin, TX: PRO-ED.

Paulson, F. L., Paulson, P. R., & Meyer, C. A. (1991). What makes a portfolio a portfolio? *Educational Leadership, 48*(5), 60–63.

Pavri, S., & Monda-Amaya, L. (2000). Loneliness and students with learning disabilities in inclusive classrooms: Self-perceptions, coping strategies, and preferred interventions. *Learning Disabilities Research & Practice, 15,* 22–33.

Payne, K. T., & Taylor, O. L. (2006). Multicultural differences in human communication and disorders. In N. B. Anderson & G. H. Shames, *Human communication disorders: An introduction* (7th ed., pp. 93–125). Boston: Allyn & Bacon/Pearson.

Pearl, R., Bryan, T., & Donahue, M. (1980). Learning disabled children's attributions for success and failure. *Learning Disability Quarterly, 3*(1), 3–9.

Peck, K. L., & Dorricott, D. (1994). Why use technology? *Educational Leadership, 51*(7), 11–14.

Pehrsson, R. S., & Denner, P. R. (1988). Semantic organizers: Implications for reading and writing. *Topics in Language Disorders, 8*(3), 24–32.

Pershey, M. G., & Clickner, P. A. (2007). Phonological awareness and working memory in children with phonological impairment. *College Reading Association Yearbook, 28,* 170–183.

Peterson, D., Taylor, B., Burnham, B., & Schock, R. (2009). Reflective coaching conversations: A missing piece. *The Reading Teacher, 62*(9), 500–509.

Phelps-Terasaki, D., & Phelps-Gunn, T. (2000). *Teaching competence in written language* (2nd ed.). Austin, TX: PRO-ED.

Phelps-Terasaki, D., & Phelps-Gunn, T. (2007). *Test of Pragmatic Language—2.* Austin, TX: PRO-ED.

Phillips, V., & McCullough, L. (1990). Consultation based programming: Instituting the collaborative ethic in schools. *Exceptional Children, 56,* 291–304.

Piaget, J. (1960). *The psychology of intelligence.* Paterson, NJ: Littlefield, Adams.

Pianta, R. C., & Hamre, B. K. (2009). Conceptualization, measurement, and improvement of classroom processes: Standardized observation can leverage capacity. *Educational Researcher, 38,* 109–119.

Pianta, R. C., La Paro, K. M., & Hamre, B. K. (2008). *Classroom assessment scoring system.* Baltimore, MD: Brookes.

Pianta, R. C., La Paro, K. M., Payne, C., Cox, M. J., & Bradley, R. (2002). The relation of kindergarten classroom environment to teacher, family, and school characteristics and child outcomes. *The Elementary School Journal, 102*, 225–238.

Piers, E. V., Harris, D. B., & Herzberg, D. S. (2002). *The Piers-Harris Children's Self-Concept Scale: Second Edition.* Austin, TX: PRO-ED.

Pinnell, G. S. (1990). Success for low achievers through Reading Recovery. *Educational Leadership, 48*(1), 17–21.

Pinnell, G. S., DeFord, D. E., & Lyons, C. A. (1988). *Reading Recovery: Early intervention for at-risk first graders.* Arlington, VA: Educational Research Service.

Polloway, E. A., Patton, J. R., & Serna, L. (2008). *Strategies for teaching learners with special needs* (9th ed.). Upper Saddle River, NJ: Merrill/Prentice Hall/Pearson.

Polsgrove, L., & McNeil, M. (1989). The consultation process: Research and practice. *Remedial and Special Education, 10*(1), 6–13, 20.

Poplin, M. S. (1988). The reductionist fallacy in learning disabilities: Replicating the past by reducing the present. *Journal of Learning Disabilities, 21*, 389–400.

Porter, A. C., & Brophy, J. (1988). Synthesis of research on good teaching: Insights from the work of the Institute for Research on Teaching. *Educational Leadership, 45*(8), 74–85.

Poteet, J. A. (1980). Informal assessment of written expression. *Learning Disability Quarterly, 3*(4), 88–98.

Potter, M. L., & Wamre, H. M. (1990). Curriculum-based measurement and developmental reading models: Opportunities for cross-validation. *Exceptional Children, 57*, 16–25.

Prater, M. A. (1993). Teaching concepts: Procedures for the design and delivery of instruction. *Remedial and Special Education, 14*(5), 51–62.

Pray, B. S., Jr., Hall, C. W., & Markley, R. P. (1992). Social skills training: An analysis of social behaviors selected for individualized education programs. *Remedial and Special Education, 13*(5), 43–49.

Premack, D. (1959). Toward empirical behavior laws: I. Positive reinforcement. *Psychological Review, 66*, 219–233.

Pressley, M., & Harris, K. R. (1990). What we really know about strategy instruction. *Educational Leadership, 48*(1), 31–34.

Pressley, M., & Rankin, J. (1994). More about whole language methods of reading instruction for students at risk for early reading failure. *Learning Disabilities Research & Practice, 9*, 157–168.

Pugach, M. C., & Johnson, L. J. (1988). Peer collaboration. *Teaching Exceptional Children, 20*, 75–77.

Pugach, M. C., & Johnson, L. J. (1990). Meeting diverse needs through professional peer collaboration. In W. Stainback & S. Stainback (Eds.), *Support networks for inclusive schooling: Interdependent integrated education* (pp. 123–137). Baltimore, MD: Paul H. Brookes.

Pullen, P. C., & Justice, L. M. (2003). Enhancing phonological awareness, print awareness, and oral language skills in preschool children. *Intervention in School and Clinic, 39*, 87–98.

Pullen, P. C., Lane, H. B., & Monaghan, M. C. (2004). Effects of a volunteer tutoring model on the literacy development of struggling first grade students. *Reading Research and Instruction, 43*(4), 21–40.

Pullen, P. C., Tuckwiller, E. D., Konold, T., Maynard, K., & Coyne, M. (2010). A response to intervention model for vocabulary instruction: The effects of tiered instruction for students at risk for reading disability. *Learning Disabilities Research & Practice, 25.*

Put reading first: The research building blocks for teaching children to read. (2001). Jessup, MD: National Institute for Literacy.

Quay, H. C., & Peterson, D. R. (1996). *Revised Behavior Problem Checklist.* Lutz, FL: Psychological Assessment Resources.

Rademacher, J. A., Callahan, K., & Pederson-Seelye, V. A. (1998). How do your classroom rules measure up? Guidelines for developing an effective rule management routine. *Intervention in School and Clinic, 33*, 284–289.

Rademacher, J. A., Deshler, D. D., Schumaker, J. B., & Lenz, B. K. (1998). *The content enhancement series: The quality assignment routine.* Lawrence, KS: Edge Enterprises.

Rampey, B. D., Dion, G. S., & Donahue, P. L. (2009). *NAEP 2008 trends in academic progress* (NCES 2009–79). Washington, DC: National Center for Education Statistics, Institute of Education Sciences, U.S. Department of Education.

Rankin, J. L., Bruning, R. H., Timme, V. L., & Katkanant, C. (1993). Is writing affected by spelling performance and beliefs about spelling? *Applied Cognitive Psychology, 7*, 155–169.

Rankin-Erickson, J. L., & Pressley, M. (2000). A survey of instructional practices of special education teachers nominated as effective teachers of literacy. *Learning Disabilities Research & Practice, 15*, 206–225.

Rasinski, T. V. (1990). Investigating measures of reading fluency. *Educational Research Quarterly, 14*(3), 34–44.

Raskind, M. H., Goldberg, R. J., Higgins, E. L., & Herman, K. L. (1999). Patterns of change and predictors of success in individuals with learning disabilities: Results from a twenty-year longitudinal study. *Learning Disabilities Research & Practice, 14*, 35–49.

Rea, P. J., McLaughlin, V. L., & Walther-Thomas, C. (2002). Outcomes for students with learning disabilities in inclusive and pullout programs. *Exceptional Children, 68*, 203–222.

Reid, D. K., Hresko, W. P., & Hammill, D. D. (2001). *Test of Early Reading Ability—3.* Austin, TX: PRO-ED.

Reiff, H. B., & deFur, S. (1992). Transition for youths with learning disabilities: A focus on developing independence. *Learning Disability Quarterly, 15*, 237–249.

Reiff, H. B., Ginsberg, R., & Gerber, P. J. (1995). New perspectives on teaching from successful adults with learning disabilities. *Remedial and Special Education, 16*(1), 29–37.

Reynolds, A. (1992). What is competent beginning teaching? A review of the literature. *Review of Educational Research, 62*, 1–35.

Reynolds, C. R., & Kamphaus, R. W. (2004). *Behavior Assessment System for Children—Second Edition.* Minneapolis, MN: Pearson.

Reynolds, M. C. (1989). An historical perspective: The delivery of special education to mildly disabled and at-risk students. *Remedial and Special Education, 10*(6), 7–11.

Reynolds, M. C., Wang, M. C., & Walberg, H. J. (1987). The necessary restructuring of special and regular education. *Exceptional Children, 53*, 391–398.

Reynolds, M. C., Wang, M. C., & Walberg, H. J. (1992). The knowledge bases for special and general education. *Remedial and Special Education, 13*(5), 6–10, 33.

Rice, D., & Zigmond, N. (2000). Co-teaching in secondary schools: Teacher reports of developments in Australian and American classrooms. *Learning Disabilities Research and Practice, 15*, 190–197.

Rich, H. L., & Ross, S. M. (1989). Student's time on learning tasks in special education. *Exceptional Children, 55*, 508–515.

Riedlinger-Ryan, K. J., & Shewan, C. M. (1984). Comparison of auditory comprehension skills in learning-disabled and academically achieving adolescents. *Language, Speech, and Hearing Services in Schools, 15*, 127–136.

Rieth, H. J., Bryant, D. P., Kinzer, C. K., Colburn, L. K., Hur, S., Hartman, P., & Choi, H. S. (2003). An analysis of the impact of anchored instruction on teaching and learning activities in two ninth-grade language arts classes. *Remedial and Special Education, 24*, 173–184.

Rieth, H. J., & Evertson, C. (1988). Variables related to the effective instruction of difficult-to-teach children. *Focus on Exceptional Children, 20*(5), 1–8.

Rieth, H. J., & Polsgrove, L. (1994). Curriculum and instructional issues in teaching secondary students with learning disabilities. *Learning Disabilities Research & Practice, 9*, 118–126.

Riggs, C. G., & Mueller, P. H. (2001). Employment and utilization of paraeducators in inclusive settings. *The Journal of Special Education, 35*, 54–62.

Ritchey, K. D., & Goeke, J. L. (2006). Orton Gillingham and Orton-Gillingham based reading instruction: A review of the literature. *The Journal of Special Education, 40*, 171–183.

Rivera, D. M. (1993). Examining mathematics reform and the implications for students with mathematics disabilities. *Remedial and Special Education, 14*(6), 24–27.

Rivera, D. M., & Bryant, B. R. (1992). Mathematics instruction for students with special needs. *Intervention in School and Clinic, 28*(2), 71–86.

Robertson, H. M. (1999). LEA and students with special needs. In O. G. Nelson & W. M. Linek (Eds.), *Practical classroom applications of language experience: Looking back, looking forward* (pp. 221–223). Boston: Allyn & Bacon.

Robinson, F. P. (1961). *Effective study.* New York: Harper & Row.

Robinson, G. E. (1990). Synthesis of research on class size. *Educational Leadership, 47*(7), 80–90.

Robinson, S. L., DePascale, C., & Roberts, F. C. (1989). Computer-delivered feedback in group-based instruction: Effects for learning disabled students in mathematics. *Learning Disabilities Focus, 5*(1), 28–35.

Roe, B. D., & Burns, P. C. (2007). *Informal Reading Inventory: Primer to twelfth grade* (7th ed.). Florence, KY: Wadsworth/Cengage Learning.

Roe, B. D., Stoodt-Hill, B. D., & Burns, P. C. (2004). *Secondary school literacy instruction: The content areas* (8th ed.). Boston: Houghton Mifflin.

Rojewski, J. W. (1992). Key components of model transition services for students with learning disabilities. *Learning Disability Quarterly, 15*, 135–150.

Rojewski, J. W., Pollard, R. R., & Meers, G. D. (1990). Grading mainstreamed special needs students: Determining practices and attitudes of secondary vocational educators using a qualitative approach. *Remedial and Special Education, 12*(1), 7–15, 28.

Rooney, K. J., & Hallahan, D. P. (1985). Future directions for cognitive behavior modification research: The quest for cognitive change. *Remedial and Special Education, 6*(2), 46–51.

Rose, L. C., & Gallup, A. M. (2006). The 38th annual Phi Delta Kappa/Gallup poll of the public's attitudes. *Phi Delta Kappan, 88*, 41–53.

Rosenberg, D. (2009). Plato's iPod: Can hand-held electronics be valuable tools of learning? *Independent School, 68*, 92–95.

Roth, F. P., & Clark, D. M. (1987). Symbolic play and social participation abilities of language-impaired and normally developing children. *Journal of Speech and Hearing Disorders, 52*, 17–29.

Ruhl, K. L., Hughes, C. A., & Gajar, A. (1990). Efficacy of the pause procedure for enhancing learning disabled and nondisabled college students' long- and short-term recall of facts presented through lecture. *Learning Disability Quarterly, 13*, 55–64.

Ruhl, K. L., & Suritsky, S. (1995). The pause procedure and/or an outline: Effect on immediate free recall and lecture notes taken by college students with learning disabilities. *Learning Disability Quarterly, 18*, 2–11.

Rupley, W. H., & Blair, T. R. (1989). *Reading diagnosis and remediation: Classroom and clinic* (3rd ed.). Upper Saddle River, NJ: Merrill/Prentice Hall.

Russell, R., & Ginsburg, H. (1984). Cognitive analysis of children's mathematical difficulties. *Cognition and Instruction, 1*, 217–244.

Ryan, J. B., Pierce, C. D., & Mooney, P. (2008). Evidence-based teaching strategies for students with EBD. *Beyond Behavior, 17*, 22–29.

Saddler, B. (2009). Sentence combining. *Perspectives on Language and Literacy, 35*(3), 27–29.

Sadoski, M., & Willson, V. L. (2006). Effects of a theoretically based large-scale reading intervention in a multicultural urban school district. *American Educational Research Journal, 43,* 137–154.

Salend S. J. (2008). *Creating inclusive classrooms: Effective and reflective practices* (6th ed.). Upper Saddle River, NJ: Merrill/Prentice Hall/Pearson.

Salend, S. J. (2009). Technology-based classroom assessments: Alternatives to testing. *Teaching Exceptional Children, 41*(6), 48–58.

Salend, S. J., & Fradd, S. (1986). Nationwide availability of services for limited English-proficient handicapped students. *The Journal of Special Education, 20,* 127–135.

Salend, S. J., & Garrick Duhaney, L. M. (2002). Grading students in inclusive settings. *Teaching Exceptional Children, 34*(3), 8–15.

Salend, S. J., Gordon, J., & Lopez-Vona, K. (2002). Evaluating cooperative teaching teams. *Intervention in School and Clinic, 37,* 195–200.

Salend, S. J., & Salinas, A. (2003). Language differences or learning difficulties: The work of the multidisciplinary team. *Teaching Exceptional Children, 35*(4), 36–43.

Salend, S. J., & Schliff, J. (1989). An examination of the homework practices of teachers of students with learning disabilities. *Journal of Learning Disabilities, 22,* 621–623.

Salvia, J., Ysseldyke, J. E., & Bolt, S. (2010). *Assessment in special and inclusive education* (11th ed.). Belmont, CA: Wadsworth.

Salvin, R. E., & Madden, N. A. (1989). What works for students at risk: A research synthesis. *Educational Leadership, 46*(5), 4–13.

Salvin, R. E., Madden, N. A., Dolan, L. J., Wasik, B. A., Ross, S. M., & Smith, L. J. (1994). "Whenever and wherever we choose": The replication of "Success for All." *Phi Delta Kappan, 75,* 639–647.

Samuels, S. J. (1997). The method of repeated readings. *The Reading Teacher, 50,* 376–381. (Originally published in 1979 in *The Reading Teacher, 32,* 403–408).

Sander, N. W. (1991). Effects of a self-management strategy on task-independent behaviors of adolescents with learning disabilities. *B.C. Journal of Special Education, 15,* 64–75.

Savage, R., Lavers, N., & Pillay, V. (2007). Working memory and reading difficulties: What we know and what we don't know about the relationship. *Educational Psychology Review, 19,* 185–221.

Schloss, P. J., Schloss, M. A., & Schloss, C. N. (2007). *Instructional methods for secondary students with learning and behavior problems* (4th ed.). Boston: Allyn & Bacon/Pearson.

Schmidt, P. R. (1999). KWLQ: Inquiry and literacy learning in science. *The Reading Teacher, 52,* 789–792.

Schumaker, J. B. (2003). *Fundamentals in the theme writing strategy.* Lawrence, KS: Edge Enterprises.

Schumaker, J. B., Bulgren, J. A., Deshler, D. D., & Lenz, B. K. (1998). *The content enhancement series: The recall enhancement routine.* Lawrence: University of Kansas Center for Research on Learning.

Schumaker, J. B., Deshler, D. D., Alley, G. R., Warner, M. M., & Denton, P. H. (1982). Multipass: A learning strategy for improving reading comprehension. *Learning Disability Quarterly, 5,* 295–304.

Schumaker, J. B., Deshler, D. D., & McKnight, P. C. (2001). Ensuring success in the secondary general education curriculum through the use of teaching routines for content areas at the secondary level. In M. R. Shinn, H. M. Walker, & G. Stover (Eds.), *Interventions for academic and behavior problems II: Preventive and remedial approaches* (pp. 791–824). Washington, DC: National Association of School Psychologists.

Schumaker, J. B., & Hazel, J. S. (1984). Social skills assessment and training for the learning disabled: Who's on first and what's on second? Part II. *Journal of Learning Disabilities, 17,* 492–499.

Schumaker, J. B., & Lyerla, K. D. (1993). *The paragraph writing strategy.* Lawrence: University of Kansas Center for Research on Learning.

Schumaker, J. B., Nolan, S. M., & Deshler, D. D. (1985). *Learning strategies curriculum: The error monitoring strategy.* Lawrence: University of Kansas Center for Research on Learning.

Schumaker, J. B., & Sheldon, J. B. (1998). *Fundamentals in the sentence writing strategy: Instructor's manual.* Lawrence: University of Kansas Center for Research on Learning.

Schumaker, J. B., & Sheldon, J. B. (1999). *Proficiency in the sentence writing strategy: Instructor's manual.* Lawrence: University of Kansas Center for Research on Learning.

Schumm, J. S., & Vaughn, S. (1995). Meaningful professional development in accommodating students with disabilities: Lessons learned. *Remedial and Special Education, 16,* 344–353.

Schumm, J. S., Vaughn, S., Haager, D., & Klinger, J. K. (1994). Literacy instruction for mainstreamed students: What suggestions are provided in basal reading series? *Remedial and Special Education 15,* 14–20.

Schumm, J. S., Vaughn, S., & Leavell, A. (1994). Planning pyramid: A framework for planning for diverse student needs during content area instruction. *The Reading Teacher, 47*(8), 608–615.

Schunk, D. H. (1981). Modeling and attributional effects on children's achievement: A self-efficacy analysis. *Journal of Educational Psychology, 73,* 93–105.

Schwabe, A. M., Olswang, L. B., & Kriegsmann, E. (1986). Requests for information: Linguistic, cognitive, pragmatic, and environmental variables. *Language, Speech, and Hearing Services in Schools, 17,* 38–55.

Scott, B. J., & Vitale, M. R. (2003). Teaching the writing process to students with LD. *Intervention in School and Clinic, 38,* 220–224.

Scott, B. J., Vitale, M. R., & Masten, W. G. (1998). Implementing instructional adaptations for students with disabilities in inclusive classrooms: A literature review. *Remedial and Special Education, 19,* 106–119.

Scott, C., & Windsor, J. (2000). General language performance measures in spoken and written discourse produced by school-age children with and without language learning disabilities. *Journal of Speech, Language, and Hearing Research, 43,* 324–339.

Scott, S. S. (1994). Determining reasonable academic adjustments for college students with learning disabilities. *Journal of Learning Disabilities, 27,* 403–412.

Scruggs, T. E., & Mastropieri, M. A. (1994). The construction of scientific knowledge by students with mild disabilities. *The Journal of Special Education, 28,* 307–321.

Scruggs, T. E., & Richter, L. (1985). Tutoring learning disabled students: A critical review. *Learning Disability Quarterly, 8,* 286–298.

Seidenberg, P. L. (1988). Cognitive and academic instructional intervention for learning-disabled adolescents. *Topics in Language Disorders, 8*(3), 56–71.

Semel, E. M., Wiig, E. H., & Secord, W. A. (2003). *Clinical Evaluation of Language Fundamentals—4.* San Antonio, TX: Pearson.

Semel, E. M., Wiig, E. H., & Secord, W. A. (2004). *Clinical Evaluation of Language Fundamentals—4: Screening Test.* San Antonio, TX: Pearson.

Shanker, A. (1994/1995). Full inclusion is neither free nor appropriate. *Educational Leadership, 52*(4), 18–21.

Shanker, J. L., & Cockrum, W. A. (2009). *Locating and correcting reading difficulties* (9th ed.). Boston: Allyn & Bacon/Pearson.

Shany, M. T., & Biemiller, A. (1995). Assisted reading practice: Effects on performance for poor readers in grades 3 and 4. *Reading Research Quarterly, 30,* 382–395.

Shapiro, E. S. (1989). Teaching self-management skills to learning disabled adolescents. *Learning Disability Quarterly, 12,* 275–287.

Shelton, T. L., Anastopoulos, A. D., & Linden, J. D. (1985). An attribution training program with learning disabled children. *Journal of Learning Disabilities, 18,* 261–265.

Shinn, M. R., Good, R. H., Knutson, N., Tilly, W. D., & Collins, V. L. (1992). Curriculum-based measurement of oral reading fluency: A confirmatory analysis of its relation to reading. *School Psychology Review, 21*(3), 459–479.

Shonkoff, J. P., & Phillips, D. A. (2000). *From neurons to neighborhoods: The science of early childhood development.* Washington, DC: National Academy Press.

Sideridis, G. D., Morgan, P. L., Botsas, G., Padeliadu, S., & Fuchs, D. (2006). Identifying students with or at risk for learning disabilities based on motivation, metacognition, and psychopathology: A ROC analysis. *Journal of Learning Disabilities, 39,* 215–229.

Sidman, M. T. (1979). The effects of group free time and contingency and individual free time contingency on spelling performance. *The Directive Teacher, 1,* 4–5.

Simmons, D. C., Chard, D., & Kame'enui, E. J. (1994). Translating research into basal reading programs. Applications of curriculum design. *LD Forum, 19*(4), 9–13.

Simmons, D. C., Fuchs, D., & Fuchs, L. S. (1991). Instructional and curricular requisites of mainstreamed students with learning disabilities. *Journal of Learning Disabilities, 24,* 354–360.

Simmons, D. C., Fuchs, D., Fuchs, L. S., Hodge, J. P., & Mathes, P. G. (1994). Importance of instructional complexity and role reciprocity to classwide peer tutoring. *Learning Disabilities Research & Practice, 9,* 203–212.

Simmons, D. C., Gunn, B., Smith, S. B., & Kame'enui, E. J. (1994). Phonological awareness: Applications on instructional design. *LD Forum, 19*(2), 7–10.

Simon, C. S. (1985). *Communication skills and classroom success.* San Diego, CA: College-Hill Press.

Simonsen, F., & Gunter, L. (2001). Best practices in spelling instruction: A research summary. *Journal of Direct Instruction, 1,* 97–105.

Simpson, R. L. (1996). *Working with parents and families of exceptional children and youth* (3rd ed.). Austin, TX: PRO-ED.

Sindelar, P. T., Smith, M., Harriman, N., Hale, R., & Wilson, R. (1986). Teacher effectiveness in special education programs. *The Journal of Special Education, 20,* 195–207.

Sitlington, P. L., Frank, A. R., & Carson, R. (1993). Adult adjustment among high school graduates with mild disabilities. *Exceptional Children, 59,* 221–233.

Sitlington, P. L., Neubert, D. A., & Clark, G. M. (2010). *Transition education and services for students with disabilities* (5th ed.). Upper Saddle River, NJ: Merrill/Pearson.

Skinner, B. F. (1957). *Verbal behavior.* New York: Appleton-Century-Crofts.

Slavin, R. E. (1978). Student teams and achievement divisions. *Journal of Research and Development in Education, 12,* 39–49.

Slavin, R. E. (1986). *Using student team learning* (3rd ed.). Baltimore, MD: Center for Research on Elementary and Middle Schools, Johns Hopkins University.

Slavin, R. E. (1988). Synthesis of research on grouping in elementary and secondary schools. *Educational Leadership, 46*(1), 67–77.

Slavin, R. E. (1989/1990). Research on cooperative learning: Consensus and controversy. *Educational Leadership, 47*(4), 52–54.

Slavin, R. E. (1991). Synthesis of research on cooperative learning. *Educational Leadership, 48*(5), 71–82.

Slavin, R. E., & Madden, N. A. (1989). What works for students at risk: A research synthesis. *Educational Leadership, 46*(5), 4–13.

Slavin, R. E., & Madden, N. A. (Eds.). (2001). *One million children; Success for All.* Thousand Oaks, CA: Corwin.

Slavin, R. E., & Madden, N. A. (2006). *Success for All: Summary of research on achievement outcomes.* Baltimore, MD: Johns Hopkins University, Center for Data-Driven Reform in Education.

Slavin, R. E., Madden, N. A., Dolan, L. J., Wasik, B. A., Ross, S., & Smith, L. (1994). *Success for All: Longitudinal effects of systemic school-by-school reform in seven districts.* Paper presented at the meeting of the American Educational Research Association, New Orleans, LA.

Slavin, R. E., Madden, N. A., Karweit, N. L., Dolan, L. J., & Wasik, B. A. (1992). *Success for All: A relentless approach to prevention and early intervention in elementary schools.* Arlington, CA: Educational Research Service.

Slavin, R. E., Madden, N. A., & Stevens, R. J. (1990). Cooperative learning models for the 3 R's. *Educational Leadership, 47*(4), 22–28.

Slavin, R. E., Stevens, R. J., & Madden, N. A. (1988). Accommodating student diversity in reading and writing instruction: A cooperative learning approach. *Remedial and Special Education, 9*(1), 60–66.

Smith, C. R. (1995, March). *Developmental progression of phonological segmentation skills.* Paper presented at the Learning Disabilities Association International Conference, Orlando, FL.

Smith, C. R. (2004). *Learning disabilities: The interaction of students and their environment* (5th ed.). Boston: Allyn & Bacon/Pearson.

Smith, D. D. (1981). *Teaching the learning disabled.* Upper Saddle River, NJ: Prentice Hall.

Smyth, J. (1989). Developing and sustaining critical reflection in teacher education. *Journal of Teacher Education, 40*(2), 2–9.

Snipes, J., Soga, K., & Uro, G. (2007). *Research brief: Improving teaching and learning for English language learners in urban schools.* Washington, DC: Council of the Great City Schools.

Snow, C. E., Burns, M. S., & Griffin, P. (Eds.). (1998). *Preventing reading difficulties in young children.* Washington, DC: National Academy Press.

Snyder, L. S. (1986). Developmental language disorders: Elementary school age. In J. M. Costello & A. L. Holland (Eds.), *Handbook of speech and language disorders* (pp. 617–700). San Diego, CA: College-Hill Press.

Sparrow, S. S., Cicchetti, D. V., & Balla, D. A. (2005). *The Vineland Adaptive Behavior Scales—Second Edition.* Minneapolis, MN: Pearson.

Spector, J. E. (2005). How reliable are informal reading inventories? *Psychology in the Schools, 42,* 593–603.

Spekman, N. J., Goldberg, R. J., & Herman, K. L. (1992). Learning disabled children grow up: A search for factors related to success in the young adult years. *Learning Disabilities Research & Practice, 7,* 161–170.

Spekman, N. J., Goldberg, R. J., & Herman, K. L. (1993). An exploration of risk and resilience in the lives of individuals with learning disabilities. *Learning Disabilities Research & Practice, 8,* 11–18.

Spekman, N. J., Herman, K. L., & Vogel, S. A. (1993). Risk and resilience in individuals with learning disabilities: A challenge to the field. *Learning Disabilities Research & Practice, 8,* 59–65.

Spillane, S. A., McGuire, J. M., & Norlander, K. A. (1992). Undergraduate admission policies, practices, and procedures for applicants with learning disabilities. *Journal of Learning Disabilities, 25,* 665–670, 677.

Sprick, R. S. (1991). *Discipline and responsibility: A team approach.* Eugene, OR: Teaching Strategies.

Sprick, R. S. (2001). *The solution book: Managing classroom behavior.* Columbus, OH: SRA/McGraw-Hill.

Sprick, R. S., Garrison, M., & Howard, L. M. (1998). *CHAMPs: A proactive and positive approach to classroom management.* Frederick, CO: Sopris West.

Sprick, R. S., & Howard, L. M. (1995). *The teacher's encyclopedia of behavior management: 100 problems/500 plans.* Frederick, CO: Sopris West.

Sridhar, D., & Vaughn, S. (2000). Bibliotherapy for all: Enhancing reading comprehension, self-concept, and behavior. *Teaching Exceptional Children, 33*(2), 74–82.

Staats, A. (1971). Linguistic-mentalistic theory versus an explanatory S-R learning theory of language development. In D. I. Slobin (Ed.), *The ontogenesis of grammar.* New York: Academic Press.

Stahl, S. A., & Miller, P. D. (1989). Whole language and language experience approaches for beginning reading: A quantitative research synthesis. *Review of Educational Research, 59,* 87–116.

Stahl, S. A., Osborn, J., & Lehr, F. (1990). *Beginning to read: Thinking and learning about print—A summary.* Urbana-Champaign, IL: University of Illinois Center for the Study of Reading.

Stainback, S., & Stainback, W. (1987). Integration versus cooperation: A commentary on "Educating children with learning problems: A shared responsibility." *Exceptional Children, 54,* 66–68.

Stainback, S., Stainback, W., East, K., & Sapon-Shevin, M. (1994). A commentary on inclusion and the development of a positive self-identity by people with disabilities. *Exceptional Children, 60,* 486–490.

Stanford Writing Assessment Program—Third Edition. (1996). San Antonio, TX: Pearson.

Stanovich, K. E. (1994). Constructivism in reading education. *The Journal of Special Education, 28,* 259–274.

Starlin, C. M., & Starlin, A. (1973a). *Guides to decision making in computational math.* Bemidji, MN: Unique Curriculums Unlimited.

Starlin, C. M., & Starlin, A. (1973b). *Guides to decision making in spelling.* Bemidji, MN: Unique Curriculums Unlimited.

Stauffer, R. G. (1970). *The language-experience approach to the teaching of reading.* New York: Harper & Row.

Stecker, P. M., Fuchs, L. S., & Fuchs, D. (2005). Using curriculum-based measurement to improve student achievement: Review of research. *Psychology in the Schools, 42,* 795–820.

Stein, M., & Dixon, R. (2001). What research tells us about writing instruction for students in the middle grades. *Journal of Direct Instruction, 1,* 107–116.

Stein, M., Kinder D., Silbert, J., & Carnine, D. W. (2006). *Designing effective mathematics instruction: A direct instruction approach* (4th ed.). Upper Saddle River, NJ: Merrill/Prentice Hall/Pearson.

Sternberg, B. J., Kaplan, K. A., & Borck, J. E. (2007). Engaging adolescent literacy achievement through integration of technology in the classroom. *Reading Research Quarterly, 42*, 416–420.

Stetson, E. G., & Stetson, R. (2001). *Stetson spelling program: Strategies that work* (2nd ed.). Austin, TX: PRO-ED.

Stewart, S. R., & Cegelka, P. T. (1995). Teaching reading and spelling. In P. T. Cegelka & W. H. Berdine, *Effective instruction for students with learning difficulties* (pp. 265–301). Boston: Allyn & Bacon.

Stipek, D. J., & Ryan, R. H. (1997). Economically disadvantaged preschoolers: Ready to learn but further to go. *Developmental Psychology, 33*, 711–723.

Stires, S. (Ed.). (1991). *With promise: Redefining reading and writing for "special students."* Portsmouth, NH: Heinemann.

Stokes, T. F., & Baer, D. M. (1977). An implicit technology of generalization. *Journal of Applied Behavior Analysis, 10*, 349–367.

Strauss, A., & Lehtinen, L. (1947). *Psychopathology and education of the brain-injured child.* New York: Grune & Stratton.

Stuckless, E. R., & Marks, C. H. (1966). *Assessment of the written language of deaf students* (USOE Cooperative Research Project 2544). Pittsburgh, PA: University of Pittsburgh.

Sugai, G., & Fuller, M. (1991). A decision model for social skills curriculum analysis. *Remedial and Special Education, 12*(4), 33–42.

Swain, K. D. (2005). CBM with goal setting: Impacting students' understanding of reading goals. *Journal of Instructional Psychology, 32*, 259–265.

Swanson, H. L. (1999a). Instructional components that predict treatment outcomes for students with learning disabilities: Support for a combined strategy and direct instruction model. *Learning Disabilities Research & Practice, 14*, 129–140.

Swanson, H. L. (1999b). Reading research for students with LD: A meta-analysis of intervention outcomes. *Journal of Learning Disabilities, 32*, 504–532.

Swanson, H. L., & Jerman, O. (2006). Math disabilities: A selective meta-analysis of the literature. *Review of Educational Research, 76*, 249–274.

Swanson, T. J., Hodson, B. W., & Schommer-Aikens, M. (2005). An examination of phonological awareness treatment outcomes for seventh-grade poor readers from a bilingual community. *Language, Speech, & Hearing Services in Schools, 36*, 336–345.

Tappenden, V. J. (1983). Analysis of the learning styles of vocational education and nonvocational education students in eleventh and twelfth grades from rural, urban, and suburban locations in Ohio. *Dissertation Abstracts International, 44*, 1326a.

Templin, E. (1960). Research and comment: Handwriting, the neglected R. *Elementary English, 37*, 386–389.

TerraNova, Third Edition. (2007). Monterey, CA: CTB/McGraw-Hill.

Therrien, W. J. (2004). Fluency and comprehension gains as a result of repeated reading: A meta-analysis. *Remedial and Special Education, 25*, 252–261.

Therrien, W. J., Hughes, C., Kapelski, C., & Mokhtari, K. (2009). Effectiveness of a test-taking strategy on achievement in essay tests for students with learning disabilities. *Journal of Learning Disabilities, 42*, 14–23.

Thomas, C. C., Englert, C. S., & Gregg, S. (1987). An analysis of errors and strategies in the expository writing of learning disabled students. *Remedial and Special Education, 8*(1), 21–30, 46.

Thornton, C. A., & Toohey, M. A. (1982–1985). *MATH FACT: An alternative program for children with special needs* (A series of four kits: *Basic Addition Facts; Basic Subtraction Facts; Basic Multiplication Facts; Basic Division Facts*). Brisbane, Australia: Queensland Division of Special Education.

Thornton, C. A., & Toohey, M. A. (1985). Basic math facts: Guidelines for teaching and learning. *Learning Disabilities Focus, 1*, 44–57.

Thorpe, H. W., & Borden, K. F. (1985). The effect of multisensory instruction upon the on-task behavior and word reading accuracy of learning disabled students. *Journal of Learning Disabilities, 18*, 279–286.

Thurber, D. N. (2008). *D'Nealian handwriting* (Rev. ed.). Glenview, IL: Scott, Foresman/Pearson.

Thurlow, M. L., Ysseldyke, J. E., & Silverstein, B. (1995). Testing accommodations for students with disabilities. *Remedial and Special Education, 16*(5), 260–270.

Tindal, G., & Marston, D. B. (1990). *Classroom-based assessment: Evaluating instructional outcomes.* Upper Saddle River, NJ: Merrill/Prentice Hall.

Tindal, G., Shinn, M. R., & Rodden-Nord, K. (1990). Contextually based school consultation: Influential variables. *Exceptional Children, 56*, 324–336.

Tompkins, G. E. (2009). *Language arts: Patterns of practice* (7th ed.). Upper Saddle River, NJ: Merrill/Pearson.

Torgesen, J. K. (1990). Studies of children with learning disabilities who perform poorly on memory span tasks. In J. K. Torgesen (Ed.), *Cognitive and behavioral characteristics of children with learning disabilities* (pp. 41–58). Austin, TX: PRO-ED.

Torgesen, J. K., Alexander, A. W., Wagner, R. K., Rashotte, C. A., Voeller, K. K. S., & Conway, T. (2001). Intensive remedial instruction for children with severe reading disabilities: Immediate and long-term outcomes from two instructional approaches. *Journal of Learning Disabilities, 34*, 33–58, 78.

Torgesen, J. K., & Barker, T. A. (1995). Computers as aids in the prevention and remediation of reading disabilities. *Learning Disability Quarterly, 18*, 76–87.

Torgesen, J. K., & Bryant, B. R. (1994). *Phonological awareness training for reading.* Austin, TX: PRO-ED.

Torgesen, J. K., & Bryant, B. R. (2004). *Test of Phonological Awareness—Second Edition Plus.* Austin, TX: PRO-ED.

Torgesen, J. K., Rashotte, C. A., & Alexander, A. W. (2001). Principles of fluency instruction in reading: Relationships with established empirical outcomes. In M. Wolf (Ed.), *Dyslexia, fluency, and the brain*. Parkton, MD: York Press.

Torgesen, J. K., & Wagner, R. K. (1998). Alternative diagnostic approaches for specific developmental reading disabilities. *Learning Disabilities Research & Practice, 13*, 220–232.

Torgesen, J. K., Wagner, R. K., & Rashotte, C. A. (1994). Longitudinal studies of phonological processing and reading. *Journal of Learning Disabilities, 27*, 276–286.

Torgesen, J. K., Wagner, R. K., Rashotte, C. A., Alexander, A. W., & Conway, T. (1997). Preventive and remedial interventions for children with severe reading disabilities. *Learning Disabilities: A Multidisciplinary Journal, 8*(1), 51–61.

Torgesen, J. K., Wagner, R. K., Rashotte, C. A., Rose, E., Lindamood, P., Conway, T., & Garvan, C. (1999). Preventing reading failure in young children with phonological processing disabilities: Group and individual responses to intervention. *Journal of Educational Psychology, 91*(4), 579–593.

Trainor, A. A. (2007). Perceptions of adolescent girls with LD regarding self-determination and postsecondary transition planning. *Learning Disability Quarterly, 30*, 31–45.

Troia, G. A. (2009). Tactics to help students use writing to express their comprehension of content area texts. *Perspectives on Language and Literacy, 35*(3), 35–41.

Tuckwiller, E. D., Pullen, P. C., & Coyne, M. (2010). An investigation of at-risk kindergarten students' response to a two-tiered vocabulary intervention: A regression discontinuity design. *Learning Disabilities Research & Practice, 25*.

Uhry, J. K. (2005). Phonemic awareness and reading: Research, activities, and instructional materials. In J. R. Birsh (Ed.), *Multisensory teaching of basic language skills* (2nd ed., pp. 83–111). Baltimore, MD: Paul H. Brookes.

U.S. Department of Education. (1994). *National transition longitudinal study: Postschool outcomes of students with disabilities* (Contract No. 300-87-0054). Washington, DC: Author.

U.S. Department of Education. (2009, January). *28th annual report to Congress on the implementation of the Individuals with Disabilities Education Act, 2006*. Washington, DC: Author.

Utley, C. A., Mortweet, S. L., & Greenwood, C. R. (1997). Peer-mediated instruction and interventions. *Focus on Exceptional Children, 29*(5), 1–23.

Valencia, S. (1990). A portfolio approach to classroom reading assessment: The whys, whats, and hows. *The Reading Teacher, 43*, 338–340.

Van Reusen, A. K., & Bos, C. S. (1994). Facilitating student participation in individualized education programs through motivation strategy instruction. *Exceptional Children, 60*, 466–475.

Van Reusen, A. K., Bos, C. S., Schumaker, J. B., & Deshler, D. D. (2002). *The self-advocacy strategy for enhancing student motivation and self-determination* (Rev. ed.). Lawrence, KS: Edge Enterprises.

Vaughn, S., & Bos, C. S. (2009). *Strategies for teaching students with learning and behavior problems* (7th ed.). Upper Saddle River, NJ: Merrill/Pearson.

Vaughn, S., Bos, C. S., & Schumm, J. S. (2007). *Teaching students who are exceptional, diverse, and at risk in the general education classroom* (4th ed.). Upper Saddle River, NJ: Merrill/Pearson.

Vaughn, S., Gersten, R., & Chard, D. J. (2000). The underlying message in LD intervention research: Findings from research syntheses. *Exceptional Children, 67*, 99–114.

Vaughn, S., & Klingner, J. K. (1998). Students' perceptions of inclusion and resource room settings. *The Journal of Special Education, 32*, 79–88.

Veerkamp, M. B., Kamps, D. M., & Cooper, L. (2007). The effects of classwide peer tutoring on the reading achievement of urban middle school students. *Education and Treatment of Children, 30*, 21–51.

Vogel, S. A., & Adelman, P. B. (2000). Adults with learning disabilities 8–15 years after college. *Learning Disabilities: A Multidisciplinary Journal, 10*, 165–182.

Wagner, M. (1990, April). *The school programs and school performance of secondary students classified as learning disabled: Findings from the national longitudinal transition study of special education students*. Paper presented at the meetings of Division G, American Educational Research Association, Boston.

Wagner, M., Newman, L., Cameto, R., Garza, N., & Levine, P. (2005). *After high school: A first look at the postschool experiences of youth with disabilities: A report from the National Longitudinal Transition Study—2 (NLTS2)*. Menlo Park, CA: SRI International.

Wagner, R. K., & Torgesen, J. K. (1987). The nature of phonological processing and its causal role in the acquisition of reading skills. *Psychological Bulletin, 101*, 192–212.

Wagner, R. K., Torgesen, J. K., & Rashotte, C. A. (1999). *Comprehensive Test of Phonological Processing*. Austin, TX: PRO-ED.

Waksman, S., & Waksman, D. D. (1998). *The Waksman social skills curriculum for adolescents: An assertive behavior program*. (4th ed.). Austin, TX: PRO-ED.

Waldron-Soler, K. M., Martella, R. C., Marchand-Martella, N. E., Warner, D. A., Miller, D. E., & Tso, M. E. (2002). Effects of a 15-week Language for Learning implementation with children in an integrated preschool. *Journal of Direct Instruction 2*(2), 75–86.

Walker, B., Shippen, M. E., Alberto, P., Houchins, D. E., & Cihak, D. F. (2005). Using the Expressive Writing program to improve the writing skills of high school students with learning disabilities. *Learning Disabilities Research & Practice, 20*, 175–183.

Walker, H. M., McConnell, S., Holmes, D., Todis, B., Walker, J., & Golden, N. (1983). *The Walker social skills curriculum: The ACCEPTS program*. Austin, TX: PRO-ED.

Walker, H. M., Todis, B., Holmes, D., & Horton, G. (1988). *The Walker social skills curriculum: The ACCESS program*. Austin, TX: PRO-ED.

Wallace, G., & Hammill, D. D. (2002). *Comprehensive Receptive and Expressive Vocabulary Test—2*. Austin, TX: PRO-ED.

Wallace, G., & Kauffman, J. M. (1986). *Teaching students with learning and behavior problems* (3rd ed.). Upper Saddle River, NJ: Merrill/Prentice Hall.

Wallace, G., Larsen, S. C., & Elksnin, L. K. (1992). *Educational assessment of learning problems: Testing for teaching* (2nd ed.). Boston: Allyn & Bacon.

Wallach, G. P. (2005). A conceptual framework in language learning disabilities: School-age language disorders. *Topics in Language Disorders, 25,* 292–301.

Walpole, S., & McKenna, M. C. (2006). The role of informal reading inventories in assessing word recognition. *The Reading Teacher, 59,* 592–594.

Walther-Thomas, C. S. (1997). Co-teaching experiences: The benefits and problems that teachers and principals report over time. *Journal of Learning Disabilities, 30,* 395–407.

Wang, M. C. (1987). Toward achieving educational excellence for all students: Program design and instructional outcomes. *Remedial and Special Education, 8*(3), 25–34.

Wang, M. C., Haertel, G. D., & Walberg, H. J. (1993/1994). Synthesis of research: What helps students learn? *Educational Leadership, 51*(4), 74–79.

Wang, M. C., Reynolds, M. C., & Walberg, H. J. (1986). Rethinking special education. *Educational Leadership, 44*(1), 26–31.

Wang, M. C., & Zollers, N. J. (1990). Adaptive instruction: An alternative service delivery approach. *Remedial and Special Education, 11*(1), 7–21.

Wanzek, J., Vaughn, S., Wexler, J., Swanson, E. A., Edmonds, M., & Kim, A. (2006). A synthesis of spelling and reading interventions and their effects on the spelling outcomes of students with LD. *Journal of Learning Disabilities, 39,* 528–543.

Warden, M. R., & Hutchinson, T. A. (1992). *Writing Process Test.* Austin, TX: PRO-ED.

Watanabe, A. (1991). *The effects of a mathematical word problem solving strategy on problem solving performance by middle school students with mild disabilities.* Unpublished doctoral dissertation, University of Florida, Gainesville.

Wayman, M. M., Wallace, T., Wiley, H. I., Ticha, R., & Espin, C. A. (2007). Literature synthesis on curriculum based measurement in reading. *The Journal of Special Education, 41*(2), 85–120.

Wehmeyer, M. L., Palmer, S. B., Agran, M., Mithaug, D. E., & Martin, J. E. (2000). Promoting causal agency: The self-determined learning model of instruction. *Exceptional Children, 66,* 439–453.

Weiner, E. S. (1980). Diagnostic evaluation of writing skills. *Journal of Learning Disabilities, 13,* 48–53.

Weinstein, G., & Cooke, N. L. (1992). The effects of two repeated reading interventions on generalization of fluency. *Learning Disability Quarterly, 15,* 21–28.

Weinstein, R. S. (1982). *Expectations in the classroom: The student perspective.* Invited address, Annual Conference of the American Educational Research Association, New York.

Weintraub, N., & Graham, S. (1998). Writing legibly and quickly: A study of children's ability to adjust their handwriting to meet common classroom demands. *Learning Disabilities Research & Practice, 13,* 146–152.

Welch, M. (1992). The PLEASE strategy: A metacognitive learning strategy for improving the paragraph writing of students with mild learning disabilities. *Learning Disability Quarterly, 15,* 119–128.

West, J. F., & Cannon, G. S. (1988). Essential collaborative consultation competencies for regular and special educators. *Journal of Learning Disabilities, 21,* 56–63.

West, J. F., & Idol, L. (1990). Collaborative consultation in the education of mildly handicapped and at-risk students. *Remedial and Special Education, 11*(1), 22–31.

West, J. F., Idol, L., & Cannon, G. (1988). *Collaboration in the schools: Communicating, interacting, and problem solving.* Austin, TX: PRO-ED.

Western, R. D. (1977). Case against cursive script. *Elementary School Journal, 78,* 1–3.

Wheelock, W. H., Campbell, C., & Silvaroli, N. J. (2009). *Classroom Reading Inventory* (11th ed.). Columbus, OH: McGraw-Hill.

Whelan, R. J. (1996). Classroom management. In E. L. Meyen, G. A. Vergason, & R. J. Whelan (Eds.), *Strategies for teaching exceptional children in inclusive settings* (pp. 303–310). Denver, CO: Love.

Whitbread, K. M., Bruder, M. B., Fleming, G., & Park, H. J. (2007). Collaborating in special education: Parent-professional training. *Teaching Exceptional Children, 39*(4), 6–14.

White, O. R. (1986). Precision teaching—Precision learning. *Exceptional Children, 52,* 522–534.

White, W. J. (1992). The postschool adjustment of persons with learning disabilities: Current status and future projections. *Journal of Learning Disabilities, 25,* 448–456.

Wiederholt, J. L., & Blalock, G. (2000). *Gray Silent Reading Tests.* Austin, TX: PRO-ED.

Wiederholt, J. L., & Bryant, B. R. (2001). *Gray Oral Reading Tests—Fourth Edition.* Austin, TX: PRO-ED.

Wiederholt, J. L., Hammill, D. D., & Brown, V. L. (2009). *Reading Observation Scale.* Austin, TX: PRO-ED.

Wiederholt, J. L., & Wolffe, K. E. (1990). Preparing problem learners for independent living. In D. D. Hammill & N. R. Bartel, *Teaching students with learning and behavior problems* (5th ed., pp. 451–501). Boston: Allyn & Bacon.

Wiig, E. H. (1990). Linguistic transitions and learning disabilities: A strategic learning perspective. *Learning Disability Quarterly, 13,* 128–140.

Wiig, E. H., & Secord, W. A. (1992). *Test of Word Knowledge.* San Antonio, TX: Psychological Corporation.

Wiig, E. H., & Secord, W. A. (1994). Language disabilities in school-age children and youth. In G. H. Shames, E. H. Wiig, & W. A. Secord (Eds.), *Human communication disorders: An introduction* (4th ed., pp. 212–247). Boston: Allyn & Bacon.

Wiig, E. H., & Semel, E. M. (1976). *Language disabilities in children and adolescents.* Boston: Allyn & Bacon.

Wiig, E. H., & Semel, E. M. (1984). *Language assessment and intervention for the learning disabled* (2nd ed.). Boston: Allyn & Bacon.

Wilcox, M. J. (1986). Development language disorders: Preschoolers. In J. M. Costello & A. L. Holland (Eds.), *Handbook of speech and language disorders* (pp. 643–670). San Diego, CA: College-Hill Press.

Wilkinson, G. S., & Robertson, G. J. (2006). *Wide Range Achievement Test—4.* Austin, TX: PRO-ED.

Will, M. C. (1986). Educating children with learning problems: A shared responsibility. *Exceptional Children, 52,* 411–415.

Wilmore, E. L. (1994/1995). When your child is special. *Educational Leadership, 52*(4), 60–62.

Wilson, B. A., & Felton, R. H. (2005). *Word Identification and Spelling Test.* Austin, TX: PRO-ED.

Wilson, C. L., & Hughes, M. (1994). Involving linguistically diverse parents. *LD Forum, 13*(3), 25–27.

Wirtz, C. L., Gardner, R., III, Weber, K., & Bullara, D. (1996). Using self-correction to improve the spelling performance of low-achieving third graders. *Remedial and Special Education, 17,* 48–58.

Witte, R. H., Philips, L., & Kakela, M. (1998). Job satisfaction of college graduates with learning disabilities. *Journal of Learning Disabilities, 31,* 259–265.

Witzel, B. S., & Mercer, C. D. (2003). Using rewards to teach students with disabilities: Implications for motivation. *Remedial and Special Education, 24,* 88–96.

Witzel, B. S., Mercer, C. D., & Miller, M. D. (2003). Teaching algebra to students with learning difficulties: An investigation of an explicit instruction model. *Learning Disabilities Research & Practice, 18,* 121–131.

Witzel, B. S., & Riccomini, P. J. (2009). *Computation of fractions: Math intervention for elementary and middle grade students.* Upper Saddle River, NJ: Merrill/Pearson.

Witzel, B. S., Smith, S. W., & Brownell, M. T. (2001). How can I help students with learning disabilities in algebra? *Intervention in School and Clinic, 37,* 101–104.

Wolf, B. J. (2005). Teaching handwriting. In J. R. Birsh (Ed.), *Multisensory teaching of basic language skills* (2nd ed., pp. 413–438). Baltimore, MD: Paul H. Brookes.

Wolgemuth, J. R., Cobb, B., & Alwell, M. (2008). The effect of mnemonic interventions on academic outcomes for youth with disabilities. *Learning Disabilities Research & Practice, 23,* 1–10.

Wong, B. Y. L. (1986). A cognitive approach to teaching spelling. *Exceptional Children, 53,* 169–173.

Wood, B. S. (1976). *Children and communications: Verbal and nonverbal language development.* Upper Saddle River, NJ: Prentice Hall.

Wood, J. W. (2006). *Teaching students in inclusive settings: Adapting and accommodating instruction* (5th ed.). Upper Saddle River, NJ: Merrill/Prentice Hall/Pearson.

Woodcock, R. W. (1998). *Woodcock Reading Mastery Tests—Revised.* Minneapolis, MN: Pearson.

Woodcock, R. W., Mather, N., & Schrank, F. A. (2004). *Woodcock-Johnson III Diagnostic Reading Battery.* Rolling Meadows, IL: Riverside.

Woodcock, R. W., McGrew, K. S., & Mather, N. (2007). *Woodcock-Johnson III Normative Update Tests of Achievement.* Rolling Meadows, IL: Riverside.

Woods, M. L., & Moe, A. J. (2007). *Analytical Reading Inventory* (8th ed.). Upper Saddle River, NJ: Merrill/Pearson.

Woodward, J. (1991). Procedural knowledge in mathematics: The role of the curriculum. *Journal of Learning Disabilities, 24,* 242–251.

Woodward, J., & Carnine, D. (1988). Antecedent knowledge and intelligent computer-assisted instruction. *Journal of Learning Disabilities, 21,* 131–139.

Woodward, J., & Gersten, R. (1992). Innovative technology for secondary students with learning disabilities. *Exceptional Children, 58,* 407–421.

Woodward, J., & Montague, M. (2002). Meeting the challenge of mathematics reform for students with LD. *The Journal of Special Education, 36,* 89–101.

Worthen, B. R. (1993). Critical issues that will determine the future of alternative assessment. *Phi Delta Kappan, 74,* 444–454.

Xin, Y. P., & Jitendra, A. K. (1999). The effects of instruction in solving mathematical word problems for students with learning problems: A meta-analysis. *The Journal of Special Education, 32,* 207–225.

Yell, M. L. (1995). Least restrictive environment, inclusion, and students with disabilities: A legal analysis. *The Journal of Special Education, 28,* 389–404.

Yoder, P. J., Kaiser, A., & Alpert, C. (1991). An exploratory study of the interaction between language teaching methods and child characteristics. *Journal of Speech and Hearing Research, 34,* 155–167.

Ysseldyke, J. E., & Christenson, S. L. (2002). *Functional Assessment of Academic Behavior: Creating successful learning environments.* Frederick, CO: Sopris West.

Ysseldyke, J. E., Christenson, S. L., & Kovaleski, J. F. (1994). Identifying students' instructional needs in the context of classroom and home environments. *Teaching Exceptional Children, 26*(3), 37–41.

Ysseldyke, J. E., & Tardrew, S. (2007). Use of a progress monitoring system to enable teachers to differentiate mathematics instruction. *Journal of Applied School Psychology, 24,* 1–28.

Zawaiza, T. R. W., & Gerber, M. M. (1993). Effects of explicit instruction on math word-problem solving by community college students with learning disabilities. *Learning Disability Quarterly, 16,* 64–79.

Zawilinski, L. (2009). HOT blogging: A framework for blogging to promote higher order thinking. *The Reading Teacher, 62,* 650–661.

Zigmond, N. (1990). Rethinking secondary school programs for students with learning disabilities. *Focus on Exceptional Children, 23*(1), 1–24.

Index

Page references followed by "f" indicate illustrated figures or photographs; followed by "t" indicates a table.